Scottish Literature since 170

Longman Literature in English Series

**General Editors: David Carroll and Michael Wheeler
Lancaster University**

For a complete list of titles see pages x–xi

Scottish Literature since 1707

Marshall Walker

Longman
London and New York

Addison Wesley Longman
Edinburgh Gate
Harlow
Essex CM20 2JE
England
and Associated Companies throughout the world.

Published in the United States of America
by Addison Wesley Longman Inc., New York.

© Addison Wesley Longman Limited 1996

First published 1996

ISBN 0 582 02893 0 CSD
ISBN 0 582 02892 2 PPR

British Library Cataloguing-in-Publication Data

A catalogue record of this book is
available from the British Library

Library of Congress Cataloging-in-Publication Data

A catalog entry for this title is available from the
Library of Congress

Set by 35 in 10/11pt Mono Bembo
Produced by Longman Singapore Publishers (Pte) Ltd.
Printed in Singapore

Contents

Editors' Preface

The multi-volume Longman Literature in English Series provides students of literature with a critical introduction to the major genres in their historical and cultural context. Each volume gives a coherent account of a clearly defined area, and the series, when complete, will offer a practical and comprehensive guide to literature written in English from Anglo-Saxon times to the present. The aim of the series as a whole is to show that the most valuable and stimulating approach to the study of literature is that based upon awareness of the relations between literary forms and their historical contexts. Thus the areas covered by most of the separate volumes are defined by period and genre. Each volume offers new and informed ways of reading literary works, and provides guidance for further reading in an extensive reference section.

In recent years, the nature of English studies has been questioned in a number of increasingly radical ways. The very terms employed to define a series of this kind – period, genre, history, context, canon – have become the focus of extensive critical debate, which has necessarily influenced in varying degrees the successive volumes published since 1985. But however fierce the debate, it rages around the traditional terms and concepts.

As well as studies on all periods of English and American literature, the series includes books on criticism and literary theory and on the intellectual and cultural context. A comprehensive series of this kind must of course include other literatures written in English, and therefore a group of volumes deals with Irish and Scottish literature, and the literatures of India, Africa, the Caribbean, Australia and Canada. The forty-seven volumes of the series cover the following areas: Pre-Renaissance English Literature, English Poetry, English Drama, English Fiction, English Prose, Criticism and Literary Theory, Intellectual and Cultural Context, American Literature, Other Literatures in English.

David Carroll
Michael Wheeler

Longman Literature in English Series

**General Editors: David Carroll and Michael Wheeler
Lancaster University**

Pre-Renaissance English Literature

* ★ English Literature before Chaucer *Michael Swanton*
  English Literature in the Age of Chaucer
* ★ English Medieval Romance *W. R. J. Barron*

English Poetry

* ★ English Poetry of the Sixteenth Century *Gary Waller*
* ★ English Poetry of the Seventeenth Century *George Parfitt*
  (*Second Edition*)
  English Poetry of the Eighteenth Century, 1700–1789
* ★ English Poetry of the Romantic Period, 1789–1830 *J. R. Watson*
  (*Second Edition*)
* ★ English Poetry of the Victorian Period, 1830–1890 *Bernard Richards*
  English Poetry of the Early Modern Period, 1890–1940
* ★ English Poetry since 1940 *Neil Corcoran*

English Drama

* English Drama before Shakespeare
* ★ English Drama: Shakespeare to the Restoration, 1590–1660
  Alexander Leggatt
* ★ English Drama: Restoration and Eighteenth Century, 1660–1789
  Richard W. Bevis
  English Drama: Romantic and Victorian, 1789–1890
* ★ English Drama of the Early Modern Period, 1890–1940
  Jean Chothia
  English Drama since 1940

English Fiction

* ★ English Fiction of the Eighteenth Century, 1700–1789
  Clive T. Probyn
* ★ English Fiction of the Romantic Period, 1789–1830 *Gary Kelly*
* ★ English Fiction of the Victorian Period, 1830–1890 *Michael Wheeler*
  (*Second Edition*)

★ English Fiction of the Early Modern Period, 1890–1940
Douglas Hewitt
English Fiction since 1940

English Prose

★ English Prose of the Seventeenth Century, 1590–1700 *Roger Pooley*
English Prose of the Eighteenth Century
English Prose of the Nineteenth Century

Criticism and Literary Theory

Criticism and Literary Theory from Sidney to Johnson
Criticism and Literary Theory from Wordsworth to Arnold
Criticism and Literary Theory from 1890 to the Present

The Intellectual and Cultural Context

The Sixteenth Century
★ The Seventeenth Century, 1603–1700 *Graham Parry*
★ The Eighteenth Century, 1700–1789 *James Sambrook* (*Second Edition*)
The Romantic Period, 1789–1830
★ The Victorian Period, 1830–1890 *Robin Gilmour*
The Twentieth Century: 1890 to the Present

American Literature

American Literature before 1880
★ American Poetry of the Twentieth Century *Richard Gray*
★ American Drama of the Twentieth Century *Gerald M. Berkowitz*
★ American Fiction 1865–1940 *Brian Lee*
★ American Fiction since 1940 *Tony Hilfer*
★ Twentieth-Century America *Douglas Tallack*

Other Literatures

Irish Literature since 1800
★ Scottish Literature since 1707 *Marshall Walker*
Australian Literature
★ Indian Literature in English *William Walsh*
African Literature in English: East and West
★ Southern African Literatures *Michael Chapman*
Caribbean Literature in English
★ Canadian Literature in English *W. J. Keith*

★ *Already published*

Author's Preface

This discussion of Scottish literature in English, and in Scots which is accessible to readers of English, takes the year 1707 as a starting point, not only because earlier literature is dealt with in another volume of this series but also because 1707 was a new beginning for Scotland. In that year, with the Union of the parliaments of Scotland and England and the inauguration of the United Kingdom, Scottish Calvinism was compounded by paranoia. Since 1707 Scottish sensibility has either touched its forelock to England's supremacy in a nominal Britain, or has resented forces which seemed to have sabotaged an ancient nation, or has functioned, at some level, in terms of awareness that it is peripheral to the cultural and economic centre of the Union. Scottish female sensibility, of course, has been doubly peripheral, marginalized by both place and sex. Other 'minority' groups have been officially invisible.

In matters of judgement it is salutary to recall what Robert Louis Stevenson says about his 'hanging judge', Lord Weir, in *Weir of Hermiston*: 'Honest all through, he did not affect the virtue of impartiality'. Like the distinguished American critic, M. H. Abrams, I confess, safely enough perhaps, to uneasiness with 'the confrontation model of criticism' whereby the paradigmatic critical situation is an isolated person confronting a single, autonomous work of art without reference to such 'external' relations as the interests of the perceiver or the truth to life, usefulness or morality of the work. More riskily, I confess partiality for a view of literary works as incontrovertibly human products manufactured by real people with visions to impart according to more or less ascertainable aesthetic devices. Such works come from authors, not merely from other texts, but all texts are related in some way to a *Zeitgeist*. Robert Burns and Catherine Carswell were real people to whom – and to whom only – authorship of 'Holy Willie's Prayer' and *Open the Door!* may reasonably be attributed. But much may and should be learned from the context of a work which is a thing of its place and time as well as an emanation of its begetter. This book, therefore, tries to sustain a double focus. Let us look at the particular work, and, where appropriate – as with Burns, Scott and Stevenson, for example – at the biography of its author; but while doing so let us

also, in the words of the novelist, Iain Banks, 'Lie back and think of
Scotland', bearing in mind that, as with all books like this, the story told
in the following pages is by its nature provisional, a map drawn from the
predilections of one fallible devotee.

The first chapter tries to provide a grid of interlocking themes, questions and perspectives, thereby offering a frame of references in which the
topics of succeeding chapters, sins of omission and ideas that come to the
reader may be set.

In addition to the life-long debt acknowledged in the dedication, I am
grateful to the following people: the University of Waikato Research
Grants Committee for subsidizing the costs of research travel and inter-
library loans; Dr Jan Pilditch for creative advice, collegial succour and
critical wisdom; Dr Alan Riach for generously sharing his understanding
of Scottish culture, for the stimulus of his own research in Scottish literature and for access to his splendid library of Scottish works; Alasdair
and Margaret Munro for warm interest and invaluable assistance; Michael
and Colleen Lascelles for their sustained votes of confidence; Peter Rodda
in London for keeping me, in New Zealand, supplied with British literary
reviews; Rodney Hamel, Professor A. Norman Jeffares and Professor
Edwin Morgan for innumerable scholarly and personal kindnesses; Pro-
fessor Guy Butler for taking a chance on a callow young Scot; Professor
Ken Arvidson, Professor R. F. Ayling, Frank Bailey, Priscilla Barlow,
Professor Peter H. Butter, Dr Winnie Crombie, Marjory Ferguson, Philip
Gibson, Robert Graham, Ian Hogg, Tom Leonard, Eric Liggett, Frederic
Lindsay, Lois Luke, Dr Anne McKim, Dr Sheila Park, Bill Paterson,
Hugh C. Rae, Harry Sim, Dr Roderick Watson, Don Whyte and Letitia
Wichman for timely suggestions; Jillene Bydder, Stephanie Clark, Rae
Riach and Adrienne Ridley for crucial help in the University of Waikato
Library; David Bank for bibliographical sleuthing to order; Hamish Whyte
of Glasgow's Mitchell Library; the staffs of the University of Glasgow
Library and the National Library of Scotland for their patience with an
expatriate in a hurry; Elizabeth Alley for the hospitality she has given
some of the following ideas in programmes for Radio New Zealand's
Concert FM station; Helen Baird and Rachel Stubbs for help with word-
processing; Stephanie Walker for hawk-eyed proof-reading and for tholing
my four years of Scotch mist.

Finally, I thank the General Editors, Professors David Carroll and Michael
Wheeler, for the opportunity to test the conviction of The Shepherd in
the *Noctes Ambrosianae* that 'Scotland has produced some bad aneuch
writers – but the verra waurst o' them hae aye a character o' originality'.

Hamilton, New Zealand, January 1996

Acknowledgements

We are grateful to the following for permission to reproduce copyright material:

Carcanet Press Ltd for extracts from poems by Iain Crichton Smith in COLLECTED POEMS (1992), ENDS AND BEGINNINGS (1994) and SEVEN POETS ed. C. Carroll (1981, Third Eye Centre – Glasgow), extracts from poems by Sorley MacLean in FROM WOOD TO RIDGE: COLLECTED POEMS IN GAELIC AND ENGLISH (1989), poems and extracts from poems by Hugh MacDiarmid in COMPLETE POEMS (1985), extracts from poems by Edwin Morgan in COLLECTED POEMS (1990); the author, Iain Crichton Smith for an extract from his poem 'Self-Portrait'; Faber & Faber Ltd/New Directions/Oxford University Press Inc for extracts from poems by Edwin Muir in COLLECTED POEMS © Willa Muir, 1960, 1979; the author, Dr Ian Hamilton Finlay for his poem 'minnie' in GLASGOW BEASTS (1961, Wild Flounder Press); Hubert Kennedy for an extract from his translation of the poem 'Nameless Love' by John Henry MacKay in AND THUS WILL I FREELY SING (1989, Polygon) © Hubert Kennedy; the author, Tom Leonard for his poems 'Good Style' in SELECTED WORK 1965–83 (1984, Galloping Dog Press, presently published by Vintage) and 'Scotland has become . . .' in REPORTS FROM THE PRESENT: Selected Poems & Prose 1982–94 (1995, Jonathan Cape Ltd); Mariscat Press, Glasgow for an extract from the poem 'A Warning' by Edwin Morgan in HOLD HANDS AMONG THE ATOMS (1991) and the poem 'The Viper' by Edwin Morgan in TALES FROM LIMERICK ZOO (1988); John Murray (Publishers) Ltd for extracts from the poems 'Chapel between Cornfield and Shore' and 'Hamnavoe' by George Mackay Brown in SELECTED POEMS (1977, Hogarth Press), 'Uranium' by George Mackay Brown in SEVEN POETS ed. Christopher Carrell (1981, Third Eye Centre – Glasgow), the poem 'Black Furrow Gray Furrow' by George Mackay Brown in FISHERMEN WITH PLOUGHS (1971; reprinted 1979, Chatto & Windus with Hogarth Press); Random House UK Ltd/the Norman MacCaig Estate for extracts from poems by Norman MacCaig in

COLLECTED POEMS (1985, Chatto & Windus); Rebel Inc Publications for the poem 'Losing It' by Alison Kermack in WRITING LIKE A BASTARD (1993); the Saltire Society for an extract from the poem 'Sisyphus' by Robert Garioch in COMPLETE POETICAL WORKS edited by R. Fulton (1983, Macdonald Publishers, Edinburgh); Wildcat Stage Productions for extracts from the songs 'The Right of Nations' and 'Babylon' in ROADWORKS: SONG LYRICS FOR WILDCAT by David Anderson & David MacLennan (1987).

We have been unable to trace the copyright holders of the poem 'Scotland' by Robert Crawford, and would appreciate any information which would enable us to do so.

TO
JACK RILLIE,
LAMPLIGHTER, KNIFEGRINDER, FISHERMAN,
FRIEND

Chapter 1
Terms of Reference: Patriotism and Change; Scottish Identity and Tradition

Patriotism and criticism

It is the scoundrel, not the critic, whom Dr Johnson's concept of patriotism affords a last refuge. The critic as scoundrel is a comparatively rare creature who, presumably, finds other bolt-holes. Exceptions might be found among Stalinist art commissars of the former Soviet Union or in the propagandists of Hitler's *Kulturpolitik* who traduced independent thought and free expression, brutally 'exempting' anything that was judged *entartet* or degenerate and therefore inimical to the Third Reich.

Ideologues, however, do not deserve to be called critics. By comparison with such cultural atrocities simple patriotism in a critic might appear merely inadequate. It might substitute Matthew Arnold's historic estimate for his real estimate or offer emotion masquerading as analysis. The patriotic critic writing a literary history of his country might attempt a geographical estimate, regressing, like a latter-day Henry Thomas Buckle, from the varieties of twentieth-century objectivism to perspectives of 'climate, food, soil, and the general aspect of nature'.[1] Yet foregrounding a national character need not be invidious unless patriotic designs were to exalt a work above its intrinsic merit simply because it was produced in a particular place or had, perhaps, made a political impact on the affairs of a country, like the effect of *Uncle Tom's Cabin* on public opinion before the American Civil War or Yevtushenko's poem, 'Babi Yar', on Soviet anti-semitism. A Scottish patriot might exalt Burns above Shakespeare because Burns wrote in Scots, expressed contempt for the 'birkie ca'd a lord', and was not English. He might go further and prefer Sorley MacLean to Burns because MacLean writes in Gaelic, or Liz Lochhead to MacLean and Burns because she is both Scottish and a woman. Any such judgement would make him or her a bad patriot as well as a bad critic in the sense that Shylock is a bad Jew. Even when allied to political conviction the creative urge does not simply march to a flag.

Any literary history of a country, nevertheless, must be motivated by a belief that there is value in considering the country's literature in terms of its national culture. The work of literature is a cultural fact, produced in a context which includes the life of the author and the background relations of social, historical, geographical and political factors. To undertake such a literary history – or to want to read one – is to acknowledge these factors and to admit the attraction of a specific context and the works of literature set in it. Is this interest less valid if it comes in part from patriotic feeling? Swift claimed that he had 'reconcil'd Divinity and Wit', but is it possible to reconcile love and criticism? The problem is real: can a secessionist Scot forgive James Thomson for the aureate Englishness of his diction in *The Seasons* (1726–30) and for providing the English composer, Thomas Arne, with the words of 'Rule Britannia' (in *The Masque of Alfred*, 1740), or those graduates of the Scottish academy shown by Robert Crawford to have collaborated (at least) in the invention of exclusive 'Eng. Lit.'?[2]

For Ben Jonson patriots were sound lovers of their country; for Samuel Johnson they were a suspect lot and in the eighteenth century the word 'patriot' was sometimes used for 'a factious disturber of the government'. A good Scottish authority, *Chambers Twentieth Century Dictionary*, defines a patriot as 'one who truly, or ostentatiously and injudiciously, loves and serves his fatherland'. The one who truly loves and serves now seems obsolete. Fashionable post–imperial cynicism sees the British patriot as a Tory jingoist with a pipe in his mouth and a book by Kipling in his pocket. The word today is inseparable from the pejoration of Dr Johnson's apothegm, or else it signifies all the love of a guided war missile. Suppose, then, we risk the charge of *faux naïf*, turn the semantic clock back to the possibility of love and service and consider the poem 'Scotland' by Hugh MacDiarmid:

> It requires great love of it deeply to read
> The configuration of a land,
> Gradually grow conscious of fine shadings,
> Of great meanings in slight symbols
> Hear at last the great voice that speaks softly,
> See the swell and fall upon the flank
> Of a statue carved out in a whole country's marble,
> Be like Spring, like a hand in a window
> Moving New and Old things carefully to and fro,
> Moving a fraction of flower here,
> Placing an inch of air there,
> And without breaking anything.[3]

This not only vindicates love but requires it. Love is needed to read 'deeply' (which, for the critic, means adequately) the configuration of a land, that is, the filigree of a culture. Love is needed if there is to be an awareness of subtleties, 'fine shadings', as well as the homogeneity of the national culture, the 'statue carved out in a whole country's marble'. Love is needed if damage is not to result from the critical rearrangement of 'New and Old things'. In other words, the monuments can only be arranged competently in a literary history if the ordering is motivated and informed by love, and without love the discriminatory act will result in breakage.

The view from Bàrr Mòr

The island of Lismore is a small piece of the whole marble of Scotland, a sliver of land in the sea of Loch Linnhe in Argyllshire. It lies off Port Appin to the north and is seven miles distant from the market town of Oban to the south. The Gaelic name means 'great garden'. It occupies the centre of a landscape created by the long-extinct volcano whose core now comprises Ben More on the island of Mull. A low-lying island, its chief marvel, ribbed by underlying folds of limestone, is its highest point, Bàrr Mòr ('Big Top'), a modest 417 feet, from which may yet be seen the whole of the Great Glen of Scotland. Today the watcher may imagine sunlight flashing on the oars of vikings when their galleys invaded Loch Linnhe twelve centuries ago, or relish the panoramic sweep from Ben Cruachan in the east to the hunched shoulder of Ben Nevis in the north and, southward, the Isles of the Sea, Scarba and the Paps of Jura. In AD 562 Moluag and Columba, natives of Ireland, arrived on the west coast of Scotland looking for a suitable place for a centre from which to disseminate Christianity. Each chose Lismore and sought to requisition it by landing there first. Tradition pictures their coracles racing towards the island, oarsmen urged on by the tonsured missionaries. As they approached the shore Moluag saw that his rival's boat would win. Picking up an axe, he placed his little finger on the gunwale, severed it from his hand, threw it on the shingle ahead and shouted, 'My flesh and blood have first possession of this island and I bless it in the name of the Lord.' Legend makes St Columba a bad loser: he cursed Moluag, saying, 'May you have the alder for your firewood.' Moluag answered with saintly equanimity, 'The Lord will make the alder burn pleasantly.' St Columba attacked again: 'May you have the jagged ridges for your pathway.' Still Moluag was beyond provocation and replied, 'The Lord will smooth them to the feet.' Columba went north to Iona. St Moluag's alleged crozier, the Bachuil Mòr ('Great Staff'), a piece of blackthorn two feet nine inches long, can be viewed on the island at the home of the Baron of Bachuil.[4]

In this piece of the configuration of Scotland a literary history might begin with a motivation born out of limestone furrows and the stones of Picts and vikings, out of the staff of a resolute saint and the copse of alder trees at the bay where he landed, out of the congregation of peaks visible from the cairn of Bàrr Mòr. History is taken back to pre-plaid blood and bone, idealism, geology and landscape. Here are the promptings of particular earth to love and enquire, to want to know how imagination has risen to the measure of the country, its people, its history, its sense of itself. As MacDiarmid says in 'On a Raised Beach': 'We must reconcile ourselves to the stones, / Not the stones to us'. Sibelius once said: 'When we see these granite rocks we know why we can treat the orchestra as we do.'[5] George Bruce speaks more personally of the same relationship between the artist, his natural environment and his past in his poem, 'The Inheritance':

> This which I write now
> Was written years ago
> Before my birth
> In the features of my father.
>
> It was stamped
> In the rock formations
> West of my home town.[6]

The connections between Ayrshire's subtle contours and the moods of Burns, or between the neo-classical terraces of Edinburgh's eighteenth-century New Town and the stylishness of Robert Louis Stevenson's prose, or between Norman MacCaig's love of the mountain called Suilven and his essential laconism may be mysteries beyond the audacity of criticism. But the view from Bàrr Mòr is a summons to try to approach the Scottish imagination by way of its own fundamentally theological habit of taking things back to first principles.

The stereotypes

Here, too, are promptings to look beyond stereotypical perceptions of Scottish culture and to be on guard against them when reading its literature. The clichés are all too familiar: the Scot is tight-fisted, brutish, maudlin, canny, repressed, volatile, alcoholic, dourly religious, a complex barbarian worth exhibiting as one of the world's ethnic sideshows. Mary Queen of Scots, Bonnie Prince Charlie, shortbread, oatcakes and whisky, quaint accents, the bonnie banks of Loch Lomond, the Massacre of Glencoe and the pibrochs James Kennaway describes as 'damp, penetrating and sad like a mist'[7] make a culture colourful enough to sustain the kitsch-encrusted tourist industry whereby Scotland has colluded in its own inferiorization.[8] John Buchan's conservatism is nowhere more evident than in Richard Hannay's comment about the sufficiency of the disguise he is given by the shepherd's wife during his flight from The Black Stone and Scotland Yard in Chapter 7 of *The Thirty-nine Steps* (1915): 'I was the living image of the kind of Scotsman you see in the illustrations to Burns's poems'. George Douglas Brown sums up 'the pundits'' version of Scottish character in Chapter 5 of *The House with the Green Shutters* (1901):

> To go back to the beginning, the Scot, as pundits will tell
> you, is an individualist. His religion alone is enough to
> make him so. For it is a scheme of personal salvation
> significantly described once by the Reverend Mr Struthers
> of Barbie. 'At the Day of Judgement, my frehnds', said
> Mr Struthers; 'at the Day of Judgement every herring
> must hang by its own tail!' Self-dependence was never
> more luridly expressed. History, climate, social conditions,
> and the national beverage have all combined (the pundits
> go on) to make the Scot an individualist, fighting for his
> own hand. The better for him if it be so; from that he
> gets the grit that tells.

The weather, as the great humourist Stephen Leacock knew, is infamous:

> It was a gloriously beautiful Scotch morning. The rain fell
> softly and quietly, bringing dampness and moisture, and
> almost a sense of wetness to the soft moss underfoot. Grey
> mists flew hither and thither, carrying with them an
> invigorating rawness that had almost a feeling of
> dampness.[9]

The harshness of the countryside is deployed by George MacDonald in the first chapter of *Castle Warlock* (1882): 'The country produced more barley than oats, more boulders than trees, and more snow than anything.'[10] If the land is somewhat redeemed by the Scottish breakfast (Loch Fyne herring, Finnan haddie, Tay salmon, scones and oatcakes), as Susan Ferrier's gourmand Dr Redgill alleges in her novel, *Marriage* (1818),[11] and romanticized by pictorial calendar photography, it is, nevertheless, as Hugh MacDiarmid says, 'easier to lo'e [love] Prince Charlie / Than Scotland – mair's the shame!'[12] Clichés beget ignorance: the visitors come and ask their questions. In 1978 an Edinburgh tourist guide reported samples.

'Excuse me,' said one visitor to John Knox's house in Edinburgh's Royal Mile, 'but where did Knox keep the bodies he bought from Burke and Hare?' (The wrong man, sir: that was Dr Robert Knox, to whom in the late 1820s the murderers Burke and Hare sold cadavers for medical study, a pithy monomaniac assured of his gruesome immortality by James Bridie's portrait of him in the 1930 play, *The Anatomist*.) Talking of *Treasure Island* (1883) the guide remarked that Robert Louis Stevenson was sickly as a boy. 'My goodness,' gushed a wide-eyed English lady, 'to think he grew up and invented the railway engine.' At Abbotsford, home of Sir Walter Scott, an American visitor wanted to see the cloak the chivalrous knight spread out for Queen Elizabeth; another remarked that Abbotsford sure was a big house for a ploughman to have lived in; and a third, doubtless wishing to highlight the ignorance of the other two, chipped in with: 'Did Scott really write all those books before he went to the South Pole?'[13] Such fatuities imply the popular impression of a tartan canon comprising Knox, Burns, Scott and Stevenson: solid testosterone, but decorously dead.

On a higher plane of error Matthew Arnold, who never toured Scotland – and in 1877 declined nomination as Rector of the University of St Andrews – commends Burns for a view of the world that is 'large, free, shrewd, benignant – truly poetic, therefore', but finds that the poet, like Chaucer, falls short of the high seriousness of the great classics. This is hardly surprising in a poetry which, Arnold says, deals 'perpetually with Scotch drink, Scotch religion, and Scotch manners'.[14] (Had he skipped the love poems or is love reducible to 'manners'? Was he deaf to song?) The drink needs no identifying, the manners derive therefrom and the religion, as demonstrated by Hector MacMillan's play, *The Sash* (1973), about the dedicated Orangeman, Bill MacWilliam, is either bigoted Protestant, bigoted Papist or, in the west of Scotland, the transposition of these into the blue and the green, Rangers and Celtic soccer teams, endemically clashing armies of an eternal cultural night. Jacobites notwithstanding, Calvin, certainly, has been more formative than the Holy See in post-Reformation Scotland, particularly since the Disruption of 1843 when some 40 per cent of the church establishment broke from the 'Auld Kirk' to form the ineptly named 'Free Church'. In the name of true Presbyterian values, the Free Church invested the good life with a gloom even Calvin would have found over-rigid. The consequences are satirized by Charles, Lord Neaves in what he calls 'A Lyric for Saturday Night':

> We zealots, made up of stiff clay,
>   The sour-looking children of sorrow,
> While not over-jolly today,
>   Resolve to be wretched tomorrow.

We can't for a certainty tell
   What mirth may molest us on Monday;
But, at least, to begin the week well,
   Let us all be unhappy on Sunday . . .

What though a good precept we strain
   Till hateful and hurtful we make it!
What though, in thus pulling the rein,
   We may draw it as tight as to break it!
Abroad we forbid folks to roam,
   For fear they get social or frisky;
But of course they can sit still at home,
   And get dismally drunk upon whisky.[15]

In Neil Gunn's novel, *The Silver Darlings* (1941), Catrine McHamish personifies the recoil from Calvinistic brimstone. She believes in God and can see 'the figure of Christ as a child in a manger or as a grown man walking down by a ripe cornfield', but thinks religion anti-life:

Religion was for death, for the unknown hereafter, and
paradise a perpetual Sunday school smothering the quick
laughter, the gay wonder of human love – should one
ever attain paradise by avoiding the brimstone loch of hell.
Better not to think about it, to keep it away, and
meantime to have life.

Arnold's 1880 assessment of Burns gives the impression of a mind programmed by the hackneyed triad – drink, religion and manners – before its engagement with the poetry: he found what he expected to find. The tartan-quilted gift-shop editions of Burns have perpetuated the sentimental cliché of the 'heaven-taught' but wayward ploughman with too soft a spot for women and 'whisky gill or penny wheep'. To make matters worse, the impression of a national proclivity to drink, uncouth manners and religion can be reinforced by modern instances.

'Butcher Boiled His Friend' proclaimed the front page of the Glasgow *Evening Times*, implying that England's Sweeney Todd had met his match at last.[16] The butcher and his friend had been sharing a Friday-evening pint. An argument led to the exchange of insults, then of blows. A pickaxe was introduced and the friend lay dead. The butcher put the folded body of his friend in the shop's boiler, went home for dinner, and returned to the scene of the crime intending to mince the remains. When the mincer proved too small he planned to take the body to his mother's house which was empty as she was on holiday. Remorse struck early on Sunday. He confessed to his employer who contacted the police. When the butcher's wife was invited to comment she was reported as saying, 'I can't understand how he came to kill Andy Kerr, with whom he was very friendly.' It is Arnold's triad again. The story begins with drink, descends to violent manners and dissipates in sabbath remorse to end with the impeccable grammatical manners of the wife's implausibly correct 'with whom'.

An antidote may be found in a Glasgow pub. Clientele is mainly working class and drinking is methodical. Lounge-bar niceties are spurned here; ladies are not banned as they were in the old days, but there are no wilting crisps, no soggy pickled onions. Men stand at the bar or sit at spartan tables, getting on with it. The pint glasses of 'Heavy' go up and down like the pistons of an old Caledonian MacBrayne ferry plugging up the Sound of Mull. A big man comes in, orders a half of whisky – 'a wee goldie' – and a pint. He wears brown dungarees, a cloth cap pushed back on his head, heavy boots. Twenty minutes later, outside three whiskies and three pints, he is forgetting the day's nipping winds on the building site. He begins to whistle, beating time to himself with his fingers on the counter. The man next to him at the bar turns his head.

> 'Heh, Jimmy, whit's that yer whistlin'?'
> The big man doesn't seem to hear. He goes on with his whistling, fingers drumming, eyes fixed on the mirror behind the bar as though it reflects the grandeur he sees inside his head.
> 'Come on, Jimmy,' the other man says, 'gie's the name o' yer tune.'
> The whistling stops. The hand pauses in its drumming and a finger is pointed at the interlocutor.
> 'D'ye no recognize it, ma friend?'
> 'Nuh. Ah doan recognize it. 'S nice, but ah doan recognize it.'
> 'It's Sibelius, ma friend. Sibelius,' the big man says, pronouncing the name as four majestic chords. 'Sibelius, Symphony Nummer Twa. That's the last bit o' it. *Allegro moderato.*'
> 'Is that right?' says the other, vaguely impressed.
> 'Sibelius,' says the big man. 'Magic. Sibelius is pure fuckin' magic.'[17]

There is no condescending to so abundant a figure. As Robert Louis Stevenson's narrator says in *Weir of Hermiston* (1896), 'He who goes fishing among the Scots peasantry with condescension for a bait will have an empty basket by evening' (Chapter 7).

The democratic strain

The Scottish peasant may be *Grand Guignol* like the butcher in his fateful flyting or, like the builder, a lord of culture even in his drink. Butcher and builder remind us that one theme on which Scottish literary history offers a series of variations is the lot of common people. A strong sense of underlying equality is part of the idiom. Expressed as 'the sons of Adam', the idea of a common humanity beyond hierarchical accident or political manoeuvring is mythologically fanciful, but the Scottish expression that we are all 'Jock Tamson's bairns' asserts equality in terms of a continuing, imaginable family. Death the leveller is tamed to assuasive inevitability by the song in *Cymbeline* which accepts that 'the sceptre, learning, physic' must, like golden lads and girls and chimney-sweepers, 'come to dust'; but the staccato closing stanzas of Charles Murray's Scots poem, 'A Green Yule', hammer home a grittier *memento mori* in which the equalizing reality of a common end is not anaesthetized by the quiet consummation of Shakespeare's consolatory music:

> Dibble them doon, the laird, the loon,   *plant/boy*
>   King an' the cadgin caird,   *hawking tinker*
> The lady fine beside the queyn,   *girl*
>   A' in the same kirkyaird.
>
> The warst, the best, they a' get rest;
>   Ane 'neath a headstane braw,
> Wi' deep-cut text; while ower the next
>   The wavin' grass is a'.
>
> Mighty o' name, unknown to fame,
>   Slippit aneth the sod;
> Greatest an' least alike face east,
>   Waitin' the trump o' God.[18]

As one of Jock Tamson's bairns, Mary Brodie tells Walter Leslie in Robert Louis Stevenson and W. E. Henley's play, *Deacon Brodie* (1880), 'It is for every man to concern himself in the common weal',[19] and there is a main vein of humane sympathy that comes up from Barbour through the moralizing of Henryson, the complaints or satires of Dunbar and Sir David Lyndsay's John the Commonweill in *Ane Pleasant Satyre of the Three Estaitis* (1540). A vigorous egalitarian strain becomes especially evident towards the end of the eighteenth century even if it does not always rise to the measure of what Hugh MacDiarmid calls 'the fearless radical spirit

of the true Scotland'.[20] The Presbyterian ideal of the Scottish Reformation was energized by a democratic impulse even if the ideal was sometimes obscured by less worthy items on the political agenda. Revolutionary
America and France conferred on this impulse the status of natural law,
emboldening the Edinburgh mob in 1792 to a three-day riot for 'Liberty,
equality and no king'. Thomas Paine's *The Rights of Man* (1791–92),
whose blend of American idealism and European enlightenment politics
made it a textbook for British reformists, was even translated into Gaelic;
but, notwithstanding Paine's influence, Scottish writers were precociously
in advance of political radicals in works which refrain on the common
good and the worth of the individual. The Ulsterman, Francis Hutcheson,
a Scot by adoption through his seventeen-year tenure of the chair of
moral philosophy at Glasgow University, anticipated by some four decades Jeremy Bentham's equation of moral right with 'the greatest happiness of the greatest number'. The democratic refrain can be heard in
David Hume, Adam Smith and Henry Mackenzie and in the work in
Scots of the poets Allan Ramsay, Robert Fergusson and Robert Burns.
It can be heard in Robert Louis Stevenson's repudiation of Edinburgh
New Town gentility and sustained contempt for the bourgeoisie. It is
most forthrightly expressed in political terms by Hugh MacDiarmid, who
says in his autobiographical memoir *Lucky Poet* (1943):

> The Social Revolution is possible sooner in Scotland than
> in England. The working-class policy ought to be to break
> up the Empire to avert war and enable the workers to
> triumph in every country and colony. Scottish separation is
> part of the process of England's Imperial disintegration and
> is a help towards the ultimate triumph of the workers of
> the world.[21]

A thesis attempting to propound a democratic or egalitarian line in
Scottish literature might seem balked by the massive presence of Sir
Walter Scott, or compelled to look in him for the exception that could
prove the rule. Scott is, certainly, an ambiguous figure, like James Hogg,
John Galt and Thomas Carlyle. All were politically conservative men.
Scott was a Tory and a Unionist whose pseudo-aristocratic nationalism
took the form of nostalgia for the Stuarts. Hogg allied himself with
writers associated with the aggressively Conservative *Blackwood's Magazine*, in which, as the constructed *persona* of 'The Shepherd' in the *Noctes
Ambrosianae*, he is imagined calling Toryism 'an innate principle o' human
nature'[22] and declaring that 'the great majority o' shepherds are Conservatives . . . a thinkin people . . . no to be taen in by the nostrums o' every
reformer that has a plan o' a new, cheap constitution'.[23] Galt attacked
Rousseau, Robert Owen and William Godwin for basing schemes and

ideas on 'the heresies of liberty and equality'.[24] The arch-dominie Carlyle, a Victorian guru of deeply Scottish temperament, vilified the reformists, feared anarchy as much as Matthew Arnold did, and stridently opposed liberal views on human rights, particularly for Negroes in *Shooting Niagara: and After?* (1867). He was a radical but never what today we would call a democrat. 'Democracy', he writes in *Chartism* (1839), 'is, by the nature of it, a self-cancelling business; and gives in the long-run a net result of *zero*' (Chapter 6). Similarly, John Davidson, that proud, tragic man of nineteenth-century Scottish writing, denounces socialism in the Epilogue to his play, *Mammon and His Message* (1908): 'Socialism is the decadence of Feudalism; that is to say, it is less than nothing. At its very utmost it is only a bad smell; rejoicing in itself very much at present as bad smells are wont to do.'[25]

We can move on through Scottish writers, noticing Margaret Oliphant's impatience with pretension in her analyses of provincial life in both England and Scotland and her illumination of the inequitous condition of women; James (B. V.) Thomson's Dantesque (and Eliotesque) vision of the great capitalist city as an alienating dystopia in *The City of Dreadful Night* (1874); George MacDonald's compassion for the sufferings of the poor, his concern 'for the good of the community' in *Phantastes* (1858) and his abhorrence of the evil city of Bulika's recognizably nineteenth-century perversions of true community in *Lilith* (1895); J. M. Barrie's definition of the oldest Scottish university in *Courage*, his Rectorial Address to the students of St Andrews in 1922:

> Mighty are the Universities of Scotland, and they will
> prevail. But even in your highest exultations never forget
> that they are not four, but five. The greatest of them is
> the poor, proud homes you come out of, which said so
> long ago: 'There shall be education in this land'. She, not
> St Andrews, is the oldest University in Scotland, and all
> the others are her whelps.[26]

Other symptoms of the democratic strain include the socialism of Lewis Grassic Gibbon in a 'world rolling fast to a hell of riches' in *Sunset Song* (1932, Chapter 2); 'the dispensation of the poor' in the mind of Sorley MacLean ('The Cuillin' / 'An Cuilithionn', Part VI)[27] and his redefinition of Calvary in terms of 'a foul-smelling backland in Glasgow' and 'a room in Edinburgh, / a room of poverty and pain' ('Calvary'/'Calbharaigh');[28] Bill Bryden's sympathy for a moderate shop steward in his 'Red Clydeside' play, *Willie Rough* (1972); the 7:84 Theatre Company's attack on capitalist exploitation of Scotland in John McGrath's *The Cheviot, the Stag and the Black, Black Oil* (1974); the television mini-series, *Edge of Darkness* (1985), Troy Kennedy Martin's realistic and mythopoeic exposé of nuclear-age capitalist cynicism towards the well-being of the planet in Margaret Thatcher's visigothic Britain; the 'copies of the *Daily Worker* . . . dove of peace . . . poster of Paul Robeson' which a pregnant woman thinks she had better hide when a social worker calls to check her suitability for a housing waiting list in Jackie Kay's poem, 'Chapter 3: The Waiting Lists'.[29] A democratic manifesto is implicit in Ian Hamilton Finlay and Tom Leonard's use of Glasgow patois to cut through to the real lives of ordinary people and in doing so to protest, as Gaelic could never quite do, against the bending of a country's mind by 'a police régime of the signifier', to co-opt a phrase of Edward Said's,[30] that is, by the undemocratic authority of a language whose insidious 'correctness' derives from the bullying power of a remote parliament and a chimerical throne. Anti-establishment linguistic iconoclasm is part of the fun of Finlay's poems in *Glasgow Beasts, an a Burd Haw, an Inseks, an, Aw, a Fush* (1961) in which the poet's sequence of 'zen' animal reincarnations from fox to coal-horse includes life as a minnow:

> anither
> time
> ah wis a
> minnie   *minnow*
> aw
> the pond
> haw
> the shoogly caur   *swaying tram car*
> gaun   *go on*
> see s   *give me*
> a frond
> fir ma wee jaur[31] *jar*

In a poem called 'Good Style' Leonard puns on the title phrase in its Scottish usage for 'vigorously or with flair' and its implication of poetic decorum. Setting out a poem in a phonetic rendering of the language of the people can make it difficult for the outsider. Leonard turns this into a gesture of defiance towards imagined objections by supercilious guardians of 'received' or 'standard' English:

> helluva hard tay read theez init   *hell of a hard to read these isn't it*
> stull   *still*
> if yi canny unnirston thim jiss   *if you can't understand them just*
>   clear aff then   *clear off then*
>
> gawn   *go on*
> get tay fuck ootma road   *get to fuck out of my road*

ahmaz goodiz thi lota yiz so ah um	*I'm as good as the lot of you so I am*
ah no whit ahm dayn tellnyi	*I know what I'm doing telling you*
jiss try enny a yir fly patir wi me	*just try any of your fly patter with me*
stick thi bootnyi good style so ah wull[32]	*stick the boot in you good style so I will*

In case the patois has made his point inaccessible to significant readers, Leonard dreams accommodatingly in English:

> Scotland has become an independent socialist republic.
> At last.
>
> Eh?
> You pinch yourself.
> Jesus Christ. You've slept in again.[33]

But still, what of Scott, Hogg, Galt, Carlyle and Davidson?

There was another side to each of these ambiguously constituted writers. Scott's aristocratic predilections are offset by his interest in the Scottish oral tradition and by the respect he feels for the independence of ordinary Scottish folk. Hogg's suspicion of reformism is balanced by sympathy for the common people terrorized by the conservative Presbyterian establishment. *The Private Memoirs and Confessions of a Justified Sinner* received hostile, uncomprehending reviews when it was published in 1824 but has come to be regarded as one of the most penetrating and original novels in the Scottish tradition for its insight into the perversion of the Scottish psyche by Calvinism and its redefinition of the devil as corrupt theology. Galt's novels attest his unsentimental love for the small Scottish town, its burghers and peasants. If men could never be equal for the hero-worshipping Carlyle, his mistrust of the masses coexists with a passionate concern for the plight of the common people. Socialism may be a bad smell to John Davidson but there is no mistaking his humanitarian anger about the mean life to which his idiomatically eloquent Cockney thirty-bob-a-week clerk is condemned, stoically 'a-scheming how to count ten bob a pound':

> It's a naked child against a hungry wolf;
>   It's playing bowls upon a splitting wreck;
> It's walking on a string across a gulf
>   With millstones fore-and-aft about your neck;
> But the thing is daily done by many and many a one;
>   And we fall, face forward, fighting, on the deck.
>   ('Thirty Bob a Week')[34]

Even Davidson's Nietzschean *Mammon and His Message* (1908) proposes a world:

> Where men are great and conscious of their greatness –
> The very meanest intimately sure
> That he himself is the whole universe
> Become intelligent and capable.[35]

Yet the apparent conflict of ideas and attitudes in Scott, Hogg, Galt, Carlyle and Davidson cannot be ignored. How is this doubleness to be understood? How Scottish is it?

The Caledonian antisyzygy

The clue to an answer is in the conflict itself and in the proposition that it is this conflict which ignites the humanitarian elements in these writers to burn so brightly. In *The Scottish Tradition in Literature* (1958) Kurt Wittig argues that a distinctive Scottish tradition in literature can be seen in terms of a peculiar quality observable in writing by Scots or authors of Scottish extraction. This quality can be described by the term, 'Caledonian antisyzygy', an awkward mouthful coined by G. Gregory Smith in his book *Scottish Literature, Character and Influence* (1919). 'Antisyzygy' means the conjunction of opposites and Smith proposes that the term be applied to Scottish life and culture:

> [It is] a reflection of the contrasts which the Scot shows at
> every turn, in his political and ecclesiastical history, in his
> polemical restlessness, in his adaptability, which is another
> way of saying that he has made allowance for new
> conditions, in his practical judgement, which is the
> admission that two sides of the matter have been
> considered. If therefore Scottish history and life are, as an
> old northern writer said of something else, 'varied with a
> clean contrair spirit', we need not be surprised to find that
> in his literature the Scot presents two aspects which appear
> contradictory. Oxymoron was ever the bravest figure, and
> we must not forget that disorderly order is order after all.[36]

According to Smith, the sharpest expressions of these two aspects are, first, a love of detailed realistic fact and, second, a love of fantasy and the grotesque; but his perception that contrasts – 'a clean contrair spirit' – go far to distinguish Scottishness is more helpful in pointing to a fundamental quality of which the coincident love of realism and fantasy is a specific example. Granting that 'antisyzygy as such can be found in *any* literature',[37] Smith's phrase does provide a useful label for what Norman MacCaig calls 'a characteristic of the Scot – a large capacity for containing in himself elements that contradict each other'.[38] It is this doubleness of the antisyzygy which allows the humanitarian sympathies of Scott, Hogg, Galt, Carlyle and Davidson to coexist with their conservatism; it underlies Robert Louis Stevenson's interest in the cabinet-making burglar, Deacon Brodie, and his studies of yoked opposites in *The Strange Case of Dr Jekyll and Mr Hyde* (1886), in the Durie brothers of *The Master of Ballantrae* (1888) and in the relationship between Adam and Archie Weir in the unfinished *Weir of Hermiston* (1896); and it is extolled by MacDiarmid in *A Drunk Man Looks at the Thistle* (1926):

> I'll ha'e nae hauf-way hoose, but aye be whaur
> Extremes meet – it's the only way I ken
> To dodge the curst conceit o' bein richt
> That damns the vast majority o' men.
>
> (ll. 141–4)[39]

George Steiner enjoins scepticism about such formulations as Gregory Smith's: 'The ontologically linguistic, discursive substance of interpretations and value-judgements in aesthetics makes verification and falsification logically as well as pragmatically impossible. No proposition in poetics and aesthetics can, in any rigorous sense, be refuted.'[40] Yet the question of what constitutes Scottish cultural identity and artistic tradition will inevitably be asked and variously answered as long as there is a Scotland. Any country's history continuously shimmers with ambiguity. A useful complement to Gregory Smith's antisyzygy is provided by the views of two artists who have attempted to define a Scottish tradition within which they have tried to give their own paintings added resonance in the life of the nation. In *Modern Scottish Painting* (1943) J. D. Fergusson writes of 'the Scots characteristic of independence, and vigour, colour and particularly quality of paint, which means paint that is living and not merely a coat of any sort of paint placed between containing lines like a map'.[41] John Bellany emphasizes human rather than formal values: 'Independence, vigour and colour are merely means to an end, which is a heightened awareness of our human potential.'[42] If Fergusson's terms were applied to literature, Smollett, who left Scotland when he was nineteen, might yet appear more essentially Scottish than Sir Walter Scott for the independence of his social criticism, the vigour of his narratives and the colour of his caricatures. This would not be to impugn Scott for lack of vigour in his prodigious output or to deny the magnitude of his imagination, but Smollett's energy is felt in the movement of his stories and the satiric animation of his characters, while Scott's reconstructions of Scottish history can seem to be elaborate costume dramas in which the map of plot seems to have preceded the addition of costume in the medium of frequently verbose and listless prose. Bellany's emphasis on human potential hits the mark with Scottish writers from Allan Ramsay and Robert Fergusson to Mary Brunton, George MacDonald, Catherine Carswell, Iain Crichton Smith and Allan Massie.

Change, the canon and 1707

Why should a new literary history of Scotland be called for now? It has been evident enough that the record of Scottish literature is not one of continuous achievement but rather a sequence of highs and lows. It has been clear that throughout Scottish literary history estimable works in all genres reflect a preoccupation with democracy and power which is probably even stronger than the more bruited preoccupations of the Presbyterian conscience with God and guilt. It has been obvious that the theme of democracy and power is typically, if tacitly, involved with the underlying theme of national identity and self-consciousness and that it is often developed in relation to the problem of England as the 'auld enemy' or as the exploiting establishment responsible for marginalizing Scotland. In the first chapter of Grassic Gibbon's *Sunset Song* young Chris Guthrie reflects:

> ... everybody knew that the English were awful mean and
> couldn't speak right and were cowards who captured
> Wallace and killed him by treachery. But they'd been
> beaten right well at Bannockburn, then, Edward the
> Second hadn't drawn rein till he was in Dunbar, and ever
> after that the English were beaten in all the wars, except
> Flodden and they won at Flodden by treachery again, just
> as it told in *The Flowers of the Forest*. Always she wanted
> to cry when she heard that played ...

These lineaments of the Scottish literary disposition are the context in which creative functions operate in Burns's assertive use of Scots, in Sir Walter Scott's mythologizing of Scottish history, in the political stance of Hugh MacDiarmid, in the markedly un-English transnational scope of Edwin Morgan and in the outlook of the Lewis-born Gaelic poet, Derick Thomson (Ruaraidh MacThómais), as revealed in his poem 'Cruaidh?' ('Steel?'):

> ... and when you reach the Promised Land,
> unless you are on your toes,
> a bland Englishman will meet you,
> and say to you that God, his uncle, has given him a title
>   to the land.[43]

But if these characteristics are already clear, and given the poet and critic Roderick Watson's encyclopedic survey of Scottish literary history in *The Literature of Scotland* (1984), why should a new evaluation of Scottish literature be called for now? What need can there be of a new account if it is merely to tell again a familiar critical and cultural story?

The justification is partly in the changes of structures and attitudes seen in the last quarter of the twentieth century. These include the altered status of the literary canon as well as changes only recently comprehensible in the nature of society, from the decline of the aristocracy charted by David Cannadine in *The Decline and Fall of the British Aristocracy* (1990)[44] to the rise of minority groups and the impact of feminism. Even more vividly present are radical changes quite suddenly visible in the political map of the world: the 'end of the American century', the rise of global cities as command points in the organization of world economy and, therefore, of world politics, and the supremely dramatic collapse of the Soviet Union into its constituent parts with all that this process more or less bloodily implies for the autonomy of the smaller cultural unit whether Chechnya, Wales, Bosnia-Herzegovina, Quebec, Palestine, the Bantustan homelands in post-1990 South Africa, Northern Ireland or Robert Crawford's 'chip of a nation' in his electronically metaphored poem, 'Scotland':

> Micro-nation. So small you cannot be forgotten,
> Bible inscribed on a ricegrain, hi-tech's key
> Locked into the earth, your televised Glasgows
> Are broadcast in Rio. Among circuitboard crowsteps
>
> To be miniaturized is not small-minded.
> To love you needs more details than the Book of Kells –
> Your harbours, your photography, your democratic intellect
> Still boundless, chip of a nation.[45]

As Prentice McHoan says in Iain Banks's novel, *The Crow Road* (1992), 'Gorby's [Gorbachev's] unleashed restructuring ... resulted in the spectacular and literal deconstruction of one of the age's most resonantly symbolic icons' (Chapter 3). Quite suddenly, as MacDiarmid puts it in 'Au Clair de la Lune', 'Earth's littered wi' larochs [fragments] o' Empires, / Muckle nations are dust'. Culturally, in the turning world which Noam

Chomsky finds increasingly surreal,[46] there are no still points because history does not permit them. Under the impact of such changes, the failures of internationalism and the disarray of resurgent nationalisms, it is time for Scots to look at themselves afresh. As Edwin Morgan says, 'CHANGE RULES is the supreme graffito'.[47] In one episode of Scottish Television's police thriller series, *Taggart*, the unregenerate Chief Inspector says, 'I remember Glasgow when culture was something that grew on walls', but cultural change in urban Scotland over the last decade might be expressed by a progression from the drunken butcher with his implausibly grammatical wife to the equally indigenous but buoyant and integrated builder whistling Sibelius's Second Symphony after three whiskies, eloquently blending Tom Leonard's low 'good-style' diction with high art. The builder is no mere noble savage but a real, non-elitist person ready for 1990 when his Glasgow will be proclaimed 'European City of Culture', and he will have been cultured well in advance of the official imprimatur with its banal, commercial implications. Here G. Gregory Smith's 'Caledonian antisyzygy' is resurgent in a new harmony, *sui generis*, impervious, tough. The new cultural self-possession is evident in the assured eclecticism of James MacMillan's music in such works as *The Confession of Isobel Gowdie* (1990) and *Veni, Veni, Emmanuel* (1992) and in the films of Bill Forsyth, *That Sinking Feeling* (1979), *Gregory's Girl* (1981), *Local Hero* (1983) and *Comfort and Joy* (1984). In Forsyth's work the Ealing Studios sentimentality that over-sweetened Compton Mackenzie's parable of colonialism in Alexander Mackendrick's film of *Whisky Galore!* (1948) has matured into confident, edged whimsy which celebrates a realistic present in Glasgow or contemporary rural Scotland.

A literary canon implies 'Great Books', but great books are not the only books, and who pronounces them great anyway? After all, even Shakespeare's inclusion in the canon has not always been secure. In 1814 Byron wrote to James Hogg, 'Shakespeare's name, you may depend on it, stands absurdly too high and will go down'.[48] Yet the canon that was still is, albeit with its pores open to receive new and newly discovered works. It is as much the business of this book to reconsider the place of Henry Mackenzie in a Scottish canon as it is to respond to the recent poetry of Norman MacCaig or the novels of James Kelman and Iain Banks. It is not a matter of the canon versus the new. The new is what it is because the canon was there first to shape the milieu in which all literatures in English are, happily, exploding. But to call a work 'epic' still invokes Homer, Virgil and their Christianized amplification in Milton; to call a work 'lyrical' implies a relation to the sonnet and to Burns, Wordsworth and Coleridge; the term 'tragic' carries a frame of reference that originates with the Greeks but is dominated by the Shakespearean form. To have a feeling for style requires a sense of the map of styles: the kennings and half-line tensions of *Beowulf*; the speed, wit and fullness

of Chaucer; the colloquial flow of Henryson; the plain-speaking of the
Geneva Bible and the orotundities of the Authorized Version; the demotic of Burns and the snap of Pope; the poetic diction against whose
antimacassar decadence Wordsworth took so decisive a stand in one generation, Pound, Eliot and MacDiarmid in another; the incisiveness and
clamour of Dickens and the labyrinthine savourings of Henry James; the
sprung rhythms and alliterations of Hopkins, Auden and Dylan Thomas.
These are places from which Derridean quarks of significance continue
to come irresistibly into the language whoever uses it now. As George
Steiner says, 'Democracy is, fundamentally, at odds with the canonic',[49]
yet canonic reassertions are inevitable when standards are invoked or a
culture looked at whole. What the canon has lost is its normative status,
its imperious prescriptive force and its exclusivity. Thanks to work by
Tom Leonard, Robert Crawford and Edwin Morgan – all poets as well
as critics – no respectable formulation of a British canon can leave out
James (B. V.) Thomson's masterpiece, *The City of Dreadful Night*. No fair
account of excellence in British women's writing can omit Jean Elliot's
'The Flowers of the Forest', Anne Barnard's 'Auld Robin Gray', the best
of Margaret Oliphant or Catherine Carswell's *Open the Door!* (1920). The
Anglocentric canon's authority as historical fact no longer has the power
to marginalize the outsider. Peripheries are asserting themselves in a
global fugue of regional accents. Received Standard English, mercifully,
is put out to grass, a museum piece, and even the BBC's World Service
news-readers irradiate daily the intonations of Scotland and the North of
England as well as the plummier tones of the Home Counties. *Taggart*
is a world-wide export success despite occasional requests for sub-titles
by English and other foreigners; Tom Leonard is read in Gdansk and
Stellenbosch. The canon's loss of its normative value as an index of
Arnoldian touchstones is liberating, but it also prompts new responsibilities. It is time for the peripheral culture to reassess itself, respecting the
canon as formative fact but shaking off fear like a handful of dust. 'On
with the Muse', says the reactionary schoolteacher of Carol Ann Duffy's
poem, 'Head of English', introducing a visiting poet to a class of girls,
'Open a window at the back. We don't / want winds of change about
the place'.[50] The poet, of course, knows that the winds have reached gale
force and can't be kept out.

Scotland has been acclimatized to change by a history which has been
a series of new beginnings. The initial union of tribes under Kenneth
MacAlpin in 844 and then, with the addition of the Strathclyde Britons,
under Malcolm Canmore in the eleventh century, promoted an early
sense of national identity which was strengthened by the wars of independence. Bannockburn was another beginning. In the sixteenth century
the Reformation brought rejection of much of the past, melting significant
edges of nationality in preparation for the first of the two most crucial

new beginnings in 1603 when James VI of Scotland became James I of
Great Britain, endowing British kingship with Arthurian status.[51] The
second equally crucial new beginning came just over a century later in
1707 with what Lord Seafield complacently called 'the end o' an auld
sang'[52] when Scottish control energies absconded into the fundamentally
English concept of Great Britain and the greater idea of empire. In 1707,
with the union of the parliaments of Scotland and England, Scotland
embarked on a career as a colony in which life was increasingly determined by a 'signifying system' imposed by England. In the language used
by theorists of Post-colonialism, England became the colonizing machine,
Scotland the 'elided' colonized subject whose subjectivity is largely wished
away.[53] Even today, to be an urban, working-class Scottish writer is, apparently, to fear assimilation into a tradition of condescension or neglect,
despite Anthony Burgess's admiration of Alasdair Gray's *Lanark* (1981),
Jeff Torrington's Whitbread Prize for *Swing Hammer Swing!* (1992), and
Sunday Times praise for Edwin Morgan's translation of *Cyrano de Bergerac*
(1992) into Glaswegian Scots. Reviewing James Kelman's essays in *Some
Recent Attacks* (1992), Douglas Dunn sees in Kelman's opinions 'a heave
from beneath, that is, an expression from a writer whose class and locale
are traditionally disparaged by the literary mainstream'.[54] Kelman himself,
accepting the Booker Prize for his novel *How Late It Was, How Late*
(1994), felt the need to say: 'There are writers all over the world saying,
"our culture is okay". It applies to places like Yorkshire and Cornwall as
much as Scotland. Your own culture is valid. My culture and my language
have the right to exist and no one has the authority to dismiss that.'[55]

Scotland, Britain and the end, perhaps, of paranoia

There is no denying Scotland's collaboration in its own elision or the
contributions made by opportunistic Scots to the building of empire. As
Frederic Lindsay puts it:

> In the building of the empire which replaced the one
> muddled away with the American War of Independence,
> the Scots had played a disproportionate share. A quick
> conversion to the Anglican Church got them into the
> Indian Civil Service; they were missionaries in Africa and
> the traders who followed them; they instigated war with
> China in defence of the opium trade and sent the profits
> home to Dumfriesshire.[56]

With the disintegration of empire, what remains that may truly be called British except a passport? As George Orwell notices in 'England Your England' (1941), 'You can see the hesitation we feel on this point by the fact that we call our islands by no less than six different names, England, Britain, Great Britain, the British Isles, the United Kingdom and, in very exalted moments, Albion.'[57] 'Britain', the weasel-word, has its contexts in officialese and on some, though by no means all, state occasions, but 'Britain' and 'British' too easily slip, slide and perish into 'England' and 'English'. A *Gramophone* review of recordings of Janáček's *Glagolitic Mass* includes the following:

> The *Glagolitic Mass* has been recorded by two British-based
> conductors, Mackerras and Rattle . . . and, of course, it is
> in no small part due to Mackerras that England has
> become, second only to his native land, a home for
> Janáček's music.[58]

The reviewer begins with good intentions – Mackerras and Rattle are 'British-based' – but when the credit is due it is carried home to England and pop goes the weasel-word.[59] In Act I of Robert McLellan's comedy of the eighteenth century, *The Flouers o Edinburgh* (1947), Captain Sidney Simkin is introduced to the company of Girzie Carmichael, Lady Athelstane and the anglicized Charles Gilchrist, younger son of Lord Stanebyres:

> LADY A: It isna my custom, sir, to entertain officers o
>   the English Army.
> CHARLES (*in a shocked undertone*): The British Army, my
>   lady.
> SIDNEY: I beg your pardon, sir?
> CHARLES: I said 'The British Army', sir.
> SIDNEY: Oh yes. Of course you're Scotch. Quite.
>   I apologize, ma'am. You were saying?
> LADY A (*As if Charles had never spoken*): I was saying, sir,
>   that it isna my custom to entertain officers o the
>   English Army, but ye're weill come if a freind sent ye.[60]

While reminding his audience of a time when Scots was the normal speech of the aristocracy, McLellan makes a joke of the Anglo-Scot's flinch from 'English' when it should be 'British', the Englishman's condescendingly flip and insincere apology, and Lady Athelstane's adherence to 'English' for non-Scottish.[61] For the majority of English people Britain is England; for many Scots Britain is an English company with too many shares in Scotland or a politically expedient fiction which, at best, protects Scotland from the ineffectuality of its own divided nationalist politicians.

Nevertheless, as Edwin Morgan puts it, 'the circle of empire is breaking, the satellites are escaping. If the 1990s are going to be the age of the periphery, Scotland too may take the plunge; not before time.'[62] Already in 1882 in his Preface to *Familiar Studies of Men and Books* Robert Louis Stevenson calls Scotland 'a country more essentially different from England than many parts of America'.[63] In 1932 Eric Linklater compressed his views on the burgeoning 'Scottish Movement' into the following:

> 1. POLITICS. I believe that small nationalities would make the world safer, sounder, and more interesting.
> 2. ECONOMICS. (a) Scotland might become practically self-supporting; Great Britain never could. (b) Contrary to a recently established belief, I think that smaller economic units could find advantages denied to larger units.
> 3. CULTURE. It would, indeed, be as well if we got some.[64]

The Glasgow-based Wildcat theatre company voices the aspirations of many Scots in 'The Right of Nations', the final song in their show, *Heather Up Your Kilt* (1986):

> We don't believe in Utopia
> We'll face the actualities
> It's not about political myopia
> We're talking practicalities.
> We're not nostalgic for the bad old days
> Of which we've been bereft
> It's a simple matter of a people
> Who feel a lot more to the left.
>
> The right of nations
> To self-determination
> The right of nations
> To self-determination.
> No more confrontation
> And militarization
> Ecological pollution.
> It's a practical solution
> The right of nations
> To self-determination.[65]

The most significant change in Scotland since 1707 is not to be found in the youth, adolescence or incipient maturity of the Scottish National Party. But it was there in the impact of a poet's life and work before the fiasco of 1979 when Scotland failed to deliver a conclusive result in the devolution referendum it had politicked to obtain from a reluctant central government. To changes in the status of the canon, in society and in the political map of the world, the great shifts in the contextual force-fields that have occurred over the last three decades, must be added changes in Scottish cultural sensibility which largely derive from Hugh MacDiarmid. He is the next and newest beginning. 'What have you lain fallow for? / Scotland, my Scotland', he asks in 'Scotland, My Scotland', bluntly rejecting the word 'British' in a late poem called 'The Difference':

> I am a Scotsman and proud of it.
> Never call me British. I'll tell you why.
> It's too near brutish, having only
> The difference between U and I.
> Scant difference, you think? Yet
> Hell-deep and Heavenhigh![66]

His pugnacious assertion of a specifically Scottish literary tradition and his subversive attitude to British (i.e. English) cultural hegemony inspired what is now generally known as the twentieth-century Scottish Renaissance in literature. His fiercely independent imagination, Edwin Morgan's Glasgow-based internationality and, among the profusion of newer talents, Allan Massie's scepticism towards socio-political trends, Alasdair Gray's anatomizing of Scottish culture, and assertive portrayals of contemporary Scottish women's experience by Liz Lochhead, Janice Galloway and A. L. Kennedy represent a ferment of cultural health, a maturing beyond the inferiorist reflex. Douglas Gifford is right to point out that a common theme in Scottish fiction and drama of the 1960s and 1970s is the impossibility of 'a viable self-fulfilment'; but the more telling symptom is that the theme of failure is handled with increasing confidence, the art itself grows more assured and, in the work of William McIlvanney, in Archie Hind's novel *The Dear Green Place* (1966) and in the fiction of Alasdair Gray, for example, 'an introverted sense of place' is juxtaposed with international ideas.[67] If the paranoia of the cultural cringe is not yet cured it is, at least, in tolerable remission. Politically Scotland may still be a colony, and perhaps, to a debatable extent, this is its own fault, but in the arts of its letters it is no longer elided. The work of the Scottish Renaissance writers and their successors is in itself justification for new assessments of Scotland's literary history since the trauma of Union and, thereby, a new account of the major portion of a Scottish canon. What T. S. Eliot calls the 'ideal order' of the existing monuments is modified by such work. The modification and its ongoing effects should be under continuous scrutiny by that critical 'great love' whose perpetual duty is to renegotiate and maintain the culture's conscious reconciliation to its stones. In 'The War with England' Hugh MacDiarmid exemplifies the right way to begin:

> I was better with the sounds of the sea
>   Than with the voices of men
> And in desolate and desert places
>   I found myself again
> For the whole of the world came from these
> And he who returns to the source
> May gauge the worth of the outcome
> And approve and perhaps reinforce
> Or disapprove and perhaps change its course.[68]

Notes

1. Henry Thomas Buckle, 'Table of Contents', *History of Civilization in England*, 2nd edn (London, 1858), I, p. vi.

2. Robert Crawford, *Devolving English Literature* (Oxford, 1992). See particularly Chapter 1, 'The Scottish Invention of English Literature'.

3. Hugh MacDiarmid, *The Complete Poems of Hugh MacDiarmid*, ed. Michael Grieve and W. R. Aitken, 2 vols (Harmondsworth, 1985), I, p. 652. The last five lines of MacDiarmid's poem are indebted to the third of e e cummings's 'Seven Poems' in & *[AND]* (1925), 'Spring is like a perhaps hand'. MacDiarmid's use of the borrowed lines is appreciative co-option rather than plagiarism: cummings supplies a metaphor by which MacDiarmid develops a theme different from and larger than cummings's own.

4. See Ian Carmichael, *Lismore in Alba* (Perth, 1947), p. 133.

5. Burnett James, *The Music of Jean Sibelius* (London, 1983), p. 133.

6. George Bruce, *The Collected Poems of George Bruce 1939–70* (Edinburgh, 1971), p. 2.

7. James Kennaway, *Tunes of Glory* (Harmondsworth, 1985), p. 30.

8. For a scholarly and alarming discussion of the Scottish 'inferiorist reflex' see Craig Beveridge and Ronald Turnbull, *The Eclipse of Scottish Culture* (Edinburgh, 1989).

9. Stephen Leacock, 'Hannah of the Highlands', *The Penguin Stephen Leacock* (Harmondsworth, 1981), p. 34.

10. George MacDonald, *Castle Warlock*, 3 vols (London, 1882), I, pp. 1–2.

11. Susan Ferrier, *Marriage*, ed. Herbert Foltinek (Oxford, 1986), p. 237.

12. Hugh MacDiarmid, 'Bonnie Prince Charlie', in *The Complete Poems of Hugh MacDiarmid*, I, p. 274.

13. 'You've Got the Wrong Man, Chum!', *Sunday Post*, 23 July 1978, p. 19.

14. Matthew Arnold, 'The Study of Poetry', in *Essays in Criticism*, Second Series, ed. S. R. Littlewood (London, 1938), pp. 26, 29.

15. Edwin Morgan (ed.), *Scottish Satirical Verse* (Manchester, 1980), pp. 105–6.

16. 'Butcher Boiled His Friend', *Evening Times*, 28 May 1980, p. 1.

17. Marshall Walker, 'Scotch Drink, Scotch Manners and Scotch Religion', in *Living Out of London*, ed. Alan Ross (London, 1984), pp. 45–6.

18. Charles Murray, *Hamewith*, with an introduction by Andrew Lang (London, 1909), pp. 39–40.

19. Robert Louis Stevenson, *Plays*, Tusitala Edition, 35 vols (London, 1923–24), XXIV, p. 7.

20. Hugh MacDiarmid, 'The Burns Cult', in Alan Riach (ed.), *Hugh MacDiarmid: Selected Prose* (Manchester, 1992), p. 105.

21. Hugh MacDiarmid, *Lucky Poet*, ed. Alan Riach (Manchester, 1994), p. 144.

22. Professor [John] Wilson, *Noctes Ambrosianae*, A New Edition, edited by his son-in-law, Professor Ferrier, 4 vols (Edinburgh and London, 1876), I, p. 76.

23. Ibid., IV, pp. 285–6.

24. John Galt, *Cursory Reflections of Political and Commercial Topics as Connected with the Regent's Accession to the Royal Authority* (London, 1812), p. iv.

25. John Davidson, *A Selection of His Poems*, ed. with an Introduction by Maurice Lindsay, with a Preface by T. S. Eliot and an essay by Hugh MacDiarmid (London, 1961), p. 34.

26. J. M. Barrie, *Courage: The Rectorial Address Delivered At St Andrews University, May 3rd 1922* (London, 1922).

27. Sorley MacLean/Somhairle MacGill-Eain, *From Wood to Ridge / O Choille gu Bearradh, Collected Poems in Gaelic and English* (Manchester, 1989), p. 107.

28. Ibid., p. 35.

29. Jackie Kay, 'Chapter 3: The Waiting Lists', *Dream State: The New Scottish Poets*, ed. Daniel O'Rourke (Edinburgh, 1994), pp. 135–7.

30. Edward Said, *Musical Elaborations* (London, 1991), p. 56.

31. Ian Hamilton Finlay, *Glasgow Beasts, an a Burd Haw, an Inseks, an, Aw, a Fush* (Edinburgh, 1961), unnumbered pages.

32. Tom Leonard, *Intimate Voices: Selected Work 1965–1983* (Newcastle upon Tyne, 1984), p. 14.

33. Tom Leonard, *Reports from the Present: Selected Work 1982–94* (London, 1995), p. 16.

34. John Davidson, 'Thirty Bob a Week', in *The Poems of John Davidson*, ed. Andrew Turnbull, 2 vols (Edinburgh and London, 1973), I, p. 65.

35. Davidson, *A Selection of His Poems*, p. 180.

36. G. Gregory Smith, *Scottish Literature, Character and Influence* (London, 1919), pp. 4–5.

37. Kenneth Buthlay, *Hugh MacDiarmid (C. M. Grieve)* (Edinburgh, 1982), p. 47.

38. Norman MacCaig, 'A Note on the Author', in Hugh MacDiarmid, *Scottish Eccentrics*, ed. Alan Riach (Manchester, 1993), p. vii.

39. *The Complete Poems of Hugh MacDiarmid*, I, p. 87.

40. George Steiner, *Real Presences* (London, 1989), p. 68.

41. J. D. Fergusson, *Modern Scottish Painting* (Glasgow, 1943), p. 31.

42. Keith Hartley, 'Scottish Art since 1900', in *Scottish Art since 1900* (London, 1989), p. 11.

43. Derick Thomson, *Creachadh Na Clàrsaich: Cruinneachadh De Bhardachd 1940–1980 (Plundering the Harp: Collected Poems 1940–1980)* (Edinburgh, 1982), p. 99. The English translation is by the poet.

44. David Cannadine, *The Decline and Fall of the British Aristocracy* (New Haven and London, 1990).

45. Robert Crawford, 'Scotland', *Dream State: The New Scottish Poets*, p. 63.

46. Noam Chomsky, *Enter a World that is Truly Surreal* (Westfield, NJ, 1993).

47. Edwin Morgan, 'Preface' to *Essays* (Cheadle, 1974), p. vii.

48. Lord Byron, *Selected Letters and Journals*, ed. Leslie A. Marchand (Cambridge, Mass., 1982), p. 100.

49. Steiner, *Real Presences*, p. 32.

50. Carol Ann Duffy, 'Head of English', *Selected Poems* (Harmondsworth, 1994), pp. 8–9 [8].

51. See Murray G. H. Pittock, *The Invention of Scotland: The Stuart myth and the Scottish identity, 1638 to the present* (London and New York, 1991), p. 4.

52. David Daiches, *Scotland and the Union* (London, 1977), p. 161.

53. David Trotter, 'Colonial Subjects', *Critical Quarterly*, 32, no. 3 (1990), pp. 3–20 [3].

54. Douglas Dunn, 'I'm right and good, you're bad', *TLS*, 1 January 1993, p. 5.

55. Mike Ellison, 'Troubled voice of Glasgow', *Guardian Weekly*, 23 October 1994, p. 29.

56. Frederic Lindsay, 'A Union that Corrupts', *Scotland on Sunday*, 29 March 1992, p. 17.

57. George Orwell, *Inside the Whale and Other Essays* (Harmondsworth, 1962), p. 72.

58. John Warrack, *Gramophone*, vol. 69 (July 1991), p. 100. It is a fine irony that *Gramophone* was founded in 1923 by a Scottish (albeit English-born) music-lover, Sir Compton Mackenzie. In 1977 Sir Simon Rattle was appointed assistant conductor of the Glasgow-based BBC Scottish Symphony Orchestra. Brought to a high level of musicianship by the Scottish conductor/composer, Ian Whyte (1901–1960), the orchestra also provided a training ground for Sir Colin Davis as well as the Scots, Sir Alexander Gibson and Bryden Thomson. Scotland's part in the development of illustrious international musical reputations is too easily forgotten, e.g. that between 1933 and 1939 Sir John Barbirolli and George Szell were principal conductors of the Scottish (now ineptly called the Royal Scottish) Orchestra.

59. On the word 'Britain' Hugh Trevor-Roper comments: 'Since the Union we have been obliged, largely in order to humour the Scots, to use the word "Britain"; and under cover of this inaccurate word (for only the Welsh and Cornish are Britons) many important differences have been concealed.' See 'Scotching the myths of devolution', *The Times*, 28 April 1976, p. 14.

60. Robert McLellan, *Collected Plays*, ed. with an introduction by Alexander Scott, 3 vols (London, 1981), I, p. 182.

61. See Donald Campbell, 'A Sense of Community; Robert McLellan: An Appreciation', *Chapman*, 43–4, 8, no. 6 and 9, no. 1 (Spring 1986), pp. 35–41 [38].

62. Edwin Morgan, 'Saturn and Other Rings', *Chapman*, 64 (Spring/Summer 1991), pp. 1–10 [10].

63. Robert Louis Stevenson, *Familiar Studies of Men and Books*, Tusitala Edition, XXVII, p. xi.

64. Eric Linklater, 'Brief and to the Point', in 'Whither Scotland? "The Free Man" Symposium', Second Instalment, *The Free Man*, I, no. 38 (22 October 1932), pp. 3–4 [3].

65. David Anderson and David MacLennan, *Roadworks: Song Lyrics for Wildcat*, selected by Edwin Morgan (Glasgow, 1987), p. 77.

66. First published in the Sir Walter Scott centennial issue of *The Week-End Scotsman*, 14 August 1971, p. 3. Included in 'Hitherto Uncollected Poems Contributed to Books and Periodicals (1920–1976)', *The Complete Poems of Hugh MacDiarmid*, II, p. 1434.

67. See Douglas Gifford, *The Dear Green Place?: The Novel in the West of Scotland* (Glasgow, 1985), pp. 10–11.

68. *The Complete Poems of Hugh MacDiarmid*, I, p. 454.

Chapter 2
Union and Enlightenment

Views of the Union

During the Scottish Parliament's debate on the Treaty of Union in 1706 there was anti-Union pamphleteering and substantial opposition to Union in Scottish cities; but on 1 May 1707 the Treaty was made law. The Act of Union united the parliaments of Scotland and England, creating the Parliament of Great Britain. The majority of Scottish nobles supported it, but in the tower of St Giles's Church in Edinburgh a sardonic carilloner struck his bells into a wedding tune with an ironic title: 'Why Should I be Sad on My Wedding Day?'[1] Towards the end of the century Robert Fergusson is less oblique in 'The Ghaists: A Kirk-yard Eclogue' (1773): 'Black be the day that e'er to England's ground / Scotland was eikit [added] by the UNION's bond'.

Scotland kept its own legal and educational systems and its Church but finally lost the nationhood which had nearly died in 1513 with James IV at Flodden and become increasingly tenuous since the Union of the Crowns in 1603. In Smollett's novel, *Humphry Clinker* (1771), the prickly Scotsman, Lismahago, is at his most factious when Matthew Bramble makes the mistake of congratulating him on the 'flourishing state of his country' as a consequence of Union. Lismahago will have none of it:

> . . . no stone was left unturned, to cajole and bribe a few
> leading men, to cram the union down the throats of the
> Scottish nation, who were surprisingly averse to the
> expedient.[2]

If the politics of Union were disreputable, their effects on Scottish people amount to dispossession and demoralization. Lismahago is adamant:

> They lost the independency of their state, the greatest
> prop of national spirit; they lost their parliament, and their
> courts of justice were subjected to the revision and
> supremacy of an English tribunal.[3]

Robert Burns castigates the treacherous Scottish commissioners as 'a parcel of rogues in a nation!'[4] Like Lismahago he rejects the argument that 'the boasted advantages which my Country reaps from a certain Union' could 'counterbalance the annihilation of her Independance, & even her very Name!'[5] Given the long incubation of parliamentary Union, the decisiveness of the Act and its long-term colonial effects, it is reasonable to be surprised that assimilation did not reduce Scotland to a barely distinguishable province of the London-dominated confederation and its swelling imperial refrain. The paradox of Scotland since 1707 is that it never lost its distinctiveness; despite what the poet Sydney Goodsir Smith calls 'the Union's faithless peace'[6] and the elisions of colonial status, it persisted in being a potential nation, a country on the cusp. The historian R. L. Mackie's classic *A Short History of Scotland* (1930; revised 1962) ends with the observation that 'after two and a half centuries of political union, and after perhaps ten centuries of southern influence, Scotland still preserves a national identity which may be difficult to define but is none the less real'.[7]

The leather-gloved fists of the St Giles carilloner proclaimed opposition to the marriage – and auspices of divorce – for all Edinburgh to hear, but for many the Act of Union was to Scotland as the birth of Christ to Christendom or Lenin's arrival at the Finland Station to the Soviet Union and world communism. Before Union all was primitive, feudal and superstitious, Scotland 'the rudest of all the European nations'.[8] After Union all was auroral promise and progress with eighteenth-century Enlightenment bringing civilization to a society of extreme backwardness, notably in politics, agriculture and, notoriously, religion. Thomas Jefferson records that Benjamin Franklin even forecast the benefits of confederation for smaller American states by referring to the Union's aggrandizement of Scotland at England's expense:

> . . . at the time of the union of England and Scotland, the Duke of Argyle was most violently opposed to that measure, and among other things predicted that, as the whale had swallowed Jonah, so Scotland would be swallowed by England. However . . . when Lord Bute came into the government, he soon brought into its administration so many of his countrymen, that it was found in the event that Jonah swallowed the whale.[9]

While some commentators appear to believe that the Act of Union was like the throwing of a switch after which an English-style utopia leapt immediately into being, others have been more cautious. Education, for example, is castigated for dragging its feet well into the twentieth century. According to the historian, Christopher Smout, writing in 1977, Scottish educators persisted in believing that 'teaching consists of trying to smash facts into children'.[10] (He adds: 'How can constructive consensus, adventure and innovation be produced in a society where phalanges of silent children arrive at the universities with their pens poised to catch truth as it drips from their teachers' lips?'[11]) Scottish agriculture was held to be a prime cause of widespread poverty because of its adherence to obsolete methods, and religion blamed for consuming Scottish energies in strife-ridden fanaticism. For Henry Thomas Buckle, writing his *History of Civilization in England* in the mid-nineteenth century, Enlightenment had failed to rescue the country from the acrid Presbyterianism of a 'badly fed, badly housed, and not over-cleanly people'. Scotland was inimical to intellect: the free-thinker could be ostracized even in Edinburgh, 'the centre of intelligence which once boasted of being the Modern Athens', where 'a whisper will quickly circulate that such an one is to be avoided'. Buckle knows his views will not be welcome in Scotland but 'deliberately' affirms that

> . . . in no civilized country is toleration so little
> understood, and that in none is the spirit of bigotry and of
> persecution so extensively diffused. Nor can any one
> wonder that such should be the case, who observes what
> is going on there. The churches are as crowded as they
> were in the Middle Ages, and are filled with devout and
> ignorant worshippers, who flock together to listen to
> opinions of which the Middle Ages alone were
> worthy . . . And the result is, that there runs through the
> entire country a sour fanatical spirit, an aversion to
> innocent gaiety, a disposition to limit the enjoyments of
> others . . . while . . . there flourishes a national creed,
> gloomy and austere to the last degree.[12]

Recent historians have taken issue with the view of an immovably dour, primitive and fanatical pre-Union Scotland, seeing it as a Unionist myth constructed by English travellers, English historians or those Scottish intellectuals who have too readily adopted a metropolitan perspective in their determination to avoid the contempt bestowed on their countrymen by superior beings from outside Scotland. In accordance with the process of cultural intimidation described by Frantz Fanon,[13] the low estimate of Scottish culture held by the colonizer, England, as the representative of civilization has been 'taken up by the *évolués*, those natives who try to escape from their backwardness by desperate identification with the culture of the metropolis'.[14] Superficiality or vested psychology are thus held responsible for the assertion that 'Scotland before 1707 was backward, bloody and barbarous, that it was saved by the Union . . . and that thereafter economic progress and civilization flowed benignly northwards from England'.[15] According to such a view, when it came to saving the benighted Scots from themselves the altruistic English could perform trans-Pennine miracles, causing their civilization to flow promptly uphill.

Certainly, Scotland was a small country of limited resources on the edge of Europe. Economic benefits undoubtedly accrued from the amalgamation with England, but there is evidence to suggest that Union coincided with an already developing spirit of change as urged, for example, by Andrew Fletcher of Saltoun who became known as 'the Patriot' for his opposition to an incorporating Union.[16] (Nigel Tranter's 1982 novel *The Patriot* is about Fletcher.) Fletcher believed that Scottish interests were invariably sacrificed to English, arguing that Scotland's trading links with Europe had been broken and that Scotland was drawn into wars fought for England's benefit. The measure of independence ostensibly safeguarded by the Act of Union was illusory: Scotland was controlled by patronage and Court appointees. Fletcher's most significant political works are *Two Discourses Concerning the Affairs of Scotland* (1698) about self-generated Scottish economic improvement, in the second of which he offers radical solutions to problems of rural poverty; the pamphlet, *State of the Controversy betwixt United and Separate Parliaments* (1706), which proposes a federation with Scotland and England retaining separate parliaments; and a Platonic dialogue entitled *An Account of a Conversation Concerning the Right Regulation of Governments for the Common Good of Mankind in A Letter to the Marquis of Montrose, the Earls of Rothes, Roxburgh and Haddington* (1704). In this imaginary conversation Fletcher has the pro-Union Earl of Cromarty argue for incorporation on the grounds that free commerce with England and a share of the English plantation trade would prove advantageous to the Scots. A century later Sir Walter Scott's Bailie Nicol Jarvie in *Rob Roy* (1818) similarly defends the Union in terms of its economic advantage to Glasgow:

> There's nathing sae gude on this side o' time but it might
> have been better, and that may be said o' the Union.
> Nane were keener against it than the Glasgow folks, wi'
> their rabblings and their risings, and their mobs, as they
> ca' them now-a-days. But it's an ill wind blaws naebody
> gude. Let ilka ane [every one] roose the ford [take their
> own way] as they find it. I say, Let Glasgow flourish!
> Whilk [which] is judiciously and elegantly putten round
> the town's arms [coat of arms], by way of by-word. Now,
> since St. Mungo catched herrings in the Clyde, what was
> ever like to gar us [cause us to] flourish like the sugar and
> tobacco trade? Will onybody tell me that, and grumble at
> a treaty that opened us a road west-awa' [westward]
> yonder?

(Chapter 27)

The prosperity of eighteenth-century Glasgow sugar, tobacco and cotton merchants vindicates Fletcher's Cromarty in economic terms[17] but debate continues about the accompanying disadvantages, particularly among intellectuals of the resurgent Scottish National Party for whom Fletcher has understandably assumed heroic proportions. In *Past and Present* (1843) Thomas Carlyle appropriates William Wallace to his programme of hero-worship but fudges the issue of Union:

> A heroic Wallace, quartered on the scaffold, cannot hinder that his Scotland become, one day, a part of England: but he does hinder that it become, on tyrannous unfair terms, a part of it; commands still, as with a god's voice, from his old Valhalla and Temple of the Brave, that there be a just real union as of brother and brother, not a false and merely semblant one as of slave and master. If the union with England be in fact one of Scotland's chief blessings, we thank Wallace withal that it was not the chief curse.
>
> (Book I, Chapter 2)

But what side of the fence does Carlyle come down on with that 'If'? Ecclefechan, or Chelsea?

A more pragmatic view is taken by the novelist and screenwriter, Alan Sharp:

> The Scots . . . made a very interesting deal with the English. A sane deal. It had a lot of problems to it but the alternative was to have these bastards come up here and kick your arse every 25 years.[18]

The relative powers of the two countries remain similar for the novelist and political commentator, Allan Massie, and the poet and critic, Alan Riach. Massie's character, Dallas Graham, in *One Night in Winter* (1984), 'couldn't take the idea of a Scottish state seriously. That was an old song, long ended, sold down the river' (Part 1, Chapter 6). In his fifteenth-century romance, *The Hanging Tree* (1990), King James I, 'who had long been held as a hostage in England . . . had grown to like and respect his jailers, and had indeed acquired a cockney accent and an English wife' (Book 1, Chapter 9). Anglicization is associated with the improvement of Scottish life, even if it is the crookback villain, Maurie, who denigrates Scotland's alliance with France in favour of closer ties with England: 'What has France to offer that can compare with the friendship of England, or that can contribute in like manner to the peace and prosperity of this kingdom?' (Book 2, Chapter 1). Geography and a different sifting

of history provide Riach with imagery that refuses to compromise the
nationalist ideal:

> – Scotland is surrounded on all sides with sea,
> Except one, to which it bears
> A proximity much like a candle
> Burning brightly in the black eye–socket
> Of a tremendous skull.[19]

The Presbyterian inheritance

William Soutar hands down his judgement of Presbyterian obsessions in
his poem, 'The Philosophic Taed':

> There was a taed wha thocht sae lang   *toad*
> On sanctity and sin;
> On what was richt, and what was wrang,
> And what was in atween –
> That he gat naething dune.[20]   *done*

If Scotland before and after Union was preternaturally fixated on matters
of religion, the only essential rigidity was in the intensity of the involvement. Debate kept going. The strengths of the Calvinist inheritance were
'moral seriousness, distrust of complacency' and, above all, 'passion for
theoretical argument'.[21] These effects of the Scottish Reformation are
well gauged by Hugh Miller, a stonemason, geologist and journalist from
Cromarty, who made his first journey south of the border in 1845 and
describes it in *First Impressions of England and its People* (1847). In a lodging
house in Newcastle he becomes embroiled in a theological discussion
about the doctrine of atonement, the reconciliation of God and man
through the shedding of Christ's blood. Unimpressed by the amateurish
quality of arguments advanced by two Methodists from Sheffield, an
English Calvinist, and a sceptical country gentleman, Miller offers a closely
reasoned proof of the doctrine, whereupon he is arraigned by a commercial traveller: 'You Scotch are a strange people . . . When I was in Scotland two years ago, I could hear of scarce anything among you but your
Church question. What good does all your theology do you?' Miller's
reply would have ingratiated him with John Henry, Cardinal Newman:

> Independently altogether of religious considerations . . . it
> has done for our people what all your Societies for the
> Diffusion of Useful Knowledge and all your Penny and

Saturday magazines will never do for yours: it has
awakened their intellects, and taught them how to think.
The development of the popular mind in Scotland is a
result of its theology.[22]

Yet theological writing in Scotland showed little distinction before
the middle of the eighteenth century,[23] when Hugh Blair published *The
Wrath of Man Praising God* (1746) and *The Importance of Religious Knowledge
to the Happiness of Mankind* (1750) and preached his unprecedentedly
popular sermons in Edinburgh, the Glasgow-based Irishman, Francis
Hutcheson, harmonized Christian Stoicism with the moral sense in his
System of Moral Philosophy (1755) and Thomas Reid postulated his theory
of common sense on the wisdom of God in *An Inquiry into the Human
Mind on the Principles of Common Sense* (1764). Nevertheless, the turbulent
'Church question' and its theological implications had dominated Scottish
cultural life at least since the signing of the National Covenant in February 1638. By the Solemn League and Covenant of 1643 the Covenanters allied themselves uneasily with English parliamentarians during the
Civil War only to find their hopes undermined by English indifference
and the pro-Royalist campaigns of James Graham, Marquis of Montrose.
After the harassment of the Covenanters' field conventicles and ten years
after their cause was crushed by John Graham of Claverhouse at the
Battle of Bothwell Brig in 1679 came, ironically, the disestablishment
of Episcopacy as a consequence of the Glorious Revolution of 1688,
although even in 1716 Episcopalian clergy in Edinburgh outnumbered
ministers of the Established Church and Episcopacy remained supreme
from rural Aberdeenshire to Ardnamurchan, Glencoe and the western
islands of Tiree and Coll.[24] In a few northern districts most people were,
as they still are, Roman Catholics. Gradually the Episcopalians were
caught in a net of penal laws, with George I ordering all Episcopal chapels
in Edinburgh to be closed. Some thirty years later, before and after the
Battle of Culloden, persecution became more severe and chapels were
systematically destroyed by the Duke of Cumberland. Invariably, throughout this tortuous history, it is an anti-authoritarian reaction that starts a
new phase. When the Patronage Act of 1712 restored the right of church
patrons to choose parish ministers it initiated the resistance to political
interference which culminated in the Disruption of 1843 and the establishment of the Free Church of Scotland.

It may be argued that Scotland's obsession with religion stunted its
growth in political debate. As Lady Clementina says to Florimel in George
MacDonald's *The Marquis of Lossie* (1877), 'The Scotch are always preaching! I believe it is in their blood. You are a nation of parsons' (Chapter
39). If there was a profligacy of parsons, ordained and amateur, there was
a shortage of committed secular political intellect to combat the arguments

for Union. Energies were deflected from major political issues into the surrogate politics of theology and the Church question, and assimilation into the state of Great Britain was facilitated by schism within and distraction by the Church: a divided Scottish Church made it easier for London to rule the northern territory. But Hugh Miller was right too: religion developed intellects and taught people how to think in terms of first principles. David Hume's reputation as a sceptic hostile to religion cost him the Chair of Moral Philosophy at the University of Edinburgh in 1744 and seven years later the Chair of Logic at the University of Glasgow, but the Scottish flair for scepticism has its roots in theological contention. There may have been too much rote learning in Scottish schools – where was there not? – but philosophical training formed the basis of university education in which, characteristically, first principles were applied to questions about human nature and society. In the logic class taught by George Jardine, a favourite pupil of Adam Smith's and Professor of Logic at the University of Glasgow from 1774 to 1827:

> the themes set are often concerned less with pure
> philosophy than with the problem of applying first or
> philosophical principles to literary, historical, linguistic and
> economic subjects. Thus Jardine speaks of the following as
> stock subjects for essays: What is the ground of distinction
> between the liberal and the mechanical arts? – How may
> the Iliad and the Odyssey be compared, and on what
> principle is the preference determined? – What was the
> state of the Highlands of Scotland as indicated by the
> poems of Ossian? . . . Jardine not merely gives titles but
> indicates clearly, with examples, that the essay writers were
> always expected to bring the subject of discussion back to
> first principles.[25]

The Scottish religious temper thus fostered the philosophical character of higher education and intellectual life more generally. This is the context in which must be set the applied philosophies of David Hume, the father of Scottish philosophy, and Adam Smith, the father of modern economics.

The Enlightenment: David Hume and Adam Smith

Early colonists of America had little time for art. The requirements of life in a new country – survival, construction, assessment – encouraged utilitarian forms of expression, the prose of reports, histories, sermons, diaries, economic and political treatises. It is not surprising, therefore, that the first distinguished literature to come from the traumatized new Scotland includes the speculative, applied work of Hume and Smith whose philosophical stock-taking was compelled outwards from parochial issues towards universal concerns by Scotland's new constitutional involvement in the rest of Britain and the wider world and by the milieu of the Enlightenment. For intellectuals the Act of Union redefined their country and their relation to the world. It was a time to question the nature of institutions, of the self and society and the relations between them. God, humanity and the universe were under review.

In hindsight, the near-simultaneity of so much varied Scottish creativity gives the period from Union to the death of Scott in 1832 the appearance of a multi-disciplinary intellectual project. While reason took palpable form in the orderly grid construction of Edinburgh's elegant New Town, science and medicine flourished and thinkers congregated in the energized city, which became known as 'The Athens of the North'. Scottish medical faculties outshone those of the hitherto pre-eminent Dutch universities, William Cullen and Joseph Black set new standards in the teaching and development of chemistry and medicine in Glasgow and Edinburgh, and James Watt, befriended and financed by Black and inspired by Black's discovery of latent heat, invented the steam condenser. Glasgow's William and John Hunter went to London to revolutionize obstetrics and anatomy, Charles Mackintosh developed his waterproofing process using naphtha, Robert Adam and his brothers achieved fame as neo-classical architects in the 1760s, and, by the end of the century, Thomas Telford, a Dumfriesshire shepherd's son, had built over 1,000 bridges in Scotland and the Menai suspension bridge to Anglesey. In portrait painting Allan Ramsay – the poet Allan Ramsay's eldest son – and Henry Raeburn were the equals of Hogarth and Gainsborough.

Philosophical and literary ideas were debated in Edinburgh's Select Society (1754–63) whose members included its instigator, Allan Ramsay junior, Alexander 'Jupiter' Carlyle whose amiable, posthumously published *Autobiography* (1860) includes an account of the more patriotic Poker Club (1762–87), David Hume, Adam Smith and the eccentric Judge James Burnett, Lord Monboddo, who, in his six-volume *Antient Metaphysics* (1779–99), not only returned to his conviction that the orang-utan initiated human history but also anticipated the C. P. Snow–F. R. Leavis crisis of confrontation between science and the humanities in the late 1950s by arguing that the advancement of culture depends on the coexistence of philosophy and the sciences. Henry Home, Lord Kames, judge, philosopher and gentleman farmer, wrote his *Essays on the Principles of Morality and Natural Religion* (1751) in opposition to the philosophy of Hume, yet among his associates were not only the popular divine Hugh Blair, James Burnett, and Dr Johnson's biographer James Boswell, but also David Hume's friend Adam Smith. Disagreements among these principals

of the Scottish Enlightenment across a range of subjects from the existence of God to the use of the Scots tongue stimulated the intellectual
effervescence of a period distinguished by a network of outstandingly
gifted minds whose common disposition was to refer questions to first
principles.

'In the long run,' says John MacQueen, 'the most influential book
written by a Scot of the earlier Enlightenment was probably David Hume's
A Treatise of Human Nature.'[26] In prose of sustained elegance Hume –
twenty-eight years old when the work was published in 1739 – amplifies
the empiricism of John Locke and Bishop George Berkeley into a passionate scepticism, replacing reason with subjective imagination. 'Men
are mightily governed by the imagination,' he writes in the *Treatise*, 'and
proportion their affections more to the light under which any object
appears to them, than to its real and intrinsic value.'[27] Laws are necessary
to curb natural partiality but absolute ideas of divine right and infallible
hierarchy are disposed of: society must be political for the collective good,
but government is 'composed of men subject to all human infirmities'.[28]
Grasping the first principles of Locke's philosophical system, that the
mind can have precise impressions of distinct facts, the problem Hume set
himself was to find a way of establishing connections between the facts.
We may see the black billiard ball hit the white one and the white one
move, but despite guesswork based on previous observation, we cannot
know that the impact of the black ball causes the movement of the white
one or that it will do so again. The supposition that the future will
resemble the past is derived not from reason but from habit.

Hume's secular and materialist insistence on subjective imagination as
an organ of limited cognition anticipates the poet Norman MacCaig's
quizzical recognition of the mystery of perception in 'An Ordinary Day':

> I took my mind a walk
> or my mind took me a walk –
> whichever was the truth of it.
>
> The light glittered on the water
> or the water glittered in the light.
> . . .
>
> and my mind observed to me,
> or I to it, how ordinary
> extraordinary things are or
>
> how extraordinary ordinary
> things are, like the nature of the mind
> and the process of observing.[29]

The modern poet can let the problem go at that, neatly contained in his provocative rhetorical circles, but the eighteenth-century empirical philosopher has a stricter obligation to the prosaic world of ordinary days and finds a way out of his *impasse* in the Association of Ideas:

> These are, therefore, the principles of union or cohesion among our simple ideas, and in the imagination supply the place of that inseparable connection by which they are united in our memory. Here is a kind of attraction, which in the mental world will be found to have as extraordinary effects as in the natural, and to show itself in as many and various forms.[30]

In *An Abstract of a Book lately Published; Entituled A Treatise of Human Nature & Etc* (1740) Hume says of the principles of association – resemblance, contiguity and causation – 'as these are the only ties of our thoughts, they are really *to us* the cement of the universe, and all the operations of the mind must, in a great measure, depend on them'.[31]

In 1879 James (B. V.) Thomson described Hume as one whose

> calm and subtle Scepticism, so irritatingly obnoxious to the dominant dogmatism of British thought, has gathered such thick clouds of prejudice about him, steamed up and steaming up evermore from those humid flats and sluggish swamps which form so large a part of the intellectual realm of our happy nation, that it requires the keenest and steadiest and strongest insight to see the philosopher and his philosophy in plainness and truth.[32]

Yet Hume's central position is clear, even if the intimidatingly logical Bertrand Russell finds it difficult to grasp. Discovering in Hume an analytical intellect superior to Locke's, Russell nevertheless says that the *Treatise* 'represents the bankruptcy of eighteenth-century reasonableness' because Hume 'arrives at the disastrous conclusion that from experience and observation nothing is to be learnt'.[33] This is mistaken. The scepticism Hume learned from his rejection of the principle of induction overthrows previously held ideas of reason but rebuilds the rational faculty with constituents previously regarded as non-rational:

> . . . all probable reasoning is nothing but a species of sensation. It is not only in poetry and music we must follow our taste and sentiment, but likewise in philosophy. When I am convinced of any principle it is only an idea which strikes more strongly upon me. When I give the

preference to one set of arguments above another, I do
nothing but decide from my feeling concerning the
superiority of their influence.[34]

Tough-minded philosophical analysis thus instates individual experience,
imagination, taste and sentiment, aligning Hume with other proponents
of the fundamentally democratic value of sympathy in the age of reason.
Among the poems of Pope it was the affecting *Elegy to the Memory of an
Unfortunate Lady* that Hume memorized. His letter of 15 October 1754
to Pope's friend Joseph Spence implies that he has used the *Elegy* to gauge
the sensibility of the blind Scottish poet, Thomas Blacklock:

> I repeated to him Mr Pope's Elegy to Memory of an
> unfortunate Lady, which I happen'd to have by heart: And
> though I be a very bad Reciter, I saw it affected him
> extremely. His eyes, indeed, the great Index of the Mind,
> cou'd express no Passion: but his whole Body was thrown
> into Agitation: That Poem was equally qualified, to touch
> the Delicacy of his Taste, and the Tenderness of his
> Feelings.[35]

Blacklock's agitation, presumably, meant that he had passed the test as a
man of feeling. Hume's philosophy of feeling brings him into a kinship
of sensibility with Adam Smith, Henry Mackenzie and Robert Burns, and
it underlies the literary theorizing of Lord Kames in his influential *Elements of Criticism* (1762). Beauty, says Kames, is not inherent in an object
but is as dependent on the percipient as on the object perceived. He
endorses the saying that 'beauty is not in the person beloved but in the
lover's eye'. Beauty, like other principles, is an idea accessible to sympathy.[36]

As tutor to the 3rd Duke of Buccleuch, David Hume's friend, Adam
Smith of Kirkcaldy, spent the years 1764–66 in Paris and Geneva. He
had already held the Chairs of both Logic and Moral Philosophy at the
University of Glasgow and in Paris was received into the company of
French economists known as the 'Physiocrats'. The group's leaders,
Quesnay and Turgot, were exponents of the principles of free trade,
holding views Smith had already formed for himself, but doubtless encouraging him to embark on the work for which he is best known, *An
Inquiry into the Nature and Causes of the Wealth of Nations* (1776), the basis
of *laissez-faire* capitalist economic theory and practice. From Smith's perception that wealth does not consist in precious metals but in goods the
book develops its argument in terms of two dominant ideas: first, that the
division of labour is fundamental to industrial progress and, second, that
government interference in the regulation of industry and trade is invariably pernicious. Adam Smith thus enters history as the apostle of free

trade or market economy. *The Wealth of Nations* is one of the world's two most influential discussions of economic theory, the other being *Das Kapital*. 'If Marx gains by passion,' as Allan Massie puts it, 'Smith has the advantage of sense.'[37]

With hindsight a socialist point of view may find against Smith for a political economy which requires a caste system, thereby degrading the indispensable working classes, but he recognizes rather than recommends the stratification of society. Both Hume and Smith insist on freedom and respect for the individual. Although Smith's *Theory of Moral Sentiments* (1759) brought him immediate fame, it has long since been eclipsed by *The Wealth of Nations*, but it should be remembered as belonging to a Scottish pedigree with its practical sense of social justice and its doctrine of natural sympathy as the instinctive bond between people in their social and ethical relations. Sympathy is not abjured in the analyses of economic forces in *The Wealth of Nations*, even if the idea of self-interest is funda-mental to Smith's theorizing. It is not the benevolence of the butcher that brings us our dinner but his regard of his own interest. The real price of everything, Smith says in Book I, Chapter 5, is the trouble to ourselves of acquiring it, hence the development of economic systems based on the self-interested relegation to others of labour we are not equipped to undertake or find disagreeable:

> What everything is really worth to the man who has
> acquired it, and who wants to dispose of it or exchange it
> for something else, is the toil and trouble which it can
> save to himself, and which it can impose on other people.
> What is bought with money or with goods is purchased
> by labour as much as what we acquire by the toil of our
> own body. That money or those goods indeed save us this
> toil.[38]

This is how self-interest determines an economic system of which the sinister side is an inevitable conspiracy against the public:

> People of the same trade seldom meet together, even for
> merriment and diversion, but the conversation ends in a
> conspiracy against the public, or in some contrivance to
> raise prices . . . But though the law cannot hinder people
> of the same trade from sometimes assembling together, it
> ought to do nothing to facilitate such assemblies, much
> less to render them necessary.[39]

Governments must beware of vested interests and treat with suspicion the advice of merchants and master manufacturers. Such advice comes 'from an order of men whose interest is never exactly the same with that of the public, who have generally an interest to deceive and oppress the public'.[40] But Smith's recognition of the ways in which self-interest operates prompts him to emphasize the social equity which must be achieved in spite of it. Central to his discussion 'Of the Wages of Labour' in Book I, Chapter 8 is the view that

> No society can surely be flourishing and happy, of which the greater part of the members are poor and miserable. It is but equity, besides, that they who feed, clothe, and lodge the whole body of the people, should have such a share of the produce of their own labour as to be themselves tolerably well fed, clothed, and lodged.[41]

Sympathy, imagination and common sense: the Byronic synthesis

The Scottish and European Enlightenments coincided and cross-pollinated. While Scottish economic theory was buttressed by French ideas, Scottish ideas about sympathy were indebted to Descartes. According to a Cartesian antithesis, sensory pain presses injuriously inwards, but outgoing emotion is a healthy and pleasurable psychological workout. The ethically ordered pain of tragedy provides an opportunity for beneficial responsory exercise in sympathetic enjoyment of the apprehension of distress.[42] Belief in the personal and social value of vigorous emotional response characterizes the views of tragic pleasure held by the Scottish *literati*. For the Aberdonian theologist and rhetorician George Campbell 'the fact itself, that the mind derives pleasure from representations of anguish, is undeniable'.[43] Joy has 'less of the attractive power than grief', which disposes the mind to take 'a mournful satisfaction in being allowed to indulge its anguish, and to immerse itself wholly in its own afflictions'.[44] 'A scene of unmixed joy in a work of art cannot give great or lasting pleasure because 'sympathetic joy is much fainter and more transient than sympathetic grief'.[45] Henry Home, Lord Kames, begins his *Essays on the Principles of Morality and Natural Religion* by considering 'our Attachment to Objects of Distress'. When the passion of grief is at its highest, 'the very nature of it is to shun and fly from every thing which tends to give ease or comfort'.[46] This reflects 'a singular phenomenon in human nature which explains the pleasure of tragedy, an appetite after pain, an inclination to render one's self miserable'.[47] Hugh Blair finds the purpose of tragedy in its power to affect the heart: 'The pathetic, it must be remembered, is the soul of Tragedy.'[48] The self goes out in compassion for the sufferer, but the emotional dividend is pleasure in the exercise of benevolent sympathy (the kind of pleasure to be had from Henry Mackenzie's 1771 novel, *The Man of Feeling*):

> The heart is warmed by kindness and humanity, at the same moment at which it is afflicted by the distresses of those with whom it sympathizes: and the pleasure arising from those kind emotions, prevails so much in the mixture, and so far counterbalances the pain, as to render the state of the mind, upon the whole, agreeable. At the same time, the immediate pleasure, which always goes along with the operation of the benevolent and sympathetic affections, derives an addition from the approbation of our own minds. We are pleased with ourselves, for feeling as we ought, and for entering with proper sorrow, into the concerns of the afflicted.[49]

Emotion was held suspect by the School of Scottish Realism – otherwise known as the 'Common-Sense' school of Scottish philosophy – in its opposition to the radical subjectivity of David Hume's theory of perception. Thomas Reid, Adam Smith's successor to the Glasgow Chair of Moral Philosophy and the principal 'Common-Sense' epistemologist, regarded the imagination as an embellishing faculty which created a barrier to knowledge, and hypotheses as mere products of imagination. Basic to common sense was the existence of God; the imagination was arrogant and vain:

> Now, though we may, in many cases, form very probable conjectures concerning the works of men, every conjecture we can form with regard to the works of GOD, has as little probability as the conjectures of a child with regard to the works of a man . . . For until the wisdom of men bears some proportion to the wisdom of GOD, their attempts to find out the structure of his works by the force of their wit and genius, will be vain.[50]

In Reid's opinion – which was upheld by his leading exponent, Dugald Stewart – hypotheses are 'the reveries of vain and fanciful men whose pride makes them conceive themselves able to unfold the mysteries of nature by the force of their genius'.[51] Thus philosophical battle was joined between individual experience, imagination and sympathy as comprising one definition of the constituents of cognitive reason, and inductive procedures as another. Against this background must be seen the splendour of Coleridge's definition of the 'esemplastic power' of imagination in Chapter 13 of *Biographia Literaria* (1817): 'the living power and prime agent of all human perception ... a repetition in the finite mind of the eternal act of creation in the infinite I AM'.[52] For a writer of Scottish descent who closes the gap between subjectivity and inductive common sense we must look forward to George Gordon, Lord Byron. His volatile subjective imagination produces the most extreme Romantic self-portraiture and the model of the Byronic hero, while a matching inductive propensity gives him 'a more observant eye for the general spectacle of the world than any of his contemporaries'.[53] Resolved to stand with neither Whigs nor Tories, he spoke as a Radical about particulars within the general spectacle in his maiden speech in the House of Lords on 27 February 1812, opposing with both practical reason and humane feeling a government-proposed bill which called for the death penalty for frame-breaking:

> Setting aside the palpable injustice and the certain
> inefficiency of the Bill, are there not capital punishments
> sufficient in your statutes? Is there not blood enough upon
> your penal code ... ? How will you carry the Bill into
> effect? Can you commit a whole country to their own
> prisons? Will you erect a gibbet in every field, and hang
> up men like scarecrows?[54]

When it came to the everyday circumstances of real people he was, when he chose, the opposite of the 'metaphysical' Shelley whom John Galt criticizes in his *Life of Lord Byron* for 'a singular incapacity of conceiving the existing state of things as it practically affects the nature and condition of man'.[55] But Byron's Radicalism developed into belief that the existing state of things proved 'the ineffectiveness of politics as such, of sway achieved by representation and persuasion'.[56] This became the subject of his play, *Sardanapalus* (1821),[57] but did not prevent him from identifying with the cause of Greece.

Byron was hard on Coleridge, although he tried to help him and admired 'Christabel'. The Dedication of *Don Juan* (1819–24), an attack on the reactionary poet laureate, Robert Southey, includes a swipe at Coleridge's theorizing:

> And Coleridge too has lately taken wing,
>   But like a hawk encumbered with his hood,
> Explaining metaphysics to the nation.
> I wish he would explain his explanation.
>
> (stanza 2)

Yet there is no more assertive or independently creative 'I AM' in literature than Byron's, even allowing for what Keats calls 'the wordsworthian or egotistical sublime'.[58] As Galt says, 'The progress of no other poet's mind can be so clearly traced to personal experience as that of Byron's.'[59] In both his erratic life and his uneven poetry he combines, at his best, an inductive grasp of the real world with a subjective imagination of the highest voltage, 'half dust, half deity' like his own Faustian hero, Manfred. Proud, given to reveries of the length of *Childe Harold's Pilgrimage* (1812–18), the untheatrical drama, *Manfred* (1817), and the unfinished epic satire, *Don Juan*, he is a 'mix'd essence', resolving the tension between Hume's philosophy of subjectivity and the opposed convictions of the Common-Sense school in a uniquely self-conscious synthesis. Subjective idealism creates the love idyll of Haidee and Don Juan, but realism – what Graham Hough calls Byron's 'simultaneous awareness of flat earthy reality'[60] – knows that the idyll must end:

> . . . for they were children still
>   And children still they should have ever been.
> They were not made in the real world to fill
>   A busy character in the dull scene,
> But like two beings born from out a rill,
>   A nymph and her belovèd, all unseen
> To pass their lives in fountains and on flowers
> And never know the weight of human hours.
> (*Don Juan*, IV, 15)

Although he was born in London, Scotland claims Byron through his mother, Catherine Gordon of Gight (a descendant of James I of Scotland), his early education at Aberdeen Grammar School, and his sense of sin. 'I was bred a canny Scot till ten years old,' he writes to Sir Walter Scott in 1822,[61] and in the calculatedly digressive *Don Juan* – a precursor of Hugh MacDiarmid's *A Drunk Man Looks at the Thistle* (1926) – says, 'I am half a Scot by birth, and bred / A whole one' (X, 17). He is the very model of a Romantic Caledonian antisyzygy, at once lyrical (if coolly so), sceptical and neo-classical. Both liberal and aristocrat, he is a 'moderate-minded bard' (*Don Juan*, I, 118) given to excess in love and politics, sickened by the failure of revolutionary egalitarian ideals in the reactionary age of Napoleon, Metternicht and the 'intellectual eunuch', Castlereagh (*Don Juan*, Dedication, 11), dreaming 'that Greece might still be free' (*Don Juan*, III, 86, iii), and dying unheroically for Greek independence of rheumatic fever in a military cot in Missolonghi. He can gorge on a full-blown Romantic image of himself as 'The wandering outlaw of his own dark mind' (*Childe Harold*, III, 3), sound as mystical as Wordsworth (whom he deplored) when he says, 'I live not in myself, but I become

/ Portion of that around me' (*Childe Harold*, III, 72) and be stirred by 'the feeling infinite' which 'makes known / Eternal harmony' (*Childe Harold*, III, 90), before declaring in the next Canto an allegiance to 'waking Reason' (*Childe Harold*, IV, 7). In *Don Juan* he swerves again with the observation that 'Man being reasonable must get drunk; / The best of life is but intoxication' (*Don Juan*, II, 179). In the Tales which began to appear in 1813, beginning with *The Giaour* and *The Bride of Abydos*, he embarked on a series of exotic poems about 'passionate young men at odds with their environment'[62] which established him as Sir Walter Scott's rival in poetry. At his centre, when we cut through the rhetoric, the preening, epigrammatic post-Augustan wit, the contrariness, voluptuousness and what Scott called 'his misanthropical ennui',[63] his ultimate appeal is the disarming honesty of his confessed perplexity and the wry sweetness of his shrugged question:

> Man's a phenomenon, one knows not what,
>   And wonderful beyond all wondrous measure.
> 'Tis pity though in this sublime world that
>   Pleasure's a sin and sometimes sin's a pleasure.
> Few mortals know what end they would be at,
>   But whether glory, power or love or treasure,
> The path is through perplexing ways, and when
> The goal is gained, we die you know — and then?
>   (*Don Juan*, I, 133)

Writing by women: realism, reticence and determination

While men were occupied with post-Union politics, philosophy, social theory, economics and the milieu of revolution, women writers maintained, often anonymously, a brief for the more immediate realities of love, rural life and the household. Women had always been less literate as a group than men and had long filled a prominent role as purveyors of oral culture, especially in the Highlands where conversation and song were central to their lives. In the seventeenth century 'women came for the first time to occupy a place as poets in the Gaelic bardic tradition, helping to shape the subject matter of the verses',[64] and Sir Walter Scott collected several of his Border ballads from women. The number of published Scottish women writers increased dramatically in the late eighteenth and early nineteenth centuries, making neglect of their work until recently a cause of critical embarrassment.

With increased literacy among women, song remained a favourite medium. Lady Grizel Baillie is remembered less for the memorabilia of her *Household Book* (1911)[65] than for her touchingly stoical and sociologically revealing song, 'Werena my heart licht, I wad dee', about blighted young love, published in 1724 in Ramsay's *The Tea-Table Miscellany*. Anne Barnard (née Lady Anne Lindsay) is remembered for her poem, 'Auld Robin Gray' (1776; composed 1771), although her letters from the Cape of Good Hope, where she accompanied her husband in 1797–1802, give an illuminating personal account of life in the South African colony to be set beside the testimony of Thomas Pringle's *African Sketches, Narrative of a Residence in South Africa* (1834) with its outspokenly anti-slavery poems. (Pringle has been called 'possibly South Africa's first white "protest" poet'.[66]) But one song or poem can be enough: no Scottish writer is more properly assured of immortality among the people of her country than Jean Elliot by her composition, based on a traditional verse fragment,[67] of 'The Flowers of the Forest', a harrowing lament for young men killed at the catastrophic Battle of Flodden, for bereaved women and fatherless children:

> I've heard them lilting, at the ewe milking,
>   Lasses a' lilting, before dawn of day;
> But now they are moaning, on ilka green   *common pasture*
>   loaning;
>   The flowers of the forest are a' wede away.[68]   *all weeded out*

The song grieves through a day from dawn to gloaming, commemorating the human loss that spoils the tranquil activities of country life – milking, shearing, harvesting and the binding of sheaves, games of chase around the corn stacks, going to the fair or to church. Its refrain, rhythm and rhymes, together with the tune first written down in 1620,[69] set up a keening tone; but the anger comes through, too, as perhaps it only could from a woman, in a protest against the impersonality of war and the auld enemy's cunning:

> Dool and wae for the order, sent our lads to the   *Grief and woe*
>   border!
>   The English for ance, by guile wan the day;   *once*
> The flowers of the forest, that fought aye the
>   foremost,
>   The prime of our land, are cauld in the clay.[70]

This flawless song was first published in David Herd's *The Ancient and Modern Scots Songs, Heroic Ballads, Etc* (1769) under the title 'Flowdenhill: or, Flowers of the Forest', but it was probably composed in 1763 or 1764.

According to Sir Walter Scott, Alison Cockburn's song of the same title, first published in 1765, refers not to Flodden but to a financial disaster in the Ettrick Forest where seven lairds were ruined in one year. Although it was at least as well known as Jean Elliot's version, it is as much less intense as its anglicized diction is more conventionally literary:

> I've seen the smiling of Fortune beguiling,
> I've felt all its favours and found its decay;
> Sweet was its blessing, kind its caressing,
> But now it is fled, fled far, far away.[71]

Not economic theory or estate management but the power of money over ordinary people is a theme common to Lady Grizel Baillie, Anne Barnard, Alison Cockburn and Joanna Baillie. The materialism of the young man's family thwarts the lovers in 'Werena my heart licht, I wad dee', and young Jamie's determination to provide sufficiently for his future wife initiates the downfall of true love in 'Auld Robin Gray':

> Young Jamie loo'd me weel, and sought me for his bride;
> But saving ae crown-piece, he'd naething else beside.
> To make the crown a pound, my Jamie gaed to sea;
> And the crown and the pound, oh! they were baith for
>   me![72]

While young Jamie is at sea, presumed drowned, Jenny yields to the courting of auld Robin Gray because he has provided, as she could not, for her parents whose misfortunes disastrously coincide with Jamie's well-intentioned absence. Jamie's return from sea to find his sweetheart out of reach points the tragic implications of an emphasis on pelf and illustrates the unenlightened social entrapment of women, with broken-hearted but resolutely self-denying Jenny as the bartered chattel and victim of emotional blackmail in a marriage of parental convenience. Alison Cockburn's elegy in her 'Flowers of the Forest' is for the distress the lairds' ruin brings not only to themselves but to people dependent on them.

The tenant farmer in Joanna Baillie's 'A Reverie' (1790)[73] has 'no dower but love' to fix on his Nelly, and envy for the man who 'toils not daily in another's field' but, owning his own 'furnished cot', earns respect at church and market and 'makes the maid he loves an easy wife'. In Baillie's 'A Disappointment' (1790), clearly influenced by 'Werena my heart licht', money lures the frustrated young man's girl into marrying 'stiff-backed Rob' while the comely but penurious jilted lover goes stolidly home to take out his frustration on his uncomprehending dog. Consumerism and the male idea of a woman's place are gloriously spoofed in 'Hooly and Fairly (Founded on an old Scotch song)' (1840, but composed earlier) in which a 'flyting' wife's devotion to expensive drink, food and clothing, interspersed with hang-overs when she neglects her housework, drives her peevish man frantic:

> I wish I were single, I wish I were freed;
> I wish I were doited, I wish I were dead,   *crazy*
> Or she in the mouls, to dement me nae   *earth of the grave*
>   mair, lay!
>   What does it 'vail to cry hooly and   *gently (i.e. 'take it easy')*
>   fairly,
>   Hooly and fairly, hooly and fairly,
> Wasting my breath to cry hooly and
>   fairly![74]

Joanna Baillie's best poems display the qualities she commends in a letter to an unknown correspondent in New Zealand: 'feeling and fancy and the gift of harmonious and easy expression'.[75] Her poems have weathered better than the cumbersome verse dramas[76] which won her a high reputation in her lifetime and the admiration of Sir Walter Scott. (She is 'our immortal Joanna Baillie' in *The Bride of Lammermoor*, Chapter 21.) Though often marred by over-zealous efforts to be refined and by the kind of flat passages the reader must plod through in Wordsworth, her poetry offers much exact observation of rural life and behaviour, like her depiction of the uxorious cockerel and young farmer's mutual reluctance to get out of bed at the beginning of 'A Winter Day' (1790), with the wife's preparation of breakfast while children, 'peeping from the bed-clothes', respond to the cheery blaze of the newly lit fire and 'bawl for leave to rise'.[77] She can record the look of nature with touching sensitivity to detail, as in the chequered lighting effects of the setting sun toward the end of 'A Summer Day' in the poem's fresher, original version. This does not suggest emotion recollected in tranquillity, but a keen-eyed on-the-spot commentator telling us what the moment is like there and then:

> The sun, far in the west, with sidelong beam
> Plays on the yellow head of the round haycock,
> And fields are chequered with fantastic shapes,
> Or tree, or shrub, or gate, or rugged stone,
> All lengthened out in antic disproportion
> Upon the darkened grass.[78]

Her psychological acumen shows in her comments about natural infant selfishness in 'A Mother to Her Waking Infant' (1790) and in the description of evening sociability at the end of 'A Winter Day' when neighbours drop in at a friend's house. Chairs are drawn into a conversational circle:

And everyone in his own native way
Does what he can to cheer the social group.
Each tells some little story of himself,
That constant subject upon which mankind,
Whether in court or country, love to dwell.[79]

While artistic merit in Joanna Baillie's verse, if patchy, raises it above merely documentary interest, the prose works of Anne Grant and Elizabeth Hamilton retain their value as reflections of a period. Sir Walter Scott's poetry kindled interest in the life of the Highlands, assuring a public for Anne Grant's reminiscent *Letters from the Mountains* (1803) and her *Essays on the Superstitions of the Highlands of Scotland* (1811). Elizabeth Hamilton's *The Cottagers of Glenburnie* (1808) is significant as a precursor of what became known as the Kailyard novel, but, within the context of current attitudes towards the proper business of women, both Grant and Hamilton are noteworthy as early examples of professionalism in Scottish women authors for most of whom writing was a furtive or sideline activity, and publication usually anonymous. Reticence, perforce, went with the gender to the point of self-effacement. Lady Grizel Baillie 'cheerfully sacrificed her literary concerns on the altar of domestic piety',[80] and both Alison Cockburn and Jean Elliot were reluctant to admit authorship of their versions of 'The Flowers of the Forest'. Cockburn said in 1775, 'I am very certain that no woman ought to write anything but from the heart to the heart; never for the public eye, without male correction', adding later, 'As for printing, never fear. I hate print.'[81] Jean Elliot was first attributed with authorship of her perfect elegy in 1800; she supplied the 'exact copy' requested by Scott, but asked that her name 'may not be mentioned'.[82] Anne Barnard, who enjoyed the popularity of 'Auld Robin Gray', abhorred the spectacle of a woman giving herself 'the *air* of wisdom, while she knows how superficial she is . . . wilfully drawing on a pair of blue stockings she has no right to wear!'[83] and confessed: 'such was *my dread* of being suspected of writing anything, perceiving the shyness it created in those who could write *nothing*, that I carefully kept my own secret'.[84] Joanna Baillie published her poems anonymously in 1790 and only in 1800 acknowledged authorship of the first volume of her *Series of Plays* on 'the human mind under the dominion of . . . strong and fixed passions' (1798). Even Carolina Oliphant (later Lady Nairne), who wrote such hit songs of the time as the sentimental Jacobite lament for Bonnie Prince Charlie, 'Will ye no' come back again?', 'The Laird o' Cockpen', and 'Caller [fresh] Herrin'' (for Nathaniel Gow, the son of the fiddler and composer, Neil Gow), used the pseudonym 'Mrs Bogan of Bogan'; yet her works, like the songs of Burns and Jean Elliot's masterpiece, have helped to instil a sense of Scottish nationhood among people of all classes.
    Long after the prestige of her novel *Marriage* was assured, Susan Ferrier

still clung to her anonymity, modestly declaring that writing the novel had 'afforded occupation and amusement for idle and solitary hours, and was published in the belief that the author's name never would be guessed at or the work heard of beyond a very limited sphere'.[85] In the Preface to her *Metrical Legends of Exalted Characters* (1823) Joanna Baillie observes that 'women may be unlearned without any implied inferiority'. She goes on:

> At the same time they may avowedly and creditably
> possess as much learning, either in science or languages as
> they can fairly and honestly attain, the neglect of more
> necessary occupations being here considered as approaching
> to a real breach of rectitude.[86]

Fairness, honesty and rectitude in a woman are synonymous with commitment to the era's notion of womanly duty as wifeliness, maternity and household management. It was, perhaps, easy for aristocratic and well-placed women to regard their writing as luxurious amateur self-indulgence with the covert savour of putting one over on the patriarchy whose voice is heard in the father's attitude towards his daughter's 'miraculous prematurity' in Mary Brunton's *Discipline* (1814):

> 'It is a confounded pity she is a girl. If she had been of
> the right sort, she might have got into Parliament, and
> made a figure with the best of them. But now what use is
> her sense of? – 'I hope it will contribute to her
> happiness', said my mother, sighing as if she had thought
> the fulfilment of her hope a little doubtful.[87]

By the ironies of class and circumstance women remote from the salons of the *literati*, compelled to fight for their homes, were passionately shedding their submissive stereotypical roles in the bloody context of the early Highland Clearances, often putting their menfolk to shame: 'When they came with eviction orders, it was always the women who fought back.'[88] The niceties of sexual hierarchy, however, demanded other than artistic skills even in a woman who was admitted to literary circles in Edinburgh or London, and serious writing doubtless appeared to be the province of the obvious male giants like Hume, Smith, Burns, Scott and Byron. But writing was not something merely done on the side by Anne Grant and Elizabeth Hamilton. When the death of her husband left Grant virtually destitute, writing became her source of living, and the philanthropic Elizabeth Hamilton wrote out of her own experience of misfortune with the passion of a reformer. Nevertheless, the habit of applying a sexist double standard to male and female writers is still fair game for Alison Kermack's satire in 'Losing It', a patois poem of 1993:

ah sayz
ahm ritin like a basturt
shi sayz
exkyooz mee?
I said
I'm writing like a bastard
she said
beg pardon?
I said
'My Muse is Upon Me'.

She said
'That's better.
More poetic.
More befitting
a woman'.[89]

Like Elizabeth Hamilton, the Orcadian Mary Brunton wrote to im-
prove. While working on her first novel, *Self Control* (1810), she sent a
letter to her encouraging friend, Mrs Izett: 'I am positive that no part —
no, not the smallest part — of my happiness can ever arise from the
popularity of my book, further than as I think it may be useful. I would
rather, as you well know, glide through the world unknown, than have
(I will not call it *enjoy*) fame, however brilliant.'[90] After the completion
of her second novel, *Discipline*, she wrote again as a professional, committed to the role of the novelist as moral preceptor, asking why novels with
worthy purposes were still regarded as inferior literature:

> Why should an epic or a tragedy be supposed to hold
> such an exalted place in composition, while a novel is
> almost a nickname for a book? Does not a novel admit of
> as noble sentiments — as lively description — as natural
> character — as perfect unity of action — and a moral as
> irresistible as either of them? I protest, I think — a fiction
> containing a just representation of human beings and of
> their actions — a connected, interesting, and probable story,
> conducting to a useful and impressive moral lesson —
> might be one of the greatest efforts of human genius.[91]

Her ethical frame of reference is strongly Christian and as conservative as
Joanna Baillie's (to whom she dedicated *Self Control*), but her purpose in
both novels is to expose the false snobbery of materialism, the vulnerability of women to bad advice and sexual harassment, and the obstacles to
female self-realization. Fathers in *Self Control* and *Discipline* are, in their

different ways, weak and incompetent with money. Laura Montreville in *Self Control* and Emma-like Ellen Percy in *Discipline* (Jane Austen's *Emma* came out two years after the publication of *Discipline*) are obliged to fend for themselves without the support systems available to men. By refusing Hargrave after his attempt to make her his mistress in a life of 'love and rapture' (*Self Control*, Chapter 1) Laura rejects marriage for material security, unpersuaded by the romantic argument that rapture is all it takes to transform a rake into a good husband. While mourning Hargrave's degeneracy, she assumes guilt for idealizing an impious suitor and concludes that 'to love . . . she must henceforth be a stranger' (Chapter 3). Her attempt to sell her paintings expresses the resolution and independence which upright Montague De Courcy innocently but patriarchically undermines by secretly buying one of her pictures and commissioning another (Chapter 10). From a twentieth-century point of view the happiness of the ending is diminished by the suppression of Laura's small, pioneering bid for professionalism. As an individual she is not allowed the escape she has earned from her father's querulous prohibition in Chapter 13: 'I cannot endure to see you degraded into an artist, and, therefore, I desire there may be no more of this traffic.' Dorothy Porter McMillan gets to the heart of the matter when she observes: 'De Courcy admires Laura for being above the vulgar prejudice against women being useful, but, nevertheless, there is no suggestion that Laura continues to paint as anything other than a recreation after she has married for love and secured a competence upon which to live.'[92] Scotland might have lost or misplaced its independence in 1707, but the majority of women still had to win theirs for the first time.

Notes

1. John Purser, *Scotland's Music* (Edinburgh, 1992), p. 155.

2. Tobias Smollett, *The Expedition of Humphry Clinker* (New York, 1929), p. 336 (letter from Matthew Bramble to Dr Lewis, 20 Sept.).

3. Ibid., p. 335.

4. Robert Burns, 'Such a parcel of rogues in a nation', in James Kinsley (ed.), *Burns: Poems and Songs* (London, 1969), p. 512.

5. James A. Mackay (ed.), *The Complete Letters of Robert Burns* (Ayr, 1987), p. 185.

6. Sydney Goodsir Smith, 'Agin Black Spats', *Collected Poems 1941–1975* (London, 1975), p. 47.

7. R. L. Mackie, *A Short History of Scotland*, ed. Gordon Donaldson (Edinburgh and London, 1962), p. 301.

8. Hugh Trevor-Roper, 'Scotching the myths of devolution', *The Times*, 28 April 1976, p. 14.

9. Thomas Jefferson, 'Biographical Sketches of Famous Men', in *The Life and Selected Writings of Thomas Jefferson* (New York, 1944), p. 177.

10. Christopher Smout, 'The Scottish Identity', *The Future of Scotland*, ed. Robert Underwood (London, 1977), p. 18.

11. Ibid., pp. 18–19.

12. Henry Thomas Buckle, *On Scotland and the Scottish Intellect*, ed. H. J. Hanham (Chicago and London, 1970), p. 394.

13. See Frantz Fanon, *The Wretched of the Earth* (London, 1965), p. 170.

14. Craig Beveridge and Ronald Turnbull, *The Eclipse of Scottish Culture* (Edinburgh, 1989), p. 6.

15. P. H. Scott, 'Scotch Myths – 1', *The Bulletin of Scottish Politics*, 1, no. 2 (Spring 1981), p. 64.

16. See Paul H. Scott, *Andrew Fletcher and the Treaty of Union* (Edinburgh, 1992).

17. See Allan Massie, 'More trap than treaty', *TLS*, 1 January 1993, p. 8.

18. Tom Shields, 'Chasing Hemingway on a galloping horse', *The Herald*, 5 September 1992, p. 13.

19. Alan Riach, 'North', *This Folding Map* (Auckland, 1990), p. 16.

20. William Soutar, *Poems in Scots and English*, selected by W. R. Aitken (Edinburgh, 1975), p. 68.

21. Beveridge and Turnbull, *The Eclipse of Scottish Culture*, p. 10.

22. Hugh Miller, *First Impressions of England and Its People*, 9th edn (Edinburgh, 1869), p. 10.

23. See Richard B. Sher, 'Literature and the Church of Scotland', Cairns Craig, general editor, *The History of Scottish Literature*, 4 vols (Aberdeen, 1987–88), II, ed. Andrew Hook, *1660–1800*, pp. 259–71.

24. See Leighton Pullan, *Religion Since the Reformation* (Oxford, 1924), p. 150.

25. George Davie, *The Democratic Intellect. Scotland and Her Universities in the Nineteenth Century* (Edinburgh, 1961; 2nd edn 1964, reprinted 1986), p. 17.

26. John MacQueen, *Progress and Poetry: The Enlightenment and Scottish Literature* (Edinburgh, 1982), p. 42.

27. David Hume, *A Treatise of Human Nature*, 2 vols (London, 1911), II, p. 235.

28. Ibid., p. 239.

29. Norman MacCaig, 'An Ordinary Day', *Collected Poems* (London, 1985), pp. 149–50.

30. Hume, *A Treatise of Human Nature*, I, p. 21.

31. Quoted in Ernest Campbell Mossner, *The Life of David Hume* (Austin, Texas, 1954), p. 127.

32. Quoted in Tom Leonard, *Places of the Mind: The Life and Work of James Thomson ('B. V.')* (London, 1993), p. 230.

33. Bertrand Russell, *History of Western Philosophy and Its Connection with Political and Social Circumstances from the Earliest Times to the Present Day* (London, 1946; New Edition, 1961), p. 645.

34. Hume, *A Treatise of Human Nature*, I, pp. 105–6.

35. Geoffrey Tillotson (ed.), *The Poems of Alexander Pope, Volume II, The Rape of the Lock and Other Poems*, 3rd edn (London and New Haven, 1962), p. 358.

36. See J. W. H. Atkins, *English Literary Criticism, 17th and 18th Centuries* (London, 1951), pp. 337–43.

37. Allan Massie, *101 Great Scots* (Edinburgh, 1987), p. 106.

38. Adam Smith, *An Inquiry into the Nature and Causes of the Wealth of Nations*, 2 vols (London, 1960), I, p. 26.

39. Ibid., p. 117.

40. Ibid., p. 232.

41. Ibid., p. 70.

42. See Earl R. Wasserman, 'The Pleasures of Tragedy', *ELH*, 14 (December 1947), pp. 283–307.

43. George Campbell, *The Philosophy of Rhetoric, A New Edition, with the Author's Last Additions and Corrections*, 2 vols (Edinburgh, 1816), I, p. 244.

44. Ibid., p. 278.

45. Ibid., p. 281.

46. Henry Home, Lord Kames, *Essays on the Principles of Morality and Natural Religion* (Edinburgh, 1751), p. 14.

47. Ibid.

48. Hugh Blair, *Lectures on Rhetoric and Belles Lettres*, 2 vols (London, 1783), II, p. 522.

49. Ibid., pp. 495–6.

50. Thomas Reid, *Essays on the Powers of the Human Mind*, 3 vols (Edinburgh, 1803), I, pp. 75, 78.

51. Ibid., p. 78.

52. Samuel Taylor Coleridge, *Biographia Literaria* (London, 1906), p. 159.

53. Graham Hough, *The Romantic Poets* (London, 1953), p. 102.

54. *Byron: Selected Prose*, ed. Peter Gunn (Harmondsworth, 1972), p. 112.

55. John Galt, *The Life of Lord Byron* (London, 1911), p. 285.

56. Cynthia Chase, *Romanticism* (London, 1993), p. 34.

57. See Jerome Christensen, 'Byron's *Sardanapalus* and the Triumph of Liberalism', in ibid., pp. 211–39.

58. John Keats, *Letters*, selected and ed. Frederick Page (London, 1954), p. 172.

59. Galt, *Byron*, p. 89.

60. Hough, *The Romantic Poets*, p. 114.

61. Letter dated 12 January 1822 in *Byron: Selected Prose*, ed. Gunn, p. 474.

62. Ian Jack, *English Literature 1815–1832* (Oxford, 1963), p. 58.

63. John Gibson Lockhart, *Memoirs of Sir Walter Scott*, 5 vols (London, 1900), II, p. 211.

64. R. A. Houston, 'Women in the Economy and Society of Scotland, 1500–1800', *Scottish Society 1500–1800*, ed. R. A. Houston and I. D. Whyte (Cambridge, 1989), p. 140.

65. R. Scott-Moncrieff (ed.), *The Household Book of Lady Grisell Baillie, 1692–1733* (Edinburgh, 1911).

66. Stephen Finn and Rosemary Gray (eds), *Broken Strings: The Politics of Poetry in South Africa* (Cape Town, 1992), p. 155.

67. The fragment is given in Sir Walter Scott's *Minstrelsy of the Scottish Border* (London, 1931), p. 493:

> I've heard them lilting at the ewes milking,
> The flowers of the forest are a' wede away.
> I ride single on my saddle,
> For the flowers of the forest are a' wede away.

See Purser, *Scotland's Music*, pp. 90, 281.

68. Roger Lonsdale, *Eighteenth-Century Women Poets* (Oxford, 1990), p. 265.

69. See Purser, *Scotland's Music*, p. 90.

70. Lonsdale, *Eighteenth-Century Women Poets*, p. 265.

71. Ibid., p. 263.

72. Ibid., p. 277.

73. Joanna Baillie's poems were first published under her own name as *Fugitive Verses* (1840) which prints revised selections from her anonymously published *Poems: Wherein it is Attempted to Describe Certain Views of Nature and of Rustic Manners* (Joseph Johnson, 1790), first identified by Roger Lonsdale in his *New Oxford Book of Eighteenth Century Verse* (Oxford, 1984). See Lonsdale, *Eighteenth-Century Women Poets*, pp. 429–30.

74. Jennifer Breen (ed.), *Women Romantic Poets 1785–1832* (London, 1992), p. 69.

75. Joanna Baillie, 'Letter to an unidentified addressee in New Zealand' (undated), MS Papers, Folder 3446, Alexander Turnbull Library, Wellington, New Zealand.

76. Joanna Baillie (but first published anonymously), *Series of Plays, in which it is Attempted to Delineate the Stronger Passions of the Mind*, 3 vols (London, 1798–1812).

77. Breen (ed.), *Women Romantic Poets*, p. 44.

78. Lonsdale, *Eighteenth-Century Women Poets*, p. 432.

79. Breen (ed.), *Women Romantic Poets*, p. 50.

80. Dorothy Porter McMillan, 'Heroines and Writers', in *Tea and Leg-Irons: New Feminist Readings from Scotland*, ed. Caroline Gonda (London, 1992), pp. 17–30 [19].

81. Lonsdale, *Eighteenth-Century Women Poets*, p. 263.

82. Ibid., p. 264.

83. Lady Anne Barnard, *South Africa a Century Ago: Letters Written from the Cape of Good Hope 1797–1801*, ed. W. H. Wilkins (London, 1901), p. 129.

84. Ibid., p. 34.

85. Susan Ferrier, 'Preface', *The Inheritance*, Standard Novels (1841). Quoted in Susan Ferrier, *Marriage*, ed. Herbert Foltinek (Oxford, 1986), p. viii.

86. Joanna Baillie, *The Dramatic and Poetical Works* (London, 1853), p. 709.

87. Mary Brunton, *Discipline* (London, 1837), Chapter 1, p. 67.

88. John McGrath, *The Cheviot, the Stag and the Black, Black Oil* (London, 1981), p. 11.

89. Alison Kermack, *Writing Like a Bastard* (Edinburgh, 1993), p. 4.

90. Alexander Brunton, 'A Memoir of Mary Brunton', in Mary Brunton, *Emmeline with Some Other Pieces* (Edinburgh, 1819), p. xxxvi.

91. Ibid., p. lxxiv. Compare Jane Austen's spirited defence of the novel in Chapter 5 of *Northanger Abbey* (begun in 1798, published 1818).

92. McMillan, 'Heroines and Writers', pp. 24–5.

Chapter 3
Satire, Sentiment and Scots

Satire and sentiment are only superficially antithetical. In the work of Pope, Swift, Burns and Byron, they co-operate towards those points of balance we know as 'An Epistle from Mr Pope to Dr Arbuthnot', Book Four of *Gulliver's Travels*, 'The Twa Dogs' and *Don Juan*. Tobias Smollett and Henry Mackenzie might seem to represent two contrasting faces of eighteenth-century sensibility but their writings are complementary and motivated by similar convictions about society. The works of both men employ satire and sentiment, though in different proportions. Smollett is ferocious in the hectic moralities of *The Adventures of Peregrine Pickle* (1751) and *The Adventures of Ferdinand Count Fathom* (1753), but emotion is generally absorbed and cooled by the stylized knockabout mechanisms of his novels. There is a profligacy of tears and sympathy in *The Man of Feeling* (1771), yet Mackenzie's book goes beyond emotional aerobics to propound a theory of moral sentiments in the form of a novel which satirizes sentimentality while also, like Smollett's works, exposing chicanery, opportunism and injustice. Romantic elitism raises the idealized sensibility of Mackenzie's quixotic hero, Harley, above the vulgarities of an uncaring world, but his 'tribute of tears' is the reaching out of humanitarian sympathy towards victims of a cynically acquisitive society, an expression of the human feelings required to make Adam Smith's ideas of equity work. If Smollett's satire is brutal, it is, Walter Allen suggests, the 'homoeopathic' brutality of 'the morbidly sensitive man who seeks to cure his contemporaries of the filth they live in by rubbing their noses in it'.[1]

Smollett's medicinal comedy

Behind Smollett's energetic picaresque novels stand the Cervantes of *Don Quixote* and Alain-René Lesage, whose genial masterpiece, *Gil Blas*, Smollett translated in 1748. Smollett's translation of *Don Quixote*, described by the Mexican writer, Carlos Fuentes, as 'the homage of a novelist to a novelist',[2] was published in 1755. Don Quixote's ideal of a golden age, when people 'were ignorant of those two words MINE and THINE ... [when] All was peace, all was harmony, and all was friendship ... [when] There was no fraud, no deceit, no malice intermixed with plain-dealing truth',[3] is the Utopia from which eighteenth-century Britain has lapsed as had Cervantes' early seventeenth-century Spain. Don Quixote lives in what he calls 'this detestable age', anachronistically employing knight-errantry 'to defend damsels, protect widows, and succour the needy and fatherless'. Instead of illusory romance and its attendant satire, Smollett makes black comedy from 'the selfishness, envy, malice, and base indifference of mankind' with the avowed intention 'to animate the reader against the sordid and vicious disposition of the world'; see the 'Preface' to *The Adventures of Roderick Random* (1748). Yet his most accomplished novel, *The Expedition of Humphry Clinker* (1771), is optimistic. His brilliance as a caricaturist almost justifies the length of *The Adventures of Peregrine Pickle* in the figure of Hawser Trunnion, a Falstaffian retired naval officer who lives ashore as if still aboard his ship. A man of scientific as well as literary disposition, Smollett believed in the interpenetration of mental and physical properties. He treats people as complex organizations in which emotion is expressed physically: accordingly his characters have physical emotions and emotional bodies, foreshadowing the creations of Samuel Beckett in his novels *Murphy*, *Watt* and *Molloy* and the tramps in *Waiting for Godot*. Thus the volatile Peregrine Pickle is driven physically out of control by the pangs of jealousy:

> ... he endeavoured to wean his eyes from the fatal object that disturbed him, but they would not obey his direction and command; he wished himself deprived of all sensation, when he heard her laugh and saw her smile upon the officer; and, in the course of country-dancing, when he was obliged to join hands with her, the touch thrilled through all his nerves, and kindled a flame within him which he could not contain. In a word, his endeavours to conceal the situation of his thoughts were so violent that his constitution could not endure the shock; the sweat ran down his forehead in a stream, the colour vanished from his cheeks, his knees began to totter, and his eyesight to fail ...
>
> (*The Adventures of Peregrine Pickle*, Chapter 86)

Boyhood near Loch Lomond and the Water of Leven gave Smollett a lifelong affection for the Scottish countryside, but the teaching of John Love, his charismatic headmaster at Dumbarton Grammar School, instilled enthusiasms for languages, the great English writers and the world beyond Dumbartonshire. After medical studies at Glasgow University and a period of apprenticeship to the surgeons William Stirling and John Gordon he left Scotland for London in 1739 in a fruitless search for a producer to stage his play *The Regicide*. Literary disappointment and financial difficulties drove him to sea as ship's surgeon to H.M.S. *Chichester* in the disastrous Cartagena expedition against the Spanish, after which he spent some time in the West Indies where he married the daughter of a Jamaican planter. Back in London he failed to make his mark as a physician and worked as a journalist and translator. Sentimental patriotism prompted him to write the poem 'Tears of Scotland', about the Battle of Culloden and its painful aftermath, and he occasionally revisited the country of his birth, most notably in 1756 when he was invited to address the Select Society. *Roderick Random*, the story of a 'North Briton' falling among thieves away from home, evokes the hardships, disease and cruelty of the naval life Smollett knew, and displays a cross-section of London grotesques. The creation of Roderick as an outsider from the time of his unhappy childhood in Scotland seems to reflect Smollett's sense of alienation as an unmatriculated student in Glasgow (in 1750 he bought his M.D. from Aberdeen University for £28 Scots) and as an honest physician excluded from London's established medical fraternity by the accident of his birth as the son of a disinherited Scotsman. Contemporary readers compared this first novel to the work of Fielding (who disliked it) and the book was an immediate success, demonstrating that in the eighteenth century, as now, there was a market for no-holds-barred satire in the depiction of a debased society. Smollett's confection of satirical farce and comedy of manners anticipates John Gibson Lockhart's *Matthew Wald* (1824) and the novels of Eric Linklater, but his portrayals of moral anarchy border on a nihilism which does not reappear in Scottish literature until the late twentieth-century fiction of Iain Banks and Irvine Welsh.

The Scottish propensity for extremes is responsible for much of the appeal of *Humphry Clinker*, Smollett's masterpiece, an epistolary novel with a happy ending which recounts the wanderings of five travellers through the Britain of George III on a round trip from Wales to London, Scotland and back again. Humphry Clinker, the sincere Methodist footman picked up along the way, plays a subordinate role as the long-lost illegitimate son of the crusty but warm-hearted Welsh squire, Matthew Bramble (Smollett himself). The rest of the party is made up of Bramble's strident sister, Tabitha, her maid, Winifred Jenkins, Bramble's nephew, Jery Melford, and his niece, Lydia. In addition to the extremes of Tabitha's voracity towards potential husbands, the ferocity of her dog, Chowder, the imprisonment of Clinker, the overturnings of the travellers' carriage, loathing for Edinburgh and praise for Glasgow, there are Smollett's hyperbolic creations of the disputatious 'weather-beaten Scotch lieutenant',

Lismahago, destined for the gratification of Tabitha's marital ambitions, and the magnificently illiterate Winifred Jenkins. First appearing as 'a tall, meagre figure, answering, with his horse, the description of Don Quixote mounted on Rozinante',[4] Lismahago is endowed with physical attributes to make him the nonpareil of Smollett's grotesques and an obvious source for Dickens's mellower creations in the same genre:

> He would have measured above six feet in height had he
> stood upright; but he stooped very much; was very
> narrow in the shoulders and very thick in the calves of his
> legs, which were cased in black spatterdashes – As for his
> thighs, they were long and slender, like those of a
> grasshopper; his face was, at least, half a yard in length,
> brown and shrivelled, with projecting cheek-bones, little
> grey eyes on the greenish hue, a large hook-nose, a
> pointed chin, a mouth from ear to ear, very ill furnished
> with teeth, and a high, narrow fore-head, well furrowed
> with wrinkles.[5]

The novel concludes with the linguistic extreme of Winifred's last letter to Molly, a servant at Brambleton Hall. Here Winifred carries malapropism to Joycean heights as she tells her friend about the three marriages that bring the expedition to a felicitous end:

> Providinch hath bin pleased to make great halteration in
> the pasture of our affairs. – We were yesterday three kiple
> chined, by the grease of God, in the holy bands of
> mattermoney, and I now subscrive myself Loyd at your
> service . . . As for madam Lashmiheygo, you nose her
> picklearities . . . The captain himself had a huge hassock of
> air, with three tails, and a tum-tawdry coat, boddered with
> sulfur. – Wan said he was a monkey-bank . . . Mr Lloyd
> was dressed in a lite frog, and checket with gould binding;
> and thof he don't enter in caparison with great folks of
> quality, yet he has got as good blood in his veins as arrow
> privet 'squire in the county; and then his pursing is far
> from contentible . . . Now, Mrs Mary, our satiety is to
> suppurate . . . Present my cumpliments to Mrs Gwyllim,
> and I hope she and I will live upon dissent terms of
> civility.[6]

The Scottish Smollett's Welsh servant is an ancestor of James Joyce's Dublin washerwomen. Winifred's 'Providinch', 'halteration', 'chined',

'grease of God', 'mattermoney', 'Lashmiheygo', 'picklearities', 'monkey-
bank', 'caparison', 'contentible', 'satiety is to suppurate' and 'dissent terms
of civility' are forerunners of the 'jocoserious' puns of *Finnegans Wake*.
This is merriment enough to endear us to confusion. Smollett's capacity
for fun has led him out of his darkness. His homoeopathy, at least, has
worked for him.

Henry Mackenzie's *The Man of Feeling*[7]

Mackenzie's short novel is about the mortal disillusionment of a sensitive
man who discovers that decency is scarce and vulnerable in a world
where 'man is an animal equally selfish and vain' (Chapter 21). The
iniquities of the social world are contrasted with the picturesque innocence of nature. When Harley stops on his way towards the corruptions
of London he looks back for 'his wonted prospect' of fields, woods and
hills but sees them 'lost in the distant clouds' (Chapter 14); and in Chapter 34 he first observes the sleeping figure of the old soldier, Edwards, in
a scene that reminds him of the stagily sentimentalist paintings of the
Neapolitan, Salvator Rosa:

> The banks on each side were covered with fantastic shrub-
> wood, and at a little distance, on the top of one of them,
> stood a finger-post, to mark the directions of two roads
> which diverged from the point where it was placed. A
> rock, with some dangling wild flowers, jutted out above
> where the soldier lay; on which grew the stump of a large
> tree, white with age, and a single twisted branch shaded
> his face as he slept. His face had the marks of manly
> comeliness impaired by time; his forehead was not
> altogether bald, but its hairs might have been numbered;
> while a few white locks behind crossed the brown of his
> neck with a contrast the most venerable to a mind like
> Harley's.

The imagery presages Wordsworth's more richly emblematic old soldier
in Book IV of *The Prelude*. Nature is benign, the human heart instinctively sympathetic but commonly twisted by society which is 'in general
selfish, interested, and unthinking, and throws the imputation of romance
or melancholy on every temper more susceptible than its own' (Chapter
55). Mackenzie's book is a protest against the discrediting of feeling and

the tyranny of semblance. Harley's mistaken faith in physiognomy is a 'foible' which delivers him into the hands of two noted card-sharpers: 'as for faces', he is advised after his fleecing in Chapter 25, 'you may look into them to know, whether a man's nose be a long or a short one' (Chapter 27). Honour, too, is reduced to a mere foible by a cynical society, revealed as an obstacle to army promotion in the story of Emily Atkins and her father (Chapter 28). The inversion of values is projected to a national scale in the reference to British conquests in India, truly a source not of pride but of shame, as Harley tells Edwards in terms that must have endeared Mackenzie to the anti-Unionists of his time. (Towards the end of the eighteenth century anti-slavery sentiment often served as a metaphor for Scottish dissatisfaction with the Union.) His rejection of specious imperialist apologetics anticipates the Conrad of 'Heart of Darkness' and should commend him still to opponents of colonialism:

> You tell me of immense territories subject to the English:
> I cannot think of their possessions, without being led to
> enquire, by what right they possess them. They came
> there as traders, bartering the commodities they brought
> for others which their purchasers could spare; and however
> great their profits were, they were then equitable. But
> what title have the subjects of another kingdom to
> establish an empire in India? to give laws to a country
> where the inhabitants received them on the terms of
> friendly commerce? You say they are happier under our
> regulations than the tyranny of their own petty princes.
> I must doubt it, from the conduct of those by whom
> these regulations have been made . . . You describe the
> victories they have gained; they are sullied by the cause in
> which they fought: you enumerate the spoils of those
> victories; they are covered with the blood of the
> vanquished!
>
> (Chapter 36)[8]

That the perverse half of the world cannot be converted to feeling seems to be taken for granted by Mackenzie's narrator. Recording Harley's joy at receiving Captain Atkins's thanks for rescuing Emily from prostitution he says:

> We would attempt to describe the joy which Harley felt
> on this occasion, did it not occur to us, that one half of
> the world could not understand it though we did; and the

other half will, by this time, have understood it without
descriptions at all.

(Chapter 29)

The moral world is irredeemably split. Harley has given to beggars; he has
sympathized with the inmates of Bedlam when others saw them only as
wild beasts for exhibition, and left money for the special care of a woman
maddened by disappointed love; he has rescued a prostitute, reconciling
her to her father; he has provided for Edwards and succoured him in the
loss of his son; he has argued for human rights. His goodness is rewarded
by failure to secure the lease for which he went to London and by failure
in love. His death is exit from 'a scene', he tells the narrator, 'in which
I never much delighted' (Chapter 55), yet the book ends neither in hate
nor in sentimentalized injustice but in the stronger protest of compassion.
The narrator sometimes visits Harley's grave:

> It is worth a thousand homilies! every nobler feeling rises
> within me! every beat of my heart awakens a virtue! – but
> will it make you hate the world – No: there is such an
> air of gentleness around, that I can hate nothing; but, as
> to the world – I pity the men of it.

(Chapter 56)

Satirical humour braces the book against the charge of mawkishness.
When the boy Harley's numerous guardians disagree about arrangements
for their ward they resort to 'the mediatory power of a dinner and a
bottle, which commonly interrupted, not ended, the dispute; and after
that interruption ceased, left the consulting parties in a condition not very
proper for adjusting it' (Chapter 12). A stranger who overheard Harley's
advisers urging him to 'a happy forwardness of disposition' would have
been led to suppose 'that in the British code there was some disqualifying
statute against any citizen who should be convicted of – modesty' (Chapter 12). At twenty-four, Miss Walton 'was now arrived at that period of
life which takes, or is supposed to take, from the flippancy of girlhood
those sprightlinesses with which some good-natured old maids oblige the
world at three-score' (Chapter 13). Among the apparently mad women
of Bedlam several gather round their female visitors to examine 'with
rather more accuracy than might have been expected, the particulars of
their dress' (Chapter 20). The pontifical misanthrope's younger brother
marries for love a young lady of similar temperament to his own 'with
whom the sagacious world pitied him for finding happiness' (Chapter 21),
an irony which the Susan Ferrier of *Marriage* would have appreciated.
Mackenzie's opinion of the dryness of the Law – reluctantly his own

profession – is sardonically reflected in the fate of 'Coke upon Lyttleton'[9] which Harley's disputatious guardians make him read:

> He profited little by the perusal; but it was not without its
> use in the family: for his maiden aunt applied it
> commonly to the laudable purpose of pressing her
> rebellious linen to the folds she had allotted them.
>
> (Chapter 12)

A manifesto for the superiority of benevolence to prudence, *The Man of Feeling* satirizes false sentiment – the young lady who kisses her lapdog's lips in Chapter 11 is an augury of Susan Ferrier's Lady Juliana and her cosseted menagerie in *Marriage* – and exposes naïveté (Harley's extenuation of hypocrisy in the confidence trickster in Chapter 25 who, despite his high moral tone, has no change for a beggar but produces ten shillings for a game of piquet). The narrator is elegantly caustic about the practical need to accommodate false values:

> Indeed I have observed one ingredient, somewhat
> necessary in a man's composition towards happiness, which
> people of feeling would do well to acquire; a certain
> respect for the follies of mankind: for there are so many
> fools whom the opinion of the world entitles to regard,
> whom accident has placed in heights of which they are
> unworthy, that he who cannot restrain his contempt or
> indignation at the sight, will be too often quarrelling with
> the disposal of things, to relish that share which is allotted
> to himself.
>
> (Chapter 12)

This kind of Swiftian acuity in *The Man of Feeling*, usually ignored by commentators who discuss the book as a tear-jerker in the genre of the novel of sentiment, makes less surprising Sir Walter Scott's note in his *Journal* for December 1825: 'No man is less well known from his writings. We would suppose a retired, modest, somewhat affected man, with a white handkerchief and a sigh ready for every sentiment. No such thing. H. M. is as alert as a contracting tailor's needle in every sort of business, a politician and a sportsman, shoots and fishes in a sort even to this day, and is the life of the company with anecdote and fun.'[10]

Prized by Burns next to the Bible (he wore out two copies) and commended by Scott for its tone of moral pathos, *The Man of Feeling* might be expected to appeal to theory-orientated twentieth-century readers for its sense of itself as involved in the revaluation of a literary kind. Readers unfamiliar with the eighteenth-century novel of sentiment exemplified by

Oliver Goldsmith's *The Vicar of Wakefield* (1766) and Laurence Sterne's *A Sentimental Journey* (1768), to both of which *The Man of Feeling* owes much, may find it difficult to accept Mackenzie's lachrymose hero who admits that he dotes on his pain in the parodic pastoral he writes to commemorate Miss Walton's apparent preference of another suitor:

> I lean on my hand with a sigh,
>   My friends the soft sadness condemn;
> Yet, methinks, tho' I cannot tell why,
>   I should hate to be merry like them.
>   (Chapter 40)

Twentieth-century taste is more attuned to Jane Austen's satires of feeling in *Sanditon* (1817) and *Sense and Sensibility* (1811). Mackenzie's book, like Sterne's, begins its story proper with a reference to France and the aim of both works is, in Sterne's words, 'to teach us to love the world and our fellow creatures'[11] – or, in Mackenzie's case, to love half the world – but both Sterne and Mackenzie make free with form. Sterne's novel begins in mid-dialogue, parodies the fashionable literature of travel and ends in mid-sentence. Mackenzie offers a tighter metafiction, a novel cast in the form of a non-novel made up of the disconnected remains of a fictitious manuscript used by a sporting curate as wadding for his gun. 'To such as may have expected the intricacies of a novel,' concedes the narrator towards the end, 'a few incidents in a life undistinguished, except by some features of the heart, cannot have afforded much entertainment.' Thus the book directs the reader to consider the purpose of its idiosyncratic form. Mackenzie drops the reader into the midst of things in Chapter 11, the first piece of the surviving manuscript, after an introduction which allows him to forgo the linearity of the novel as practised by Richardson and Fielding, dodging the constraints regretfully acknowledged by E. M. Forster in his *cri de coeur*, 'Yes – oh dear yes – the novel tells a story',[12] to focus on the moral significance of his fragmentary episodes without the distraction of mere narrative detail. The formal strength of the book is its compression. Its understated Scottish frame of reference is evident not merely in the location of heartlessness in England but in an early critical allusion to David Hume's discussion of taste, sentiment and idea in the *Treatise of Human Nature*:

> Though I am not of opinion with some wise men, that
> the existence of objects depends on idea; yet I am
> convinced, that their appearance is not a little influenced
> by it. The optics of some minds are in so unlucky a
> perspective, as to throw a certain shade on every picture
> that is presented to them; while those of others (of which

number was Harley) like the mirrors of the ladies, have a
wonderful effect in bettering their complexions.

(Chapter 19)

Poetry in Scots: Allan Ramsay and Robert Fergusson[13]

While Scottish prose addressed social, moral and political questions in a
rapidly changing world, poets were engaging with the lives of real people.
Allan Ramsay's work is uneven but he put heart into the Scots language
and makes a fresh, prophetic annunciation about a specifically Scottish
relation of language to life, preparing the way for a more aggressive
prophet in Robert Fergusson and then the messiah, Robert Burns.

First a wig-maker, then a bookseller, Allan Ramsay established Britain's
first circulating library in 1725 at his shop in a tenement at the east end
of the Luckenbooths (i.e. the closed shops) in Edinburgh's High Street.
(Subscribers to his *Poems* of 1721 included Pope and Steele.) In 1724 he
put the case for Scots in his pioneering two-volume anthology of early
Scottish poetry, *The Ever Green* (1724), including the inauthentic ballad
fragment 'Hardyknute' by Elizabeth Wardlaw. From 1725 to 1737 the
five popular volumes of Ramsay's *The Tea-Table Miscellany: a Collection of
Choice Songs, Scots and English* (1724) stimulated fresh interest in the words
and music of Scottish ballad tradition at a time when Scottish cultural
identity was endangered by the pressures of Union. In 1727 he contributed to current debate on the 'lawfulness' of the stage with *Some Few
Hints, in Defence of Dramatical Entertainments*, meeting fundamentalist Presbyterian bigotry head-on by arguing that if theatres and plays were unlaw-
ful it was surprising that the apostles had not inveighed against them:

> That these Missionaries of Salvation should travel thro' so
> many Nations and meet at every Turn Theatres and Stage-
> players staring them in the Face, and not once reprimand
> them, is Matter of very serious reflection.
>
>   Had the Playhouse been the *Seat of Infection*, the *Chair
> of Pestilence*, or the *Devil's own Ground*, 'tis rational to
> think, that those Divine Monitors that set Bars to the Eye,
> Ear and Tongue, to every smallest Avenue that might
> admit the Tempter, would hardly have left the broad
> Gates to the Playhouse so open, without one Warning to
> the unwary Christian, in so direct a Road to Perdition.[14]

Even Ramsay could not prevail against the Licensing Act of 1737 which banned performances of plays outside the City of Westminster. Unmoved by his wit, the 'unco guid' of the Edinburgh Presbytery used the Act to close his theatre in Carrubber's Close and at fifty-five Ramsay retired from civic life to his octagonal house, the 'Goose-Pie', on Castle Hill.

Ramsay was an anti-Union Scottish nationalist with moderate Jacobite sympathies, although he did not participate in the rebellion of 1715 and was judiciously absent from Edinburgh in September and October 1745 when the city was briefly occupied by the army of Prince Charles Edward Stuart. His unjustly neglected poem 'The Vision', first published in *The Ever Green*, opposes thraldom to England, suggesting that Unionists were bribed. The vision of the poem is a wanderer's patriotic dream in which he laments English depredations and meets Scotland's guardian spirit, 'The Warden of this auntient nation', whom he asks about the future. All will be well, says the Warden, when true Scottish hearts forsake materialism and learn to 'slicht [slight] Saxon gold'. The process will be humiliating and painful but Scotland is tough enough to break from England and survive both priests and lawyers:

> . . . Scotland maun be made an ass
> To set her jugment richt.
> Theyil jade her and blad her,   *abuse/beat*
> Untill scho brak hir tether,   *she*
> Thocht auld schois, yet bauld schois,   *Though she is old yet she is bold*
> And teuch lyke barkit lether.   *tough/hardened leather*
> (XIV)

Another Bannockburn is prophesied:

> The faes sall tak the feild neir Forthe, *foes*
>   And think the day their ain:
> But burns that day sall rin with blude   *shall run*
>   Of them that now oppress;
> Their carcasses be corbys fude,   *ravens' food*
>   By thousands on the gres.   *grass*
> (XV)

Ramsay's nationalistic optimism was unjustified: instead of a second Bannockburn came the Duke of Cumberland's defeat of Prince Charles's army at Culloden which marked the end of the Jacobite uprising of 1745–46, the failure of the Stuart cause and the impending collapse of traditional Highland society; but the fervour, satirical punch and cutting edge of its Scots language merit a place for 'The Vision' beside Ramsay's better known comic poems. Of these the most accomplished is 'The Monk and the Miller's Wife: A Tale' (1728), based on a Chaucerian idea in an anonymous late fifteenth-century poem, 'The Freris of Berwick'. His most immediately attractive poems are the amiable exchange of letters, 'Familiar Epistles between Lieutenant William Hamilton and Allan Ramsay', written with William Hamilton of Gilbertfield, and the spirited mock elegies with which Ramsay entertained fellow members of the Easy Club which he helped to found in 1712. The elegies commemorate kenspeckle Edinburgh characters like Maggy Johnston who had 'The pauky knack / Of brewing ale amaist [almost] like wine' ('Elegy on Maggy Johnston'), Lucky Wood who kept a tavern in the Canongate distinguished for its cleanliness and hospitality ('Elegy on Lucky Wood in the Canongate'), and John Cowper, the Kirk-Treasurer's Man responsible for uncovering immoral behaviour and reporting offenders to the Treasurer who would then exact appropriate fines ('Elegy on John Cowper, Kirk-Treasurer's Man'). Cowper had a sharp nose for 'sculdudry' or prostitution, and with him out of the way the whores fearlessly plie their trade:

> But now they may scoure up and
>   down,
> And safely gang their wakes
>   arown,   *walk about*
> Spreading the clap throw a' the
>   town,
>   But fear or dread;
> For that great kow to bawd and   *awe-inspiring person/young*
>   lown,   *man*
>   John Cowper's dead.

The most richly characterized elegy is 'Lucky Spence's Last Advice', a dramatic monologue in memory of a notorious bawd who, according to Ramsay's note on the poem, 'made many a benefit night to herself by putting a trade in the hands of young lasses that had a little pertness, strong passions, abundance of laziness, and no fore-thought'.[15] The expiring madam demands a last drink, then another, gives her blessing to 'good Doers / Who spend their cash on bawds and whores' and dispenses practical wisdom to her working girls:

> When e'er ye meet a fool that's fow,   *full (of drink)*
> That ye're a maiden gar him trow,   *make him believe*
> Seem nice, but stick to him like glew;
>   And whan set down,
> Drive at the jango till he spew,   *liquor*
>   Syne he'll sleep soun.   *Then/soundly*

With the client sated and unconscious 'black-ey'd Bess and mim-mou'd Meg' and their co-workers may safely relieve him of his rings, his watch and the considerable cash that even a small wallet may yield:

Cleek a' ye can be hook or crook,	*Catch*
Ryp ilky poutch frae nook to nook;	*Search every pocket*
Be sure to truff his pocket-book,	
Saxty pounds Scots	
Is nae deaf nits: In little bouk	*no 'chicken feed'*
Lie great bank-notes.	

The Gentle Shepherd, a pastoral play in verse derived from two of Ramsay's earlier eclogues, was first published in 1725 and revised in 1729 to make a ballad opera for the boys of Haddington Grammar School. This is the basis, a century later, of The Shepherd's reference to Theocritus as 'the Allan Ramsay o' Sicily' in one of John Wilson's dialogues in the *Noctes Ambrosianae* (originally published in *Blackwood's Magazine*, 1822–35).[16] The play's meagre plot involves the love of the shepherds Patie and Roger for Peggy and Jenny with the return of Sir William Worthy to his estate, the discovery that Patie is Sir William's son and Peggy his niece, and that there is, therefore, no class obstacle to the marriage of Patie and Peggy. The dramatic action is slight and the piece is often criticized for its uneasy mixture of Scots and English – as felicity approaches the Scots recedes – but a twentieth-century audience could enjoy this as part of the play's genial satire. Only sympathetic production and well-chosen music are needed to bring it to life again, possibly using sur-titles to help today's Anglicized audiences with the less familiar Scots vocabulary. Ramsay's insight into the country girl's recoil from the decorative airs and graces by which the nervous suitor attempts to disguise his natural gaucherie is evident in Jenny's expression of her feelings for Roger:

I dinna like him, Peggy, there's an end;	
A herd mair sheepish yet I never kend.	*shepherd*
He kaims his hair indeed, and gaes right snug,	*combs*
With ribbon-knots at his blew bonnet-lug;	*bonnet flap*
Whilk pensily he wears a thought a-jee,	*Which affectedly/at a bit of an angle*
And spreads his garters diced beneath his knee.	

He falds his owrlay down his   *cravat*
  breast with care;
And few gang trigger to the   *go more handsomely*
  kirk or fair.
For a' that, he can neither sing
  nor say,
Except 'How d'ye' – or,
  'There's a bonny day'.
          (I, ii, ll. 35–44)

Peggy's resistance to Jenny's gloomy view of marriage puts the case for love, family, and shared old age with a simple eloquence in which Ramsay's blend of Scots and English diction sets the heart-felt conviction of the peasant girl in the context of natural process:

Bairns, and their bairns, make sure a firmer ty,   *bond*
Than ought in love the like of us can spy,
See yon twa elms that grow up side by side,
Suppose them, some years syne, bridegroom   *ago*
  and bride;
Nearer and nearer ilka year they've prest,
Till wide their spreading branches are increast,
And in their mixture now are fully blest.
This shields the other frae the eastlin blast,
That in return defends it frae the west.
Sic as stand single, – a state sae liked by you!   *Such*
Beneath ilk storm, frae ev'ry airth, maun bow.   *every/direction/must*
          (I, ii, ll. 191–201)

Ramsay's significance in the Scottish tradition is much greater than the handful of his poems that deserve a secure place in academies and living rooms. Fergusson's originality and range are more impressive than Ramsay's and his craft more consistent, but neither achieved the scope of Burns or the best poets of the twentieth-century Scottish literary renaissance. Their works should not be over-valued, but their impact can hardly be over-estimated. They both made the living Scots language work in literature for the people, and Ramsay's diverse activities brought crucial stimulus to the influential cultural life of Edinburgh.

  The young Fergusson quickly found his feet as a writer when he abandoned English pastoral style in favour of a Scots that blends Edinburgh dialect with usages from rural Aberdeen. From the High School of Edinburgh he went as a bursar to the High School of Dundee and matriculated in 1765 at the University of St Andrews where he began writing poetry, including the comic 'Elegy on the Death of Mr David Gregory, late Professor of Mathematics in the University of St Andrews':

> By numbers too he cou'd divine,
> > Whan he did read,
> That three times three just made up nine;
> > But now he's dead.

After his father's death in 1767 he left the university without taking a degree to support his mother and sister in Edinburgh by his tedious, poorly paid employment in the Commissary Office. As a member of the debating society called the Cape Club he found encouragement to write and took the pseudonym 'Sir Precenter', marking his own ability as a singer and the concern for music which prompted his 'Elegy, On the Death of Scots Music'. Like Ramsay and Burns he objected to the distortion of native songs by over-decorated arrangements in the Italian style:

> Now foreign sonnets bear the gree,   *carry off the prize*
> And crabbit queer variety   *perverse*
> Of sound fresh sprung frae Italy,
> > A bastard breed!
> Unlike that saft-tongu'd melody
> > Which now lies dead.

The verse is typically well turned but more patriotic than accurate. Native melody was alive and valued as never before, with the preservation of Scottish poetry and song a growing passion among such collectors as James Watson, Allan Ramsay and David Herd as well as George Thomson, James Johnson, Robert Burns and the controversial James Macpherson, who based his 'translations' of Ossian's alleged epic *Fingal* (1762) and other poems on Gaelic and pseudo-Gaelic ballad material which he collected in the Highlands.[17] Burns's development as a lyric poet exemplifies the feeding of a creative gift by the antiquarian movement. Compelled by sickness and depression to resign from his job, Fergusson experienced a slight improvement in health but in June 1774 fell down a flight of stairs, struck his head and was taken as a 'pauper lunatic' to the Edinburgh Bedlam where he died on 17 October, a few weeks after his twenty-fourth birthday, leaving thirty-three poems in Scots of consistently high quality and fifty comparatively pallid poems in English.

The high spirits of Fergusson's genius are most infectious in 'The Daft-Days' (the New Year holiday period) during which Edinburgh escapes from 'mirk December's dowie face' into mirth and 'blithesome innocence' with assistance from 'the great god of *Aqa Vitae!* / Wha sways the empire of this city', and in 'To the Principal and Professors of the University of

St Andrews, On Their Superb Treat to Dr Samuel Johnson'. The treat was a banquet given in Johnson's honour on 19 August 1773, James Boswell noting that 'the professors entertained us with a very good dinner'.[18] The occasion gave Fergusson an opportunity to mock the Regents of the university's culinary sycophancy towards the eminent Scotophobe. If Fergusson had organized it he would have changed the menu from continental delicacies to Scottish haggis, sheep's head and trotters, brose and oatcakes. Revenge should be taken for Johnson's offensively patronizing reference in his *Dictionary* to oatmeal as the diet of English horses and the Scottish people:

How I wad trimm'd the bill o' fare!	
For ne'er sic surly wight as he	*such a*
Had met wi' sic respect frae me.	
Mind ye what Sam, the lying loun!	*rascal*
Has in his Dictionar laid down?	
That aits in England are a feast	*oats*
To cow and horse, an' sican beast,	*such a*
While in Scots ground this growth was common	
To gust the gab o' man and woman.	*please the palate*

Though small in volume and relatively narrow in scope, Fergusson's work 'is unquestionably the finest body of poetry produced in Scotland during the eighteenth century before Burns'.[19] Without the examples of Fergusson Burns might not have found the forms that best suited him and enabled him to become Scotland's national poet. Auguries of Burns are clear in 'The Lee Rigg', Fergusson's one attempt at Scots song and acknowledged by Burns as a source of his own 'The lea-rig', as well as in 'Ode to the Bee', 'Ode to the Gowdspink' (goldfinch) and 'To My Auld Breeks', respected protectors of the poet's hurdies 'frae wind and weet, frae snaw and hail' but, like him, governed by physical limitations:

For you I car'd, as lang's ye dow'd	*could*
Be lin'd wi' siller or wi' gowd:	*silver or with gold*
Now to befriend, it wad be folly,	
Your raggit hide an' pouches holey;	
For wha but kens a poet's placks	*Scots coins worth a third of a penny (i.e. small change)*
Get mony weary flaws an' cracks,	
And canna thole to hae them tint,	*lost*
As he sae seenil sees the mint?	*seldom*
Yet round the warld keek and see,	*look*
That ithers fare as ill as thee.	

Like Ramsay, Fergusson loves his Edinburgh, castigating its dirt, smells, libertinism and hypocrisy in his long poem, *Auld Reikie*, but doing so with a Hogarthian savour of detail. After an invocation to 'Auld Reikie!' (i.e. 'Old Smoky', a traditionally popular name for Edinburgh) the poet's eye pans across the city's day from the early-morning stirrings of servant lasses and barefoot housemaids emptying their chamber-pots, to schools at play, glowering traders and strutting lawyers. Darkness brings out the night life of the streets: an ex-prostitute sings a sad song by a lamp-post and a pugilist erupts drunkenly from a tavern with his dandified hangers-on:

> Frae joyous tavern, reeling drunk,
> Wi' fiery phizz, and ein half sunk,   *eyes*
> Behald the bruiser, fae to a'   *foe to all*
> That in the reek o' gardies fa':   *That fall within reach of his arms*
>
> Close by his side, a feckless race
> O' macaronies shew their face,   *fops*
> And think they're free frae skaith   *injury*
>   or harm,
> While pith befriends their leaders
>   arm.
>   (ll. 99–106)

In contrast with the lively secular miscellany of the weekday, Sunday's 'alter'd scene / O' men and manners' provokes a caustically logical reprimand to the sabbath hypocrisies of those who change their faces with their clothes:

> Why should religion make us sad,
> If good frae virtue's to be had?
> Na, rather gleefu' turn your face;
> Forsake hypocrisy, grimace;
> And never have it understood
> You fleg mankind frae being good.   *frighten*
>   (ll. 241–6)

The hypocrisy of appearance is also Fergusson's subject in 'Braid Claith', where the fun the poet is having is evident in the way he plays with the six-line 'Standard Habbie' stanza[20] in rhymes worthy of MacGonagall:

> For thof ye had as wise a snout on   *although*
> As Shakespear or Sir Isaac Newton,

> Your judgement fouk wou'd hae a doubt on,   *folk*
>   I'll tak my aith,   *oath*
> Till they cou'd see ye wi' a suit on
> O' gude Braid Claith.

Here the jocose Fergusson's satire on clothing as a measure of human worth anticipates Burns's more Swiftian contempt for 'tinsel show . . . silks . . . riband, star and a' that' in 'A Man's a Man for a' That'. Fergusson enjoys the folly where Burns is scathing about the superficiality of rank in his affirmation of the radical ideals of liberty, equality and fraternity. Nevertheless, Burns felt a strong affinity with Fergusson as his 'elder brother in Misfortune' and in the Muse.[21] The spirit of Fergusson is revived in the twentieth century in the Scots poetry of Robert Garioch. Robert Louis Stevenson, another rebel against the hypocrisies of Edinburgh gentility, also felt close to Fergusson. Shortly before he died he told his friend, Charles Baxter:

> I had always a great sense of kinship with poor Robert Fergusson – so clever a boy, so wild, of such a mixed strain, so unfortunate, born in the same town with me, and, as I always felt, rather by express intimation than from evidence, so like myself.[22]

Attitudes to the Scots language

Despite the successes of Ramsay and Fergusson, Scots was a threatened language. In 1707 the Act of Union installed English as the official language of Scotland, now part of the United Kingdom, and standard southern English soon became the language written by Scots people who wished to appear cultivated even if they still spoke their native Scots in informal situations. The patriotic revival of interest in early Scots poetry and song was partly a reaction to attempts by Scottish Enlightenment *literati* to purge Scoticisms from the language used in Scotland. The most significant communication was now with London and Scots who visited the capital did not wish to be thought bumpkins because of their outlandish speech. On her journey through northern England in *The Heart of Midlothian* (1818) Sir Walter Scott's Jeanie Deans replaces her tartan screen with an English-style bonnet and conforms to 'the national extravagance of wearing shoes and stockings for the whole day' but is made to suffer for her language:

. . . her accent and language drew down on her so many
jests and gibes, couched in a worse *patois* by far than her
own, that she soon found it was her interest to talk as
little and as seldom as possible.

(Chapter 28)

The language of government was the language of civilization, though
poets might think differently. In the 'Preface' to *The Ever Green* (1724)[23]
Allan Ramsay extols 'that natural Strength of Thought and Simplicity of
Stile our Forefathers practised'. Naturalness means fidelity to home: 'Their
Images are native, and their *Landskips* domestick; copied from those Fields
and Meadows we every Day behold.' Truth to native soil requires allegiance to native language: 'There is nothing can be heard more silly than
one's expressing his *Ignorance* of his *native Language*.' Yet a goal of the
Select Society founded by Ramsay's artist son was to upgrade, i.e. An-
glicize, the speech of its members and in 1761 they invited the Irish actor,
Thomas Sheridan, to Edinburgh to teach elocution. Although Henry
Mackenzie hailed Burns as 'this heaven-taught ploughman' when he
reviewed the Kilmarnock Edition of *Poems, Chiefly in the Scottish Dialect*
(1786) in his magazine *The Lounger* on 9 December 1786, he campaigned
in *The Mirror* (1779) and its successor, *The Lounger* (1785–7), for an
English style free of Scots idioms. Henry Home, Lord Kames, was one
of the last Scottish judges to use Scots in the courts until his famous
valediction to fellow members of the bench: 'Fare ye weel, ye bitches!',[24]
but he was one of a crusty, valiant minority among Edinburgh intellectuals. The Aberdeen poet, James Beattie, compiled his popular *Scoticisms,
Arranged in Alphabetical Order, Designed to Correct Improprieties of Speech and
Writing* (1799), listing 200 words which might be used by those who 'had
no opportunity of learning English from the company they kept'.[25]

David Hume, Hugh Blair and the strongly pro-government historian
William Robertson agreed with Beattie and Mackenzie, seeking to rid
their language of Scoticisms, though a contemporary of Burns who heard
both Hume and Burns speak in Edinburgh reported that the citified
Hume sounded more Scottish than the country poet,[26] and it is said
of Hume, who admired all things English, that 'he died confessing not his
sins but his Scotticisms'.[27] On paper, in England, Burns's dialect could be
too Scottish for his own good. According to William Cowper in 1787:
'Poor Burns loses much of his deserved praise in this country, through
our ignorance of his language. I despair of meeting with any Englishman
who will take the pains that I have taken to understand him. His candle
is bright, but shut up in a dark lantern.'[28] Scottish writers who wished
their work to sell in England realized that a linguistic accommodation
must be found. Even in the later work of Scott the Scots language becomes 'in the theatrical sense, a "property" and most in use in what may

be called the "costume" kind of narrative',[29] employed for 'a special spectacular purpose, to strike a note or differentiate a character' by sprinklings
from what G. Gregory Smith calls 'the glossarial pepper-pot'.[30] Susan
Ferrier's 'costume' Highlanders in *Marriage* (1818) speak in broad Scots to
dramatize the differences between their gutsy provincial manners and the
cold suavities of the English society into which the heroine, Mary Douglas,
is transplanted.

As Roderick Watson says, 'the Leddy [Lady] of Grippy' stands out as
a vernacular *tour de force* in John Galt's novel *The Entail* (1823).[31] The
sprinklings of Scots in Galt's *Annals of the Parish* (1821) and *The Provost*
(1822) give cause for regret that such tangily expressive language has
fallen into literary desuetude. In *Annals of the Parish* there are 'grulshy [fat
and clumsy] bairns', 'birky' (sharp) girls and ladies who are 'tozy and cosh'
(tipsy and happy); the minister's servants squander his stipend with their
'galravitching' (extravagance); disputation is 'argol-bargling' and altercation is 'stramash'; untidy is 'untrig' and excessively rigid politeness is
'overly perjinct'. Corruptible Deans of Guild in *The Provost* have 'their
loofs creeshed' (their palms greased); secret information is 'spunkit' (sparked)
out; and a boozy party is a 'gavawlling'. In Chapter XXX of *Annals of
the Parish* a visiting preacher is criticized by the incumbent minister, the
Rev. Micah Balwhidder, and his congregation:

> the elderly people thought his language rather too
> Englified, which I thought likewise, for I never could
> abide that the plain auld Kirk of Scotland, with her sober
> presbyterian simplicity, should borrow, either in word or
> in deed, from the language of the prelatic hierarchy of
> England.[32]

Like the volume of Moral Essays he goes on to publish, the young
preacher's sermon lacks 'birr and smeddum' (force and mettle), implying
that he is deficient in evangelical energy; but fault is also being found
with his over-Anglicized language. Galt, however, kept his Scots 'unnaturally light',[33] rationalizing his practice by arguing that 'there is such an
idiomatic difference in the structure of the national dialects of England
and Scotland, that very good Scotch might be couched in the purest
English terms, and without the employment of a single Scottish word'.[34]
While many of Scott's most memorable characters speak in a fully authentic Scots, with 'Wandering Willie's Tale' in *Redgauntlet* (1824) his
masterpiece of broad Scots, in Galt's work Scoticism is 'rather a matter
of accent than of vocabulary'.[35] Yet Galt can achieve by his formula the
flavour of a Scottish ballad. Madge Wildfire's song, 'Proud Maisie', in *The
Heart of Midlothian* is echoed in the lament of simple-minded Meg Gaffaw,
rejected in love in *Annals of the Parish*:

The worm – the worm is my bonny bridegroom, and
Jenny with the many feet [the centipede] my bridal maid.
The mill-dam's water the wine o' the wedding, and the
clay and the clod shall be my bedding. A lang night is
meet for a bridal, but none shall be langer than mine.[36]

In his preface to the collected *Noctes Ambrosianae* John Wilson's son-
in-law, James Frederick Ferrier, introduces the language of The Shepherd
(the persona Wilson and his associates created for James Hogg) as a last
stand for written Scots:

> ... the dialect of the Shepherd ... is thoroughly Scottish,
> and it could not be Anglicized without losing its raciness
> and spoiling entirely the dramatic propriety of his character
> ... the author of the *Noctes Ambrosianae* wields it with a
> copiousness, flexibility, and splendour which never have
> been, and probably never will be, equalled ... the last
> specimen, then, on a large scale of the national language
> of Scotland which the world is ever likely to see.[37]

Standard English could not suppress spoken Scots, as the Scottish Language Resource Centre is proud to point out:

> In spite o twa hunner year o Standart English bein learnt
> in the schules the lenth an breadth o Scotland – aw ye
> need tae dae is tae keep yer lugs cockit an ye'll hear that
> Scots is still aboot, whither ye're argyin in Ayr or
> Aiberdeenshire, bidin in Buckie or Biggar, crackin in
> Castlemilk or Crieff or daunderin roon Dumbarton or
> Dundee.[38]

Scots continued to be spoken, and George MacDonald's realistic use of
it is an attractive feature of his once popular romantic novels. While
'Scotch was quite discouraged at home' in *Alec Forbes of Howglen* (1865,
Chapter 14), Alec's 'immaculate' mother falls 'into the slough of the
vernacular' when speaking her mind to Murdoch Malison, the psychotic
schoolteacher, in Chapter 24, thereby giving MacDonald an opportunity
to pronounce on the virtues of patois:

> The fact is, it is easier to speak the truth in a *patois*, for it
> lies nearer to the simple realities than a more conventional
> speech ... I do not however allow that the Scotch is a
> *patois* in the ordinary sense of the word. For had not
> Scotland a living literature, and that a high one, when

England could produce none, or next to none – I mean
in the fifteenth century? But old age, and the introduction
of a more polished form of utterance, have given to the
Scotch all the other advantages of a *patois*, in addition to
its own directness and simplicity.

The natural use of dialect was, nevertheless, still unacceptable in the
typical turn-of-the-century Scottish classroom. In William McIlvanney's
Docherty (1975) young Conn Docherty's teacher asks the boy what's
wrong with his face:

> 'Skint ma nose, sur.'
> 'How?'
> 'Ah fell an' bumped ma heid in the sheuch [gutter], sur.'
> 'I beg your pardon?'
> 'Ah fell an' bumped ma heid in the sheuch, sur.'
> 'I beg your pardon?'
> In the pause Conn understands the nature of the choice,
> tremblingly, compulsively, makes it.
> 'Ah fell an' bumped ma heid in the sheuch, sur.'
> The blow is instant . . .
> 'That, Docherty, is impertinence. You will translate,
> please, into the mother-tongue.'
>
> (Book 1, Chapter 15)

Ironically, Conn's father, Tam, out of conditioned belief in the inferiority
of his class, holds up this teacher as a model his son should emulate: 'See
Mr Pirrie. He's aff the same kinna folk as oorselves, Ah hear. An' ye see
whit he's made o' himself. Noo is that no' an example fur ye?' (Book 2,
Chapter 7).
   Lewis Carroll records in his diary (16 January 1866) that he enjoyed
the story of *Alec Forbes of Howglen*, and that the 'Scotch dialect, too, is
pleasant enough when one gets a little used to it';[39] but for almost a
century after the *Noctes Ambrosianae* it looked as if Ferrier had been right
about the written language until the publication of Charles Murray's
north-east dialect poems (most of them written in South Africa) in *Hamewith*
(1900), the first in a series of collections leading to *Hamewith and Other
Poems: Collected Edition* (1927).[40] Despite such lapses into sugary sentimentality as his evocation of 'a wee, wee glen in the Hielan's' in 'Hame',
Murray's command of a vigorous Aberdeenshire Scots derived from country
life and the oral tradition deserves to be better known than merely by the
few poems that occasionally find their way into anthologies. His strength
is most evident in the vernacular compressions of his familiar Scots idiom.
Thus, in 'Spring in the Howe o' Alford': 'The sheep are aff to the hills

again / As hard as the lambs are able'; and in 'The Hills an' Her': 'By
nicht, by day, my dream's the same / The warl' at peace an' me at hame'.
An irresistibly pawky apologia for drinking concludes 'The Miller Explains':

> Fae forbears my thirst I inherit,
>   As others get red hair or gout;
> The heirship's expensive: mair merit
>   To me that I never cry out.
> An' sae, man, I canna help thinkin'
>   The neighbours unkindly; in truth,
> Afore they can judge o' my drinkin'
>   They first maun consider my drooth.   *thirst*

'Gin I were God' exemplifies Murray's characteristically bittersweet blend
of wit and sentiment. The poet imagines himself as God, 'Deaved [deaf-
ened] wi' harps an' hymns' and tired 'o' the flockin' angels hairse wi'
singin', looking down on earth from the edge of a convenient cloud:

> Syne, gin I saw hoo men I'd made mysel'   *Then if*
> Had startit in to pooshan, sheet an' fell,   *shoot and kill*
> To reive an' rape, an' fairly mak' a hell   *plunder*
> O' my braw birlin' Earth, – a hale week's wark –
> I'd cast my coat again, rowe up my sark –
> An', or they'd time to lench a second ark,
> Tak' back my word an' sen' anither spate,
> Droon oot the hale hypothec, dicht the sklate,
> Own my mistak', an', aince I'd cleared the brod,
> Start a' thing owre again, gin I was God.

In 1925 Murray wondered if a Scots poet might appear 'who could
handle the vernacular and bring back some of our ancient greatness'.[41]
Then, in 1926, came the 2,685 lines of Hugh MacDiarmid's philosophical
poem *A Drunk Man Looks at the Thistle* expressly designed to show 'that
Braid Scots is adaptable to all kinds of poetry, and to a much greater
variety of measures than might be supposed from the restricted practice
of the last hundred years'.[42] Lewis Grassic Gibbon uses an accessibly
Anglicized version of the Scots of his native north-east Lowlands to
convey 'the speak' of Kincardineshire in *A Scots Quair* (1932–4). Reading
and schooling commend English, but Gibbon's heroine, Chris Guthrie,
is repeatedly pulled back to the language of her place and people:

> you wanted the words they'd known and used, forgotten
> in the far-off youngness of their lives, Scots words to tell
> to your heart, how they wrung it and held it, the toil of

their days and unendingly their fight. And the next minute
that passed from you, you were English, back to the
English words so sharp and clean and true – for a while,
for a while, till they slid so smooth from your throat you
knew they could never say anything that was worth the
saying at all.

(Sunset Song, Chapter 1)

By the 1930s the use of Scots was a political affirmation of un-
Englishness. So it remained for Robert Garioch, the bulk of whose poetry
is in Scots. When asked in 1980 why he wrote in Scots, Garioch replied:

> Well, it is my native tongue . . . I remember the conscious
> effort I had to make at school to adapt my speech to the
> requirements of the teachers. This is different nowadays,
> because people don't speak as my father and mother
> did . . . They spoke Scots. That is to say, Scottish English,
> with a pretty good Scottish vocabulary. So that was the
> predicament I was conscious of – and I did it deliberately,
> as a reaction, almost, against a very English upbringing.[43]

A tougher mood brings a more political answer to the same question:
'Like everyone else, I suffer more or less from belonging to a half-nation
betrayed to and taken over by the English government of 1707. So there
is a political reason for writing in Scots, but poetical reasons come first
in poetry, I hope.'[44] For Garioch language is not a matter of choice:
he writes in his 'native tongue', relishing the political statement he un-
avoidably makes by being true to his upbringing and producing several
enduring Scots poems of satire and sentiment as well as his translations
of 'Roman Sonnets Frae Giuseppe Belli'. The theme of freedom is developed into the image of humanity 'birlan [whirling round] in wretched-
ness' in 'The Wire', a long poem based on Garioch's experience as a
prisoner in the Second World War. The same theme receives comic
treatment in 'Sisyphus'. Disliking all attempts in English to translate Homer's
description of Sisyphus, Garioch tried it in Scots, satirizing the king's
perpetual torment as a case of misplaced ingenuity. His Sisyphus collab-
orates in his own humiliation, sacrificing freedom for the certainty of his
pay cheque at the end of the month. The poem deploys the rich ono-
matopoeic resources of Scots and the idiom's genius for understatement:

Bumpity doun in the corrie gaed	*hollow/went rushing*
whuddran the pitiless whun stane.	*lump of hard rock (e.g. basalt)*
Sisyphus, pechan and sweitan, disjaskit,	*panting/worn out*
forfeuchan and broun'd-aff,	*exhausted*

sat on the heather a hanlawhile,	*short time*
houpan the Boss didna spy him,	
seein the terms of his contract includit	
nae mention of tea-breaks,	
syne at the muckle big scunnersom	*disgusting*
boulder he trauchlit aince mair.	*struggled*

When the boulder unexpectedly stands firm at the top of the hill, Sisyphus stretches out and takes a break, hoping the Boss isn't looking, eats a pie and a cheese sandwich, and perversely sets the process in motion again:

> Whit was he thinkin about, that he jist gied the boulder a
>   wee shove?
> Bumpity doun in the corrie gaed whuddran the pitiless
>   whun stane,
> Sisyphus dodderan eftir it, shair of his cheque at the
>   month's end.[45]

Edwin Morgan thinks Hugh MacDiarmid's ideal of 'a national language for Scotland, which won't be English . . . far from practicability'.[46] He usually writes in English or in the kind of Scots that is spoken in most parts of the country, a language which is English coloured by 'local varieties'[47] of vocabulary and idiom, but not so highly coloured as to be inaccessible to the majority of Scots or to other users of English. But he can enjoy the tension between Scots and English. In 'Canedolia, an off-concrete Scotch fantasia' he imagines a perplexed South Briton getting his come-uppance from an irrepressibly mischievous Scots vocabulary. A glossary is no help here:

> *what is it like there?*
> och it's freuchie, it's faifley, it's wamphray, it's frandy, it's
> sliddery.

> *what do you do?*
> we foindle and fungle, we bonkle and meigle and
> maxpoffle. we scotstarvit, armit, wormit, and even whifflet.
> we play at crosstobs, leuchars, gorbals, and finfan. we
> scavaig, and there's aye a bit of tilquhilly. if it's wet,
> treshnish and mishnish.[48]

Overwhelming the condescending outsider by nonsensical explosions of a wildly self-generating un-English, Morgan takes his place with Ramsay and Fergusson, Burns, The Shepherd of the *Noctes Ambrosianae*, Murray,

MacDiarmid, Lewis Grassic Gibbon, the Scots playwright Robert McLellan, Violet Jacob, Robert Garioch and other defenders of one of the Scottish languages.

Notes

1. Walter Allen, *The English Novel, A Short Critical History* (Harmondsworth, 1958), p. 69.

2. Miguel de Cervantes, *Don Quixote De La Mancha*, trans. Tobias Smollett with an Introduction by Carlos Fuentes (London, 1986), p. xiii.

3. Ibid., pp. 79–80.

4. Tobias Smollett, *The Expedition of Humphry Clinker* (New York, 1929), p. 225.

5. Ibid., p. 226.

6. Ibid., p. 429.

7. The following quotations from *The Man of Feeling* are taken from Henry Mackenzie, *The Man of Feeling*, ed. Brian Vickers (London, 1967).

8. Mackenzie's liberalism in attacking British conquests in India is ahead of his time. The first parliamentary report on Indian affairs did not appear until two years later, and it took a fairly neutral position. See Vickers, p. 137.

9. 'Coke upon Lyttleton' is the lawyers' name for the reprint and translation of Littleton's *Tenures* (c. 1465) published with a commentary by Sir Edward Coke, 1628–44.

10. W. E. K. Anderson (ed.), *The Journal of Sir Walter Scott* (Oxford, 1972), p. 26.

11. See Laurence Sterne, *The Life and Opinions of Tristram Shandy, Gentleman*, edited by James Aiken Work (New York, 1940), p. lxxvii.

12. E. M. Forster, *Aspects of the Novel* (London, 1927), p. 27.

13. The following quotations from Ramsay and Fergusson are from *Poems by Allan Ramsay and Robert Fergusson*, ed. Alexander Manson Kinghorn and Alexander Law for the Association for Scottish Literary Studies (Edinburgh and London, 1974).

14. Allan Ramsay, *Some Few Hints, in Defence of Dramatical Entertainments*, in *Mr Law's Unlawfulness of the Stage Entertainment Examin'd, etc.*, ed. Arthur Freeman for *The English Stage, Attack and Defense 1577–1730* (New York and London, 1974), pp. 4–5.

15. Kinghorn and Law, *Poems*, p. 13.

16. Professor Wilson, *Noctes Ambrosianae*, A New Edition, edited by his son-in-law, Professor Ferrier, 4 vols (Edinburgh and London, 1876), I, p. 174.

17. John Purser, *Scotland's Music* (Edinburgh, 1992), pp. 200–1.

18. See Roderick Watson (ed.), *The Poetry of Scotland: Gaelic, Scots and English 1380–1980* (Edinburgh, 1995), p. 347.

19. Allan H. MacLaine, *Robert Fergusson* (New York, 1965), pp. 162–3.

20. Standard Habbie is the verse form used by many Scottish poets during the eighteenth century and particularly favoured by Ramsay and Fergusson. The name derives from its use in Robert Sempill's (c. 1595–1665) poem, 'The Life and Death of Habbie Simpson, the Piper of Kilbarchan'.

21. Robert Burns, 'On Fergusson', *Poems and Songs*, ed. James Kinsley (Oxford, 1969), p. 258.

22. Robert Louis Stevenson, *Letters, Volume V*, Tusitala Edition, 35 vols (London, 1923–4), XXXV, p. 126.

23. Quoted in Kinghorn and Law, *Poems*, p. x.

24. Trevor Royle, *The Macmillan Companion to Scottish Literature* (London and Basingstoke, 1983), p. 145.

25. Ibid., p. 256.

26. David Daiches, *Robert Burns and His World* (London, 1971), p. 12.

27. Robert McCrum, William Cran, Robert MacNeil, *The Story of English*, new and revised edn (London, 1992), p. 151.

28. Letter from William Cowper to Samuel Rose, 27 August 1787, in *The Life and Works of William Cowper*, ed. Robert Southey, 15 vols (London, 1836), VI, pp. 56–7.

29. G. Gregory Smith, *Scottish Literature, Character and Influence* (London, 1919), p. 127.

30. Ibid., p. 129.

31. Roderick Watson, *The Literature of Scotland* (Basingstoke, 1984), p. 279.

32. John Galt, *Annals of the Parish*, ed. James Kinsley (London, 1967), p. 132.

33. Ibid., p. xix.

34. John Galt, *Ringan Gilhaize or The Covenanters*, ed. Patricia J. Wilson (Edinburgh, 1984), p. 323.

35. Gregory Smith, *Scottish Literature*, p. 127.

36. Galt, *Annals of the Parish*, ed. Kinsley, p. 160.

37. Wilson, *Noctes Ambrosianae*, I, p. xix. Ferrier's Preface is dated 18 July 1855.

38. 'See Scots!', *The Scots Language Resource Centre*, brochure (Perth, 1993).

39. See Raphael B. Shaberman, *George MacDonald: A Bibliographical Study* (Winchester and Detroit, 1990), p. 24.

40. This edition is superseded by *Hamewith: The Complete Poems of Charles Murray* (Aberdeen, 1979) which includes Murray's last poems with notes by Alexander Keith and an introductory essay, 'Charles Murray', by Nan Shepherd. Quotations are from this edition.

41. 'Buchan's Bard Honoured', *Glasgow Herald*, 30 October 1925.

42. 'Braid Scots in Verse', *Glasgow Herald*, 13 February 1926, p. 4.

43. Robert Garioch interviewed by Marshall Walker, 28 September 1980, in *Seven Poets*, ed. Christopher Carrell (Glasgow, 1981), p. 60.

44. Ibid., p. 67.

45. Robert Garioch, *Complete Poetical Works*, ed. Robin Fulton (Edinburgh, 1983), p. 28.

46. 'Edwin Morgan interviewed by Robin Hamilton', selection from transcript published in *Eboracum*, 11$^{1/2}$ (1972), pp. [5, 7, 8], full transcript printed in Edwin Morgan, *Nothing Not Giving Messages: reflections on work and life*, ed. Hamish Whyte (Edinburgh, 1990), pp. 22–45 [30].

47. Ibid., p. 31.

48. Edwin Morgan, *Collected Poems* (Manchester, 1990), p. 156.

Chapter 4

Robert Burns: the Myth and the Gift

'Auld lang syne'

Robert Burns has been long accorded the status of a mythical hero, an apostle of liberty and equality, the 'giant Original Man' of Thomas Carlyle's 'The Hero as Man of Letters' in Lecture V, *On Heroes, Hero-Worship & the Heroic in History* (1841). All too often the myth takes precedence over the poetry. Hugh MacDiarmid's excoriation of Burns cult bardolatry, written in 1934, is still regrettably apposite:

> It has denied his spirit to honour his name.
> It has denied his poetry to laud his amours.
> It has preserved his furniture and repelled his message.
> It has built itself up on the progressive refusal of his lead
>   in regard to Scottish politics, Scottish literature, and the
>   Scottish tongue.[1]

Every Hogmanay (New Year's Eve) drink and sentimentality transcend accuracy in what Lewis Grassic Gibbon calls 'the sugary surge' (*Sunset Song*, Chapter 3) of 'Auld Lang Syne' (K, 240),[2] progress seldom being made beyond the first quatrain and chorus to the lyrical perfection of what follows:

> We twa hae run about the braes,
>   And pou'd the gowans fine;   *pulled daisies*
> But we've wander'd mony a weary fitt,   *foot*
>   Sin auld lang syne.   *long ago*
>
> We twa hae paidl'd in the burn,
>   Frae morning sun till dine;   *dinner time*
> But seas between us braid hae roar'd,   *broad*
>   Sin auld lang syne.

The childhood that kept companions playing together on familiar hills has passed. Adult feet have taken their separate ways and the shared miniature waters of the burn have been immersed in the vastness of sundering oceans. So let us commemorate the bonding, companionable burn of innocence that flowed, as it must, into the severing seas of distance, experience and time with a draught of good fellowship, the 'willie-waught' in our raised glasses, as we toast again the emotionally tenacious past from which the present has come. These are the implications by which Burns raises the power of an old song from facile sentimentality to the exactness of universal sentiment.

In a letter of 17 December 1788 Burns complimented his friend Mrs Frances Anna Dunlop on her description in a letter to him of a meeting with an old friend from her school days:

> Your meeting which you so well describe with your old
> Schoolfellow & friend, was truly interesting. – Out upon
> the ways of the World! They spoil these 'Social Offspring
> of the heart' . . . Apropos, is not the Scots phrase, 'Auld
> lang syne', exceedingly expressive. – There is an old song
> & tune which has often thrilled thro' my soul. – You
> know I am an enthusiast in old Scots songs. – I shall give
> you the verses on the other sheet . . . Light be the turf on
> the breast of the heaven-inspired Poet who composed this
> glorious Fragment! There is more of the fire of native
> genius in it, than in half a dozen of English
> Bacchanalians.[3]

The 'verses on the other sheet' were Burns's first version of 'Auld Lang Syne', derived from 'the old Song of the olden times' which he 'took down from an old man's singing'.[4] He sent the verses, slightly emended, to James Johnson, an Edinburgh engraver and music seller who had begun publication of the *Scots Musical Museum*, a five-volume anthology of words and music of all the Scottish songs he could find. (This is where Max Bruch found the folk tunes he used in the composition of 1880's *Scottish Fantasy for Violin and Orchestra*.) Despite Burns's enthusiastic collaboration with him, Johnson delayed publication of 'Auld Lang Syne' until the fifth volume of the *Museum* which appeared some six months after Burns's death, presumably because he had already printed Allan Ramsay's inferior poem with the same title and the opening words, 'Should auld acquaintance be forgot', together with the mediocre air supplied again by Burns. In September 1793 Burns sent the verses to another collector, George Thomson, who published them in *Select Scotish Airs* (1799) matched with the tune to which they are now sung everywhere. Aptly described as 'the song that nobody knows'[5] – apart from the

first stanza and chorus – 'Auld Lang Syne' is essential Burns in its demonstration of the poet's gift for poetry as song, his passion for the Scottish
tradition, his talent for reworking folk material, his feeling for human
connection, and his use of Scots. Lionized after the appearance of the
Kilmarnock Edition, Burns might have given in completely to the Anglicized tastes of the *literati* if only to show that a ploughman could
graduate from his rustic background and beat the English at their own
language. Occasionally he succumbed, in the generally second-rate poems
written in English; but he was never long deflected from his idiom. The
most striking aspect of Burns's character is his independence. This is the
point of contact between the myth of Burns and his gift.

The myth

The myth is fed by colourful background and salty incident. There is the
poet's humble Ayrshire origin in 'the auld clay biggin' – 'The Vision' (K,
62) – the two-roomed thatched Alloway cottage, now picturesque to
tourist expectations ('O the flummery of a birth place!' Keats exclaimed
on his visit to the house in 1818[6]) but then rudimentary, built by his
father, William Burnes, with his own hands. There are the unpropitious
farms at Mount Oliphant and Lochlea where he helped his industrious
but unlucky father until 1784 when with his brother, Gilbert, he took
the family to Mossgiel in the parish of Mauchline. There is his attempt
to rescue the family fortunes by learning the trade of flax-dressing, the
scheme aborted by the burning of the Irvine flax-dressing shop, set alight
'by the drunken carelessness' of his thieving partner's wife and reduced
to ashes, leaving Burns 'like a true Poet, not worth sixpence'.[7] There is
his plan to escape from personal and financial difficulties by emigrating to
Jamaica with 'Highland' Mary Campbell, his hiding from the wrath of
James Armour, father of the pregnant Jean, then his decision to stand his
ground in Scotland after the publication of the Kilmarnock Edition elic-
ited praise from the blind poet and critic Thomas Blacklock which 'over-
threw all my schemes by rousing my poetic ambition'.[8] There are the
children by Elizabeth Paton, Jean Armour, May Cameron, Jenny Clow
and Anna Park, and the amours with Mary Campbell (who may have
died giving premature birth to his child) and Margaret Chalmers, perhaps
the love of his life, who rejected him. There is the largely epistolary affair
with Agnes Craig McLehose, the 'Clarinda' to his implausibly Arcadian
'Sylvander' and the 'Nancy' of 'Ae Fond Kiss' (K, 337) which commemorates their final parting in the compact expression of Burns at his
most intense, the amoral rawness of commanding love and the hurt of
disjunction simply set down with the art that conceals art:

I'll ne'er blame my partial fancy,
Naething could resist my Nancy:
But to see her, was to love her;
Love but her, and love for ever. –

Had we never lov'd sae kindly,
Had we never lov'd sae blindly!
Never met – or never parted,
We had ne'er been broken-hearted.

There is the fall from his horse, Jenny Geddes (named after the woman who in 1637 is supposed to have thrown her stool at the Dean of St Giles's Church when he began to read from Archbishop Laud's English prayer book), during an inebriated race at Loch Lomond: 'Jenny Geddes trode over me with such cautious reverence that matters were not so bad as might well have been expected; so I came off with a few cuts and bruises, and a thorough resolution to be a pattern of sobriety for the future.'[9] The resolution was less than thorough, for in 1793 there is the social gaffe of his career when, encouraged to drink too much by his host, Robert Riddell of Friar's Carse in Nithsdale, he apparently acted out the Rape of the Sabine Women all too graphically with Riddell's wife Elizabeth and was ordered from the house. Despite persistent financial needs and the responsibilities of his marriage to Jean Armour in 1788 there is his likeable disregard for money: in 1792 he offered the publisher, William Creech, material for a new edition of his poems, saying, 'A few Books which I very much want, are all the recompence I crave, together with as many copies of this new edition of my own works as Friendship or Gratitude shall prompt me to *present*.'[10] A five-pound note from George Thomson drew the response, 'I assure you, Sir, that you truly hurt me with your pecuniary parcel. – It degrades me in my own eyes.'[11] Sadly, he was to write to Thomson a few days before he died, asking for five pounds to settle an account with 'a cruel scoundrel of a Haberdasher'.[12] Then there is the overworked exciseman, wearied by a life of emotional, intellectual and sexual intensity, riding up to forty miles a day, incongruously a figure of the establishment but still temperamentally attuned to the free spirits on the other side of the line of his profession, as he makes clear in 'The De'il's awa wi' th' Exciseman' (K, 386):

The deil's awa the deil's awa
   The deil's awa wi th' Exciseman,
He's danc'd awa he's danc'd awa
   He's danc'd awa wi' th' Exciseman.

We'll mak our maut and we'll brew our drink,   *malt*
   We'll laugh, sing, and rejoice, man;
And mony braw thanks to the meikle black deil,   *great*
   That danc'd awa wi' th' Exciseman.

It is said that in the search for illicit stills Burns would 'arrive at the door of an old widow woman with his hat off, thus making it unofficial, to tell her that he would be back shortly with his hat on, which would make it official. She would then have time to make appropriate arrangements!'[13] Finally, there is the disappointed tenant of Ellisland Farm near Dumfries, 'this accursed farm' as he called it,[14] whose position on the river Nith was visually pleasing, but whose soil was too exhausted to yield profit from his crops.[15]

Sources of the gift

These are pieces of the furniture of the myth. What, then, of the gift and the message? What of the mixture of tenderness and bawdy, calculation and spontaneity, vulgarity and exaltation? Byron, reading Burns's letters in 1813, marvels at the contraries in the poet's make-up:

What an antithetical mind! – tenderness, roughness –
delicacy, coarseness – sentiment, sensuality – soaring and
grovelling, dirt and deity – all mixed up in that one
compound of inspired clay![16]

Byron catches the range and variety of the poet's antisyzygy, but Burns, of course, was no more or less 'inspired' or 'heaven-taught' than any other genius. Writing to Byron about the greater disadvantages of James Hogg's peasant background for a man of literary ambition, Scott observes: 'Burns . . . had an education not much worse than the sons of many gentlemen in Scotland'.[17] His schooling, mostly supplied by John Murdoch, the Alloway teacher hired co-operatively by his father and four neighbours to educate their children, and enlarged by William Burnes himself, was essentially English, although he did learn to read French and acquired the basic elements of Latin. In the summer of 1775 he went to Kirkoswald to learn mathematics from Hugh Rodger, the parish schoolteacher and local surveyor, making 'pretty good progress' until 'set off in a tangent' from his studies by Peggy Thomson – the 'lovely charmer' of 'Now westlin winds' (K, 2) – who lived next door to the school, also making 'greater

progress in the knowledge of mankind' and learning 'to look unconcern-
edly on a large tavern-bill'.[18]

He read the prominent eighteenth-century English writers as well as
Shakespeare, Milton and Dryden. Gilbert Burns recalls that in 1772 'a
bookish acquaintance of my father's procured for us a reading of two
volumes of Richardson's *Pamela*, which was the first novel we ever read'.[19]
Pamela remained a favourite with the poet along with Smollett's *The
Adventures of Ferdinand Count Fathom*, Sterne's *Tristram Shandy* and Mackenzie's *The Man of Feeling*; but the two books that galvanized him –
Blind Harry's *Wallace*[20] and Robert Fergusson's *Poems* – were more specifically Scottish than either Smollett or Mackenzie. From the blacksmith
who shod the Burns horses he borrowed an abridged, Anglicized version
of Blind Harry's late fifteenth-century poem published in 1722 by William
Hamilton of Gilbertfield. Although this popular modernization of the
heroic poem was a symptom of the decline of Scots as a literary medium
it cast its patriotic spell on the young poet: 'the story of Wallace poured
a Scotish prejudice in my veins which will boil along there till the flood-
gates of life shut in eternal rest'.[21] In 1793 the prejudice boiled over into
the nationalist verse of 'Robert Bruce's March to Bannockburn' (K, 425)
or 'Scots, wha hae', the 'most thrilling and defiant of all the battle-songs
of the nation'.[22] On 26 August 1787 Burns had visited the site of the
Battle of Bannockburn where, against fearful odds, Robert the Bruce
achieved his great victory over Edward II on 24 June 1314. Now his
historical nostalgia was associated with sympathy for the revolutions in
America and France. Especially forceful are the central stanzas in which
Bruce challenges any cowards in his army to flee the field and equates
freedom with the Scottish cause:

> Wha will be a traitor-knave?
> Wha can fill a coward's grave?
> Wha sae base as be a Slave?
> – Let him turn and flie: –
>
> Wha for SCOTLAND'S king and law,
> Freedom's sword will strongly draw,
> FREE-MAN stand, or FREE-MAN fa',
>   Let him follow me.

In the autobiographical letter he wrote to Dr John Moore on 2 August
1787 Burns says, 'Rhyme, except some religious poems which are in
print, I had given up; but meeting with Fergusson's Scotch poems, I
strung anew my wildly-sounding rustic lyre with emulating vigour.'[23]
The raised consciousness of Scottish feeling instilled by *Wallace* was now
enhanced by Fergusson's models of native expression, and Burns was soon

developing his own Scots synthesis of diction from the Scottish tradition, English and the spoken language of Ayrshire, acknowledging Fergusson as 'my elder brother in Misfortune, / By far my elder Brother in the muse' (K, 143). In 1787 he commissioned a stone to be erected on Fergusson's unmarked grave and in the verse epistle 'To W. S*****n [William Simson], Ochiltree' (K, 59) extols Fergusson's virtues with those of Ramsay and Gilbertfield, berating the Edinburgh gentry for their neglect of the talent in their midst:

> O *Ferguson*! thy glorious *parts*,
> Ill-suited *law's* dry, musty arts!
> My curse upon your whunstane hearts,   *whinstone*
>   Ye Enbrugh Gentry!
> The tythe o' what ye waste at *cartes*   *cards*
>   Wad stow'd his pantry!   *would have filled*

The model of Fergusson was crucial: 'had it not been for Fergusson's achievement, Burns would not have been the Burns that we know as the great national poet of Scotland. Part of Burns's glory belongs, in a very real sense, to Robert Fergusson.'[24]

Love, nature, sex

Even before his encounter with Fergusson's poems Burns learned to use Scots confidently. At fifteen he 'first committed the sin of RHYME' in 'O once I lov'd' (K, 1), a song praising Nelly Kilpatrick who initiated him 'in a certain delicious Passion, which in spite of acid Disappointment, gin-horse Prudence and bookworm Philosophy, I hold to be the first of human joys, our dearest pleasure here below'.[25] The piece is fluent like other early poems written in an English tinged with Scots, and mannered in its pious focus on the girl's moral character rather than on the physical magnetism which doubtless attracted the young Burns. (Compare the twenty-six-year-old Yeats's similar but more disingenuous romantic pose in his poem to Maud Gonne, 'When you are old'):

> A gaudy dress and gentle air
>   May lightly touch the heart,
> But it's innocence and modesty
>   That polishes the dart.

'Thus with me began Love and Poesy,' Burns recalls.[26] A year and a girl (Peggy Thomson) later love and poesy jointly advanced to the technically maturer and emotionally richer song, 'Now westlin winds' (K, 2), an early masterpiece in which 'the charms of nature' complete the trinity of elements characteristic of Burns's best songs, the gentleness of love harmonizing with the clear evening, blue sky and skimming swallow in contrast to the turbulence of the rough westerly and the murderous guns of autumn sportsmen. (No lover of Scots song should fail to hear the folk singer Dick Gaughan's recording of 'Now westlin winds' in his album, *Handful of Earth*.[27]) The naturalness of free love is the theme of the 'Song' (K, 8) to the tune of 'Corn rigs are bonie', and the naturalness of fatherhood the poet's pride in 'A Poet's Welcome to his love-begotten Daughter; the first instance that entitled him to the venerable appellation of Father' (K, 60). Here Burns's use of Scots is as full-blooded as his defiance of conventional propriety and Calvinistic name-calling:

> Tho' now they ca' me, Fornicator,
> And tease my name in kintra clatter,   *country gossip*
> The mair they talk, I'm kend the better;
>   E'en let them clash!
> An auld wife's tongue's a feckless matter
>   To gie ane fash.   *annoyance*

Landscape and love suffuse each other in 'I love my Jean' (K, 227) and in the haunting song (K, 456) 'Ca' the yowes to the knowes'. (If poets were accorded poetic justice Burns would have lived two centuries longer to hear the singer Kathleen Ferrier's impeccable interpretation of 'Ca' the yowes'.[28]) In 'My bony Mary' (K, 242) neither war nor 'the roar o' sea or shore' holds intimidation equal to the pain of parting. In 'The Banks o' Doon' (K, 328B) the beauty of nature, impervious to the poet's unhappiness, expresses more simply than W. H. Auden's 'Musée Des Beaux Arts' a similar truth about the exacerbation of anguish by a world that goes heedlessly on:

> Ye banks and braes o' bonie Doon,
>   How can ye bloom sae fresh and fair;
> How can ye chant, ye little birds,
>   And I sae weary, fu' o' care!
> Thou'll break my heart, thou warbling bird,
>   That wantons thro' the flowering thorn:
> Thou minds me o' departed joys,
>   Departed, never to return.

If this third of Burns's versions of 'The Banks o' Doon' is more calculatedly literary than its plainer predecessors (the second version is K, 328A), the decorative lengthening of the lines can be condoned for the sake of fitting the verses to the traditional melody, 'The Caledonian Hunt's Delight'. The perfect match achieved is most expressively realized in the piano arrangement by Roger Quilter.[29]

In 'Fair Eliza' (K, 370) the pang of love is lightly reckoned in terms of bees and fairies, even superseding the rapturous, sharp moment of poetic inspiration:

> Not the bee upon the blossom
>   In the pride o' sinny noon;   *sunny*
> Not the little sporting fairy,
>   All beneath the simmer moon;   *summer*
> Not the Poet in the moment
>   Fancy lightens in his e'e,
> Kens the pleasure, feels the rapture,
>   That thy presence gies to me.

The last farewell to 'Highland Mary' (K, 389) is taken amidst the 'banks, and braes, and streams', woods and flowers of the castle of Montgomery, and the lover meets his girl in 'The lea-rig' (K, 392) 'Down by the burn where scented birks / Wi' dew are hanging'. In 'A red, red Rose' (K, 453) love is measured against vast imagined natural processes which the lover vows he will conquer. The evidence for Burns's hand in the song is inconclusive. Thomas Crawford considers it in terms of 'archetypal images' defined as 'the concentrated experiences and feelings of many generations, organized by language and handed down over a long period'. He concludes:

> it is from socially-transmitted emotional patterns of this
> sort that Burns's song derives its peculiar beauty. Another
> way of stating the same conclusion is to say that 'A red,
> red Rose' is a lyric of genius, made out of the common
> inherited material of folk-song by an author whose name
> we happen to know.[30]

James Kinsley thinks it more probable that the song is just as Burns heard and recorded it: 'Editors have turned up chapbook models for every stanza, and almost every line, of this song; and have treated it as an exquisite example of Burns's art in raising folksong to perfection . . . We may, however, be doing an injustice to oral tradition in regarding ['A red, red Rose'] even as a reconstruction by Burns.'[31] As Alan Bold demonstrates in *A Burns Companion* (1991), there was rich source material available to the poet, but 'the song has touches of genius usually associated with Burns'.[32] There has never been doubt about the eloquence of the song in asserting the power of love, fragile like the flower and delicate like the melody 'that's sweetly play'd in tune' but, with the fiery energy of the rose's colour, perhaps more enduring than seas and rocks in its power to 'come again' not only after a journey but after death itself.

A connoisseur of tenderness in love, Burns also relishes the coarseness of blatant sex in his bawdy poems, many of which remained unpublished until the appearance in 1800 of *The Merry Muses of Caledonia*, both publisher and place of publication unspecified, based on the poet's private collection of songs and poems, some written or reworked by himself. (An edition of the book by James Barke and Sydney Goodsir Smith became generally available in 1965.[33]) Among the poems attributable to Burns are jauntily obscene tributes to 'Bonie Mary' (K, 435) whose 'face it was fine, and her bosom divine, / And her cunt it was theekit wi' glory', and to the 'hidden mine o' pleasure' reserved for the poet in 'O saw ye my Maggie' (K, 614). In 'Come rede me, dame' (K, 252) a country woman's answer to the poet's question about the ideal length for a penis stresses the importance of technique over size: 'It's no the length that maks me loup, / But it's the double drivin'. The 'Ode to Spring' (K, 481) is more polished bawdry. In a letter to George Thomson in January 1785 Burns refers to a 'belle lettre' friend who bet him 'that it was impossible to produce an Ode to Spring on an original plan. – I accepted it; & pledged myself to bring in the verdant fields, – the budding flowers, – the chrystal streams, – the melody of the groves – & a love-story into the bargain, & yet be original.'[34] The mock-pastoral love-story shows the effect of 'Dame Nature's impètus' on the intercourse of Damon and Sylvia. Nature and lovers are one harmony and rhythm until Damon spoils the perfection:

> First, wi' the thrush, his thrust and push
>   Had compass large and long, Sir;
> The blackbird next, his tuneful text,
>   Was bolder, clear and strong, Sir:
> The linnet's lay came then in play,
>   And the lark that soar'd aboon, Sir;
> Till Damon, fierce, mistim'd his arse,
>   And fuck'd quite out o' tune, Sir.

Coarseness almost turns nasty in the sexually frustrated wife Rachel's laceration of her husband, Jacob, in the biblical spoof, 'The Patriarch' (K, 609), but comedy prevails when Jacob explains his connubial dilatoriness. He has, it seems, been more than fair by Old Testament standards, if not according to those upheld by the Church of Scotland:

> 'I mow you as I mow the lave,   *fuck/the others*
>   'And night and day I'm bisy.

'I've bairn'd the servant gypsies baith,
   'Forbye your titty Leah;   *sister*
'Ye barren jad, ye put me mad,   *hussy*
   'Whit mair can I do wi' you.

'There's ne'er a mow I've gi'en the lave,
   'But ye ha'e got a dizzen;   *dozen*
'And damn'd a ane ye'se get again,
   'Altho' your cunt should gizzen.'   *wither*

This is enough to make Rachel grateful for what she can get; com-
plimenting her husband on his expertise she 'claps him on the waulies'
and advises him not to heed a woman's idle chatter. Jacob's anger spent,
sexual relations are vigorously restored. The range of Burns's sexual moods
is deducible from the variations on 'Green grow the Rashes' (K, 45)[35]
entered in his first Common Place Book in August 1784 and beginning
with the chorus:

   Green grow the rashes, O;
   Green grow the rashes, O;
   The sweetest hours that e'er I spend,
      Are spent amang the lasses, O.

Two years later the poet sent a friend cheerfully lewd particulars of one
sweet hour:

   I dought na speak – ye was na fley'd –   *frightened*
      My heart play'd duntie, duntie, O
   An ceremony laid aside,
      I fairly fun' her cuntie, O.

If the love songs pull at the heart, the bawdy poems tickle the risibles,
Burns having fun with sex as earthy leveller in the human situation.

Satire

The instinctively democratic strain in Burns's character links his love
to his satire. The lover exercises his natural right to negotiate freely for
himself regardless of church or social pressure (even if he does submit
to public penance in kirk for child-bearing extra-marital relations with
Elizabeth Paton and Jean Armour). The satirist exposes the falsities of

unegalitarian systems which try to curb people's freedom in order to
protect positions of unnatural privilege. Burns noticed inequality early:

> I formed many connections with other Youngkers who
> possessed superior advantages; the youngling Actors who
> were busy with the rehearsal of PARTS in which they
> were shortly to appear on that STAGE where, Alas! I was
> destined to druge behind the SCENES. – It is not
> commonly at these green years that the young Noblesse
> and gentry have a just sense of the immense distance
> between them and their ragged Playfellows.[36]

Never losing touch with his 'ploughboy carcase', there was in Burns even
a thrawn delight in remaining the 'ragged Playfellow', keeping his distance from the generalized 'Great Man' typified by what he sarcastically
calls 'that proper, decent, unnoticing disregard for the poor, insignificant,
stupid devils, the mechanics and peasantry around him'.[37] It is said that
John Wilson, printer of the Kilmarnock Edition, shook his head at Burns
and said, 'Ah, Rab, it winna do unless ye begin your buik wi' mair
sprinklins o' serious bits';[38] but the volume showed what the mischievous,
ragged Playfellow could do with satire in its first poem, 'The Twa Dogs',
as well as in 'The Holy Fair' and 'Address to the Deil'.

A year earlier he had written the satirical masterpiece, 'Holy Willie's
Prayer' (K, 53), but judged it too incendiary to include in the collection.
First published anonymously in 1789, the poem is based on the figure
of William Fisher, an 'Auld Licht' (i.e. conservative) elder of Mauchline
Kirk, who instigated an action against Burns's friend, Gavin Hamilton,
accusing him of religious dereliction. The Ayr Presbytery found in Hamilton's favour, to the delight of Burns who riskily circulated his poem:
'Holy Willie's Prayer . . . alarmed the kirk-Session so much that they held
three several meetings to look over their holy artillery, if any of it was
pointed against profane Rhymers'.[39] A dramatic monologue in which the
speaker unwittingly reveals the unsavoury truth about himself (compare
Browning's 'My Last Duchess' or 'The Bishop orders his tomb in St
Praxed's Church'), the poem opens as 'the Muse' overhears Willie ad-
dressing God in terms whose matter-of-factness ridicules the extreme
Calvinist doctrine of predestination and Divine Election:

> O THOU that in the heavens does dwell!
> Wha', as it pleases best thysel,
> Sends ane to heaven and ten to hell,
>   A' for thy glory!
> And no for ony gude or ill
>   They've done before thee.

Here Burns is referring to the Confession of Faith approved by the General Assembly of the Church of Scotland in 1647 which was read and memorized throughout Scottish schools and homes along with the Shorter and Larger Catechisms. The doctrine of Divine Election is expressed uncompromisingly in Chapter Three, Section Six of *The Confession of Faith; the Larger and Shorter Catechisms, with the Scripture Proofs at Large: together with The Sum of Saving Knowledge, etc*:

> As God hath appointed the elect unto glory, so hath he,
> by the eternal and most free purpose of his will, fore-
> ordained all the means thereunto. Wherefore they who are
> elected being fallen in Adam, are redeemed by Christ; are
> effectually called unto faith in Christ by his Spirit working
> in due season; are justified, adopted, sanctified, and kept
> by his power through faith unto salvation. Neither are any
> other redeemed by Christ, effectually called, justified,
> adopted, sanctified and saved, but the elect only.[40]

The absurd arbitrariness of the doctrine is brought out when Willie acknowledges that, if God had been so disposed, even he might have been dropped at infancy into an eternity of hell:

> When from my mother's womb I fell,
> Thou might hae plunged me deep in hell,
> To gnash my gooms, and weep, and wail,
>   In burning lakes,
> Where damned devils roar and yell
>   Chained to their stakes.

The image of a toothless baby in perpetual torment expresses Burns's outrage at a system of belief that could doom even a newly born child to everlasting agonies in its lovingly constructed hell. The Calvinist position is mocked by the excesses of the pictured hell and by Willie's fawning on a sadistic God who allocates such enormities to others, whether deserved or not, but exempts so gross an egotist as himself. Willie's politic humility is soon replaced by self-righteousness so complete that he can find evidence of his own election even in his yieldings to sexual temptation. After calling down the wrath of God on Gavin Hamilton, the Presbytery of Ayr and Robert Aiken, Hamilton's counsel, he combines avarice and sanctimony, instructing God to signify his election to the life hereafter by making him manifestly a winner in this one:

> But Lord, remember me and mine
> Wi' mercies temporal and divine!

> That I for grace and gear may shine,
> Excell'd by nane!
> And a' the glory shall be thine!
> AMEN! AMEN!

The poem is an object lesson in the vanity of a kind of egotism fostered by Calvinism and an artistic triumph for Burns, as the vindication of Hamilton was a victory for the 'New Lichts', the liberals of the Scottish Church. As John Cairney puts it, the laughter caused by Burns's poem 'loosened the hitherto tyrannical grip of the Kirk and its Elders, not only in Ayrshire but all over Scotland. Precisely and with deadly effect, a man, an attitude, a whole age and a persistent Scottish tradition was captured in its entirety and nailed to the page.'[41] In 1863 George MacDonald nails it to the page again in *Alec Forbes of Howglen* when the kind minister, Mr Cowie, tries to comfort young Annie Anderson who is panicking at the thought that she may not be one of 'the eleck'. Mr Cowie reflects that 'this terrible doctrine was perfectly developed in the creed of the Scottish Church; the assembly of divines having sat upon the Scripture egg till they had hatched it in their own likeness' (Chapter 27). In 'Scotland 1941' Edwin Muir recalls a time when Scots 'were a tribe, a family, a people' and 'A simple sky roofed in that rustic day, / The busy corn-fields and the haunted holms'. Calvin's disciples destroyed all this:

> Knox and Melville clapped their preaching palms
> And bundled all the harvesters away,
> Hoodicrow Peden in the blighted corn
> Hacked with his rusty beak the starving haulms.
> Out of that desolation we were born.[42]

In his poem, 'The Ship' ('An Saothach'), Sorley MacLean includes Calvin among the forces that have steered the ship of Gaeldom off course, 'the black hardness, the bald grey head, / and the Election tight in his eyes'.[43] But it would take more than Burns, MacDonald, Muir and MacLean to beat the terrible doctrine into permanent retreat. In her novel, *Looking for the Possible Dance* (1993), A. L. Kennedy defines 'THE SCOTTISH METHOD (FOR THE PERFECTION OF CHILDREN)'. The ten points of her summary include:

> 1. Guilt is good.
> 6. Pain and fear will teach us to hurt and petrify ourselves.
> 7. Joy is fleeting and the forerunner of despair.
> 9. God hates us. In word, thought, in deed we are hateful before God and we may do no greater good than to hate ourselves.[44]

Although Burns would rather be 'an atheist clean' than subscribe to 'three-mile prayers, an' hauf-mile graces', he is not hostile to religion which he hails as a 'maid divine!' threatened by the 'rotten, hollow hearts' of the Auld Lichts in the epistle 'To the Rev. John McMath' (K, 68):

> Tho' blotch't an' foul wi' mony a stain,
> An' far unworthy of thy train,
> With trembling voice I tune my strain
>   To join with those,
> Who boldly dare thy cause maintain
>   In spite of foes.

Here, of course, he is writing to a New Licht minister whom he liked. In a review of Stopford A. Brooke's *Theology in the English Poets*[45] Henry James extracts the appropriate summing-up from Brooke's discussion of theology in Burns: 'He was always – like the Prodigal Son . . . coming to himself and saying, "I will arise and go to my Father"; but he never got more than half-way in this world.'[46] His finest touch in 'The Cotter's Saturday Night' (K, 72) is the depiction of simple family worship in stanza xii which stimulated David Wilkie, 'the most successful artist of his time and, too, next to Hogarth, the British artist with the most far-reaching European influence',[47] to paint his masterpiece with the same title as Burns's poem.

In 'The Death and Dying Words of Poor Mailie, The Author's only Pet Yowe, An Unco Mournfu' Tale' (K, 24) Burns discovered the humorous potential of the beast fable which endows animals with human attributes. Humour is sharpened to satire in the ironic inversions of 'The Twa Dogs' (K, 71) where the aristocratic dog exposes the futilities and cruelties of his class of humans. Caesar, a laird's dog, 'whalpet [whelped] some place far abroad, / Where sailors gang to fish for Cod' (i.e. Newfoundland), and the ploughman's collie, Luath, a home-grown 'gash [shrewd] an' faithfu' *tyke* [mongrel]', compare the self-indulgent lives of the rich to the homely, fulfilling decencies of the hard-working peasantry. Although a 'locked, letter'd, braw brass-collar, / Show'd him the *gentleman* an' *scholar*', Caesar's high degree has not made him proud:

> Nae tawtied *tyke*, tho' e'er sae duddie,   *shaggy mongrel/tattered*
> But he wad stan't, as glad to see him,
> An' stroan't on stanes an' hillocks wi'   *pissed*
>   him.

The human invention of class distinction cannot prevent the two dogs from being 'fain o' ither [fond of each other], / An' unco pack [very intimate] an' thick the gither [together]': thus the animals are morally

superior to the accident of social circumstance. Caesar's experience of
the profligacies of the privileged rich makes him question Luath about
the lives of the poor, 'huff'd, an' cuff'd, an' disrespeket!' especially by the
factor, the steward who administered an estate on behalf of its owner,
supervising tenants and collecting rents:

> How they maun thole a *factor*'s snash;   *endure/abuse*
> He'll stamp an' threaten, curse an' swear,
> He'll *apprehend* them, *poind* their gear,   *distrain*
> While they maun stand, wi' aspect humble,
> An' hear it a', an' fear an' tremble!

This sharp portrait of the factor is heartfelt: at Mount Oliphant the Burns
family 'fell into the hands of a Factor who sat for the picture I have drawn
of one of my Tale of two dogs'.[48] Burns's picture, in turn, inspired David
Wilkie's paintings 'The Rent Day' (1807) and 'Distraining for Rent'
(1815). Luath turns the tables on Caesar's preconceived ideas and the
reader's expectations. Practice in living on the brink of poverty makes the
poor unafraid; comfort is forthcoming from their 'grushie [lusty] weans,
an' faithfu' wives', a shilling's worth of ale and the social merriment of
seasonal festivities. Caesar is right up to a point: the poor are sometimes
cruelly treated, but this is surely balanced in the scheme of things by the
self-sacrifice of the Member of Parliament who indents his soul for his
country. This ingenuous notion of Luath's is Caesar's cue to an indictment of his own class. 'Britain's guid' is merely a pretext for further
'dissipation, feud an' faction'. Luath's idealized parliamentarian is a self-
centred fop who weakly submits to the whim of his 'Premier', parades
at operas and plays, and learns '*bon ton*':

> There, at VIENNA or VERSAILLES,
> He rives his father's auld entails;
> Or by MADRID he takes the rout,   *road, way*
> To thrum *guitarres* an' fecht wi' *nowt*;   *cattle, oxen*
> Or down *Italian Vista* startles,
> Whore-hunting amang groves o' myrtles.

Contempt for the vacuous amusements of the capricious rich is brilliantly
conveyed in the line, 'To thrum *guitarres* an' fecht wi' *nowt*', where 'the
homely Scots word for cattle [*nowt*] reduces at once the ritual splendour
of bull-fighting to a meaningless brawl with a beast'.[49] The poem's culminating stroke is to expose the advantaged class as incapable of achieving
the pleasure to which they dedicate their selfish energies. Caesar grows
heated, demolishing the rich in terms ironically derived from Luath's
account of the resilience of the poor. Peasants work and rest content; the
rich are neurotic insomniacs:

> Gentlemen an' Ladies warst,
> Wi' ev'n down *want o' wark*   *cursed by having no work to do*
>   they're curst.
> They loiter, lounging, lank an' lazy;
> Tho' deil-haet ails them, yet uneasy;   *devil a bit, ie 'damn all'*
> Their days, insipid, dull an' tasteless,
> Their nights, unquiet, lang an'
>   restless.

Discussing the differences between the haves and have-nots, Caesar and Luath have shown that the poor are the haves and the rich contemptibly ineffectual. Their conversation over, they can part, 'Rejoic'd they were na *men* but *dogs*', immune to the human follies whose absurdities they have recognized and 'Resolv'd to meet some ither day'.

In 'The Holy Fair' (K, 70) the poet meets three young women – Fun, Superstition and Hypocrisy – on the way to Mauchline Fair. Fun guides him round the sights of the Fair as he observes the rival preachers, their tipsy audiences, whores, roistering weaver lads from Kilmarnock, 'some thinkan on their sins, / An' some upo' their claes', and well-adjusted lads and lasses unintimidated by 'tidings o' damnation', 'blythely bent / To mind baith *saul* an' *body*'. In Burns's time such holy fairs, mass Communions in which several parishes combined, were 'a mixture of the austere and the Rabelaisian, the devotional and the Bacchanalian, that could hardly be paralleled outside the ancient Greek cults of Dionysos'.[50] The satirical force of the poem is in its panoramic display of varied human behaviour whose exuberance defies regulation; the holiness of the fair is the pagan sanctity of life itself. The day sees many conversions, some religious, some decidedly fleshly, and the scrambling of biblical and secular vocabulary in the last stanza expresses the poet's delight in life's system-resistant volatility:

> How monie hearts this day converts,
>   O' Sinners and o' Lasses!
> Their hearts o' stane, gin night are gane
>   As saft as ony flesh is.
> There's some are fou o' *love divine*;
>   There's some are fou o' *brandy*;
> An' monie jobs that day begin,
>   May end in *Houghmagandie*   *fornication*
>   Some ither day.

In 'piercin words, like highlan swords' a hell-fire preacher divides the 'joints and marrow' of his listeners in stanza xxi of 'The Holy Fair' before evoking the Calvinist hell in the next stanza:

> A vast, unbottom'd, boundless *Pit*,
>   Fill'd fou o' *lowan brunstane*.   *fiery brimstone*
> Whase raging flame, an' scorching heat,
>   Wad melt the hardest whunstane!   *whinstone*

In 'Address to the Deil' (K, 76) Burns cuts Satan down to size with aggressive familiarity, amiably calling him 'Auld Hornie, Satan, Nick or Clootie' in mock-heroic contrast to Milton's 'great Personage' in *Paradise Lost*. The Devil is fetched from hell – now diminished from the 'burning lakes' of 'Holy Willie's Prayer' and the 'raging flame' of 'The Holy Fair' to a 'brunstane cootie' (a brimstone tub) – and domesticated out of theological evil into the mischievous world of mere witchcraft, spoiling the butter in the churn, depriving the ardent bridegroom of his erection, luring night travellers to destruction with assistance from 'Water-kelpies' (water demons in the shape of horses). Even the seduction of Adam and Eve to original sin is deflated from cosmic villainy to a mean trick that didn't quite work:

> Then you, ye auld, snick-drawing dog!   *crafty*
> Ye cam to Paradise incog,   *incognito*
> An' play'd on a man a cursed brogue,   *trick*
>   (Black be your fa'!)
> An' gied the infant warld a shog,
>   'Maist ruin'd a'.

As he brings his cheeky apostrophe to a close the poet concedes, then defies, the Devil's point of view:

> An' now, auld *Cloots*, I ken ye're thinkan, *(Cloven-footed) Devil*
> A certain *Bardie*'s rantin, drinkin,
> Some luckless hour will send him linkan,   *skipping*
>   To your black pit;
> But faith! he'll turn a corner jinkan,   *dodging*
>   An' cheat you yet.

The satires, together with 'To a Mouse' and 'To a Louse', are the best of the Kilmarnock Edition, coming from the same democratic impulse as the great 'Song – For a' that and a' that –' (K, 482) and disproving the view of Edwin Muir that Scots 'was to [Burns] a language for sentiment but not for thought'.[51] Beside them 'The Cotter's Saturday Night' (K, 72), much praised by Burns's contemporaries and described by William Hazlitt as 'a noble and pathetic picture of human manners, mingled with a fine religious awe',[52] is sentimentally idyllic, a moralizing exercise in the Augustan manner, adroitly executed in Spenserian stanzas. As Catherine

Carswell observes in *The Life of Robert Burns*, 'It is noteworthy that Burns, who was a good judge of his own work, could never be induced to make another effort of the kind. "The Cotter's Saturday Night" succeeded as he had intended it should succeed, as an exhibition piece.'[53] 'To a Mountain Daisy' (K, 92) is pompous and mawkish, the poet sliding self-indulgently away from the fact of the initiating flower into his contrived analogies. The strength of 'To a Mouse' and 'To a Louse' is in the steady eye he keeps on the creatures. The famous lines in 'To a Mouse' (K, 69) arise from the detailed apprehension of a miniature fellow-being in a moment keenly felt. Breaking up the mouse's 'wee-bit housie' prompts the expansion of the poet's speculation into regret that 'Man's dominion / Has broken Nature's social union' (an ironic solemnity is achieved by the abrupt, momentary shift from colloquial Scots into formal English), his identification with the vanity of the mouse's foresight warrants the reflection that 'The best laid schemes o' *Mice* and *Men* / Gang aft agley [awry]', and his focus on the mouse's unenviable situation leads logically to a final comparison of their lives in which the parallel of the second-last stanza prompts a concluding sense of the crucial difference between them:

> Still, thou art blest, compar'd wi' *me*!
> Thy *present* only toucheth thee:
> But Och! I *backward* cast my e'e,
>   On prospects drear!
> An' *forward*, tho' I canna *see*,
>   I *guess* an' *fear*!

Again in 'To a Louse' (K, 83), while Burns is more obviously relishing the flavours of his language for their own sake, he refers to the 'crowlan ferlie' (the crawling prodigy) throughout the poem, noticing the vainglorious particulars of sartorial pretension, present and imagined, and earning his aphorism: 'O wad some Pow'r the giftie gie us / *To see ourels as others see us!*'

Burns thought 'Tam o' Shanter. A Tale' (K, 321) showed 'a finishing polish that I despair of ever excelling'[54] and called the poem his 'own favourite'[55] of his works. Certainly, none of his works has been in such danger of losing its character under the weight of critical acclaim. Neither Sir Walter Scott's comparison of Burns with Shakespeare[56] nor Byron's calling 'Tam o' Shanter' Burns's 'opus magnum'[57] catches the poem's wit, fluency, pace and irony. Reviewing the poem negatively, Thomas Carlyle is weighed down by his own leaden criteria: 'the heart and body of the story lies hard and dead. He has not gone back, much less carried us back, into that dark, earnest, wondering age, when the tradition was believed, and when it took its rise . . . the piece does not properly cohere . . . the Tragedy of the adventure becomes a mere drunken phantasmagoria, or many-coloured spectrum painted on ale-vapours.'[58] Nothing could be further than tragedy from the intentions of Burns's incandescent frolic. Thomas Crawford gives the most comprehensive list of ingredients: 'its synthesis of rapid motion, high energy, pure comedy, imaginative fantasy, and a sense of the stubborn realities of everyday life'.[59] The poem is a mock-heroic variation on the *topos* of the homeward journey, with Tam crossing the 'mosses, waters, slaps, and styles' between Ayr and Kirkoswald where his 'sulky, sullen dame' awaits to berate him again for being a 'skellum', no Penelope to his Ulysses but, perhaps, a grumpy Calvinist Molly to his tipsily returning Bloom. Rapid motion begins in the opening lines, the octosyllabic couplets already anticipating Tam's hectic ride through the night, propelling him from the convivial ingle with Souter Johnny into the real storm he must face as a prelude to the 'gathering storm' waiting at home. Ostensibly a warning against the evils of drink, the poem is a denial of its own posture, being a celebration of 'Inspiring bold *John Barleycorn*' and vitality which undercuts its own po-faced moralizing:

> Whene'er to drink you are inclin'd,
> Or cutty-sarks run in your mind,   *(girls wearing) short shirts*
> Think, ye may buy the joys o'er dear,
> Remember Tam o' Shanter's mare.

The throw-away ending is pure ironic bathos: the reader is teasingly enjoined to repudiate the pleasures of the tavern, illicit adventure and a glimpse of a girl who can make the Devil wriggle all because a horse has lost its tail. No reader capable of joys, Burns knows, is that sort of fool. The anti-climax of the conclusion turns the reader back into the contradictory life of the poem: the crackle of its witticisms, the sweetly hair-raising fear of bogles, the grisly associations of the district (ll. 90–96), the hyperbolic piling-up of horrors on the illuminated 'haly table' in the Kirk-Alloway (ll. 130–42), the open coffins and the wild satanic dance to piped music from Auld Nick (ll. 120–24). That the moral is doomed from the beginning Burns makes clear by the smugly pompous English couplets and pulpit gravity of lines 59–67. After such a night Tam can have nothing to fear either from such glib homiletics or from his killjoy Kate. 'Kings may be blest', but Tam is still glorious, 'O'er a' the ills o' life victorious!' Burns's mock-heroic, like his work as a whole, is as affirming as the final 'Yes' of Joyce's *Ulysses*.

Scotland has mythologized him but fallen short of his affirmations. The misty-eyed fervour of the cult comes not only from a sentimental Celtic disposition but also from a discomfiting sense that the culture has whinged too long for the liking of 'Rab, the Ranter' as he calls himself in the third verse epistle 'To J. Lapraik' (K, 67) and that Scots have failed to realize the ideals of their 'simple, contra bardie' (epistle 'To the Rev. John McMath', K, 68). The sentimentality of the cult which was such anathema to Hugh MacDiarmid is nostalgia for an unachieved Scotland in the poet's image, an expression of guilt. (In a letter to the American critic, Hugh Kenner, Ian Hamilton Finlay says: '*You* probably have no idea of the terrible things for which the Scotch have managed to forgive themselves by invoking their "guilt".'[60]) But the poet Burns is beyond psycho-political degradation; as Wordsworth says in 'Thoughts Suggested the Day Following [a visit to the grave of Burns in 1803], on the Banks of Nith, near the Poet's Residence': 'Deep in the general heart of men / His power survives'.

Notes

1. Hugh MacDiarmid, 'The Burns Cult', in Alan Riach (ed.), *Hugh MacDiarmid: Selected Prose* (Manchester, 1992), p. 104.

2. Burns's poems are cited with reference to the numbers used in James Kinsley's three-volume *The Poems and Songs of Robert Burns* (Oxford, 1968) and his one-volume *Burns: Poems and Songs* (Oxford, 1969); thus (K, 240) refers to 'Auld Lang Syne' as number 240 in Kinsley's editions.

3. James A. Mackay (ed.), *The Complete Letters of Robert Burns* (Ayr, 1987), pp. 161–3.

4. Ibid., p. 646.

5. Maurice Lindsay, *The Burns Encyclopedia*, 3rd edn (New York and London, 1980), p. 14.

6. Letter to John Hamilton Reynolds dated 11 July 1818, in Frederick Page (ed.), *Letters of John Keats* (London, 1954), p. 143.

7. Letter of 2 August 1787 from Burns to Dr John Moore, in Mackay, *The Complete Letters*, p. 254. Reprinted in Alan Bold, *A Burns Companion* (Basingstoke and London, 1991), p. 415.

8. Mackay, *The Complete Letters*, p. 256.

9. Ibid., p. 120.

10. Ibid., p. 306.

11. Ibid., p. 631.

12. Ibid., p. 679.

13. John Cairney, '*A Moment White . . .*': 200 years of the Glasgow Herald, Scotland's Newspaper and Scotland's National Bard (Glasgow, 1986), p. 13.

14. Mackay, *The Complete Letters*, p. 358.

15. Bold, *A Burns Companion*, p. 72.

16. Byron's *Journal* for Monday 13 December 1813, in Leslie A. Marchand (ed.), *Lord Byron: Selected Letters and Journals* (Cambridge, Mass., 1982), p. 93.

17. John Gibson Lockhart, *Memoirs of Sir Walter Scott*, 5 vols (London, 1900), II, p. 306.

18. Mackay, *The Complete Letters*, p. 253.

19. 'Gilbert's Narrative' in Bold, *A Burns Companion*, p. 422.

20. The full title of Blind Harry's poem, written circa 1477, is *The Actes and Deidis of the Illustre and Vallyeant Campioun Schir William Wallace*.

21. Mackay, *The Complete Letters*, p. 250.

22. Franklyn Bliss Snyder, *The Life of Robert Burns* (New York, 1932), p. 419.

23. Mackay, *The Complete Letters*, p. 254.

24. Allan H. Maclaine, *Robert Fergusson* (New York, 1965), p. 162.

25. Mackay, *The Complete Letters*, p. 251.

26. Ibid.

27. Dick Gaughan, *Handful of Earth*, track 2, Topic Records Ltd, 1989, CD TSCD 419.

28. Kathleen Ferrier, *Blow the Wind Southerly*, track 9, Decca CD 417 192-2 (1988).

29. Ibid., track 18.

30. Thomas Crawford, *Burns: A Study of the Poems and Songs* (Edinburgh, 1960), p. 281.

31. James Kinsley (ed.), *The Poems and Songs of Robert Burns*, 3 vols (Oxford, 1968), I, p. 455.

32. Bold, *A Burns Companion*, p. 343.

33. James Barke and Sydney Goodsir Smith (eds), *Robert Burns: The Merry Muses of Caledonia* (London, 1965).

34. Mackay, *The Complete Letters*, p. 669.

35. Bold, *A Burns Companion*, p. 141.

36. Mackay, *The Complete Letters*, p. 250.

37. Ibid.

38. Catherine Carswell, *The Life of Robert Burns* (London, 1930), p. 187. Reviewing a Canongate Classics reprint (Edinburgh, 1992), Iain Crichton Smith comments: 'Apparently the book caused a stushie when first published in 1930, and a correspondent sent [Carswell] a bullet through the post with a suggestion on how to use it. I found her version of Burns entirely credible, a portrait of a highly intelligent, role-playing protean character. It makes him much more interesting than the sturdy peasant we used to keep in our heads' (*Glasgow Herald*, 2 January 1992, p. 16).

39. Mackay, *The Complete Letters*, p. 255.

40. *The Confession of Faith; the Larger and Shorter Catechisms, with the Scripture Proofs at Large: together with The Sum of Saving Knowledge; Covenants, National and*

Solemn League; Acknowledgement of Sins, and Engagement to Duties; Directories for Public and Family Worship; Form of Public Authority in the Church of Scotland, with Acts of Assembly and Parliament Relative to, and approbative of, the same (Edinburgh, 1855), pp. 29–30.

41. Cairney, '*A Moment White . . .*', p. 10.

42. Edwin Muir, *The Complete Poems of Edwin Muir*, an annotated edition by Peter Butter for The Association for Scottish Literary Studies (Aberdeen, 1991), p. 100.

43. Sorley MacLean/Somhairle MacGill-Eain, *From Wood to Ridge / O Choille gu Bearradh, Collected Poems in Gaelic and English* (Manchester, 1989), p. 35.

44. A. L. Kennedy, *Looking for the Possible Dance* (London, 1993), pp. 15–16.

45. Stopford A. Brooke, *Theology in the English Poets* (New York, 1875).

46. Henry James, *Literary Criticism: Essays on Literature, American Writers, English Writers* (The Library of America, New York, 1984), p. 771.

47. Duncan Macmillan, *Scottish Art 1460–1990* (Edinburgh, 1990), p. 165.

48. Mackay, *The Complete Letters*, p. 250.

49. David Daiches, *Robert Burns* (London, 1957), p. 20.

50. Douglas Young, *Scotland* (London, 1971), p. 10.

51. Edwin Muir, *Scott and Scotland* (London, 1936), p. 29.

52. Donald A. Low (ed.), *Robert Burns: The Critical Heritage* (London, 1974), p. 303.

53. Carswell, *The Life*, p. 168.

54. Mackay, *The Complete Letters*, p. 194.

55. Ibid., p. 578.

56. Low (ed.), *The Critical Heritage*, p. 207.

57. Ibid., p. 326.

58. Ibid., pp. 367–8.

59. Crawford, *Poems and Songs*, p. 221.

60. Ian Hamilton Finlay, 'Letter to Hugh Kenner', *Chapman*, nos. 78–9 (1994), 39–41 [39–40].

Chapter 5
Sir Walter Scott and the Supreme Fiction

Fame and fortune

Summing up his life in 1821, Scott wrote to a friend: 'I have had . . . more of fame and fortune than mere literature ever procured for a man before'.[1] Fame arrived spectacularly in 1805 when *The Lay of the Last Minstrel* made him the most popular poet in Britain. Although he was a pro-Union Tory all his life[2] his poem called to a bruised post-Union Scottish psyche in the fervently nationalistic lines that begin Canto Six:

> Breathes there the man, with soul so dead,
> Who never to himself hath said,
>   This is my own, my native land!
> Whose heart hath ne'er within him burn'd,
> As home his footsteps he hath turn'd,
>   From wandering on a foreign strand!

Unprecedented prominence came when he was identified as 'The Great Unknown', author of the anonymously published 'Waverley' novels, although the secret was not officially revealed until a public dinner at the Assembly Rooms in Edinburgh in 1827. His fortune and credit-rating were grandiosely visible in the estate of Abbotsford near Melrose which he bought in 1811 when his imagination was still full of the faery-castle fantasy he had created in *The Lady of the Lake* (1810). Lavishing money on additions and improvements to the property ('Builders and planners have drained my purse,' he wrote to Joanna Baillie in January 1823[3]) he pursued his ambition to create a dynasty and to become a living, land-scaped part of his own subject matter, the pageant of Scottish history. He was Laird of Abbotsford and Sheriff-Depute of Selkirkshire – 'his devotion for titled rank', says James Hogg, 'amounted almost to adoration'[4] – but when Lord Henry Cockburn visited him in the already legendary house in September 1828 he saw in him both the hospitable farmer and the smuggler captain of *Guy Mannering*:

> When fitted up for dinner, he was like any other
> comfortably ill-dressed gentleman. But in the morning,
> with the large coarse jacket, great stick, and leathern cap,
> he was Dandy Dinmont, or Dick Hattrick [i.e. Dirk
> Hatteraick] – a smuggler or a poacher. Would that his
> money and his care had been given to a better subject
> than Abbotsford.[5]

He might be the Laird, but he retained the common touch. Similarly, his novels relate the elevated platforms of history to the works and days of common folk, so providing a model for later writers of historical fiction from Galt and Stevenson to Neil Munro and Nigel Tranter.

Fortune left him first. In 1826 his unexpected bankruptcy on the failure of the publishing companies of Constable, Hurst and Robinson and of the printing firm of James Ballantyne was a 'thunderbolt which . . . fell on Edinburgh'.[6] Cockburn describes Scott's first appearance after the crash in the Edinburgh Court of Session where he had served as Clerk since 1806:

> There was no affectation, and no reality, of *facing it*; no
> look of indifference or defiance; but the manly and
> modest air of a gentleman conscious of some folly, but of
> perfect rectitude, and of most heroic and honourable
> resolutions. It was on that very day, I believe, that he said
> a very fine thing. Some of his friends offered him, or
> rather proposed to offer him, enough of money, as was
> supposed to enable him to arrange with his creditors. He
> paused for a moment; and then, recollecting his powers,
> said proudly – 'No! this right hand shall work it all off!'[7]

It was more than a proud boast: he literally wrote off the bulk of his debts before he died and those remaining were settled by the sale of copyrights. For Thomas Carlyle 'the great fact' about the Waverley novels is 'that they were faster written and better paid for than any other books in the world'.[8] By the time of his death in 1832 he had achieved heroic dimensions as 'the Wizard of the North' for three reasons: his output of work, much of it produced under extreme financial pressure, was prodigious; his portrayal of Scotland was a supreme fiction which determined the world's perception of the country and its people; and he made the novel respectable as the dominant literary form of his own age and of time to come, even if Charlotte Brontë thought that the novel of quality climaxed and stopped with him. 'For fiction,' she wrote to Ellen Nussey in 1834, 'read Scott alone; all novels after his are worthless.'[9]

Fame, or more accurately reputation and readership, left him more gradually than the sudden desertion of fortune. In 1824 William Hazlitt, at the height of his powers as a critic, observed that 'Sir Walter Scott is undoubtedly the most popular writer of the age', cannily adding that he 'is "lord of the ascendant" for the time being'.[10] Despite growing competition, especially from Dickens, Scott's time lasted for almost another century, during which he remained a favourite of the reading public and crucially influenced writers in America and Europe. 'It was odd,' says Elizabeth Grant of Rothiemurcus in her sprightly *Memoirs of a Highland Lady* (1898), 'but Sir Walter never had the reputation in Edinburgh he had elsewhere – was not the Lion, I mean. His wonderful works were looked for, read with avidity, praised on all hands, still the Authour made far less noise at home than he did abroad.'[11] Praised by Heine, Goethe, Sainte-Beuve, Balzac, the Russian Vissarion Belinsky and the Italian Alessandro Manzoni, today he is largely unread, despite erudite homage from the Hungarian Marxist critic Georg Lukács,[12] dogged prescription of *Ivanhoe* in school reading syllabuses,[13] and brave cases made for him by critics who enjoy the amplitude of his work, finding in the loose, baggy monsters of his novels not only garrulity, clumsy plotting, and unheavenly length, but the strengths of balladry, memorable characters – especially those who speak in Scots – Scottish history vividly brought to life, political acumen and an impressive contribution to the debate between romantic and realistic views of the world. 'A wordy big tumphy', as Alan Riach calls him,[14] he is, still, the most copious and problematic of Scottish writers. Venerated, mythologized and left on the shelf, what are the qualities that might induce us to take him down again?

Ballads and romances: problems of the long poem

Scott was, above all, a story-teller. Essentially, his long poems and novels are ballad narratives expanded by accretions of history, politics, characterization and descriptions of nature, and marinated in nostalgia. His literary imagination was formed by the ballad and his development 'was a progress from ballad collection to ballad imitation; from ballad imitation to the making of ballad epics; and from ballad epics . . . to prose fiction'.[15] At the age of about eighteen months poliomyelitis made him lame in his right leg. In 1773 his parents despatched him to his grandfather's Border farm at Sandyknowe in Tweeddale for the good of his health. The stories that he collected in what Hazlitt calls 'the vast cells of his memory'[16] began here with the folk-poetry he heard recited and sung by his grandmother, by Sandy Ormiston the cow bailiff and by others who joined the family circle, as he recalls in the Introduction to Canto Three of *Marmion*:

> And ever, by the winter hearth,
> Old tales I heard of woe or mirth,
> Of lovers' slights, of ladies' charms,
> Of witches' spells, of warriors' arms;
> Of patriot battles, won of old
> By Wallace wight and Bruce the bold;
> Of later fields of feud and fight,
> When, pouring from their Highland height,
> The Scottish clans, in headlong sway,
> Had swept the scarlet ranks away.

To this legendary lore he added Lady Wardlaw's persuasive imitation ballad, 'Hardyknute', from Allan Ramsay's *Tea-Table Miscellany*, the songs from Ramsay's *The Ever Green*, Percy's *Reliques of Ancient English Poetry* and the voluminous, random reading he commemorates in 'the desultory studies'[17] of Edward Waverley who drives 'like a vessel without a pilot or a rudder' through 'a sea of books' in Chapter 3 of *Waverley* (1814). Scott's rudder was his developing engagement with the matter of Scotland and his interest in history. Some months in Kelso awakened his feelings for nature, and his study of law at Edinburgh University alerted him to Scottish social history. He was already aware of Scottish religious history through his solicitor father's interest in the Calvinist Church. By July 1792, when he was admitted to the Bar, he possessed the apparatus he needed for writing.

He also possessed extraordinary energy, in spite of the polio virus and his resulting limp. (Hogg describes him as 'the best formed man I ever saw and laying his weak limb out of the question a perfect model of a man for gigantic strength'.[18]) 'He was *makin' himsell* a' the time,' remembered Robert Shortreed[19] with whom Scott went on what he called his annual 'raids' into Liddesdale to look for the material of old ballads as it could still be found in a living oral tradition. With assistance from the scholar and poet John Leyden the raids yielded *The Minstrelsy of the Scottish Border* (Volumes 1 and 2, 1802; Volume 3, 1803) which is still regarded as the greatest of the Scottish ballad collections despite Scott's editorial tinkerings. Of the 72 ballads printed, 38 were published for the first time, and the collection includes such masterpieces of the form as 'The Twa Corbies', 'Kinmont Willie' and 'The Wife of Usher's Well'.

In 1796 Scott's first publication was *The Chase, and William and Helen: Two Ballads from the German of Gottfried Augustus Bürger*. On the impetus of his work for *The Minstrelsy* he progressed from translating and collecting to extended original composition with the first of his metrical romances,

The Lay of the Last Minstrel (1805), based on a story of the goblin or brownie, Gilpin Horner. The model of Coleridge's 'Christabel' gave him a flexible stanzaic form and drew his poem towards the world of Border enmities in a romantic narrative blend of chivalry and the supernatural. The role of the mysterious brownie, waspish, malignant and forlorn, was reduced, but 'Lord Cranstoun's Goblin-Page' remains one of the poem's most memorable ingredients as a Spenserian expression of nature's inimical, eruptive magic:

> That Dwarf was scarce an earthly man,
> If the tales were true that of him ran
>   Through all the Border, far and near.
> 'Twas said, when the Baron a-hunting rode
> Through Reedsdale's glens, but rarely trod,
>   He heard a voice cry, 'Lost! lost! lost!'
> And, like tennis-ball by racket toss'd,
>   A leap, of thirty feet and three,
> Made from the gorse this elfin shape,
> Distorted like some dwarfish ape,
>   And lighted at Lord Cranstoun's knee.
>   (Canto Two, XXXI)

The *Lay*'s simple Montague–Capulet pattern of forbidden love between Margaret Buccleuch of Branksome and Lord Cranstoun, ornamented by Scots–English rivalry and the kidnapping of the young Buccleuch heir, was followed by a self-defeatingly convoluted plot in *Marmion* (1808) whose main interest for the modern reader is not so much its melodramatic tale of James IV and Flodden as the moral doubleness of its hero's character. At once gallant and treacherous, Marmion's mixture of contradictory qualities – by comparison young Lochinvar, though tricky, is all valour – anticipates the complexities of character later to be found in Edward Waverley and Fergus Mac-Ivor Vich Ian Vohr of Glennaquoich in *Waverley*, George Staunton, 'the most consciously designed romantic hero in the Waverley novels',[20] in *The Heart of Midlothian*, Leicester in *Kenilworth*, Redgauntlet and, in the maturer blend of elements that make up the blacksmith, Henry Gow in *The Fair Maid of Perth*. The last of Scott's popularly successful long poems, *The Lady of the Lake* (1810), tells a straightforward story of love requited during the reign of James V but achieves supremacy among the metrical romances by its evocation of the landscape of the Trossachs and its romanticized Highlanders. The poem did wonders for the tourist trade of the day. As David Daiches says:

> Tourists from the south had of course visited the
> Highlands before Scott – indeed as early as July 1810

Scott, with considerable exaggeration, called the age one in which 'every London citizen makes Loch Lomond his washpot and throws his shoe over Ben Nevis' – but it was Scott who made touring, first in the Trossachs and then in other parts of the Highlands, a really popular activity.[21]

All Scott's long poems suffer from what C. S. Lewis calls 'dry information' in his discussion of Spenser's poetic styles in *The Faerie Queene*.[22] Rhymes are often perfunctory or bathetic where the story is simply being moved forward or the poet feels a sudden incumbency to appear sage. In *The Lay of the Last Minstrel* Canto Three, II the bard pontificates:

In peace, Love tunes the shepherd's reed;
In war, he mounts the warrior's steed;
In halls, in gay attire is seen;
In hamlets, dances on the green.

Facile rhyme and rhythmic monotony threaten to undermine the rough nobility of Tantallon Castle in *Marmion*, Canto Six, II:

I said Tantallon's dizzy steep
Hung o'er the margin of the deep.
Many a rude tower and rampart there
Repell'd the insult of the air,
Which, when the tempest vex'd the sky,
Half breeze, half spray, came whistling by.

Arthurian soap-opera is suggested by Canto Two, XVIII of *The Bridal of Triermain* (1813), a variant of the Sleeping Beauty story starring Merlin, Sir Roland de Vaux of Triermain and an early nineteenth-century minstrel:

The champions, arm'd in martial sort,
    Have throng'd into the list,
And but three knights of Arthur's court
    Are from the tourney miss'd.
And still these lovers' fame survives
    For faith so constant shown, –
There were two who lov'd their neighbours' wives,
    And one who loved his own.

It is easy to deride such banalities, but do they contaminate Scott's metrical romances so badly that the poems should be consigned to critical perdition?

It is the besetting fault of all critical approaches that they favour works which yield most to their own branded methods of analysis and evaluation. A good work is one which validates the critical instruments. The long poem – Milton's *Paradise Lost*, Wordsworth's *The Prelude*, MacDiarmid's *In Memoriam James Joyce*, Edwin Morgan's 'Memories of Earth' or a metrical romance by Scott – does not show to advantage when measured by the criteria made fashionable by reading techniques which equate excellence with unflagging intensity, irony and semantic fibrillation. Neither *The Faerie Queene* (which Scott loved) nor *The Lady of the Lake* can be read appropriately, that is, according to its literary nature, as if it were a sonnet by Donne or a Keatsian ode, and it may be that the capacity to enjoy the pace and texture of a long poem has been permanently damaged by the aesthetic and moral priorities of such influential 'new' critics as I. A. Richards, F. R. Leavis and Cleanth Brooks. For Charlotte Brontë's Jane Eyre *Marmion* is 'one of those genuine productions so often vouchsafed to the fortunate public of those days – the golden age of modern literature' (*Jane Eyre*, Chapter 32), whereas, today, intolerance of the slack in Scott's writing and the frequent banality of his rhymes and rhythms can forestall appreciation of the cumulative effect of his extended ballads in their creation of richly imagined worlds of action and romantic-historical colour. Scott is like the balladists, 'who were concerned to tell a tale vividly and picturesquely and were content to let the poetry look after itself, welling up unexpectedly, like water in a dry, parched land'.[23] In the age of the short poem readers have become as short-winded as the poetry promoted by the high priests of close reading and Scott's long-winded romances are gutted for their extractable ballad-like lyric inserts, such as Albert Graeme's song, 'It was an English ladye bright' (*The Lay of the Last Minstrel*, Canto Six, XI–XII), the 'Hymn for the Dead', Scott's translation of *Dies Irae* (*The Lay of the Last Minstrel*, Canto Six, XXXI), Fitz-Eustace's song, 'Where shall the lover rest' (*Marmion*, Canto Three, X–XI), and the redoubtable 'Lochinvar' (*Marmion*, Canto Five, XII). *Rokeby* (1813), set in Yorkshire during the English Civil War, *The Lord of the Isles* (1815), which recounts the adventures of Bruce culminating in the Battle of Bannockburn, and *Harold the Dauntless* (1817), a tale of father–son conflict, are unlikely ever again to win even as many readers as they did among disappointed admirers of Scott's work when they were first published; but Canto Three of *Rokeby*, for example, yields 'O, Brignal banks are wild and fair' (XVI–XVIII), 'A weary lot is thine, fair maid' (XXVIII) and 'Allen-a-Dale' (XXX).

Whether allegorical, philosophical or relatively straightforward narrative, the long poem, metabolically, cannot easily be great according to Ezra Pound's imagist definition of greatness in literature as 'language charged with meaning to the utmost possible degree'.[24] There are, clearly, generic differences between Milton's epic 'heavenly theme', Spenser's multi-layered 'elfin dream' (*Marmion*, 'Introduction to Canto First') and

Scott's romantic lays – Wordsworth deprecated them as 'amusing stories in verse'[25] – but the charge of meaning fluctuates in any long poem which takes its time, its pace slackening between moments of intensity. *The Prelude* oscillates between Wordsworth's reflective passages, many of them flat and verbose, and his crystallizing 'spots of time' which key the meditative stretches. In Scott's three best romances the poetic troughs, stanzas of basic narrative function, and the poet's characteristic prolixity offset those more vivid passages of action, description and philosophizing through which his story passes. Action can be succinctly impressionistic as in the imagery of blood and claymore in the single combat between Richard of Musgrave and Lord Cranstoun in *The Lay of the Last Minstrel*, Canto Five, XXI, or panoramic as in the extended account of the Battle of Flodden in *Marmion*, where Scott's camera eye sweeps across the 'full array' of the Scottish and English armies and the 'battle on the plain' before zooming in on the dying Marmion (Canto Six, XXIX–XXXII). Splendour falls conventionally enough on Norham Castle's walls (*Marmion*, Canto One, I), but the 'battled towers' take on solidity from the precisely imagined visual effect of the setting sun on the armour of its soldiery:

> The warriors on the turrets high,
> Moving athwart the evening sky,
>   Seem'd forms of giant height:
> Their armour, as it caught the rays,
> Flash'd back again the western blaze,
>   In lines of dazzling light.

The Introduction to Canto Two of *Marmion* includes the description of 'lone Saint Mary's silent lake' which prompted James Hogg to tell Scott, 'there never was any thing more graphic written in this world'.[26] The speed and excitement of the stag-hunt which begins *The Lady of the Lake* impart a dynamic to the earth itself in the scene-painting of the first Canto. The foiled hunter looks down on Loch Katrine set in a landscape felt as massively alive:

> Loch Katrine lay beneath him roll'd;
> In all her length far winding lay,
> With promontory, creek, and bay,
> And islands that, empurpled bright,
> Floated amid the livelier light,
> And mountains, that like giants stand,
> To sentinel enchanted land.
> High on the south, huge Benvenue
> Down to the lake in masses threw
> Crags, knolls, and mounds, confusedly hurl'd,

The fragments of an earlier world;
A wildering forest feather'd o'er
His ruin'd sides and summit hoar,
While on the north, through middle air,
Ben-an heaved high his forehead bare.

His brisk philosophizing can build a perdurable monument in verse to
Nelson, Pitt and Fox in *Marmion*'s 'Introduction to Canto First', the
sadness of the loss to Britain of Pitt's death implicit in the silence of the
well-known lines: 'The trumpet's silver sound is still, / The warder silent
on the hill!' In gnomic mood he defines love:

It liveth not in fierce desire,
     With dead desire it doth not die;
It is the secret sympathy,
The silver link, the silken tie,
Which heart to heart, and mind to mind
In body and in soul can bind.
                    (*The Lay of the Last Minstrel*,
                         Canto Five, XIII)

or reflects pawkily on the waywardness of women:

We hold our greyhound in our hand,
     Our falcon on our glove;
But where shall we find leash or band
For dame that loves to rove?
          (*Marmion*, Canto One, XVII)

or appreciates a capricious woman's instinct for practical sympathy in
times of trouble:

O Woman! in our hours of ease,
Uncertain, coy, and hard to please,
And variable as the shade
By the light quivering aspen made;
When pain and anguish wring the brow,
A ministering angel thou!
          (*Marmion*, Canto Six, XXX)

Scott's later, hastily written romances fail because their rickety plots
and predictable rhymes are too seldom lifted by the atmospheric and
descriptive felicities of the first three and the charged moments are too
few to compensate for their flat passages. In the 'Introduction to Canto
First' of *Marmion* 'the legendary lay / O'er poet's bosom holds its sway'

and 'on the ancient minstrel strain / Time lays his palsied hand in vain'; but in *The Vision of Don Roderick* (1811) Scott seems to realize that the palsy is taking hold, that he is losing the winning formula:

> Minstrel, the fame of whose romantic lyre,
> Capricious-swelling now, may soon be lost,
> Like the light flickering of a cottage fire.
>> (Canto One, VII)

Byron, too, was taking hold, usurping Scott's position as the best-selling poet of the day. In a letter of 1821 Scott refers with pragmatism and generosity to Byron's impact on public taste and on his own prospects of further success as a poet:

> I had my day with the public and being no great believer in poetical immortality I was very well pleased to rise a winner without continuing the game till I was beggard of any credit I had acquired with the public. Besides I felt the prudence of giving way before the more forcible and powerful genius of Byron.[27]

After *The Lady of the Lake*, as he says himself, Scott 'declined as a poet to figure as a novelist'.[28] Searching a desk in Abbotsford for fishing flies, he found the manuscript of a novel he had begun and abandoned in 1805. In 1814 he published the finished work as *Waverley* and the first edition of 1,000 copies sold out in five weeks. The best-selling poet would now become the best-selling novelist, though the poet contributed to the novelist's success, especially in the earlier novels, with such verses as Davie Gellatley's 'False love, and hast thou played me thus' based on a traditional lyric fragment in *Waverley* (Chapter 9) and, in the same novel, his song, 'Young men will love thee more fair and more fast' (Chapter 14); Elspeth Mucklebackit's 'wild and doleful recitative' of 'the red Harlaw' in *The Antiquary* (1816, Chapter 40); the secretly romantic Lucy Ashton's premonitory repudiation of 'the tinsel of worldly pleasure' in 'Look not thou on beauty's charming' in *The Bride of Lammermoor* (Chapter 3), and the stirring song 'March, march Ettrick and Teviotdale' in *The Monastery* (1820, Chapter 25). Best of all, in *The Heart of Midlothian*, are Madge Wildfire's songs including the stark perfection of 'Proud Maisie' (Chapter 40), a projection of the abused and deranged Madge's own pathetic situation in the novel. As Madge, a Scottish Ophelia, is now without hope and on the point of death, the 'Sweet Robin' has a sour message for Maisie, shattering her hope and pride by equating her marriage with her funeral. Her groomsmen are her pall-bearers, her bridal bed the grave. The poignancy of the poem comes from the discrepancy between Maisie's blithe questions and the bird's cryptically mordant answers:

'Tell me, thou bonny bird,
    When shall I marry me?'
'When six braw gentlemen,
    Kirkward shall carry ye.'

'Who makes the bridal bed,
    Birdie, say truly?' –
'The grey-headed sexton,
    That delves the grave duly.'

The novelist

Waverley; or 'Tis Sixty Years Since (1814) is the most thoroughly integrated of Scott's novels about history and stands aesthetically with *The Heart of Midlothian* (1818) as his best work in the genre. *Redgauntlet* (1824) is a subtler meditation on history and change, free-will and determinism but an inferior novel as a whole, despite some of his finest passages including the showdown between Prince Charles and his supporters in Chapter 22, the moving account in Chapter 23 of the Pretender's final, dignified departure for France with a sad but resigned Redgauntlet, and 'Wandering Willie's Tale' of Steenie Steenson's supernatural dealings with two former generations of Redgauntlets which Scott incorporates into the story of Darsie Latimer's search for himself. Goethe thought highly of *The Fair Maid of Perth* (1828) and relished Scott's qualities in general but insisted that *Waverley* stood alone: 'After reading Waverley, you will understand why Walter Scott still designates himself the author of that work; for there he showed what he could do, and he has never since written anything to surpass, or even equal, that first published novel.'[29] A historical novel about the impact of history on its unheroic hero and on a large, varied cast of supporting characters, *Waverley* argues for moderation in personal life as well as in politics. Young Edward Waverley chances to fall into history and is seduced by the glamour of the Jacobites on the eve of the 1745 rebellion. His immersion in history matures him into chastened, moderate, domesticated adulthood not so much by the exertion of his own will as by the pressures of historical circumstance and accident on his malleable sensibility and fundamental decency. The process makes Waverley an expression of the history he lives through and of

Scott's conception of an individual's relation to history as an amalgam of determining socio-political forces and acts of more or less conscious choice.

The autobiographical impulse behind the story is evident from an entry in Scott's *Journal* for December 1825 which summarizes the author's life in terms that could almost apply to his hero:

> What a life mine has been. Half educated, almost wholly neglected or left to myself – stuffing my head with most nonsensical trash and undervalued in society for a time by most of my companions – getting forward and held a bold and clever fellow, contrary to the opinion of all who thought me a mere dreamer – Broken-hearted for two years.[30]

Waverley recovers from his broken heart more quickly than Scott did from his unsuccessful wooing of Williamina Belsches, but his character is determined by the combination of his unguided, epicurean reading and the political division in his family background between his uncle's 'Tory or High-Church predilections and prejudices' and his father's choice of the Whig persuasion as 'a political creed more consonant both to reason and his own interest' (Chapter 2). The split expresses Scott's own divided sympathies for Tory politics, the Hanoverian succession – he was responsible for George IV's visit to Scotland in 1822 – and the Jacobite cause as well as his sense of the opposed appeals of romanticism and Enlightenment reason. Reconciling such contradictions could not be easy, as Scott admits in a letter of 1813:

> I am very glad I did not live in 1745 for though as a lawyer I could not have pleaded Charles's right and as a clergyman I could not have prayed for him yet as a soldier I would I am sure against the convictions of my better reason have fought for him even to the bottom of the gallows.[31]

It was a serious dilemma for a patriot, but Scott can incorporate it into the comic characterization of the Baron of Bradwardine who toasts the health of the King, 'politely leaving to the consciences of his guests to drink to the sovereign *de facto* or *de jure*, as their politics inclined' (*Waverley*, Chapter 11). In *The Antiquary* the egregious Sir Arthur Wardour is a 'melancholy instance of human inconsistency' close enough to Scott's own:

> Sir Arthur continued to pray for the house of Stewart even after the family had been extinct, and when, in

truth, though in his theoretical loyalty he was pleased to regard them as alive, yet, in all actual service and practical exertion, he was a most zealous and devoted subject of George III.

(Chapter 5)

The achievement of *Waverley* is precisely that it does reconcile these conflicting sympathies, thereby reflecting the pragmatic point of balance Scott reached himself: 'I am not the least afraid nowadays of making my feelings walk hand in hand with my judgement though the former are Jacobitical the latter inclined for public weal to the present succession.'[32] For Redgauntlet being a Jacobite means a romantic preference for 'honour and principle to fortune, and even to life'; but for his nephew, Darsie Latimer, English-born representative of the new order, Jacobitism is 'an antiquated and desperate line of politics' (*Redgauntlet*, Chapter 9). Scott both celebrates Redgauntlet's idealism and endorses Darsie's judgement. Redgauntlet stands alone at the end of his story, 'splendid, heroic, courageous, romantic and absurd'.[33] Compared to the energy and passion of Redgauntlet, the ordered routine of the Solway Quakers exhibits 'a uniformity, a want of interest, a helpless and hopeless languor, which rendered life insipid' (*Redgauntlet*, Letter 10); but Joshua Geddes is the practical man of a commercial future, and the 'manly sport' of fishing must give way to the more productive stake-nets of the Tide-net Fishing Company.

E. M. Forster's celebrated hatchet job on the story of *The Antiquary* in *Aspects of the Novel* is justifiable and good critical fun, but it is imperceptive of Forster to say in general of Scott: 'He cannot construct. He has neither artistic detachment nor passion.'[34] Certainly, he 'made no rules for himself'.[35] Fielding, for example, keeps, in Robert Louis Stevenson's phrase, 'a far firmer hold upon the tiller of his story'.[36] *The Bride of Lammermoor* (1819) begins and ends effectively, but fails to satisfy as a whole because Scott's control wavers in the middle. With well-judged acceleration of the action in its last five chapters the novel moves towards the tragic climax that has been implicit in the legend of the ruined Gothic fountain (Chapter 5), the warnings of Alice Gray (Chapter 19), and the dead raven whose blood stains Lucy Ashton's dress (Chapter 20). As Ralph Waldo Emerson puts it in his essay, 'History', Lucy Ashton 'is another name for fidelity, which is always beautiful and always liable to calamity in this world',[37] but the sense of tragic inevitability is dissipated in over-elaborate characterization and too much talk. Unlike young Lochinvar, Edgar Ravenswood arrives too late, and so does the dénouement. As Dick Tinto tells Peter Pattieson in Scott's otiose first chapter, the characters '*patter* too much', and so does the narrator. The Whig–Tory sub-plot appears tacked on and is, therefore, more trivializing than contextualizing. Working on the same story with the compressions of opera in *Lucia Di Lammermoor* (1835), Donizetti overgoes his source. Scott is often heedless if not incapable of effective construction as in the wandering plot of *The Antiquary*, the snail's pace of *The Talisman* and *The Betrothed*, which he published together in 1825 as *Tales of the Crusaders*, and the laboured use of the epistolary form in the thirteen letters between Alan Fairford and Darsie Latimer that make up the first third of *Redgauntlet*. The twentieth-century reader is unlikely to be disarmed by Scott's admission in Chapter 1 of *Redgauntlet* that 'various prolixities and redundancies occur in the course of an interchange of letters, which must hang as a dead weight on the progress of the narrative'. Such coyness merits the observation that conceding a dead weight does not lighten it.

The ponderous narrative framework he constructed for the four series of novels published between 1816 and 1831 as *Tales of My Landlord* requires the story of *The Heart of Midlothian* to be prefaced not only by the author's explanatory Introduction and Postscript, but also by the bombastic Jebediah Cleishbotham's dedicatory address to the reader and the introductory first chapter purporting to follow the superfluous Peter Pattieson's fictitious manuscript. Clearly akin to the imaginative frameworks supplied by the Last Minstrel in *The Lay of the Last Minstrel* and the 'Harp of the North' in *The Lady of the Lake*, these are mannered, unattractively complacent manipulative games, even if a technical case can be made for them as Scott's 'devices for distancing his reader from the past through layers of memory'.[38] (How much more sensitively Nathaniel Hawthorne invokes the past and relates it to his 1850 story of *The Scarlet Letter* in the introductory chapter entitled 'The Custom-House'.) A technical rationale does not extenuate a boring effect any more than Scott's likening himself to 'the digressive poet Ariosto' (*The Heart of Midlothian*, Chapter 16) can ingratiate his wayward narrative method with a reader brought up on the tighter controls of the later Dickens, or the economies of Joseph Conrad, Robert Louis Stevenson and Henry James. Yet the last twenty chapters of *The Heart of Midlothian* are unjustly castigated on the ground that Scott carried the story beyond its proper ending because he wanted payment for a big novel. This criticism first apeared anonymously in the *British Review* for November 1818:

> Repetition, tautology, with clumsiness of every species and degree meet our eyes in almost every page; and we have, moreover, some reason to be dissatisfied with [Scott] for attacking so unmercifully our patience and our purses, by protracting so doggedly and heavily an exhausted subject, merely, as it should seem, to comply with the mercenary condition of extending the tale to four volumes.[39]

It is true that 'we cannot cut short *The Heart of Midlothian* at that point where its older readers found it still so highly praiseworthy – the point where Jeanie obtains the pardon; we must judge the book at its full length without commiseration for Scott's financial needs in building Abbotsford'.[40] The novel was extended from three to four volumes to fulfil the contract for a four-volume second series of *Tales of My Landlord*;[41] but neither Scott's undeniable interest in money nor the perfunctory melodrama of George Staunton's death at the hand of his and Effie Deans's son invalidates John Buchan's judgement that 'the conception of the Roseneath chapters is right. Scott was always social historian as well as novelist, and he wanted to show Scottish life passing into a mellower phase in which old unhappy things were forgotten. Artistically, too, the instinct was sound. The figures, who have danced so wildly at the bidding of fate, should find reward in a gentle, bright, leisurely old age. Even so Tolstoy rounded off his *War and Peace*.'[42]

The simple linear construction of *Waverley* is sufficient to its chronological purpose and the novel is its author's declaration that he does care passionately about his country's history. He understands history's counterpoint of loss and progress from 'the destruction of the patriarchal power of the Highland chiefs' and the eradication of the Jacobite party to the 'gradual influx of wealth', 'the extension of commerce' and the disappearance of 'folks of the old leaven' who were 'living examples of singular and disinterested attachment to the principles of loyalty which they received from their fathers, and of old Scottish faith, hospitality, worth, and honour'. Irrespective of class or party, Scott respects such values. His Scottish novels are a recognition, informed, proud and tender, of the traumas of social change and resulting problems of judgement: 'There is no European nation which, within the course of half a century, or little more, has undergone so complete a change as this kingdom of Scotland' ('A Postscript, which should have been a Preface', *Waverley*, Chapter 72). His sensitivity to the social conditions of the common people in the era before 'the now universal potato' is nowhere more evident than in the carefully balanced description of the straggling village of Tully-Veolan (*Waverley*, Chapter 8). At first glance the place suggests 'a stagnation of industry, and perhaps of intellect'. He notices effects of poverty and 'indolence, its too frequent companion', but penetrates to virtues discernible below the depressing surfaces of the scene:

> Yet the physiognomy of the people, when more closely
> examined, was far from exhibiting the indifference of
> stupidity: their features were rough, but remarkably
> intelligent; grave, but the very reverse of stupid; and from
> among the young women, an artist might have chosen

more than one model, whose features and form resembled those of Minerva.

Scott also exposes the moral values that underlie political surfaces in *Waverley*. Jacobite braggadocios and volatility are forgotten in Fergus Mac-Ivor's dignified acceptance of the death sentence and in Evan Dhu Maccombich's proposal that six clansmen should replace Fergus on the gallows (Chapter 68). A reader inclined to dismiss the offer as romantic bluster is rebuked by the judge along with the 'sort of laugh' heard in the court, and Evan shames both the insensitive reader and the court audience in a speech that makes real the romantic principles of self-sacrifice and honour:

> If the Saxon gentlemen are laughing . . . because a poor
> man, such as me, thinks my life, or the life of six of my
> degree, is worth that of Vich Ian Vohr, it's like enough
> they may be very right; but if they laugh because they
> think I would not keep my word . . . I can tell them they
> ken neither the heart of a Hielandman, nor the honour of
> a gentleman.

Highland honour is the subject of 'The Two Drovers', an impeccably paced and focused short story about the fatal cultural clash between the Englishman, Harry Wakefield, and Robin Oig McCombich which was first published in *Chronicles of the Canongate* (1827). The legal case, as the venerable judge lucidly explains without the digressions to which Scott's lawyers are typically prone, hinges on the pre-determination of Robin Oig's revenge. After being knocked down by his former friend and mocked by the crowd in Heskett's inn he walks twelve miles to retrieve the dirk he needs to kill Wakefield. For Robin Oig the mandatory restoration of his honour requires his openly killing Wakefield before surrendering himself to the penalty of the law. This is honourable, tragic equity. As he says at his execution: 'I give a life for the life I took . . . and what can I do more?'

Scott makes a point of saying that he does not intend to emulate Cervantes in *Waverley*. His hero does not tilt quixotically at windmills, but evinces 'that more common aberration from sound judgement' which communicates to real occurrences 'a tincture of its own romantic tone and colouring' (Chapter 5). (The tinctures of Catherine Morland's romantic projections were not revealed until the publication of *Northanger Abbey* in 1818, although Jane Austen had begun work on the novel in 1798.) But romanticism needs a kick-start, even in a man who 'can admire the moon and quote a stanza from Tasso' (Chapter 52). Rose

Bradwardine is 'too frank, too confiding, too kind; amiable qualities undoubtedly, but destructive of the marvellous, with which a youth of imagination delights to address the empress of his affections' (Chapter 14). Waverley's encounter with Donald Bean Lean and Fergus Mac-Ivor leads him to Fergus's single-minded sister Flora, 'precisely the character to fascinate a youth of romantic imagination' (Chapter 24), and to his head-long plunge into history on the Jacobite side by which he joins forces not only with the suave Chevalier, who finds him 'perhaps somewhat roman-tic', but also with the ladies of Scotland who 'very generally espoused the cause of the gallant and handsome young Prince, who threw himself upon the mercy of his countrymen rather like a hero of romance than a calculating politician' (Chapter 43).

Yet the plot's cleverest twist is Flora's treatment of Waverley. Despite her idealistic fervour for the Jacobite cause, she is untainted by her brother's opportunism, and will not exploit Waverley's infatuation with her to enlist him more deeply than is good for him. Aware of Fergus's short-comings, she also realizes that Waverley's disposition, 'notwithstanding his dreams of tented fields and military honour, seemed exclusively do-mestic' (Chapter 52). His Jacobite episode has been a symptom of his own lack of self-knowledge, a stage in his development. 'Blown about with every wind of doctrine' (Chapter 50), Waverley comes to see him-self as a 'very child of caprice' (Chapter 54). 'You are not celebrated for knowing your own mind very pointedly,' Fergus tells him (Chapter 59), but he is, like Henry Mackenzie's lachrymose hero, a 'man of feeling'. Impulses of 'general philanthropy' more instinctive than the vanity grati-fied by Jacobite approval or the mirrored reflection of himself in High-land dress (Chapter 42) prompt him to tend the dying soldier, Houghton (Chapter 45), to rescue the English Colonel Talbot from certain death at the Battle of Prestonpans and to want to save Colonel Gardiner, his former commanding officer (Chapter 47). His government pardon is thus his earned absolution from romantic illusion and political dilettantism, his passport to the mature, prosaic world of domesticity and realistic com-promise. In the aftermath of Prestonpans and the Highlanders' decision at Derby to evade the Duke of Cumberland by retreating northward, Waverley feels himself 'entitled to say firmly, though perhaps with a sigh, that the romance of his life was ended, and that its real history had now commenced' (Chapter 60). His marriage to the devoted Rose signifies that he has come through his initiations, though Scott is too shrewd a psychologist to strip him entirely of egotism. To Waverley, Rose Brad-wardine 'possessed an attraction which few men can resist, from the marked interest which she took in everything that affected him' (Chapter 52). As V. S. Pritchett says, Scott 'asserts the normal man'.[43]

The Antiquary's 'Advertisement' reveals that Scott regarded his first three novels as a trilogy:

> . . . a series of narratives, intended to illustrate the manners
> of Scotland at three different periods. WAVERLEY
> embraced the age of our fathers, GUY MANNERING
> that of our own youth, and the ANTIQUARY refers to
> the last ten years of the eighteenth century.

Waverley is the most successful of the three both structurally and in its
unsentimental animation of a bygone Scotland. It works as a moral fable
not because Scott endows Edward Waverley with what a twentieth-
century reader would recognize as three-dimensional life – the character,
like most of Scott's people, is always felt as a construct under authorial
manipulation, a puppet of the novel's thesis – but because the history in
which Waverley's *Bildungsroman* is set comes alive in the portrayal of the
Highlanders, the appearances of the Chevalier himself, and the Battle of
Prestonpans and its consequences. There is also a cast of ancillary characters, several of them comic, whose variety fills out a comprehensively
realized world: Fergus Mac-Ivor's foxy retainer, Callum; the Baron of
Bradwardine and his factor, Duncan Macwheeble; the headstrong Laird
of Balmawhapple, finally stopped in his quarrelsome tracks by the English
dragoons who, 'cleaving his skull with their broadswords, satisfied the
world that the unfortunate gentleman had actually brains, the end of his
life thus giving proof of a fact greatly doubted during its progress' (Chapter 47). *Guy Mannering; or The Astrologer* (1815) may entertain the reader
looking for a passably romantic yarn wordily told, but fails in its intention
to illuminate the friction between Scotland's past and the country of
Scott's youth because the theme of the missing heir on which the plot
turns is trite, the hero, Harry Bertram, is pasteboard and the secondary
characters are stiff, except for the farmer, Dandie Dinmont, and the
splendidly wild, self-sacrificing gypsy, Meg Merrilies, who represents the
best indigenous qualities of the unregenerate, older Scotland and deserves
to be in a better book. Admired by Wordsworth,[44] she is 'a sort of picturesque reincarnation of the Last Minstrel, lamenting the changes that
have befallen Scotland as the feudal order has been hurried towards its
end'.[45] The anonymous critic of the *Augustan Review* for July 1815 rightly
singles her out: 'Meg Merrilies is, however, the great agent – the genius
of the author shines forth in every line she utters and every scene in
which she appears.'[46] The diatribe Meg delivers to the Laird of Ellangowan
in the attitude of 'a sibyl in frenzy' after the ejection of the Derncleugh
gypsies from their 'city of refuge' cottages in Chapter 8 is an aria of
denunciation in true demotic Scots:

> 'Ride your ways', said the gipsy, 'ride your ways, Laird of
> Ellangowan – ride your ways, Godfrey Bertram! – This
> day have ye quenched seven smoking hearths – see if the

fire in your ain parlour burn the blyther for that. Ye have
riven the thack off seven cottar houses – look if your ain
roof-tree stand the faster. – Ye may stable your stirks in
the shealings at Derncleugh – see that the hare does not
couch on the hearthstane at Ellangowan. – Ride your
ways, Godfrey Bertram – what do ye glower after our folk
for? – There's thirty hearts there, that wad hae wanted
bread ere ye had wanted sunkets, and spent their lifeblood
ere ye had scratched your finger.

Despite the tedious Dousterswivel plot, a heavy-handed anti-Gothic
joke which outstays its welcome,[47] *The Antiquary* (1816) is full of good
invention and acute social observation. In Chapter 11 the fisherfolk of the
east coast are portrayed in terms of their settlement of huts with its smells
of melting boat-pitch and fish. A keen sense of their lives comes through
Maggie Mucklebackit's unequal contest with the Antiquary of the title,
Jonathan Oldbuck, Laird of Monkbarns, when they haggle over the price
of her fish. Oldbuck has the buying power, but Maggie has principle on
her side as well as the sharp eloquence of Scots:

And div ye think . . . that my man and my sons are to gae
to the sea in weather like yestreen and the day – sic a sea
as it's yet outby – and get naething for their fish, and be
misca'd into the bargain, Monkbarns? It's no fish ye're
buying – it's men's lives.

The inside story of the fishers' huts is given in Chapter 26 when Scott
takes us into the Mucklebackits' cottage, and in Chapter 29 when news
of Steenie Mucklebackit's drowning interrupts a tranquil evening game of
village longbowls, tragically vindicating Maggie's equation of fish and
men's lives. There is the chorus of gossips in the back-parlour of the post-
master's house at Fairport, 'forming conjectures about the correspondence
and affairs of their neighbours':

'But look here, lasses,' interrupted Mrs Mailsetter, 'here's a
sight for sair e'en! What wad ye gie to ken what's in the
inside o' this – For William Lovel, Esquire, at Mrs
Hadoway's, High-Street, Fairport, by Edinburgh, N. B.
This is just the second letter he has had since he was
here.'

(Chapter 15)

There is the traditional German legend touched up by Isabella Wardour
into 'The Fortunes of Martin Waldeck' (Chapter 18), and, above all,
there is the engagingly idiomatic character of Edie Ochiltree, the King's

bedesman. He is the natural antiquary, who carries the past unpedantically within him and knows how to function usefully in the present, 'the oracle of the district through which he travels – their genealogist, their newsman, their master of the revels, their doctor at a pinch, or their divine'. But *The Antiquary* fails to gel because of Scott's now full-blown loquacity. The wisdom of old Scotland is supposedly embodied in the maddeningly digressive Oldbuck who acts as adviser, arbiter and buffer state between gullible, bigoted Sir Arthur Wardour and the English Major Neville, alias Lovel, who is still not good enough for Sir Arthur's emotionally constipated daughter, Isabella, when he has rescued her and her father from death by high tide and tempest (Chapters 7–8) but becomes acceptable when he turns out to be heir to the estate of Glenallan.

Both *Old Mortality* (1816) and *Rob Roy* (1817) follow *Waverley*'s pattern of opposites. Like Edward Waverley, both Henry Morton and Francis Osbaldistone are moderate men propelled into a conflict generated by historical forces. Each becomes involved in the anti-government side of his story and each eventually returns to respectable domestic felicity within the establishment. Morton's unpartisan protection of Tillietudlem Castle against his own side and his efforts to save Lord Evandale, his rival for the hand of Edith Bellenden, parallel Waverley's efforts on behalf of Houghton, Colonel Gardiner and Colonel Talbot. *Old Mortality* is set in the time of the Covenanting wars, the 'killing-time' between 1679, the year in which John Graham of Claverhouse crushed the Covenanters' rebellion at the Battle of Bothwell Brig, and the period of 'prudent tolerance' introduced by the bloodless or Glorious Revolution of 1688 when 'the blessed licht shone upon the kingdom', as Robert Louis Stevenson's narrator recalls in his story, 'Thrawn Janet'. Scott well understands the irony of the religious extremist's dislike of toleration when it is extended to those of another persuasion:

> The triumphant Whigs, while they reestablished Presbytery
> as the national religion, and assigned to the General
> Assemblies of the Kirk their natural influence, were very
> far from going to the lengths which the Cameronians and
> the more extravagant portion of the nonconformists under
> Charles and James loudly demanded . . . Those who had
> expected to find in King William a zealous covenanted
> monarch were grievously disappointed when he intimated
> his intention to tolerate all forms of religion consistent
> with the safety of the state.
>
> (Chapter 37)

The novel's main attractions are Scott's balanced treatment of the Covenanters[48] and his portrait of Claverhouse, 1st Viscount Dundee, whom he reverentially brings back from the dead six years later in the devil's replica of Redgauntlet Castle in 'Wandering Willie's Tale': 'And there was Claverhouse, as beautiful as when he lived' (*Redgauntlet*, Letter XI). This is the 'Bonnie Dundee' who inspired Scott's popular song in his late, otherwise forgettable play, *The Doom of Devorgoil* (1830):

> Come fill up my cup, come fill up my can,
> Come saddle your horses, and call up the men,
> Come open your gates, and let me gae free,
> For it's up with the bonnets of Bonny Dundee!
> (II, ii)

Scott uses historical materials confidently but drily in *Old Mortality*. During his confinement at Tillietudlem, 'Morton's "cold fits" over Edith's return of his affections become an impelling force in his rebellion against the government', which is 'not only an attempt by Scott to stitch together disparate levels of human life' but 'an effort as well to show how Morton's subjective life affects his decision to participate in the ongoing struggle'.[49] But Morton's predicament is more moral theorem than flesh-and-blood dilemma and the novel, therefore, lacks human pulse. It is history without a centre. Set in the aftermath of the Jacobite rebellion of 1715, *Rob Roy* is more full-blooded, yet neither Rob Roy's flight from government troops nor Frank's love for the compelling Diana Vernon, whom he finally marries, stays in the mind as brightly as Frank's kindly, self-important companion, the pragmatic, pro-Unionist Glasgow merchant, Bailie Nicol Jarvie, and Andrew Fairservice, the garrulous, untrustworthy gardener at Osbaldistone Hall, whose name exactly indicates what he does not render.

One consequence of being a genuinely historical novelist – that is, a novelist for whom history is subject, not merely setting – is an inevitable problem with foreground because history simultaneously pulls towards the sprawl of panorama and draws attention to the minutiae of life on the edges, to the detriment of that focus on the pre-determined 'special case' which Henry James insists is the novel's peculiar business. In *Kenilworth* (1821) the special case is the relationship between Leicester and Amy, but the real subject is the effect of historical force personified by the jealous Queen Elizabeth. The Queen's absolute power moderates romance by inversion: because of Elizabeth, Amy is a damsel who needs rescuing from her prince, and Leicester is finally responsible for her death. Scott's history repeatedly pushes the peripheral to centre stage. Edie Ochiltree and the Mucklebackits displace Major Neville and Isabella Wardour in *The Antiquary*; Jeanie Deans is almost upstaged by her foil, Madge Wildfire, in *The Heart of Midlothian*; Richie Moniplies eclipses George Heriot in *The Fortunes of Nigel* (1822), Scott's most amiable novel. In *Ivanhoe* (1820), the most widely read of the historical romances, Ivanhoe and Rowena are themselves part of a background which is further enriched by Gurth the swineherd, Wamba the jester, the Knights Templar and the tournament at Ashby-de-la-Zouche. In *The Pirate* (1822) cardboard characterization and leaden-paced action are no match for Scott's vivid evocation of Shetland's landscape and customs.

The Heart of Midlothian; Scott's appeal then and now

The stark clarity and moral weight of Jeanie Deans's dilemma prevent her from being swamped by the teeming life of *The Heart of Midlothian* (1818), through which she walks at the rate of 'five-and-twenty miles and a bittock' towards one of fiction's most implausible resolutions, her meeting with Queen Caroline. The novel takes its title from Edinburgh's Old Tolbooth or prison, known as 'the heart of Midlothian'. (After the building was demolished in 1817 its door was presented by the city magistrates to Scott who had it set into an upper wall of Abbotsford House.) Jeanie Deans's appeal, therefore, is in her achievement of moral independence in a world presided over by the image of punishment by law and inhibited by the prospect, fundamental to her father's system of belief, of punishment by God. David Deans's 'true-blue' Cameronian inflexibility – despite his disclaimers to Mr Middleburgh in Chapter 18 – makes lying a sin under any circumstances. The acknowledged injustice of the law by which Effie Deans is condemned to death for child-murder[50] cannot justify a lie or mitigate a lie's everlasting injury to the liar's immortal soul. Scott emphasizes the rigidity of Jeanie's inherited absolute by placing it in a context of ironic moral ambiguities. The law's agent, Captain John Porteous of the Edinburgh City Guard, 'is said to have been a man of profligate habits, an unnatural son, and a brutal husband' (Chapter 3); the smuggler, Andrew Wilson, is a criminal but 'bold, stout-hearted, generous' (Chapter 33); the adventurer, George Staunton alias Robertson, abuses Madge Wildfire but loves Effie Deans; the Tolbooth turnkey and former thief, James Ratcliffe, declines the money Jeanie offers him to do what he can for Effie's comfort in prison, urging her to lie for her sister's sake with the classic tax-dodger's rationalization, 'deil a hair ill there is in it, if ye are rapping again the crown' (Chapter 20). Such moral relativities are no help to Jeanie: she is stuck with her unyielding principle, though she wrestles with it:

> Roaming from thought to thought, she at one time
> imagined her father understood the ninth commandment

literally, as prohibiting false witness *against* our neighbour, without extending the denunciation against falsehood uttered *in favour* of the criminal. But her clear and unsophisticated power of discriminating between good and evil, instantly rejected an interpretation so limited, and so unworthy of the Author of the law.

(Chapter 19)

In facing her problem – to lie to save Effie's life, or not to lie – Jeanie is completely alone, 'cruelly sted between God's laws and man's laws' (Chapter 19). David Deans is immovably resolved not to see Effie again 'if her gude name be gone' (Chapter 18); George Staunton can only urge Jeanie to lie; the pallid Reuben Butler is short on passion, well-meaning and ineffectual. The good Mrs Saddletree is sympathetic, but her amateur-lawyer husband – one of Scott's best caricatures – is an 'intrusive ass' about whom 'there is a great question whether the gratification of playing the person of importance, inquiring, investigating, and laying down the law on the whole affair, did not offer, to say the least, full consolation for the pain which pure sympathy gave him on account of his wife's kinswoman' (Chapter 12). Ironically, it is Jeanie's comically uncouth rejected suitor, the laconic Laird of Dumbiedikes, who gives her money for her journey to London without understanding her at all: it is not a romantic wind that fills her sails. To make matters worse, the Porteous riots of 1736 have brought Edinburgh into royal disfavour as 'a very disaffected and intractable metropolis'. (The government fined the city council £2,000 in 1737.) On every level – personal, ideological and political – Jeanie is alone in a hostile world. Her distinction is that she acts, drawing a strength from her adherence to principle and her belief in Effie's innocence that carries her across England to the sympathetic Duke of Argyle in London and into her ringing plea for Effie's life to Queen Caroline:

'Oh, madam, if ever ye kend what it was to sorrow for and with a sinning and a suffering creature, whose mind is sae tossed that she can be neither ca'd fit to live or die, have some compassion on our misery! – Save an honest house from dishonour, and an unhappy girl, not eighteen years of age, from an early and dreadful death! Alas! it is not when we sleep soft and wake merrily ourselves, that we think on other people's sufferings. Our hearts are waxed light within us then, and we are for righting our ain wrangs and fighting our ain battles. But when the hour of trouble comes to the mind or to the body – and seldom may it visit your Leddyship – and when the hour of death comes, that comes to high and low – lang and late may it be yours – Oh, my Leddy, then it isna what we hae dune for oursells, but what we hae dune for others, that we think on maist pleasantly.'

(Chapter 37)

'This is eloquence,' says the outclassed Queen with regal succinctness to the Duke of Argyle, yet Jeanie's eloquence is not merely in her impassioned, well-chosen words but in her unswervingly straight moral path through forbidding complications. Georg Lukács astutely finds Scott's greatness 'in his capacity to give living embodiment to historical-social types'.[51] Edward Waverley, the Chevalier of *Waverley* and *Redgauntlet*, Harry Bertram, Henry Morton and Lord Evandale, Frank Osbaldistone and Rob Roy, Jeanie Deans and Redgauntlet are all characters 'who, in their psychology and destiny, always represent social trends and historical forces'[52] in their maker's construction of Scotland's supreme, nostalgic fiction. Mr Redgauntlet, alias Herries of Birrenswork, virtually hands Lukács his theory ready-made when he tells Darsie Latimer:

The privilege of free action belongs to no mortal – we are tied down by the fetters of duty – our moral path is limited by the regulations of honour – our most indifferent actions are but meshes of the web of destiny by which we are all surrounded.

(*Redgauntlet*, Chapter 9)

But Sir Arthur Darsie Redgauntlet rejects his atavistic uncle's 'Destiny' or historical determinism, and Jeanie Deans is more than a compendium of Cameronian religion, moral crisis and historical circumstance. She preserves her immortal soul from the sin of lying; she also has guts. Scott endows her with a conception of morality 'that admits of greater human sympathy than absolute principles usually allow'.[53] If she is the mother of Scott's peace-loving Catherine Glover in *The Fair Maid of Perth*, she is also the mother of Charlotte Brontë's Jane Eyre. Finding what Lukács calls 'the middle way'[54] and bringing out the good in others, she stays in the mind as one of the great literary heroines.

In his own time Scott the novelist reigned supreme as 'the perennial fatherly baronet of the folk imagination'.[55] Maggie Tulliver in George Eliot's *The Mill on the Floss* sometimes longs for 'all Scott's novels and all Byron's poems', aware that they may provide the 'absorbing fancies' of a 'dream-world' and 'dull her sensibility' (Book 4, Chapter 3). In St Louis, Missouri, the young Kate Chopin read Scott to escape into his past from the present anguish of the American Civil War.[56] Yet Scott's mass appeal was more than escapist. After Union the positive past available to Scots

was 'the past not of their own country but of England. It was English
history that provided the model for the evolution of a modern, stable,
commercially successful and freedom-loving society.'[57] The Waverley
novels, with their apparatus of historical notes and ballad fragments both
authentic and invented, gave post-Union Scotland its own native chronicles, and gave the world a Scotland 'released . . . from the limbo of the
secret places of the mind'.[58] In America they gave James Fenimore Cooper
in the north and William Gilmore Simms in the south the model they
needed for their own pseudo-historical canvases,[59] and influenced the
work of writers as diverse as Washington Irving, Harriet Beecher Stowe,
Frank Norris, Ellen Glasgow[60] and William Faulkner. Mark Twain loathed
them. In Chapter 40 of *Life on the Mississippi* (1883) he supposes that Scott
has 'run the people mad' as the source of a degenerate romanticism whose
'windy humbuggeries' are absurdly memorialized in the Capitol building
at Baton Rouge, Louisiana, a 'sham castle . . . with turrets and things'.
Twain would have liked Havelock Ellis's sneer at the 'jerry-built, pseudo-
medieval structures which [Scott] raised so rapidly and so easily'.[61] In
Chapter 46 of *Life on the Mississippi* Twain accuses Scott and his 'enchant-
ments' of doing 'measureless harm' to the progress of civilization and of
being 'in great measure responsible' for the Civil War. It may not be
strictly true that Scott's novels gave the American South its social ideal,
but W. J. Cash is sure that 'they did become the inspiration for such
extravaganzas as the *opéra bouffe* title of "the chivalry" by which the ruling
class, including the Virginians, habitually designated itself'.[62]

'They have always a charm for me,' Henry James wrote of the novels
in his Notebook, 'but I was amazed at the badness of R. [i.e. *Redgauntlet*]:
l'enfance de l'art.'[63] Most of the novels are 'ramshackle wholes with magnificent parts'[64] and they are usually long: 'given the sense of time that
he inherited from his culture, [Scott] had little need to clip, skip, focus.
Pageants are not to be rushed.'[65] The historical events on which the
novels depend have largely receded from common knowledge, even in
Scotland, and Scott's essentially eighteenth-century genteel style with its
mannered periphrases is blamed for 'lassitude of language and tedium of
depiction'.[66] C. S. Lewis's comment on the texture of George MacDonald's
writing might also be applied to Scott's: 'Bad pulpit traditions cling to it;
there is sometimes a nonconformist verbosity, sometimes an old Scotch
weakness for florid ornament (it runs right through them from Dunbar
to the Waverley Novels).'[67] As Stendhal predicted, the nineteenth century
moved on 'towards a more true and natural form of expression'.[68] Yet
there is an appeal to twentieth-century sensibility in his heroes: 'The
actions and commitment of the passive hero in the Waverley Novels are
so restricted that any activity depends upon other sources of energy.'[69]
This is a foretaste of the twentieth-century anti-hero, from Joseph Heller's
Yossarian in *Catch-22* to Alasdair Gray's Lanark, tyrannized by politics,

economics and the machinations of media-manufactured figures glimpsed floating down their corridors of power in television newscasts. Scott's real hero is the people, history's irrepressible constant: the villagers of Tully-Veolan, the Mucklebackits, Meg Merrilies, Madge Wildfire, Alice Gray, Wandering Willie and Peter Peebles, the zany, eternal litigant of *Redgauntlet*. As David Daiches puts it, 'The ordinary folk win in the end.'[70] So there is pleasing appropriateness in the quirk of history by which the distinguished American ex-slave who began life as Frederick Bailey changed his name to Frederick Douglass in 1838, the year of his escape to freedom, on advice from his abolitionist protector who 'had just been reading the *Lady of the Lake*'.[71] Scott's fundamentally balladist appeal to commonalty transcends both his pageantry and his verbosity and is the most deeply Scottish of his qualities. In this he offers corrective example to cruder expressions of nationalism in any era.

Notes

1. Sir Walter Scott, *Letters*, ed. H. J. C. Grierson, Centenary Edition, 12 vols (London, 1932–7), VI, pp. 507–8.

2. In Allan Massie's novel, *The Ragged Lion* (London, 1994), largely based on Sir Walter Scott's *Journal*, Scott says: 'I have never indulged in the folly of contemning our southern neighbours. On the contrary, I have loved England . . . second only to Scotland, and curiously this love was never shaken by what I learned of the long and heroic resistance which throughout more than two centuries my ancestral compatriots conducted against the threat of English dominance' (p. 8).

3. Scott, *Letters*, VII, p. 297.

4. James Hogg, *Memoir of the Author's Life and Familiar Anecdotes of Sir Walter Scott*, ed. Douglas S. Mack (Edinburgh and London, 1972), p. 95.

5. Lord Henry Cockburn, *Memorials of His Time by Henry Cockburn, New Edition with Introduction by his Grandson Harry A. Cockburn* (Edinburgh and London, 1909), p. 424.

6. Ibid., p. 402.

7. Ibid., p. 403.

8. John O. Hayden, *Scott: The Critical Heritage* (London, 1970), pp. 363–4.

9. Thomas James Wise and John Alexander Symington, *The Brontës: Their Lives, Friendships and Correspondence*, 4 vols bound as 2 (Oxford, 1980), I–II, p. 122.

10. William Hazlitt, 'Sir Walter Scott', *Lectures on the English Poets – The Spirit of the Age* (London, 1964), p. 223. Essay first published as 'The Spirits of the Age', *New Monthly Magazine*, No. IV, April, 1824, X, pp. 297–304. Included as 'Sir Walter Scott' in *The Spirit of the Age* (London, 1825).

11. Elizabeth Grant of Rothiemurcus, *Memoirs of a Highland Lady*, ed. with an introduction by Andrew Tod, 2 vols bound together (Edinburgh, 1988), II, p. 74.

12. Georg Lukács, *The Historical Novel* (Harmondsworth, 1969), pp. 29–69.

13. Poor strategy if the aim is the promotion of Scott, to judge from Catherine Carswell who says that she never 'worshipped at the Waverley shrine' because '*Ivanhoe*, set as a class-book at school, had engendered a lasting coolness'. See Catherine Carswell, 'John Buchan: A Perspective', in *John Buchan by His Wife and Friends* (London, 1947), p. 148.

14. Alan Riach, 'The Gothic Search: Maurice Shadbolt and *The Lovelock Version*', in Ralph J. Crane (ed.), *Ending the Silences: Critical Essays on the Works of Maurice Shadbolt* (Auckland, 1995), pp. 83–99 [84].

15. Thomas Crawford, *Scott* (Edinburgh, 1982), p. 21.

16. Hazlitt, 'Sir Walter Scott', p. 224.

17. Sir Walter Scott, 'General Preface, 1829', *Waverley*, ed. Andrew Hook (Harmondsworth, 1972), p. 521.

18. Hogg, *Memoir*, p. 130.

19. J. G. Lockhart, *Memoirs of Sir Walter Scott*, 5 vols (London, 1900), I, p. 168.

20. Alexander Welsh, *The Hero of the Waverley Novels: With New Essays on Scott* (Princeton, 1992), p. 41.

21. David Daiches, *Sir Walter Scott and His World* (London, 1971), p. 83.

22. C. S. Lewis, *English Literature in the Sixteenth Century Excluding Drama* (Oxford, 1954), p. 390.

23. John W. Oliver, 'Scottish Poetry in the Earlier Nineteenth Century', in *Scottish Poetry: A Critical Survey*, ed. James Kinsley (London, 1955), p. 221.

24. Ezra Pound, *Literary Essays of Ezra Pound*, ed. T. S. Eliot (London, 1954), p. 23.

25. Hayden, *The Critical Heritage*, p. 381.

26. Hogg, *Memoir*, p. 111.

27. Scott, *Letters*, VI, p. 506.

28. Sir Walter Scott, 'Introduction and Notes to *The Lady of the Lake*; Introduction to the Edition of 1830', *The Poetical Works of Sir Walter Scott*, ed. J. Logie Robertson (London, 1904), p. 276.

29. Hayden, *The Critical Heritage*, p. 308.

30. W. E. K. Anderson (ed.), *The Journal of Sir Walter Scott* (Oxford, 1972), p. 42.

31. Scott, *Letters*, III, p. 302.

32. Ibid., pp. 302–3.

33. D. D. Devlin, *The Author of Waverley: A Critical Study of Sir Walter Scott* (London and Basingstoke, 1971), p. 131.

34. E. M. Forster, *Aspects of the Novel* (London, 1949), p. 32.

35. Angus and Jenni Calder, *Scott* (London, 1969), p. 58.

36. Hayden, *The Critical Heritage*, p. 476.

37. Ralph Waldo Emerson, *Works*, ed. with an introduction by J. P. (Edinburgh, 1906), p. 13.

38. James Kerr, *Fiction against History: Scott as Storyteller* (Cambridge, 1989), p. 103.

39. Hayden, *The Critical Heritage*, p. 166.

40. Dorothy Van Ghent, *The English Novel: Form and Function* (New York, 1961), p. 115.

41. See Anderson (ed.), *The Journal of Sir Walter Scott*, p. 32.

42. John Buchan, *Sir Walter Scott* (London, 1932), p. 188.

43. V. S. Pritchett, *The Living Novel* (London, 1946), p. 45.

44. Hayden, *The Critical Heritage*, p. 86.

45. Ian Jack, *Sir Walter Scott* (London, 1958), p. 17.

46. Hayden, *The Critical Heritage*, pp. 88–9.

47. Scott also disliked the Gothic style in architecture. In a letter of 1821 to William Laidlaw he refers to 'modern Gothic, a style I hold to be equally false and foolish' (*Letters*, VI, p. 323).

48. John Galt would not have agreed. He objects to *Old Mortality* because he thought that Scott 'treated the defenders of the Presbyterian Church with too much levity, and not according to my impressions derived from the history of that time' (*Literary Life and Miscellanies*, I, p. 254). Galt gives his own impressions of Covenanting history in his novel *Ringan Gilhaize* (1823).

49. Kerr, *Fiction against History*, p. 52.

50. The law is both unjust and wrongly administered. Effie's guilt strictly depends on the counsel for the crown's proof that she 'communicated her pregnancy to no one' (Chapter 22); but Robertson's letter, exhibited in court, obviously proves that she told him and that he told 'a woman who is well-qualified to assist you in your approaching streight' (Meg Murdockson). Effie refuses to name the writer of the letter, 'but enough of the story was now known, to ascertain that it came from Robertson' (Chapter 23).

51. Lukács, *The Historical Novel*, p. 34.

52. Ibid., p. 33.

53. A. Fleishman, *The English Historical Novel* (Baltimore, 1971), p. 89.

54. Lukács, *The Historical Novel*, p. 32.

55. Karl Miller, 'Walter Scott: Laird of the gang', *The Times*, 4 January 1969, p. 15.

56. Anne Rowe, 'Kate Chopin', *The History of Southern Literature*, ed. Louis D. Rubin (Baton Rouge and London, 1985), p. 229.

57. Andrew Hook, 'The death of history', *TLS*, 17 December 1993, p. 24.

58. Paul Henderson Scott, *Walter Scott and Scotland* (Edinburgh, 1981), p. 96.

59. Cooper was widely known as 'the American Sir Walter Scott' which could have pleased neither writer. Cooper and Scott never really liked one another, though they were diplomatically friendly. Cooper thought Scott 'hopelessly

lacking in seriousness'. See Arthur Mizener, *Twelve Great American Novels* (London, 1968), p. 1.

60. Ellen Glasgow (1874–1945) learned her alphabet from *Old Mortality* and was led to learn to read from hearing an aunt relate the plots of the Waverley novels. When she first visited Scotland she said, 'I felt that I had come to my home in the past, because of my childish adoration of Sir Walter.' See C. Hugh Holman, *Windows on the World: Essays on American Social Fiction* (Knoxville, Tennessee, 1979), p. 122.

61. Havelock Ellis, 'Concerning Jude the Obscure' (*Savoy*, no. 6, October 1896, pp. 35–49), in John Charles Olmsted, *A Victorian Art of Fiction: Essays on the Novel in British Periodicals, 1870–1900* (New York and London, 1979), p. 579.

62. W. J. Cash, *The Mind of the South* (New York, 1941), pp. 67–8.

63. F. O. Matthiessen and Kenneth B. Murdock (eds), *The Notebooks of Henry James* (New York, 1961), p. 37.

64. Jack, *Sir Walter Scott*, p. 26.

65. Irving Howe, 'Falling Out of the Canon', *The New Republic*, 17 & 24 August 1992, p. 37.

66. Ibid., p. 36.

67. C. S. Lewis, 'Preface', *George MacDonald: An Anthology* (London, 1946), p. 14.

68. Hayden, *The Critical Heritage*, p. 319.

69. Welsh, *The Hero of the Waverley Novels*, p. 40.

70. David Daiches, 'Scott's Achievement as a Novelist', in *Scott's Mind and Art*, compiled and ed. A. Norman Jeffares (Edinburgh, 1969), p. 52.

71. Frederick Douglass, *Narrative of the Life of Frederick Douglass, an American Slave, Written by Himself*, ed. Benjamin Quarles (Cambridge, Mass., and London, 1960), p. 148.

Chapter 6

Calvin's Scottish Devil, the End of Rural Sleep and Practical Christianity

While Scott paid his bills and remythologized Scottish history his contemporaries, James Hogg and John Galt, illuminated Scotland's capacity for religious fanaticism, studied regional country and small-town life under the impact of economic and political change, and took creative liberties with the form of the novel. Susan Ferrier satirized prejudice in the attitudes of the Scots and the English towards each other and in the social and sexual clichés governing current views of marriage. Scottish fiction would never lose its sense of the past but its focus was shifting from consideration of history to analysis of contemporary social mores and conditions.

James Hogg, 'the Ettrick Shepherd'

Hogg insisted that he was born on 25 January 1772, thereby sharing a birthday with Robert Burns, but parish records give his date of baptism as 9 December 1770. A contemporary of Wordsworth, Scott and Beethoven, he may be approached as a Romantic phenomenon, as a poet, and as a writer of prose works, of which *The Private Memoirs and Confessions of a Justified Sinner* (1824) is the most accomplished. His genius is evident in what he became, a literary figure better known in Scotland than any of his contemporaries except Sir Walter Scott, in spite of an almost total lack of formal schooling. Born at Ettrickhall Farm in the Ettrick Forest sixteen miles from Selkirk in a remote district of the Borders, he was the son of a tenant-farmer who went bankrupt in 1777. As a result Hogg's formal education at the parish school-house ended when he was only six. In his *Memoir of the Author's Life* (1807) he tells how he 'was hired by a farmer in the neighbourhood to herd a few cows; my wages for the half year being a ewe lamb and a pair of new shoes'.[1] Some further schooling came from a boy who was teaching a neighbouring farmer's children. Hogg progressed to the class which read the Bible, but never mastered hand-writing. 'Thus terminated my education. After this I was never another day at any school whatever. In all I had spent about half a year at it.'[2]

From his parents Hogg learned traditional tales, songs and ballads of the Borders, and in 1802 he was able to assist with Scott's collection of traditional ballads for the third volume of his *Minstrelsy of the Scottish Border*. In 1807 Scott persuaded Archibald Constable to publish Hogg's *The Mountain Bard*, a collection of imitation ballads, and with profits from the book Hogg financed himself as a farmer. By 1810 he was bankrupt. He abandoned farming and, at the age of forty, set out for Edinburgh, 'determined, since no better could be, to push my fortune as a literary man'.[3] Finding that his 'poetical talents were rated nearly as low there as my shepherd qualities were in Ettrick', he fell foul of polite literary fashion with his weekly literary magazine, *The Spy*, which ceased pub-lication after a year. ('It was considered too coarse. When girls were pregnant, Hogg said so directly.'[4]) Associating with Walter Scott's son-in-law, John Gibson Lockhart, John Wilson (alias Christopher North) and other writers involved in the newly established pro-Tory *Blackwood's Magazine* (originally the *Edinburgh Monthly Magazine*), he persevered with his writing and became widely known by his pseudonym, 'the Ettrick Shepherd'. His image as an outspoken, well-read rustic incongruously but vividly holding his own in cultivated conservative society was promoted by the characterization of him by John Wilson and others as The Shepherd for *Blackwood's* in the *Noctes Ambrosianae*, records of a series of imaginary conversations held at Ambrose's Tavern in Edinburgh, which appeared in the magazine between March 1822 and February 1835. Scott refers to him as 'the great Caledonian Boar',[5] but The Shepherd of the *Noctes* is 'a complex embodiment of profoundly intuitive responses to experience, standing in a teasing relationship with his original',[6] and demonstrating the autodidact's gifts of independence and the power to entertain.

As Edwin Morgan says, Hogg 'was willing to try anything'.[7] He first achieved fame as 'a true national poet' in 1813 with a book-length poem called *The Queen's Wake*, which includes 'Kilmeny', the story of 'a virgin in her prime' who disappears and is given up for lost. When she returns briefly to human life it is from a visionary 'land of thought' which could be either the Christian heaven or fairyland:

> . . . where the cock never crew,
> Where the rain never fell, and the wind never blew,
> But it seemed as the harp of the sky had rung,
> And the airs of heaven played round her tongue
> When she spoke of the lovely forms she had seen,
> In a land where sin had never been.

There is the ballad grotesquerie and rich Scots of 'The Witch of Fife', and the jaunty suggestiveness of the shorter poem of the same title where the witch carries implications of sexuality and the poet's muse. Satire uses apt sarcasm in the portrayal of a conceited young minister's 'simpering seriousness' and the 'blare' of his preaching in 'The First Sermon', and absurdity in 'The Great Muckle Village of Balmaquhapple':

> D' ye ken the big village of Balmaquhapple,
> The great muckle village of Balmaquhapple?
> 'Tis steep'd in iniquity up to the thrapple,
> An' what's to become o' poor Balmaquhapple?

There is the directness of lovers' complaints in 'I'm a' gane wrang' and 'I hae lost my love' and the hilariously distracting love which 'winna let a poor body / Gang about his biziness' in 'Love is like a dizziness':

> To tell my feats this single week
>   Wad mak a daft-like diary, O!
> I drave my cart outow'r a dike,
>   My horses in a miry, O!
> I wear my stockings white and blue,
>   My love's sae fierce an' fiery, O!
> I drill the land that I should plough,
>   An' plough the drills entirely, O!

He is best known as a poet for the unaffected lyricism of 'A Boy's Song':

> Where the pools are bright and deep
> Where the grey trout lies asleep
> Up the river and o'er the lea
> That's the way for Billy and me.

Such innocence is vexed by the world of experience in the relationship between little Benjy and his dog, Cocket, in Hogg's short story, 'The Poachers'. There are parodies of Wordsworth, Coleridge, Scott, Byron and others in *The Poetic Mirror* (1816–31). Colloquial raciness energizes 'The True Story of a Glasgow Tailor', 'The Dominie' and 'Disagreeables'. This range of styles, tones and effects is symptomatic, for one of the strongest features of *The Confessions* is its startlingly modern amalgamation of comedy, satire, pathos, violence and the supernatural which undermines conventional genre expectations as confidently as the cinema of Luis Bunuel or David Lynch's 1990s American television series *Twin Peaks*. Hogg belittles himself by his claim to be 'king o' the mountain an' fairy school'[8] of writing, for he is much more. Strongly indebted to the

Scottish ballad tradition, he blends realism and fantasy, combining the world of peasant superstition with the angels and devils of Christian iconography, notably in *The Confessions* and 'The Witches of Traquair', whose narrator says that the tale seems 'to have been moulded on the bones of some ancient religious allegory, and . . . transformed into a nursery tale'.[9] Fusing these elements, Hogg anticipates the work of Robert Louis Stevenson in such stories as 'The Merry Men', 'Will o' the Mill', 'Markheim' and 'Thrawn Janet'. In all moods and kinds his style is forthright, unembellished and quick, invariably suggesting speech. John Wilson appropriately makes The Shepherd in the *Noctes Ambrosianae* refer to 'ma style o' colloquial oratory',[10] for in Hogg's work 'fine writing and the fine sentiments that go with it are cast aside as insincere'.[11] Writing against the background of the so-called age of reason, his repeated message is that people are deprived of reason by perverted religion, twisted love, or, in the story called 'Some Terrible Letters from Scotland', by disease in a world partly supernatural.

In 1818 Hogg turned to prose, publishing a two-volume collection of stories which included a short novel about Border life in the covenanting period, *The Brownie of Bodsbeck* (1818), probably drafted before *Old Mortality* (1816), Sir Walter Scott's treatment of a similar subject. Larger prose works followed, notably *Winter Evening Tales* (1820) and *The Three Perils of Man: War, Women and Witchcraft* (1822), a sprawling, exuberant *mélange* of history, allegory, comedy and epic in which Hogg both celebrates and undercuts romantic attitudes. An unwieldy entertainment of blowsy extravagance, the book derives from an uninhibited relish of the varieties of Scottish culture. Its companion volume, *The Three Perils of Woman, or Love, Leasing and Jealousy* (1823), is much less fun, a clumsy novel of manners which turns sourly Gothic.

The Private Memoirs and Confessions of a Justified Sinner

The apparent waywardness of Hogg's imagination and his disregard of literary decorum prepared critics to be hard on *The Private Memoirs and Confessions of a Justified Sinner*. Contemporary reviewers judged the work 'uncouth and unpleasant', 'extraordinary trash', and lacking 'one single attribute of a good and useful book'.[12] An edition of the novel published in 1947 printed an introduction by André Gide which hails the book as 'astounding', 'an extraordinary achievement', wonders why it had failed to become famous and hopes to have helped awaken the work's 'belated glory'.[13] In *The English Novel* (1954) Walter Allen judges it 'a remarkable work by any standard . . . a psychological document compared with which Stevenson's *Dr Jekyll and Mr Hyde* is a crude morality'.[14] Stephen Prickett calls it a 'brilliant metaphysical thriller'.[15] Hogg's study of the psychology of fanaticism – a theme visible in his early story, 'A Singular Dream' – anticipates Goethe's *Faust* (1832), the most celebrated account of a man who surrenders his soul to the Devil, and foreshadows many subsequent Scottish variations on the theme of the double self, the best known of which is Stevenson's famous tale. The Devil of the *Confessions* reappears as a master of polemics in James Bridie's play, *Mr Bolfry* (1943), and again as the shadowy figure of Tod in George Friel's novel, *Mr Alfred M.A.* (1972). Emma Tennant's exploration of duality and obsession in *The Bad Sister* (1978)[16] transposes Hogg's story into the twentieth-century world of sexual politics, suggesting that 'to pursue the feminist position, to become aware of the loss of the masculine principle in you, and then to murder it . . . is self-defeating, just as in Hogg's *Confessions* it's self-defeating to go around murdering people in order to be told that you are one of the elect'.[17] In *Faustine* (1992) Tennant craftily reworks the Faust legend, recalling Hogg's magical realism in an astringent twentieth-century parable about a woman who tries 'to reverse the natural order of things' (Part 3, Chapter 15) by selling her soul to the Devil in exchange for twenty-four years of youth, beauty and wealth. Beyond men's victimizing classification of women into 'sexy' and 'plain' (or 'of a certain age' and therefore 'invisible'), the larger object of Tennant's satire is a patriarchal society's fanatical worship of consumerism as Hogg's subject is fanaticism in religion. It is Tennant's Devil himself who remarks, 'souls cannot co-exist with consumerism' (Book 4, Chapter 19). That's the trouble with the Devil: he's often right, though Tennant's can also be satanically – if provocatively – wrong:

> . . . the real nature of women . . . is to grab love, to feed voraciously on the affections of the children they dominate and raise, and to demand attention and obedience at all times.
>
> (Book 4, Chapter 19)

André Gide says that the Devil in Hogg's book is 'the exteriorized development of our own desires, of our pride, of our most secret thoughts. It consists throughout in the indulgence we accord to our own selves.'[18] There are two sets of doubles in *Confessions*. First, there is Robert Wringhim's malevolent shadowing of George Colwan the younger by which he compels his brother to acknowledge the power of his own antithesis (George is extraverted, genial and gregarious while Robert is introverted, spiteful and solitary). Second, there is the duality of Robert

Wringhim and Gil-Martin, the sinister friend who is revealed as the Devil. Hogg uses the idea of the *doppelgänger* to portray the near-extinction of conscience by a combination of pride and fanaticism, Robert Wringhim being most disturbed when a residual conscience asserts itself. After taking possession of the Dalcastle estates he says:

> I felt so much gratified that I immediately set about doing
> all the good I was able, hoping to meet with all
> approbation and encouragement from my friend. I was
> mistaken. He checked the very first impulses towards such
> a procedure, questioned my motives, and uniformly made
> them out to be wrong.
>
> (p. 173)

Thus begins the last phase of the novel, in which the anti-hero finds himself an outcast, abjectly killing himself in a suicide pact with his satanic friend to escape retribution for his crimes on earth and enter into the company of the elect in Heaven. But the last stroke of Hogg's brilliantly engineered narrative is to end the book with a reverberating chord of pulpit hell-fire which pronounces the judgement of orthodox Christianity: the unforgivable sin of suicide has 'consigned his memory and his name to everlasting detestation'. The duality of Wringhim, self-justifying Calvinist Christian, and his devilish counterpart is finally resolved as the perverted Christian is fully satanized and *en route* to hell.

Hogg uses several narrative layers to persuade the reader that his story is true. First, history supplies basic information about the Colwan family and the lands of Dalcastle, though only tradition is the source of the rest of the Editor's Narrative. Second, the Editor imposes on tradition a quasi-historical authority and manipulates disbelief into suspension by saying:

> in recording the hideous events which follow, I am only
> relating to the greater part of the inhabitants of at least
> four counties of Scotland matters of which they were
> before perfectly well informed.
>
> (p. 1)

By inviting the reader to catch up with common knowledge the Editor allays scepticism while insinuating the enticement of something 'hideous'. He reminds us of his documentary scrupulousness and further whets expectations shortly after the Arthur's Seat episode by saying that he cannot give further details without forestalling Robert Wringhim's account of events which is 'of higher value than anything that can be retailed out of the stories of tradition and old registers'. Another strategic reminder comes at the end of his narrative with a reference to the death of Thomas Drummond in 1715, adding that 'this is all with which history, judiciary records, and tradition, furnish me in relating to these matters'. The factual authority of both the Editor's Narrative and Wringhim's confessions is reinforced after the end of the Memoir by the extract from 'an authentic letter', published in *Blackwood's Magazine* for August 1823. This is a real letter describing the digging up of a suicide's grave, signed by James Hogg, published in the magazine under the heading 'A Scots Mummy'.[19] The letter is deployed to authenticate the narrative; it had already acted as a wily advertisement for the forthcoming book.

Hogg's book may have been influenced by a story which also appeared in *Blackwood's Magazine* in 1823 entitled 'The Confessions of an English Glutton'.[20] Unlike Robert Wringhim, the Glutton does not expect the reader to sympathize with his voracity. Inveighing against the egotism of the times, he offers his confession as a self-sacrifice for which he expects a different kind of approbation from that sought by Wringhim:

> with all the chances of public odium and private
> reprobation impending over me, I hasten to the
> performance of my duty, and I am proud to consider
> myself a kind of literary Curtius, leaping willingly into the
> gulf, to save my fellow-citizens by my own sacrifice.[21]

After illustrating his constitutional gluttony and recounting his sufferings, the Glutton describes the moment when he first saw himself as obese at a public exhibition of a person called 'fat Lambert':

> The very instant I saw him, the notion struck me that I
> had become his second-self − his ditto − his palpable echo
> − his substantial shadow − that the observers laughed at
> our 'double transformation', for he was become me at the
> same time − that I was exhibiting as he then was, − and,
> finally, that I was dying of excessive fat . . . in one
> moment I felt that the double identity was completed
> . . . that I, in short, was Lambert, and Lambert me![22]

This passage may have influenced the moment in the *Confessions* when Wringhim begins to fear that Gil-Martin is his 'second self': 'to shake him off was impossible − we were incorporated together − identified with one another, as it were'. Like Wringhim, the Glutton flees in despair from his second self and both characters attempt suicide, the Glutton unsuccessfully.

Whatever Hogg may owe to an English Glutton, there is no gainsaying the peculiarly Scottish character of his work. André Gide quotes his friend and translator Dorothy Bussy's telling him: 'This book is Scottish to its very marrow; no Englishman could possibly have written it. Its whole atmosphere, the very form and substance of its Puritanism, is essentially Scottish.'[23] Contemporary Scottish interest in the psychology of sin is illustrated by John Gibson Lockhart's novels, *Adam Blair* (1822) and *Matthew Wald* (1824). Adulterous love for his married housekeeper, Charlotte Campbell, drives Adam Blair, a Presbyterian minister, to all the torments of horrified remorse, dreams that suggest the possible influence of De Quincey, and contemplated suicide. The specifically Scottish atmosphere of Hogg's psychological study in *The Confessions* is substantiated by his introducing historical people and events, meticulously setting the story in a period of political and religious controversy when the distribution of power between Scotland and England was disputed under the threat of Jacobitism which sought to restore the House of Stuart to the throne after the bloodless revolution of 1688 replaced the deposed Catholic James II with his Protestant daughter, Mary, in conjunction with her Dutch husband, William of Orange. In reaction to the Reverend Wringhim's power over Lady Dalcastle, the laird 'began to set himself against them [the extreme Presbyterians], joining with the Cavalier party', but as a Government supporter he would have voted for the English Act of Occasional Conformity which was designed to disenfranchise dissenters and safeguard the episcopacy. The Reverend Wringhim would have taken the opposing side, and as Colwan's and Wringhim's sons accompany their fathers to Edinburgh, 'the story of the persecution of George by Robert, the blighting of his life and finally his murder, is rooted in a situation of enmity like that of Montagu and Capulet'.[24]

The second paragraph of the Editor's Narrative sets the story – in particular the marriage of George Colwan senior to Baillie Orde's fanatical daughter – in the context of 'Reformation principles'. Contrasted to the 'free principles cherished by the court party' are the 'stern doctrines of the reformers' which included belief in election by predestination rather than by works or merit. Hogg is not an opponent of religion or of the Reformation itself. It is the blatantly physical, man-eating Jessie Armstrong who scorns religion when she quotes 'He that prays is ne'er to trust' from Hogg's song, 'The Laird o' Lamington', in the story, 'Love Adventures of Mr George Cochrane', which contrasts the ideal harmony of marriage with the fracturing of Scottish society by sectarianism and class. *The Brownie of Bodsbeck* is not hostile to religion but towards the brutalities of Claverhouse and the Royalists. Although some of the Covenanters in *The Brownie* 'said violent and culpable things, and did worse', Hogg appreciates 'the scattered prowling way in which they were driven to subsist'[25] and he is plainly pro-Covenanter in the story 'A Tale of the Martyrs'. His target in *The Confessions* is the extreme Antinomian form of 'Auld Licht' Protestantism and its hellish Calvinist doctrine of Election. It is out of his understanding of the sado-masochistic intensities of Scottish religious extremism that he says through Samuel Scrape of Penpunt:

'Nothing in the world delights a truly religious people so much as con-
signing them to eternal damnation.'

Antinomians carried the Calvinist doctrine of Election to the extreme
position that the moral law was transcended by faith and the Elect free
to act as they wished, even beyond the law. On this basis Robert
Wringhim's murders of Mr Blanchard and George Colwan are 'justified'
by faith as Mary Shelley's Frankenstein and Stevenson's Dr Jekyll are
justified by science. British Antinomians were not confined to Scotland:
in his *Journal* for 22 March 1746 the Methodist leader, John Wesley,
records a debate with an Antinomian:

> 'Do you believe you have nothing to do with the law
> of God?'
> 'I have not; I am not under the law; I live by faith.'
> 'Have you, as living by faith, a right to everything in
> the world?'
> 'I have. All is mine since Christ is mine.'
> 'May you then take any thing you will, any where,
> (suppose out of a shop,) without the consent or
> knowledge of the owner?'
> 'I may, if I want it; for it is mine; only I will not give
> offence.'
> 'Have you also a right to all the women in the world?'
> 'Yes, if they consent.'
> 'And is that not a sin?'
> 'Yes, to him that thinks it is a sin; but not to those
> whose hearts are free.'[26]

In Lady Dalcastle and the Wringhims Hogg satirizes the comparable
excesses of Scottish reformist bigotry: Lady Dalcastle's beliefs 'were not
the tenets of the great reformers, but theirs mightily overstrained and
deformed'. As propounded by John Knox, the doctrine of predestination
gained a large following in Scotland, occasioning the satire of Burns's
'Holy Willie's Prayer'. Willie's worst characteristics are echoed in the
sanctimonious festivity by which Robert Wringhim, his mother and
adopted father give thanks for Robert's accession to Dalcastle:

> ... which thanks, by the by, consisted wholly in telling
> the Almighty what he was; and informing, with very
> particular precision, what *they* were who addressed him;
> for Wringhim's whole system of popular declamation
> consisted, it seems, in this – to denounce all men and
> women to destruction, and then hold out hopes to his
> adherents that they were the chosen few, included in the

promises, and who could never fall away. It would appear
that this pharisaical doctrine is a very delicious one, and
the most grateful of all others to the worst characters.

(pp. 55–6)

The book progressively intensifies its focus on the horrific psychological and social effects of the doctrine of Election, but there is much satire
in the earlier stages of the story, as in the 'marvellous' conversation between Lady Dalcastle and the Rev. Mr Wringhim:

> Wringhim had held in his doctrines that there were eight
> different kinds of FAITH, all perfectly distinct in their
> operations and effects. But the lady, in her secluded state,
> had discovered another five, making twelve [*sic*] in all: the
> adjusting of the existence or fallacy of these five faiths
> served for a most enlightened discussion of nearly
> seventeen hours; in the course of which the two got
> warm in their arguments, always in proportion as they
> receded from nature, utility, and common sense.
>
> (p. 12)

Such quibbling discredits the religion. The Editor comments that these
two pettifogging zealots spent their time on 'points of such minor importance that a true Christian would blush to hear them mentioned, and the
infidel and profane make a handle of them to turn our religion to scorn'.
The absurdity of the religious convictions imparted to young Robert is
nowhere clearer or funnier than when he says that he was confounded
by the multitude of his sins – well over a hundred and fifty thousand –
and the endless series of repentances to which he had subjected himself:

> A life-time was nothing to enable me to accomplish the
> sum, and then being, for anything I was certain of, in my
> state of nature, and the grace of repentance withheld from
> me – what was I to do, or what was to become of me?
> In the meantime, I went on sinning without measure.
>
> (pp. 107–8)

His inner conflict appears resolved when his reverend father announces
that Robert is a 'justified person' who can do no wrong, and the prompt
entrance of the Devil – 'the same being as myself' – is the exteriorized
personification of the evil he is now free to commit.

Initially feigning respect for Robert as his spiritual brother, Gil-Martin
begins deferentially as his 'humble disciple' and friend – reminding us that
there is no more satanic character in Dickens than the unctuous Uriah
Heep in *David Copperfield* – then makes Robert so dependent on him that

the doomed young man comes to dread his presence and counsels more than Hell. (A modern variation on the theme of such a shift of power is Joseph Losey's 1963 film, *The Servant*, scripted by Harold Pinter, in which a crafty manservant effects a diabolical role-reversal with his wealthy, upper-class master. More recently – 1984 – the surrealist atmosphere of the *Confessions* and the characters of Wringhim and Gil-Martin were powerfully recalled in the ambiguous relationship between the student and the mysterious Anders Brond in Frederic Lindsay's political thriller, *Brond*.) Wringhim's repulsion by the tones of Gil-Martin's voice is expressed in imagery that might have come from Edgar Allan Poe: 'They were the sounds of the pit, wheezed through a grated cranny.' Despite Robert's pleadings his formidable friend will not abandon him: 'Our beings are amalgamated,' Gil-Martin says, 'and consociated in one, and never shall I depart from this country until I can carry you in triumph with me.' This speech would have been chilling enough if Gil-Martin *had* been the Czar of Russia; from the Devil it is an intimation of Robert's inevitable destruction. Robert's corrosion by the pernicious doctrine is graded by the escalation of his sins into the crimes of fratricide and matricide. He begins by breaking vows, engineers the dismissal of John Barnet, habitually lies, contrives a flogging and expulsion for his school rival McGill, murders Mr Blanchard, and harasses his brother into public disgrace before he kills him. If Gil-Martin is technically responsible for killing Lady Dalcastle, the moral and psychological responsibility is Robert's. Her death at the hand of his *alter ego* is the consummation of his admitted contempt for her, in accordance with the vainglorious belief that his dislike of her 'was a judgement from heaven inflicted on her for some sin of former days, and that I had no power to have acted otherwise towards her than I did'. Of course, Hogg would have enjoyed despatching Lady Dalcastle, to judge by the comment about women like her by the narrator of 'Love Adventures of Mr George Cochrane': 'I have an aversion to those ladies who make extravagant pretensions to religion, and am more afraid of them than any set of reformers in the realm.'

T. S. Eliot says that Ben Jonson's satire 'is merely the means which leads to the aesthetic result, the impulse which projects a new world into a new orbit'.[27] Hogg's satire projects into orbit a world of inverted values. Righteousness becomes evil; good-heartedness as in the George Colwans, father and son, is destroyed; John Barnet's honesty is his undoing, although he leaves the Reverend Wringhim's employment with peasant dignity; merit is turned into disgrace for the schoolboy, McGill. The Lady of Dalcastle is a manic bigot, and decency is to be found below stairs in old Colwan's housekeeper/mistress, Arabella Logan, in Arabella Calvert, the whore with a heart of gold, and in Bessy Gillies, Arabella Logan's maid, whose irreverent flippancies in court expose the law's concern for its own procedures before the truth of a case brought before it. This moral confusion is embodied in a work which deploys generic confusion. A dark vision is constructed out of satire and the supernatural, melodrama and social iniquity, perverted theology and psychological collapse to present a conflict of good and evil which is shot through with comedy. This fugue of incongruous elements is a refinement of impulses discernible in *The Three Perils of Man* and *The Three Perils of Woman*, mirroring the intransigent messiness of experience, its immunity to the constraints of religious and political dogmas and its resistance to the artificialities of generic literary regulation. It constitutes the realism of Hogg's projected world.

The opening of the book is strongly comic, with the laird of Dalcastle capering at his wedding while his disapproving bride talks theology with the odious Mr Wringhim; then there are the inebriated laird's vivid wedding-night dreams, the bugle calls of his snores and his triumphant morning retrieval of his new wife rolled in a blanket. There is Lady Dalcastle's father's pretence of revenge on the laird for ill-treating his unlovely daughter by punishing her in her persona as the wicked laird's wife. On a social scale there is the comic chaos of the combat between Whigs and Cavaliers with the mob thrown in to underline Hogg's satirical point about the farce of sectarian politics in which doctrinaire party lines are quickly obscured by the gratifications of violence. There are the comic excesses of the Reverend Wringhim as in his visit to chastise Lord Dalcastle, his vicious psalm, 'Set thou the wicked over him', and his gullibility in Robert's manipulation of the John Barnet episode. There is the mixture of candour, precision and cunning in court of Bessy Gillies, Hogg's working-class Portia. In contrast to the theological hair-splitting of Lady Dalcastle and Mr Wringhim, Bessy's pedantry on points of law is to the humane purpose of being kind to the much abused Arabella Calvert:

> '. . . Did you ever see these silver spoons before?'
> 'I hae seen some very like them, and whaever has seen siller spoons has done the same.'
> 'Can you swear you never saw them before?'
> 'Na, na, I wadna swear to ony siller spoons that ever war made, unless I had put a private mark on them wi' my ain hand, an' that's what I never did to ane.'
> 'See, they are all marked with a C.'
> 'Sae are a' the spoons in Argyle, an' the half o' them in Edinburgh I think. A C is a very common letter, an' so are a' the names that begin wi't. Lay them by, lay them by, an' gie the poor woman her spoons again. They are marked wi' her ain name, an' I hae little doubt they are hers, an' that she has seen better days.'
>
> (pp. 66–7)

In Robert Wringhim's 'Private Memoirs and Confessions' there are comic moments too. Robert's persistent crowding of his bewildered, good-natured brother is diabolic in motivation and effect, but there is something inherently comic in Robert's waiting until George has profaned his Maker's name three times, then kicking him and ingenuously remarking out of the hubris of his twisted faith that this 'had . . . the effect of rousing up [George's] corrupt nature to quarrelling and strife, instead of taking the chastisement of the Lord in humility and meekness'. There is the comedy of the rigidly righteous people of Auchtermuchty and the Devil whose cloven feet are revealed just in time by Robin Ruthven in the folk-tale *exemplum* retailed by Samuel Scrape (pp. 198–203). Thus there is more than one valency even in this predominantly dark section of the book, and a basically comic stiffness in the mechanism of Robert's fearful sanctimony. The moral, then, is that if you believe yourself redeemed 'by grace, preordination, and eternal purpose' you have gone to the Devil. There may be tragic consequences, but they will not exalt you to tragic stature: you are, after all, an essentially comic object. Hogg's assessment of the Church's damage to the lives of people of all classes anticipates the view expressed by William Soutar in 1932: 'the disintegration of the Church may be a pointer; a necessary preliminary to our faith in MAN'.[28]

John Galt: theoretical history

Comedy, usually in the ironic mode, is the key to John Galt's most memorable creations, the Rev. Micah Balwhidder of Dalmailing in *Annals of the Parish* and Provost James Pawkie in *The Provost*. Son of a sea-captain, then a London businessman who turned entrepreneur in an abortive scheme to set up a trading company in Gibraltar, Galt became Secretary to the Canada Company which was involved in developing unexplored areas of Canada. His life in Britain and Canada and his travels in Europe might have been expected to yield literary works on a grand scale, but he found his *métier* in portrayals of small-town Scotland as surely as Jane Austen found hers in '3 or 4 Families in a Country Village'.[29] Yet the sense of global implications is there in Galt's work, from *The Ayrshire Legatees* (1821) with its background in India to his American novel, *Lawrie Todd; or the Settlers in the Wood* (1830), making him 'the most cosmopoli-tan of parochial writers'.[30] India and Virginia have greater local significance than Edinburgh or London for the Rev. Micah Balwhidder in *Annals of the Parish*. In *The Steamboat* (1822), *The Member* (1832) and *The Radical* (1832) he deals with British politics of the period which included the passage of the first Reform Bill. *Ringan Gilhaize* (1823) is an ambitious attempt at realistic folk history on an epic scale, written to redress the wrong Galt thought Scott had done the Covenanters in *Old Mortality*. Like the best work in his six 'Tales of the West' – the novels he wrote for William Blackwood between 1820 and 1822 – *Ringan Gilhaize* is a study of self-revelation in the form of imagined autobiography. Galt's only obviously passionate book, its strengths are in his reanimation of a critical phase of Scottish history in relation to several generations of the Gilhaize family and his creation of an appropriately grave, biblically measured style for the zealous Ringan. Galt runs his characteristic risk of making his narrator unpalatably egotistical. Ringan's obsession with the divine right of resistance and the odour of sanctity in his language almost alienate the reader's sympathy, yet his despatch of the brutal John Graham of Claverhouse (the historical 'Bloody Clavers' was killed at the Battle of Killiecrankie on 27 July 1689) to meet 'the audit of his crimes' is felt as a triumph for a man who loses himself in his cause, sustains the psychological injuries of his fanaticism, and puts faith before self. 'A terrible beauty is born,' as Yeats says of the Irish resistance fighters petrified by political conviction in 'Easter 1916'. This man is no Robert Wringhim:

> I took off my bonnet, and kneeling with the gun in my
> hand, cried, 'Lord, remember David and all his afflictions';
> and having so prayed, I took aim as I knelt, and
> Claverhouse raising his arm in command, I fired. In the
> same moment I looked up, and there was a vision in the
> air as if all the angels of brightness, and the martyrs in
> their vestments of glory, were assembled on the walls and
> battlements of heaven to witness the event, – and I started
> up and cried, 'I have delivered my native land!' But in the
> same instant I remembered to whom the victory was due,
> and falling again on my knees, I raised my hands and
> bowed my head as I said, 'Not mine, O Lord, but thine
> is the victory!'
>
> (Chapter XXXIII)

Prolixity, Galt's besetting fault, damages the art of *Ringan Gilhaize*, though the novel deserves to be grouped with Hogg's *The Brownie of Bodsbeck* and Scott's *Old Mortality* as a literary reconstruction of a tense, ambiguous era in Scottish history. Wordiness, however, is essential to the garrulous self-revelations of 'old doited [simple-mindedly confused as in dotage]'[31] Micah Balwhidder in *Annals of the Parish* and smug, self-made Mr Pawkie in *The Provost*.

After the serial success in *Blackwood's Magazine* of *The Ayrshire Legatees* (1821), an epistolary novel modelled on Smollett's *Humphry Clinker* about the impact on the Pringle family and their correspondents of a journey to London, Galt recovered from the failure of his 'European' novel, *The Earthquake* (1820), with the stories of *The Steamboat* (1821), notable for an account of George IV's coronation, and his finest book, *Annals of the Parish*. In 1822 he added to his set of Blackwood novels *Sir Andrew Wylie* (1822) and *The Provost* (1822) which ends with James Pawkie's considered opinion 'that there is a reforming spirit abroad among men, and that really the world is gradually growing better'. The world, certainly, has grown steadily better for Mr Pawkie of Gudetown who has progressed from apprentice to shop-owner to Dean of Guild to Bailie to Provost, collecting substantial property on the way. *The Entail* (1823), which, with *The Provost*, prompted Coleridge to put Galt 'in the front rank of contemporary Novellists – and second only to Sir W Scott in technique',[32] is an indictment of the materialism that motivates the sly Provost and of a world increasingly submissive to the tyranny of economic forces. An essentially political novel, *The Provost* should be compulsory reading for anyone contemplating a career in municipal politics. It is both a manual of manipulative technique and a warning of what one may become in such a world. It is with 'a sense of appropriateness', comments Ian Jack, 'that we discover that Galt was a great admirer of Machiavelli' and decided that *The Prince* should be read as satire.[33] 'Galt's irony never falters,' says Ian A. Gordon,[34] noticing that it is Pawkie's growing older and wealthier that comfortably enables him not 'to be so grippy' and 'to partake of the purer spirit which the great mutations of the age had conjured into public affairs'. *The Entail*, a study of materialism's power to corrupt and victimize and of the capacity of some to rise above it, is an ironic refutation of the Provost's complacency.

Galt was displeased by the public reception of *Annals of the Parish* and *The Provost* as novels. His intention was 'to exhibit a kind of local theoretical history, by examples, the truth of which would at once be acknowledged'.[35] Read as an inter-connected series, the Blackwood books comprise 'a complex tableau of a society which could not be encompassed within the limits of a single work, nor understood from a single point of view'.[36] Critics have tended to agree with his own judgement that the *Annals* 'is so void of any thing like a plot, that it lacks in the most material feature of the novel'.[37] Yet his contemporary, Susan Ferrier, could see beyond the genre's orthodox mechanical requirements, appraising Jane Austen's *Emma* in terms appropriate to one of Galt's studies of small-town life: 'there is no story whatever, and the heroine is no better than other people; but the characters are all so true to life, and the style so piquant, that it does not require the adventitious aids of mystery and adventure'.[38] Like Jane Austen, Galt was changing the scope of the novel by parodying 'the fad of memoir',[39] but if plot is simply defined as narrative pattern, *Annals of the Parish* clearly has one, and if Aristotle's requirements for *mythos* are the criteria, it also presents a beginning, a middle, an end, and obvious wholeness. After giving us the text of his last sermon – worthy of anthologizing with such literary imitations of the form as Father Mapple's sermon in Melville's *Moby Dick*, Robert Colquohoun's last sermon in Lewis Grassic Gibbon's *Cloud Howe* and the Easter sermon in Faulkner's *The Sound and the Fury* – Mr Balwhidder begins on the fifty years of his ministry (1760–1810) with an account of his abuse by 'mad and vicious' people on the occasion of his 'placing' in the parish kirk of Dalmailing. The middle of the memoir is Chapter XX for the year 1779, by which time the minister has won over his congregation, developed a rudimentary sense of humour sufficient to recognize the absurdity of Lady Macadam's revenge on Betty Wudrife in Chapter XVI, and reached the peak of his career as delegate to the General Assembly (the annual supreme court of the Kirk), commanded to preach before his Grace the Commissioner (the king's representative at the Assembly). The end of the action is Balwhidder's last sermon, his receipt of a silver server from a grateful congregation, and his comically matter-of-fact anticipation of pleasant reunions after death, especially with the first and second Mrs Balwhidders.

The microcosm of Dalmailing reverberates to events in the greater world beyond the parish as Scotland wakes 'from a long rural sleep to the promise of industry and commerce'.[40] In his annal for 1809 (Chapter L) Balwhidder says that he writes 'to testify to posterity anent [about] the great changes that have happened in my day and generation – a period which all the best informed writers say, has not had its match in the history of the world, since the beginning of time'. In the same year Byron comments on the pace of change in *English Bards and Scotch Reviewers*:

> Thus saith the Preacher; 'nought beneath the sun
> Is new', yet still from change to change we run.
> What varied wonders tempt us as they pass!
> The Cow-pox, Tractors, Galvanism, and Gas
> In turns appear to make the vulgar stare,
> Till the swoln bubble bursts – and all is air!

With commercial promise comes the caprice of market forces and new vulnerability: in Dalmailing the industrial bubble swells and bursts when the cotton mill built in Chapter XXIX is sold in Chapter XLIX, Mr and Mrs Dwining despair and commit suicide. For a time the town is 'suddenly thrown out of bread' as it is drawn into 'the great web of commercial reciprocities'. National politics encroach on the rural idyll: some parishioners panic in 1780 when news reaches them of the anti-Catholic Gordon Riots and the rabble-rousing Lord George Gordon's committal to the Tower of London on a charge of high treason (Chapter XXI); the wars with France become parish business in 1782 when Charles Malcolm is killed in the Battle of the Saints (Chapter XXIII); and the parish children turn from their victory merry-making to enact a touching lesson in true community. Mr Balwhidder has broken the news of her son's death to his revered Mrs Malcolm, and they leave the Manse together:

> All the weans were out parading with napkins and kail-
> blades [leaves of green kale or cabbage] on sticks, rejoicing
> and triumphing in the glad tidings of victory. But when
> they saw me and Mrs Malcolm coming slowly along, they
> guessed what had happened, and threw away their banners
> of joy; and, standing all up in a row, with silence and
> sadness, along the kirk-yard wall as we passed, shewed an
> instinct of compassion that penetrated to my very soul.
> The poor mother burst into fresh affliction, and some of
> the bairns into an audible weeping; and, taking one
> another by the hand, they followed us to her door, like
> mourners at a funeral.
>
> (Chapter XXIII)

The changing world converts Balwhidder from abhorrence of smuggling (Chapter III) to sympathy with the 'poor smugglers' (Chapter XXI) harried by the relentless, bounty-hunting exciseman, Mungo Argyle. Canny Presbyterian materialism, which assesses the state of the world in terms of local prosperity and condones the second Mrs Balwhidder's purchase of a silver teapot (Chapter XX), gives way to apprehension of the 'evil and vanity of riches' and prescient sermonizing: '. . . in that same spirit of improvement, which was so busy every where, I could discern something like a shadow, that shewed it was not altogether of that pure advantage, which avarice led all so eagerly to believe' (Chapter XXXII). With industrial progress come the division of the parish into Government men and Jacobins, and a new crisis for the Rev. Balwhidder when he preaches against materialism only to be accused of being a 'leveller' (Chapter XXXIII).

Scott's attempts to be realistic are invariably thwarted, to some degree, by his histrionics even when he achieves psychological or social truth. By comparison Galt's less gesticulant art, despite its bias towards caricature, comes closer to the surfaces of recognizable life. Yet the chamber music of Galt's *Annals* is not as far removed as it might seem from the grand opera of Scott. As Francis Russell Hart says, 'Galt was as much interested as Scott in the end of the past'.[41] As original and successful an adaptation of the form of the novel as Hogg's *Confessions*, Galt's *Annals* tells of the evolving world of middle to late eighteenth-century and early nineteenth-century small-town Scotland in the characterful voice of a plausibly conceived minister of the time (and a type by no means extinct). The book contains 'no false note and not a surplus page'; it is at once 'an evocation of a period . . . an illustration of a theory of social change', and 'a highly entertaining comedy'.[42] If twentieth-century sensibility cannot easily warm to the egotism, 'humdrum preaching' and self-delusion of the Rev. Micah Balwhidder it should, at least, experience no difficulty in laughing at them. He is, after all, a good man who does the best he can, and his vanities are small. The Scottish literary canon holds a secure place for Galt's minister in his small symptomatic place. Galt's friend and first biographer, David Macbeth Moir's *The Life of Mansie Wauch Tailor in Dalkeith* (1828), is a lively imitation of the Galt formula, but lacks the portrayal of enveloping social transition by which life in Dalmailing or Gudetown is implicated in the wider world.

Susan Ferrier: pride, prejudice and Christianity

Susan Ferrier's work retains its documentary value both as period fiction and as an informed appraisal of the contemporary circumstances of women. At least Galt's equal in psychological penetration, she fails to achieve his coherent economy of art; but her false notes and surplus pages are offset by her humour – particularly in the first volume of *Marriage* (1818) – her social satire, her eye for prejudice and her sturdily Christian resolution of the competing claims of sense and sensibility.

First impressions of her three novels – *Marriage* (1818), *The Inheritance* (1824) and *Destiny* (1831) – suggest a novelist of manners. Her infectious enjoyment of the contrast between provincial Scottish behaviour and English suavity is responsible for much of the appeal of *Marriage*. Modelled on the beginning of *Pride and Prejudice*, the first sentence of *The Inheritance* is a deliberate reminder of Jane Austen's world: 'It is a truth universally acknowledged, that there is no passion so deeply rooted in human nature as that of pride.' The liveliest part of the novel is garrulous Miss Pratt, cast in the same mould as Jane Austen's Miss Bates in *Emma*:

> Every body wearied of her, or said they wearied of her,
> and every body abused her; while yet she was more
> sought after and asked about, than she would have been
> had she possessed the wisdom of a More or the
> benevolence of a Fry. She was, in fact, the very heart of
> the shire, and gave life and energy to all the pulses of the
> parish. She supplied it with streams of gossip and chit-chat
> in others, and subject of ridicule and abuse in herself.[43]

(I, 10)

The opening pages of *Destiny* exhibit a colourful digest of Highland life in the decadent chief of Glenroy, his parasitical kinsman, Benbowie, and the genuinely pious widowed housekeeper, Mrs Macauley. Ferrier's pleasure in drawing character is evident in her scheme for *Marriage*: 'the sudden transition of a high-bred English beauty, who thinks she can sacrifice all for love, to an uncomfortable solitary Highland dwelling among tall red-haired sisters and grim-faced aunts'.[44] High-born Lady Juliana's horrified encounter with her husband's aunts ('three long-chinned spinsters'), with his sisters ('five awkward purple girls'), with his forthright, Scots-speaking father, the Laird of Glenfern, and with the omniscient Lady Maclaughlan and her petulant, disintegrating husband, Sir Sampson, is rich comedy of manners, influenced by Maria Edgeworth's *Castle Rackrent* (1800), but based on Susan Ferrier's own shrewd observation of types. Ferrier's caricatures are very funny, but, like Mary Brunton, she is a Christian moralist and the comedy is there to serve the homily. In *The Inheritance* and *Destiny* the moralist is too much with us. *Marriage* is her most successful novel because it achieves the most effective balance of morals and manners with an impressive range of realized life to carry its didacticism. The title of each novel proclaims its topic, but Ferrier's message, common to the three, is the equation of full humanity with the difficult life of intelligent Christianity.

Susan Ferrier resembles Jane Austen only superficially. Her novels lean much further than Austen's towards the moral tract and her observation, judged aesthetically, takes too much 'the form of description and explicit comment rather than that of dramatic portrayal'.[45] Thematically, however, *Marriage* does recall Jane Austen in combining the topics of *Sense and Sensibility* with those of *Pride and Prejudice*. In a world of aggressive stupidity and vulgar prejudice Mary Douglas's task, like her foster-mother's before her,[46] is to resolve the tension in herself between the dutiful promptings of sense and the heart's sensibility. The novel's satirical humour largely derives from its display of prejudice. 'Destitute of every resource in herself', Lady Juliana is briefly prejudiced in favour of marrying for love, rejects her aristocratic moneyed suitor − 'a hunchback of fifty-three' − but is converted by cold-comfort Glenfern and her invertebrate husband's inconsiderate penury to the opposite persuasion whereby, as her father had told her, 'it was very well for ploughmen and dairymaids to marry for love, but for a young woman of rank to think of such a thing, was plebeian in the extreme' (I, 1).[47] Accordingly she rejects one of her twin daughters, disastrously schools the other in her own view of marital felicity and social propriety, and is parodied in her prejudice by Lady Maclaughlan's remark: 'Miss McKraken has bounced away with her father's footman − I hope he will clean his knives on her' (I, 16). National prejudice makes the Laird reckon 'all foreign music, *i.e.* every thing that was not Scotch, an outrage upon his ears'; Miss Nicky exclaims, 'The

Englishwomen are all poor droichs [dwarfs]' on the basis of having 'seen three in the course of her life'; and Miss Grizzy is astonished to find Mary so improved in appearance since she left Lochmarlie because 'she had always understood Scotland was the place for beauty, and that nobody ever came to anything in England' (III, 10). Scottish national prejudice is matched by English. Lady Audley accuses Alicia Malcolm of 'base Scotch blood' and Lady Juliana contemplates the arrival of Mary Douglas with deep ethnic revulsion:

> . . . what can I do with a girl who has been educated in Scotland? She must be vulgar – all Scotchwomen are so. They have red hands and rough voices; they yawn, and blow their noses, and talk, and laugh loud, and do a thousand shocking things. Then, to hear the Scotch brogue – oh, heavens! I should expire every time she opened her mouth!
>
> (II, 6)

A conversation between Mary's attractively sharp-tongued cousin, Emily, and Dr Redgill exposes the inanity of standards by which another country may be judged. Culinary expertise proves the superiority of the French to the gluttonous Dr Redgill:

> 'Every man in France is a first rate cook – in fact they are a nation of cooks; and one of our late travellers assures us, that they have discovered three hundred methods of dressing eggs, for one thing.'
> 'That is just two hundred and ninety-nine ways more than enough,' said Lady Emily; 'give me a plain boiled egg, and I desire no other variety of the produce of a hen, till it takes the form of a chicken.'
>
> (II, 15)

Miss Becky's incarceration by sartorial fashion – 'her arms had been strapped back till her elbows met, and her respiration seemed suspended' (I, 16) – is an expression of the constraints imposed on women and accepted by them, while male prejudice about the ordained role of women is satirized in the Laird's expostulation to his son about Lady Juliana's education:

> Edication! what has her edication been, to mak her different frae other women? If a woman can nurse her bairns, mak their claes, and manage her hooss, what mair need she do? If she can play a tune on the spinnet and

dance a reel, and play a rubber at whist – nae doot these
are accomplishments, but they're soon learnt. Edication!
pooh!

(I, 13)

Mary's role in *Marriage* is to exemplify true values against the pressures
of a society where status-conscious materialism passes for prudence and
infatuation for love. Ferrier uses the sparky, independent Emily as a foil
to protect her heroine from the charge of being too good to be true.
Mary's insistence on preferring duty to amusement irks Emily:

> O hang duties! they are odious things. And as for your
> amiable, dutiful, virtuous Goody Two-Shoes[48] characters,
> I detest them. They never would go down with me, even
> in the nursery, with all the attractions of a gold watch,
> and a coach and six. They were ever my abhorrence, as
> every species of canting and hypocrisy still is.

(II, 16)

The protective device is necessary. As with Gertrude in *The Inheritance*,
'social satire and presbyterian piety join'[49] in Mary's experience, but while
the authorial voice advises us that Mary is 'no rigid moralist', her angelic
nature and unswerving devotion to 'the Creator as the engrossing principle
of the soul' tremble on the brink of implausibility. Yet Mary's humanity
engages the reader, as in her kindness to blind Mrs Lennox (who, we are
told, 'never complained' but does so constantly), her affectionate tolerance of empty-headed but good-natured Aunt Grizzy, and her scruples
about marrying the man she loves for fear that he has been instructed to
love her out of gratitude for her care of his mother. Mary's Christianity
is practical: her values work, she gets her man, and it is clear that he will
be the greater beneficiary of the marriage. Her womanly prudence, tolerance, selflessness and love redeem Scottish religion from its submission
to Calvin's Devil.

Notes

1. James Hogg, *Memoir of the Author's Life and Familiar Anecdotes of Sir Walter
   Scott*, ed. Douglas S. Mack (Edinburgh, 1972), p. 5.

2. Ibid.

3. Ibid., p. 18.

4. Douglas Gifford, *James Hogg* (Edinburgh, 1976), p. 72.

5. Sir Walter Scott, *The Letters of Sir Walter Scott*, ed. H. J. C. Grierson, Centenary Edition, 12 vols (London, 1932–7), VI, p. 487.

6. J. H. Alexander (ed.), *The Tavern Sages, Selections from the Noctes Ambrosianae* (Aberdeen, 1992), p. viii.

7. Edwin Morgan, *Crossing the Border: Essays on Scottish Literature* (Manchester, 1990), p. 94.

8. Hogg, *Memoir*, ed. Mack, p. 118.

9. Judy Steel (ed.), *A Shepherd's Delight: A James Hogg Anthology* (Edinburgh, 1985), p. 161.

10. Professor Wilson, *Noctes Ambrosianae*, A New Edition, edited by his son-in-law, Professor Ferrier, 4 vols (Edinburgh and London, 1876), II, p. 338.

11. Louis Simpson, *James Hogg, A Critical Study* (Edinburgh and London, 1962), p. 126.

12. James Hogg, *The Private Memoirs and Confessions of a Justified Sinner*, ed. John Carey (Oxford, 1981), p. 256. Page references in the text are to this edition.

13. André Gide, 'Introduction' to James Hogg, *The Confessions of a Justified Sinner* (London, 1970), pp. 7, 13.

14. Walter Allen, *The English Novel* (Harmondsworth, 1958), pp. 130–31.

15. Stephen Prickett, *The Romantics* (London, 1981), p. 133.

16. See Carol Anderson, 'Listening to the Women Talk', Gavin Wallace and Randall Stevenson (eds), *The Scottish Novel Since the Seventies: New Visions, Old Dreams* (Edinburgh, 1993), pp. 170–86 [175–80].

17. Interview with Emma Tennant in John Haffenden (ed.), *Novelists in Interview* (London, 1985), pp. 281–304 [291].

18. Gide, 'Introduction' to Hogg, *Confessions*, p. 12.

19. James Hogg, 'A Scots Mummy', *Blackwood's Magazine*, xiv (August 1823), pp. 188–90.

20. See David Groves, ' "Confessions of an English Glutton": A (Probable) Source for James Hogg's *Confessions*', *Notes and Queries*, March 1993, pp. 46–7.

21. Anon., 'The Confessions of an English Glutton', *Blackwood's Magazine*, 13 (January 1823), pp. 86–93 [87].

22. Ibid., pp. 92–3.

23. Gide, 'Introduction' to Hogg, *Confessions*, p. 8.

24. James Hogg, *The Private Memoirs and Confessions of a Justified Sinner*, ed. John Wain (Harmondsworth, 1986), p. 11.

25. James Hogg, *The Brownie of Bodsbeck*, ed. Douglas S. Mack (Edinburgh and London, 1976), p. 75.

26. Cited by Jack Lindsay, *William Blake* (London, 1978), p. 278.

27. T. S. Eliot, 'Ben Jonson', in *Selected Essays*, 3rd edn (London, 1951), p. 159.

28. William Soutar, 'Towards an Indigenous Communism', 'Whither Scotland? "The Free Man" Symposium', Second Instalment, *The Free Man*, 1, no. 38 (22 October 1932), pp. 3–4 [3].

29. Jane Austen, *Jane Austen's Letters to her sister Cassandra and others*, collected and ed. R. W. Chapman, 2nd edn (London, 1952), p. 401.

30. John MacQueen, 'Scott and His Scottish Contemporaries', *The Week-End Scotsman*, 14 August 1971, p. 3.

31. Letter from John Galt to William Blackwood, 27 February 1821, cited in John Galt, *Annals of the Parish*, ed. James Kinsley (London, 1967), p. 206.

32. See letter from A. J. Ashley, 'Coleridge on Galt', *TLS*, 25 September 1930, p. 757.

33. Ian Jack, *English Literature 1815–1832* (Oxford, 1963), p. 230.

34. John Galt, *The Provost*, ed. Ian A. Gordon (London, 1973), p. xv.

35. Galt, *Literary Life, and Miscellanies*, 3 vols (Edinburgh and London, 1834), I, p. 226.

36. Keith M. Costain, 'The Scottish Fiction of John Galt', *The History of Scottish Literature, Volume 3, The Nineteenth Century*, ed. Douglas Gifford (Aberdeen, 1988), pp. 107–22 [114].

37. Galt, *Literary Life, and Miscellanies*, I, p. 156.

38. Susan Ferrier, *Memoir and Correspondence of Susan Ferrier, 1782–1854, based on her private correspondence in the possession of and collected by her grand-nephew John Ferrier*, ed. John A. Doyle (1898), p. 128.

39. Francis Russell Hart, *The Scottish Novel: A Critical Survey* (London, 1978), p. 53.

40. Galt, *The Provost*, ed. Gordon, pp. xii–xiii.

41. Hart, *The Scottish Novel*, p. 43.

42. P. H. Scott, *John Galt* (Edinburgh, 1985), p. 36.

43. Susan Ferrier, *The Inheritance*, 3 vols (Edinburgh, 1824), I, p. 102.

44. Jack, *English Literature*, p. 237.

45. Ibid., p. 238.

46. The background of Mrs Douglas's life prior to the action of the novel is given in 'History of Mrs. Douglas' in Vol. I, Chapter 14. This is all that certainly remains of the contribution to *Marriage* of Charlotte Clavering, the niece of the Duke of Argyll, with whom Susan Ferrier originally intended to write the novel jointly.

47. Quotations from *Marriage* are taken from Susan Ferrier, *Marriage*, ed. Herbert Foltinek (Oxford, 1986).

48. Goody Two-Shoes is the eponymous heroine of an improving nursery tale published in 1765 and said to be by Oliver Goldsmith.

49. Hart, *The Scottish Novel*, p. 63.

Chapter 7
Didacts and Doomsters: Nineteenth-Century Prophecy, Fantasy and Nightmare

Thomas Carlyle and the condition of 'England'

If the eighteenth century was enlightened, reasoning and increasingly sure of itself, the first half at least of the nineteenth was opinionated, impetuous and unsure. Protesting too much its 'confidence in the power of the mind to resolve every problem and of the individual to influence the course of events regardless of political or economic forces',[1] the century grew in cultural neurosis and self-doubt. Coming to terms with the Industrial and French Revolutions, it was an age of transition which resisted change. Gluttonous for material prosperity, it was caught unprepared for the accelerating growth of industry and the expansion of cities. John Galt's Rev. Balwhidder had been right to see a shadow in the spirit of improvement (*Annals of the Parish*, Chapter XXXII). The consequent problems of unemployment and urban poverty bred slums on an unprecedented scale. In his broadside against the workhouses in the first chapter of *Past and Present* (1843) Thomas Carlyle passes from an indignant description of the unemployed at the workhouse of St Ives in Huntingdonshire to the observation that while 'many hundred thousands sit in workhouses', there are 'other hundred thousands [who] have not yet got workhouses':

> . . . and in thrifty Scotland itself, in Glasgow or Edinburgh
> City, in their dark lanes, hidden from all but the eye of
> God, and of rare Benevolence the minister of God, there
> are scenes of woe and destitution and desolation, such as,
> one may hope, the Sun never saw before in the most
> barbarous regions where men dwelt . . . Not in sharp fever-
> fits, but in chronic gangrene of this kind is Scotland
> suffering.

The bases of traditional social assumptions and religious faith were shaken by a bombardment of movements and 'isms': Socialism, Puseyism and the Oxford Movement, Evangelicalism, Utilitarianism and Chartism. The age was sceptical and nothing if not ambiguous, even after the Great Exhibition of 1851 seemed to call for certainty and confidence in its assertion of the triumph of British industry and production. While castigating the dehumanizing effects of social mechanisms Carlyle can recognize the benefits of industrial creativity in *Chartism* (1839) and relish the 'awakening of a Manchester', its cotton-mills starting up in the morning 'like the boom of an Atlantic tide':

> Cotton-spinning is the clothing of the naked in its result;
> the triumph of man over matter in its means. Soot and
> despair are not the essence of it; they are divisible from it,
> – at this hour, are they not crying fiercely to be divided?
>
> (Chapter 8)

A similarly ambivalent attitude is found in John Davidson's 'Ballad in Blank Verse of the Making of a Poet', where affection for the poet's Greenock rises above pollution, industrial din and class inequality:

> . . . this grey town
> That pipes the morning up before the lark
> With shrieking steam, and from a hundred stalks
> Lacquers the sooty sky; where hammers clang
> On iron hulls, and cranes in harbours creak
> Rattle and swing, whole cargoes on their necks;
> Where men sweat gold that others hoard or spend
> And lurk like vermin in their narrow streets.

But how were soot and despair to be eliminated from industrial processes and expelled from the lives of blighted workers who, if lucky enough to be employed, needed the wages that came from the manufacturing boom even if their conditions of work damaged them physically, broke their spirits and condemned them to 'lurk like vermin'? Nobody seemed to know. 'Things, if it be not mere cotton and iron things, are growing disobedient to man,' Carlyle says in *Past and Present* (Book I, Chapter 1), and across the Atlantic his Transcendentalist admirer, Ralph Waldo Emerson, was characterizing the times in terms that applied as much to Britain as to America: 'The merchant serves the purse / . . . 'Tis the day of the chattel, / . . . Things are in the saddle, / And ride mankind' ('Ode, Inscribed to W. H. Channing', 1846). Throughout the United Kingdom society had lost its bearings, even if the imperial theme was assiduously whistled in the dark of social confusion. The times were ripe for visionaries and prophets. England had John Stuart Mill, Dickens, Ruskin, Matthew Arnold and William Morris, but Carlyle was the biggest shaman of them all. London was the intellectual centre of British cultural ferment, and, sooner or later, to London went the liveliest Scottish writers. Thomas Carlyle began to be famous as 'The Sage of Ecclefechan' in Annandale where he was born, but, after a short residence in Edinburgh and six bleak years at Craigenputtoch farm near Dumfries, graduated to the title of 'The Sage of Chelsea'.

Major Scottish contributions to British nineteenth-century debate about the human situation begin with Carlyle's jeremiads and include George MacDonald's symbolic interpretations of life as a quest for spiritual and sexual fulfilment under God. Margaret Oliphant develops her own amateur theology of the supernatural, contemplates provincial life and sharpens awareness of the condition of women, notably in her novels *Hester: A Story of Contemporary Life* (1883), *Effie Ogilvie* (1886), *Kirsteen* (1890) and *The Railway Man and His Children* (1891). But, despite improvements in social conditions from the early 1850s, towards the close of the century the expanding tyrannies of economics and science, continued inequalities and metaphysical gloom infuse MacDonald's evil city of Bulika in *Lilith* (1895) and darken the London of John Davidson as well as Mrs Oliphant's Dantesque 'cities of the night' in her fantastic story, 'The Land of Darkness' (1887), and James (B. V.) Thomson's 'City of Night; perchance of Death' in *The City of Dreadful Night* (1874). Ahead, in the early years of the next century, lay the tragic, endemically Scottish disintegrations of George Douglas Brown's *The House with the Green Shutters* (1901) and John Macdougall Hay's blood-curdling *Gillespie* (1914). These novels, at once specific to Scotland and expressive of the general malaise that still underlay the new prosperities, give the lie to the Kailyard ('cabbage patch') rural Scottish sentimentality of novels by S. R. Crockett, J. M. Barrie and John Watson ('Ian Maclaren'). Kailyard writing celebrates the parish minister and his flock of village worthies, the honest farmer and the everyday decencies of a church-going community. Although death, disease and unacceptable outsiders intrude, the Kailyard world is remote from the tentacles of nineteenth-century industrialism with its poverty, alienation and high mortality rate. Essentially nostalgic, such writing is an idealized projection of early Romantic views of the beneficent power of nature over people who were disposed to live simply and morally in an achievable, detached Arcadia. The poetry of Thomson and Davidson and the novels of Brown and Hay complete the movement of Scottish imagination from sentimental miniaturism and ameliorist didacticism to recognition that centres were not holding and that Arcadia was an illusion. Carlyle's rasping *Latter-Day Pamphlets* (1850) pronounce the moral and social doom of the age. That the nightmare of Thomson's apocalyptic vision was latent in Carlyle's earlier response to the world is evident in

a passage from Carlyle's journal for 1835 which might almost be Thomson
writing about his 'dolent city' some forty years later:

> The world . . . looks often quite spectral to me; sometimes,
> as in Regent Street the other night (my nerves being all
> shattered), quite hideous, discordant, almost infernal. I had
> been at Mrs. Austin's, heard Sydney Smith for the first
> time guffawing, other persons prating, jargoning. To me
> through these thin cobwebs Death and Eternity sate
> glaring. Coming homewards along Regent Street, through
> street-walkers, through – *Ach Gott!* unspeakable pity
> swallowed up unspeakable abhorrence of it and of myself.[2]

This, too, is the London of John Davidson's 'St Valentine's Eve' from his
Fleet Street Eclogues (1893): 'a darksome cell where men go mad'.

Leslie Stephen's observation that 'Mr Carlyle is both a man of genius
and a Scotchman'[3] states more than the obvious. 'To hear Englishmen
talk', says Tarmillan in *The House with the Green Shutters*, 'you would
think Carlyle was unique for the word that sends the picture home – they
give the man the credit of his race' (Chapter 17). Carlyle's genius and the
interlaced ideas with which he became obsessed are crucially Scottish.
While a student at Edinburgh University he lost the creed of his pious
Calvinist upbringing but retained the pressure of its Puritan intensity.
Similarly, John Davidson rebelled against his father's Scottish Evangelicalism but never lost its ideological earnestness and missionary-mindedness;
his later poems celebrating a godless universe – in particular the projected
dramatic trilogy, *God and Mammon* – 'are as remarkable for their narrow
fervour and their denunciation of different points of view as the polemics
of Knox three and a half centuries earlier'.[4] Carlyle's inbred belief in
transcendental purpose and the fallacies of mere reason was endorsed and
amplified by his reading of German literature, Goethe in particular but
also Schiller, Kant, Fichte, Novalis and Jean Paul Richter. His first contribution to the *Edinburgh Review*, the essay 'Jean Paul Friedrich Richter'
(1827), expresses admiration for an intellect 'vehement, rugged, irresist-
ible' like his own as revealed in *Sartor Resartus* (1836), 'an imagination
vague, sombre, splendid or appalling: brooding over the abysses of Being
. . . a humourist from his inmost soul . . . a Titan in his sport as in his
earnestness'. ('In his graphic description of Richter's style, Carlyle describes his own pretty nearly,' observes Henry David Thoreau in 1847.[5])
At once didactic novel and satirical extravaganza, *Sartor Resartus* rejoices
in generic freedoms learned from Sterne's *Tristram Shandy*, presenting the
life and opinions of Diogenes (i.e. God-born) Teufelsdröckh (i.e. Devil's
dung), 'Professor of Things in General' at the New University of Weiss-
nichtwo (i.e. know-not-where).

'In my own heterodox heart,' Carlyle wrote to his brother John, 'there is yearly growing up the strangest crabbed one-sided persuasion, that all Art is but a reminiscence now, that for us in these days *Prophecy* (well understood) not Poetry is the thing wanted; how can we *sing* and *paint* when we do not yet *believe* and *see*?'[6] *Sartor Resartus* (i.e. The Tailor Re-tailored) is a prophetic book, Blakean in its intention to illuminate the path to moral deliverance for a society that had lost its way. First pub-lished in instalments in *Fraser's Magazine* in autumn 1833, it found only a small audience among the circle of Carlyle's admirers and, until it appeared in America as a book in 1836 thanks to Emerson's influence, seemed destined to sink into obscurity. Even in 1837 Thomas's gifted and endlessly supportive wife, Jane Welsh Carlyle, could write in exasperation to her husband's friend, John Sterling: 'Is it not curious that my husband's writings should be only completely understood and adequately appreci-ated by women and mad people?'[7] A year later, following the success of *The French Revolution*, a British edition was published. Undeniably a dif-ficult book, *Sartor Resartus* engages the reader by the story of Teufelsdröckh's life, love, and the evolution of his speculative radicalism, by the humour and earnestness of the Swiftian conceit which perceives the material universe as a clothing of the Divine Idea – what Carlyle calls 'the *vesture*' that makes the divine mystery visible in Lecture III of *On Heroes, Hero-Worship & the Heroic in History* (1841) – and by the multi-toned ebullience of its language. The constituents of its heterodoxy are the relatively few basic ideas that occupied Carlyle throughout his life. They are all Calvinistic in origin:[8] his indomitably religious belief in a transcendent scheme of values beyond physical nature; his contempt for the mechanistic operations of a world brutalized by materialism; his gospel of work with its emphasis on action as the way to personal and social salvation; and his hero-worship.

Calvinism concentrates on eternity and so does Carlyle, hence Profes-sor Teufelsdröckh's insistence on wonder as the instinctive 'basis of Wor-ship' (*Sartor Resartus*, Book I, Chapter 10) which reason and 'the progress of Science' seek to destroy by 'Mensuration and Numeration'. Although Carlyle derides existing churches as systems of cant, 'Christianity must ever be regarded as the crowning glory, or rather the life and soul, of our whole modern culture', he asserts in 'Signs of the Times' (1829). Damage to the 'Pericardial Nervous Tissue' of religion has produced a society 'long pining, diabetic, consumptive' which can now be regarded as 'defunct' (*Sartor Resartus*, Book III, Chapter 5). Human unhappiness, Teufelsdröckh explains, comes from the 'Infinite' in man 'which with all his cunning he cannot quite bury under the Finite' (*Sartor Resartus*, Book II, Chapter 9). Rational assessment of his own life and the present human condition leads Teufelsdröckh, as some years earlier it had led Carlyle himself,[9] to the 'Everlasting No' (Book II, Chapter 7), a complete loss of hope and belief. Discovering his inner resources of consciousness, heart and freedom, he raises himself from despair, reinstating his own 'Infinite' and embracing the 'Everlasting Yea' in a Nietzschean outcry of religio-romantic defiance:

> What *art* thou afraid of? Wherefore, like a coward, dost thou forever pip and whimper, and go cowering and trembling? Despicable biped! what is the sum-total of the worst that lies before thee? Death? Well, Death; and say the pangs of Tophet[10] too, and all that the Devil and Man may, will or can do against thee! Hast thou not a heart; canst thou not suffer whatsoever it be; and, as a Child of Freedom, though outcast, trample Tophet itself under thy feet, while it consumes thee? Let it come, then; I will meet it and defy it! And as I so thought, there rushed like a stream of fire over my whole soul; and I shook base Fear away from me forever. I was strong, of unknown strength; a spirit, almost a god. Ever from that time, the temper of my misery was changed: not Fear or whining Sorrow was it, but Indignation and grim fire-eyed Defiance.
>
> (*Sartor Resartus*, Book II, Chapter 7)

From his earliest essays to the affectionate biography of his ill-starred friend in *The Life of John Sterling* (1851) Carlyle inveighs against what he calls the 'demon of Mechanism' (*Chartism*, Chapter 4). It is on this theme that he speaks most prophetically to the defining feature of the late twentieth century. 'It is not by Mechanism,' he writes in 'Characteristics', 'but by Religion; not by Self-interest, but by Loyalty, that men are governed or governable.' Notwithstanding a deeply instilled Calvinistic rage for order, he rejects the false order produced by so-called rational methods which belie human instinct for the true, transcendent values of the inner world. The age's scourge is machinery which not only manages the external and physical but has also taken over the internal and spiritual, thereby corroding people's capacity for true feeling and right action. 'We have machines for education . . . Religious machines . . . Royal Academies.' Literature should be 'a "continuous revelation" of the Godlike in the Terrestrial and Common' (*On Heroes*, Lecture V) but it, too, has been commandeered by 'Paternoster-row mechanism . . . so that books are not only printed, but in great measure, written and sold, by machinery' ('Signs of the Times'). Professor Teufelsdröckh's darkest hour is his vision of an indifferent, mechanical universe:

> To me the Universe was all void of Life, of Purpose, of Volition, even of Hostility: it was one huge, dead

immeasurable Steam-engine, rolling on, in its dead
indifference, to grind me limb from limb.

(*Sartor Resartus*, Book II, Chapter 7)

While Teufelsdröckh is temporarily reduced to fear and trembling nihil-
ism by the mechanical universe, poor people are crushed by it. The
Professor's 'saddest spectacle' in Book III, Chapter 5 is really Carlyle's
summing-up of 'the condition of England' (for England read Britain): 'the
Poor perishing, like neglected, foundered Draught Cattle, of Hunger
and Over-work; the Rich, still more wretchedly, of Idleness, Satiety, and
Over-growth'. No one benefits from material wealth alone. Passionately,
Carlyle resents the illusion of prosperity and the reality of waste:

> This successful industry of England, with its plethoric
> wealth, has as yet made nobody rich; it is an enchanted
> wealth, and belongs yet to nobody. We might ask, Which
> of us has it enriched? We can spend thousands where we
> once spent hundreds; but can purchase nothing good with
> them. In Poor and Rich, instead of noble thrift and
> plenty, there is idle luxury alternating with mean scarcity
> and inability. We have sumptuous garnitures for our Life,
> but have forgotten to *live* in the middle of them. It is an
> enchanted wealth; no man of us can yet touch it. The
> class of men who feel that they are truly better off by
> means of it, let them give us their names!

(*Past and Present*, Chapter 1)

In a godless, morally barren society under the mismanagement of self-
interested 'Mammonists' and 'Dilettantes', as he calls the industrial middle
class and the land-owning aristocracy in Book III of *Past and Present*, the
Midas-touch is a curse which nourishes the Chartist movement in Britain
as aristocratic self-indulgence had recently caused the Revolution in France.
Carlyle's historical masterpiece, *The French Revolution* (1837), is another
prophetic book. His brilliantly vivid and authoritatively detailed evocation of events before and during the Revolution is his next warning to
Britain. 'Awakening . . . to consciousness in deep misery', the French people
believed themselves 'within reach of a Fraternal Heaven-on-Earth' (Book
III, Chapter 1), but saw their utopian hopes shredded by what Carlyle
ironically calls 'the all-healing Guillotine' (Book VI, Chapter 6). The
same tragic explosion could happen in Britain if action is not taken to
alleviate the distresses of the working classes. The ultimatum is generally
implied, but Carlyle's anger on behalf of the underdog can suddenly sting
through the racy news-documentary idiom of his history, as in his account
of the death of Louis XVI's young heir, the Dauphin, who died obscurely
in prison:

> ... the poor boy, hidden in a tower of the Temple [i.e.
> the Temple Prison], from which in his fright and
> bewilderment and early decrepitude he wishes not to stir
> out, lies perishing, 'his shirt not changed for six months';
> amid squalor and darkness, lamentably, – so as none but
> poor Factory Children and the like are wont to perish,
> and *not* be lamented!
>
> (*The French Revolution*, III [*The Guillotine*],
> Book VI, Chapter 3)

The late twentieth century wants just this fearlessly outspoken, unabating alertness to the cruelties of social injustice to bring home the significance of human catastrophes in Somalia, Bosnia, Rwanda and East Timor.

Calvinism's grimly discriminatory doctrine of the Elect is transformed into Carlyle's hero-worship. Evaluation of Sir Walter Scott in his essay of 1838 prompts the dictum: 'Veneration of great men is perennial in the nature of man; this, in all times, especially in these, is one of the blessedest facts predictable of him.' *On Heroes, Hero-Worship & the Heroic in History* derives from a series of lectures Carlyle gave in 1840, but the germinal ideas frequently appear many years earlier. In 'Signs of the Times', the first essay in which he openly expresses views hitherto implicit chiefly in his writings about German literature, a passage which begins by attacking the mechanistic society moves seamlessly into his conception of divinely inspired heroic superiority, showing how each of his basic ideas entails the others. Here the conception of society as a machine is held to be absurd because it postulates arithmetically quantifiable mental capacities, different degrees and kinds of mental ability as units of the same thing, thereby failing to appreciate the incalculable mystery of superior, divinely ordained powers:

> We figure Society as a 'Machine', and that mind is
> opposed to mind, as body is to body; whereby two, or at
> most ten, little minds must be stronger than one great
> mind. Notable absurdity! For the plain truth, very plain,
> we think is, that minds are opposed to minds in quite a
> different way; and *one* man that has a higher Wisdom, a
> hitherto unknown spiritual Truth in him, is stronger, not
> than ten men that have it not, or than ten thousand,
> but than *all* men that have it not; and stands among them
> with a quite ethereal, angelic power, as with a sword out
> of Heaven's own armory, sky-tempered, which no
> buckler, and no tower of brass, will finally withstand.

The thought pattern displayed in the passage is not logical, but a sequence of assertions in which each one is sealed in by the next. Once drawn in, the reader is caught and the rhetoric does its work. So Teufelsdröckh's predilection for great men in *Sartor Resartus* (Book II, Chapter 8) heralds his defence of the divine right of kings, his equation of freedom with 'Obedience to the Heaven-chosen' (Book III, Chapter 7) and his climactic pronouncement that hero-worship is natural:

> In which fact, that Hero-worship exists, has existed, and
> will forever exist, universally among Mankind, mayest thou
> discern the corner-stone of living-rock, whereon all
> Polities for the remotest time may stand secure.
> *(Sartor Resartus*, Book III, Chapter 7)

This is the basis of Carlyle's message in *On Heroes* that 'Universal History, the history of what man has accomplished in this world, is at bottom the History of the Great Men who have worked here' (Lecture 1). The hero and history 'are perfect mates: what better solution than that which discovers both unity and continuity in the hero and the divine substance to which he bears witness and with which he is in special contact?'[11] To prove his thesis the six lectures exhibit six classes of heroic men: the hero as divinity (the Scandinavian god, Odin); the hero as prophet (Mahomet); the hero as poet (Dante and Shakespeare); the hero as priest (Martin Luther and John Knox); the hero as man of letters (Dr Johnson, Rousseau and Burns); and the hero as king, lord protector or emperor (Cromwell and Napoleon). Since hero-worship 'is the soul of all social business among men' it is imperative that we, in spiritually asphyxiated Britain, 'learn to do our Hero-Worship better' (*Past and Present*, Book, I, Chapter 6) if 'the condition of England' is to be cured. In Britain, as in pre-Revolutionary France, politically inert aristocracies have failed in their duty to be heroically responsible for the people. The governing class has inspired no nation-forming belief, preferring 'Donothingism and *Laissez-faire*' (*Chartism*, Chapter 7) to the responsibilities of governing, but 'change is universal and inevitable' ('Characteristics') and 'government of the under classes by the upper on a principle of *Let-alone* is no longer possible' (*Chartism*, Chapter 6).

All heroes inspire belief, and 'the history of a nation becomes fruitful, soul-elevating, great, so soon as it believes' (*On Heroes*, Lecture 2). This is Carlyle at his most disconcertingly Nietzschean; the mesmerizing oratory has turned as potentially toxic as the Calvinism he thought he had abandoned. To urge hero-worship and belief in the raw without defining the belief and specifying the qualities of the hero the hour requires is to extend *carte blanche* to a Napoleon, a Franco, a Hitler, a Stalin, a Verwoerd. The demagogic power of his rhetoric, his command of history and the vigour of his commitment give the impression of a 'humane Jeremiah', a social prophet who not only sees what has gone wrong but knows what

must be done to bring about a new order, yet he fails to offer a programme of reform. He is as incapable as Dickens or Charlotte Brontë
were of conceiving a time when workers – 'the great dumb, deep-buried
class' (*Chartism*, Chapter 9) – might govern themselves. All will be well,
he says, if we believe in the Divine Idea and follow our leaders, provided
that the elect ruling class stops luxuriating in its advantages, stops attending to its game preserves, assumes its responsibilities and discharges them
heroically like a true 'corporation of the Best, of the Bravest' (*Chartism*,
Chapter 6). Carlyle's labourer struggles neither for workhouses and doles,
nor to seize control of his own destiny from the aristocratic club of
enlightened despots, but ' "for justice" . . . "for just wages", – not in
money alone! An ever-toiling inferior, he would fain . . . find for himself
a superior that should lovingly and wisely govern' (*Chartism*, Chapter 3).
If such marmoreal conservatism in a radical is chilling, especially to the
ever-toiling inferior, it grows harsh and grating in his demand for restoration of the 'beneficent whip' to coerce idle West Indian slaves into work
in 'Occasional Discourse on the Negro Question' (1849), in the collection of *Latter-Day Pamphlets* and in his monumental six-volume tribute to
the bullying Frederick the Great of Prussia in *History of Friedrich II. of
Prussia, called Frederick the Great* (1858–65). Yet Carlyle's genuine sympathy for the oppressed and suffering keeps him from being a Fascist's
fascist: the obverse of his hero-worship is compassion for the people who
need a hero to help them. His style now seems badly dated: 'Its energy
seems obstructed by its heavily biblical language, and its involved structures (often concealing irony) difficult to analyse without painful effort.'[12]
But it is still worth making the effort to get at the spiritual electricity, at
the 'energy which is capable of violating ideas, of subjugating them without
inducing them to obedience or discipline',[13] and at the prophetic flashes
that still illuminate our own mechanistic age of consumer economies and
perishable values. No one has caught him better than Swinburne in his
elegy, 'On the Deaths of Thomas Carlyle and George Eliot':

> The stormy sophist with his mouth of thunder,
> Clothed with loud words and mantled in the might
> Of darkness and magnificence of night.

It is enough, perhaps, that he will always be a writer's writer.

George MacDonald: spiritual geology

George MacDonald read deeply in Carlyle and absorbed many of the
same German influences, Novalis in particular. Both Scotsmen were mystics,

and both anticipated Freud with similar beliefs in the unconscious. MacDonald suggests that artistic forms come from 'the unconscious portion' of human nature, 'that chamber of our being in which the candle of our consciousness goes out in darkness'.[14] God sits in the chamber. Whereas Carlyle's mysticism came from writers of the eighteenth- and early nineteenth-century German Renaissance, MacDonald's was essentially if unconventionally Christian. In his masterpiece, *Lilith, A Romance* (1895), the cryptic librarian/bird/sexton, Mr Raven, tells the hero, Mr Vane: 'We are often unable to tell people what they *need* to know, because they *want* to know something else' (Chapter 9). Writing at a time when people wanted to know about science, empire, politics and economics, MacDonald believed they needed to know about God and the moral life. Education in these matters involved an appeal to the imagination which, in terms reminiscent of Coleridge, MacDonald defines as 'that faculty which gives form to thought . . . that faculty in man which is likest to the prime operation of the power of God'.[15] Defining the main function of the imagination, he says:

> It is aroused by facts, is nourished by facts, seeks for
> higher and yet higher laws in those facts; but refuses to
> regard science as the sole interpreter of nature, or the laws
> of science as the only region of discovery.[16]

With what he somewhat disingenuously calls his 'plain-talking pen' in the poem, 'Were I a Skilful Painter', he tried to tell people what he thought they needed to know about 'higher and yet higher laws' in conventional novels compounded of realism, didacticism and sentimentality.

He also tried to tell them in fantastic stories for both children and adults which were much admired by his friend Charles Dodgson (Lewis Carroll) whom MacDonald and his family encouraged to publish *Alice's Adventures in Wonderland* (1865). Passages in MacDonald's *Phantastes: A Faerie Romance for Men and Women* (1858)[17] undoubtedly influenced the *Alice* books.[18] Alice's descent underground is similar to MacDonald's hero, Anodos's, descent down a perpendicular hole 'like a roughly excavated well' in Chapter 17 of *Phantastes*, and while Anodos is in pursuit of a white lady, not a white rabbit, he does meet 'a large white rabbit with red eyes' in Chapter 5. Lewis Carroll's mirror in *Through the Looking Glass and What Alice Found There* (1872) is strongly reminiscent of the enchanted mirror in *Phantastes*, Chapter 13 which prompts Cosmo von Wehrstahl to exclaim, as Lewis Carroll might have done: 'What a strange thing a mirror is! and what a wondrous affinity exists between it and a man's imagination.' The success of *Alice* has been attributed to its lack of a moral – pre-Freudian children could read it without feeling they were being got at – but the popularity of MacDonald's novels and neglect of his adult

176 SCOTTISH LITERATURE SINCE 1707

fantasies during his own lifetime were largely owing to the marketable sentimentality and moral saturation of his orthodox fiction and the off-putting obliquities of the symbolic works. In the fantasies he is like Anodos, 'a geologist', turning up 'to the light some of the buried strata of the human world, with its fossil remains charred by passion and petrified by tears' (*Phantastes*, Chapter 1).

The twentieth century has preferred the fantasies, which have been praised by H. G. Wells, A. A. Milne, W. H. Auden and C. S. Lewis whose 'Narnia' stories for children and strongly Christian science fiction novels owe much to MacDonald's example, as do the works of David Lindsay, Mervyn Peake, J. R. R. Tolkien and Charles Williams. What Auden calls MacDonald's 'dream realism'[19] derives not only from British sources like Spenser and the ballads but also from Novalis, Goethe and other German Romantic writers. It anticipates the magical realism of Kafka, Jorge Luis Borges, Italo Calvino and Dennis Potter, as well as that of Scotland's Alasdair Gray and Iain Banks. On the basis of MacDonald's 'originality of outlook' G. K. Chesterton's magnificent obituary tribute refers to him as 'one of the three or four greatest men of 19th century Britain', belonging to the class of 'the sage, the sayer of things'.[20] In his preface to *George MacDonald: An Anthology* (1946), a collection of 365 passages mostly culled from the three volumes of MacDonald's expository *Unspoken Sermons* (1867, 1885, 1889) and presumably designed to provide a year's worth of daily readings, C. S. Lewis says: 'I have never concealed the fact that I regarded him as my master.'[21] Lewis appreciates that 'Necessity made MacDonald a novelist . . . few of his novels are good and none is very good.'[22] The novels were written to support MacDonald's family after he was forced to give up his Congregationalist pulpit at Arundel in Sussex following disputes with the church elders about the liberal content of his sermons. (An Arundel deacon who gave him 'a good deal of trouble' was the basis of Appleditch the grocer in *David Elginbrod*.[23]) Anodos's willingness to sacrifice his life to expose the bestial rottenness of the mysterious ceremonial in Chapter 23 of *Phantastes* is readily interpreted as an expression of MacDonald's revulsion from prevailing religious orthodoxy. Throughout his career, if one eye was necessarily on income, the other was always kept steadily on 'the urgent religious message which he felt called upon to disseminate, pulpit or no pulpit'.[24]

Of his twenty-nine novels *Alec Forbes of Howglen* (1865) and *Sir Gibbie* (1879) are likeliest to survive MacDonald's verbosity and melodrama and the vagaries of changing taste. Alec Forbes's protection of young Annie Anderson is touching because it is psychologically credible and skilfully dramatized, as are the petty cruelties of Robert Bruce's family towards the orphaned heroine. Kate Fraser and Patrick Beauchamp are creditable variations of Dickens's Estella and Bentley Drummle in *Great Expectations*

(1860) and both Murdoch Malison, the sadistic schoolteacher who personifies 'the God of a corrupt Calvinism' (Chapter 9), and old Cupples,
the alcoholic librarian, are lifelike, fully realized characters. The schoolroom
scenes are among MacDonald's finest passages, and genuine tension is
achieved in Chapter 76 when Cupples offers to sacrifice his own addic-
tion if it will save Alec ('Bantam') from the demon drink.

> 'Bantam,' said Mr Cupples solemnly, 'I sweir to God,
> gin ye'll gie ower the drink and the lave o'yer ill gaits, I'll
> gie ower the drink as weel. I hae naething ither to gie
> ower. But that winna be easy,' he added with a sigh,
> stretching his hand towards his glass.
>   From a sudden influx of energy, Alec stretched his hand
> likewise towards the same glass, and laying hold on it as
> Mr Cupples was rasing it to his lips, cried:
>   'I sweir to God likewise – And noo,' he added, leaving
> his hold of the glass, 'ye daurna drink it.'
>   Mr Cupples threw his glass and all into the fire.

If the realistic novels are too formulaically replete with noble artisans, do-
gooders, aristocratic villains, morally weighted violence, natural disasters
and implausibly happy endings, what Lewis calls 'a queer, awkward charm'[25]
enlivens parts of *David Elginbrod* (1863) and *Robert Falconer* (1868) – both
largely autobiographical – *Malcolm* (1875) and its sequel *The Marquis of
Lossie* (1877), *Paul Faber, Surgeon* (1879) and *Castle Warlock* (1882; entitled
Warlock O'Glenwarlock in some later editions). MacDonald knew his market
well enough to exploit topics of current interest: hypnotism in *David
Elginbrod*, body-snatching in *Alec Forbes of Howglen*, 'stickit' (i.e. failed)
ministers in *Malcolm* and *The Marquis of Lossie*, vivisection, blood transfusion
and atheism in *Paul Faber, Surgeon*. Greville MacDonald, the author's son,
thought *Sir Gibbie* 'the most direct and the most beautiful' of his father's
novels: 'His life's warfare against vulgarity in art, professionalism in religion, wage estimate of labour, dogmatic interpretations of the Infinite
Love, class-worship and spiritual wickedness in high places, marches through
the pages of this book with bagpipes and bonnet and broadsword.'[26]
    MacDonald's poetry is voluminous and mostly bad, a rich seam for a
mischievous anthologist of flaccid verse. There are some cleverly, if more
often cloyingly, fey verses in the fantasies, including Little Diamond's
song in *At the Back of the North Wind* (1871), the first of MacDonald's
longer fairy stories to be published in book form, which became a staple
recitation piece of the Victorian parlour:

> Where did you come from, baby dear?
> Out of the everywhere into here.

Where did you get your eyes so blue?
Out of the sky as I came through.

What makes the light in them sparkle and spin?
Some of the starry spikes left in.

Where did you get that little tear?
I found it waiting when I got here.

At the Back of the North Wind is a fable written to allay the fear of death
– Little Diamond appears dead but the narrator knows that 'he had gone
to the back of the north wind' (Chapter 38) – so the song's message that
the baby is a cherubic emanation of God and therefore eternally safe is,
at least, germane to one of MacDonald's favourite themes. The four-line
epitaph for the hero's ancestor which became the germ of *David Elginbrod*
is not MacDonald's own but was supplied by Charles Manby Smith,
a journalist he met at a supper party.[27] The jingle does, however, call
attention to MacDonald's sense of humour, a quality of his prose writings
often overlooked:

> Here lie I, Martin Elginbrodde:
> Hae mercy o' my soul, Lord God;
> As I wad do, were I Lord God,
> And ye were Martin Elginbrodde.
> (Book I, Chapter 13)

In the first chapter of *Phantastes* he pokes fun at the sexism of his time.
When the miniature woman who emerges from his late father's desk
transforms herself into a tall, gracious lady, Anodos is overcome by her
beauty. He reaches impulsively for her, only to be repelled by the astonishing news that she was 'two hundred and thirty-seven years old, last
Midsummer eve' and her observation that 'a man must not fall in love
with his grandmother':

> 'But you are not my grandmother,' said I.
> 'How do you know that?' she retorted. 'I dare say you
> know something of your great-grandfathers a good deal
> further back than that; but you know very little about
> your great-grandmothers on either side.'

In *Lilith* his matrix of archetypes includes Lilith, Lona, Mara and Eve, 'all
aspects of the feminine'.[28]
    MacDonald reveres physical detail. Like Carlyle, and partly in the
manner of Fichte and Novalis, he considers the appearances of things as

a vesture of the eternal and all nature evidence of a divine spirit at work. Combining an insistence on 'the *factitude* of things . . . the recognition of inexorable reality' in *What's Mine's Mine* (1886), Chapter 30 with a talent for mythopoeic fantasy, he is a prime example of G. Gregory Smith's 'Caledonian antisyzygy',[29] but, like Carlyle, it is in his relation to Calvinism that he is most Scottish. With Calvinist passion he consistently repudiates Scottish Calvinist doctrine, in particular the doctrine of divine Election. 'I did not care for God to love me if He did not love everybody,' he writes in *Weighed and Wanting* (1882).[30] As for William Blake, theology for MacDonald is a clarification of the vision of life as sanctified, 'a washing down of the doors of perception'.[31] God must be perceived as a loving Father, not as the martinet God projected in their own image by the Calvinists:

> They yield the idea of the Ancient of Days, 'the glad creator' and put in its stead a miserable, puritanical martinet of a God, caring not for righteousness, but for his rights; not for the eternal purities, but the goodly properties. The prophets of such a God take all the glow, all the hope, all the colour, all the worth, out of life on earth, and offer you instead what they call eternal bliss – a pale, tearless hell.
>
> (*Unspoken Sermons*, 3rd Series, p. 161)

Pleasure and tears are not only permissible in MacDonald's worlds, they are encouraged. As Chesterton puts it, 'MacDonald was a mystic who was half mad with joy'.[32] So the princess whose recovery of her gravity and the ability to weep mark her emergence into freely sexual womanhood in 'The Light Princess' (1864 in *Adela Cathcart*) tumbles with her prince into the liberating lake as often as she pleases, 'and the splash they made before was nothing to the splash they made now'. The phallic key Mossy finds at 'the place where the end of the rainbow stands' unlocks an eternity of happiness for him and Tangle at the end of 'The Golden Key' (1867 in *Dealings with the Fairies*).[33] There is Curdie's pleasure in his mother and father in *The Princess and the Goblin* (1872) which Auden thought 'the only English children's book in the same class as the Alice books'.[34] Above all, in the fantasies, there is the pleasure to be had from 'the sheer experience of entering the domain which MacDonald's imagination has created'.[35]

MacDonald also outmanoeuvres Calvinism's terrorist deployment of guilt and death. Recurrent guilt is Anodos's most potent and evil adversary in *Phantastes*, symbolized by the Shadow that follows him on his picaresque twenty-one-day journey towards his true self through the initiatory moral, psychological and sexual challenges of Fairy Land. He is

'joyously delivered' from it in Chapter 25. The more concentrated symbolism of *Lilith* presents the universe as 'a riddle trying to get out'. ('It
seems to me that there is nothing very obscure in it that is worth finding
out,' MacDonald wrote to a friend, 'though I hope there are some things
in it not therefore shallow.'[36]) 'You *must* answer the riddles,' Mr Raven
tells the impatient, bewildered Mr Vane in Chapter 9. In answering the
central riddle, the meaning of death, by surviving his encounters with
'Death Absolute' personified by Lilith (Chapter 39) and with the corrupt
city of Bulika, Mr Vane earns the repose that comes after right action.
Like Joyce's Leopold Bloom in the 'Ithaca' chapter of *Ulysses* 'He rests.
He has travelled'; like the eponymous hero of Saul Bellow's *Herzog*
(1964) he ends his pilgrim's progress in Chapter 46 suspended, expectant,
resigned: 'I wait; asleep or awake, I wait'. Intimations of truth seek him:
'they come, and I let them go'. He is, in Simone Weil's phrase, 'waiting
for God'.[37] Like MacDonald himself he is, theologically, ahead of his
time.

Margaret Oliphant: woman's place and God's supervision

Mrs Margaret Oliphant, née Wilson, was also ahead of her time. As a
widow of exemplary courage and independence who lived well enough
by her pen to pay for her two sons' education at Eton and Oxford, and
to provide for two feckless brothers, she is one of the great success stories
of the century. Of her ninety-three published novels she was most acclaimed, albeit briefly, for *The Chronicles of Carlingford*, stories of provincial
English social and religious life in the style of Anthony Trollope's tales of
Barsetshire. *Salem Chapel* (1863) and *Miss Marjoribanks* (1866) are the two
chronicles of her series most likely to live beyond the specialist interests
of the literary historian or biographer, who must also take account of
her histories, her critical work and the two volumes she contributed to
her publisher, William Blackwood's, *Annals of a Publishing House: William
Blackwood and His Sons, Their Magazine and Friends* (1897). Despite its
sensationalist element, attributable to Mrs Oliphant's liking for the work
of Wilkie Collins, *Salem Chapel* is notable for its insight into Congregationalist non-conformism, *Miss Marjoribanks* for its sustained ironic comedy and a heroine, Lucilla, insubordinate to men, who wins praise from
Q. D. Leavis as 'a triumphant intermediary' between Jane Austen's *Emma*
and the Dorothea of George Eliot's *Middlemarch*.[38] For the late twentieth-
century reader Mrs Oliphant's claims as a writer of enduring value are

most apparent in *Kirsteen* (1890), in her excursions into what she calls in her story, 'The Secret Chamber' (1876), the 'debatable land between the seen and the unseen', and in the fragmentary autobiographical narrative published in 1899 with a selection of her letters in an arrangement by Mrs Harry Coghill as *The Autobiography and Letters of Mrs M. O. W. Oliphant*.[39] From her enormous output, these make up a minimal core of her work which should be kept continuously in print by the custodians of Scottish literature in English.

The distinction of the *Autobiography* is not only its testimony to Mrs Oliphant's victory over financial adversity (her husband died in 1859 leaving her £1,000 in debt) and bereavement (her three children predeceased her), but also in its total lack of affectation. It reads like a letter frankly addressed to the reader by a brave, perceptive, cultivated friend. In the first part, begun in 1885 and expanded as the notion took her, she looks back on the practical difficulties a woman writer faced in a society which condoned her precocity but had no thought for the need for privacy that would be taken for granted today:

> ... up to this date, 1888, I have never been shut up in a separate room, or hedged off with any observances. My study, all the study I have ever attained to, is the little second drawing-room, the first being where all the (feminine) life of the house goes on; and I don't think I have ever had two hours undisturbed (except at night, when everybody is in bed) during my whole literary life. Miss Austen, I believe, wrote in the same way, and very much for the same reason; but at her period the natural flow of life took another form. The family were half ashamed to have it known that she was not just a young lady like the others, doing her embroidery. Mine were quite pleased to magnify me, and to be proud of my work, but always with a hidden sense that it was an admirable joke, and no idea that any special facilities or retirement was necessary.[40]

She knows that her writing career has been handicapped by circumstances as George Eliot's was not, that she has experienced 'all the ways of mental suffering' and 'lived a laborious life' of 'incessant work, incessant anxiety'. She thinks of Lady Grizel Baillie's line, 'Werena my heart licht, I wad dee',[41] but there is no rancour in her memoir. Early in the second part of the *Autobiography*, dated 1891, she exemplifies her remembered happy moments in terms that are as touching as they are mildly and conventionally those of a contented wife and mother:

It was the moment after dinner when I used to run up-
stairs to see that all was well in the nursery, and then to
turn into my room on my way down again to wash my
hands, as I had a way of doing before I took up my
evening work, which was generally needlework, something
to make for the children. My bedroom had three windows
in it, one looking out upon the gardens . . . the other two
into the road. It was light enough with the lamplight
outside for all I wanted. I can see it now, the glimmer of
the outside lights, the room dark, the faint reflection in
the glasses, and my heart full of joy and peace – for what?
– for nothing – that there was no harm anywhere, the
children well above stairs and their father below. I had
few of the pleasures of society, no gaiety at all. I was
eight-and-twenty, going down-stairs as light as a feather to
the little frock I was making. My husband also gone back
for an hour or two after dinner to his work, and well –
and the bairnies well. I can feel now the sensation of that
sweet calm and ease and peace.[42]

In *Kirsteen*, however, her view of the condition of women is neither
mild nor conventional. Morally and psychologically the novel transposes
into more overtly feminist terms Margaret Maitland's defiance of world-
liness in Mrs Oliphant's first novel, *Some Passages in the Life of Mrs Margaret
Maitland* (1849). Set in a decaying patriarchal Scotland at the time of
the Napoleonic Wars, *Kirsteen* is a protest against female subservience to
male-dominated social orthodoxies. Setting and theme are well matched,
given the historian, T. C. Smout's, description of Scottish society as
'exceptionally male-dominated'.[43] Kirsteen's chief obstacle to happiness
is her ultimately murderous father, Mr Douglas of Drumcarro, a former
slave-trader addicted to the pretensions of Highland aristocracy, contemp-
tuous of women and forerunner of both Robert Louis Stevenson's Adam
Weir in *Weir of Hermiston* (1896) and George Douglas Brown's brutish
John Gourlay, in *The House with the Green Shutters* (1901). Attitudes in
Scotland 'were strongly coloured by a characterization of women' whereby
'the function of women was presented primarily in terms of supporting
their menfolk'.[44] Like Mrs Oliphant, who toiled to support her menfolk,
Kirsteen is allowed little time to herself. As the male-orientated family's
trusty drudge, she is constantly at the beck and call of her frail, complain-
ing mother, a female type amplified into the terrorized wife of Stevenson's
Lord Weir and Douglas Brown's abused Mrs Gourlay. Escaping to London from an arranged marriage to John Campbell of Glendochart, a
kindly but vain suitor old enough to be her father, Kirsteen becomes a
spectacularly successful dressmaker and woman of business, but when she

makes enough money to enable her father to buy back the Douglas lands she is still an object of disapproval in her own family. In contrast to her prosaic and opportunistic sister, Mary, who neatly scoops up Glendochart, her sister, Anne, who has eloped into the middle-class citadel of marriage, and her vulnerably sensual, spoiled sister, Jeanie, she has remained 'the stand-by of the family, she who had fled from it to find a shelter among strangers' (Chapter 38). But she has remained single, faithful to the memory of her youthful lover killed in India, and she has done man's work. She is, therefore, 'a rare and not very welcome visitor in the house she had redeemed. They all deplored the miserable way of life she had chosen, and that she had no man' (Chapter 46). Mrs Oliphant also deplores Scottish parochialism:

> 'Glasgow!' said Miss Jean with disdain. 'Glasgow has no more right to be named with London than the big lamp at Hyde Park Corner, which burns just tons of oil, with the little cruse in my kitchen. It's one of the points on which the Scots are just very foolish. They will bring forward Edinburgh, or that drookit hole of a Glasgow, as if they were fit to be compared with the real metropolis. In some ways the Scots, our country-folks, have more sense than all the rest of the world, but in others they're just ridiculous.'
>
> (Chapter 25)

A didactic novel without being strident, *Kirsteen* offers a persuasive vision of a trapped woman's winning free from the prejudices of her up-bringing – even in her escape from Drumcarro Kirsteen is morally encumbered with snobbishness about her pedigree as a Douglas – and succeeding in a bigoted world. Granting that 'a faultless style is like a faultless person, highly exasperating', as Mrs Oliphant remarks in a letter to John Blackwood,[45] her novel's slack passages do, nevertheless, provoke impatience. Yet its thesis, that a determined, principled woman can liberate herself, albeit at the terrible cost of her sexuality, works imaginatively because Mrs Oliphant establishes Kirsteen as a realistically complex character in conflict with herself as well as with the false values embodied in her extravagantly coarse father and in the stereotypically rakish Lord John. The element of caricature in both Drumcarro and Lord John enhances the sense of Kirsteen's reality: her aesthetic and moral superiorities coincide, while her resolution and fidelity make her kin both to Scott's Jeanie Deans and Catherine Carswell's Joanna Bannerman in *Open the Door!* (1920). Paradoxically, however, Mrs Oliphant conveys a sense of reality most consistently when she writes about the supernatural in stories whose didactic purpose is fundamentally theological.[46]

Her gift for writing in the supernatural genre, evident in *The Be-leaguered City* (1880) and in the over-sentimental *A Little Pilgrim in the Unseen* (1882), is best represented by the tightly executed fables recently published as *Selected Short Stories of the Supernatural.*[47] They all react against the dominant secularisms of the period. Although she drew away from the narrowness of the Free Church, she retained, like Carlyle and MacDonald, the intensely religious disposition of her background. As Henry James saw, her 'instrument was essentially a Scotch one'.[48] She believed in a loving and forgiving God and in 'the light of the perfect day' which finally receives the narrator's ghostly mother in 'The Portrait' (1885), when her injunctions from the spirit world have been brought tellingly to bear on difficult topical questions of social responsibility. 'You are asking me to believe in purgatory,' the Vicar says to 'little Mary' in 'Old Lady Mary' (1884). Mrs Oliphant takes from Catholicism and from Dante the concept of purgatory as a place of spiritual rehabilitation pre-paratory to heavenly peace. A loving deity presides over a system that allows Lady Mary to return to the living in order to make anguished amends for her vaguely arrogant belief in her own immortality and her failure to provide efficiently for her all-forgiving ward. We are not told that eventual discovery of Lady Mary's will in the secret drawer of her old Italian cabinet brings due material prosperity to little Mary, but we are told that 'everything is included in pardon and love'. The genius of the story is that, for a space, we accept this just as willingly in our suspension of disbelief as we believe in the solidity of evil portrayed by the 'Appearance' of Earl Robert Randolph as a satanic wizard in 'The Secret Chamber' (1876). The earthbound spirit of 'The Library Window', many of whose effects anticipate by two years Henry James's 'The Turn of the Screw' (1898), brings comfort to the bereft descendant of his murderers.

Evil is a metaphysical object of fact for Mrs Oliphant, with the worship of science its wickedest contemporary expression. This is the conviction at the heart of her toughest and most intricately visionary story, 'The Land of Darkness' (1887), in which the narrator travels through three nightmare cities which are like three successive infernal circles derived from Dante's *Inferno*. The freedom of the first city, where strangers are met with curses, results in the vicious disorder of unbridled selfishness; beyond the frenzy of the goldfields – materialism gone insane – the second city is inhumanly ordered; the third city, dedicated to pleasure, is the most subtly soul-destroying of all. The narrator meets 'a lady very fair and richly dressed, but with a look of great weariness in her eyes':

> 'Are you so new to this place', she said, 'and have not
> learned even yet what is the height of all misery and all
> weariness: what is worse than pain and trouble, more

dreadful than the lawless streets and the burning mines, and the torture of the great hall and the misery of the lazar-house –'

'Oh, lady!' I said, 'have you been there?'

She answered me with her eyes alone: there was no need of more. 'But pleasure is more terrible than all,' she said; and I knew in my heart that what she said was true.

The reductive, smug brutality of scientific enquiry into the human condition is horrifically exemplified in the first city by the vivisection of a man to demonstrate the working of his nerves 'as a lesson in construction and the calculation of possibilities', and in the second city by the dumping of 'bruised and broken creatures' used in experiments. In the story's prophetic conclusion the narrator meets the master of a place 'full of furnaces and clanking machinery and endless work'. Admiring his godlike powers in general and his robots in particular, the narrator asks why the master does not 'shake the universe . . . and break all our bonds'. The answer is simple: the ingenuity of science is vanity for 'God rules over all'. The case for God is brilliantly made by the irony that it is the scientist who longs to 'find Him again', the narrator who turns back to the waste land, fleeing from 'hope that is torment, and from the awful Name'.

Poets of apocalypse: James (B. V.) Thomson and John Davidson

The reality of God, which Mrs Oliphant's narrator confirms by trying to escape it, is repudiated by Scotland's two most original late nineteenth-century poets. Both James (B. V.) Thomson – he assumed the *nom de plume*, 'Bysshe Vanolis', out of admiration for Shelley and Novalis – and John Davidson were pathological outsiders who became exiles in London. Rejection of the religious upbringing they experienced during their early years in Scotland accounts, at least partly, for the darkness and austerity of their poetic visions: Thomson's mother was a disciple of the apocalyptic secessionist preacher, Edward Irving, and Davidson's father was a minister of the Evangelical Union. Thomson rejected both secular and religious utopias, and died of poverty, pessimism and dipsomania. Poems like 'Sunday up the River' and 'Sunday at Hampstead (An Idle Idyll by a Very Humble Member of the Great and Noble London Mob)' show that he had his lighter moments, but he became increasingly affected by the pessimism of the Italian poet, Giacamo Leopardi, whom he translated and whose life he told in his *Memoir of Leopardi* published in *The National Reformer* (1869–70). The major achievement of his maturity is *The City of Dreadful Night* (1874) which tells of 'a city in one aspect like a reverse picture of the New Jerusalem of *Revelation*'.[49] Davidson, taking his own life, died of poverty, neglect, fear of physical decline and that quality of despair which is akin to pride: like the threadbare figure of his poem, 'A Loafer', he 'conquered fate',[50] rejecting in the manner of his death as in his life what Hugh MacDiarmid calls 'the horrible humility of mediocrity'.[51] A God who could consign humanity to so dolorous a world would have to be 'wicked, foolish, and insane', suggests one of Thomson's shadowy speakers in section VIII of *The City of Dreadful Night*,[52] and God's non-existence is eerily proclaimed by a 'head . . . of enormous size' from the dark pulpit of the 'mighty fane' in section XIV. There is no 'living Person' to 'curse for cursing us with life'; God 'was the dark delusion of a dream':

> And now at last authentic word I bring,
> Witnessed by every dead and living thing;
>   Good tidings of great joy for you, for all:
> There is no God; no Fiend with names divine
> Made us and tortures us; if we must pine,
>   It is to satiate no Being's gall.

The 'proto-modernist'[53] Davidson outgrew his association with Yeats's 'Companions of the Cheshire Cheese'[54] in the Rhymers Club to become a lonely prophet in clamorous verse testaments which propound an idiosyncratic materialist philosophy, a kind of defiantly atheistical, Nietzschean corollary to Carlyle's hero-worship by which he made a 'vain but courageous attempt . . . to fuse the disconnected, conflicting ideas of his age into an acceptable system'.[55] 'Get thee behind me, God' is the unflinching message of his last, nobly flawed apocalyptic plays in which established religion is battered to death by hectoring, intermittently magnificent blank verse. God is 'The cowardice of men flung forth to fill / With welcome shadow an imagined void' in *Mammon and His Message* (1908).[56] In *The Triumph of Mammon* (1907), as the personification of a new order of vital materialism, Davidson's mouthpiece, Mammon, issues a summons to the present, to the body and to energy:

> I want you to begin a world with me,
> Not for posterity, but for ourselves.
> Prophets have told that there has seized on us
> An agony of labour and design
> For those that shall come after such as no age
> Endured before. I, Mammon, tell you, No!
> *We* have come after! We *are* posterity!

And time it is we had another world
Than this in which mankind excreted soul,
Sexless and used and immaterial
Upon the very threshold of the sun,
To wonder why the earth should stink so! Men
Belov'd, women adored, my people, come,
Devise with me a world worth living in –
Not for our children and our children's children,
But for our own renown, our own delight![57]

T. S. Eliot found Davidson's materialist philosophy uncongenial and
would not have liked Thomson's brand of nihilism, but he acknowledges
Davidson's 'Thirty Bob a Week' and *The City of Dreadful Night* as two
poems which influenced him in his formative years and helped him with
the 'good many dingy urban images [he had] to reveal'.[58] The brevity of
his reference to Thomson is surprising. It is tempting to surmise that
George MacDonald's *Phantastes* lies behind Parts I and V of *The Waste
Land*, if only on the basis of the image cluster that opens Chapter 10 with
'a desert region of dry sand and glittering rocks', mocking goblin-fairies,
shadow, and the 'small spring' which bursts healingly from 'the heart of
a sun-heated rock'. But, even allowing for Thomson and Eliot's sharing
the models of Dante's *Inferno* and *Purgatorio*, Thomson's whole poem
markedly prefigures Eliot's in imagery, idea and determining state of
mind.[59] The nocturnal people of Thomson's apocalyptic city 'murmur to
themselves' and brood 'maddeningly inward', each 'wrapt in his own
doom' (section I) like many of Eliot's figures in *The Waste Land*; death,
the 'One anodyne for torture and despair' (section I) is as desirable to
Thomson's alienated people as the deadening 'forgetful snow' of winter
is to Eliot's in 'The Burial of the Dead'; Thomson's narrator speaks of a
'drear pilgrimage to ruined shrines' (section II), a premonition of Eliot's
ruined Grail chapel in 'What the Thunder said'; after listening to the
desert traveller's story in section IV Thomson's protagonist sits 'forlornly
by the river-side' (section VI) as Eliot's Tiresias sits exhausted on the
shore with the desert behind him at the end of *The Waste Land*; in
Thomson's portentous streets 'The booming and the jar of ponderous
wheels' (section IX) anticipate Eliot's 'sound of horns and motors' in
'The Fire Sermon'. *The City of Dreadful Night* is most obviously a precursor and likely source of *The Waste Land* in Thomson's use of the desert
sequence of section IV to express desolation, menace, spiritual desiccation
and panic in a vision of essentially urban alienation:

As I came through the desert thus it was,
As I came through the desert: All was black
In heaven no single star, on earth no track;

A brooding hush without a stir or note,
The air so thick it clotted in my throat;
And thus for hours; then some enormous things
Swooped past with savage cries and clanking wings:
But I strode on austere;
No hope could have no fear.[60]

This City of insomniac night is, in the words of Thomson's best
informed and most sensitive commentator, the poet Tom Leonard, 'a
place of relentless thought and consciousness, where the only certainty is
the certainty of death'.[61] After the Proem the sections of *The City of
Dreadful Night* are organized in two alternating sequences. The first (eleven
odd-numbered sections in present tense) portrays and interprets the City;
the second (ten even-numbered sections in past tense) presents illustrative
episodes and characters. Thomson's narrator functions like Eliot's Tiresias
who 'although a mere spectator and not indeed a "character", is yet the
most important personage in the poem, uniting all the rest'.[62] Thomson's
narrator is similarly a unifying zone of consciousness mapped out cumu-
latively by the poem's succession of personages: the frail man in section
II who endlessly traces out the deaths of Faith, Love and Hope; the desert
traveller of section IV who splits into two selves, one apparently journey-
ing into *Liebestod* with the woman carrying the lamp of her heart, the
other left blood-stained and forlorn to 'dree his weird' (follow his destiny)
in section V; the despairing people in section VI who seek admission to
a Dantesque hell, preferring 'That positive eternity of pain / Instead of
this insufferable inane', but have no hope left with which to pay their
entrance fees; the lover keeping his grieving vigil at the deathbed of the
Lady of the images in section X; the 'isolated units' questioned in turn
by the shrouded figure in the porch of the great cathedral of section XII;
the savage, piteous creature that 'had been a man' in section XVIII who
searches for the 'long-lost broken golden thread' that will lead him out
of nightmare back to the oblivion of the womb. With the shattering of
the sworded stone angel in section XX the sphinx remains as a pointer
to the summation of Thomson's vision in the 'bronze sublimity' of the
'City's sombre Patroness and Queen' in section XXI, a transcript of 'the
pure, sad artist', Albrecht Dürer's etching, *Melencolia I* (1514). The massive, winged woman's book and compasses, the scales, hour-glass, bell,
magic-square and household keys symbolize all human endeavour, now
demoralized by 'The sense that every struggle brings defeat'. Her laurel
wreath weighs her down; she is a synthesis of paralysed human skills of
control and organization. She inspires endurance in some, but all who
look up to her gain 'renewed assurance / And confirmation of the old
despair'. The City of Dreadful Night has conquered even her 'indomitable will'. The tense is present; this is now.

Like *King Lear* and Beckett's *Endgame*, Thomson's great poem of despair uplifts by the poetic sufficiency of its imagery of 'the promised end'. For the initiate Thomson addresses in the Proem the horror is mitigated by the art which gives 'some sense of power and passion' in its shaping of 'Our woe in living words howe'er uncouth'. John Davidson, too, is full of woe and no subtle theologian, but his spiritual daring, reminiscent of the mad grandeur of Melville's solipsistic Ahab, must bring special pleasure to anyone who has suffered from the cruder intimidations of Scottish Calvinism. When Mammon says 'I'll carve the world / In my own image' (*Mammon and His Message*)[63] he echoes the iconoclastic son's urgent words to his dying mother in the superbly conceived 'A Woman and Her Son' ('I am God. I shall create / The heaven of your desires') and foreshadows the megalomania of *The Testament of John Davidson* (1908) in which the hero is Davidson himself. The most winning poetry of this last testament is its 'Epilogue – The Last Journey', a premonition of Davidson's suicidal exit from the world he saw as 'A sink and overflow of decadence / With slimy rags and greasy fragments stopped' (*Mammon and His Message*)[64] into the sea off Penzance:

> My feet are heavy now, but on I go,
>   My head erect beneath the tragic years.
> The way is steep, but I would have it so;
>   And dusty, but I lay the dust with tears,
> Though none can see me weep: alone I climb
> The rugged path that leads me out of time –
>   Out of time and out of all,
>   Singing yet in sun and rain,
>   'Heel and toe from dawn to dusk,
>   Round the world and home again'.

Blank verse enabled Davidson to develop his eccentric ideas in grandiose dramatic if untheatrical form, but his poetic talent is best represented by the imitation ballads and eclogues which brought him lamentably short-lived reputation and modest financial reward, particularly the poems collected in *Fleet Street Eclogues* (1893), *Ballads and Songs* (1894) and *New Ballads* (1897). Understandably, 'A Runnable Stag' from *Holiday and Other Poems* (1906) has become an anthology piece. Its immediate attraction is its rhythmic evocation of the chase but the poem is also Davidson's personal allegory, depicting the fate of a splendid, solitary creature harried to suicide by 300 sportsmen out for fun from 'a stag of warrant'. The animal has his 'hoofs on fire, his horns like flame'; the sportsmen have their racketing 'tally-ho' jargon. At last the hunters are cheated of their prey while, under the sea, their superior, the stag, is glorified by its 'jewelled bed', free from what Burns calls 'Tyrannic man's dominion' in 'Now westlin winds'.

Davidson's feeling for disadvantaged city people is evident in 'Thirty Bob a Week', a poem in the social protest tradition of Thomas Hood's 'The Song of the Shirt' and Thomson's 'Low Life', and in the pathos of 'A Loafer':

> I move from eastern wretchedness
>   Through Fleet Street and the Strand;
> And as the pleasant people press
>   I touch them softly with my hand,
> Perhaps to know that still I go
>   Alive about a living land.

He understands the quality of working-class life in the suburbs where 'the whetted fangs of change' have made shoddy terraces 'In gaudy yellow brick and red, / With rooting pipes, like creepers rank' ('A Northern Suburb'). He can bring awake the detail of a London cityscape – huddled wharfs, barges at anchor, figureheads that are 'bosoms thrown / Against the storm' – under 'blots of faintest bronze / The stains of daybreak' in 'The Thames Embankment', and make scientific appraisal of water-crystals a panegyric to snow ('Snow'). He exposes religious and anti-religious bigotry in 'A Woman and Her Son', sexual bigotry in 'A Ballad of a Nun', and artistic bigotry in 'A Ballad of a Poet Born'. Davidson's achievement 'in "Thirty Bob a Week", in a few lyrics, and in *Fleet Street and Other Poems* (1909) takes his work . . . into the realm of major poetry'.[65] Like Thomson's his verse abjures mere polish and is often rough as well as unpredictable. The aesthetic roughness of both poets is inseparable from their work's peculiar strengths.

Notes

1. Walter E. Houghton, *The Victorian Frame of Mind 1830–1870* (New Haven, 1957), p. 261.

2. J. A. Froude, *Thomas Carlyle: A History of His Life in London, 1834–1881*, 2 vols (London, 1885), I, p. 54.

3. John O. Hayden, *Scott: The Critical Heritage* (London, 1970), p. 442.

4. Maurice Lindsay, 'Introduction' to *John Davidson: A Selection of His Poems*, ed. with an introduction by Maurice Lindsay, Preface by T. S. Eliot, with an essay by Hugh MacDiarmid (London, 1961), p. 20.

5. Jules Paul Seigel, *Thomas Carlyle: The Critical Heritage* (London, 1971), p. 283.

6. Charles Eliot Norton (ed.), *Letters of Thomas Carlyle: 1826–1836* (London, 1889), p. 378.

7. Letter to John Sterling, 1 February 1837, in Trudy Bliss (ed.), *Jane Welsh Carlyle: A Selection of Her Letters* (London, 1959), p. 60.

8. See C. F. Harrold, 'The Nature of Carlyle's Calvinism', *Studies in Philology*, XXXIII (1936), pp. 475–86.

9. Froude quotes Carlyle's description of his 'conversion' or 'new birth', when he 'authentically took the Devil by the nose': 'Nothing in "Sartor Resartus" . . . is fact; symbolical myth all, except that of the incident in the Rue St. Thomas de l'Enfer, which occurred quite literally to myself in Leith Walk, during three weeks of total sleeplessness, in which almost my one solace was that of a daily bathe on the sands between Leith and Portobello. Incident was as I went down; coming up I generally felt refreshed for the hour. I remember it well, and could go straight to about the place.' See J. A. Froude, *Thomas Carlyle: A History of the First Forty Years of His Life 1795–1835*, 2 vols (London, 1882), I, p. 101.

10. A favourite word of Carlyle's from Hebrew *Topheth*, an Old Testament term of uncertain etymology and meaning. Used by Milton as another name for Gehenna or for Hinnom, the valley near Jerusalem where some of the Israelites sacrificed their children to Moloch. By association a place of abomination where fires were burned perpetually to prevent pestilence, hence a kind of hell.

11. Albert J. LaValley, *Carlyle and the Idea of the Modern* (New Haven and London, 1968), pp. 239–40.

12. Ian Campbell, *Thomas Carlyle* (London, 1974), p. 193.

13. Louis Cazamian, *Carlyle*, trans. E. K. Brown (New York, 1932), p. 286.

14. George MacDonald, *A Dish of Orts* (London, 1893), pp. 24–5.

15. George MacDonald, 'The Imagination: Its Functions and Its Culture', *Orts* (London, 1882), p. 2.

16. Ibid.

17. Phantastes is the name of a character who represents fancy in *The Purple Island* (1633), an allegorical poem by Phineas Fletcher (1582–1650). MacDonald misquotes two lines from this poem on his title page, giving 'Phantastes from "their fount" all shapes deriving' instead of Fletcher's 'Phantastes from the first all shapes deriving'. Presumably the substituted words are meant to stress that the shapes Phantastes meets on his journey come from the original, divine source. The name of MacDonald's hero, Anodos, 'is presumably Greek, meaning "pathless"' – see Robert Lee Wolff, *The Golden Key: A Study of the Fiction of George MacDonald* (New Haven, 1961), p. 47 – but also implying 'a way back'.

18. See Raphael B. Shaberman, *George MacDonald: A Bibliographical Study* (Winchester and Detroit, 1990), pp. 119–22.

19. W. H. Auden, 'Introduction', *The Visionary Novels of George MacDonald*, ed. Anne Fremantle (New York, 1954), p. vii.

20. G. K. Chesterton, 'George MacDonald', *The Daily News* (London), 23 September 1905, p. 6.

21. C. S. Lewis, *George MacDonald: An Anthology* (London, 1946), p. 20.

22. Ibid., p. 17.

23. John Malcolm Bulloch, *A Centennial Bibliography of George MacDonald* (Aberdeen, 1925), p. 16.

24. Richard H. Reis, *George MacDonald* (New York, 1972), p. 24.

25. Lewis, *An Anthology*, p. 17.

26. Greville MacDonald, introduction to the 'Everyman' edition (London, 1914). See Shaberman, *A Bibliographical Study*, p. 61.

27. See Greville MacDonald, *George MacDonald and His Wife* (London, 1924), p. 321.

28. William Raeper, *George MacDonald* (Tring, 1987), p. 383.

29. For a discussion of the 'Caledonian antisyzygy' see Chapter 1, p. 14.

30. George MacDonald, *Weighed and Wanting*, 3 vols (London, 1882), I, p. 47.

31. Raeper, *George MacDonald*, p. 242.

32. Chesterton, 'George MacDonald'.

33. For a systematically Freudian reading of MacDonald see Wolff, *The Golden Key*.

34. Auden, 'Introduction' to *The Visionary Novels*, ed. Fremantle, p. vi.

35. David S. Robb, *George MacDonald* (Edinburgh, 1987), p. 86.

36. Letter to Henry Sutton, 14 March 1897, in *An Expression of Character: The Letters of George MacDonald*, ed. Glenn Edward Sadler (Grand Rapids, Michigan, 1994), pp. 366–7.

37. See Simone Weil, *Waiting for God*, trans. Emma Craufurd (New York, 1951).

38. Q. D. Leavis, 'Introduction' to Mrs Oliphant, *Miss Marjoribanks* (London, 1969), p. 1.

39. A modern edition is *The Autobiography of Margaret Oliphant: The Complete Text*, ed. and introduced by Elisabeth Jay (Oxford, 1990).

40. Mrs M. O. W. Oliphant, *The Autobiography and Letters of Mrs M. O. W. Oliphant*, arranged and ed. Mrs Harry Coghill, 3rd edn, rev. (Edinburgh and London, 1899), p. 22.

41. Ibid., p. 2.

42. Ibid., pp. 42–3.

43. T. C. Smout, *A Century of the Scottish People 1830–1950* (New Haven and London, 1986), p. 292.

44. Jenni Calder, 'Heroes and Hero-makers: Women in Nineteenth-Century Scottish Fiction', in *The History of Scottish Literature*, 4 vols, III, *The Nineteenth Century*, ed. Douglas Gifford (Aberdeen, 1988), pp. 261–73 [264].

45. Mrs M. O. W. Oliphant, *The Autobiography and Letters*, p. 170.

46. See Vineta Colby and Robert A. Colby, *The Equivocal Virtue: Mrs Oliphant and the Victorian Literary Market Place* (Archon, 1966), p. 87.

47. Margaret Oliphant, *Selected Short Stories of the Supernatural*, ed. Margaret K. Gray (Edinburgh, 1985).

48. Henry James, 'London, August 1897', *Harper's Weekly*, XLI (21 August 1897), p. 834; reprinted in *Literary Criticism: Essays on Literature; American Writers; English Writers* (New York, 1984), p. 1413.

49. Tom Leonard, *Places of the Mind: The Life and Work of James Thomson (B. V.)* (London, 1993), p. 144.

50. Quotations of Davidson's poems are taken from *The Poems of John Davidson*, ed. Andrew Turnbull, 2 vols (Edinburgh and London, 1973). Extracts from his plays are quoted from Lindsay (ed.), *John Davidson: A Selection of His Poems*.

51. Hugh MacDiarmid, 'John Davidson: Influences and Influence', in Lindsay (ed.), *John Davidson: A Selection of His Poems*, p. 52.

52. Thomson expresses a similar point of view in his notebook for 15 May 1873: 'There may or may not be beings superior to us. But I cannot think so ill of any possible supreme being as to accuse him of the guilt and folly of the voluntary creation of such a world and of such lives as ours. I cannot accuse a possible Devil of this, much less a possible God.' See James Thomson, *Poems, Essays, and Fragments*, ed. J. M. Robertson (London, 1892), p. 262.

53. Douglas Dunn, *The Faber Book of Twentieth-Century Scottish Poetry* (London, 1992), p. xvii.

54. W. B. Yeats, 'The Grey Rock'. The Cheshire Cheese is the tavern in Fleet Street where a group of poets called The Rhymers Club met between 1891 and 1894. The most notable members of the group were its founder, Ernest Rhys, Yeats, Richard Le Gallienne, Ernest Dowson, Lionel Johnson, Arthur Symons and John Davidson.

55. J. Benjamin Townsend, *John Davidson: Poet of Armageddon* (New Haven, 1961), p. 495.

56. Lindsay (ed.), *John Davidson: A Selection of His Poems*, p. 172.

57. Ibid., pp. 166–7.

58. T. S. Eliot, 'Preface' to Lindsay (ed.), *John Davidson: A Selection of His Poems*. Oddly, there is no reference to either Davidson or Thomson in the relevant period of Eliot's correspondence. See *The Letters of T. S. Eliot, Volume 1 1898–1922*, ed. Valerie Eliot (London, 1988).

59. Eliot's 'three districts' in 'Little Gidding', II echo the 'three close lanes' of Thomson's *The City of Dreadful Night*, section XVIII, and his meeting with 'a familiar compound ghost' is strongly reminiscent of Thomson's encounter with the 'wounded creature' that 'had been a man'. See T. S. Eliot, *The Complete Poems and Plays* (London, 1969), p. 193. For further discussion of the relation between Thomson and Eliot see Robert Crawford, *The Savage and the City in the Work of T. S. Eliot* (Oxford, 1987), Chapter 2.

60. Quotations from *The City of Dreadful Night* are taken from James Thomson, *The City of Dreadful Night*, introduced by Edwin Morgan (Edinburgh, 1993).

61. Leonard, *Places of the Mind*, p. 146.

62. T. S. Eliot, 'Notes on the *Waste Land*', *The Complete Poems and Plays*, p. 78.

63. Lindsay (ed.), *John Davidson: A Selection of His Poems*, p. 173.

64. Ibid., p. 179.

65. Mary O'Connor, *John Davidson* (Edinburgh, 1987), p. 134.

Chapter 8

Robert Louis Stevenson and the War in the Members

The figure, RLS: from proto-hippy to Tusitala

Summing up Robert Louis Stevenson's career, his friend, Henry James, concludes: 'It has been his fortune (whether or not the greatest that can befall a man of letters) to have had to consent to become, by a process not purely mystic and not wholly untraceable – what shall we call it? – a Figure.'[1] A specialist in fable, Stevenson became in his lifetime the most fabulous of Victorian writers, as colourful a figure in the nineteenth century as Ernest Hemingway and Alexander Solzhenitsyn in the twentieth. The year before he died another friend, Edmund Gosse, wrote to him in Samoa:

> . . . the gossip-columns of the newspapers pullulate with
> gossip about you that cannot be true, such as: 'All our
> readers will rejoice to learn that the aged fictionist L R
> [*sic*] Stevenson has ascended the throne of Tahiti of which
> island he is now a native' . . . Since Byron was in Greece,
> nothing has appealed to the ordinary literary man as so
> picturesque as that you should be in the South Seas.[2]

The sequence of events by which Stevenson became the legendary figure known as RLS began with a sickly childhood. Often invalided to 'the land of counterpane' by the bronchial problems that plagued him all his life, he soon learned to live in his imagination in ways recalled in the poems of *A Child's Garden of Verses* (1885). As a reluctant student first of engineering then of law, he became what Anthony Burgess calls 'a proto-hippy'[3] in a velvet coat, frequenting the dives of old Edinburgh, drinking and whoring among the alleys and chimney-pots. He learned an avant-garde respect for women as much from prostitutes as from his gentle mother, Margaret, née Balfour, and his devoted, influential nurse, Alison

Cunningham, whom he called Cummy, 'the angel of my infant life'.[4] When he escaped from the study of engineering by which his father, Thomas, a lighthouse engineer and Commissioner of Northern Lights, hoped he would find a profession, he ostensibly embarked on an alternative career in law. Passing his final exams for admission to the Bar, he celebrated the success by driving flamboyantly through Edinburgh in an open carriage, hailing all who cared to notice him, and by promptly abandoning law for good. ('Give me', he says in 1881's *Virginibus Puerisque*, 'the young man who has brains enough to make a fool of himself.') His father was disappointed and both parents were deeply hurt by his turning agnostic, yet they recognized his true vocation and supported him through his early efforts to succeed as a writer, through his moves from Scotland to France and England in search of a healthy climate, and even in America where in May 1880 in San Francisco he married his resourceful lover, Fanny Vandegrift Osbourne, an American born in Indianapolis, ten years his senior and the divorced mother of two surviving children, Lloyd and Belle. The quest for a benign environment took him to Strathpeffer, Davos Platz in Switzerland, Pitlochry, Braemar, Hyères, Bournemouth, Saranac Lake in the Adirondack Mountains and to the Pacific. He sampled the Marquesas, Fakarava, Tahiti and Hawaii, but finally bought 400 acres of land on the slopes of Mount Vaea near Apia on the island of Upolu in Samoa and built his last home, Vailima ('Five streams'). To the watching world he had become as exotic as a character from his own *Treasure Island*.

In the balance of life and art, commentators sometimes find the figure more vivid and the life more commanding than the work: 'His genius lay in who and what he was, rather than in the products of his pen.'[5] For others Stevenson the man 'remains so lovable, a creature of innocence and integrity at odds with convention, the footloose romantic unencumbered with aesthetic dogma or imperialist preachiness, that we are ready to forgive him *Prince Otto*, *St Ives* or the more twaddling passages of *Travels With a Donkey*'.[6] The story of Stevenson's triumph over chronic bronchial illness to become a distinguished Samoan – 'Tusitala', or 'teller of tales' – and international best-seller, is certainly that of a man with a genius for life against often fearful odds; but it is unlikely that it would have attracted so much notice without the products of his pen, even if products of the highest calibre are relatively few in proportion to the size of an output heroically voluminous for a man who died three weeks after his forty-fourth birthday. The fashion started by his friend, Sidney Colvin, of regarding the unfinished *Weir of Hermiston* (1896) as the best of Stevenson[7] is symptomatic of a common perception that none of the finished works quite measures up to the legendary figure of the man. Certainly, the *Weir* fragment is rich in promising material: the dark character of the Lord Justice-Clerk ascending 'the great, bare staircase of his duty' (Chapter 2),

alien to his timorous wife and renegade son; the sensual and moral grandeur of Kirstie Elliott; the treachery of Frank Innes and the strong presence of the Scottish landscape. Stevenson did write to Colvin, 'I expect
The Justice-Clerk to be my masterpiece';[8] but, given the completed works,
it is niggardly to rest the critical case on a might-have-been.

The making of a stylist

Nothing was lost on Stevenson even in the professions he tried and
rejected. As an apprentice lighthouse engineer, at least in his father's expectation, he accompanied Thomas Stevenson in 1870 to the Isle of Erraid
off the Ross of Mull, acquiring a setting for his ballad-like tale of the
supernatural, 'The Merry Men' (1882), and first-hand knowledge of the
island on which David Balfour thinks himself marooned in *Kidnapped*
(1886), unaware that he can walk across to Mull at low tide. From his
knowledge of law and lawyers he makes credible minor characters such
as William Lawson, the Procurator-Fiscal with his incontinent quoting of
law Latin in *Deacon Brodie or The Double Life* (1880), the 'shrewd, ruddy,
kindly, consequential' Mr Rankeillor in *Kidnapped*, and in *Catriona* (1893)
Charles Stewart the Writer and the Lord Advocate Prestongrange who in
scale, temper and relationship to David Balfour foreshadows the monstrous Adam Weir and his treatment of his son, Archie, in *Weir of Hermiston*.
He had the true writer's eye for detail and worked so assiduously at style
that Joseph Conrad – who never wrote a book as popular as *Treasure
Island* or *Kidnapped* – could say, 'When it comes to popularity I stand
much nearer the public mind than Stevenson, who was super-literary, a
conscious virtuoso of style.'[9] A letter to his friend Mrs Frances Sitwell in
1873 shows the young Stevenson's sensitivity to style even in the informal
context of affectionate correspondence:

> I hope you don't dislike reading bad style like this as
> much as I do writing it: it hurts me when neither words
> nor clauses fall into their places, much as it would hurt
> you to sing when you had a bad cold and your voice
> deceived you and missed every other note. I do feel so
> inclined to break the pen and write no more.[10]

Most early products of his pen, and some later ones, offer more elegance than thematic meat. Complete professionalism and stylistic accom-
plishment are his only consistencies. Edmund Gosse thought of him as
resembling Anatole France, the Anglo-Irish novelist George Moore, and

Laurence Sterne in being 'a *pure* writer'.[11] If plotting creaks as it does in
The Master of Ballantrae (1888) or loses direction as in *Catriona*, the quality
of the writing is never in serious doubt, but there is often paucity of
content. Profoundly influenced by Stevenson in his youth, John Buchan
admits, 'His fastidiousness came to repel me.'[12] Even so, Compton Mackenzie's impatience with Stevenson's detractors is soundly based on appreciation of Stevenson's craftsmanly way with language: 'None of those
who profess to dispose of Stevenson is capable of handling the English
language with a fraction of his control. That such perfect control should
parody itself occasionally was inevitable whenever manner was called
upon to conceal lack of matter.'[13] To read any writer whole is to become
aware of an *oeuvre* with its peculiar system of consiliences and reverbera-
tions. It is also to experience, in the curving of one mind and its art,
literature as process rather than product. Stevenson's process was an oscil-
lation between professional writing, which can be insipid, and writing to
a thematic imperative, still as the professional, but fired. Apart from the
pleasure of learning as much as possible about the RLS figure the chief
delight of reading him entire is coming upon felicities beyond *Treasure
Island*, *A Child's Garden of Verses* and *Kidnapped*, and the discovery that
reference to the characteristics of a 'Jekyll and Hyde' alludes to a meticulously wrought novella whose excellence as literary art has too often been
underestimated because of the deceptive simplicity of its idea. For those
in search of Stevenson the figure there is biographical interest in *The
Amateur Emigrant* (1895), in which he describes his first journey to America
in 1879, and in *The Silverado Squatters* (1883), his memoir of life with
Fanny in their shack in a disused Californian mining camp, but there are
only intermittent satisfactions in these earlier works which, despite sharp
observation and stylistic polish, seldom advance beyond the belletristic.
By 1880 he was aware of the shortcomings of his travel books. When
Sidney Colvin criticized *The Amateur Emigrant* Stevenson wrote to him:
'My sympathies and interests are changed. There shall be no more travel
books for me. I care for nothing but the moral and the dramatic.'[14]

The pursuit of style made him a great phrase-maker. No book of
quotations would be complete without a selection from *Virginibus Puerisque*
in which he dispenses mischievous *aperçus* in the manner of a renegade
dominie. The chapter entitled 'El Dorado' yields his most famous
dictum: 'To travel hopefully is a better thing than to arrive, and the true
success is to labour.' Though he frequently doubted his own prospect
of success he was aware of the labour required to become a writer. He
was often depressed. 'I am, unhappily, off my style, and can do nothing
well,' he writes to Mrs Sitwell on 12 September 1873,[15] but reports a
slight improvement on 4 October: 'I made a little more out of my work
than I have made for a long while back: though even now I cannot make
things fall into sentences – they only sprawl over the paper in bald orphan

clauses.'[16] On 30 Novermber he is ready to quit: 'I have given up all hope, all fancy rather, of making literature my hold: I see that I have not capacity enough.'[17] Yet the following May he is telling Mrs Sitwell that writing is his sole pleasure and the best way of forgetting his physical insecurity:

> my body is most decrepit, and I can just manage to be
> cheery and tread down hypochondria under foot by work.
> I lead such a funny life, utterly without interest or
> pleasure outside of my work: nothing, indeed, but work
> all day long, except a short walk alone on the cold hills,
> and meals, and a couple of pipes with my father in the
> evening. It is surprising how it suits me, and how happy I
> keep.[18]

In 1887, looking back on his early days, he recalls training himself systematically to become an author:

> All through my boyhood and youth, I was known and
> pointed out for the pattern of an idler; and yet I was
> always busy on my own private end, which was to learn
> to write. I always kept two books in my pocket, one to
> read, one to write in. As I walked, my mind was busy
> fitting what I saw with appropriate words; when I sat by
> the roadside, I would either read, or a pencil and a penny
> version-book would be in my hand, to note down the
> features of the scene or commemorate some halting
> stanzas. Thus I lived with words. And what I thus wrote
> was for no ulterior use, it was written consciously for
> practice. It was not so much that I wished to be an
> author (though I wished that too) as that I had vowed
> that I would learn to write. That was a proficiency that
> tempted me; and I practised to acquire it, as men learn to
> whittle, in a wager with myself.[19]

At a period when literature was unsure of its own function in a world that was being redefined by industrialization, Darwin, the assorted mechanisms anathematized by Carlyle and the effects of the colonial enterprise, the most reliable way into publication for a new writer was the essay. This suited Stevenson, for although his career is one of unremitting dedication to writing he is almost as shortwinded artistically as he was physically. He had bursts of enthusiasm for drama, for playing the flageolet, and for Pacific politics, which helped him to move imaginatively from Scotland's past into the present life of the South Seas. He excels in the epigrammatic pronouncement, the short poem and the short story. Billy Bones, Blind Pew, the 'Admiral Benbow', Long John Silver and Ben Gunn will always come alive for readers who care nothing for the style of *Treasure Island* or go any further with RLS. The house of Shaws, Ebenezer Balfour and Alan Breck Stewart deserve almost as much of a life beyond the pages of *Kidnapped*; but among Stevenson's full-length novels only *Kidnapped* sustains its energy and art on the same level as 'Thrawn Janet' (1881), 'Markheim' (1885), 'The Suicide Club' in *New Arabian Nights* (1882), *The Strange Case of Dr Jekyll and Mr Hyde* (1886), *The Beach of Falesá* (1892) and *The Ebb-Tide* (1894), which is the best of his collaborations with his stepson, Lloyd Osbourne. If not quite a miniaturist, his true strength is the compactness of moral fable, and he wrote nothing more perfect than 'The House of Eld', posthumously published in the collection of *Fables* (1924). A precursor of the moralistic symbolic fantasies of George MacDonald, the story is a biblically cadenced parable of Scottish religious sado-masochism and personal guilt which implicitly acknowledges the violence done to Stevenson's parents by his renunciation of the church. When Jack kills the wizard responsible for shackling children at birth, he kills in turn the apparitions of his uncle, his father and his mother. He is in the right, for as his uncle and father fall to the ground, 'a little bloodless white thing fled from the room', a consummately expressive image of evil that holds its own in the imagination with Ridley Scott and James Cameron's gruesome special effects in their *Alien* films. But when Jack goes home he finds 'the uncle smitten on the head, and his father pierced through the heart, and his mother cloven through the midst. And he sat in the lone house and wept beside the bodies.'[20] The shackles that have fallen from the right ankles of his countrymen have become fastened to the left. So even when the cause is just, guilt is inevitable, the past inescapable, and who is to say which shackle is preferable? The story is an example of the dualism that preoccupied Stevenson. It is hardly surprising that Henry James, a connoisseur of ambiguity, should have been so drawn to the work of his Scottish friend.

Both *An Inland Voyage* (1878) and *Travels with a Donkey in the Cevennes* (1879) are essentially collections of stylish essays which demonstrate that style alone is not sufficient. In 1876 Stevenson and his friend, Walter Simpson, paddled their two canoes, 'Arethusa' and 'Cigarette', from the river Scheldt at Antwerp by canals and the river Oise to the valley of the Loing. Stevenson's account of the journey includes observations on Belgian food, the psychological effects of spectating, the pleasures of maps and the silent preaching of cathedrals:

> I could never fathom how a man dares to lift up his voice
> to preach in a cathedral. What is he to say that will not
> be an anti-climax? For though I have heard a considerable

variety of sermons, I never yet heard one that was so expressive as a cathedral. 'Tis the best preacher itself, and preaches day and night; not only telling you of man's art and aspirations in the past, but convicting your own soul of ardent sympathies; or rather, like all good preachers, it sets you preaching to yourself, – and every man is his own doctor of divinity in the last resort.[21]

There are sketches of inns along the route and of appealing characters like M. Bazin, the connubial innkeeper of La Fère, and M. de Vauversin, a prodigiously versatile strolling player described in the chapter 'Précy and the Marionettes'. 'It was agreeable on the river,' Stevenson says, echoing Huckleberry Finn's tribute to life on a raft, but neither the journey nor Stevenson's revealed personality is substantial enough to make the book more than merely agreeable. The same may be said about *Travels with a Donkey* in which Stevenson's frustration with the refractory donkey, Modestine, becomes a tedious refrain – though his parting from her is touching – and the narrative comes to life only when he reaches Pont de Montvert in the country of the Camisards, the French equivalent of the Scottish Covenanters. Beyond the religious parallel Stevenson's interest is caught by the revenge of 'Spirit Séguier' on François de Langlade du Châyla who survived persecution for his faith in China to become a persecutor in France. A brisk account of violent action leads to the description of du Châyla, 'A poor, brave, besotted, hateful man, who had done his duty resolutely according to his light both in the Cevennes and in China',[22] thus hinting at Stevenson's later studies of contrary moral qualities in human character.

The moralist

The enquiring moralist is evident even in the heavy-handed plays he wrote with William Ernest Henley and with Fanny Stevenson. According to Lloyd Osbourne, Stevenson embarked 'with his underlying Scotch caution'[23] on the collaboration with Henley, whose purpose was to make them both rich by effecting a revolution in British drama. Stevenson had been attracted to drama since the age of six when an aunt presented him with a toy theatre, and his projection of himself as a romantic bohemian was itself a theatrical performance sustained throughout his life. 'I wish that life was an opera,' he wrote to his mother from Frankfurt in August 1872, adding, 'I should like to *live* in one.'[24] Success in creating theatre from the materials of his own life was not matched by success as a dramatist for the stage. The plays, in Ian Bell's opinion:

... are perhaps the least Stevensonian of the works to
which Louis's name is attached ... Their authors'
ignorance of the stage is obvious; the dialogue is almost
unrelievedly risible; the plots are hackneyed. *Brodie* is the
worst sort of melodramatic amateur psychology; *Macaire* is
Louis's love for French wit gone haywire; *Guinea* says
something about slavery, but not much. All swarm with
dull prose, as though woodworm had been let loose on
the rickety structure of Victorian drama.[25]

This is fair to the plays as texts for the theatre, but fails to notice that,
with the exception of *Macaire* (1885) – a silly mixture of farce and melodrama set in the confusions of a French country wedding – the plays
touch on complexities of character from which Stevenson's best subjects
come. Obscure motivation undermines the attempt of *Deacon Brodie or
The Double Life* to portray the psychological subtleties of the divided self,
but the play is a clear precursor of *The Strange Case of Dr Jekyll and Mr
Hyde*. Deacon of the Incorporation of Edinburgh Wrights by day and
housebreaker by night, Brodie reveals his doubleness as he prepares to
exit from respectability through his bedroom window into his darker,
truer self:

> On with the new coat and into the new life! Down with
> the Deacon and up with the robber! ... If we were as
> good as we seem, what would the world be! ... Shall a
> man not have half a life of his own? ... (*Addressing the
> bed.*) Lie there, Deacon! sleep and be well tomorrow. As
> for me, I'm a man once more till morning. (*Gets out of
> the window.*)
>
> (Tableau I, ix)

Beau Austin (1884), written in four days, depicts the change of heart in
an ageing roué, and *Admiral Guinea* (1884) the victory of true feeling over
the malevolence of a sinful past represented by Blind Pew – to be used
again in *Treasure Island* – and the guilt of the Admiral whose recoil from
his own life as a slave-trader determines him to shield his daughter from
evil by denying her the risk of love. Fortunately for everyone the daughter, Arethusa's, view of the need to accept the hazards of a mixed world
prevails over the Admiral's life-denying guilt:

> Let my life ... flow like common lives, each pain
> rewarded with some pleasure, each pleasure linked with
> some pain: nothing pure whether for good or evil: and

my husband, like myself and all the rest of us, only a
poor, kind-hearted sinner, striving for the better part.

(III, i)

The Hanging Judge (1887), a turgid collaboration between Stevenson and
his wife, portrays two men with double lives in the characters of Justice
Harlowe, who exploits his position as a judge to protect his wife from the
shame of bigamy by condemning her first husband to the gallows, and
Malone, a gentleman gone to seed, whose moral nature cannot bear the
Judge's abuse of power.

The Sea Cook, or *Treasure Island* as it was renamed at the suggestion of
the proprietor of *Young Folks* magazine in which it was serialized from
July 1881 to June 1882, was based not on a moral idea but on a map
which Stevenson devised with Lloyd Osbourne. Like all great books for
the young the novel infuses the appeal to youth with adult vision. Lloyd
Osbourne says that Stevenson spoke of his belief that children should be
helped to face reality:

> A child should early gain some perception of what the
> world really is like – its baseness, its treacheries, its thinly
> veneered brutalities; he should learn to judge people, and
> discount human frailty and weakness, and be in some
> degree prepared and armed for taking his part later in life.
> I have no patience with this fairy-tale training that makes
> ignorance a virtue.[26]

As much a tale of initiation as *The Adventures of Huckleberry Finn*, though
without Twain's specific satire, *Treasure Island* uses the search for hidden
treasure to show Jim Hawkins the impurities of a world where romantic
expectation is constantly menaced by the likes of Blind Pew, Long John
Silver and Israel Hands, with Ben Gunn the best *deus ex machina* life can
offer. Even Billy Bones's 'eternal song' in Chapter One, 'Fifteen men on
the dead man's chest', probably alludes to the pirate, Edward Teach's,
lingering revenge on a mutinous crew.[27] The villainous Silver's hypnotic
attraction is the toughest part of Jim's education. Stevenson uses the
moral issue in 'A Fable: The Persons of the Tale' in a dialogue worthy
of John Fowles or Dennis Potter. Two of his puppets, Silver and Captain
Smollett, discuss the story in which they find themselves. Smollett is
bewildered, Silver cocky:

> What I know is this: if there is sich a thing as a Author,
> I'm his favourite chara'ter. He does me fathoms better'n
> he does you – fathoms, he does. And he likes doing me.
> He keeps me on deck mostly all the time, crutch and all;

and he leaves you measling in the hold, where nobody
can't see you, nor wants to, and you may lay to that! If
there is a Author, by thunder, but he's on my side, and
you may lay to it![28]

In reply, Captain Smollett admits his own unattractiveness – 'I'm not a
very popular man at home' – but insists: 'I know the Author's on the side
of good; he tells me so, it runs out of his pen as he writes.' The worthy
Captain is right, of course; the author is on the side of good but, like
Ben Jonson and most of us, enjoys a clever rogue. Despite the perverse
appeal of the satanic James Durie in *The Master of Ballantrae*, Stevenson
is not of the Devil's party; but, like Burns and Hogg, he is fascinated by
the opposition.

Alan Breck Stewart is to David Balfour as Long John Silver is to Jim
Hawkins. Stevenson's most polished novel on Scottish themes, and a
dramatic artistic recovery from the vagaries of *Prince Otto* and his toy
kingdom, *Kidnapped* is set against the background of the failure of the
1745 Jacobite rebellion when 'the men of the clans were broken at Culloden, and the good cause went down'. Crossing the Isle of Mull David
sees the humiliations of the Highlanders, most visible in their dress:

> The Highland dress being forbidden by law since the
> rebellion, and the people condemned to the Lowland
> habit, which they much disliked, it was strange to see the
> variety of their array. Some went bare, only for a hanging
> cloak or a great coat, and carried their trousers on their
> backs like a useless burthen; some had made an imitation
> of the tartan with little parti-coloured stripes patched
> together like an old wife's quilt; others, again, still wore
> the Highland philabeg, but by putting a few stitches
> between the legs, transformed it into a pair of trousers like
> a Dutchman's. All those makeshifts were condemned and
> punished, for the law was harshly applied, in hopes to
> break up the clan spirit.
>
> (Chapter 15)

David is dropped into history like Scott's Edward Waverley, Quentin
Durward and Frank Osbaldistone. David's journey, like those of Edward
Waverley and Jim Hawkins, is one of initiation. Like Waverley, David is
discovering his country as he finds himself. Cheated of his inheritance by
his miserly, homicidal uncle, he is refined by experience into the young
man who reclaims it at the end of the novel. Experience is the tangle of
clan hatred, conflicting loyalties and personal danger centred on the Appin
murder of Colin Campbell of Glenure, the 'Red Fox', after the forfeiture

of Stewart and Cameron land to the Campbells. Superficially a romance, the book is historically accurate and psychologically realistic. Jacobite glamour is undercut by tipsy toasts and maudlin Gaelic songs in the house of Hector Maclean and by hot-headed egotism in Alan Breck, Robin Oig (son of Rob Roy Macgregor) and Cluny Macpherson. Stevenson would have known the Introduction to *Redgauntlet*, where Scott refers to 'McPherson of Cluny, chief of the clan Vourich, whom the Chevalier had left behind at his departure from Scotland in 1746, and who remained during ten years of proscription and danger, skulking from place to place in the Highlands, and maintaining an uninterrupted correspondence between Charles and his friends'. Scott also writes of the Young Pretender's decline from being 'the leader of a race of pristine valour' into 'those humiliating habits of intoxication, in which the meanest mortals seek to drown the recollection of their disappointments and miseries'. From Cluny David receives unromantic information about Prince Charlie:

> I gathered the Prince was a gracious, spirited boy, like the
> son of a race of polite kings, but not so wise as Solomon.
> I gathered, too, that while he was in the Cage [Cluny's
> lair], he was often drunk; so the fault that has since, by all
> accounts, made such a wreck of him, had even then
> begun to show itself.
>
> (Chapter 23)

The 'good cause' had its decadence; but if Alan Breck's vanity can make him quarrelsome or cold-blooded as he surveys the corpses of his attackers in 'The Siege of the Round-House', he is also 'a bonny fighter', a 'doughty friend', and a man of principle, an imaginatively maturer instance of the mixed man than Long John Silver, illuminating a more subtly ambiguous world than *Treasure Island*'s, and forebear of the more neurotically complicated Robert Herrick in *The Ebb-Tide*. The orchestration of moral issues in such a precisely realized historical setting makes the romantic adventure of *Kidnapped* a masterpiece whose deeper implications may be better recognized by late twentieth-century readers comfortable with the generic varieties of contemporary fiction and not strait-jacketed by grim Dr Leavis's repressive Great Tradition. That tradition, of course, pretended to be English despite its greedy appropriation of the American Henry James and the Polish Joseph Conrad.

Apart from the interest of what happens next to David Balfour and the spooky Scots 'Tale of Tod Lapraik', *Catriona*, the sequel to *Kidnapped*, is a disappointment, muddled both in plot and psychology. In the speed and adult tension of its opening pages *The Master of Ballantrae* promises a further advance on *Kidnapped* in the portrayal of peculiarly Scottish moral conflict. Essentially a ballad of intended epic proportions, the novel achieves a thematic grandeur second only to *Dr Jekyll and Mr Hyde*, and the narrative voice of Ephraim Mackellar is one of Stevenson's best inventions; but, despite the psychological interest of Henry Durie's feeding on his vengeance, the power of the moral fable is diminished by the supernatural in the heavily implicit equation of James Durie with the Devil, the clumsy mechanism of the Chevalier de Burke's narrative and the forced, melodramatic ending.

Jekyll and Hyde

There is nothing clumsy about *The Strange Case of Dr Jekyll and Mr Hyde* which, Henry James suggests, 'would generally be called the most serious of the author's tales':

> It deals with the relation of the baser parts of man to his
> nobler, of the capacity for evil that exists in the most
> generous natures; and it expresses these things in a fable
> which is a wonderfully happy invention. The subject is
> endlessly interesting, and rich in all sorts of provocation,
> and Mr Stevenson is to be congratulated on having
> touched the core of it.[29]

That James's imagination was fed by the core of Stevenson's subject – 'man is not truly one, but truly two' – is evident in his own psychological ghost stories, 'The Private Life' (1891) and 'The Jolly Corner' (1908). References to double, divided or hidden selves 'pervade Victorian literature'.[30] In *The City of Dreadful Night*, section IV, James (B. V.) Thomson says, 'I was twain, / Two selves distinct that cannot join again'. In 'The Buried Life' (1852) Matthew Arnold repines that most people, separated from their true selves, hunger for the mystery of the buried, wild self. In lines that could speak for Henry Jekyll he says:

> But often, in the world's most crowded streets,
> But often, in the din of strife,
> There rises an unspeakable desire,
> After the knowledge of our buried life,
> A thirst to spend our fire and restless force
> In tracking out our true, original course;
> A longing to inquire
> Into the mystery of this heart that beats
> So wild, so deep in us.

Similarly, in a sequence of poems entitled 'Blank Misgivings of a Creature moving around in Worlds not realized' (1839–41), Arthur Hugh Clough laments the inaccessibility of 'The buried world below'. Dickens's interest in doubleness appears in Chapter 3 of *The Mystery of Edwin Drood* (1870) where he introduces a description of Miss Twinkleton's 'two distinct and separate phases of being' with the observation that:

> As, in some cases of drunkenness, and in others of animal
> magnetism, there are two states of consciousness which
> never clash, but each of which pursues its separate course
> as though it were continuous instead of broken.

Behind Stevenson's story of duality in its Victorian context lay Mary Shelley's *Frankenstein; or, the Modern Prometheus* (1818) in which Frankenstein's pathetically humanoid *alter ego* creature inspires loathing, commits murder and declares that Frankenstein will be his last victim, as, in a sense, Jekyll is Hyde's. In Melville's *Moby Dick* (1851) Captain Ahab re-creates the white whale in the image of the demonism within himself. The deformed cretin child in Charlotte Brontë's *Villette* (1853) embodies the deformity of Lucy Snowe's repressed passional self. Out of Calvinist obsession with the conflict of eternal opposites Scottish literature had produced Hogg's *The Private Memoirs and Confessions of a Justified Sinner*, precursor of many variations on the theme of the double self including Edgar Allan Poe's short story, 'William Wilson' (1839),[31] and what Stevenson called his 'fine bogy tale'. In 1890 Oscar Wilde published *The Picture of Dorian Gray* in which Dorian's essential doubleness is split into his tempter, Lord Henry Wotton, and his good angel or conscience, Basil Hallward, the portrait painter whom Dorian murders. Both Stevenson and Wilde make fables out of a culture they perceive as divided against itself: on the surface urbane and civilized, but underneath degraded and bestial. As a young man Stevenson had found relief from the 'draughty parallelograms' of middle-class New Town Edinburgh in the classless candour of human need in the city's bars and brothels. *Dr Jekyll and Mr Hyde* splits the moral atom to strike at the hypocrisy of a society in which the outwardly respectable Victorian drank and fornicated discreetly out of the public eye. In *The Time Machine* (1895) H. G. Wells projects this dichotomy into a future when the human race has separated into two antithetical species, the decadent, upper-class Eloi and the brutish, subterranean Morlocks who do the dirty work of society. Emma Tennant's *Two Women of London: The Strange Case of Ms Jekyll and Mrs Hyde* (1989) adapts Stevenson's story to the new Victorian social circumstances of Thatcher's Britain when 'rapaciousness and a "loadsamoney" economy have come to represent the highest values in the land' ('Editor's Introduction'). There is still what the lawyer, Jean Hastie, calls 'evil' in the case, but child-worn

Mrs Hyde's use of the drug 'Ecstasy' to transform her into the attractive Eliza Jekyll, fondled and promoted by a consumerist society, expresses the desperation of a solo mother in an uncaring system:

> it is incontestably true that the stress and discrimination suffered by a single mother in an environment growing daily more hostile in both financial and psychological terms can cause defensive violence as well as misery and frustration.
>
> (Part 2, 'Afterword by Jean Hastie')

Like Hogg's novel and Poe's story, Stevenson's novella is about conscience. When Jekyll discovers the drug that allows his personality to be split, thereby liberating his repressed desires, the grasp of his conscience is at first 'insidiously relaxed', then jolted into conflict with the illicit pleasures he enjoys as Mr Hyde. In Hogg's story the Calvinist doctrine of Election is discredited by its justification of Robert Wringhim's crimes, and the godlike presumptions of nineteenth-century science are called in question by Frankenstein and Dr Jekyll. (Stevenson's attitude towards science is ambiguous: Dr Lanyon's medical conservatism is punished by despair and death.) Like Robert Wringhim, Dr Jekyll loses control; overcome by his metamorphoses, he confesses before Hyde kills himself to escape the gallows.

In a letter to J. A. Symonds in spring 1886 Stevenson refers to '*Jekyll*' as 'a dreadful thing . . . that damned old business of the war in the members'.[32] The phrase is echoed in Dr Jekyll's 'consciousness of the perennial war among my members', and again in Stevenson's reference to 'that double law of the members and the will' in the essay, 'Pulvis et Umbra' (1888).[33] If the ambivalence of human character is the principal motif in his work, it is closely followed by the power of evil, which is the subject of 'Thrawn Janet' (1881) and 'Markheim' (1884) in both of which the Devil appears. Written in the vernacular of the Pitlochry district where Stevenson was spending a wet summer, 'Thrawn Janet' tells how a minister's mind is turned by contact with Janet, a witch possessed by the Devil. Stevenson's cousin and biographer, Graham Balfour, believes that the story has two defects: 'it is true only historically, true for a hill parish in Scotland in old days, not true for mankind and the world'.[34] Yet 'Thrawn Janet' illustrates a valid general truth about the incapacity of fanaticism to cope with an extreme situation for which its rules make no provision, breaking because it cannot bend. Published shortly before *Dr Jekyll and Mr Hyde*, 'Markheim' is a distinctively Scottish elaboration of Poe's theme in 'The Black Cat' (1843) and 'The Imp of the Perverse' (1845). While Poe treats perversity as a psychological phenomenon, Stevenson's Presbyterian sensibility associates it with the theological condition of original sin and 'the war between the members' of good and evil. Once an enthusiastic participant in revivalist meetings, his voice 'the loudest in the hymn', Markheim, like Jekyll, recognizes the opposites that make up his own moral nature and that of others:

> Evil and good run strong in me, haling me both ways. I do not love the one thing, I love all. I can conceive great deeds, renunciations, martyrdoms; and though I be fallen to such a crime as murder, pity is no stranger to my thoughts. I pity the poor; who knows their trials better than myself? I pity and help them; I prize love, I love honest laughter; there is no good thing nor true thing on earth but I love it from my heart. And are my vices only to direct my life, and my virtues to lie without effect, like some passive lumber of the mind? Not so; good, also, is a spring of acts . . . I have in some degree complied with evil. But it is so with all: the very saints, in the mere exercise of living, grow less dainty and take on the tone of their surroundings.[35]

The story achieves the universality of fable because we recognize Markheim in ourselves: as Wayne C. Booth says, 'Markheim murders the pawnbroker, and we hope for Markheim's salvation'.[36] For the same reason we hope for Jekyll's.

While Dr Jekyll is haled like Markheim by good and evil, austere Mr Utterson is the perfect foil, 'a lover of the sane and customary sides of life'. Yet the lawyer, too, has his duality which he keeps under control, mortifying 'a taste for vintages' by drinking gin, denying himself the pleasures of the theatre, taking his regular, dull walks with Mr Enfield and ending his Sundays with 'a volume of some dry divinity on his reading desk, until the clock in the neighbouring church rang out the hour of twelve, when he would go soberly and gratefully to bed'. Thus duplicity in Dr Jekyll is matched by repression in Mr Utterson and in Mr Enfield who refrains from asking about the mysterious door, telling Mr Utterson, 'I make it a rule of mine: the more it looks like Queer Street, the less I ask.' Mr Utterson approves the rule. If he betrays symptoms of depressive withdrawal, Markheim and Jekyll exemplify features of *dementia praecox* or schizophrenia as it was known after Eugen Bleuler introduced the word in 1911 to denote forms of mental illness characterized by splitting of the mind. Towards the end of the nineteenth century the German psychiatrist, Emil Kraepelin, distinguished between *dementia praecox* and manic-depression. The split in Jekyll particularly suggests the bi-polar illness of manic-depressive psychosis as well as a classically Freudian conflict between the interdependent super-ego and the id. It also demonstrates the

Jungian coexistence of persona (Jekyll) and shadow (Hyde), 'the shadow compensating for the pretensions of the persona, the persona compensating for the antisocial propensities of the shadow'.[37]

Markheim is possessed by a compulsion to kill, then in defiance of a smoothly manipulative Devil, to confess and give himself up. Jekyll, too, is finally repelled by the evil he has released and confesses to the representatives of morality and respectability. Yet the attraction of evil is what lingers in the mind at the end of *Dr Jekyll and Mr Hyde* (as James rather than Henry Durie stays in the mind at the end of *The Master of Ballantrae*), which implies that good is restriction, evil freedom, and that shedding the 'load of genial respectability' to become pure evil is to 'spring headlong into the sea of liberty'. After the racking pangs of his first transformation, Jekyll's sensations as Mr Hyde are 'incredibly sweet':

> I felt younger, lighter, happier in body; within I was
> conscious of a heady recklessness, a current of disordered
> sensual images running like a millrace in my fancy, a
> solution of the bonds of obligation, an unknown but not
> an innocent freedom of the soul. I knew myself, at the
> first breath of this new life, to be more wicked, tenfold
> more wicked, sold a slave to my original evil; and the
> thought, in that moment, braced and delighted me like
> wine.
>
> ('Henry Jekyll's Full Statement of the Case')

But this manic, evil side of Jekyll's dual nature is housed in a small, deformed body. His evil side is 'less developed than the good', and good asserts itself in Jekyll's depressive revulsion from his *alter ego*. The book's acutest insight into the psychology of moral consciousness is in the passage which defines the problem of choosing between circumscribed Jekyll and autonomous Hyde:

> To cast in my lot with Jekyll, was to die to those
> appetites which I had long secretly indulged and had of
> late begun to pamper. To cast it in with Hyde, was to die
> to a thousand interests and aspirations, and to become, at a
> blow and forever, despised and friendless. The bargain
> might appear unequal; but there was still another
> consideration in the scales; for while Jekyll would suffer
> smartingly in the fires of abstinence, Hyde would be not
> even conscious of all that he had lost.
>
> ('Henry Jekyll's Full Statement of the Case')

It is not remorse that makes Hyde seek refuge in the person of Jekyll after the murder of Sir Danvers Carew has screwed his love of life 'to the topmost peg'; in the 'divided ecstasy of his mind' he is torn between gloating and fear of 'the avenger'. Hyde is 'a being inherently malign and villainous', in Vladimir Nabokov's phrase 'a concentrate of pure evil';[38] conscience is the preserve and solitary torment of Markheim's descendant, the morally composite Jekyll.

Henry James was struck not so much by 'the profundity of the idea' in *Dr Jekyll and Mr Hyde* as by 'the art of the presentation – the extremely successful form' of Stevenson's 'short, rapid, concentrated story, which is really a masterpiece of concision'.[39] Gerard Manley Hopkins disagreed with Robert Bridges's criticism of 'the gross absurdity' of the interchange between Jekyll and Hyde: 'Enough that it is impossible and might perhaps have been a little better masked: it must be connived at, and it gives rise to a fine situation. It is not more impossible than fairies, giants, heathen gods, and lots of things that literature teems with.'[40] Underlying the enduring appeal of its theme, the book's strength comes from its narrative method, its use of atmosphere and its evocation of the affective power of evil. 'Backward in sentiment', Mr Utterson, 'to whom the fanciful was the immodest', is skilfully installed as a reliable commentator trusted by both Dr Jekyll and Dr Lanyon, and trustworthy to the point of respecting Dr Lanyon's direction that his letter is not to be opened until Jekyll's death or disappearance. Opposite in character to 'lean, long, dusty, dreary' Mr Utterson is Dr Lanyon, 'a healthy, dapper, red-faced gentleman, with a shock of hair prematurely white, and a boisterous and decided manner'. The impossible truth seems plausible when two such different temperaments converge on it. With Dr Lanyon's letter the relationship between Jekyll and Hyde is revealed from the outside by a qualified observer in preparation for Jekyll's 'Full Statement of the Case' in which the truth is finally clarified from the inside.

Dickensian effects of atmosphere and imagery are used with perfectly judged economy. Like the doctor himself, Jekyll's house is composite, respectable at one end with an imposing Victorian front hall and corridors leading to the laboratory where Jekyll becomes Hyde, entering the world by a door 'blistered and distained'. The eerily church-like, lamplit street described by Enfield implies blasphemy in the cruelty of Hyde's trampling the child. Sound is used dramatically in the silence of the night when Utterson sees Hyde's face after the approach of swift, ominous footsteps and Hyde's satanically serpentine 'hissing intake of the breath'. Fog infects Soho with dismal mystery. The darkened moon and puffs of wind agitating the flame of Utterson and Poole's candle as they prepare to break down the door of Jekyll's cabinet make conspirators of nature and the supernatural.

The force of Hyde's evil is conveyed by its impact on others, as summed up by Dr Lanyon:

> I was struck . . . with the odd, subjective disturbance
> caused by his neighbourhood. This bore some resemblance
> to incipient rigour, and was accompanied by a marked
> sinking of the pulse. At the time, I set it down to some
> idiosyncratic, personal distaste, and merely wondered at the
> acuteness of the symptoms; but I have since had reason to
> believe the cause to lie much deeper in the nature of
> man, and to turn on some nobler hinge than the principle
> of hatred.
>
> ('Dr Lanyon's Narrative')

The 'nobler hinge' is the principle of goodness to which Hyde is constitutionally inimical, hence his compulsion to murder the emblematic Sir Danvers Carew, 'an aged beautiful gentleman with white hair', whose face seems to breathe 'an innocent and old world kindness of disposition'. The 'troglodytic' Hyde is perceived as 'particularly small and wicked-looking' by the maid who witnesses the killing of Sir Danvers, a 'masked thing like a monkey' by Poole, and he inspires Mr Utterson with 'a nausea and distaste of life'. According to Enfield he is like Satan, and Utterson's exclamation, 'God forgive us, God forgive us' at the end of 'Incident at the Window' is like the sign of the cross made in the presence of evil. In a work so precisely written there can be no doubt about Hyde's theological value when Dr Jekyll calls him 'my devil' and 'that child of Hell', indications of Stevenson's 'absorption of the devil–ridden folklore of Scotland'.[41] (Of James Durie he writes to Sidney Colvin in 1887: 'The Master is all I know of the devil.'[42])

Stevenson's fable implies that evil is potentially stronger than good: Hyde is, after all, the death of Jekyll, the embodiment of evil which 'will not die until it has corrupted the good to its own image and brought it down by its side to a common grave'.[43] His realistic descendant is Huish, Stevenson's 'trivial hell-hound'[44] with a 'precedency in evil'[45] in The Ebb-Tide, whose final and fatal prospect of pleasure is to throw vitriol into the eyes of Attwater, the ambiguous Christian pearl-fisher. The final assertion of good implicit in Jekyll's judgement of himself comes from panic that the evil side of his nature is taking over, that his natural, morally composite identity may be lost to him. The message is that we are inescapably forked creatures: the 'war in the members' is 'the doom and burthen of our life' and 'when the attempt is made to cast it off, it but returns upon us with more unfamiliar and more awful pressure'. The Pyrrhic victory of good is the intolerable pressure Jekyll feels in the prospect of losing his capacity for virtue. The book is thus no more or less optimistic than the view Stevenson takes of virtue in 'Pulvis et Umbra' where he finds men and women, however wretched their circumstances,

> without hope, without help, without thanks, still obscurely fighting the lost fight of virtue, still clinging, in the brothel or on the scaffold, to some rag of honour, the poor jewel of their souls! They may seek to escape, and yet they cannot; it is not alone their privilege and glory, but their doom; they are condemned to some nobility; all their lives long, the desire of good is at their heels, the implacable hunter.[46]

Here Stevenson's stoical view of the moral life on what Matthew Arnold in 'Dover Beach' (1867) calls the 'darkling plain' develops Carlyle's belief in Chapter 4 of *Chartism* that, whatever the obstacles, 'Every mortal can and shall himself be a true man.' It also resembles Joseph Conrad's stoical imperative in Chapter 20 of *Lord Jim* (1900) where Stein explains the difference between the tragic circumstance of life in 'the destructive element' and the futility of trying to escape it:

> A man that is born falls into a dream like a man who falls into the sea. If he tries to climb out into the air as inexperienced people endeavour to do, he drowns – *nicht wahr?* . . . No! I tell you! The way is to the destructive element submit yourself, and with the exertions of your hands and feet in the water make the deep, deep sea keep you up.

The dream will destroy a man who attempts to deny it by living only on the dry land of the unprincipled, naturalistic world, in recoil from the idealistic imperatives of full humanity. As Robert Penn Warren glosses the passage, man, being a natural creature, 'is not born to swim in the dream, with gills and fins, but if he submits in his own imperfect, "natural" way he can learn to swim and keep himself up, however painfully, in the destructive element'.[47] Warren expresses the idea – a secular approximation to Francis Thompson's implacable hunter in 'The Hound of Heaven' (1893) – more earthily in his long poem, *Brother to Dragons* (1953):

> . . . despite all naturalistic considerations,
> Or in the end because of naturalistic considerations,
> We must believe in virtue. There is no
> Escape. No inland path around that rocky
> And spume-nagged promontory. There is no
> Escape: dead-fall on trail, noose on track, bear-trap

Under the carefully rearranged twigs. There is no
Escape, for virtue is
More dogged than Pinkerton, more scientific than the
    F.B.I.,
And that is why you wake sweating toward dawn.[48]

To attempt to live naturalistically, abjuring the dream, that mandate of principle which our mixed moral natures must obey, is to die, like Jekyll and Hyde, sooner rather than later. The power of the idea in *The Beach of Falesá* is personified in the love of Uma which converts Wiltshire from an opportunistic trader beholden to the manipulative Case into the man of feeling and principle who abandons his dream of owning a pub in favour of loyalty to his wife and half-caste children. It is Attwater, the sophisticated man of ideas, who gets the better of the three derelicts in *The Ebb-Tide*. Yet the supreme tragic irony is that the idea cannot save us from eventual destruction by the element in which we must swim to be fully human. At the end of *The Ebb-Tide* Attwater's religion salvages what is left of Captain Davis, but represents the final unresolved menace for Robert Herrick. The diabolical James Durie's cruellest taunting of Ephraim Mackellar is when he says, 'Recognize in each of us a common strain: that we both live for an idea' (*The Master of Ballantrae*, Chapter IX). As every Presbyterian knows, the Devil, too, has his dream.

Notes

1. Henry James, *Literary Criticism: Essays on Literature, American Writers, English Writers* (The Library of America, New York, 1984), p. 1273.

2. Evan Charteris, *The Life and Letters of Sir Edmund Gosse* (London, 1931), pp. 232–3.

3. Anthony Burgess, 'The Wandering Star', *The Observer*, 9 May 1993.

4. Robert Louis Stevenson, 'To Alison Cunningham from Her Boy', the dedication to *A Child's Garden of Verses* in *Poems*, Tusitala Edition, 35 vols (London, 1923), I, p. xxi, and in *Collected Poems*, ed. Janet Adam Smith (London, 1971), p. 361. References are to the Tusitala Edition whenever possible.

5. Jenni Calder, *RLS: A Life Study* (London, 1980), p. 66.

6. Jonathan Keates, 'An innocent abroad', *The Observer Review*, 11 December 1994, p. 16.

7. See 'Editorial Note' by Sir Sidney Colvin in Robert Louis Stevenson, *Weir of Hermiston; Some Unfinished Stories*, Tusitala Edition, XVI, pp. 125–36.

8. Ibid., p. 133.

9. Letter from Joseph Conrad to Alfred A. Knopf, 20 July 1913, in G. Jean-Aubry, *Joseph Conrad: Life and Letters*, 2 vols (London, 1927), II, p. 147.

10. Robert Louis Stevenson, *Letters, Vol. 1*, Tusitala Edition, XXXI, p. 91.

11. Charteris, *Sir Edmund Gosse*, p. 434.

12. John Buchan, *Memory Hold-the-Door* (London, 1940), p. 43.

13. Compton Mackenzie, *Literature in My Time* (London, 1933), p. 30.

14. Robert Louis Stevenson, *Letters, Vol. 2*, Tusitala Edition, XXXII, pp. 99–100.

15. Robert Louis Stevenson, *Letters, Vol. 1*, Tusitala Edition, XXXI, p. 73.

16. Ibid., p. 82.

17. Ibid., p. 100.

18. Ibid., p. 160.

19. Robert Louis Stevenson, 'A College Magazine', in *Memories and Portraits of Himself; Selections from His Notebook*, Tusitala Edition, XXIX, p. 28.

20. Robert Louis Stevenson, *The Strange Case of Dr Jekyll and Mr Hyde; Fables*, Tusitala Edition, V, p. 92.

21. Robert Louis Stevenson, *An Inland Voyage; Travels with a Donkey in the Cevennes*, Tusitala Edition, XVII, p. 80.

22. Ibid., p. 222.

23. Robert Louis Stevenson, *Plays*, Tusitala Edition, XXIV, p. ix.

24. Robert Louis Stevenson, *Letters, Vol. 1*, Tusitala Edition, XXXI, p. 51.

25. Ian Bell, *Dreams of Exile* (Edinburgh, 1992), pp. 176–7.

26. Robert Louis Stevenson, *Treasure Island*, Tusitala Edition, II, pp. xv–xvi.

27. In the early 1700s Edward Teach, alias Blackbeard, punished a mutinous crew by marooning them on the tiny waterless island of Dead Man's Chest, part of the British Virgin Islands (BVI). Inhabited by mosquitoes, fire ants and inedible soldier crabs, navigation charts list it as 'Dead Chest Island', and it has been called 'the dustbin of the BVI'. Each man was given a cutlass and a bottle of rum. Teach hoped that they would kill each other, but when he returned thirty days later he found that fifteen men had survived. Hence, 'Drink and devil had done for the rest – / Yo-ho-ho, and a bottle of rum!' See Quentin van Marle, 'Island Life', *Geographical*, 67, no. 4 (April, 1995), pp. 34–5.

28. Stevenson, *Treasure Island*, p. 224.

29. James, *Literary Criticism*, pp. 1251–2.

30. Tony Tanner, 'In two voices', *TLS*, 2 July 1993, p. 12.

31. Stevenson's review of Poe's works edited in seven volumes by J. H. Ingram appeared in *The Academy* for 2 January 1875.

32. Robert Louis Stevenson, *Letters, Vol. 3*, Tusitala Edition, XXXIII, pp. 80–81.

33. Robert Louis Stevenson, 'Pulvis et Umbra', *Ethical Studies: Edinburgh; Picturesque Notes*, Tusitala Edition, XXVI, p. 66.

34. Graham Balfour, *The Life of Robert Louis Stevenson*, 6th edn (London, 1911), p. 134.

35. Robert Louis Stevenson, 'Markheim', *The Merry Men and Other Tales*, Tusitala Edition, VIII, pp. 104–5.

36. Wayne C. Booth, *The Rhetoric of Fiction* (Chicago and London, 1961), p. 113.

37. Anthony Stevens, *On Jung* (Harmondsworth, 1991), p. 43.

38. Vladimir Nabokov, 'Robert Louis Stevenson: The Strange Case of Dr Jekyll and Mr Hyde', in *Lectures on Literature*, ed. Fredson Bowers (New York, 1980), p. 182.

39. James, *Literary Criticism*, p. 1252.

40. Gerard Manley Hopkins, letter to Robert Bridges, 28 October 1886, in Gerard Manley Hopkins, *Selected Letters*, ed. Catherine Phillips (Oxford, 1990), p. 243.

41. Calder, *RLS*, p. 222.

42. Robert Louis Stevenson, *Letters, Vol. 3*, Tusitala Edition, XXXIII, p. 171.

43. Leslie A. Fiedler, 'The Master of Ballantrae', introduction to *The Master of Ballantrae*, Rinehart Edition, 1954. Reprinted in Austin Wright (ed.), *Victorian Literature* (New York, 1961), p. 292.

44. Robert Louis Stevenson, *The Ebb-Tide; The Story of a Lie*, Tusitala Edition, XIV, p. 24.

45. Ibid., p. 126.

46. Stevenson, 'Pulvis et Umbra', pp. 64–5.

47. Robert Penn Warren, *Selected Essays* (New York, 1966), p. 44.

48. Robert Penn Warren, *Brother to Dragons: A Tale in Verse and Voices* (New York, 1953), p. 29.

Chapter 9

Tragedy, Epic and Entertainment: Early Twentieth-Century Fiction

Scottish writers of fiction in the first half of the twentieth century divide into two groups. It would be wrong to call them 'serious' and 'popular' but there are authors whose themes are obviously and consistently serious, and others whose intentions may, at least sometimes, have been equally serious but who, like Sir Arthur Conan Doyle, Neil Munro, John Buchan, Compton Mackenzie and A. J. Cronin, have secured their places in Scottish literature as entertainers.

In the unequivocally serious category George Douglas Brown, John Macdougall Hay, Neil Gunn and Lewis Grassic Gibbon (the pen-name of James Leslie Mitchell) write from an essentially proletarian, post-Victorian impulse about the relation between people and place, social change and the power of money. Both Douglas Brown and Macdougall Hay are turn-of-the-century one-book writers, each achieving a single, grimly tragic masterpiece – Brown's *The House with the Green Shutters* (1901) and Hay's *Gillespie* (1914) – in a short life which produced only relatively minor other work. Neil Gunn's reputation as 'the most import-ant Scottish novelist of the twentieth century',[1] based on a corpus of some twenty volumes of fiction mainly centred on life in the Scottish Highlands, has been largely eclipsed by growing appreciation of Grassic Gibbon's epic achievement in the trilogy, *A Scots Quair* (1932–4), whose stature has increased with each new generation of readers. Gibbon emerges as the most distinguished novelist of the Scottish Literary Renaissance, while Gunn is now generally known by one novel, *The Silver Darlings* (1941).

Catherine Carswell has long commanded respect as a critic for *The Savage Pilgrimage: a Narrative of D. H. Lawrence* (1932),[2] based on her exceptionally harmonious and mutually sustaining friendship with Lawrence, and, after initial denunciation by orthodox Burnsites, her carefully researched *Life of Robert Burns* (1930). She should be extolled for her first novel, *Open the Door!*, which draws on experiences described in her unfinished autobiography, *Lying Awake* (1950), for the story of Joanna Bannerman's escape from the confinements of an oppressive United Free Church background and the smotheringly Calvinistic yet emotionally intense attitudes of middle-class Glasgow. Carswell's book belongs to the

tradition of Scottish feminist moral fiction with Mary Brunton, the Susan
Ferrier of *Marriage*, the Margaret Oliphant of *Kirsteen*, Elspeth Davie, Joan
Lingard, Emma Tennant, Janice Galloway and A. L. Kennedy. This tradition can be distinguished from that of the novel-of-manners developed
by Jane Findlater and her sister Mary, best known for their jointly written
village romance, *Crossriggs* (1908), and by Jane Duncan's popular 'My
Friends' series of novels.

    In Germany, under the pseudonym 'Sagitta', the Greenock-born anar-
chist John Henry Mackay was also engaged with themes of repression,
confinement and freedom. His stories of homosexual love culminated in
his novel *The Hustler* (*Der Puppenjunge*, 1926),[3] an evocation of the sub-
culture of 1920s Berlin. Mackay's account of Gunther and the boys of
Friedrich Street's notorious alley, 'The Passage', is part of his campaign
for the recognition of what he calls 'The Nameless Love' in his poem of
that title:

> Yet since you think it a dirty thing
>   Have dragged it through mud and infamy
>   And kept in the dark under lock and key –
>
> This love will I freely sing.
>
> To love's persecuted my song I bring
>   And to the outcasts of our time
>   Since happy or not this love is mine –
>
> This love dare I loudly sing.[4]

Infatuated with the street-wise Gunther, Hermann Graff thinks about 'his
[own] orientation' in a passage which exposes Mackay's novel's missionary intention:

> He knew his orientation. He knew how it stood with
> him. He still read a great deal, but did not trouble himself
> for an explanation when there was nothing to explain.
> What was self-evident, natural, and not in the least sick
> did not require an excuse through an explanation. Many
> of the theories now posed he held to be false and
> dangerous.
>   It was love just like any other love. Whoever could not
> or would not accept it as love was mistaken. The mistake
> reflected onto those who were mistaken.
>   They were still in the majority, those who were
> mistaken. And therefore in possession of force.
>
>   (Part 3, Chapter 6)

Thirty years later Compton Mackenzie's *Thin Ice* (1956) treats the problem of 'wild risks' in the life of Henry Fortescue, a homosexual Member of Parliament, with equally pioneering insight and a moral delicacy the more affecting because the field of experience is for Mackenzie as for the narrator, George Gaymer, 'all outside my imagination' (Chapter 16). Stresses of potentially explosive homosexual relationship are further illuminated by Candia McWilliam's story of Lucas Salik and the sadistic Hal Darbo in the manipulative intrigues of her first novel, *A Case of Knives* (1988).

The popularity of science fiction and fantasy has won new enthusiasm for London-born David Lindsay's symbolic novel, *A Voyage to Arcturus* (1920), and prompted a long overdue reprinting of Grassic Gibbon's briskly written Wellsian post-projected holocaust, anti-Fascist morality novel, *Gay Hunter* (1934).[5] Gibbon proposes that there still could be a return to a Golden Age of co-operative, pastoral society despite the refreshingly forthright Gay's distaste for the anti-urban sentimentality of life conceived as 'an eternal picnic' (Chapter 5), especially after she has been pursued by a boar amidst a herd of wild pigs, 'an ungenteel and odoriferous encounter' (Chapter 4).

Tragedy: George Douglas Brown and John Macdougall Hay

'There is a megalomaniac in every parish in Scotland,' says George Douglas Brown in *The House with the Green Shutters* (published in 1901 under Brown's pseudonym, George Douglas). He adds:

> Well, not so much as that; they're owre canny for that to
> be said of them. But in every district, almost, you may
> find a poor creature who for thirty years has cherished a
> great scheme by which he means to revolutionize the
> world's commerce, and amass a fortune in monstrous
> degree.
>
> (Chapter 11)

'Monstrous' would have been the operative word for R. B. Cunninghame Graham. In 'Calvary', one of his *Thirteen Stories* (1900), Graham has only vitriol for 'holy commerce . . . which makes the whole world kin, reducing all men to the lowest common multiple; commerce that curses equally both him who buys and him who sells'. Brown concedes the merits of

Scottish commercial ingenuity, but John Gourlay in *The House with the Green Shutters* and the eponymous protagonist of Macdougall Hay's *Gillespie* are megalomaniacs whose rise and fall carry their authors' indictments of the cult of property. Economic and entrepreneurial power makes Gourlay 'the big man of Barbie' (the 'petty burgh' based on Brown's birthplace of Ochiltree in Ayrshire) and Gillespie 'gigantic' in Brieston (modelled on Tarbert, Loch Fyne, Argyll, where Hay was born and raised). Both men 'amass a fortune in monstrous degree' and gain control over the lives of their townspeople who, for the most part, hold them in a combination of fear and loathing, acting as reflectors and choruses in the two narratives, commenting on the two men's decline to melodramatic ruin. Each novel's massive anti-hero causes the deaths of his wife and children and dies horribly himself. Both novels are intensely claustrophobic: even when Gourlay and Gillespie are not centre-stage, as in the chapters in *The House with the Green Shutters* that deal with young Gourlay at Edinburgh University and the account of Eoghan Strang grappling with his drink-crazed mother's degradation in the last Book of *Gillespie*, their malign presences are felt. Yet, despite common themes and the similarities between their obsessed, pervasive central figures, the two novels are as different as they are alike. Patterned on Greek tragedy,[6] *The House with the Green Shutters* is tightly shaped and unerringly paced with no superfluous matter, while the scale and tempo of *Gillespie* suggest the expansiveness of Dostoevsky or Theodore Dreiser. Brown's style is analytical with passages of almost painful lyricism. *Gillespie* opens crisply with the story of the 'Ghost' inn and its ominously creaking sign, but as the action gathers momentum towards the final catastrophe Hay piles up blocks of strenuously expressive language lit by his proselytizing urge to show that 'the growing spirit of materialism in Scotland needed a Gillespie'.[7] Hay's novel is over-written, particularly in Book III, but gets away with it through sheer intensity.

Gillespie Strang's power derives not only from adamantine egotism and tireless application but also from his ability to employ cold-bloodedly rapacious capitalist business methods against an entrepreneurially primitive community. He is particularly astute in exploiting the outlawed ringnetting of herring in anticipation of its legalization, falsely appearing to be 'the fisherman's friend' (Book II, Chapter 9). John Gourlay is driven by a comparably obsessive strength of purpose but fails in business because his methods are outdated. He cannot compete with his wily rival, James Wilson, the new economic man who, abetted by the cunning of Gibson the builder, masters the capitalist techniques necessary for commercial success in an era of rapid change. In Chapter 12 the description of Gourlay and Wilson externalizes the contrast between them by their physical differences and Brown's antipathy to both types is expressed further in the extension of the two men's characters into their sons. Jimmy Wilson has 'no more real ability than young Gourlay, but infinitely more caution. He was one of the gimlet characters who, by diligence and memory, gain prizes in their schooldays – and are fools for the rest of their lives' (Chapter 14); young Gourlay is 'cursed with impressions which he couldn't intellectualize' (Chapter 16). The senior Gourlay is as solid as the 'bluff' house with green shutters which is 'his character in stone and lime' (Chapter 24), 'a material means by which he could hold his own and reassert himself' (Chapter 3), and 'the perfect god of his idolatry' (Chapter 5).[8] Gillespie Strang requires no such objective correlative to prove the force of his manipulative genius. Gourlay is a 'resolute dullard' (Chapter 1), a 'donkey' without 'gumption' possessing only 'a dour kind of abeelity . . . that has no cleverness, but just gangs trampling on' until beaten by Wilson's 'flank attack' (Chapter 2).[9] In his 'stupeedity o' spite' he is no match for the innuendos and gibes of Barbie's 'nesty bodies', either 'adepts at the under stroke' (Chapter 5) like the lisping 'artist in spite', Deacon Allardyce (Chapter 21), or stridently vicious like Tam Brodie who stabs young Gourlay 'like an awl' (Chapter 25).

While Gourlay uses commerce as a way of rising above the slicker citizens of Barbie, Gillespie is the pure materialist, a true 'worshipper of things' (Book I, Chapter 4) and, therefore, 'impervious to the common tongue' (Book II, Chapter 4). 'Without bowels of pity, immovable as granite' (Book I, Chapter 20), he is unaware – and wouldn't have cared if he had known – that Mrs Galbraith imagines him a snake (Book I, Chapter 12), a 'predatory beast' and a 'pirate with his carrion eyes and expressionless face' (Book I, Chapter 14). Committed to her hatred for him, Mrs Galbraith neglects her philosophy, poetry and music to become a vindictive 'machine of steel, constantly running' (Book II, Chapter 12), and enter into a compact of revenge with Gillespie's disillusioned partner, Hector Lonend, who sees him as a 'damn wolf' (Book I, Chapter 13) and 'a cuttlefish, impenetrable behind the ink of his dissembling' (Book I, Chapter 20). To his maddened alcoholic wife in the hour of her death, poised for the moment when she can draw the blade of his razor across the throat of her too-loving son, 'Gillespie Strang is hell' (Book IV, Chapter 16). Both Gourlay and Gillespie exemplify in a secular scheme of values the perverse tenacity of the corrupting doctrine of Election. Dispensing with God – Gillespie's substitution of the stars which he 'conceived were fighting for him' (Book I, Chapters 6 and 11) would be, for the ordained Presbyterian Hay, the ultimate hubris – they assume, like Burns's Holy Willie, that they 'for . . . gear may shine / Excell'd by nane'. Grace does not interest them.

The two novels are full of anger, yet Brown and Hay invite pity for Gourlay and Gillespie. Both writers seem fearful that they may appear to have been brutalized out of compassion by involvement with the monstrous psychopathologies they have created. Brown's diagnosis of Gourlay's brutishness in Chapter 4 of *The House with the Green Shutters* dilutes his guilt to inadequacy: 'Yet he was not wilfully cruel; only a stupid man with a strong character, in which he took a dogged pride. Stupidity and pride provoked the brute in him.' Extenuation is almost explicit in the part played by gossip in Gourlay's downfall:

> The bodies of Barbie became not only the chorus to
> Gourlay's tragedy, buzzing it abroad and discussing his
> downfall; they became also, merely by their maddening
> tattle, a villain of the piece and an active cause of the
> catastrophe. Their gossip seemed to materialize into a
> single entity, a something propelling, that spurred Gourlay
> on to the schemes that ruined him. He was not to be
> done, he said; he would show the dogs what he thought
> of them.
>
> (Chapter 11)

This is enough to refute J. B. Priestley's criticism that Brown spoils his tragic drama by mixing it with a social novel's exhibition of 'Scotsmen in small towns'.[10] These gossiping, spiteful Scotsmen are part of the cause and effect of the tragic process. But even Brown cannot finally submit the bodies' goading of Gourlay in mitigation of his guilt when he, in turn, mercilessly goads his son, sweating punishment out of him:

> To bring a beaten and degraded look into a man's face,
> rend manhood out of him in fear, is a sight that makes
> decent men wince in pain; for it is an outrage on the
> decency of life, an offence to natural religion, a violation
> of the human sanctities. Yet Gourlay had done it once
> and again.
>
> (Chapter 25)

Similarly, Hay is ambivalent about Gillespie, saying of him, 'His fate deserves some pity' (Book IV, Chapter 18). It is difficult to see why, notwithstanding the determinism of his father's denying him books and schooling in the belief that 'if the lad got no stupid stories into his head he was safe' from the ancestral doom predicted by Mrs Strang (Book I, Chapter 2).[11] True judgement of Gillespie is pronounced in Book II, Chapter 30 and it can stand for Gourlay too:

> Gillespie was punished because he had derided the
> permanent things in life, which humanity have learned to
> prize through centuries of the discipline of immitigable
> sorrow, vicissitude, and blood. To deride those permanent
> things is to flout the hope and ideals which in the breast

of mankind have borne privation, suffering, and death with fortitude and patience. For innocence, youth, laughter, friendship, natural ties, and even death Gillespie had neither bowels of sympathy nor compassion. He had been self-centred in rearing his house of life and filling it with his own peculiar idols. The precious things of man's soul outraged took their inevitable revenge.

The oppressive atmosphere of Brown's anti-Kailyard burgh is a little alleviated by the small group of 'harmless bodies': thoughtful Johnny Coe who, when drinking, believes Gourlay 'the only gentleman' in Barbie, easy-going Tam Wylie and Tom, the Burns-loving baker who is kind to young Gourlay during the storm in Chapter 14. The darkness of *Gillespie* is lightened by the good Dr Maclean, by Kennedy the schoolteacher, by 'Topsail' Janet Morgan who tenderly nurses back to strength and freedom the broken-winged solan goose gifted to her by the north wind before she becomes devoted companion and nurse to the similarly broken Morag Strang, and by Barbara's steady love for the doomed Eoghan. But it is nature, tranquil or turbulent yet constant in its mutability, which provides the real locus of whatever hope there can be in the humanly rent worlds of these novels. Aloof from the fury and mire of human striving, nature can make Barbie 'a very pleasing place to look down at on a summer evening' (Chapter 1) and impart to Brieston 'at sunset a shining peace' (Book II, Chapter 19). In different mood, as it is to young John Gourlay, guiltily a truant from Skeighan High School, nature can be the lightning that 'stabbed the world in vicious and repeated hate' (Chapter 14), and equinoctial gales come to Gillespie's Brieston in 'a savage nihilism of storms' (Book II, Chapter 23). The beauty of countryside and sky highlights the ugliness of 'the human pismires' stinging Gourlay with their gibes in the brake (Chapter 15) and the splendour of the sky seems to Eoghan to mock the search for Iain Strang's drowned body in *Gillespie* (Book III, Chapter 9). But nature is impersonal; its apparent nihilism, reprimand or mockery are human projections. Lewis Grassic Gibbon says as much when Chris Guthrie reflects in *Sunset Song* that the land 'didn't rise up and torment your heart' (Chapter 4). Brown, Hay and Gibbon all recognize the distance between what Brown calls 'the suave enveloping greatness of the world' (Chapter 15) and human action. Neither benign nor maleficent, the natural world simply is. The obduracy that makes these three writers angry is the persistence with which people fail to measure up to nature. The 'radiant arch of the dawn' above Gourlay's deadly house at the end of *The House with the Green Shutters* (Chapter 27) and the 'transitory ploughman' coaxing new life from the earth on the last page of *Gillespie* express the hope that inheres in the continuity of great creating nature despite the worst that Gourlays and Gillespies may do.

Epic fantasy: David Lindsay

The certainty of continuous epic conflict between mighty opposites is the only answer granted to David Lindsay's protagonist in a world of questions at the end of *A Voyage to Arcturus* (1920; originally entitled *Nightspore in Tormance*). As escapist fantasy the novel allures with an enigmatic tower in Scotland – launching-pad for a crystal space-rocket – characters with other-worldly names like Joiwind, Corpang, Polecrab and Dreamsinter, a provocative theory of music, bizarre physical transformations which jolt stereotypical earthly assumptions, new sense organs and colours called ulfire, jale and dolm. As a moral fable of love, duty and pain it hooks the susceptible reader on the epic paradigm of the hero Maskull's situation on the planet Tormance under the double star of Arcturus: 'He was a naked stranger in a huge, foreign, mystical world, and whichever way he turned, unknown and threatening forces were glaring at him' (Chapter 14). Maskull has volunteered for his predicament. Typifying the quester, he tells Krag, the arch-manipulator:

> You talk about a certain journey. Well, if that journey
> were a possible one, and I were given the chance of
> making it, I would be willing never to come back. For
> twenty-four hours on that Arcturian planet, I would give
> my life. That is my attitude towards that journey . . .
>
> (Chapter 2)

Life is a fair price for knowledge. Maskull duly travels to Tormance, learns from its codes about the complexities of his own human potential, occluded on earth, and dies to become Nightspore, his *alter ego*. Interplanetary personality melt-down opens him to the experience of approved homosexual bonding in his meeting with Joiwind's husband, Panawe: 'She put him in her husband's arms with gentle force, and stood back, gazing and smiling. Maskull felt rather embarrassed at being embraced by a man, but submitted to it; a sense of cool, pleasant languor passed through him in the act' (Chapter 7). The 'Belle Dame Sans Merci' theme is developed through associations of sex and death in Maskull's encounters with the women, Oceaxe, Tydomin and Sullenbode, who subverts the false pretences in which Tormance abounds – dualism is predictably rife under a double star – by her definition of love: 'Love is that which is perfectly willing to disappear and become nothing, for the sake of the beloved' (Chapter 19). Such simple apothegms often acquire fresh authority from inclusion in the surprises of Lindsay's imagined world, but can also be diminished by a context of over-intricate philosophizing and too many detailed but indecipherable symbolic alien landscapes.

From Spadevil, one of his many guides, Maskull learns of Hator who used pain to shield himself from the snares of pleasure and of the people of Sant who cultivate pain 'for the sake of vanity and pride' (Chapter 12). Calvin, apparently, has colonized outer space. From Tydomin he learns of the egotism of humility: 'Do not be humble, for humility is only self-judgement, and while we are thinking of self, we must be neglecting some action we could be planning or shaping in our mind' (Chapter 12). But the abuse of pain does not detract from its reality. As Nightspore the reincarnated Maskull is granted a vision of the source of divine light, Muspel, joined in cosmic struggle with the satanically leering Crystalman, shaper of worlds (Chapter 21). Krag, the initiator of Maskull's journey into the light, reveals himself: his name on earth is 'pain'. Though far from Christ-like, only he is stronger than Crystalman. Thus Lindsay's highly decorated philosophical rhapsody ends with the dourly fundamentalist proposition that pain is the necessary instrument by which forces hostile to spiritual truth will be conquered eventually. Among the jottings Lindsay extracted from his notebooks for the typescript of his unpublished *Philosophical Notes* is an observation that would have won approval from Mrs Oliphant's weary lady in 'The Land of Darkness':

> There is one thing worse than pain, and that is pleasure.
> So long as men suffer, there is still room for sublimity,
> but in the happy society of the sociologists, men will
> think and feel in battalions, and no one will any more feel
> himself an individual, rooted in Eternity.[12]

Linday's double-starred Arcturus projects the puritanism of his own way of life and reformulates the Presbyterian Manichaeism inherited from his Scottish-born Presbyterian forebears. To those who claim that he was a visionary genius others respond with allegations of clumsiness, but 'it is possible to be both a genius and a clumsy writer . . . Lindsay was not a clumsy writer so much as a *peculiar* one. Once the nature of the peculiarity is accepted, the qualities can be perceived.'[13]

Epic self: Catherine Carswell

'She's like a person in a book,' Mabel says of Joanna Bannerman to Bob Ranken in Catherine Carswell's *Open the Door!* (1920, Book, I, Chapter 5 [7]). To those governed by repressive middle-class Presbyterian forms of behaviour and modes of feeling Joanna is an exotic. Bob recognizes Mabel's 'trifling, feminine humbug' but is at ease with her, preferring

conventional flirtation and the pleasure of manly contempt for her 'tricki-
ness' to the demands made on him by an assertive, indecorously passionate Joanna. In her self-infatuation Joanna tries to control a Bob Ranken of
her own invention, magisterially challenging him at 'her carefully planned
betrothal feast' to love her more vigorously by presenting him with the
bogus gift of equal freedoms:

> If people love each other they shouldn't make bargains or
> tie each other down (much less of course if they don't
> love each other). I want you to feel quite, quite free. And
> if you should ever stop wanting me, you aren't to feel bad
> or anything. You are just to tell me straight out. That is
> to be *our* sort of engagement.
>
> (Book I, Chapter 5 [6])

Already her giving is as spurious as Lawrence Urquhart defines it to her
years later: 'Your kind of giving, if you only knew, is sheer robbery.
Give, give, give – to the poor man, when in reality it all goes to feed
your own egoism' (Book III, Chapter 3 [4]). He's right: even the kiss she
gives the blind woman beggar comes from 'feeling obscurely something
of that strangest envy of the human soul – the envy of utter misfortune'
(Book I, Chapter 2 [4]). To the destitute woman the kiss is no substitute
for the penny which Joanna, in her ecstasy of self-gratifying charity,
forgets to bring. ('The poor, one might say, were our pets,' Carswell
remembers of her Glasgow childhood in Chapter 2 of *Lying Awake*.[14]) Yet
Joanna never loses the reader's sympathy because, for all her mistakes, she
does not repeat her disappointed mother's lie which she thinks of, in a
phrase that expresses the thematic kernel of the novel, as 'a shirking of
the personal issue' (Book III, Chapter 3 [3]). Therefore we applaud her
when, resisting the atavistic power she still feels in the language and
formulae of her upbringing and in the minatory Eva Gedge, she dismisses
sister Georgie's religiose cant with 'I don't believe a single word of all you
have said to-day' (Book III, Chapter 3 [3]).

Bent on 'heroic love' with her 'deep-set human longing for wings',
Joanna is the next generation of her Italianized, manic-depressive Aunt
Perdy who opens her first 'unsuspected door of escape' (Book I, Chapter
6 [1]). 'Will freedom give you what you hunger for?' asks her first
husband (Book I, Chapter 6 [5]), the exigent Mario Rasponi, caging her
in his possessiveness as she had tried to cage Bob in her falsifying drama
of self. Mario's accidental death bequeaths to an awakened Joanna the
freedom to seek the answer to his question. Carswell's account of a
woman in love is clearly influenced by D. H. Lawrence whose themes
she understood and whose novels she reviewed for *The Glasgow Herald*.
Joanna's epiphany of the interpenetration of flesh and spirit (Book III,

Chapter 3 [10]) is essential Lawrence. So is the pre-empting of the political by the personal. Although Joanna goes to art school and her 'quest
for personal space and freedom coincides with the suffragists' struggles
which in Glasgow centred on the activities of students and teachers at the
College of Art', these political struggles are not part of her story.[15] But
Carswell's novel is no mere imitation of Lawrence. Expansively set in
Glasgow, Italy and London, *Open the Door!* is an exhilaratingly original
psychological epic of self-awakening and hard-won self-fulfilment, told
from the point of view of a woman who empathizes with the yearnings
of both sexes, including the longing to cease from compulsive competition, and who never undersells the complexities of male–female interaction on either personal or social levels.

Joanna's loves – Gerald, Bob, Mario, Louis, Lawrence Urquhart – are
stages in her progress towards self through a series of broken connections
and false freedoms. The novel's crucial images are those of the cage and
the door. Even when she is in motion with her family on the train to
Edinburgh (Book I, Chapter 1 [2]), the young Joanna is caged by the
trellised metal structure of Glasgow's Jamaica Bridge over the river Clyde.
Under the bridge she sees an image of flight in the 'giant liner that made
her slow way seaward' with a solitary figure on deck: 'Only a negro leaned,
gazing, upon a rail astern.' The point is clear: you have to be or become
an outsider to get away. Ironically, getting away to Italy with Mario takes
her into deeper captivity. Unsympathetic to his wife's desire for liberated
movement, Rasponi thinks a woman should be grateful for caged security:

> 'How would you like to live in a cage, a cage full of
> sunshine and beauty and delight, a cage of which the man
> you loved kept the key?'
> 'I don't think I should like it, thank you.'
> 'Why not?'
> 'A cage is a prison, isn't it?'
> 'A prison!' Mario made a gesture of despair. 'Oh, you
> English women with your phrases!'
> 'I'm not English, I'm Scotch.'
>
> (Book I, Chapter 6 [5])

Sympathy with Phemie Pringle's panic at the prospect of emigration and
with the afflicted Moon family frees Joanna from self-entrapment, showing her the quality of love that can survive crisis. In her discovery that
her true partner is Lawrence Urquhart, she finds at last the 'little sunken
door' once pointed out by Mario in the wall of the courtesan's villa, *La
Porziuncola*: 'It was that door in the garden wall of a villa through which
a famous woman was said to have welcomed her lover' (Book II, Chapter
2 [3]).

Freed of Mario, she is next caged by love for the artist, Louis Pender. Within the constraints of his thraldom to convention and the loveless marriage he cannot bring himself to abandon, he seems to promise freedom and the kind of 'utter union' her self-denying mother had craved in vain with the admonishing Sholto 'through all the years of a marriage physically fruitful' (Book II, Chapter 5 [1]). Nothing in Lawrence Urquhart's personality damages his prospects in the competition with Louis Pender so much as the stifling character of his formidable mother. Classily armour-plated in cashmere and gold, she is a portrait of refined moral ugliness. Carswell's precisely expressive style evokes Mrs Urquhart's insidious mixing of condescension with venomous innuendo till the flesh creeps and the spirit gasps for breath:

> Here was the source of suffocation in the house. Here in this woman with the large, pale, comely face, the beautiful snow-white hair, of an astonishing thickness (at one time no doubt, black like her son's), and the great, cashmere bosom, surmounted by a heavy, gold brooch like a snake coiled and knotted. In her large, comely whiteness Mrs Urquhart seemed to Joanna to absorb light and oxygen as might some powerfully succulent plant. Anything staying beside her for long, must surely yield up its share and languish. Though one of the two windows was open at the top, Joanna could have cried out for air as her hostess bore down upon her.
>
> (Book II, Chapter 3 [5])

Pender is not evil; but Joanna is in danger of suffocation by the insufficiency of his essential, aesthetic detachment. Lacking 'either the certainty or the courage of his love . . . this infirmity of spirit in him imposed sin upon her also' (Book II, Chapter 4 [3]). Their ecstasy is not only made to feel sinful by his lack of conviction, it is also barren. There is no prospect of the self-justifying 'utter union'. Louis keeps himself 'almost wholly inviolate' – a reminder of 'the pathos of incapacity' in Juley Bannerman's Sholto (Book III, Chapter 3 [3]) – and in being 'straight' ironically extends to Joanna, out of his own self-uncertainty, an adult version of the freedom she had once histrionically proposed to Bob Ranken. Something has 'just gone *phut*' in him by the time the trip to Edinburgh in Book III might have closed the gap between his covert love for Joanna and his public self. At least he cannot deceive her: 'the proof that her virtue was stronger than her falseness lay in the fact that no man she attracted could act falsely toward her. Punish them she might, but she drew the truth from them' (Book II, Chapter 4, [2]).

If Louis's truth is derived from Joanna's moral virtue, Lawrence

Urquhart's is his own, though Joanna is the agent of his self-awareness. Even the African sun cannot burn away Bob Ranken's 'spiritual indecision' (Book III, Chapter 4 [1]), but Joanna's insistence on the need for happiness in oneself (Book III, Chapter 2 [3]) decisively clarifies both Lawrence's sense of himself and his imperative need of her which distinguishes him from her other men. 'Joanna's self is not endowed upon her by Urquhart: that self must be complete before her final run. Joanna comes to terms first with her father . . . then with Louis . . . and, perhaps, most of all, with her own geography, the terrain of her earliest longings.'[16] The emotional and psychological logic of the novel persists despite the blemish of its hurried melodramatic ending, Joanna's breathless pursuit of Urquhart over the Duntarvie moor with which Carswell completes her intricate theorem of selfhood and love. 'It needs a man and a woman to create anything,' D. H. Lawrence wrote to Carswell in 1916, 'there is nothing can be created save of two, a two-fold spirit.'[17] Only desert and darkness would remain if this man and woman, ripened by experience into coherent selves and mutual need, did not come together:

> 'If I hadn't caught up on you,' she said, 'I should have died.'
> 'And I', said Lawrence, 'should never have lived.'
> (Book III, Chapter 5 [5])

The happy ending has been earned.

Epic earth: Neil M. Gunn and Lewis Grassic Gibbon

By the end of Lewis Grassic Gibbon's *A Scots Quair* (the trilogy was first published under its collective title in 1946) Chris Guthrie has been widowed twice and has parted amicably from her third husband. She is politically and spiritually at odds with her son, although the connection between them is still loving. In addition to losses from war with Germany and war against capitalism, her pagan relationship to the earth established in *Sunset Song* (1932) has been curtailed by the Manse in her marriage to the idealistic, liberal Reverend Robert Colquohoun. After his death at the end of *Cloud Howe* (1933) it is interrupted by her co-management of Ma Cleghorn's Duncairn boarding-house. But it is to the earth of her beginnings that Chris returns on the last page of *Grey Granite* (1934). From the summit of the Barmekin she looks out over the land as she had used to survey it from the cobwebbed, immemorial Standing Stones above Blawearie, Druidical symbols of cleaner ways of life before 'the dirt of gentry' (*Sunset Song*, Prelude). Rain and darkness fall on her:

> Lights had sprung up far in the hills, in little touns for a sunset minute while the folk tirred and went off to their beds, miles away, thin peeks in the summer dark.
> Time she went home herself.
> But she still sat on as one by one the lights went out and the rain came beating the stones about her, and falling all that night while she still sat there, presently feeling no longer the touch of the rain or hearing the sound of the lapwings going by.

Chris does not move because she is already home, absorbed back into the elemental truth of the land, beyond the human epic of love and war, political strife, religion and mortality. This, for Gibbon, is the only resolution of life's conflicts, a stark neo-Wordsworthian assimilation to 'earth's diurnal course / With rocks, and stones, and trees'.

Neil Gunn's earth is as solidly there as Gibbon's – 'The land, the quiet land, which for ever endures' (*The Silver Darlings*, Chapter 5) – but it is also metaphysically charged with a numinous quality from which Gunn acquires a serenity that distinguishes his vision from the Celtic fatalism found in the novels of Fiona Macleod (the pen-name of William Sharp) and from the angry anti-Presbyterian undertow of Fionn MacColla's (the pen-name of Tom Macdonald) highland novels, *The Albannach* ('The Highlander', 1932) and *And the Cock Crew* (1945). Writing of his beloved Caithness and the northern sea-coasts in 'My Bit of Britain', an essay for *The Field* in 1941, Gunn equates feeling for place with spiritual integrity:

> This is my corner of the Highlands, here my earliest memories were formed, and so, for better or worse, richer or poorer, I stick by it. It is the way the blood argues. And in itself it is perhaps not a bad way, for its springs out of affection and loyalty. All the theorists who argue so nobly against nationalism and for peace miss this simple point, it seems to me. When the blood fondly says, 'This is my land', it is at that moment profoundly in harmony and at peace. When it cannot say that, something has gone wrong, and it is that something that is the evil thing.[18]

The enforced migrations and relocations of the Highland Clearances that began with the destruction of the clan system of land ownership after the Jacobite rebellion of 1745 and were intensified throughout the nineteenth

century until the late 1880s violated this primal need, coming 'between
one and the sweet freedom of life' like the violence of Colonel Hicks's
attitude of mind as it seems to Clare in *The Lost Glen* (1932), 'a shadow
on thought . . . an insidious destruction of humour, a corrosive taint'
(Part 3, Chapter 1, [3]). Clearance disruption of crofter life is the real beginning of *The Silver Darlings*:

> They had come from beyond the mountain which rose up
> behind them, from inland valleys and swelling pastures,
> where they and their people before them had lived from
> time immemorial. The landlord had driven them from
> these valleys and pastures, and burned their houses, and set
> them here against the sea-shore to live if they could, and,
> if not, to die.
>
> (Chapter 1)

Gunn's belief in the sanctity of belonging led to his involvement with the
Scottish National Party and, despite their differences, cemented his friendship with Hugh MacDiarmid. In Gibbon the pathos of the epic effort to
live well is felt in the contrast between human action, which is fallible
and transient, and the land, which is aloof, impersonal and enduring; in
Gunn's novels the earth is full of messages, part of the action in a set of
variations on the epic theme of the relation between land and people. As
Ewan Macleod realizes towards the end of *The Lost Glen*, 'True environment gives to a man's actions an eternal significance. A native's natural
movement is part of land and sea and sky; it has in it the history of his
race; it is authentic . . . The unconscious held in common – that was race'
(Part 3, Chapter 3, [3]).

  The antitheses in Gunn's fiction are country and city (*Wild Geese
Overhead*, 1939; *The Key of the Chest*, 1945), urban alienation (notably in
his dystopian fable, *The Green Isle of the Great Deep*, 1944) and post-
Clearance communal Highland life (*The Silver Darlings*). Within this thematic frame he considers the oppositions between love and power (the
contest between Jeems and the landowner, Donald Tait, in *The Grey
Coast*, 1926), truly cognitive feeling and arid intellect (the superiority of
Harry's spiritual vision to the 'menacing forces of modern intelligence'[19]
represented by Geoffrey Smith in *Second Sight*, 1940). In *The Drinking
Well* (1946) love of the land (bannocks and butter) saves Iain Cattanach
from urban depletion (the tainted eggs served by his Edinburgh landlady)[20] and personal discord, but it is a love toughly earned in opposition
to his mother's hatred of the land and the economic arguments of Davidson,
the socialist orator. It is Douglas, the romantic historian, who prompts in
Iain the shock of recognition that makes him say, 'You talk out of the
blood. And – and that's where the music comes from' (Part 2, Chapter

20). In *Sun Circle* (1933) the same music 'sets a man brooding or walking in defiance, and the memory of it can in a lonely place make him shout with defiance and laugh, for he knows the challenge of his own creation against the immortality of the jealous gods' (Chapter 4, [4]). Cities are subject to time and change but this regenerative music lasts, even when the land itself seems to be 'settling down into decay' as in *The Lost Glen* (Part 1, Chapter 2, [1]). Will's vision of wild geese in *Wild Geese Overhead* draws him out of Glasgow to 'put a pastoral distance between himself and the murderous cruelty of city life'.[21] He is looking for the meaning of 'something which it was hardly right he should see, something out of occult books, out of magic. He should have been better prepared. It was going from him; and he had not got it all. He had missed something. What he had missed, he wondered over' (Chapter 1). After losing his fight with Jake in the street violence that flares at the end of Chapter 8, the answer comes to him during his recuperation in hospital when he realizes that Jenny Baird's strength comes from the earth through the rock garden at his landlady's farm. Her reticence is like the elm-tree's 'listening silence, like the silence in the heart of a harp' (Chapter 9). Even in his novels of Highland boyhood Gunn's ruralism abjures 'the distortions of agrarian romanticism'.[22] The boy of *Morning Tide* (1931) is initiated into rivalries, sexual distances and economic necessity. In *Highland River* (1937), technically Gunn's most original treatment of the fluid, unchronological interrelation of past and present, the boy Kenn's river with its salmon 'all-father' rises to archetypal value under the scrutiny of Kenn the adult physicist and damaged veteran of the First World War. In *Young Art and Old Hector* (1942) Art is located on both realistic and metaphysical levels by the unassailable matter-of-factness that earths Old Hector's wisdom of the heart:

> You see, I know every corner of this land, every little
> burn and stream, and even the boulders in the stream.
> And I know the moors and every lochan on them. And I
> know the hills, and the passes, and the ruins, and I know
> of things that happened here on our land long long
> ago . . . It's not the size of the knowing that matters, I
> think . . . it's the kind of the knowing. If, when you know
> a thing, it warms your heart, then it's a friendly knowing
> and worth the having.
>
> (Chapter 17)

Propulsion towards self-consciousness is fundamental in all Gunn's work. The central experience of his own boyhood, recounted in his autobiography, *The Atom of Delight* (1956), is the epiphany he experienced while sitting on a river boulder cracking hazelnuts:

Then the next thing happened, and happened, so far as I
can remember, for the first time. I have tried hard but can
find no simpler way of expressing what happened than by
saying: *I came upon myself sitting there.*

Within the mood of content, as I have tried to recreate
it, was this self and the self was me.

The state of content deepened wonderfully and
everything around was embraced in it.

(Chapter 4)[23]

A calmly vigilant sense of self is the contented state of being for which
Gunn's metaphor provides his title, *Sun Circle*:

As the Sun put a circle round the earth and all that it
contained, so a man by his vision put a circle round
himself. At the centre of this circle his spirit sat, and at
the centre of his spirit was a serenity for ever watchful.
Sometimes the watchfulness gave an edged joy in holding
at bay the demons and even the vengeful lesser gods, and
sometimes it merged with the Sun's light into pure
timeless joy.

(Chapter 8)

As with Lewis Grassic Gibbon, Catherine Carswell and the John Buchan
of *Sick Heart River* (1941), Gunn's quest in his fiction 'is for *self*; what
makes *a* self, what evidence can we find that we as humans have identity,
value, permanence, immortality?'[24] *The Silver Darlings* is the story of Finn's
quest for himself as a member of a community struggling for survival over
economic hardship, plague and the sea which, since the Clearances, has
become its principal source of income. The picture is animated by some
of Gunn's most fully realized characters – Catrine, Robbie, Kirsty and
Finn himself. It is raised to epic scale both by the continual interaction
between the people and the elements and by a dominantly heroic quality[25] exemplified by Catrine's dignity as solo mother after her husband,
Tormad, has been press-ganged and by her walk from Helmsdale to
Dunster – an echo of heroic walks undertaken by Scott's Jeanie Deans
and Mrs Oliphant's Kirsteen. The epic journey is a recurrent motif with
Roddie Sinclair's herring-fishing expedition to Stornoway providing a
pivotal episode whose consequences are felt by all the main characters
(Chapters 14–18). Finn's name associates him with Finn MacCoul, and
in Chapter 20 he reminds the drover of the legendary Celtic hero. Killing
the butterfly in Chapter 5 introduces him to 'the terrible knowledge of
good and evil', initiating his personal journey. By stages he finds adult

self-definition through his walk to Wick in search of the cholera doctor (Chapter 12), climbing the precipice to bring water to Roddie's fishermen aboard the *Seafoam* (Chapter 15), his rescue of Oscar and Duncan from the wreck (Chapter 23), his own expedition to Stornoway (Chapter 24) – by which he matches Roddie's heroism as his walk to Wick matches his mother's – his love for Una against competition by other fancies, and the maturing of his bond with Catrine from dependence and denial into a stable 'relationship of the blood' as 'imperceptible as a sleeping instinct' (Chapter 26).

The success of Finn's journey is assured by the approval of his story by Finn-son-of-Angus, the old story-teller on North Uist whose name guarantees appreciation of the genuinely heroic, in a passage which reveals Gunn's ideal of narrative art:[26]

> You told the story well. You brought us into the far
> deeps of the sea and we were lost with you in the
> Beyond where no land is, only wind and wave and the
> howling of the darkness. You kept us in suspense on the
> cliffs, and you had some art in the way you referred to
> our familiars of the other world before you told of the
> figure of the man you felt by the little stone house. There
> you saw no-one and you were anxious to make this clear,
> smiling at your fancy. It was well enough done. It was all
> well done. It was done, too, with the humour that is the
> play of drift on the wave. And you were modest.
>
> (Chapter 24)

All Gunn's ingredients are here, including, in the phrase 'smiling at your fancy', a reference to the gentle, even tentative character of a writer who always wonders if he's got it right and unflinchingly looks beyond the horizon of his own comprehension. His work is uneven and he over-writes, a Scottish failing since Scott, giving excessive information even in such a passage as his description of Kenn's 'saga of a fight' with the salmon in Chapter 1 of *Highland River*. He often labours the obvious. Lyricism and idiosyncratic philosophy can overshadow his characters and burden his narrative with ponderous reverie. His values are humane, his reading of history and vexed questioning of post-Second World War society are scrupulous, his love of his country is constant, critically responsible and proud. Scotland has produced no writer more likeable. *Highland River* and *The Silver Darlings* are his best books. Readers attracted by these towards his other works will find not only their incidental felicities, but also the stimulus of a wondering companion of the mind with a deeply earthed philosophy of hope.

Epic austerity: *A Scots Quair*

In *A Scots Quair* Gibbon[27] offers a bleaker vision with greater art than Gunn's. ('Quair' is an archaic word for 'quire', meaning gathered pages.) '*Oh Chris Caledonia,*' exclaims Robert Colquohoun to his wife in *Cloud Howe*, '*I've married a nation!*' (Chapter 3). The trilogy moves from legend to history, emerging from the days of William the Lyon and Cospatric de Gondeshil, Knight of Kinraddie, 'when gryphons and suchlike beasts still roamed the Scots countryside' (*Sunset Song*, Prelude) into a chronicle of the Scots nation from 1911 to the General Strike of 1926 and the hunger marches of 1932. Dot Allan's novel *Hunger March* (1934) describes the day of one of the marches in a city identifiable as Glasgow from various class and occupational perspectives. A more complex figure than Gibbon's young Ewan Tavendale, Allan's revolutionary character, Hamish Nimrod, is the novel's point of reference although seldom directly presented in the action. Nimrod seems to embody 'all that was most vital in the revolutionary movement in Scotland today',[28] but towards the end of the novel there is the suggestion that he may be a double agent who manipulates the hungry and unemployed into mass protest as a safety valve for the protection of an obtuse regime (Chapter 10). Stylistically dated but politically subtle, Allan's book should be remembered with George Blake's attempts to portray revolutionary politics in *The Wild Men* (1925) and *Young Malcolm* (1926) and with Blake's depiction of Glasgow during the Depression in *The Shipbuilders* (1935).

Chris Guthrie is the point of moral reference throughout the *Quair*, even in *Grey Granite*, the third book, in which her son Ewan's political career provides the main story. Gibbon's flowing style, derived from north-east Scottish idiom, gives the effect of one speaker talking, 'the voice of Scotland itself'.[29] 'In all three books,' wrote Eric Linklater, 'the rendering of the anonymous voice of the countryside is miraculously evocative and quintessentially true.'[30] Like the similarly unremitting prose style of William Faulkner, Gibbon's narrative rhythms keep 'the form – and the idea – fluid and unfinished, still in motion, as it were, and unknown, until the dropping into place of the very last syllable'.[31] Idiomatic humour, especially in *Sunset Song*, palliates the work's fundamental austerity. Like the combination of affection and bite in his Scottish short stories,[32] in *Scottish Scene: or the Intelligent Man's Guide to Albyn* (1934, written in collaboration with Hugh MacDiarmid), and in the fragment of *The Speak of the Mearns* (1982) left at his death,[33] his humour is both acerbic and warm. He gives us a bottomless loch which is like 'the depths of a parson's depravity'; Mistress Munro who, suspecting an ill word about herself, would 'redden up like a stalk of rhubarb in a dung patch'; the ministers offering up prayers for rain 'in between the bit about the

Army and the Prince of Wales' rheumatics'; the Tory who fights a by-election 'with a funny bit squeak of a voice, like a bairn that's wet its breeks'; Long Rob of the Mill's pipe-smoking defiance of the Exemption Board. In *Cloud Howe* there is the Segget War Memorial, 'an angel set on a block of stone, decent and sonsy in its stone night-gown', and the story of Dite Peat and Jim the Sourock's pig. In *Grey Granite* the Reverend Edward MacShilluck is a caricature of church bigotry, another Holy Willie.

Each book of the *Quair* culminates in Chris's survival over the failures of others. *Sunset Song* focuses on the life of farming. Chris's love of her land and its folk alternates with hatred:

> two Chrisses there were that fought for her heart and
> tormented her. You hated the land and the coarse speak
> of the folk and learning was brave and fine one day and
> the next you'd awaken with the peewits crying across the
> hills, deep and deep, crying in the heart of you and the
> smell of the earth in your face, almost you'd cry for that,
> the beauty of it and the sweetness of the Scottish land and
> skies.
>
> (Chapter 1)

The split of feeling in Chris reflects Gibbon's own ambivalence towards the life of the Mearns. In an essay entitled 'The Land' he writes:

> *That* is The Land out there, under the sleet, churned and
> pelted there in the dark, the long rigs upturning their
> clayey faces to the spear-onset of the sleet. That is The
> Land, a dim vision this night of laggard fences and long
> stretching rigs. And the voice of it – the true and
> unforgettable voice – you can hear even such a night as
> this as the dark comes down, the immemorial plaint of the
> peewit, flying lost. *That* is The Land – though not quite
> all. Those folk in the byre whose lantern light is a
> glimmer through the sleet as they muck and bed and tend
> the kye, and milk the milk into tin pails, in curling froth
> – they are The Land in as great a measure . . . I like to
> remember I am of peasant rearing and peasant stock.[34]

But a few lines later he says: 'Once I had a very bitter detestation for all this life of the land and the folk upon it.'[35] Chris's achievement in the first book of Gibbon's epic sequence is a capacity for joy that withstands a series of primal shocks as well as her moods of recoil from her environment: John Guthrie treats her mother 'like a breeding sow'; pregnant again and unable 'to thole it longer', Jean Guthrie poisons herself and her twins (Chapter 2); Guthrie terrifies Chris with urgent demands for incestuous sex (*'You're my flesh and blood, I can do with you what I will, come to me, Chris, do you hear?'* Chapter 3); her husband, Ewan Tavendale, treats her like a recalcitrant whore when he comes home on leave from the First World War, 'the foulness dripping from the dream that devoured him', and is executed in France as a deserter who only wanted to go home to his farm, the cry of the peewits and his sleeping wife (Chapter 4). In *Cloud Howe* Chris survives the failure of religion to make a better world either by her energetic second husband's practical Christianity or by his gloomily apocalyptic Christian mysticism. In *Grey Granite* she survives the failure of politics. (A talent for survival and non-conformity similar to Chris's characterizes Janie McVean in Jessie Kesson's *The White Bird Passes*, written in 1959.)

Young Ewan replaces his stepfather's God with the Communist ideal of freedom from capitalist controls. Beaten up by the police, he feels his identity melt into 'a hundred broken and tortured bodies all over the world' as Gibbon's anger builds a litany of contemporary injustices and political hypocrisies:

> . . . in Scotland, in England, in the torture-dens of the
> Nazis in Germany, in the torment-pits of the Polish
> Ukraine, a livid, twisted thing in the prisons where they
> tortured the Nanking Communists, a Negro boy in an
> Alabama cell while they thrust the razors into his flesh,
> castrating with a lingering cruelty and care. He was one
> with them all, a long wail of sobbing mouths and wrung
> flesh, tortured and tormented by the world's Masters while
> those Masters lied about Progress through Peace,
> Democracy, Justice, the Heritage of Culture – even as
> they'd lied in the days of Spartacus, lying now through
> their hacks in pulpit and press, in the slobberings of
> middle-class pacifists, the tawdry promisings of Labourites,
> Douglasites . . .
>
> (*Grey Granite*, Chapter 3)

Notwithstanding the righteous ecstasy of his own outrage, Gibbon understands the psychology of the political fanatic. Ewan is not to be idealized, although his character closely resembles the revolutionary Mitchell's. As a boy he collects Bronze Age flints. His mother watches him become 'rather like a flint himself . . . grey granite down to the core' (*Cloud Howe*, Chapter 3). Chris may represent the Earth-Goddess, but Ewan 'is something deeper: mineral . . . still natural, but part of a different and slower time-process'.[36] The rock-like purity of his political commitment is at once the source of his strength and of his cruelty to Ellen Johns – '*I can get a prostitute anywhere,*' he tells her – when she leaves the Communist Party, tired and disillusioned (Chapter 4). At the end of the Gowans and Gloag strike Big Jim Trease, the Party Agitator, says, '*A hell of a thing to be history, Ewan*' (Chapter 3). He has become 'the Just Man made Perfect, or History, in the Marxist sense, incarnate; in other words, a heroic concept'.[37] But a concept is in danger of remaining an abstraction, unreal as well as coldly inhuman. Ewan knows that his mother is still real: '*Didn't you know you were real, Chris, realer than ever?*' (Chapter 4). Gibbon knows that 'his [Ewan's] conception can neither compete with nor replace hers'.[38] Whether she would have kept her reality if she had not folded up her books and dreams 'and laid them away by the dark, quiet corpse that was [her] childhood' (*Sunset Song*, Chapter 2) is an open question. Roderick Watson notices that the first of Nan Shepherd's three novels, *The Quarry Wood* (1928), gives an idea of 'what might have happened to Chris Guthrie, had she decided to go to university after all, for Martha Ironside makes the same difficult journey towards intellectual and emotional maturity at a time when such space was seldom freely given to women'.[39] 'Mostly nerves and temper' as a child (Chapter 1), Martha manages to integrate 'what Chris Guthrie felt to be the division between her "English" and her "Scottish" selves'.[40] The two sides of a likely post-feminist Chris are to be found in practical Rona and introspective Cassie, Janice Galloway's fellow-travellers in her prize-winning novel, *Foreign Parts* (1994).

As the trilogy unfolds 'Gibbon is seized more and more by an overweening compassion for his kind – chivvied and trodden under by wars, capitalist farming, slump, and by the sheer brute pain and brevity of human life',[41] but Chris's reality is untouched by religious or political faction and impervious to the gossip which gives Gibbon's panorama its anecdotal vitality. Yet, 'SHE HAD NOTHING AT ALL', she thinks in *Grey Granite*, 'she never had anything, nothing in the world she believed in but change . . . Nothing endured' (Chapter 2). The theme of change is a refrain throughout the three novels. 'Nothing endures,' she thinks when Marget Strachan instructs her in love-making; 'nothing ever stayed the same', she decides, observing her careworn mother's sadness (*Sunset Song*, Chapter 1). 'Nothing endured at all,' she thinks again after the death of her father, 'nothing but the land' (*Sunset Song*, Chapter 3). The land is what she has had from the beginning, 'her surety unshaken' in 'the moors and the sun and the sea' (*Cloud Howe*, Chapter 4). It is the land that mortally calls her husband back from the insanity of war and out of his perverse attitude towards her. She can take pride in her grim, tormented father in relation to the land because he 'could farm other folk off the earth' (*Cloud Howe*, Chapter 1). All the other characters in *Sunset Song* are subsidiary to Chris's evolution and nature's unbiddable variety, from the June moors 'yellow with broom and powdered with purple', the 'shoom-shoom' of the sea by Bervie, the whistle of blackbirds in Blawearie's trees, the wail of peesies (lapwings), night coming over the Grampian Hills and the snipe crying in their hundreds, to rain on the roof, the batter of sleet, the lightning that strikes the barbed wire, killing Old Bob, and the rats she finds 'maybe kissing' on her wedding day. Gibbon's – and Chris's – song of the earth is muffled by Robert's intensities in *Cloud Howe*. In *Grey Granite* it is almost silenced, except in Chris's mind, by the urban life of Duncairn until her final return to Cairndhu. Her brother Will had been right after all:

> Scotland lived, she could never die, the land would outlast
> them all, their wars and their Argentines, and the winds
> come sailing over the Grampians still with their storms and
> rain and the dew that ripened the crops – long and long
> after all their little vexings in the evening light were dead
> and done.
>
> (*Sunset Song*, Chapter 4)

This 'unending morning' (*Grey Granite*, Chapter 4) is Gibbon's best hope, but it is scarcely human. According to his wife he believed 'in the Golden Age of prehistory and was not unhopeful of a Golden Age yet to come',[42] but at the end of the *Quair* Chris neither feels the rain nor hears the lapwings. She has become as the stones about her on which the rain also beats.

The entertainers: Conan Doyle, John Buchan and others

Richard Hannay, doyen of British action-men and amateur forefather of Ian Fleming's professional James Bond, is in pursuit of The Black Stone gang. A prominent politician is due to be assassinated. Time is running out. The stability of Europe is at stake. From the murdered American agent, Franklin P. Scudder's, coded notebook he deduces that 'the three cleverest rogues in Europe' will leave England for Germany from a place on the south-east coast where there are thirty-nine steps down to the sea. 'All this was very loose guessing,' Hannay admits with the inbred, coy self-deprecation of the ex-colonial Anglo-Scottish gentleman – the Great War is coming and he is clearly officer material – 'and I don't pretend it was ingenious or scientific. I wasn't any kind of Sherlock Holmes.' So, in Chapter 9 of his best-selling 'shocker', *The Thirty-nine Steps* (1915), John Buchan defers to Sir Arthur Conan Doyle, inventor of 'the most perfect reasoning and observing machine that the world has ever seen' ('A Scandal in Bohemia'[43]) and his bluff accomplice and foil, Dr Watson, the intellectual fall-guy of limited 'frontal development' to whom nothing is ever as elementary as Holmes makes out.

Like Neil Munro, the best of whose historical romances – *John Splendid* (1898) and *The New Road* (1915) – lack the vitality and easy craft of his humorous Para Handy tales (first collected in *The Vital Spark*, 1906) about a West of Scotland steam puffer and its shrewd, rascally skipper, both Doyle and Buchan wrote more ambitiously literary and scholarly works than those that won them enduring popularity. Similarly, Compton Mackenzie bid for high literary stakes with the autobiographical novel, *Sinister Street* (1913), and again with *The Four Winds of Love* (1937–45), an elaborate four-volume social, political and philosophical saga of the modern world. He displays moral distinction in the more sparingly written *Thin Ice*, but won hearts, fame, and a film contract with *Whisky Galore* (1947), the best of his light-hearted skits on the Scottish character in which the islanders of 'Todday', sharing their devotion to Scotland's peerless amber fluid, conspire against the imperialist excisemen. Kenneth Grahame made his name with gently satirical child's-eye perceptions of the adult world in *The Golden Age* (1895) and *Dream Days* (1898) – 'Grown-up people really ought to be more careful'[44] – but *The Wind in the Willows* (1908) with its anthropomorphic animals is his masterpiece, an entertainment that delivers much more than expected. Norman Douglas holds his corner on the outskirts of Scottish literature with the sophisticated Italian sketches of *Old Calabria* (1915) and, particularly, with *South Wind* (1917) which is less a novel than an episodic display of high-acidity sarcasm and camp amorality on the fictitious island of Nepenthe ('distilled out of Capri . . . as it always should have been and as it never, alas! yet was or will be'[45]). Like an antic minister of the Devil's party Douglas preaches a seductively anti-Calvinist gospel of hard-boiled hedonism through his inimitably bitchy character-portraits and by such actions as 'when Mrs Meadows pushes her scoundrelly first husband off a cliff [Chapter 42] and her cousin Bishop Heard condones it, his Northern sense of morality beginning to dissolve in the warm Mediterranean sun'.[46] Eric Linklater's best work is the comedy of *Poet's Pub* (1929), the lightly sustained anti-establishment satire of *Private Angelo* (1946) and his riotous extravaganza for children, *The Wind on the Moon* (1944), rather than the more stagily contrived picaresque critique of *Juan in America* (1931) or the epic pretensions of *The Men of Ness* (1932).[47]

Both Conan Doyle and Buchan were drawn to history. Notable among Doyle's historical romances are his idealizing story of fourteenth-century chivalry, *The White Company* (1891), *The Exploits of Brigadier Gerard* (1896)

– the first of his tales about a debonair, comically egotistical Napoleonic soldier and *raconteur* – and *Sir Nigel* (1906), a companion piece to *The White Company* designed to 'reproduce the Middle Ages in all their Gothic richness'.[48] In *The Lost World* (1912) his Professor Challenger's journey into preserved pre-history foreshadows Michael Crichton's science-fiction fantasy of genetically engineered dinosaurs in *Jurassic Park* (1993). From his experiences as Boer War correspondent came *The Great Boer War* (1900) and *The War in South Africa: Its Causes and Conclusions* (1902). His later interest in spiritualism produced *The History of Spiritualism* (1926). But it was the publication of *A Study in Scarlet* (1887) with its introduction of Sherlock Holmes (based on the forensic expert, Dr Joseph Bell, one of Doyle's teachers at Edinburgh University) that led to the stories in the *Strand Magazine* which made him and his detective famous by popularizing the recipe devised by Edgar Allan Poe in such stories as 'The Murders in the Rue Morgue' (1841) and 'The Purloined Letter' (1845). Poe's unflappably ratiocinative detective, Monsieur Dupin, and his narrator's role as a comparatively slow-witted intermediary between detective and reader, give the model for the Holmes–Watson formula. Conan Doyle also admired Emile Gaboriau, French creator of the professional detective Monsieur Lecoq and the amateur Le Père Tabaret ('Wilkie Collins, but more so', Doyle noted[49]). His own skill in portraying memorable characters is more responsible for his success than the ingenious plots of his 'children's stories for grown-ups'.[50] Holmes's violin, deerstalker, hypodermic and dottles smoked before breakfast guarantee a continuing readership for *The Sign of Four* (1890), *The Hound of the Baskervilles* (1902) and the stories leading up to the great confrontation at the falls of Reichenbach with his arch-enemy, Professor Moriarty ('The Final Problem'[51]).

The fertility of Doyle's imagination is less widely recognized than it deserves to be because Holmes's unique magnetism as the world's 'only unofficial consulting detective . . . the last and highest court of appeal in detection' (*The Sign of Four*, Chapter 1) has deflected attention from stories in which he does not appear. The variety of Doyle's interests is reflected in the headings under which *The Conan Doyle Stories* (1929) arranges its contents into tales of the Ring, the Camp, Pirates, Blue Water, Terror, Mystery, Twilight and the Unseen, Adventure, Medical life and – his own favourite group – 'Tales of Long Ago'. He is an expert in the shock ending ('The Case of Lady Sannox'; 'How It Happened'), the tale of horror ('The Pot of Caviare'; 'The Striped Chest', a gruesome variation of the *Marie Celeste* theme), and the mixture of scientific and supernatural ideas ('The Horror of the Heights'; 'Lot 249'). His Captain Sharkey of the barque *Happy Delivery* is an irresistibly villainous model of insolent cunning, slicing wit and inventive cruelty among those who 'hoisted the Jolly Roger at the mizzen and the bloody flag at the main, declaring a private war upon their own account against the whole human race' ('Captain Sharkey: How the Governor of Saint Kitt's came Home'[52]).

John Buchan's fluent narrative style and personal conviction enliven his subjects and their times in *Montrose* (1928), *Sir Walter Scott* (1932), *Oliver Cromwell* (1934) and *The Path of the King* (1921), a historical fantasy on the theme of 'kingly blood' which traces the charismatic ingredient from a young Viking to Abraham Lincoln. But it is the characters he called his 'group of musketeers'[53] who save him from becoming merely an honourable footnote to the histories of Scottish and English literature. The popularity of *The Thirty-nine Steps* encouraged Buchan to follow it with a series of novels[54] in which Richard Hannay reappears with his comrades – Pieter Pienaar, Sandy Arbuthnot (Lord Clanroyden), Sir Archibald Roylance, Sir Edward Leithen and John S. Blenkiron, the bulky American indebted to Hannay for the Turkish escapade in *Greenmantle* (1916) which cures his dyspepsia. If they now seem like humanoid editions of Kenneth Grahame's Mole, Ratty, Badger and Toad at play on a *Boy's Own Paper* riverbank, these are the 'puppets' who became for Buchan and the English-reading world 'very real flesh and blood'.[55] His retired Glasgow grocer, Dickson McCunn, is a more original invention than Hannay, but the novels in which he appears with his Gorbals Diehard boys – *Huntingtower* (1922), *Castle Gay* (1930) and *The House of the Four Winds* (1935) – are more loosely constructed than the Hannay books and less successful in projecting a coherent world for the reader to escape to.

The Hannay stories specialize in action – even if urgency is often jeopardized by Buchan's lingering too long in Hannay's decently prosaic mind – and compelling villains. Hannay's admiration for brutal Colonel von Stumm ('The German of caricature, the real German . . . I couldn't help admiring him') and Hilda von Einem ('Mad and bad she might be, but she was also great') in *Greenmantle* and Dominick Medina ('a devil . . . but . . . a great devil') in *The Three Hostages* (1924) smacks of the sado-masochism pornographically deployed by Ian Fleming in his suavely commercial James Bond novels. The racism of Buchan's musketeers towards Jews, blacks, Bolsheviks and the Irish is even more discomfiting than his smugly clubbable imperialism. Inadvertent self-parody is never far away:

> We met in a room on the second floor of a little
> restaurant in Mervyn Street . . . The Club had its own
> cook and butler, and I swear a better dinner was never
> produced in London, starting with preposterously early
> plovers' eggs and finishing with fruit from Burminster's
> houses. There were a dozen present including myself
> . . . Collatt was there, and Pugh, and a wizened little man
> who had just returned from bird-hunting at the mouth of
> the Mackenzie. There was Palliser-Yeates, the banker, who

didn't look thirty, and Fulleylove, the Arabian traveller,
who was really thirty and looked fifty. I was specially
interested in Nightingale, a slim, peering fellow with
double glasses, who had gone back to Greek manuscripts
and his Cambridge fellowship after captaining a Bedouin
tribe. Leithen was there, too, the Attorney-General, who
had been a private in the Guards at the start of the War
and had finished up a G.S.O.I. . . . I should think there
must have been more varied and solid brains in that dozen
than you would find in an average Parliament.

(*The Three Hostages*, Chapter 5)

All he claimed for his writings was that they were 'pure minstrelsy',[56] yet
behind the butlers, plovers' eggs, country estates and jolly good fellows,
Buchan writes as committedly as William Golding about the fragility of
civilization. As the icily urbane Andrew Lumley tells Edward Leithen in
The Power-House (1916), 'Civilization needs more than the law to hold
it together . . . Civilization is a conspiracy . . . Modern life is the silent
compact of comfortable folk to keep up pretences' (Chapter 3). Golding's
Lord of the Flies (1954) endorses the position. As a son of the Manse
Buchan believed in human susceptibility to evil. Sandy Arbuthnot's speech
about Ram Dass's opinion of propaganda in *The Three Hostages* is to be
taken seriously: 'He said that the great offensives of the future would be
psychological, and he thought the Governments should get busy about it
and prepare their defence . . . He considered that the most deadly weapon
in the world was the power of mass-persuasion' (Chapter 5).

Leithen's flight from acedia into northern Canada in *Sick Heart River*
(1941; published in the USA as *Mountain Meadow*) to rescue Francis
Galliard from despair, finding his God in the process and sacrificing
himself for the sake of the mortally dispirited Hare Indians, is part of the
'contest between Death and Life' (Part III, Chapter 18) which finds its
greater theatre in the Second World War. Leithen and Galliard organize
their guides, Lew and Johnny Frizel, 'to *hunt* for the Hare's meat: to
recreate in Canadian terms the pre-agricultural idyll. Leithen's last act
places him with the fishermen in Gunn and the innocent hunters in
Gibbon's "dawn of time".'[57] This most personal of Buchan's novels is
marred by travelogue scenic indulgence and excessive self-important in-
trospection by the physically afflicted Leithen, yet Leithen's elemental
search for himself persuades, touches the heart and shows that the basis
of Buchan the entertainer is Buchan the son of a Free Church minister,
preoccupied with the good of the soul. Buchan's adventure stories, like
the best-sellers of Alistair MacLean, demonstrate that for good entertainment something must be at stake. Serious and popular need not be too
far apart.

Notes

1. Trevor Royle, *The Macmillan Companion to Scottish Literature* (London, 1983), p. 133.

2. F. R. Leavis calls it 'Admirable and indispensable' in his *D. H. Lawrence: Novelist* (Harmondsworth, 1955), p. 11.

3. John Henry Mackay, *The Hustler, The Story of a Nameless Love from Friedrich Street*, translated from the German by Hubert Kennedy (Boston, 1985). The first English translation of *Der Puppenjunge*.

4. Toni Davidson (ed.), *And Thus Will I Freely Sing: An Anthology of Gay and Lesbian Writing from Scotland* (Edinburgh, 1989), p. [5].

5. J. Leslie Mitchell (Lewis Grassic Gibbon), *Gay Hunter*, with an introduction 'Lewis Grassic Gibbon and Science Fiction' by Edwin Morgan (Edinburgh, 1989).

6. See George Douglas Brown, *The House with the Green Shutters*, ed. with an Introduction, Notes and Glossary by J. T. Low (Edinburgh, 1974), pp. xvi–xxii.

7. J. Macdougall Hay, *Gillespie*, with an Introduction by Bob Tait and Isobel Murray (Edinburgh and Vancouver, 1979), p. vii.

8. Lewis Grassic Gibbon alludes to Brown's novel in the Prelude of *Sunset Song*. A new minister calls Kinraddie 'the Scots countryside itself, fathered between a kailyard and a bonny brier bush in the lee of a house with green shutters. And what he meant by that you could guess at yourself if you'd a mind for puzzles and dirt, there wasn't a house with green shutters in the whole of Kinraddie.' The allusion is repeated in Chapter 2. The people of the Mearns, presumably, would not have tolerated a Gourlay.

9. George Douglas Brown's description of Paul Kruger, the Boer president, foreshadows his characterization of John Gourlay. From November 1899 to February 1900, in consultation with his friend, Andrew Melrose, Brown published in twenty-seven episodes *The Life of Paul Kruger, the Most Remarkable Character in Modern History* in the *Morning Herald*, nos. 184–260. A passage about Kruger's stubbornness in the issue of 20 December 1899 presages the same trait in Gourlay: 'his is not a quick, facile, and easily-altered mind, but a sullen and heavily-pondering one. Thus an impression which he once receives is retained for ever. "Hard as it is to get an idea into his mind," says one friend who knows him well, "it is a thousand times harder to get it out when once you get it in."' See Patrick Scott, 'The Kailyard on the Veldt: George Douglas Brown's Life of Paul Kruger', *Scottish Literary Journal*, 12, no. 1 (May 1985), pp. 40–52 [50].

10. George Douglas Brown, *The House with the Green Shutters*, with an Introduction by J. B. Priestley (London, 1929), p. 8.

11. See Ian Spring, 'Determinism in John MacDougall Hay's *Gillespie*', *Scottish Literary Journal*, 6, no. 2 (December, 1979), pp. 55–68.

12. David Lindsay, 'From *Philosophical Notes*', *Lines Review*, no. 40 (March 1972), pp. 22–7 [23].

13. J. B. Pick, untitled note in *Lines Review*, no. 40 (March 1972), p. 2.

14. Catherine Carswell, *Lying Awake: An Unfinished Autobiography and Other Posthumous Papers*, ed. with an introduction by John Carswell (London, 1950), p. 15.

15. Pam Morris, *Literature and Feminism* (Oxford, 1993), p. 143.

16. Jan Pilditch, 'Opening the door on Catherine Carswell', *Scotlands*, 2 (1994), pp. 53–65 [63].

17. Catherine Carswell, *The Savage Pilgrimage: A Narrative of D. H. Lawrence*, with a memoir of the author by John Carswell (Cambridge, 1981), p. 71.

18. Neil M. Gunn, *The Man Who Came Back: Short Stories and Essays*, ed. Margery McCulloch (Edinburgh, 1991), p. 64.

19. Francis Russell Hart, *The Scottish Novel, A Critical Survey* (London, 1978), p. 352.

20. J. B. Caird, 'Neil M. Gunn, Novelist of the North', David Morrison (ed.), *Essays on Neil M. Gunn* (Thurso, 1971), p. 41.

21. F. R. Hart and J. B. Pick, *Neil M. Gunn, A Highland Life* (London, 1981; reissued Edinburgh, 1985), p. 168.

22. Douglas Dunn, 'Critics' silver darling', *Glasgow Herald*, 11 July 1987, p. 13.

23. Referring to this passage in a letter to Francis Russell Hart, Gunn writes: '. . . there is a condition of the mind "on the way" to what the Japanese Zen masters call *satori*. All tensions (mental and muscular) vanish and you rise out of yourself into freedom – an atom of delight.' See Neil M. Gunn, *Selected Letters*, ed. J. B. Pick (Edinburgh, 1987), p. 199.

24. Douglas Gifford, *Neil M. Gunn and Lewis Grassic Gibbon* (Edinburgh, 1983), p. 15.

25. See Margery McCulloch, *The Novels of Neil M. Gunn: A Critical Study* (Edinburgh, 1987), p. 87.

26. Hart, *The Scottish Novel*, p. 359.

27. Explaining his pseudonym, J. Leslie Mitchell said: 'It was necessary for *Sunset Song* . . . Mitchell is primarily an archaeologist and a Diffusionist. He's not "national". But *Sunset Song*, as a realism-romance of Scotland, needed another personality and a different style of writing to bud it forth. Hence Gibbon – which, by the way, is a family name.' See Louis Katin, 'Author of *Sunset Song*', *Glasgow Evening News*, 16 February 1933, p. 6.

28. Dot Allan, *Hunger March* (London, 1934), p. 36.

29. Ivor Brown, 'Foreword', Lewis Grassic Gibbon, *A Scots Quair*, 2nd impression (London, 1950), p. 9.

30. Letter to Ray Mitchell, 19 February 1935, quoted in Ian S. Munro, *Leslie Mitchell: Lewis Grassic Gibbon* (Edinburgh, 1966), p. 213.

31. Conrad Aiken, 'William Faulkner (1939)', *A Reviewer's ABC: Collected Criticism of Conrad Aiken from 1916 to the Present* (London, 1961), p. 203.

32. See Lewis Grassic Gibbon, *A Scots Hairst: Essays and Short Stories*, ed. and introduced by Ian S. Munro (London, 1967).

33. Lewis Grassic Gibbon, *The Speak of the Mearns*, ed. and introduced by Ian Campbell (Edinburgh, 1982). Munro prints parts of Gibbon's unfinished typescript in *A Scots Hairst*.

34. Gibbon, *A Scots Hairst*, ed. Munro, pp. 67–8.

35. Ibid., p. 68.

36. Gifford, *Gunn and Gibbon*, p. 112.

37. Walter Allen, *Tradition and Dream: The English and American Novel from the Twenties to Our Time* (London, 1964), p. 231.

38. D. M. Roskies, 'Lewis Grassic Gibbon and *A Scots Quair*: Ideology, Literary Form, and Social History', *Southern Review*, 15, no. 2 (July 1982), pp. 178–204 [199].

39. Nan Shepherd, *The Quarry Wood*, introduced by Roderick Watson (Edinburgh, 1987), pp. vii–viii.

40. Ibid., p. viii.

41. 'Homeward Bound', *TLS*, 18 August 1966, p. 748.

42. 'So Well Remembered: Lewis Grassic Gibbon by His Wife', *New Scot*, 4, no. 6 (June 1948), pp. 16–17 [17].

43. The first story in Sir Arthur Conan Doyle, *The Adventures of Sherlock Holmes* (London, 1892).

44. Kenneth Grahame, 'The Magic Ring', *Dream Days* (Edinburgh, 1983), p. 71.

45. Norman Douglas, *South Wind* (London, 1946), p. vi.

46. Edwin Morgan, *Twentieth-Century Scottish Classics* (Glasgow, 1987), p. 4.

47. Allan Massie would deplore this relegation of Linklater who he believes 'has strong claims to be considered Scotland's best novelist since Stevenson'. See Allan Massie, *101 Great Scots* (Edinburgh, 1987), p. 280.

48. John Dickson Carr, *The Life of Sir Arthur Conan Doyle* (London, 1953), p. 180.

49. Ibid., p. 51.

50. Sean French, 'The game's afoot', *The Observer Review*, 12 December 1993, p. 21.

51. The last story in *The Memoirs of Sherlock Holmes* (London, 1894). The encounter was not as fatal for Holmes as Conan Doyle intended it to be. Public demand compelled him to resurrect Holmes in *The Hound of the Baskervilles*.

52. Story number 13 in Sir Arthur Conan Doyle, *The Conan Doyle Stories* (London, 1929).

53. John Buchan, *Memory Hold-the-Door* (London, 1940), p. 195. (Published in the USA as *Pilgrim's Way*, Boston, 1940.)

54. *Greenmantle* (1916), *Mr Standfast* (1919), *The Three Hostages* (1924), *The Courts of the Morning* (1929). Hannay also appears in the stories of *The Runagates Club* (1928) and *The Gap in the Curtain* (1932).

55. Buchan, *Memory Hold-the-Door*, p. 195.

56. Alastair Buchan, 'J. B.', *John Buchan by His Wife and Friends* (London, 1947), p. 290.

57. Christopher Harvie, 'Second Thoughts of a Scotsman on the Make: Politics, Nationalism and Myth in John Buchan', *The Scottish Historical Review*, 70, 1: no. 188 (April 1991), pp. 31–54 [54].

Chapter 10

'Whaur's yer Wullie Shakespeare?' The Return of Scottish Drama

There is no paucity of Scottish theatrical heritage, but there is a shortage of durable Scottish plays. Drama is the genre in which Scottish writers have shown least distinction. This is partly explained by the circumstances of theatrical history. From the thirteenth to the eighteenth century theatrical activity was plagued by suppression and censorship. In 1214 Alexander II forbade both plays and banquets at court after the death of his father.[1] Folk plays survived and theatrical entertainment returned to the Scottish court, but encouragement and patronage of theatre under James VI absconded when the court moved to London in 1603, and the Reformation dourly favoured plays with a devotional message. Above this dreich theatrical landscape towers Sir David Lyndsay's verse morality play, *Ane Pleasant Satyre of the Three Estaitis, in Commendation of Vertew and Vituperation of Vyce*, performed at the Palace of Linlithgow in 1540. Its trenchant commentary on Lords, Commons and Clergy, racy interludes, lively use of stage business and metrical variety make it, still, Scotland's one indisputably great dramatic achievement. Its exposure of the abuses of power, its blend of formality, satire and comedy, tirades and turns, the role of John the Commonweill as *vox populi*, and, most of all, its topicality make it a prototype of the most successful Scottish plays produced in the twentieth century. Joe Corrie's working-class drama – best represented by his first full-length script, the 1926 General Strike play, *In Time of Strife* (1928), and the one-acter, *Hewers of Coal* (1937) – Robert McLellan's 'historical comedy' *Jamie the Saxt* (1937), the 7:84 Theatre Company's *The Cheviot, the Stag and the Black, Black Oil* (1973) arranged and directed by John McGrath, Liz Lochhead's *Mary Queen of Scots Got Her Head Chopped Off* (1987), and even Tony Roper's *The Steamie* (1987) are among the various ideological if not formal descendants of Lyndsay's masterpiece.

Sir Robert Walpole's notorious Licensing Act of 1737 closed Allan Ramsay's Carrubber's Close playhouse in Edinburgh, though Ramsay's *The Gentle Shepherd* remained popular in performance. If the reception of John Home's *Douglas* (1756) can be gauged by the enthusiast in the audience who called out, 'Whaur's yer Wullie Shakespeare noo?', its success was greater than its merit, though it did wonders for the Scottish reputation of Mrs Sarah Siddons as the despairing, suicidal Lady Randolph. A Gothic concoction of gesticulant heroics and melodramatic pathos, it remains a curiosity, as does the nineteenth-century vogue for sensation-alist adaptations of Scott's novels. Despite the favourable reception accorded Joanna Baillie's historical romance, *De Montfort* (1800), and praise of her drama by John Wilson, Byron, Scott and Wordsworth, the only reason why her plays 'should be rescued from the midden of oblivion' is their demonstration 'that it was possible for a woman to handle themes till then supposed to be the province of male genius only',[2] even if 'not even the greatest actor could lift [her] passion-dominated heroes into the realms of humanity'.[3] Nothing in Scottish 'legitimate' theatre compared for vitality with the developing music-hall or variety theatre until J. M. Barrie's success on the London stage with *The Little Minister* (1897) seemed to augur a new playwright of exceptional promise.

The failure of J. M. Barrie and the success of *Peter Pan*

Apart from his one masterpiece, *Peter Pan* (1904), Barrie defied the au-gury. Applauded by an undernourished theatre-going public in what Barrie calls his 'beloved solitary London that was so hard to reach',[4] his plays, though 'human and humorous',[5] lack depth except as reflections of his complicated personality. A few of his inventions – the perfect butler of *The Admirable Crichton* (1902), Peter Pan, Wendy, Tinker Bell, Captain Hook and 'The Island that Likes to be Visited' in *Mary Rose* (1920) – have attained a permanence detached from their scripts, and Barrie's gift for a smart turn of phrase takes him into Oscar Wilde territory.

'There is a satisfaction about living in *Quality Street* which even religion cannot give,' announces the opening stage direction for *Quality Street* (1901), in which Susan Throssel reprimands Miss Willoughby's disap-proval of Miss Phoebe, who is expected to marry soon, with ''Tis all jealousy to the bride and good wishes to the corpse' (I); *The Admirable Crichton* (1902) introduces the sporadically philanthropic Earl of Loam as 'really the reformed House of Lords which will come some day' and sends up the smug Hon. Ernest Woolley by the blank response accorded his choicest epigram, 'Agatha, I'm not young enough to know every-thing' (I); *What Every Woman Knows* (1908) furnishes the Wylie living room with 'a bookcase of pitch pine, which contains six hundred books, with glass doors to prevent your getting at them' (I) and includes David

Wylie's deathless observation to the Comtesse de la Brière: 'My lady, there are few more impressive sights in the world than a Scotsman on the make' (II); in *The Twelve-Pound Look* (1910) Kate tells Sir Harry, 'One's religion is whatever he is most interested in, and yours is Success', and the stage direction for Act I of *Dear Brutus* (1917) observes that 'Every woman who pronounces *r* as *w* will find a mate; it appeals to all that is chivalrous in man.' Barrie is aware that 'the strange days when it was considered "unwomanly" for women to have minds' were not over yet (*What Every Woman Knows*, III). Like Robert Louis Stevenson he is a stylist, but his style has made him obsolete. The knowingness at first ingratiates by mild surprise, then seems cheap. Facility degrades sentiment. Maturing stagecraft and, even in the early plays, a nimbler epigrammatic wit than the Hon. Ernest Woolley's cannot disguise complacent Edwardian sentimentality and matinée triviality. While George Douglas Brown and Macdougall Hay confront the realities of a changing world in their fiction, Barrie is discovered 'playing hide and seek with angels',[6] flirting with the *Zeitgeist* in chintzy divertimenti which titillatingly raise contemporary social issues only to run away from them. He gives the impression of a mind that thinks it is too clever to care enough about the vulgar business of sorting something out.

Quality Street is set during the Napoleonic Wars among provincial manners like those of Thrums, Barrie's fictionalized Kirriemuir in the Kailyard sketches of *Auld Licht Idylls* (1888) and *A Window in Thrums* (1889), whose blending of mockery and sentimentality, rooted in Barrie's pathological melancholia, anticipates the characteristic tone of the plays. Assumptions supported by established masque conventions in the Elizabethan theatre are unsustainable on a realistic stage, so the disguise by which Phoebe gives Valentine Brown's male chauvinism its come-uppance by attracting him, among others, to herself as Livvy, her non-existent niece, is too implausible a device to carry even this play's lightweight action. There is an adroitly theatrical turning of the tables when the chastened Dr Brown advises Livvy in Act II to desist from indiscriminate flirting before he goes on to declare his love for her supposed aunt – Phoebe had expected him to propose to her manufactured Livvy – but Barrie's stage mechanics creak embarrassingly and his characters are too visibly puppets. Valentine's conversion and the pluck of the Throssel sisters – blustering but educable man and obscurely soldiering women – are potentially serious themes amenable to genuinely satirical treatment. Barrie's candy-floss is sticky and demeaning.

The Admirable Crichton turns more securely on the irony that it is the butler who 'can't help being a Conservative', dissenting from the aristocrat's Radical views – while rendering his lordship impeccable service – maintaining strict hierarchical etiquette in the servants' hall and abhorring 'his lordship's compelling his servants to be his equals – once a month'

(Act I). 'No condescension', Lord Loam admonishes his fashionably in-
dolent daughters, Catherine, Agatha and Mary, 'The first who conde-
scends recites', getting a laugh but missing the point that his monthly
equality charade is the soul of condescension. The island of Acts II and
III proves the sham. 'There must always, my lady, be one to command
and others to obey,' announces Crichton in Act II as though serving his
apothegm on a silver tray. In any situation the leader will naturally emerge,
though it takes a while for Lord Loam to appreciate his peerless butler's
Radical Conservatism:

> LORD LOAM. Well, well. This question of the
>   leadership; what do you think now, Crichton?
> CRICHTON. My lord, I feel it is a matter with which I
>   have nothing to do.
> LORD LOAM. Excellent. Ha, Mary? That settles it,
>   I think.
> LADY MARY. It seems to, but – I'm not sure.
> CRICHTON. It will settle itself naturally, my lord,
>   without any interference from us.
> (*The reference to Nature gives general dissatisfaction.*)
>
> (II)

Rescue brings the second reversal by which Crichton, natural dictator on
the island, is all too predictably returned to his fitting station in the
artificial class system of 'the other island' which unnaturally prefers Lord
Loam and his kind by the natural accident of birth. The paradoxes are
clear and they are lucidly dramatized, but 'Barrie's position is strictly
neutralist in dealing with the class system',[7] and the story which *The
Admirable Crichton* stimulates the audience to want is the play that might
have followed it, not the mincing pantomime on which the curtain falls.
As Granville-Barker puts it, referring to Barrie's need to keep sympathy
for Crichton as well as for Lady Mary, 'The issue is shirked, very cleverly
shirked; but the shirking of an obvious issue must always be a deadly
weakness in a play.'[8] The play that might have been is implicit in the final
exchange between Lady Mary and Crichton:

> LADY MARY. Do you despise me, Crichton? (*The man
>   who could never tell a lie makes no answer.*) You are the
>   best man among us.
> CRICHTON. On an island, my lady, perhaps; but in
>   England, no.
> LADY MARY. Then there's something wrong with
>   England.

CRICHTON. My lady, not even from you can I listen to
a word against England.

(IV)

Barrie tries to be tougher in *What Every Woman Knows* and almost
succeeds in the arrestingly Pinteresque first Act with its atmosphere of
unspoken conspiracy, jerky dialogue and David's startling proposal to
John Shand, apprehended in the act of burgling knowledge from the
locked bookcase:

DAVID (*sternly*). . . . Mr Shand, we're willing, the three of
us, to lay out £300 on your education . . . On
condition that five years from now, Maggie Wylie, if
still unmarried, can claim to marry you, should such be
her wish; the thing to be perfectly open on her side,
but you to be strictly tied down.

(I)

However, after John Shand's 'great hour has come' at the beginning of
Act II the play collapses into situation comedy on the unexceptional
theme of the clever woman discernible behind any successful man. It is
a motif in Barrie's work; even in *Mary Rose* he tells us that 'Mrs Morland
knows everything about her husband except that she does nearly all his
work for him' (I). Maggie Wylie does know that she is the source of her
husband's 'pluck to divide the House' (III) and responsible for 'the little
things' that transform a dull, vain man into a successful MP. The trouble
is that the audience has known it too, since the beginning, and the play
holds no surprises except, perhaps, that Maggie's powers extend to
coaxing stolid John into laughter at the end. Slick stage-management, the
worldly Comtesse, the 'naughty little impediment' in Lady Sybil's voice
when she is most alluring, and Charles Venables, the courtly diplomat
with a heart of steel and Leeds in his gift for Maggie's version of John
decorate the theme without developing it. As with *The Admirable Crichton*,
it is when the play ends that we wish for one to begin.

Whimsy and the supernatural make *Peter Pan* (1904), *Dear Brutus* and
Mary Rose Barrie's most distinctive works, each play coming from emotional and psychological elements of his personal history. His mother
retreated into grief when her favourite son David was killed at the age
of thirteen. Sympathizing with her anguish, wounded by her withdrawal,
guiltily jealous of his dead brother, the seven-year-old James Matthew, a
Scots boy emotionally on the make, seized the opportunity to earn his
mother's affection. *Margaret Ogilvy by Her Son* (1896) describes his painful
attempts to replace David by becoming so like him that his mother would
not see the difference:

> . . . one day after I had learned his whistle . . . from boys
> who had been his comrades, I secretly put on a suit of his
> clothes . . . and thus disguised I slipped . . . into my
> mother's room. Quaking, I doubt not, yet so pleased, I
> stood still until she saw me, and then – how it must have
> hurt her! 'Listen' I cried in a glow of triumph, and I
> stretched my legs wide apart and plunged my hands into
> the pockets of my knickerbockers, and began to whistle.
>
> (Chapter 1)

'There was always something of the child in her,' Barrie says, and his
memoir ends with a fancy that heralds Mary Rose, the mother who could
not grow up, perceived by a son with the same condition:

> And if I also live to a time when age must dim my mind
> and the past comes sweeping back like the shades of night
> over the bare road of the present it will not, I believe, be
> my youth I shall see but hers, not a boy clinging to his
> mother's skirt and crying, 'Wait till I'm a man, and you'll
> lie on feathers', but a little girl in a magenta frock and a
> white pinafore, who comes toward me through the long
> parks, singing to herself, and carrying her father's dinner in
> a flagon.
>
> (Chapter 10)

The ostensibly religious drama of *The Boy David* (1936) is a metaphor
of reconciliation between himself as Jonathan and his brother as the
young King David of the play. David's death gave him a second chance
with his formidable, girlish mother and he took it, unlike the more cor-
roded beings shown in Act II of *Dear Brutus* 'groping terribly' if not quite
credibly for a second chance with new selves in Lob's Midsummer Eve's
wood. *Dear Brutus*, for G. K. Chesterton Barrie's 'most perfect . . . elvish
comedy',[9] eventually gives its title away:

> PURDIE. . . . Shakespeare knew what he was talking about –
>
>> 'The fault, dear Brutus, is not in our stars,
>>   But in ourselves, that we are underlings.'
>
> JOANNA. For 'dear Brutus' we are to read 'dear
>   audience', I suppose?
> PURDIE. You have it.
> JOANNA. Meaning that we have the power to shape
>   ourselves?

PURDIE. We have the power right enough.
JOANNA. But isn't that rather splendid?
PURDIE. For those who have the grit in them, yes.

(III)

Most of the characters in *Dear Brutus* take the same turnings as they did before, though there is hope for the Dearths, but Barrie had the grit to reshape himself. Although he could not make her forget 'the bit of her that was dead', the neglected son became his mother's intimate and the Free Kirk, working-class boy from Kirriemuir became the Lob of London's theatrical West End. If dead brother David is Mr Dearth's might-have-been Margaret as well as part of the ephemeral child-mother in *Mary Rose*, he is also Peter Pan; but so is Barrie himself, his 'fear of going out of existence'[10] momentarily overcome by the creation of an immortal boy who loses his shadow but finds it again and cleaves to the fun his maker found through his intense friendship with the five sons of the Llewelyn Davies family whose guardian he became.[11]

The fantasy of *Peter Pan* stands out in Barrie's work not only because of its enduring popularity. *Dear Brutus* and *Mary Rose* are plays of one core idea – the second chance; the childish other-worldliness of love – but the inspired central concept of *Peter Pan* – Peter himself – is ingeniously set in a bright tumble of ambiguous inventions. The Darlings seem at first a faultlessly cosy family, if a little impecunious and eccentric in their choice of nanny, but Mr Darling is merely 'a good man as breadwinners go', can't take his medicine and retires to his kennel of remorse leaving in charge Mrs Darling, a playtime sibling to Phoebe Throssel, Lady Mary in Act IV of *The Admirable Crichton*, Maggie Wylie, the redoubtable Mrs Dowey of *The Old Lady Shows Her Medals* (1917), Mabel Pringle in *Dear Brutus* and Mrs Morland. Peter Pan's freedom of flight is enviable and we are grateful to him for taking us to enchanted places, but he is indomitably self-centred, has to be reminded not to bite his nails, and declines even to play at being a husband. James Bridie is being uncharacteristically literalist when he castigates Barrie for obscuring 'the cruelty, irresponsibility and lies which were the principal features of this matchless boy'.[12] Like Barrie, Peter prefers to be a son; like Hook in Act III he cannot define a mother. Tinker Bell carries a robust human psyche in her flitting point of light, sacrifices herself for Peter but is spiteful to Wendy. It is, therefore, easy enough for anyone to believe in fairies if they are all so human. Captain Hook's claw chills the spine with such reassuring evidence that wickedness is recognizable that we don't really want the crocodile to get him, and pirates can't be all bad with the domesticated Smee in the crew, though decidedly undergraduate redskins, alas, are rather boring.

Wendy's death and resurrection enact the ritual of the child-mother lost and found, finally to be lost in time to the time-defying son in Peter as Mary Rose, a late Edwardian echo of the virgin spirited away in James Hogg's 'Kilmeny', is lost to her Australian Harry. The substitution of thimbles and acorn buttons for kisses and the 'something' (I) which prevents the meeting of Peter's and Wendy's faces cannot hold Wendy much beyond Act IV. The girl is melting into the woman, but Peter is evasive:

> WENDY (*knowing she ought not to probe but driven to it by something within*). What are your exact feelings for me, Peter?
> PETER (*in the class-room*). Those of a devoted son, Wendy.
> WENDY (*turning away*). I thought so.
> PETER. You are so puzzling. Tiger Lily is just the same; there is something or other she wants me to be, but she says it is not my mother.
> WENDY (*with spirit*). No, indeed it isn't.
> PETER. Then what is it?
> WENDY. It isn't for a lady to tell.
>
> (IV)

For Wendy, at least, Peter's flightpath is not the expected stairway to paradise – sex with mortality is preferable to the sanitary infantilism of Never Land – and even the lost boys choose the protection of a real mother instead of Hook's resourceful nemesis, 'Peter Pan the avenger' (IV). If Peter 'could get the hang of the thing', Barrie surmises in his concluding stage direction, 'his cry might become "To live would be an awfully big adventure"'. Self-protective knowingness and saccharin are not absent from *Peter Pan*: Barrie himself never quite got the hang of the thing, but his great play for all ages and every wondering generation provokes questions not only about the adventures that might have been but also about the way we live here and now.

Good intentions: playwrights of the Scottish Renaissance

A French professor of English is often accredited with coining the term 'Scottish Renaissance' in its current usage to signify the cultural movement led by Hugh MacDiarmid.[13] In 1924 Denis Saurat of the University of Bordeaux referred to poets composing in Scots as 'le groupe de "la

Renaissance écossaise"'.[14] Certainly, Saurat was influential, but he did not invent the phrase. In the February 1923 issue of his magazine, *The Scottish Chapbook*, MacDiarmid had already proclaimed his belief in the possibility of a Scottish Literary Renaissance,[15] making the phrase a battle-cry for Scottish culture in general and poetry in particular. In Scottish theatre new leads were given by John Brandane (the pen-name of John MacIntyre), his friend James Bridie (the pen-name of O. H. Mavor), Robert McLellan, Alexander Reid and Robert Kemp. As writers and spokesmen for Scottish theatre they raised public consciousness of theatre, contributed to the milieu of the renaissance and helped to foster a climate in which concerted efforts were made to organize and advance theatrical activity through the Scottish National Theatre Society and Tyrone Guthrie's Scottish National Players.

Their plays have not worn well. John Brandane's best-known work *The Glen is Mine* (1923) dramatizes the real conflict between Highland traditions and modern values, but is vitiated by sentimentality and a well-intentioned but awkward use of Gaelic speech rhythms. McLellan, Reid and Kemp took their plays more deeply into the MacDiarmid camp by writing in Scots. McLellan enjoyed his greatest success with his sardonic historical comedy *Jamie the Saxt* (1937) about the power struggle between Francis Stewart, Earl of Bothwell, and King James VI. The king is presented as 'one of the most vital characters ever to appear on the Scottish stage, a physical coward, a scholastic pedant, and a mistrustful husband who is also a skilled manipulator of political forces, adept at playing off one side against another in a power struggle where he himself has no power at all'.[16] Cornered in argument by the preacher, Robert Bruce, in Act II, James gives an unanswerable defence of kingship's divine responsibility followed by a glancing blow at the vanity of the Kirk:

> BRUCE. A King's pouer is temporal!
> THE KING. It's temporal and speeritual baith! A king's
> the faither o his subjects, responsible for the weilfare o
> their minds and bodies in the same wey as ony ordinary
> faither's responsible for the weilfare o his bairns! He is,
> I tell ye, for his bluid rins awa back through a lang line
> o kings and patriarchs to its fountain-heid in the first
> faither o mankind! And the first faither o mankind was
> Adam wha gat his authority straucht [straight] frae the
> Lord wha made him in His ain image, efter His ain
> likeness!
> BRUCE. Ye forget that Adam sinned and fell frae grace!
> There was nae salvation till the Saviour cam! And He
> invesitit his Authority in His twelve Disciples, whause
> speeritual descendants are the Preachers o the Kirk!

> THE KING. What richt hae ye to say that? Ye're heids
> are aa that swalt [swollen] wi conceit that I woner
> [wonder that] ye acknowledge ony God at aa![17]

Reid won short-lived popularity with *The Lass wi' the Muckle Mou'* (1950) and *The Warld's Wonder* (1953), both set in medieval times. Although McLellan and Reid's plays were well received, especially when the lantern-jawed, quintessentially Scottish actor Duncan Macrae took the leads – and *Jamie the Saxt* has had four successful revivals – the combination of historical material with the use of Scots seemed to confirm the Scots tongue as outdated, a relic of the past instead of the living language MacDiarmid and his associates wanted it to be. A language artificially resuscitated against the pressure of the English spoken by the majority of Scots might work for comedy, but who would take it seriously enough as a vehicle for serious drama about present concerns? Scots was associated with a pastoral past, but Scotland had become urbanized. Suspicion that the language's range was limited and its relevance and commercial prospects questionable discouraged other writers from following the example of playwrights like McLellan, Reid and Kemp, but their committed use of Scots helped to break the exclusive norm of standard or discreetly tinctured English and encouraged younger artists to bring the vernacular to the stage.

Doctor dominie: James Bridie

James Bridie worked tirelessly for the development of Scottish theatre as chairman of both the Glasgow Citizens' Theatre[18] and the Scottish Arts Council, founder of the Royal Scottish College of Drama and author of forty-two plays which seemed to many to make him Scotland's answer to Shaw. Critics found 'Shavian echoes' in the Birmingham première of *The Switchback* (1929) when 'they should have detected the ringing tones of Bridie's own voice'.[19] Certainly his plays, like Shaw's, are full of clever talk. Like *The Anatomist* (1930), which uses caricature and melodrama in its morally challenging account of the obsessionally scientific Dr Robert Knox's connection with the Burke and Hare body-snatching scandal, they typically employ the set speech as dramatic aria in the operatic Shavian style. Thus, in Act I, the pathologically histrionic Dr Knox rounds on the moral nicety of the Misses Amelia and Mary Belle Dishart:

> KNOX. My dear, we all seek to explain ourselves in big
> words and windy notions. The wise disregard these
> things . . . The vulgarian, the quack and the theologian

are confronted with the Universe. They at once begin
to talk and talk and talk. They have no curiosity. They
know all about it. They build a mean structure of
foolish words and phrases, and say to us, 'This is the
World.' The comparative anatomist *has* curiosity. He
institutes a divine search for facts. He is unconcerned
with explanations and theories. In time, when you and
I are dead, his facts will be collected and their sum will
be the Truth. Truth that will show the noblest thing in
creation, how to live. Truth that will shatter the idol
Mumbo Jumbo, before which man daily debases his
magnificence. Truth . . .

MARY. No doubt that is very fine. But it is all words,
too.

Bridie's words are less polished and his plays less fluently projected than
Shaw's but his ideas are more provocatively original. His 'Author's Note'
to *The Anatomist* alerts us to a perennial problem beyond the medical
monomaniac in the grip of his avocation: 'If it illustrates anything it is the
shifts to which men of science are drawn when they are ahead of their
times. The "mob" should be very careful in its choice of objects for
persecution; for stoning the prophets is not so good for their morale as
many adepts of martyrdom would have us believe.' With *The Anatomist*
Bridie 'ceased to be a minority playwright, becoming instead one of the
most popular West End authors, and it is as such he will chiefly be
remembered'.[20]

Tobias and the Angel (1930), based on the Apocryphal *Book of Tobit*,
dramatizes Tobias's journey with the archangel Raphael (played by Tyrone
Guthrie in the first production) to Gabael of Rages and marriage to Sara
of Ecbatana as the pattern of a young man's progress from callow innocence to adulthood via the discovery that he is braver and more lovable
than he thought he was. Pleasure in life is defined as extending beyond
the self into the fortune Tobias and Raphael take back to Tobias's parents
and the restoration of old Tobit's eyesight. *Mr Bolfry* (1943) introduces
a more insidiously elegant devil than the pantomime 'Stinker' Asmoday,
Raphael's fallen fellow graduate of the College of Cherubim (*Tobias and
the Angel*, II, i). Bridie's anti-Calvinist theorem takes the form of a rhetorical duel between the Devil as Dr Bolfry and the Rev. Mr McCrimmon
which cures the minister of smug theological polemics by exposing
the devil in himself. As the Devil, Bolfry infernally annihilates the self-
righteousness of Calvinist repression:

I love repression. You repress your passion to intensify it;
to have it more abundantly; to joy in its abundance. The

prisoner cannot leap to loose his chains unless he has been chained.

(iii)

In *A Sleeping Clergyman* (1933) the genetic determinism implicit in a simplistic 'bad seed' view of heredity is denied by the representatives of modern medicine, though it can still make Dr Marshall uneasy when faced with the brilliant but dissolute young Charles Cameron:

> MARSHALL. Laddie, you're the son of a bad man and a
> foolish girl. And it gets worse as it goes back. If I had
> been one of those eugenic madmen I'd have drowned
> you when you were a pup. It would be better I had
> you by the leg than your heredity.
> CAMERON. Heredity's all rot.
> MARSHALL. Is it? You've your grandfather's eyes and
> ears and hands and mouth. You've your mother's trick
> of tossing your head back. Thank God I see little of
> your father in you but your obstinacy and your infernal
> love of an argument . . . though he was a methodical
> brute, too, damn him! and so are you . . . It's not that
> we're like our fathers and mothers. We *are* our fathers
> and mothers.

(II, i)

Charles's sister, Hope, develops the theme. She knows her forebears' virtues as well as their vices:

> HOPE. I am . . . on my father's side, a liar, a hypocrite, a
> thief, a seducer and a blackmailer. On my mother's side
> I am a harlot and a murderess . . . And my grandmother
> Marshall was a sensual fool, and my grandmother
> Hannah was a corpse-fed maggot, and my grandmother
> Cameron was a whisky-sodden blackguard . . . But my
> father could work and slave and eat dirt and have
> patience and wait. And my mother had the courage to
> do what was to be done and the courage to kill and
> the courage to die. And my grandfather had the key to
> all the mysteries.

(II, ii)

Dr Marshall's professional stance and Hope's assessment of her background are justified by the emergence of Charles and Hope from three generations of disease, blackmail, murder and suicide into lives of distinguished service on a global scale, with Charles becoming the dedicated medical researcher who saves the world from a pandemic of polio-encephalo-myelitis and Hope appointed principal secretary of the League of Nations. The 'huge, white-bearded clergyman' who sleeps throughout the action 'with the *Spectator* spread on his abdomen' ('Chorus to Act I') suggests an unheeding, absentee God who takes no interest in the refutation of obsolete orthodoxies by new intelligences about to inherit the earth. As Bridie says in his genial autobiography, *One Way of Living* (1939), 'I showed a wild horse after three generations or incarnations finally harnessing itself to the world for the world's good. God, who had set it all going, took his ease in an armchair throughout the play.'[21] 'Anything to do with gods and god-men was anathema,'[22] reports Ronald Mavor, the playwright's son, but there is seldom a last word with Bridie. In *Jonah and the Whale* (1932) God's refusal to destroy the city of Nineveh leaves the disappointed Jonah wincing at the idea 'that Jahveh may have a sense of humour' (III, ii).

The schoolteacher's story in *Mr Gillie* (1950) reworks the moral ques-tion posed by *The Anatomist*. Dr Knox sacrifices his moral nature and, perhaps, his prospects with Miss Amelia by condoning murder for the sake of medical science, thereby bringing discredit on himself and his profession; Mr Gillie devotes his life 'to opening cages and letting pris-oners fly free' (Epilogue), encouraging his students 'with a bit of natural talent' to escape from their provincialism only to see them 'hawking Communist pamphlets on Glasgow Green', 'singing in the chapel choir at Wormwood Scrubbs' (I) or, like Tom Donnelly, seduced by London sleaze and easy money. Yet, as the abused, altruistic Dr Mallaby cries at the end of *The Switchback* (1929) before the curtain falls on his quotation from the epic ending of *Paradise Lost*, 'Nothing a man does with his whole soul is ever lost' (III). Both Knox and Gillie deny themselves in the service of ideals which let them down. On the point of finding a cure for tuberculosis, Dr Mallaby is similarly betrayed by representatives of the press, high finance – the 'serpent' Burmeister is the play's devil (II) – his wife, and the president of the Royal College of Surgeons; but in the Prologue to his play Mr William Wotherspoon Gillie of the mining village of Crult is 'a candidate for immortality' with 'Bridie . . . Dramatic author. Writer of one or two West End successes' as his sponsor, and it is not stretching the point too far to suggest that Mallaby, the emblem-atically one-eyed Knox, and Charlie Cameron, who gives his DSO medal to a prostitute, should be judged worthy candidates too.

Bridie's is the subtlest and most enquiring Scottish mind so far given expression on the stage, and he is one of the most intellectually fertile contributors to Scottish literature in any genre. His work deserves 'regular revival so that each age may have a chance to pass judgement on its relevance and dramatic effectiveness'.[23] Yet, as Roderick Watson says, 'there have been no successors to his style'.[24] The narrowness and philistinism he found in the Scottish bourgeoisie are 'the most important aspects of his work and ones which do require further development in Scottish dramatic writing. We have yet to see that development.'[25] Despite occasionally adverse critical reception, of *The Black Eye* (1935) for example, he is never dull, 'the only word that can damn a play',[26] and his work is always morally engaging, but his sportive intelligence is verbal[27] and philosophical at the expense of being theatrical. A medical practitioner until the age of fifty, he is the doctor dominie, telling us what's good for us if we wish to elude what Joey Mascara in Act II of *The Baikie Charivari* (1952) calls 'Bewilderment, doubt and a fog of the mind'. He knows that 'the absence of a moral . . . is difficult for a Scotsman to condone',[28] but the frequently unresolved endings of his theatrical diagnoses stop short of prescription partly, at least, because what he implicitly prescribes is ambiguity – tolerance in reaction to the Presbyterian Manichaeism which cut the world into two mutually exclusive categories of value. His frequent choice of biblical themes, from *The Amazed Evangelist* (1932) to *The Dragon and the Dove* (1942), and his over-elaborate Punch and Judy 'miracle play', *The Baikie Charivari or The Seven Prophets*, reveal a determination to probe scripturally derived tenets which had so long deformed the Scottish psyche.

'His mission', says Ronald Mavor, 'was to cherish the human race. And to forgive God.'[29] This God, presumably, is the Jupiter of *The Queen's Comedy* (1950) who does not understand his own creation ('I am still working on its permutations and combinations'). The Free Kirk's God 'is really the Devil', Jean tells Cully in *Mr Bolfry*, 'All this holiness and censoriousness is to save their skins from boils and leprosy and their souls from damnation' (i), or, as Mr Bolfry puts it more succinctly to the pixilated Morag, 'Life . . . is one long smutty story' (iii). The Devil may be 'endless enmity to humanity and all its works',[30] but Bridie's Devil is also linked to the rebel in us all, and Bridie is in favour of rebellion, hence his approval of Lady Katherine Pitts, the middle-aged nymph, Daphne, of *Daphne Laureola* (1949), who marries her dead husband's chauffeur, preferring the earthy risks of a 'nice clean pig-sty' (IV) to being merely possessed again as the laurel crown of the self-styled Polish Apollo, Ernest Piaste. As Bolfry says, 'We cannot conceive the Universe except as a pattern of reciprocating opposites' (*Mr Bolfry*, iii). It is Blake's position in *The Marriage of Heaven and Hell*: 'Without Contraries is no progression'.

Although the significance of Bridie's characters is never in question, they do not attract the kind of theatrical sympathy that must be generated if an audience is to be drawn fully into the total action of a play. Notwithstanding his mixture of realism and fantasy and the audacious tripartite staging (heaven, earth and Neptune's underwater realm) of *The Queen's Comedy* which juxtaposes the intrigues of Olympus with the realities of modern warfare in a scheme of things grimly short of rebels, his plays are invariably bravura intellectual shows recessed behind an actual or felt proscenium. And after Bridie? In 1956 Christopher Small, drama critic for the *Glasgow Herald*, was prompted to ask, 'Is there really such a thing as the Scottish theatre?' Post-war theatre was threatened by public indifference even in parts of the world where once it flourished, whereas in Scotland 'it has never been much better than a tentative growth'.[31] While appreciating the efforts of such writers as Ian Hamilton Finlay, Cecil Taylor and Stewart Conn, in 1967 Edwin Morgan felt obliged to write: 'In spite of these and other fairly hopeful growing-points, it must be said that Scottish drama still has a long way to go.'[32] The political and working-class plays of the 1970s and 1980s did eventually dissolve the formal distance between play and auditorium, breaking, as Bridie had failed to do, the technical hiatus in theatrical development. Using production styles influenced by the rapidly developing techniques of television drama, they brought new life to Scottish theatre and created audiences who wanted more of the involvement that only live theatre can provide.

7:84, politics, protest and patter

In 1971 John McGrath founded the 7:84 Theatre Company, taking the name from a statistic published in *The Economist* in 1966 which located 84 per cent of British capital wealth in 7 per cent of the population.[33] In a note about the Company written in 1974 McGrath comments:

> Although this proportion may have fluctuated marginally over the years, we continue to use it because it points to the basic economic structure of the society we live in, from which all the political, social and cultural structures grow. The company opposes this set-up, and tries to present in its work a socialist perspective on our society, and to indicate socialist alternatives to the capitalist system that dominates all our lives today.[34]

A Scottish 7:84 Theatre Company was formed in 1973. It promptly scored its major triumph with *The Cheviot, the Stag and the Black, Black Oil* (1973) using Scottish actors and musicians who collaborated with McGrath on the research, text, presentation and music of the play.[35] James Bridie had given a precedent for this kind of communal production in his co-operative work with the actor, Alastair Sim, and Tyrone Guthrie and in the composition of his pantomimes *The Tintock Cup* (1949) and

Red Riding Hood (1950) with contributions from members of their Glasgow Citizens' Theatre casts.

Modelled on the Gaelic ceilidh with its ingredients of song, dance, poetry and story, *The Cheviot* toured the crofting communities of Scotland taking its documentary exposé of successive capitalist exploitations of the Highlands to some 30,000 people in a blend of dramatized narrative sketch and song stylistically derived from variety theatre, the homiletic folk play and the social analysis of Sir David Lyndsay. Its talent for immediacy was often startling:

> The night after Fred Olsen (UK) Ltd announced plans for a £6 million oil development at a public meeting in Stornoway, a rather bigger crowd turned up for a performance of *The Cheviot, the Stag and the Black, Black Oil* by the 7:84 Theatre Company. The two events might not seem connected, but they were. A reference to the Stornoway Trust, involved in negotiations with Olsen, had already been written into the substantial part of the play that deals with the effects of the oil industry on the West Coast.[36]

The play pulls no punches, anatomizing a set of connected issues in order to agitate its audiences of 'little Scottish people' (p. 66) into an empowering awareness of the socio-economic imbalance at the root of Scottish life and the iniquity whereby 'a whole culture was systematically destroyed – by economic power' (p. 52). The main issues are summed up shortly before the play concludes its evening of tuition through entertainment:

> ALL. Have we learned anything from the Clearances?
>
> When the Cheviot came, only the landlords benefited.
>
> When the Stag came, only the upper-class sportsmen benefited.
>
> Now the Black Black Oil is coming. And must come. It could benefit everybody. But if it is developed in the capitalist way, only the multi-national corporations and local speculators will benefit.
>
> (p. 73)

Improvisatory staging immediately implicates the assembling audience in the performance, with The Fiddler playing in the bar and foyer while the

Company openly prepares props and costumes and John Byrne's ingeniously portable pop-up-book scenery. The involving bustle of these activities leads into the audience's singing 'These are My Mountains' along
with the Company to establish a shared sense of identification with Scotland and the story about to be told. The song is satirically recalled throughout the play as when Queen Victoria fits the tune to her own proprietory
words:

> QUEEN VICTORIA. These are our mountains
> And this is our glen
> The braes of your childhood
> Are English again
>
> Though wide is our Empire
> Balmoral is best
> Yes these are our mountains
> And we are impressed
>
> (pp. 37–8)

Stark documentary is juxtaposed with Gaelic lament and satirical vaude-
ville routines to give a Brechtian display of cruelty, courage and absurdity
from different intellectual and emotional perspectives in 'a story that has
a beginning, a middle, but, as yet, no end' (p. 2). Thus one sequence
begins with an account of the international effects of the Clearances.
While Scots settlers in Canada are attacked by Indians, harassed by the
French and manipulated by shareholders of the Hudson's Bay Company,
the Scottish situation is shown to be a paradigm of remorseless, world-
wide capitalism:

> STURDY HIGHLANDER (*out of character*). . . . The
> highland exploitation chain-reacted around the world; in
> Australia the aborigines were hunted like animals; in
> Tasmania not one aborigine was left alive; all over
> Africa, black men were massacred and brought to heel.
> In America the plains were emptied of men and buffalo,
> and the seeds of the next century's imperialist power
> were firmly planted.
>
> (p. 29)

After a Gaelic poem about the deracination of transplanted Scots, the
quick music-hall repartee of two Highlanders spoofs the stereotype of the
drunken Scotsman and exemplifies the resilience that could not be crushed
even by Lord Macdonald, notorious for his brutal treatment of the people
of the Glendale and Braes districts of Skye:

HIGHLANDER 2. Now at that time, Lord Macdonald
was driving the people down to the shores . . .
HIGHLANDER 1. What shores?
HIGHLANDER 2. Oh, I'll have a wee dram!
Roll on drum.
No, but seriously though, he was having a bit of an
altercation about the grazing rights on a little moor . . .
HIGHLANDER 1. A little moor?
HIGHLANDER 2. Oh well, that's very civil of you!
HIGHLANDER 1. Oh, Sandy, you're a great one for the
drink.
HIGHLANDER 2. Oh Angus, I am that, I am.
HIGHLANDER 1. I tell you what, when I'm dead will
you pour a bottle of the Talisker[37] over my dead body?
HIGHLANDER 2. Certainly, certainly, you won't mind if
I pass it through the kidneys first.

(p. 30)

The archetypal traitor to his heritage is Texas Jim, *aka* Elmer Y.
MacAlpine the Fourth, who keeps up the rapport between stage and hall
by shaking hands with the audience before breaking into his parodic
square dance calls. We have heard about the Duke of Sutherland's brutal
displacement of people to make way for the profitable Cheviot sheep, and
about stag and grouse shooting by the likes of Lord Crask and Lady
Phosphate with her sten-gun capacity overkill and gentrified accent ('Oh it's
awfully, frightfully ni-i-ce, / Shooting stags, my dear, and grice', p. 41).
We have met Andy McChuckemup, the Glasgow Property-operator's
man ('So – picture it, if you will – a drive-in clachan on every hill-top
where formerly there was hee-haw but scenery', p. 49), raucous proof
that 'Nationalism is not enough. The enemy of the Scottish people is
Scottish capital, as much as the foreign exploiter' (p. 66). Now it is oil's
turn, the third era of major exploitation:

TEXAS JIM. Take your oil-rigs by the score,
Drill a little well just a little off-shore,
Pipe that oil in from the sea,
Pipe those profits – home to me.

I'll bring work that's hard and good –
A little oil costs a lot of blood.

Your union men just cut no ice
You work for me – I name the price.

So leave your fishing, and leave your soil,
Come work for me, I want your oil.

Screw your landscape, screw your bays
I'll screw you in a hundred ways.

(p. 59)

Before the closing Gaelic song, a political call-to-arms, the Company
spells out the moral of the play:

> ALL. At the time of the Clearances, the resistance failed
> because it was not organized. The victories came as a
> result of militant organization – in Coigeach, The Braes,
> and the places that formed Land Leagues. We too must
> organize, and fight – not with stones, but politically,
> with the help of the working class in the towns, for a
> government that will control the oil development for
> the benefit of everybody.

(p. 73)

The Cheviot, the Stag and the Black, Black Oil was Scotland's most vital
theatrical event since Lyndsay's Ane Pleasant Satyre of the Three Estaitis
spoke out some 400 years earlier for the rights of the folk against corruption in Church and state. The best of subsequent Scottish 7:84 shows are
The Game's a Bogey (1974), based on the career of the Glasgow socialist
and republican, John Maclean, and Little Red Hen (1975), in which Scottish left-wing and nationalist activism of the 1970s is reviewed in terms
of the high but disappointed political hopes of the 1920s. Wildcat, a
popular off-shoot of 7:84 begun in 1978, is also left-wing and hard-
hitting but less exclusively working-class in orientation. Class is seen as
a social fact which is often a problem, but the song, 'Babylon', in Dummies defines the problem as well as the recurrent theme on which the
company's productions are a series of variations:

> The message is simple
> Needs no explanation
> The Devil's disciple
> Is alienation
> Of people from people
> Of mind from emotion
> Of man from the temple
> Of his own creation
> Of the slum from the castle
> We call this situation

Babylon![38]

Scripts principally by David Anderson and David MacLennan use an adaptation of the Bertolt Brecht/Kurt Weill cabaret format of narrative and song to address a broad range of social topics including victimization of the mentally ill by pharmaceutical interests (*The Painted Bird*, 1978), 'a dossers' eye view of Thatcher's Britain'[39] (*Dummies*, 1979), unemployment (*Blooter*, 1980), the nuclear menace and the arms race (*1982 or Any Minute Now*, 1982), the mass media (*His Master's Voice*, 1982), the National Health (*Bed Pan Alley*, 1984), Nicaragua's fight for freedom (*Business in the Back Yard*, 1985) and ecology (*Heather Up Your Kilt*, 1986). Like 7:84 Wildcat is an agit-prop group, tending to preach to the converted. While John McGrath, Anderson, MacLennan and their co-writers offer theatre which 'demands of its audiences affirmation rather than exploration',[40] other recent playwrights protest less directly against the 'set-up', leaving more scope for differences in audience response and interpretation of their material.

There is something wrong with a society in which life on the shop-floor of a glass works is as harsh as Roddy Macmillan portrays it in *The Bevellers* (1973), but protest is implicit in the sympathy evoked for his apprentice's initiation into a rough world. Questions rather than certainties are posed by Hector MacMillan's portrayal of Protestant bigotry and Irish socialist sentiment in *The Sash* (1973), by Donald Campbell's *The Jesuit* (1976) about the imprisonment, torture and trial of the Roman Catholic martyr, John Ogilvie, and by the controversial, box-office-record-breaking story of Johnny Byrne in Tom McGrath's *The Hard Man* (1977), based on the life of his collaborator, Jimmy Boyle,[41] from juvenile thief and street-fighter to gang leader, convicted murderer and ultimate, transcendent judge of himself and society. In a speech to the audience in Act II Paisley, 'the bad screw', defines the problem faced by McGrath's consummately stagecrafted play:

> PAISLEY. . . . You people out there . . . you've got a crime
> problem so you just flush it away one thug after
> another in behind bars and safely locked away. The
> cistern's clanked and you can think you can leave it
> floating away from you to the depths of the sea. Well,
> ah've goat news fur you − it's pollution. Yir gonnae
> huv tae look ut it. Because if yae don't, wun day it's
> gonnae destroy yae.

McGrath sees beneath the symmetrical brutalities of street and prison. His moral penetration is most impressive when Paisley, the prison's 'hard man', who has first goaded then almost drowned Byrne in a sink, turns to the audience again, showing that McGrath has anticipated the danger inherent in too facile a swing of sympathy towards Byrne. Both criminal and screw are products of a defective system:

> PAISLEY (*to audience*). Listen, if you excuse him (*indicates BYRNE*) on the grounds that he's a product of this shit-heap system, then you'd better excuse me on the same grounds.
>
> (II)

Tracing the career of Francis Seneca McDade, 'illegitimate issue of one Otto Dusselfurt, a peripatetic "physician" from The Hague' in *Writer's Cramp* (1977), John Byrne turns pretentiousness about 'the deciduous tree of Scottish literature' (I, i) into satirical farce, and in *Colquhoun and MacBryde* (1992) he indicts the two painters' turning themselves into caricature Scotsmen as a tawdry reaction to English hostility and the risen star of Jackson Pollock. In *Dead Dad Dog* (1988) John McKay combines comic treatment of the father–son relationship with sharp if understated allegorical comment on Scotland's flair for getting hung up on its past:

> ECK (*to audience*). Diggin up aw that stuff from the past. I dinnae need that. Makin me feel like a three-year-old. That slippy-slidey in the gut family feeling. That's today to a tee. No hope. No change. No nuthin. Hell, that's this whole place to a tee. Well, screw that . . .[42]

Socialist stereotypes and 'slum drama' expectations are ingeniously subverted by the unheroic heroine of Chris Hannan's *Elizabeth Gordon Quinn* (1985) who defiantly veils her poverty and her husband in the formality of her language and her indomitable refusal to be part of a mob or 'to learn how to be poor' (Part 2, viii). In the closing moment of the play her individualism puts to shame the over-simplifying party lines along which the condition of Britain has become defined. Her daughter, Maura, wears a Union Jack around her shoulders: '*She's conscious of it – it's grandiose, bombastic . . . She takes it off*'.[43] Questions about the historical and contemporary estate of women are raised with virtuoso theatricality in eclectic Scots by Liz Lochhead's meticulously researched *Mary Queen of Scots Got Her Head Chopped Off* (1987), despite over-complicated stage business her most accomplished play, first produced by Communicado Theatre. In I, iii the 'chorus', La Corbie, asks, 'when's a queen a queen / And when's a queen juist a wummin?' Male sexual opportunism, John Knox's 'trumpet against the monstrous regiment o' women' (I, iv), Scots–English politics and Protestant–Catholic rivalry marginalize the woman in Mary, the doomed *femme fatale*, and in her tougher cousin, Queen Elizabeth. Both Queens are conditioned and victimized by the same attitudes that Lochhead satirizes in modern society in her 'Rap' poem, 'Page Three Dollies',[44] and in 'Almost Miss Scotland': 'How would *thae guys* like to be a prize — /A cake everybody wanted a slice of . . . ?'[45] The nation will not allow Elizabeth her Leicester and the Scots nobles square off factionally, irrespective of Mary's personal preference:

> SCOTS NOBLE 1 (*To MARY*). The Queen should
> mairry a Hamilton!
> SCOTS NOBLE 2. No she shouldnae! She should mairry
> a Douglas.
> SCOTS NOBLE 3. A Gordon!
> SCOTS NOBLE 2. By God and she better no'!
> SCOTS NOBLE 3. Wha says she'll no'?
> SCOTS NOBLE 2. I dae!
> LA CORBIE. A Lennox-Stewart, that's wha she should
> mairry!
> (*SCOTS NOBLES, 1, 2, and 3 all draw their swords.*)
> SCOTS NOBLES 1, 2 and 3 (*Together*). Ower ma deid
> body!

(I, ii)

The doublings of Mary and Elizabeth with the maids, Marian and Bessie, the beggar urchins, Mairn and Leezie, and the modern children, Marie and Wee Betty, emphasize the continuity of prejudice, sexism, harassment and cruelty, so that the play functions effectively as 'a metaphor for the Scots today'.[46] The entrapment of the two Queens is updated to the frustrations of Verena, the Glasgow housewife in Lochhead's male–female black-comedy duet, *Quelques Fleurs* (1991).

After the use of urban vernacular brought audiences fresh pleasures of recognition in Bill Bryden's *Willie Rough* (1972), an accurately detailed portrait of working-class graft, confusion and bravery, political tension and capitalist hypocrisy set in a Clydeside shipyard during the First World War, and *Benny Lynch* (1974) about the rapid, tragic decline of Scotland's most famous boxer, colloquial speech became increasingly common in plays of the 1970s and 1980s. The 7:84 Theatre Company's 1982 revival of Ena Lamont Stewart's *Men Should Weep* (1947) introduced a new generation of theatre-goers to a faultlessly crafted earlier play whose energy comes from the vitality of its Glasgow speech. In the revised version for which Stewart rewrote Act III the play's essential strengths are its balanced moral judgement, its economic use of precisely individuated minor characters in a choric role, and the stature of its heroine, Maggie Morrison, comparable in her resilience to Sean O'Casey's Juno Boyle in *Juno and the Paycock* (1924).[47] If there's 'nae work for the men' in the depression of the 1930s, 'there's aye plenty for the women' (II, ii). Grateful for a tin of baked beans from her unmarried sister, Maggie copes single-handedly with her whingeing mother-in-law, her tubercular son and Alec, the spoiled son in thrall to a tarty wife, but her case is never desperate enough to extinguish her love for her family or her sense of humour. Her unemployed ex-alcoholic husband, John, reads library books and reacts violently against Maggie's suggestion that he might help to keep the house tidy: 'Tae Hell wi this Jessie business every time I'm oot o a job! I'm no turnin masel intae a bloomin skivvy! I'm a man' (II, ii). Yet John is a sympathetic character, victimized like his womenfolk by 'they dirty rotten buggers in Parliament' (I, i) and trapped by circumstance:

JOHN. If I could hae jist . . . jist done better by ye a. If I could hae . . . (*Head in hands, eyes on floor*) . . . If! If! . . . Every time I've had tae say 'no' tae you an the weans it's doubled me up like a kick in the stomach.

He lifts his head and cries out:

Christ Almighty! A we've din wrong is tae be born intae poverty!

Whit dae they think this kind o a life dis tae a man?

Whiles it turns ye intae a wild animal. Whiles ye're a human question mark, aye askin why? Why? *Why?*

There's nae answer. Ye end up a bent back and a heid hanging in shame for whit ye canna help.

(II, i)

In a final scene whose intense sentiment is achieved by Maggie's ability to transcend male sentimentality, she mothers her bewildered husband out of his pride and prejudice. By accepting their daughter, Jenny's, offer of the money needed for a new house despite John's bigoted contempt for it as a 'whore's winnins', she brings her family the promise of 'Four rooms . . . an a park forbye' with 'flowers come the spring!' (III). This must not be underestimated: they are about to escape from the kind of environment that filled the poet, Edwin Muir, with 'an immense, blind dejection'.[48]

Repartee in idiomatic Glaswegian 'patter' upstages plot in John Byrne's *The Slab Boys Trilogy* (1987) about carpet-factory employees,[49] and in his popular television drama series, *Tutti Frutti* (1987). Tony Roper's ear for the patter and sensitivity to working-class sentiment are as sharp as Ena Lamont Stewart's. His play, *The Steamie*, was first staged by Wildcat in

1987 with songs by David Anderson. Set in a Glasgow 'steamie' or public wash-house on Hogmanay, Roper's play blends New Year's Eve senti-mentality with a humorous but sympathetically exact depiction of the conditions of working-class women to dramatize a vindication, as moving as it is funny, of the community feeling, particularly among women, that was destroyed by the demolition of old neighbourhoods, the urban kailyards that were replaced by the alienating high-rise estates favoured by town-planners in the 1950s and 1960s. Mrs Culfeathers, whose obsession with mince from the Glasgow butcher, Galloway's, in Act II has passed into Scottish theatrical mythology,[50] rises to lyrical heights of vernacular nostalgia when she recalls visits to the steamie of her childhood as the hey-day of Glasgow life when '*naebody* seemed to be lonely':

> MRS CULFEATHERS. . . . Ah kin aye mind, as a wee
> lassie, gaun [going] wi' ma mother, and d'y'e know whit
> was lovely? Seein' Glesca [Glasgow] Green wi' aw the
> washin' hingin fae the lines. Yon was a marvellous
> sight . . . Of course we had real summers then, fae May
> right ontae September. It was that hot the tar used tae
> stick tae yer feet, and the whole of Glesca Green was like
> a sea of colour, sheets and mattress covers and the men's
> shirts. White as snow as far as ye could see, and lovely
> coloured silks and woollens, aw dancin' in the dryin'
> wind.
>   At that age ah always thought they looked kinna [kind
> of] happy, it sounds daft ah know hen, but it was the
> men's shirts and women's dresses. Ye see, they aw have
> arms and when the wind blew them aboot, they aw
> seemed tae be wavin' tae each other. It wis as if the claes
> [clothes] had a life o' their ain . . . and underneath them
> the women were aw movin' aboot, laughin' and jokin' wi'
> wan another . . . it was noisy but tae me then,
> somehow . . . thrillin'.
>
>   (I)

The laundrette is no substitute – 'they don't even speak tae wan another right?' The steamie was a place for gossip, for joking, for acting out dreams of a posh house with all mod cons, for doing an impromptu tango with a pal, for resigned bitching about feckless, football-crazy menfolk, most of all for sharing a common lot. Roper catches the frustration, the tenderness, the wistfulness and the buoyancy of such people. If there is, so far, no sign of a 'Wullie Shakespeare' – such magnitude would require a playwright made up of Bridie, the two McGraths, Tony Roper, David Anderson, Ena Lamont Stewart and Liz Lochhead for their analytical wit and vivacity of language as well as for political correctness and their distinctively female voices – the plays of the last two decades show Scottish drama back on track with Sir David Lyndsay.

Notes

1. See Alasdair Cameron, 'Theatre in Scotland: 1214 to the Present', *Scotland: A Concise Cultural History*, ed. Paul H. Scott (Edinburgh, 1993), pp. 145–58.

2. John Wylie, 'Our Greatest Dramatist', *Northern Review*, 1, no. 1 (May 1924), pp. 51–2.

3. M. Norton, 'The Plays of Joanna Baillie', *The Review of English Studies*, 23, no. 90 (April 1947), pp. 131–43 [143].

4. J. M. Barrie, 'To the Five: A Dedication', *Peter Pan, or The Boy who Would Not Grow Up, The Plays of J. M. Barrie* (London, 1928), p. 6.

5. Arthur Symons, 'A Theory of the Stage', in Eric Bentley, *The Theory of the Modern Stage: An Introduction to Modern Theatre and Drama* (Harmondsworth, 1968), pp. 339–45 [343].

6. J. M. Barrie, *Courage: The Rectorial Address Delivered at St Andrews University*, 3 May 1922 (London, 1922), p. 7.

7. Harry M. Geduld, *Sir James Barrie* (New York, 1971), p. 118.

8. Granville Barker, 'J. M. Barrie as a Dramatist', *The Bookman*, 39, no. 229 (October 1910), pp. 13–21 [19].

9. G. K. Chesterton, 'Barrie as an Artist', *The Bookman*, 59, no. 350 (December 1920), pp. 105–6 [105].

10. David Holbrook, 'Woman, Death and Meaning in *Peter Pan* and *Mary Rose*', Chapter 5 of his *Images of Woman in Literature* (New York and London, 1989), pp. 71–114 [75].

11. See Andrew Birkin, *J. M. Barrie and the Lost Boys* (London, 1979).

12. James Bridie, *One Way of Living* (London, 1939), p. 109.

13. See Kenneth Buthlay, *Hugh MacDiarmid (C. M. Grieve)* (Edinburgh, 1964), p. 21.

14. 'Un nouveau mouvement littéraire se prononce en Ecosse, qui est une des choses les plus intéressantes et les plus riches en promesses dans le groupe des littératures anglo-saxonnes à l'heure présente. Tout récent, ce mouvement a déjà produit une quantité d'oeuvres assez considérable, particulièrement dans la poésie lyrique . . . L'idée centrale qui a groupé plus de cinquante écrivains – dont quelques-uns déjà célèbres – est l'idée de l'autonomie écossaise.' Denis Saurat, 'Le Groupe de "La Renaissance Ecossaise"', *Revue Anglo-Américaine* (April 1924), pp. 295–307 [295].

15. Hugh MacDiarmid, 'A Theory of Scots Letters', in *Selected Prose*, ed. Alan Riach (Manchester, 1992), pp. 16–33 [19].

16. Alexander Scott, 'Introduction', in Robert McLellan, *Collected Plays Volume One* (London, 1981), p. viii.

17. Robert McLellan, *Jamie the Saxt: A Historical Comedy*, ed. Ian Campbell and Ronald D. S. Jack (London, 1970), p. 61.

18. See Tony Paterson, 'James Bridie: Playwright as Impresario?', *Chapman*, 11, nos. 2–3 (1989), pp. 139–45.

19. Winifred Bannister, *James Bridie and His Theatre* (London, 1955), p. 57.

20. Allardyce Nicoll, *English Drama 1900–1930* (Cambridge, 1973), p. 266.

21. James Bridie, *One Way of Living*, p. 278.

22. Ronald Mavor, *Dr Mavor and Mr Bridie* (Edinburgh, 1988), p. 124.

23. John Thomas Low, *Doctors, Devils, Saints and Sinners: A Critical Study of the Major Plays of James Bridie* (Edinburgh, 1980), p. 26. Low makes this comment with reference to *A Sleeping Clergyman*.

24. Roderick Watson, *The Literature of Scotland* (Basingstoke, 1984), p. 412.

25. David Hutchison, *The Modern Scottish Theatre* (Glasgow, 1977), p. 97.

26. James Bridie, 'Preface: The Anatomy of Failure', *Moral Plays* (London, 1936), p. vii.

27. Helen L. Luyben thinks that '*Jonah and the Whale, The Last Trump, It Depends What You Mean*, and *Dr. Angelus* deserve to be criticized for, respectively, their prolixity, acres of talk, unabashed garrulity, and longwindedness'. See Helen L. Luyben, *James Bridie: Clown and Philosopher* (Philadelphia, 1965), pp. 22–3.

28. James Bridie, 'Preface', *Colonel Wotherspoon and Other Plays* (London, 1934), p. x.

29. Ronald Mavor, 'Bridie Revisited', *Chapman*, 11, nos. 2–3 (1989), pp. 146–51 [147].

30. Walter Elliott, 'Bridie's Last Play', Preface to James Bridie, *The Baikie Charivari* (London, 1953), p. vi.

31. Christopher Small, 'Theatre and Audience', *Saltire Review*, 3, no. 9 (Winter 1956), pp. 75–6 [75].

32. Edwin Morgan, 'Scottish Writing Today, II. The Novel and the Drama', *English*, 16, no. 96 (Autumn 1967), pp. 227–9 [229].

33. 'Taxing Britain's Wealth – I: The Indefensible Status Quo', *The Economist*, 15 January 1966, pp. 217–19 [218]: '. . . about 84 per cent of wealth seems to be owned by the top 7 per cent of taxpayers; indeed, as much as 55 per cent is owned by the top 2 per cent of taxpayers. This shows an even more uneven distribution than the Inland Revenue estimates. And the reason for this extreme concentration is not that a few have such vast wealth. It is that so many have virtually no wealth.'

34. John McGrath, *The Cheviot, the Stag and the Black, Black Oil* (London, 1981), p. 76. As the play is not divided into acts and scenes, references in the text are to pages of this edition.

35. 'Although John McGrath had been working on the idea of the play, and the historical background to it, for fifteen years, the whole company was drawn

into the process of making it. Each member checked some areas of research and was free to throw in ideas, gags, musical suggestions and to question everything being written. The final result, therefore, represents the talents, skills and beliefs of the company as a whole.' Ibid., p. 77.

36. Bob Tait, 'Highland jaunt with the 7:84 Company', *The Weekend Scotsman*, 6 October 1973, p. 1.

37. 'Talisker' is the brand name of a single-malt whisky distilled on the island of Skye.

38. David Anderson and David MacLennan, *Roadworks: Song Lyrics for Wildcat*, selected by Edwin Morgan (Glasgow, 1987), p. 16.

39. Ibid., p. 14.

40. David Hutchison, 'Theatre, Politics and Culture', *The Media Education Journal*, 14 (Summer, 1993), pp. 25–7 [27].

41. McGrath insists that Byrne is not simply a stage version of Boyle: 'Certainly, Jimmy Boyle provided much of the information underlying the character's behaviour and . . . the entire closing section of the play was directly dramatized out of a letter from Jimmy to myself describing his experience in the Cage. But Byrne carried more than Boyle in him . . . I knew, for instance, that he carried aspects of myself and of other hardmen I had known about.' See *The Riverside Interviews: 6. Tom McGrath* (London, 1983), pp. 187–8.

42. *Scot-Free: New Scottish Plays*, selected and introduced by Alasdair Cameron (London, 1990; reprinted 1993), xii, p. 172.

43. Ibid., p. 146.

44. Liz Lochhead, *True Confessions & New Clichés* (Edinburgh, 1985; revised and reprinted 1986), pp. 40–41.

45. Liz Lochhead, *Bagpipe Muzak* (Harmondsworth, 1991), p. 3.

46. See Anne Varty, 'Scripts and Performances', *Liz Lochhead's Voices*, ed. Robert Crawford and Anne Varty (Edinburgh, 1993), pp. 148–69 [162].

47. See also Robert McLeish, *The Gorbals Story* (Edinburgh, 1946), which portrays living conditions in Glasgow's notorious slums.

48. Edwin Muir, *An Autobiography* (London, 1954), p. 92.

49. A 'slab boy' is a colour mixer. The plays comprising Byrne's trilogy are *The Slab Boys* (1978), *Cuttin' a Rug*, originally titled *The Loveliest Night of the Year* (1979), and *Still Life* (1982).

50. See Cameron (ed.), *Scot-Free*, p. xv.

Chapter 11

Poets of the Scottish Renaissance from Hugh MacDiarmid to Edwin Morgan

Hugh MacDiarmid: reading the stones

In Jeff Torrington's novel *Swing Hammer Swing!* (1992) the hero, Tam Clay, is caustic about a display of model figures 'purporting to be typical members of a Japanese family' in Glasgow's Kelvingrove Art Gallery and Museum. The exhibit prompts him to wonder

> . . . what would they be palming off on the public a couple of centuries hence as your 'typical Scots'? Wee tartan bendy gnomes, maybe, with their eyeballs glued to their assholes to guard against any new poets who might be on their way to disturb the kailyard calm.
>   Aye, twad fair mak ye grieve Christopher, wad it no?
>
>   (Chapter 29)

The pun on the name of Christopher Murray Grieve signifies his enduring presence among contemporary literate Scots with a sense of nationhood. His withering repudiations of falsifying cultural stereotypes (judged by resolutely Scotocentric standards), his individual brands of Scottish Nationalism (having helped to found the Scottish National Party in 1928 he was expelled from it in 1933 for being a Communist) and Communism (he was also expelled from the Communist Party in 1938 for being too nationalist, but rejoined in 1956 after the Soviet invasion of Hungary), made him uniquely kenspeckle and notorious. His book on *Scottish Eccentrics* (1936) is written from the inestimable advantage of his being one himself. Abhorred or revered, he was and remains incontrovertibly momentous in the development of Scotland's sense of itself, seeing his function 'as that of the cat-fish that vitalizes the other torpid denizens of the aquarium'[1] and ending his cornucopian memoir, *Lucky Poet* (1943), with characteristic cheek:

my last word here is that, if I had to choose a motto to
be engraved under my name and the dates of my birth
and death on my tombstone, it would be:
   'A disgrace to the community' – Mr. Justice Mugge.[2]

   In 1920 he opposed the foundation of the Vernacular Circle of the
London Burns Club on the ground that the Scots language 'is, and will
remain . . . a backwater of the true river of Scottish national expression'.[3]
Soon afterwards, as Norman MacCaig tells it, 'he got hold of Jamieson's
Etymological Dictionary of the Scottish Language and – Christopher Murray
Grieve dived in at one end and Hugh MacDiarmid clambered ashore at
the other'.[4] Henceforth his pseudonym – and *nom de guerre* – would be
linked to the revival of poetry in vernacular Scots or 'Lallans' (the 'Doric'
language of Lowland Scotland) although after 1934 he chose more often
to write in English. Thus in his later works he tacitly accepted Edwin
Muir's opinion that the predicament of the Scottish writer 'cannot be
solved by writing poems in Scots'[5] because 'Scottish poetry exists in a
vacuum'.[6] But he would never have admitted it and couldn't forgive
Muir for saying so.
   In the February 1923 issue of his journal, *Scottish Chapbook*, MacDiarmid
declares his faith in the possibility of 'a great Scottish Literary Renaissance, deriving its strength from the resources that lie latent and almost
unsuspected in the Vernacular'.[7] These resources were soon empowered
in his own verse as

> – Coorse words that shamble thro' oor minds   *coarse*
>   like stots,   *bullocks*
> Syne turn on's muckle een wi' doonsin'   *dazzling emeralds*
>   emerauds lit.
>   ('Gairmscoile' ['Poets' School'])[8]

In 1925, after a poem which envisages the planet Earth as a neglected,
tear-stained child whom the poet encourages to drown in the tears of its
suffering an unfeelingly garish crimson ('crammasy') Mars, a green, silken
Venus and a golden-feathered moon ('The Bonnie Broukit Bairn'), the
collection *Sangschaw* (nicely translated by Edwin Morgan as 'Songfest'[9])
heralded the poetic rebirth by an enigmatic rainbow on a cold summer
evening:

> Ae weet forenicht i' the yow-   *wet evening during cold July*
>   trummle   *weather after sheep-shearing*
> I saw yon antrin thing,   *unusual*
> A watergaw wi' its chitterin' licht   *faint rainbow/shivering*
> Ayont the on-ding;   *Beyond the downpour*

An' I thocht o' the last wild look ye
   gied
Afore ye deed!
                          ('The Watergaw'
                    ['The Indistinct Rainbow'])

The chittering light becomes a shiver of cold, for as there is no smoke
('reek') in the lark's ('laverock's') house in the second stanza so there is
no source of comforting warmth in the speaker's. The look of death is
chilling, even if 'the dying man [possibly MacDiarmid's father] closes his
eyes on a world full of a natural beauty that may foreshadow an after-
life',[10] but the concentrated lyric gift of the poet is quick with 'Gairmscoile's'
bullock strength and emerald dazzle.

In a succession of similarly compact, radiant verses ranging from the
whimsical to the tersely philosophical MacDiarmid combines freshly home-
spun Lallans with the cosmic, sending out from the unforgiving disappointment of his atheism playful or intensely searching feelers to the space
where God was. A 'licht-lookin' craw [crow] o' a body', the moon sits
on the four cross-winds and leaps 'clean on the quick o' my heart', lifting
him to transcendence of earthly sounds and human time in 'Moonstruck';
the Earth quivers in the deathly silence of space, its meaning indecipherable even to God in 'The Eemis [unsteady] Stane'; God returns to the sea
from which he once produced life, 'free / Frae a' that's happened since'
in 'God Takes a Rest', but in 'The Innumerable Christ' Earth is the star
of Bethlehem to countless worlds where 'the Babe maun cry / An' the
Crucified maun [must] bleed'. In the folkish comedy of 'The Last Trump'
the dead are reluctantly awakened when 'Gabriel mak's hullaballoo. /
Hark his trumpet's awfu' toot', and in 'Crowdieknowe' (the name of a
graveyard near the poet's birthplace of Langholm) the same last trumpet
calls forth big men with tousled beards to 'glower at God an' a' his gang'.
In the Wordsworthian 'Empty Vessel' a girl sings to her dead baby more
sweetly than 'Wunds [winds] wi' warlds to swing' and more intensely
than the eternal 'licht that bends owre a' thing'. Thus the connection
between the bleakness of the girl's situation and the illumination it brings
the poet anticipates the observation that 'deep surroondin' darkness . . .
Is aye the price o' licht' with which MacDiarmid ends 'Milk-Wort and
Bog-Cotton', one of many poems set to music by his friend and former
teacher, Francis George Scott, and the light that seems a 'queer extension
o' the dark' in *A Drunk Man Looks at the Thistle* (l. 2128). Such poems come
from the lyrical core of an irreducibly Scottish, God-bereft and therefore
insatiably humanist intellectual who, in the most eloquent poem of *Penny
Wheep* ('Small Beer', 1926), still seizes on the Ophite myth of the supreme
being's primal serpent not as a way of daring God out of his heaven but
of petitioning the almighty deserter on behalf of His weeping earth:

> O Thou that we'd fain be ane wi' again
> Frae the weary lapses o' self set free,
> Be to oor lives as life is to Daith,
> And lift and licht us eternally.   *light*
> Frae the howe o' the sea to the heich o' the   *hollow/height*
>   lift,   *sky*
> To the licht as licht to the darkness is,
> Spring fresh and fair frae the spirit o' God
> Like the a'e first thocht that He kent was His.   *thought/knew*
>   ('Sea-Serpent')

The serpentine spirit didn't respond. MacDiarmid abandoned sobriety and got drunk on Scotland, politics, literature and science, though God, if gone, was never forgotten. '*I'm fu' o' a stickit* [inadequate] *God*', he confesses in *A Drunk Man Looks at the Thistle*, 'THAT'S *what's the maitter wi' me*' (ll. 1632–3). Under the alliterative crust of objectifying words 'assembled like sea stones'[11] at the beginning of 'On a Raised Beach' in *Stony Limits and Other Poems* (1934) the authority of the stones' eternal vibrations is clinched by the assertion: 'Nothing can replace them / Except a new creation of God'.[12] The meaning of 'the words cut oot i' the stane' earlier described in 'The Eemis Stane' as buried in 'the fug o' fame' and 'history's hazelraw [lichen]' is now given in the vocabulary of traditional religious discourse:

> . . . the kindred form I am conscious of here
> Is the beginning and end of the world,
> The unsearchable masterpiece, the music of the spheres,
> Alpha and Omega, the Omnific Word.[13]

The poignancy of this valiant poem comes not primarily from its injunction to see the poetry inherent in scientific terminology but from the interfusion of two ways of looking at the world, the tension and interplay between the categorical fixities of science and the porous, atavistic yearnings of the poet's proudly questing spirit:

> These stones go through Man, straight to God, if there is
>   one.
> What have they not gone through already?
> Empires, civilizations, aeons. Only in them
> If in anything, can His creation confront Him.
> They came so far out of the water and halted forever.
> That larking dallier, the sun, has only been able to play
> With superficial by-products since;
> The moon moves the waters backwards and forwards,

But the stones cannot be lured an inch farther
Either on this side of eternity or the other.
Who thinks God is easier to know than they are?[14]

'Larking dallier' is jarringly archaic diction but we condone it for the sake
not merely of the ideas in the passage, which are quite straightforward,
but for the urgent emotion of MacDiarmid's apprehension in a moment
when the poetry happens precisely because, in T. S. Eliot's phrase, 'the
poetry does not matter' (*East Coker*, II). In the last line MacDiarmid effectively brings God down to earth – confrontation indeed.

David Daiches remembers that *A Drunk Man Looks at the Thistle* (1926)
broke 'on a startled and incredulous Scotland with all the shock of a
childbirth in church'.[15] The shock came from the form as much as from
the eldritch thought processes, the admiration of Russia or the sexual
daring of the passage beginning, 'O wha's been here afore me, lass / And
hoo did he get in?' (ll. 620–21). MacDiarmid advises the reader that his
poem is a 'gallimaufry': it invokes the mental state of drunkenness which
'has a logic of its own' and deliberately avoids the kind of intelligibility
susceptible to division into sections or signposting by thematic 'hand-rails'
for rationally minded readers.[16] 'Your whisky has made you original,'
Byron says of Burns and James Hogg in a letter to Hogg,[17] and Mac-
Diarmid's inebriate originality in *A Drunk Man* is that of a modernist
Byronic miscellany presented in a manner that can be traced back to the
freely associating loquacity of The Shepherd in the *Noctes Ambrosianae*.
'Like a' thing else ca'd Scottish nooadays' (l. 19) the adulterated whisky
flowing through the poem is 'no' the real Mackay' (l. 9), but it works
well enough to remind the poet that 'whiles when I'm alowe [ablaze] wi'
booze, / I'm like God's sel' and clad in fire' (ll. 1393–4).

While the watered-down wine of his country is both a symbol of the
national condition and pretext for the work's digressive method, abrupt
transitions and shifting metres, the poet's ego is the unifying suspension
in which the poem hangs over its central images of thistle, rose, whisky
and moon. There it swings from the expostulatory opening barrage (resemblances here to Pope's Moral Essays) on the theme of '*Sic transit gloria
Scotia*' (l. 33) to the poet's vision of himself (ll. 121–68) and his 'Auld
Scottish instincts' (l. 152), adaptations of Alexander Blok (ll. 169–220,
241–52), a dig at T. S. Eliot who should have gone to Scotland 'Afore
he wrote "The Waste Land"' (ll. 345–8) – a parody of Eliot's Sweeney
poems is introduced at line 2184 – and a captivating address to the thistle
in which the appearance of the national emblem evokes the sounds of the
national instrument:

Plant, what are you then? Your leafs
Mind me o' the pipes' lood drone

>   – And a' your purple tops
>   Are the pirly-wirly notes   *grace notes*
>   That gang staggerin' owre them as they groan.
>   (ll. 411–15)

The thistle is reared to eight feet (l. 461) for the ritual of the Common Riding 'in the Muckle Toon' (MacDiarmid's Langholm) but withers to a 'ghaistly stick' (l. 1173) and shivers 'like / A horse's skin aneth a cleg [under a gadfly]' (l. 1438) before accreting enough ambiguity to become 'A symbol o' the puzzle o' man's soul' (l. 2065). The solution to the puzzles of the poem and the soul of MacDiarmid himself is in the poet's kinship to the 'Appallin' genius' of Dostoevsky (l. 1752), who also had his land in his blood (l. 1985), and in the idea of unity. While the poem lurches through its songs, reveries, comic turns and pontifications, Yggdrasil (l. 1457), the unifying world-tree of Scandinavian mythology, becomes the skeleton of the moonlit thistle which in turn becomes a candelabra analogous to the 'Octopus of Creation'. The poet becomes them all:

>   A mony-brainchin' candelabra fills
>   The lift and's lowin' wi' the stars;   *sky/flaming*
>   The Octopus Creation is wallopin'   *writhing*
>   In coontless faddoms o' a nameless sea.
>   I am the candelabra, and burn
>   My endless candles to an Unkent God.
>   I am the mind and meanin' o' the octopus
>   That thraws its empty airms through a' th' Inane.
>   (ll. 2089–95)

Centring these conflated images in the poet affirms his sufficiency for the task of making unifying sense of the disparate Inane and his capacity to evolve into an artist with the only purpose that matters:

>   And organs may develop syne
>   Responsive to the need divine
>   O' single-minded humankin'.
>
>   The function, as it seems to me,
>   O' Poetry is to bring to be
>   At lang, lang last that unity . . .
>   (ll. 2581–6)

Who could fail to be intoxicated by the prospect? Even Lenin is invited to join in the excitement. In 'First Hymn to Lenin' the poet salutes the revolutionary politician in whom he sees 'that mightier poo'er / Than

fashes [troubles] wi' the laurels and the bays', but in 'Second Hymn to
Lenin' poetry is ranked above politics: 'Ah, Lenin, you were richt. / But
I'm a poet . . . Aimin' at mair than you aimed at'. The art of the politician, in some sense, 'comes first', but though 'Poetry like politics maun
cut / The cackle and pursue real ends', poetry's nature 'better tends' to
the job. What's wanted to rid the world of the *breid-and-butter problems*
in 'Second Hymn to Lenin' is a combination of political and poetic
genius, exactly the unity MacDiarmid tried to achieve himself:

> Wi' Lenin's vision equal poet's gift
> And what unparallelled force was there!
> Nocht in a' literature wi' that
> Begins to compare.[18]

Reading the stones of his raised beach, MacDiarmid sees beneath them
'a stupendous unity'[19] and tries to achieve just that in each of his long
poems from *To Circumjack Cencrastus or The Curly Snake* (1930) to *In
Memoriam James Joyce* (1955) and *The Kind of Poetry I Want* (1961). None
of these poems is in any conventional sense a success, yet all are laudable
attempts to create 'A poetry that has developed to a high degree / An
uncanny sense of direction',[20] rooted in fact. Here is a poet who made
Scots lyrical masterpieces of the calibre of Burns, yet instead of sticking
to an applauded *métier* moves on, driven by conviction that the world
needed a different kind of poetry. 'The poet's hame is in the serpent's
mooth', he says in *To Circumjack Cencrastus*,[21] installing the poet as the
voice of the cosmic world-serpent; but the voice utters only learned,
rambling, occasionally felicitous chatter in which the poem's ostensible
theme of the unifying 'Gaelic Idea'[22] is drowned out. *In Memoriam James
Joyce* loses the unity that might have come from 'a vision of world language' in digressions, catalogues, indigestibly recondite information tipped
from the poet's filing cabinets on to the page and shaped into lines but
into no useful coherence, recalling the question raised in 'A Four Year's
Harvest', one of the prose sketches in *Annals of the Five Senses* (1923):

> There was so much to be read that there was hardly time
> to think. How could he digest the marvellous, the epoch-
> making truths which every day put before him! And the
> still more marvellous lies! The war-time lies, the press
> bureau lies, the eye-witness lies, the lies of accusation and
> the lies of defence; thousands of liars, nations of liars,
> conscience-impelled liars and liars for the love of art![23]

The answer is that he couldn't do it – nobody could – without a clinically
deviant digestive tract. He tried to be super-human, believing that his

work sprang 'from the deeps of the destined'.[24] Yet the long poems do
have their grandeur as witnesses to the unremitting attentiveness of an
omnivorously life-celebrating mind which could be content with nothing
short of an epic effort to broadcast the message of the stones. This effort
MacDiarmid titanically made when he left his miniatures behind and aimed
for stupendous unities on the scale of Wagner, Dostoevsky, Pound and
Joyce.

His literary preferences and his Anglophobia can be as quirky, cantan-
kerous and splenetic as his arrogance can be embarrassing. Neil Gunn
more or less told him so: '. . . your violence, qua violence or anent that
which you are violent against, may not enthuse me. And occasionally it
leads you not merely astray but betrays you into the damnedest non-
sense.'[25] Douglas Dunn finds him as C. M. Grieve guilty of cultivating
'Nietzschean cerebral solitude and super-élitism as a platform for the lofty
intellectual superstructure of his alter ego, Hugh MacDiarmid'.[26] He is
accused of coldness, even of cruelty, yet praises Dylan Thomas's 'buoyant
flashing geniality',[27] warmly introduces 'the sweetness and abundant zest'[28]
of the polio-stricken journalist Don Whyte's *On the Lonely Shore* (1977),
a classic of Scottish autobiography, and enjoyed a long-lasting friendship
with Sean O'Casey, that unswervingly humane Irish man of the people.[29]
'Man does not cease to interest me' he declares in 'Reflections in a Slum',
a poem of focused human pity if ever there was one:

> A lot of the old folk here – all that's left
> Of them after a lifetime's infernal thrall
> Remind me of a Bolshie the 'Whites' buried alive
> Up to his nose, just able to breathe, that's all.
>
> Watch them. You'll see what I mean. When found
> His eyes had lost their former gay twinkle.
> Ants had eaten *that* away; but there was still
> Some life in him . . . his forehead *would* wrinkle!

While wisely observing that 'the dialect of Burns, or the synthetic
Lowlands . . . of MacDiarmid and his collaborators, does not take the
authors concerned out of English literature any more than William Barnes
is outside because he wrote in the language of Dorset', C. H. Sisson
concedes that 'there is a sort of moral impropriety about including him
in a history of *English* poetry'.[30] A large proportion of his work is in the
lingua franca, but it is his poetry in Scots that metabolizes his idiosyncrasies
into the observant, emotional powers of the language he revived to suit
his and his country's needs as he understood them. However his work
and his nationalism finally may be judged there is no disputing that he
became a prime cause of what is now called the Scottish Renaissance in

literature of the twentieth century,[31] a still generally under-valued composite *geist* made up of individual writers who came to maturity during the MacDiarmid era: Sorley MacLean and Iain Crichton Smith (the northwest), George Bruce (the north-east), George Mackay Brown (Orkney), Norman MacCaig and Robert Garioch (Edinburgh) and Edwin Morgan (Glasgow). Tartan poetry which used Scots for sentimental or homiletic effect was discredited by the intellectual strength and craft of William Soutar, Robert Garioch, New Zealand-born Sydney Goodsir Smith and Alexander Scott. Among younger poets MacDiarmid's influence, often transmitted by Edwin Morgan's teaching and example, persists in Tom Leonard and Liz Lochhead's concerns with language, power and politics, Veronica Forrest-Thomson's interest in extending the exploration of language into the universe of nuclear and astrophysics, the meditative strength of James Aitchison, the declaratory lyricism of Alan Bold, the essentially Scottish intellectuality of Roderick Watson and Robert Crawford, and Alan Riach's receptivity to disparate areas of experience, emotional, cerebral and geographical.

Edwin Muir and George Mackay Brown: Orcadian wayside stations

Early childhood on the small Orkney island of Wyre was Edwin Muir's induction to an uncompetitive pastoral society steeped in legend and tradition. People lived in harmony with nature and the boy was safe:

> Long time he lay upon the sunny hill,
>   To his father's house below securely bound.
> Far off the silent, changing sound was still,
>   With the black islands lying thick around.
>   ('Childhood')[32]

His loss of this Eden, which was followed by the deaths of his parents and two brothers within two years after the Muirs moved to Glasgow, became the fixation that informs his best poetry. 'The life of every man is an endlessly repeated performance of the life of man,' he says in *An Autobiography* (1954).[33] Within the particulars of every individual life is a fable of all lives. His own life became devoted to expressing the fable in terms of symbols by which the randomness of events, the surface story, might be shaped into universality.

In *Scott and Scotland* (1936) Muir explains why he chooses to write in

English. Unlike MacDiarmid he believes that 'If we are to have a com-
plete and homogeneous Scottish literature it is necessary that we should
have a complete and homogeneous language . . . To say this is to say that
Scotland can only create a national literature by writing in English.'[34]
For many years he tried to replace the religion of his childhood with
Nietzschean philosophy, Guild Socialism – a tempered but firmly rooted
socialism is the ideological centre from which he sets out on his *Scottish
Journey* (1935) – and literary criticism, but in 1939 recovered his sense
'that Christ was the turning-point of time and the meaning of life to
everyone, no matter what his conscious beliefs'.[35] The gate to Eden was
locked for the present, but it would open again when Christ returned to
redeem the labyrinthine story of human history:

> . . . for all things,
> Beasts of the field, and woods, and rocks, and seas,
> And all mankind from end to end of the earth
> Will call him with one voice. In our own time,
> Some say, or at a time when time is ripe.
> Then he will come, Christ the uncrucified,
> Christ the discrucified, his death undone,
> His agony unmade, his cross dismantled –
> Glad to be so – and the tormented wood
> Will cure its hurt and grow into a tree
> In a green springing corner of young Eden,
> And Judas damned take his long journey backward
> From darkness into light and be a child
> Beside his mother's knee, and the betrayal
> Be quite undone and never more be done.
> ('The Transfiguration')

Some readers may be repelled by Muir's expression of faith – or his
wishful thinking – or feel that 'the chaste, unshowy quality of the verse
is a virtue more appropriate to the cloister than the page'[36] or resent being
got at emotionally by his chant of primary terms: mankind, beasts and
seas, earth, time, agony, darkness, light, mother. Like it or not, however,
his poetry 'had integrity; it was never facile'[37] and for many readers it
retains its power to sanctify. He remained a socialist, continued to write
literary criticism and, with his wife, produced forty-three volumes of translation including the first English versions of Kafka, but poetry increasingly
took over.

Kafka's world of perplexity, loneliness and impersonal menace is clearly
an influence in the dream-like 'tall and echoing passages' of Muir's 'The
Labyrinth' and in the occasional similarity of the 'lovely world' to the
twilight nothingness of the maze he has escaped from:

> . . . all the roads
> That run through the noisy world, deceiving streets
> That meet and part and meet, and rooms that open
> Into each other – and never a final room –
> Stairways and corridors and antechambers
> That vacantly wait for some great audience,
> The smooth sea-tracks that open and close again,
> Tracks undiscoverable, indecipherable,
> Paths on the earth and tunnels underground,
> And bird-tracks in the air – all seemed a part
> Of the great labyrinth.

The labyrinth of what Muir in this poem calls the world of 'illusion' – though we might call it the real one – includes 'The Good Town', an image of destruction caused by the 1948 Communist *coup* in Czechoslovakia where Muir had lived and worked as a British Council officer in Prague. It is not only the 'mounds of rubble', 'shattered piers, half-windows, broken arches' and 'gaping bridges' that distress the poet but the mystery of how the town could 'grow wicked in a moment':

> What is the answer? Perhaps no more than this,
> That once the good men swayed our lives, and those
> Who copied them took a while the hue of goodness,
> A passing loan; while now the bad are up,
> And we, poor ordinary neutral stuff,
> Not good nor bad, must ape them as we can,
> In sullen rage or vile obsequiousness.

His compassion for a Scotland 'that is kingless and songless and whose people are spiritually dead'[38] is evident in 'Scotland's Winter' in which Percy, Douglas and Bruce, sleeping dead heroes of Scottish history, can hear from the living world above them only mocking sounds of a stultifying way of life ignorantly resigned to its exclusion from the values they fought for:

> Listening [they] can hear no more
> Than a hard tapping on the sounding floor
> A little overhead
> Of common heels that do not know
> Whence they come or where they go
> And are content
> With their poor frozen life and shallow banishment.

Although out of the mainstream of predominantly secular twentieth-century thinking, watching the world from 'The Wayside Station' of his belief in Christ and immortality as he implies in the poem of that title,

Muir engages with the anxieties of his time. He writes about the horrors of atomic war in 'The Horses' ('That old bad world that swallowed its children quick / At one great gulp'), in 'The Last War' ('No place at all for bravery in that war') and in 'The Day Before the Last Day' ('Mechanical parody of the Judgement Day / That does not judge but only deals damnation'). In the finest of these, 'The Horses', the coming of the 'fabulous steeds' is a new beginning for the dispossessed survivors, a redemptive turning back to the 'free servitude' of an Edenesque way of life before the rule of the tractor led to the age of the nuclear bomb. Even as 'the world's great day' was 'growing late', Muir still stood with 'One Foot in Eden' and kept the fable going.

The largest of the Orkney islands, called Hrossey ('horse island') by the Vikings, is marked insipidly 'Mainland' on modern maps. It has two towns, Kirkwall in the centre and in the west George Mackay Brown's home town, Stromness. After a serious attack of tuberculosis in his twenties Brown attended Newbattle Abbey College for residential education in 1951, coming under the tutelage of Edwin Muir who had been appointed Warden in the previous year. Brown, who converted to Roman Catholicism in 1961 (rejecting the effects of what he calls John Knox's 'wild hogmanay'[39]), was profoundly affected by Muir's sacramental view of life and by the religious vision and alliterative, word-compounding diction of Gerard Manley Hopkins whose poetry he read as a graduate student at Edinburgh University.[40] Settled back in Stromness he immersed himself in Orkney history and the mythologizing stories of the *Orkneyinga Saga*, developing a conception of time as a loom weaving past and present together. He has a special interest in Magnus Erlendson, the martyred and canonized twelfth-century earl who became a political victim of his cousin, Hakon Paulson's, ambition to be sole ruler of Orkney instead of sharing the earldom with Magnus. In Chapter 7 of Brown's most poetical and inventive novel, *Magnus* (1973), the saint's reluctant executioner, a cook called Lifolf, is transposed into the Second World War as chef in a German concentration camp, compelled to butcher a Magnus updated to resemble the German theologian, Dietrich Bonhoeffer, who was hanged by the Gestapo in 1945. Brown's story of the day-dreaming crofter's son, Thorfinn Ragnarson, in his recent novel, *Beside the Ocean of Time* (1994), also interweaves past and present but is merely charming by comparison with *Magnus* which suggests an equivalence calculated to distress – are we incapable of learning from history, fated to repeat our evil mistakes?

Brown cherishes Orcadian continuities that go further back than the Vikings to the Picts, the broch-builders who came before them, and the neolithic people who erected the standing stones of Stenness and Brodgar, the chambered burial mound of Maes Howe and Skara Brae, the best preserved prehistoric village in northern Europe. Stones are sacred to him. His poetic ideal, as Alan Bold notices, 'is the permanence of runic cuttings in stone',[41] his poems and stories celebrating what he calls 'A solid round of stone and ritual' in the sonnet, 'Chapel Between Cornfield and Shore'.[42] His miraculous staples are earth, sea, 'King Barleycorn' ('The Scarecrow in the Schoolmaster's Oats'[43]) and fish:

> From the black furrow, a fecund
> Whisper of dust,
> From the gray furrow, a sudden
> Gleam and thrust,
> Crossings of net and ploughshare,
> Fishbone and crust.
> ('Black Furrow, Gray Furrow'[44])

The old name for Stromness was 'Hamnavoe', the title of a poem in which Brown memorializes his father, a tailor and postman, ritualizing a typical day in the life of the town into panels of imagery that do for Stromness what Dylan Thomas did more expansively for his 'Llareggub' in *Under Milk Wood*. Morning breaks to the sound of gulls and herring boats 'puffing red sails' for the horizon. At noon 'four bearded merchants' stroll past the pier 'holy with greed . . . chanting / Their slow grave jargon'. As the 'amber day' ebbs, drinkers' beards are 'spumy with porter' in 'The Arctic Whaler', fishing boats drive 'furrows homeward, like ploughmen / In blizzards of gulls', and fisher girls gut and clean the day's catch, flashing 'knife and dirge / Over drifts of herring'. The picture ends with a house going 'blind' with grief for someone lost at sea, with church-going, love, the postman's last call for the day and the son's gratitude for his father's protection:

> He quenched his lantern, leaving the last door.
> Because of his gay poverty that kept
>   My seapink innocence
>   From the worm and black wind;
>
> And because, under equality's sun,
> All things wear now to a common soiling,
>   In the fire of images
>   Gladly I put my hand
>   To save that day for him.[45]

In his own northerly wayside station of Stromness much of what is normally meant by progress is anathema to Brown. He makes his position clear in *An Orkney Tapestry* (1969) where Progress is 'a rootless utilitarian faith, without beauty or mystery; a kind of blind unquestioning belief that men and their material circumstances will go on improving until some kind of nirvana is reached and everyone will be rich, free, fulfilled, well-informed, masterful . . . Word and name are drained of their ancient power. Number, statistic, graph are everything.'[46] The possibility of humanity's mass self-immolation on the altar of progress is one of the themes in the novel, *Greenvoe* (1972), where a secret nuclear development is called 'Operation Black Star'. In *Fishermen with Ploughs* (1971) the poet's fear of 'the bedlam and cinders of A Black Pentecost' ('Dead Fires') is realized in 'Landfall', a prose sequence in which modern civilization has been destroyed by 'The Black Flame' ('Fire bowed through the door, a mad inspector', recalls the blind schoolteacher). In the same volume the poem, 'Love Letter', refers to girls who are nothing but 'giggles, lipstick, and gramophone records' instead of being the 'walking wombs' or 'seed jars'[47] crucial to the continuity of a life Brown sees as gracefully elemental, even if his terminology is likely to affront a political correctness he could not have foreseen. Pessimistic about a secular future, he re-enacts in 'Stations of the Cross (for a chapel in the fields)'[48] Jesus's journey from Pilate to the cross in terms that proclaim a spiritual hunger for Christ as basic as the physiological hunger for food. When uranium deposits were found on Orkney, shops in Stromness and Kirkwall displayed stickers urging citizens to 'Say No to Uranium'. Brown's poem, 'Uranium', sets the new era of unimaginable energies in the continuity of earlier ages. The ending of the poem is ambiguous. The ages of stone, bronze and salt are succeeded by a harmonious age of agriculture, but the tribe is destined to move on:

> This, we are assured,
> Is not the place still
> Where the tribe
> Will write history on skins
> And seal it in a jar, cave-kept.
> A horseman
> Returned across the desert this morning.
> On the far side
> He had stood before the magnificent Door of Fire.[49]

There is recognition of vast potential in the measured fatefulness of that last line; but what will the tribe do with it? Like Brown, we wait to see.

Two Gaels: Sorley MacLean (Somhairle MacGill-Eain) and Iain Crichton Smith (Iain Mac a'Ghobhainn)

MacDiarmid resuscitated Scots and Sorley MacLean rejuvenated literary Gaelic. By writing in Gaelic MacLean limits the immediate audience for his poetry to approximately 80,000 speakers of the language, but makes much of his work available to a wider public through versions in which truth to the originals prevails over English-idiom elegance of the translated line. The foremost Gaelic poet of this century — some say of any century — he was born on the isle of Raasay which lies between Skye and the Applecross peninsula on the mainland of Wester Ross, the son of a 'tailor-crofter-fisherman'.[50] While a student at Edinburgh University he abandoned the English styles of Eliot and Pound, and turned to Gaelic as truer to himself, drawing on a memory stored with Gaelic poetry and song by a family of tradition-bearers, singers and pipers. There is a Yeatsian mystical grandeur in MacLean's work; while always persuasive, it absolutely resists the worst that explication can do, even when the explicator has the Gaelic, and his impregnable linguistic identity prevents his work from ever appearing to be 'English poetry dressed up in Gaelic'.[51] His poems are bardic, marmoreal, sometimes as barely scrutable as the meditation on the fate of Gaelic culture and Highland life in 'The Cave of Gold' ('Uamha 'n Òir')[52] where the music of two MacCrimmon pipers seems to represent an art of transcendent ordering power although it is beyond the understanding of the men who make it:

> as he went on in his perplexity
>
> with no struggle but the plea of the music,
> he did not let go his pipe.
> The sword was useless,
> it was the music that strengthened his step,
> it was the music itself that strove.
>
> The pipe itself had the power . . .
>
> its genesis, purpose and meaning,
> the argument that was in its cry,
> though weak yet stronger than the strongest
> hero ever seen on field
> wrestling with the green bitch of death.
>
> ('The Cave of Gold', III)

In an essay entitled 'The Poetry of the Clearances' MacLean says, 'The Highland Clearances constitute one of the saddest tragedies that has ever come on a people, and one of the most astounding of all the successes of landlord capitalism in Western Europe, such a triumph over the workers and peasants of a country as has rarely been achieved with such ease, cruelty and cynicism.'[53] In 1846 the last MacLeod, or MacGille Chaluim, of Raasay sold the island to an Edinburgh man who despatched 129 families to Australia and exiled others to the small island of Rona.[54] In the visionary poem, 'Hallaig', the poet revisits the cleared townships, asserting a ghostly continuity of 'every single generation gone', their lives now transformed into birches, hazels and rowans, yet supernaturally alive:

> They are still in Hallaig,
> MacLeans and MacLeods,
> all who were there in the time of Mac Gille Chaluim
> the dead have been seen alive.

In an astonishing final image which refers back to the poem's epigraph – 'Time, the deer, is in the wood of Hallaig' – the poet kills the deer with the force of his love, imaginatively preserving his island from the spoliations of history, and getting away with it:

> . . . when the sun goes down behind Dun Cana
> a vehement bullet will come from the gun of Love;

> and will strike the deer that goes dizzily,
> sniffing at the grass-grown ruined homes;
> his eye will freeze in the wood,
> his blood will not be traced while I live.

In 'Screapadal' (the title is the name of a place on Raasay facing Applecross) an ultimate, nuclear clearance is threatened by 'the death / that killed the thousands of Nagasaki'. Instead of seal and basking-shark:

> . . . today in the sea-sound
> a submarine lifts its turret
> and its black sleek back
> threatening the thing that would make
> dross of wood, of meadows and of rocks
> that would leave Screapadal without beauty
> just as it was left without people.

While he belongs to an ancient Gaelic tradition, MacLean is also driven by a modern imagination which brings together the heterogeneous elements of love and politics, personal passion and social responsibility. 'The Choice' ('An Roghainn'), from the collection *Poems to Eimhir and Other Poems* (*Dàin do Eimhir agus Dàin Eile*, 1943),[55] expresses his conviction that participation in the human community is a prerequisite for personal success in love. If you dodge the call to righteous arms in the Spanish Civil War, don't expect to get the girl:

I followed only a way
that was small, mean, low, dry, lukewarm,
and how then should I meet
the thunderbolt of love?

But if I had the choice again
and stood on that headland,
I would leap from heaven or hell
with a whole spirit and heart.

In 'The Turmoil' ('Am Buaireadh'), a love poem from the same collection, the poet's passion for a woman obscures his sense of wounded humanity and the historical significance of Christ and Lenin. 'The Blue Rampart' ('Am Mùr Gorm') from the sequence 'The Haunted Ebb' ('An Tràigh Thathaich') refers to the 'Tree of Strings', an old Gaelic kenning for the harp, a symbol for music and by extension for poetry. Love changes everything, interfering with nature's capacity to exalt the imagination to the sufficiency of reason. The poem loses some of its complexity of meaning in translation. In the last stanza the phrase 'luxuriant summit' fails to bring out an oxymoron of the original where the Gaelic word 'creachainn' means 'bare summit' or 'bare wind-swept summit':[56]

But for you the oceans
in their unrest and their repose
would raise the wave-crests of my mind
and settle them on a high serenity.

And the brown brindled moorland
and my reason would co-extend –
but you imposed on them an edict
above my own pain.

And on a distant luxuriant Summit
there blossomed the Tree of Strings,
among its leafy branches your face,
my reason and the likeness of a star.

In 'A Highland Woman' ('Ban-Ghàidheal') MacLean excoriates the doctrine of Election. Here the phrase 'Black Labour' originally referred to days of work done for a landlord partly in lieu of rent; it came to mean any arduous physical work in the fields, much of which devolved on women when their men were at sea, fishing. MacLean remembers that it was common in his youth to see women prematurely aged by these harsh circumstances, and abandoned by Christ, the 'great Jew' and 'King of Glory', who remains pitilessly aloof from peasant anguish:

And every twenty Autumns gone
she has lost the golden summer of her bloom,
and the Black Labour has ploughed the furrow
across the white smoothness of her forehead.

And Thy gentle church has spoken
about the lost state of her miserable soul,
and the unremitting toil has lowered
her body to a black peace in a grave.

And her time has gone like a black sludge
seeping through the thatch of a poor dwelling:
the hard Black Labour was her inheritance;
grey is her sleep to-night.

Many modern poets have tended to separate reason from feeling. There is T. S. Eliot's coinage, 'dissociation of sensibility', and in the essay 'Tradition and the Individual Talent' (1917) his split between 'the man who suffers and the mind which creates'.[57] There is Yeats's distinction between perfection of the life and perfection of the work, and Wallace Stevens's imperialist imagination as a faculty for shaping a surrogate poetical world. MacLean can admire these poets but insists on a balance of intellect and feeling. In 'The Knife' ('An Sgian') love saves him from the intellectual incision that would cut off brain from heart:

Dear, if my heart love
of you were not like the hardness of the jewel
surely it could be cut
by a hard sharp brain.

Born on the island of Lewis in 1928, Iain Crichton Smith writes poetry, novels and short stories both in English and his native Gaelic, translating much of his Gaelic work for English readers. Like MacLean he finds a ready theme in the Clearances. An early poem registers the Highlander's anger towards the house of Sutherland (the English family of George Leveson-Gower), held responsible for causing much of the suffering:

Though hate is evil we cannot
but hope your courtier's heels in hell

are burning: that to hear
the thatch sizzling in tanged smoke
your hot ears slowly learn.
                              ('Clearances')[58]

Smith writes obliquely about the Clearances in *The Emigrants* (1983) but more directly in *Consider the Lilies* (1968), a beautifully controlled novel about an old woman confronted by eviction, in which Smith chooses a 'simple and almost transparent' style to portray events 'as if through the mind of the old woman'.[59] The title poem of *The Exiles* (1984)[60] commemorates the deracination of people banished to Canada:

> The many ships that left our country
> with white wings for Canada.
> They are like handkerchiefs in our memories
> and the brine like tears
> and in their masts sailors singing
> like birds on branches.

In 'Australia' even dingos are agitated by the spirits of the exiles:

> Sometimes I hear graves singing
> their Gaelic songs to the dingos
> which scrabble furiously at the clay.
> Then tenderly in white they come towards me,
> drifting in white, the far exiles
> buried in the heart of brown deserts.

Smith prefers 'poetry which contains fighting tensions' to 'poetry of statement'.[61] A poem of 1980, 'Self-portrait', expresses the tension between the poet's secular adult outlook and his Scottish Free Church background:

> Whose is this Free Church face?
> Surely it's someone else, from my childhood,
> making its endless principled demands
> through the round glasses' twin gun-barrels.
> There was a time I would have mocked you, face,
> in your gaunt heaven fixed, so smug and clear,
> now I bear you with me like a penance.[62]

The Free Church face is no mask; it belongs inescapably to the poet, the 'twin gun-barrels' proclaiming one who shoots for truth. The image also suggests that he is now armed against a system that has become inimical to him. While abjuring the religion of his forefathers, he can admire those who live by it and acknowledges its formative influence as part of his composition, separable from the Church which institutionalized it, enduring in its effect and verbalized here without a trace of satire when he refers to 'those secret moral waters' that surely made him. In the poem 'Old Woman' from *Thistles and Roses* (1961) there is a fighting tension between life and death, religion and nature, the poet and his past. In a house on Lewis an old woman is lying on a bed attended by her husband, a Free Church elder. The woman is so old and weak that her husband has to feed her. He puts the plate in front of her and spoons the food into her 'blindly searching' mouth. As the husband stoically prays the poet formulates his bitter imagery:

> I saw the teeth
> tighten their grip around a delicate death.
> And nothing moved within the knotted head
>
> but only a few poor veins as one might see
> vague wishless seaweed floating on a tide
> of all the salty waters where had died
> too many waves to mark two more or three.

Outside the brave, degraded house 'the grass was raging', as though nature itself is made angry by its own diminishment within, and the poet rages too. These 'few poor veins' are acceptable in seaweed, but not in a human head.

While envying the religious certainty of his forebears, Smith's sense of 'the infinitely complex' precludes it for himself.[63] In the volume *The Law and the Grace* (1965) 'A Note on Puritans' recognizes the courage of people whose faith put 'no curtain between them and fire' but understands that 'certain truths can make men brutish too', the supreme brutality for Smith being denial of complexity. In the sequence 'Deer on the High Hills' freedom to negotiate complexity is the essence of an art symbolized by the deer and constructed from natural elements:

> You must build from the rain and stones
> till you can make
> a stylish deer on the high hills,
> and let its leaps be unpredictable!
>
> (V)

An artistic spirit responsive to the 'flow' of life that frightens the typical preacher in 'A Day without Dogma'[64] must be as unconstrained and unpredictable as the flow itself. This sensitive freedom is Smith's idea of the inner law of grace which the Puritans forswore. 'Hume' declares the insufficiency of 'the reasonable mind' and the treachery of 'diplomacies' that 'displace / the inner law'. 'Lenin' clarifies the poet's exclusion from even the secular certainties of Communism: the truth about Lenin, 'that troubling man / "who never read a book for pleasure" ' – another graceless puritan – is a distorting simplicity of mind:

> . . . the true dialectic is to turn
> in the infinitely complex, like a chain
> we steadily burn through, steadily forge and burn
> not to be dismissed in any poem
>
> by admiration for the ruthless man
> nor for the saint but for the moving on
> into the endlessly various, real, human,
> world which is no new era, shining dawn.

'Russian Poem' is blunter: Lenin has 'simplified the world like an assassin / Where his barrel points is where evil is'. In Smith's most recent collection, *Ends and Beginnings* (1994), largely inspired by a visit to the Golan Heights, dogma is still 'perfidious' ('Dogmas'[65]), 'the defence against reality' which creates 'Blood, death and terror' and 'a measure of our inability to live' ('A Day without Dogma'). The victims of biblical dogma 'have black faces and its saints have batons' ('The Bible'[66]). How can the heart be cosmopolitan when only 'wasteful commonness' is shared and the dogma of nationalism is asserted by flags which are merely 'unreasoning rags'? ('Turkey'[67]).

More 'a contemplator of the world than one who . . . aspires to change it',[68] his view of life is reminiscent of Conrad's – the Reverend Donald Black's African experience in 'The Missionary'[69] is a variation on Kurtz's in 'Heart of Darkness' – and conveys 'a deep-seated unease with the contemporary world'.[70] He can be humorous, as in the hilariously anarchic early sections of 'Murdo', the story of a bank clerk who reneges against conformity until his father's death convinces him that 'there are no angels'.[71] Often tempted by pessimism, Smith yields to it on the Golan Heights where the fighting tension between 'unexploded mines' and 'sweet red flowers'[72] induces the dogma of despair; but the surrender is temporary. 'Conversion', the long final poem in *Ends and Beginnings*, leaves him freed of history, books, symbol and language, 'a voyeur / of final uncluttered pure humanity'.[73]

Three stylists: Norman MacCaig; W. S. Graham; Douglas Dunn

'A threequarter Gael',[74] Norman MacCaig feels at home both in Edinburgh and in the village of Inverkirkaig near Lochinver in Sutherland. His favourite mountain is Suilven. 'I love Suilven', he says, 'because from the

West it looks like the top joint of your thumb. But he cons you: there's a ridge and there's a pinky at the far end . . . so that when you get on to the ridge, suddenly you see miles and miles instead of just what was under you.'[75] His idea of a miracle in 'Above Inverkirkaig'[76] is the coupling of the mountains, Suilven and Cul Mor, to produce 'a litter of tiny Suilvens, each one / the dead spit of his father'. In 'Climbing Suilven' a dizzying shift of scales and perspectives intensifies the poet's sense of physical self:

> Parishes dwindle. But my parish is
> This stone, that tuft, this stone
> And the cramped quarters of my flesh and bone.
> I claw that tall horizon down to this;
> And suddenly
> My shadow jumps huge miles away from me.

This poem is from the volume *Riding Lights* (1955), in which MacCaig abandons the New Apocalypse surrealist practices of his earlier work, a major step in what he calls his 'long haul towards lucidity'.[77] His triumph is to have developed a style which can tackle anything without needing to be obscure in poetry which 'makes none of the usual bids for attention, denying itself the hieratic tone, the high rhetoric, the incantations which homogenize mass feelings'.[78] Yet there is a tension in a MacCaig poem that comes from the sense that each word, each line has passed a rigorous test of validity in competition with the appeal to the poet of leaving the subject alone without interference from him. Impelled to use words, he remains suspicious of them: 'the ones I use', he says, 'often look at me / with a look that whispers, *Liar*' ('Ineducable me'). There are no lies in the non-verbal realm of the thrush, the newt and the gannet, 'A free world, a world without hypocrisy, without masks' ('Hard Division').

He is often wryly aware of his own act of perception as in the poem 'An ordinary day' in which either he takes 'his mind a walk' or his mind takes him a walk, whichever is the elusive truth of it, and in the earlier 'No consolation' from the volume *Surroundings* (1966):

> I consoled myself for not being able to describe
> water trickling down a wall or
> a wall being trickled down by water
> by reflecting that I can see
> these two things are not the same thing:
> which is more than a wall can do,
> or water.

Referring to what he cannot describe, the poet consoles himself with the thought that, unlike the wall and the water, he is a discriminating consciousness. He can describe his own inventions, but consciousness cannot feed on itself. What the imagination can do is elicit strangeness from ordinary reality, heightening perception by making water into a wall, or making the wall trickle like water. (Dylan Thomas does the same thing in 'Fern Hill' when he writes of 'fire green as grass'.) Nature or reality is like one's wife. The poet has a promiscuous imagination and can be loyal to his wife by transforming her into somebody else, making her new; MacCaig's genius specializes in charging the ordinary – landscapes, animals, people – with celebratory newness, revealing a world of 'teeming unpredictables' ('Centre of centres') which he exposes but never appropriates or binds.

Few poets are so unegotistical, so lacking in posture. The 'miraculous declarations' he shows us are always out there to be wondered at for themselves, not to be applauded as an attribute of the poet's skill in divulging them. So, straws lie on grass 'like tame lightnings' and 'a hen stares at nothing with one eye / Then picks it up' ('Summer farm'); sprinting plover 'have no acceleration / and no brakes' ('Ringed plover by a water's edge'); a dog flows 'through fences like a piece of black wind' ('Praise of a collie'); he thinks about a loved one 'in as many ways as rain comes' ('No choice'); a toad looks 'like a purse' and crawls 'like a Japanese wrestler' ('Toad'); the lochs of his beloved north-west may be 'just H_2O in a hollow' but they stand 'huge mountains on their watery heads' ('Small lochs'). In darker mood he trembles for the stag who will be 'an old rug rotting in the heather' ('Two focuses'); the hearts of world leaders conceal the devil who 'sits crosslegged, / grinning and cracking his finger joints' ('Leaders of men');[79] American skyscrapers walk around 'with atom bombs slung at their hips' ('Rewards and furies'); and in the circus of life outside the 'Big Top' crowds panic 'towards exits / that aren't there'. The Duke of Sutherland is a thief who steals the land from the people, driving them from their homes to the shore, where the tide steals it again, and on to Canada ('Two thieves'). In 'A man in Assynt' metaphor gives way to undecorated anger about the depopulation of the Highlands first by the Clearances, later by 'English businessmen and the indifference / of a remote and ignorant government':

Who owns this landscape?
The millionaire who bought it or
the poacher staggering downhill in the early morning
with a deer on his back?

If MacCaig contemplates his own darkness – midnight blood 'bubbles / into ferocious flowers that eat the darkness and crawl / on the sleeper's skin' ('Midnights') – he objectifies it, hating the word 'confessional'. In 'Go away, Ariel', he finds the grid of himself in Shakespeare's *The Tempest* from whose cast of characters Caliban is a more welcome visitor than 'heartless, musical . . . supersonic Ariel', even if he does blubber about Miranda and go on about his mother:

> Phone a bat, Ariel. Leave us
> to have a good cry – to stare at each other
> with recognition and loathing.

He detests cant. In response to a ponderous critical comment about his work he once replied, 'Oh, I think that kind of talk stinks the joint up, as Ellington said when they asked him if he was influenced by Debussy.'[80] The academic is 'the tone-deaf man in the orchestra', the 'frog / who wouldn't a-wooing go' ('An academic'). Socio-psychological cant gets no quarter either. He does not hide his contempt for the excuses people make for their evil blunders: '"Wisnae me, came from a broken home" – all that stuff. "I had a black-out" – this is after sawing a woman in quadruplets.'[81] His poem about the abrogation of responsibility is called 'The first of them', the title referring to the snake which has been blamed and hated since Adam and Eve:

> Poor snake. He crawls on his belly
> dropping amber tears in the dust and whining
> *I was only obeying orders.*

Religion, too, is cant in a world which mixes adders and butterflies, torture and Schubert. God is 'an absentee landlord' in 'The Kirk', reaching down from 'some Bahamas in the sky' to collect 'the price of suffering with which to pay / a pittance to his estate workers'. (Wickedly, he professes to believe in the Devil but not in God, which makes him, he says, 'a Zen Calvinist'.[82]) The effort of balancing beauty and suffering shakes his mind in 'Assisi' and 'Equilibrist':

> I had a difficulty in being friendly
> to the Lord, who gave us these burdens,
> so I returned him to other people
> and totter without help
> among his careless inventions.
> > ('Equilibrist')

The reported totter is internal, never public and rarely aesthetic, in a body of poetry in which language does an inimitable version of its best.

W. S. Graham and Douglas Dunn stand out among poets of their successive generations as isolated twentieth-century figures whose work achieves universality in diametrically opposed styles. Graham's poetry is densely figured and strongly textured by syntactical dislocations – like the young Norman MacCaig he was associated with the New Apocalypse Movement – while Dunn's verse is lucid and ungesticulant. Though Graham 'was disenchanted with the 1920–45 Scottish Renaissance movement *as such*, he by no means lost sight of the Scotland of his hard childhood and early years'.[83] He writes about 'Blantyre seasons' and the river Calder in 'The Search by a Town'[84] and recalls the pavements of his birthplace 'shouting games and faces' on a 'Clydeside, / Webbed in its foundries and loud blood' in 'The Children of Greenock'. Meditating on the lives of islanders, he walks 'beside the subsided herds / Of water' watching children and the sun wading in 'Gigha'; but his real preoccupation is with the world as words. His particular message is that reality itself is the language it becomes. For Graham as for Wallace Stevens 'the real is only the base',[85] the poem not merely an act of description but 'Part of the res itself and not about it'.[86] It is 'the word's crest' as well as Ben Narnain's that he scales with his mind and hobnail in 'Since All My Steps Taken' and, in a neat inversion, springtime 'sheepdogs' his 'fertile heel to word' in 'The Children of Lanarkshire'. In his most powerful poem, 'The Nightfishing', his sea, like Melville's, is at once literal – 'deep and shifting seams of water' – and a metaphor for the mind which experiences 'grace of change' as 'Words break' into fresh waves of language that name him 'to the bone' and bring a reconstitution of consciousness.

'Brainy, cerebral poetry seldom recommends itself' to Douglas Dunn.[87] In fastidiously pruned diction through which imagery seems to speak for itself he writes about Clydeside cranes coming down to enjoy their reflections in the river ('Landscape with One Figure'[88]), 'Caledonian Moonlight',[89] Glasgow schoolboys and the odds the future stacks against them ('Glasgow Schoolboys, Running Backwards'[90]), Dundee and the 'rain-misted, subtle Tay' ('Leaving Dundee'[91]), the burning of a witch in Dornoch and the harrowing tale of her lame daughter ('Witch-girl'[92]). 'St Kilda's Parliament: 1879–1979' is a monumental elegy to a 'remote democracy' which ended when the islanders were evacuated in 1930 and the island returned 'to its naked self, / Its archaeology of hazelraw [lichen] / And footprints stratified beneath the lichen'.[93] The volume *Elegies* (1985) presents thirty-nine poems as a monument to his dead wife. Keenly felt but devoid of breast-beating ego, the poems combine into the emotional 'aerial photograph' the lark takes of the poet in 'Larksong', subtly commemorating 'the private grace of man and wife' ('Land Love') without breaking the decorums of that privacy:

> I can feel history close
> Its bedroom door. It reads,
> Then switches the lamp off.
>   ('Snow Days')

The appeal of Dunn's poems comes partly from the sense that they follow no agenda, though a recurrent motif is the distances between people
he has seen and can't forget, like the rough-chinned old men pedalling
their bikes 'on low gear' and white-scarved for one another's funerals in
'The Patricians',[94] or the 'winey down-and-out', shuffling simpleton and
other passengers 'Loitering, discontent and ghetto-blasting' in the Country
Bus Station of 'Broughty Ferry'.[95] A winter sky's roselight perfection
might neutralize the pathos of such lives in the 'mind-aggrandized' vision
of the poet, but he is aware of the danger: 'I won't disfigure loveliness
I see / With an avoidance of its politics'. Notwithstanding his anger on
behalf of Scotland as 'a posthumous Nation' in 'At Falkland Palace',[96] his
habit is to leave politics eloquently implicit and his ironies gentle. 'They
will not leave me, the lives of other people', he says in 'The Hunched',[97]
'I wear them near my eyes like spectacles'.

Poems and spaceships: Edwin Morgan

An *honnête homme* involved with books and humankind, Edwin Morgan
is Scotland's most distinguished person of letters after MacDiarmid. In
1990 he chose the occasion of his seventieth birthday to confirm his
position as a homosexual writer.[98] The decision to publish an explicit
interview[99] and an autobiographical poem, 'Epilogue: Seven Decades',[100]
completed a coming-out process in which the habits of secrecy formerly
required by law or enjoined by social convention yielded to his wish to
'record the truthful emotional basis of the poetry'.[101] The forthright poem
ends *Collected Poems* (1990),[102] illuminating the constriction within which
he had lived and suppressed, but always managed to work:

> At thirty I thought life had passed me by,
> translated *Beowulf* for want of love.
> And one night stands in city centre lanes –
> they were dark in those days – were wild but bleak.
> Sydney Graham in London said 'you know
> I always thought so', kissed me on the cheek.
> And I translated Rilke's *Loneliness*
> *is like a rain*, and week after week after week
> strained to unbind myself,
> sweated to speak.

The variety of his work includes love poems, concrete poems, Glasgow
poems and Scottish sonnets, emergent poems – the most famous of these

being the much-discussed 'Message Clear' evolved from the line 'I am the resurrection and the life' – poster poems, sound poems, science-fiction poems and libretti. His critical writing is erudite without pomp and never sectarian. He is the most holistic, enlanguaged and internationalist of contemporary British poets. The internationalism is evident in his range of styles and in his translations of European and Russian writers. In the Second World War he joined the Royal Army Medical Corps – as MacDiarmid had done in the First – and served at the 42nd General Hospital at El Ballah in the Egyptian desert as quartermaster's clerk and stretcher-bearer. The liking he acquired for Arab culture is evident in his 1977 sequence of poems, 'The New Divan'. In 1992 his Glasgow-based Scots version of Edmond Rostand's *Cyrano de Bergerac* was staged to nation-wide acclaim at the Edinburgh Festival. Against stiff competition his 1952 translation of *Beowulf* has been called 'the most satisfactory of all the attempts to reduce *Beowulf* to modern English verse'.[103]

Morgan does not like 'systems of thought or systems of belief'.[104] A Blakean prose-poem called 'The Fifth Gospel' says:

> I have come to overthrow the law and the prophets:
>   I have not come to fulfil, but to overthrow . . .
> It is not those that are sick who need a doctor, but
>   those that are healthy. I have not come to call sinners,
>   but the virtuous and law-abiding, to repentance.

There is an echo here of the 'piece of wisdom' Sullenbode shares with Maskull in David Lindsay's *A Voyage to Arcturus*:

> Men who live by laws and rules are parasites. Others shed
> their strength to bring these laws out of nothing into the
> light of day, but the law-abiders live at their ease – they
> have conquered nothing for themselves . . . there is no
> longer any spirit of adventure among the Earthmen.
> Everything is safe, vulgar, and completed.
>
> (Chapter 19)

Hugh MacDiarmid had taken a similar position, adopting as his motto Thomas Hardy's declaration, 'Literature is the written expression of revolt against accepted things.'[105] This anti-establishment strain is the anarchic side of Morgan's relish of life in its fullness. *Wi the Haill Voice* ('With the Whole Voice') is the title of his volume (1972) of translations into Scots of poems by Vladimir Mayakovsky, and it is the wholeness of his own voice that best testifies to the generosity of his imagination. It is the voice of a romantic and intellectual sensibility in constant touch with a world which is 'everything that is the case' ('Wittgenstein on Egdon Heath')

as it endows with speech an apple, a hyena, a centaur, a Mercurian, the
Loch Ness Monster, Glasgow's hard men, or the mummy of Rameses II.
It speaks of the vitality of the city and of its pathos; yet even in works
which present the dark side of urban life ('Glasgow Green') or the
cruelties of mid-century South African politics ('Starryveldt') or the ironies
of events in the Gulf ('An Iraqi Student'[106]) there is compassion in the
poetry, between the lines or like a heartbeat under them to be felt as
part of what Charles Olson calls the poem's 'energy-discharge'.[107] With
the break-up of the USSR and 'the body of socialism' dragged 'into a
common grave' the '*novus ordo*' prompts 'A Warning' in *Hold Hands
Among the Atoms* (1991). The poem's fuse of feeling rises through an
empathic choice of detail to a poise of sadness and irony in which
political realism and humane concern are perfectly combined:

> . . . Take your string bag. An orange
> for strippers. Don't feel bought, you're buying, buying.
> – And if, oh, any should stint the euphoria
> for a moment, watching the snow falling slowly
> over shot-pocked facades, there'd only be some
> muffled echo of the better life that
> never seems to come, like a faint singing
> heard in the pauses of snoring out of cardboard
> or waiters' shouts from bursting blood-red kitchens.
> They must listen so very hard, the freed ones![108]

Morgan's work offers the hope that comes from the intrinsic optimism
of curiosity and it is the passion of that hope which can take us on our
grey days to the Wordsworthian altitude of 'Thoughts that do often lie
too deep for tears'.[109] For Robert Frost a poem gives 'a momentary stay
against confusion';[110] for T. S. Eliot in 'East Coker', IV, 'the whole earth
is our hospital'; for Wallace Stevens 'reality is a cliché from which we
escape by metaphor'.[111] Confusion, hospital, escape – a doleful trio. Morgan's Glaswegian 'Trio', in the poem of that name, wind in their arms
'the life of men and beasts, and music, / laughter ringing them round like
a guard', and for him poetry and life are not to be defined in the negative
terms often favoured by other twentieth-century masters. 'I think of
poetry as partly an instrument of exploration,' he says, 'like a spaceship,
into new fields of feeling or experience (or old fields which become new
in new contexts or environments).'[112] Neophiliac enjoyment of science
and technology is evident throughout his writing, but the sonnet 'Computer Error: Neutron Strike' graphically faces the supreme peril of
modern science in a poem to be set beside Edwin Muir's 'The Horses',
though without Muir's redemptive conclusion. The removal of the Berlin
Wall in 1989 signalled the official end of the Cold War, but the nuclear

threat remains. The possibility of total annihilation is still the nightmare distinction of our time:

> No one was left to hear the long All Clear.
> Hot wind swept through the streets of Aberdeen
> and stirred the corpse-clogged harbour. Each machine,
> each building, tank, car, college, crane, stood sheer
> and clean but that a shred of skin, a hand,
> a blackened child driven like tumbleweed
> would give the lack of ruins leave to feed
> on horrors we were slow to understand
> but did.

His sense of fun can be whimsical as in the 'concrete' poems, 'French Persian Cats Having a Ball' and 'Siesta of a Hungarian Snake', or grotesque as in his guidance about the right way to throw a dwarf. 'Rules for Dwarf-Throwing' include:

> 4. If a dwarf is to be thrown across the path of an
> oncoming train, the thrower must previously satisfy the
> organizers that he bears no personal malice to the
> throwee.

> 10. It is strictly forbidden, in dwarf-throwing literature and
> publicity, to refer to dwarfs as 'persons of restricted
> growth' or 'small people'.

'The Hanging Gardens of Babylon (for John Furnival's 50th birthday)' deconstructs from 'the hanging gravids of babyland' via 'the hamfisted gasfitters of hyderabad' to a birthday compliment in 'the halcyon galleys of furnival'. ('remains turn happy', endorses 'The Computer's First Birthday Card'). In 'Not Marble: A Reconstruction' Shakespeare is co-opted to give Wallace Stevens's Tennessean jar (in 'Anecdote of the Jar') a run for its jungle:

> A Sqezy bottle in Tennessee,
> if you want permanence, will press
> a dozen jars into the wilderness.

All W. H. Auden's conversations about art, Stravinsky observes, were 'so to speak, *sub specie ludi*:[113] creating poetry and music was a game to be played in a magic circle. Such a view can be meretricious if it consigns the arts to a zone of rarefied precocity, obscuring the fact that the arts are, somehow, news of life, not intellectual larks to be shared by members of an inner ring. But fun is what first commends a Carroll or a Lear and the surreal is a truth not only of the semi-conscious or nightmare kind Morgan writes about in the sequence 'Waking on a Dark Morning', but of the comic kinds he celebrates in 'The Computer's First Christmas Card', 'Little Blue Blue', 'The Glasgow Subway Poems' or in his *Tales from the Limerick Zoo* (1988):

> A viper with contact lenses
> Was subject to murderous frenzies.
> He bit the Mackays
> From ankles to thighs,
> Thinking the fools were Mackenzies.[114]

The fun can be sharp-edged. 'Rules for Dwarf-Throwing' strikes both at racism and the sanctimonies of political correctness. In 'Save the Whale Ball' trophy fetishism has made a huge ball of whalebones, 'a gigantic hyperborean scrimshaw / perched on a scarp at Angmagssalik'. The Whale Ball is crumbling, people are concerned, but too late, and the poem finally kicks in its reproach:

> Some would re-cast it in stainless steel; others
> would pulverize it for talismans.
> Some say we should have saved whales instead.

In the collection called *Instamatic Poems* (1972)[115] Morgan shows his responsiveness to fact, the cool hand of the poet interfering with the material of news clippings only to adjust them into the surprises generated by their arrangement as verse. *Themes on a Variation* (1988) includes 'Newspoems', an earlier group of poems derived from newspapers where the whimsical effect largely depends on the poet's success in completing the unexpected message with an appropriate title or caption. 'Notice in Hell' is the caption for 'HALT COMMIT ADULTERY' and the title 'Joe's Bar' is just right for the wistful:

> SORT OF PLACE YOU
>   SORT OF
>   YOU WISH
>   until Midnight[116]

The Styx will not easily regain its solemnity after 'Charon's Song'. Morgan's caption recalls Charles Murray's poem of the same title ('Another boat-load for the Further Shore, / Heap them up high in the stern'[117]) but his 'Newspoem' overgoes Murray's mordant whimsy with a jokey hint of necrophilia:

'I place
the
dead
ahead
of me,
and bong'

If the 'Newspoems' are a species of light verse, modern life on wry, they are also reifications of unexpected ideas, arrests of attention belonging to the same constellation of aesthetic and moral purposes as the concrete poems, epigrammatic inscriptions, sculptures and sundials with which Ian Hamilton Finlay has created the tangible question-marks of 'Little Sparta', his symbolic garden at Stonypath in Lanarkshire. The poems arise from Morgan's interest in the power of the media which he explores in the sequence of twenty-seven poems called 'From the Video Box' based on the technology by which viewers can record their reactions to television broadcasts. They comprise a study of the uses and impact of television through a range of individual reactions from that of a man prospecting in Patagonia who is infuriated by the image on his wrist-watch television of an astronaut probing for water and life on Mars ('Good God, we've got life galore – / twenty million sheep in Patagonia') to the disgruntlement of the owner of the biggest satellite dish in Perthshire. The 'Burning of the Books, in China / I don't know how many centuries BC' is 'first-class entertainment' for one viewer, while to another the burning of the Library at Alexandria is 'barbarous philistinism' foisted on a million homes. For a third viewer

. . . the display of that conflagration
which laid the new British Library in ashes
must rate as quite unusually riveting.

The sequence considers the power of television to impose its own values on the material it selects. The opportunity to appear on television by way of the Video Box, to become authenticated by the ruling medium of the age, inspires a Glasgow flasher ('Big yin, innit? . . . Wave / goodbye, Willie') and brings hope to the owner of a lost marmalade cat called Robertson ('I know you won't mind if I use your box / for a *cri de coeur*'). Violence on the screen becomes gore in the living room as a television set oozes blood and the anonymous, controlling power of the medium is spoofed:

. . . what sort of programme was that
and who lets these things happen?
Look, I didn't wipe it off. See that, camera.

You think I'm crazy? Think again.
I know we get our mail through the set, bills,
Bank balances, but blood is ridiculous.
I want a clean dry screen from now on.
Let them bleed elsewhere, whoever they are.

The capricious medium touches the heart in the seventh poem where the
speaker tells of an abstract blue image which grows on the screen to
'kick-start hope racing forward / into I don't know what roads of years',
and in the seventeenth poem a woman tells of her impression that her
dead son has appeared in a blizzard of images:

his fist in a revolutionary salute,
a letter sticking from his pocket
with writing I saw as mine.
Oh how little we know
of those we love!

His science-fiction poetry confirms Morgan as a futurist with Mac-
Diarmid's faith in 'the third factor between Man and Nature – the
Machine'.[118] He takes 'a hopeful or even a *very* hopeful long-term view
of the possibilities of the human race',[119] relishing the capabilities of the
machines we've got – computers, space stations, modules, videos – and
the machines yet to come, like the de-/re-materialization apparatus used
in 'In Sobieski's Shield', or the 'demagnification banks' in 'Memories of
Earth'. In the second of his collected *Essays* (1974), 'The Poet and the
Particle', he recalls C. P. Snow's Rede Lecture on *The Two Cultures and
the Scientific Revolution*: 'It is bizarre how very little of twentieth-century
science has been assimilated into twentieth-century art.'[120] If the poet is
'the man who traditionally finds links and resemblances, dissolves rather
than erects barriers, moves among the various worlds of his time',[121] how
can the contemporary poet responsibly ignore technology? As shaman the
artist has a duty to 'record what is happening, telling the tribe's history'.[122]
The tribe uses computers, goes up in rockets, lands on the moon, links
vehicles in space. It is time poetry rose to such occasions. The problem
of technological language is no excuse for not trying. Two kinds of
poetry might be produced:

. . . there could be a simple, even perhaps romantic kind
of poetry of space exploration where things would not be
described in technical terms . . . but there might also be a
different kind of poetry which was more willing to use
the specifics in the situation as far as possible and therefore
to have to use technological language.[123]

In 'A Home in Space' from the sequence 'Star Gate' Morgan fuses these
two kinds. The language is as technical as it has to be: lift-off, key-ins,
food-tubes, screens, lenses, station, capsule. The jump of adrenalin in the
astronauts as they agree to sever their connection with earth and launch
themselves outwards in their mobile home is felt through the accelerating
repetitions of the run-on lines:

> . . . and it must be said they were –
> were cool and clear as they dismantled the station and –
> and gave their capsule such power that –
> that they launched themselves outwards –
> outwards in an impeccable trajectory, that band –
> that band of tranquil defiers, not to plant any –
> any home with roots but to keep a –
> a voyaging generation voyaging . . .

The epic assertion at the end of the poem is refurbished by the use of
technical language familiar to any reader with a basic knowledge of space
hardware.

Anti-sexist humour goes into orbit in the 'Instamatic' poem
'TRANSLUNAR SPACE MARCH 1972' and 'The First Men on
Mercury' shatters imperialist vanities by setting a pompous astronaut against
a mind-bendingly superior Mercurian. The close-encounters situation opens
with the earthman's stiff greeting:

> – We come in peace from the third planet.
> Would you take us to your leader?

Earthly self-importance vaporizes to comedy when the Mercurian forces
the earthling to swap languages:

> – I am the yuleeda. You see my hands,
> We carry no benner, we come in peace.
> The spaceways are all stretterhawn.

In rapidly mastered English the Mercurian tells the stuffy earthman to
push off home, a sadder and wiser man now ironically fluent in Mercurian.
The moral – don't condescend to the natives – is refreshed by Morgan's
dramatizing it in the comic interplay of languages. Already in the sequence of nine poems called 'Interferences' he had experimented with
language in relation to alien existence. The idea for the sequence comes
from the phenomenon of tektites, small glassy objects of unexplained
origin, and the science-fiction element is the analogously small linguistic
disruption in each poem. The moments of interference include the flight
of an arrow ('straight to its / targjx'), and a failed lift-off for a mission to

Saturn ('wo de nat hove loft-iff'). The key idea of the poems – 'the conception "of other eyes watching" or intersecting worlds or planes of existence'[124] – is the central notion in Morgan's three most haunting science-fiction narrative poems: 'In Sobieski's Shield', 'From the Domain of Arnheim', which takes off from Poe's story, 'The Domain of Arnheim', and 'Memories of Earth'.

'In Sobieski's Shield' is based on the postulate that a person can be beamed through space by the method used in the television series, *Star Trek*. Morgan uses the idea to trigger a meditation on change, identity and the relationship between past and present. Is the narrator the same person still, even with only four fingers on his left hand? Apparently he is. Despite his traumatic rebirth he continues, evincing in the alien context of his 'second life' the best of human qualities. Above all there is his resilience as he prepares to leave the protective 'dome' and fare forward into the unknown world of iron hills and lakes of mercury. We can adapt to what lies ahead, the poem says, life goes on even out there; we can, with a will, be masters of the universe. In 'Memories of Earth' Morgan achieves both astounding science fiction and an artistic hat-trick. It is a science-fiction poem; it is a relatively long narrative poem; its verse, though free, is subtly braced by an iambic underbeat. As in 'From the Domain of Arnheim' with its 'fires of trash and mammoths' bones' and new-born child, it is recognizable earth which is the alien place and again it is the alien visitors who are chastened and enlarged by what they find. Beauty is to be seen in the sight and sound of Wordsworth musing upon Snowdon in the company of Robert Jones and the shepherd with his lurcher (the reference is to *The Prelude*, Book Fourteen), in the love that even Auschwitz cannot extinguish, in the frailty of a white butterfly, and in a canoe of Polynesians crossing the Pacific.

Morgan sports with physics in the sequence of six 'Particle Poems'; in 'Memories of Earth' he uses the idea of the particle scientifically, given that even a complicated system like the earth may be treated astronomically as a particle. The invention of the poem begins with a shift in scale that makes the earth a sub-atomic stone particle. Signals emitted by the stone have been detected by the Council of a cold-blooded, authoritarian society. Like the crew of the *Nostromo* in Ridley Scott's film, *Alien*, Hlad, Kort, Hazmon, Baltaz and the narrator, Erlkon, have been despatched to investigate. Their instructions are clear:

> Keep your report formal, said the Council,
> your evidence is for the memory-banks,
> not for crude wonder or cruder appraisal.

So the discredited explorers meet in secret, listen to the tapes of their expedition and 'study how to change this life', home safely but, like T. S.

Eliot's Magi, aliens in the old dispensation. The imaginative power of 'Memories of Earth' is first felt in the narrator's effort to describe the miniaturization that shrinks the Brobdignagian travellers to micro-Lilli-putian size, allowing them to enter first the stone, then the smaller entities inside it:

> The shrinking must be done by stages, but
> even so it comes with a rush, doesn't
> feel like shrinking. Rather it's the landscape
> explodes upwards, outwards, the waves rise up
> and loom like waterfalls, and where we stand
> our stone blots out the light above us, a crag
> pitted with caves and tunnels, immovable
> yet somehow less solid.

Once the travellers are inside the stone the narrative focuses on the conflict between the Council's demand for objective documentation and the pull of earth's gravity of beauty and passion. The special successes of the poem are the exactness with which Morgan describes complex pro-cesses and the victory over cold injunction of this spinning particle of earth, intransigently ambiguous, beautiful, violent, frail, self-tormenting and self-renewing. His planetary stone is as full of messages as the 'lithogenesis' of MacDiarmid's raised beach.

In *Sonnets from Scotland* (1984) science fiction's malleabilities of time and space are used to give surprising perspectives of Scotland and the planet Earth. In 'The Coin' a visitor finds a £1 coin bearing the head of a red deer and the words *Respublica Scotorum*. A machine has brought space travellers to land on the earth of a remotely future Scotland at a time when an independent Scottish state has been in existence long enough for a coin of its realm to have had its date rubbed off by successive fingers. The race is now 'silent', which suggests that the state may have had its day, but can we be sure? The poem ends:

> . . . Yet nothing seemed ill-starred.
> And least of all the realm the coin contained.

A star suggests destiny, a future. Perhaps the race is only silent because the people are hidden. The visitors may look up from the well-worn coin to confront Scots whose 'yuleeda' will be waiting to try languages with them in Edinburgh. 'On Jupiter' offers a less sanguine prospect where 'a simulacrum, a dissolving view' of Scotland is found:

> . . . as solid as a terrier
> shaking itself dry from a brisk swim

in the reservoir of Jupiter's grim
crimson trustless eye.

If the gods or people of Jupiter have made this Scotland, they have abandoned it to a 'sea of doubt', though the 'terrier' gives it vitality, implying that doubt is external to the country and self-doubt not necessarily the Scottish problem; but will the terrier catch the stick the untrusting 'launchers' have thrown, or will the prospect of such a possibility just dissolve like so many promises of Scottish self-determination, and if it does, who will be to blame? Again Morgan uses the idiom of science fiction to ask questions about the reality of Scotland, its gods, its people, the sea of doubt that encircles it and the questionable national will, 'the strong sick dirkless Angel' which groans and shivers in 'Post-Referendum'. In the last of the *Sonnets from Scotland*, 'The Summons', visitors to Earth are surprised that they find it difficult to leave the planet ('Despite our countdown, we were loath to go'). 'They have', says Morgan, 'become more involved than they thought they would. They don't understand their emotional reaction. They take with them perhaps a kind of love.'[125] The love is Morgan's own commitment to his country and to the 'Earth . . . the favoured place'[126] where 'nothing is not giving messages'[127] and which he has made so vocal.

Notes

1. Hugh MacDiarmid, 'Author's Note: On Being a Hippopotamus', *Lucky Poet: A Self Study in Literature and Political Ideas*, ed. Alan Riach (Manchester, 1994), p. xxv.

2. MacDiarmid, *Lucky Poet*, p. 426.

3. Kenneth Buthlay, *Hugh MacDiarmid (C. M. Grieve)* (Edinburgh, 1982), p. 14.

4. Norman MacCaig, 'A Note on the Author', Hugh MacDiarmid, *Scottish Eccentrics*, ed. Alan Riach (Manchester, 1993), p. ix.

5. Edwin Muir, *Scott and Scotland: The Predicament of the Scottish Writer* (London, 1936), p. 15.

6. Ibid., p. 21.

7. See Hugh MacDiarmid, *Selected Prose*, ed. Alan Riach (Manchester, 1992), p. 19.

8. With the exception of *A Drunk Man Looks at the Thistle*, quotations of MacDiarmid's poetry are taken from Hugh MacDiarmid, *Complete Poems*, ed. Michael Grieve and W. R. Aitken, 2 vols (Manchester, 1993–4), which reprints the text of *Complete Poems* (Harmondsworth, 1985) with additional poems discovered since the first edition of 1978. Quotations from *A Drunk*

Man Looks at the Thistle are taken from Hugh MacDiarmid, *Selected Poetry*, ed. Alan Riach and Michael Grieve (Manchester, 1992), which numbers the lines of the poem, as does Kenneth Buthlay's annotated edition for the Association for Scottish Literary Studies (Edinburgh, 1987). Footnoted page references in my text are given for passages in the longer poems whose lines are not numbered.

 9. Edwin Morgan, *Hugh MacDiarmid* (Harlow, 1976), p. 9.

10. Alan Bold, *MacDiarmid: A Critical Biography* (London, 1988), p. 139. Bold points out that the words for 'The Watergaw' came not from Jamieson but from two pages of Sir James Wilson's *Lowland Scotch as Spoken in the Lower Strathearn District of Perthshire* (1915). See Bold, pp. 137–8.

11. Ruth McQuillan, 'Hugh MacDiarmid's "On a Raised Beach" ', *Akros*, 12, nos. 34–5 (August 1977), Special Double Hugh MacDiarmid Issue, pp. 89–97 [96].

12. MacDiarmid, *Complete Poems*, I, p. 426.

13. Ibid., pp. 428–9.

14. Ibid., p. 429.

15. David Daiches, 'Appendix B', Hugh MacDiarmid, *A Drunk Man Looks at the Thistle*, 200 Burns Club 4th edn (Edinburgh, 1962), p. 103.

16. MacDiarmid, 'Author's Note', *A Drunk Man Looks at the Thistle*, in *Selected Poetry*, pp. vii–viii.

17. Lord Byron, letter to James Hogg, 24 March 1814, *Selected Letters and Journals*, ed. Leslie A. Marchand (Cambridge, Mass., 1982), p. 101.

18. MacDiarmid, *Complete Poems*, I, p. 324.

19. Ibid., p. 426.

20. Ibid., p. 614.

21. Ibid., p. 186.

22. Ibid., p. 222.

23. C. M. Grieve, *Annals of the Five Senses*, with an introduction by Alan Bold (Edinburgh, 1983), p. 95.

24. Hugh MacDiarmid, *The Letters of Hugh MacDiarmid*, ed. Alan Bold (London, 1984), p. 298.

25. Letter to C. M. Grieve, 9 July 1932, in Neil M. Gunn, *Selected Letters*, ed. J. B. Peck (Edinburgh, 1987), p. 19.

26. Douglas Dunn, 'Language and Liberty', introduction to *The Faber Book of Twentieth-Century Scottish Poetry*, ed. Douglas Dunn, paperback edn (London, 1993), p. xviii.

27. Hugh MacDiarmid, 'On the Death of Dylan Thomas', *Lines Review*, no. 4 (January 1954), pp. 30–31 [31].

28. Don Whyte, *On the Lonely Shore: An Autobiography*, Foreword by Hugh MacDiarmid (London, 1977), p. 11.

29. See Ronald Ayling, 'An Almighty Epistolary Performer' – review of David Krause (ed.), *The Letters of Sean O'Casey: Volume IV, 1959–1964* – *Irish Literary Suplement*, 12, no. 2 (Fall 1993), pp. 15–18 [15].

30. C. H. Sisson, *English Poetry 1900–1950: An Assessment* (London, 1971), p. 235.

31. As Naomi Mitchison puts it, MacDiarmid 'did get what at the beginning was called the Scottish Renaissance really seething'. See Naomi Mitchison, 'MacDiarmid and the Scottish Renaissance', in Nancy Gish (ed.), *Hugh MacDiarmid: Man and Poet* (Maine and Edinburgh, 1992), pp. 39–41 [39].

32. Quotations from Edwin Muir's poems are taken from *The Complete Poems of Edwin Muir*, an annotated edition by Peter Butter for the Association for Scottish Literary Studies (Aberdeen, 1991).

33. Edwin Muir, *An Autobiography* (London, 1954), p. 49.

34. Muir, *Scott and Scotland*, p. 178.

35. Muir, *An Autobiography*, p. 247.

36. Patrick Crotty, 'The vision thing', *TLS*, 1 January 1993, p. 6.

37. P. H. Butter, *Edwin Muir* (Edinburgh, 1962), p. 49.

38. Thomas Crawford, 'Edwin Muir as a Political Poet', *Literature of the North*, ed. David Hewitt and Michael Spiller (Aberdeen, 1983), pp. 121–33 [123].

39. George Mackay Brown, 'Chapel Between Cornfield and Shore', *Selected Poems* (London, 1977), p. 23.

40. See Colin Nicholson, 'Unlocking Time's Labyrinth: George Mackay Brown', *Poem, Purpose and Place: Shaping Identity in Contemporary Scottish Verse* (Edinburgh, 1992), pp. 96–113 [98].

41. Alan Bold, *George Mackay Brown* (Edinburgh, 1978), p. 9.

42. George Mackay Brown, *Selected Poems*, p. 23.

43. Ibid., p. 57.

44. George Mackay Brown, *Fishermen with Ploughs: A Poem Cycle* (London, 1979), p. 38.

45. George Mackay Brown, *Selected Poems*, pp. 14–15.

46. George Mackay Brown, *An Orkney Tapestry* (London, 1973), pp. 20–21.

47. George Mackay Brown, *Fishermen with Ploughs*, p. 94.

48. Ibid., pp. 15–16.

49. George Mackay Brown, 'Uranium', in *Seven Poets*, ed. Christopher Carrell (Glasgow, 1981), p. 58.

50. Christopher Carrell (ed.), *Seven Poets* (Glasgow, 1981), p. 77.

51. See Derick Thomson, 'Scottish Gaelic Poetry: A Many-faceted Tradition', *Scottish Literary Journal*, 18, no. 2 (November 1991), pp. 5–26 [24].

52. References to MacLean's poetry are to Sorley MacLean/Somhairle MacGill-Eain, *From Wood to Ridge/O Choille gu Bearradh, Collected Poems in Gaelic and English* (Manchester, 1989).

53. Sorley MacLean/Somhairle MacGill-Eain, *Ris A' Bhruthaich: Criticism and Prose Writings*, ed. William Gillies (Stornoway, 1985), p. 48.

54. See Douglas Sealy, 'Out from Skye to the World: Literature, History and the Poet', *Sorley MacLean: Critical Essays*, ed. Raymond J. Ross and Joy Hendry (Edinburgh, 1986), pp. 53–79 [60].

55. Joy Hendry discusses the identity, or identities, of the woman referred to in this sequence in 'Sorley MacLean: the Man and His Work', *Sorley MacLean: Critical Essays*, pp. 9–38. Eimhir was the most beautiful of the Ulster heroes' women in the Early Irish sagas. Poems from the sequence referred to here are included in *From Wood to Ridge*.

56. See Carrell (ed.), *Seven Poets*, p. 69.

57. T. S. Eliot, 'Tradition and the Individual Talent', *Selected Essays*, 3rd edn (London, 1951), pp. 17–18.

58. References are to Iain Crichton Smith, *Collected Poems* (Manchester, 1992), except where indicated otherwise.

59. Iain Crichton Smith, Preface, *Consider the Lilies* (Edinburgh, 1987), p. v.

60. Selections from *The Emigrants* (1983) and *The Exiles* (1984) are included in *Collected Poems,* as are selections from the earlier volumes, *Thistles and Roses* (1961) and *The Law and the Grace* (1965).

61. 'Iain Crichton Smith interviewed by Marshall Walker', in Carrell (ed.), *Seven Poets*, p. 51.

62. Ibid., p. 43.

63. Ibid., p. 44.

64. Iain Crichton Smith, *Ends and Beginnings* (Manchester, 1994), pp. 22–3.

65. Ibid., p. 21.

66. Ibid., p. 6.

67. Ibid., pp. 60–63.

68. Sorley MacLean, 'Foreword', *Iain Crichton Smith: Critical Essays*, ed. Colin Nicholson (Edinburgh, 1992), p. v.

69. Ibid., pp. 15–50.

70. Gerald Dawe, 'Law and Grace: A Note on the Poetry of Iain Crichton Smith', *Iain Crichton Smith: Critical Essays*, pp. 73–81 [74].

71. Iain Crichton Smith, *Murdo and other stories* (London, 1981), p. 140.

72. Iain Crichton Smith, 'On the Golan Heights', *Ends and Beginnings*, p. 66.

73. Iain Crichton Smith, *Ends and Beginnings*, p. 152.

74. Norman MacCaig, 'My Way of It', in *As I Remember: Ten Scottish Authors Recall How Writing Began for Them*, ed. Maurice Lindsay (London, 1979), pp. 79–88 [81].

75. 'Norman MacCaig interviewed by Marshall Walker', in Carrell (ed.), *Seven Poets*, p. 34.

76. Unless otherwise indicated references are to Norman MacCaig, *Collected Poems* (London, 1985), which includes selections from *Riding Lights* (1955) and *Surroundings* (1966).

77. MacCaig, 'My Way of It', in *As I Remember*, p. 85.

78. Jack Rillie, 'Net of Kins, Web of Ilks: MacCaig's Phantasmagoria', *Chapman*, 66 (Autumn 1991), pp. 46–51 [46].

79. Carrell (ed.), *Seven Poets*, p. 39.

80. Ibid., p. 36.

81. Ibid.

82. Ibid., p. 35.

83. Tony Lopez, 'W. S. Graham: An Introduction', *Edinburgh Review*, Issue 75 (1987), pp. 7–23 [20].

84. W. S. Graham's poems are quoted from *Collected Poems 1942–1977* (London, 1979).

85. Wallace Stevens, 'Adagia', *Opus Posthumous* (New York, 1957), p. 160.

86. Wallace Stevens, 'An Ordinary Evening in New Haven', *The Collected Poems of Wallace Stevens*, 7th Printing (New York, 1965), p. 473.

87. Charles King and Iain Crichton Smith (eds), *Twelve More Modern Scottish Poets* (London, 1986), p. 116.

88. Douglas Dunn, *Terry Street* (London, 1969), p. 55.

89. Douglas Dunn, *Love or Nothing* (London, 1974), p. 38.

90. Douglas Dunn, *Barbarians* (London, 1979), p. 39.

91. Douglas Dunn, *Elegies* (London, 1985), p. 64.

92. Douglas Dunn, *St. Kilda's Parliament* (London, 1981), pp. 22–3.

93. Ibid., pp. 13–15 [14].

94. Douglas Dunn, *Selected Poems 1964–1983* (London, 1986), p. 5.

95. Douglas Dunn, *Northlight* (London, 1988), pp. 24–5.

96. Ibid., pp. 1–2.

97. Douglas Dunn, *The Happier Life* (London, 1972), p. 38.

98. For a discussion of Morgan as a homosexual writer see Christopher Whyte, ' "Now you see it, now you don't": The Love Poetry of Edwin Morgan', *The Glasgow Review*, Issue Two (Autumn 1993), pp. 82–93.

99. Christopher Whyte, 'Power from things not declared', in Edwin Morgan, *Nothing Not Giving Messages: reflections on work and life*, ed. Hamish Whyte (Edinburgh, 1990), pp. 144–87.

100. First published as 'Seven Decades' (the text marred by several misprints), in *Felt-Tipped Hosannas: for Edwin Morgan on his 70th Birthday*, ed. Susan Stewart and Hamish Whyte (Glasgow, 1990), p. 5.

101. John Linklater, 'Morgan's last step to openness at seventy', *Glasgow Herald*, 27 April 1990, p. 11.

102. Edwin Morgan, *Collected Poems* (Manchester, 1990). References are to this edition wherever possible. Other sources are footnoted.

103. Eric Stanley, 'Translation from Old English: "The Garbaging War-Hawk", or, The Literal Materials from Which the Reader Can Re-create the Poem', *Acts of Interpretation, The Text in Its Contexts 700–1600: Essays on Medieval and Renaissance Literature in Honour of E. Talbot Donaldson*, ed. Mary J. Carruthers and Elizabeth D. Kirk (Norman, Oklahoma, 1982), pp. 70–71.

104. Colin Nicholson, 'Living in the Utterance: Edwin Morgan', *Poem, Purpose and Place: Shaping Identity in Contemporary Scottish Verse* (Edinburgh, 1992), pp. 57–79 [62].

105. MacDiarmid, *Selected Prose*, p. 206.

106. Edwin Morgan, *Hold Hands Among the Atoms* (Glasgow, 1991), p. 76; reprinted in a selection from this volume in *Sweeping out the Dark* (Manchester, 1994), p. 87.

107. Charles Olson, 'Projective Verse', *Selected Writings of Charles Olson*, ed. with an Introduction by Robert Creeley (New York, 1966), pp. 15–26 [16].

108. Morgan, *Hold Hands Among the Atoms*, p. 41; *Sweeping out the Dark*, p. 61.

109. William Wordsworth, 'Ode: Intimations of Immortality from Recollections of Early Childhood' stanza 11.

110. Robert Frost, 'The Figure a Poem Makes', *Complete Poems of Robert Frost 1949* (New York, 1949), p. vi.

111. Wallace Stevens, *Opus Posthumous* (New York, 1957), p. 179.

112. Geoffrey Summerfield, 'Edwin Morgan', *Worlds: Seven Modern Poets* (Harmondsworth, 1974), pp. 228–78 [229].

113. Igor Stravinsky, *Stravinsky in Conversation with Robert Craft* (Harmondsworth, 1962), p. 281.

114. Edwin Morgan, 'The Viper', *Tales from the Limerick Zoo* (Glasgow, 1988), unnumbered pages.

115. Edwin Morgan, *Instamatic Poems* (London, 1972). Of the fifty-two poems a selection of twenty-four is reprinted in *Collected Poems*.

116. Edwin Morgan, *Themes on a Variation* (Manchester, 1988), p. 70.

117. Charles Murray, *Hamewith: The Complete Poems of Charles Murray*, ed. Nan Shepherd (Aberdeen, 1979), p. 52.

118. MacDiarmid, *Lucky Poet*, p. 3.

119. Marshall Walker, *Edwin Morgan: An Interview* (Preston, 1977), p. 22; reprinted as 'Let's go' in Edwin Morgan, *Nothing Not Giving Messages*, pp. 54–85 [84].

120. C. P. Snow, *The Two Cultures and the Scientific Revolution* (London, 1959), p. 16.

121. Edwin Morgan, *Essays* (Cheadle, 1974), p. 17.

122. Morgan, *Nothing Not Giving Messages*, p. 67.

123. Ibid.

124. Explanatory note by Morgan for *Interferences*, pamphlet (Poetry Glasgow 3), (Glasgow, 1970). Renumbered and without the note the poems are included in *From Glasgow to Saturn* (1973), *Poems of Thirty Years* (1982) and *Collected Poems*.

125. Lesley Duncan, 'Poet's place for looking out at the universe', *Glasgow Herald*, 1 December 1984, p. 7.

126. Edwin Morgan, 'The Worlds', *Collected Poems*, pp. 383–4 [384].

127. Robert Crawford, 'An interview with Edwin Morgan', *Verse*, 5, no. 1 (February 1988), pp. 27–42; reprinted as 'Nothing is not giving messages' in Morgan, *Nothing Not Giving Messages*, pp. 118–43 [131].

Chapter 12
Post-war Fiction:
Realism, Violence and Magic

Suppressed into the British role in Allied opposition to the Fascisms of Nazi Germany, Italy and Japan, Scottish national consciousness gradually realized in the early post-war years that if the northern part of the United Kingdom had helped to win the victory it had also lost, for the second time in thirty years, a lion's share of the peace. The Festival of Britain on London's South Bank in 1951 (marking the centenary of the 'Great Exhibition' of 1851) and the coronation of Queen Elizabeth II in June 1953 proclaimed Britain's determination to overcome post-war austerities, but for many people, especially in Scotland and the north of England, such junketings seemed remote from a dour world of recent ration books and unconvincing socialism.

Early post-war Scottish fiction favours realism, although the works of two practitioners, Robin Jenkins and Muriel Spark, come from such idiosyncratic personal beliefs that they touch only intermittently on common experience. The more conventional realism practised by James Kennaway and William McIlvanney intensifies into the violent metaphors of Hugh C. Rae and Frederic Lindsay, while socio-political protest gathers momentum in the satire of Alasdair Gray and the fierce, vernacular fiction of James Kelman. Allan Massie casts a sceptical eye over moral and political trends in novels which refresh traditional forms. Realism alternates with surrealism in Alasdair Gray's *Lanark* (1981), Iain Banks's *The Bridge* (1986) and Irvine Welsh's *Marabou Stork Nightmares* (1995) and becomes magical in works by Emma Tennant, Gray's *Poor Things* (1992) and in A. L. Kennedy's novel *So I am Glad* (1995). Thus, as the end of the twentieth century approaches, an increasingly complex postmodern world elicits a profusion of fictional styles in an age of unprecedented diversity. The recurrent theme is disillusionment, but hope inheres in the writers' alertness, energy, analytical intelligence and aesthetic independence.

Post-war pibroch: James Kennaway

While America's Norman Mailer and James Jones and England's Nicholas Monsarrat wrote panoramically about the entrapments and chaos of wartime action in *The Naked and the Dead* (1948), *From Here to Eternity* (1951) and *The Cruel Sea* (1951), James Kennaway followed the example of Carson McCullers's insular Southern fort in *Reflections in a Golden Eye* (1941), setting his *Tunes of Glory* (1956) in the claustrophobic peace-time microcosm of 'Campbell Barracks' to focus on a specifically Scottish post-war conflict between two representative men. Kennaway's novels depict tense relationships between people whose identities are threatened by each other in the context of corrupt or disintegrating value systems. In *Tunes of Glory*, the taut, realistic story of fatal antagonism between Acting Lieutenant-Colonel Jock Sinclair DSO (and bar) and Colonel Basil Barrow symbolizes the tragic consequences of the divided state of the sometime Scottish nation. War has made a hero of Jock and a Battalion historian of Barrow. Jock's background is Sauchiehall Street, Barlinnie gaol and El Alamein. 'Barrow Boy' is the product of Eton, private tuition, Oxford and Sandhurst and his only claim to post-graduate experience is as an officer-class prisoner in a Japanese POW camp. Class discrepancy is reinforced by physical difference. Jock does 'not look broad because he was also deep', his meaty face is 'big and smooth and red and thick' and his trews skin-tight so that 'it looked as if he need only brace his muscles to tear the seams apart' (Book 1, Chapter 1). Barrow is a small greying man with 'a yellowish shadow of tiredness' round his eyes (Book 1, Chapter 2). Corporal Fraser is a scapegoat. When Jock strikes him for drinking with Morag (Book 1, Chapter 11) he is not punishing his daughter for lying to him about being out with a girlfriend so much as hitting back at the Brigade and the system by which he has lived for the greater betrayal of taking command of the Battalion away from him after nearly five years and giving it to a man like Barrow.

Jock's outrage is partly justified by 'a hint of an analogy with a clan and its chief'.[1] 'I'll tell you why he's [i.e. Barrow] the better Colonel,' says the obtuse RSM, 'Because he's a gentleman' (Book 1, Chapter 6); but the gentleman is afraid of the legendary soldier's 'authority, his unpredictability, his bluntness' (Book 2, Chapter 3). Incapable of decisive action – whether to report Jock for court-martial or deal discreetly with the matter himself – Barrow commits suicide 'by the bank of the river' (Book 2, Chapter 7), at which point in the novel the ironic connection between the antagonists is made vivid by MacKinnon's finding Jock on a bridge over the same river, ritually attired for his own death in full dress uniform. Instead of killing himself Jock attempts to drown the Battalion in his sense of loss, his pity for Barrow and in the hyperbolic pomp of a funeral with full military honours. Both men love the Battalion, but neither knows how to deal with the other though each needs the other's strengths. The post-war regime buries 'the whole bloody glory' (Book 3, Chapter 1) by divisively advancing the educated, Englished bureaucrat (whose manners never could have won a war) over the proletarian, coarse, instinctively traditional man of action (whose manners did) and by pre-ferring paper-pushing, decorum and brandy to guts, bacchanalian country dancing and whisky. Neither man can work alone in the post-war era of 'anxious and ambitious men' (Book I, Chapter 5). Divided they fall in a mutual, beautifully executed tragedy of continuing relevance, Scotland the brave – and tragically inelastic – brought low by Scotland adminis-tered from Whitehall. As Jock the piper says, the pibroch is 'no just grieving. There's something angry about it too' (Book 1, Chapter 3). As the pibroch, so the novel.

Tangents: Robin Jenkins and Muriel Spark

'Never bottle up your feelings, laddie,' Jock advises MacKinnon (*Tunes of Glory*, Book 3, Chapter 7). Robin Jenkins's novels have failed to attract a readership commensurate with his imaginative effort because he bottles up his feelings in elusive symbolism and complex philosophy, making much of his work seem tangential both to the condition of Scotland and to twentieth-century life more generally. This opacity is surprising in a writer who consciously 'shed the showing off with words' for the sake of clarity: 'Words are there as servants to show the reader what is hap-pening in the story. If the words are flashing at you on the page, they will distract.'[2] His two most striking and substantial works are *The Cone-Gatherers* (1955) and *Fergus Lamont* (1979), both novels of tension without clear resolution. If the opposition between Calum, the Christ-like hunch-back of *The Cone-Gatherers*, and Duror, the gamekeeper, is plainly enough an expression of the conflict between good and evil or regeneration and death both in Lady Runcie-Campbell's forest and in the war beyond her estate, the motives of the novel's characters are, in Iain Crichton Smith's phrase, 'knotted like roots'.[3] This can be defended as moral realism, but the tormented Duror's suicide in Chapter 16 remains unsatisfactorily ambiguous despite the implied power of the natural world to withstand the hostile spirit he represents. As with many of Jenkins's novels the action is oddly static, like a moral fresco in the author's mind which fails to come accessibly alive on the page.

The admirable intention behind *Fergus Lamont* seems to be to write an anti-romantic novel about a self-deluded, wronged yet vainglorious man who sees himself as a justified sinner in his bid to achieve 'status as an officer and a gentleman' (Part 3, Chapter 12). Calvinist and class forces are held responsible for shaping an unengaging hero predestined for failure. Look, the novel seems to say, you can't expect good to come from such a warped, endemically Scottish background: Fergus Lamont distils the moral poisons of his cultural heritage. But it is hard, in this diffusive work, to maintain interest in the career of someone so irredeemably egotistical. 'Why am I not wanted?' Fergus asks his unfaithful wife, Betty, who replies, 'Because you yourself want no one. I don't think you ever have' (Part 4, Chapter 6). The problem with Jenkins's ambitious, vexing novel is that he has made it too difficult for the reader to want Fergus imaginatively even as the embodiment of a problem.

According to Alan Bold 'only two truly great Scottish novels have been produced, so far, in the twentieth century'.[4] The first is George Douglas Brown's *The House with the Green Shutters* (1901), the second Muriel Spark's *The Prime of Miss Jean Brodie* (1961), a cool satirical entertainment about early twentieth-century Edinburgh vanities and frustrations, with a special dig at the pretensions of Scottish education – ironically similar to those of the Calvinist doctrine of Election. In her other books the expatriate Spark's offhandedly mischievous world of alienations and false pretences has little to say about peculiarly Scottish experience, despite references in *Symposium* (1990) to Calvinism, the Border Ballads and *Jekyll and Hyde* and the use of *Peter Pan* in *The Hothouse by the East River* (1973). Admittedly, Scots must assent with other readers to the universal truth of Donald Cloete's pronouncement in the title story of Spark's *The Go-Away Bird* (1957): 'I grant you we have the natives under control. I grant you we have the leopards under control . . . We are getting control over malaria. But we haven't got *the savage in ourselves* under control.'[5] With 'an almost irresponsible impertinence towards everyday reality'[6] Spark controls her savages by making their worlds slippery – Jean Brodie's Protestant (and Fascist) prime and pretensions are betrayed by her favourite *crème de la crème* pupil, Sandy Stranger, who, 'destined to be the great lover', prefers to become a nun – and by deadpan irony. Nobody's thoughts are just their own in *The Comforters* (1957) as Laurence Manders discovers in a conversation with his mother:

> 'To think that our old trusted servant should do a thing like this.'
> He thought that a bit of hypocrisy – that 'old trusted servant' phrase.
> 'You think I'm a hypocrite, don't you?' his mother said.
> 'Of course not,' he replied, 'Why should I?'

> (Chapter 4)

The flying saucer of 'Miss Pinkerton's Apocalypse' (1967) leads to typically Sparkish argument between Laura Pinkerton and George Lake:

> 'The thing might be radio-active. It might be
> dangerous.' George was breathless. The saucer had
> climbed, was circling high above his head, and now made
> for him again, but missed.
> 'It's not radio-active,' said Miss Pinkerton, 'it is Spode.'[7]

English sexuality is caustically pondered in *The Public Image* (1968):

> It was somehow felt that the typical Englishman . . . was,
> had always really concealed a foundry of smouldering sex
> beneath all that expressionless reserve. It was suggested
> . . . that this was a fact long known to the English
> themselves, but only now articulated. Later, even some
> English came to believe it, and certain English wives
> began to romp in bed far beyond the call of their
> husbands, or the capacities of their years, or any of the
> realities of the situation.
>
> (Chapter 2)

Lise's improbable quest for someone to kill her in *The Driver's Seat* (1970), a razor-edged fable based on the idea that victims are self-elected and destroy other people, leads to her encounter with the opinionated Mrs Fiedke from Nova Scotia ('I never trust the airlines from those countries where the pilots believe in the after-life' [Chapter 4]), who turns out to be a Jehovah's Witness and the ultimate Women's Lib. vigilante:

> 'The male sex . . . are demanding equal rights with us . . .
> Perfume, jewellery, hair down to their shoulders . . . if God
> had intended them to be as good as us he wouldn't have
> made them different from us to the naked eye . . . Fur
> coats and flowered poplin shirts on their backs . . . If we
> don't look lively . . . they will be taking over the homes
> and the children, and sitting about having chats while we
> go and fight to defend them and work to keep them.
> They won't be content with equal rights only. Next thing
> they'll want the upper hand, mark my words.
>
> (Chapter 5)

The Abbess of Crewe (1974) parodies America's Watergate scandal (the serene, elected abbess has beaten her rival by bugging the abbey and its sacred Avenue of Meditation), but there is invariably real murk under

Spark's frugal, dryly witty style: fraud and attempted murder in *Robinson* (1958), blackmail and murder in *Memento Mori* (1959), forgery and attempted murder in *The Bachelors* (1961), madness and immolation in *The Girls of Slender Means* (1963), vindictive suicide in *The Public Image* (1968), media marketing of death and sex in the ghoulish servants' hall of *Not to Disturb* (1972), something suspiciously like Purgatory in *The Hothouse by the East River*, a buried corpse and more blackmail in *Territorial Rights* (1979), and the seductiveness of active evil in *Symposium*. Early in *The Driver's Seat* we are told that Lise 'will be found tomorrow morning dead from multiple stab-wounds, her wrists bound with a silk scarf and her ankles bound with a man's necktie, in the grounds of an empty villa, in a park of the foreign city to which she is travelling on the flight now boarding at Gate 14' (Chapter 3). Lacking relationships to give her life moral and emotional shape in a callous world, Lise 'is reduced to making drama out of the most elemental plot of all, the knowledge that her life will end'.[8] So it goes, for a Catholic novelist, in a sinful scheme of things whose evil, no matter how hard it tries, fails to be grandiose, and where 'the best terrestrial image of divine order is, perhaps, that dementia of the imagination which makes the human mess but is also its solvent'.[9] In the eyes of God and Muriel Spark, as in James Hogg's, the wickedness of egotism, however damaging it may be, is basically absurd. Spark gives her own spirited game away when she recalls her preference, among the first issue of Penguin books in 1935, for Eric Linklater's *Poet's Pub*: 'In tone, there was a throw-away quality of liberty and humour, so far absent in the modern fiction I was used to; at the same time it was a serious book.'[10] Like the works of Jenkins and Linklater, Spark's novels spin in an orbit of their own.

Realisms: Alan Sharp, Hugh C. Rae, William McIlvanney, James Kelman and others

What was the literary imagination to make of bleak, victorious Scotland? How had a second world war moved life on since Eddy MacDonnel travelled from the tenement warrens of the Gorbals to the First World War blackout in a conscientious objector's cell in Edward Gaitens's novel, *The Dance of the Apprentices* (1948), about working-class sensibility trying 'like a being defying evil and death' (Chapter 1) to break free from capitalist determinants by way of pacifism and socialism? Like MacDonnel in relation to the First World War Scotland needed to interpret the

Second not only according to the rights and wrongs of fighting but also in terms of peace-time problems. 'To the victor the spoils,' pontificates the grandfather, Old Conn, in William McIlvanney's *Docherty* (1975), to which Mick, who has lost an eye and an arm in First World War trenches, replies, 'Hoo much o' the spoils are you gettin', gran'feyther?' (Book 2, Chapter 18). The question had come up again, prompted by the same feelings as those McIlvanney attributes to a weary Jenny Docherty: 'They were all trapped. All they could do was wait, while the government invented the weather, visited crises on them like hurricanes, out of no-where, never to be understood' (Book 3, Chapter 4).

'Where did the past go, what happened to its reality?' John Moseby wonders in the first chapter of Alan Sharp's *A Green Tree in Gedde* (1965); but the answer was to be found neither in the historic past, despite the underlying contemporary relevance of Naomi Mitchison's saga of the aftermath of the Jacobite Rebellions in her *The Bull Calves* (1947), nor in the tranquillizing Kailyard charm and anecdotal pawkiness of Cliff Hanley's beguiling childhood memoir, *Dancing in the Streets* (1958). Post-war stock-taking demanded facing up to the present with the kind of paint-stripping realisms employed by Sharp and McIlvanney as well as Gordon Williams, Archie Hind and Hugh C. Rae. For these writers grace is not to be found through a transcending literary sensibility as, to a limited extent, it is for the eponymous, lonely teacher-hero ('a wallflower since puberty') of *Mr Alfred M.A.* (1972), George Friel's novel of Glasgow and modern Scottish society at their bleakest, or by way of the subtly implied spiritual dimension available to Alan Spence's charac-ters in the thirteen linked stories of *Its Colours They are Fine* (1977) and, under the gentle aegis of Krishna, in his novel, *The Magic Flute* (1990).[11] In Archie Hind's *The Dear Green Place* (1966) Mat Craig has a stab at the transcendental but gets himself into an 'awful mess on behalf of literature', his pursuit of 'the rapturous, the hopeful, the exploratory, the courageous' taking him from the security of collar-and-tie prospects to immersion in the gross material processes of a graphically rendered slaughter-house and a feeling of affinity with Glasgow's negative escutcheon:

> *This is the tree that never grew,*
> *This is the bird that never flew,*
> *This is the fish that never swam,*
> *This is the bell that never rang.*
> (Chapter 16)

Sensational when it first appeared, Alan Sharp's unrelievedly strenuous, semi-autobiographical story of the interwoven quests for identity of Moseby, Gibbon, Ruth and Cuffee in *A Green Tree in Gedde* now seems dated, its macho electricity too often cut by the author's sensually pedantic dwelling on his over-blown perceptions. Sharp's writing is like the kind of football he prefers: 'an over-ornate style, an embellished way of playing which is not efficient but is awfy nice to watch'.[12] Sadly – for the novel came as linguistic and moral refreshment in 1965 – the reader tires of watching Sharp manipulate his resolutely adolescent characters despite the perkiness of what in the first chapter he calls his 'cod joycery' ('Many a true word spoken incest', Peter Cuffee reminds his sister/lover, Ruth, in Chapter 3) and the magnificence of the book's opening evocation of Greenock's monolithic tenements set on their abiding hills. The prolific Hugh C. Rae's compelling first novel, *Skinner* (1965), uses the technique of multiple points of view as practised by Faulkner in *The Sound and the Fury* (1929) and *As I Lay Dying* (1930) and by Lawrence Durrell in *The Alexandria Quartet* (1957–60) to build, in his dauntingly believable portrait of a psychopathic killer (based on the actual crimes of Peter Manuel) and the people who come under his spell, a composite image of a sick Scottish society.

In his second, equally hard-boiled, novel of sex, sin, guilt and vengeance, *Night Pillow* (1967), Rae moves from the psychopathology of a murderer to the pathology of a city, taking his title from Blake's *Visions of the Daughters of Albion* (1793) which supplies the epigraph's[13] allusion to the sadistic ravishment and sexual arousal of Oothoon by Bromion. The novel dissects post-war Glasgow with impressive aural and visual accuracy in terms of 'the austerity incurred by the war and the lean years of the wake' (Part 1, Chapter 3), the violence and cynicism promoted by post-war social conditions, and the alienating town-planning alluded to by Tony Roper in *The Steamie* and William McIlvanney in the slum and motorway background of his second novel, *A Gift from Nessus* (1968). 'Skyscrapers; it's a damn' crime. You'd think it was America,' complains Matt Leishman, nodding towards the new high flats blocking the green view from his cherished council house and garden. 'Well, there's nothin' the likes of us can do about it,' says his wife (Part 1, Chapter 3). The Leishmans accordingly flit to the eleventh floor of their allocated jerry-built 'Sing Sing' in parallel with the Farrells who are transplanted to new flats 'from the heart of the dark clan country along the south bank of the Clyde, where in wide pockets and gulches the slums were coming down to make way for new housing schemes and modern factories' (Part 2, Chapter 1). Drainage of people into the new developments leaves behind the dank, echoing tenement stairs and industrial dereliction of Frederic Lindsay's Kafkaesque *Brond*, and the 'façades of mean dullness . . . pubs, betting shops, gap sites and boarded windows' of his Moirhill in *Jill Rips* (1987, Chapter 6). Jacko Farrell's rape of Alice Leishman in *Night Pillow* dramatizes on a personal level the violating impersonality of 'the rape of the parkland' symbolized by the new housing scheme at dusk:

The lights going on up and down them made the whole
area resemble a vast computer, winking and shuttering out
its inhuman formula, balancing time and space and capital
in neat economy.

(Part 1, Chapter 3)

But the economy is not as neat as the planners assume and Rae's city
can't be computerized out of its inimical energies. Men are brutish,
selfish, treacherous or ineffectual; women are abused, stoical or predatory.
Laughter splits silence 'like the blade of an axe' (Part 1, Chapter 1); the
portrait of a Presbyterian minister looks out with 'eyes set hard and almost
sneering, glittering, even through the dusty glass, like industrial diamonds'
(Part 1, Chapter 9), implying that the Church has gone cold-bloodedly
over to the authorities; a steelworks accident melts hands 'like two stumps
of candle-wax' (Part 2, Chapter 2); Jacko Farrell wakes up on New Year's
Day to find that 'a wedge of sunlight, like gelatine, sat on his face' (Part
3, Chapter 4). Alice Leishman strikes up a liaison with Jacko's brother,
George, in an attempt to get back to her rapist – she has become Jacko's
as Oothoon becomes 'Bromion's harlot'[14] – and the moment of 'witless
delight, divorced from all thought of consequence and, if only for an
instant, of self' (Part 1, Chapter 1), which is, appallingly, the best thing
going in a morally entropic system.

There is in Kennaway and Rae none of the self-indulgence that flaws
the work of Sharp or William McIlvanney's first, *Hamlet*-patterned novel,
Remedy is None (1966), whose lingering over the details of Charlie Grant's
father's death and burial gives the impression that the author thinks he has
invented funerals (Part 1, Chapters 4 and 5). In this book McIlvanney
appears as a talented writer flexing an uncertain style in search of a subject
beyond himself. In *Docherty* (1975) he triumphantly finds his theme and
his style in Graithnock, 'an industrial town under siege from farmland'
(Book 1, Chapter 18), loosely based on Kilmarnock, his home town. The
distinctive quality of *Docherty* is not so much in the fine portrait of Tam
Docherty, the 'awesome wee man' at the novel's centre who dies 'wi'
his balls on' (Book 3, Chapter 16) saving the life of a fellow miner, as
in McIlvanney's informed respect for the range and subtlety of human
nature evinced by his representative cast of working-class characters. The
book presents McIlvanney's nostalgic and realistic annals of a cherished
social and geographical parish where life, from the opening birth of Conn
the son to the concluding death of Tam the father, is made up of
moments 'ordinary yet profound, such as are found in long-established
rituals' by physical people who, when the body starts to go at the end of
'a lifetime's darg' (toil), 'had no recourse in the occupational therapy of
art, the bathchair of intellect, the artificial stimuli of theories' (Book 2,
Chapter 19). What such people do have recourse to, as Miss Gilfillan can

tell from her window of vantage over the High Street, is 'independence' (Prologue).

Paradoxically, they also have, and need, community. 'Why did even the most natural things you did have to pivot on economy?' asks Charlie Grant in *Remedy is None*, torn like a spiritual sibling of Grassic Gibbon's Chris Guthrie between his Scots-speaking working-class background and the English-speaking, bourgeois life to which university education will admit him, 'Money. Mon-ey! God of our fathers, we worship thee in all thy glorious manifestations, from the mighty fiver to the sterling pound, yea even to the little pennies of the pocket. Without thee, what is man?' (*Remedy is None*, Part 1, Chapter 1). For the workers of *Docherty*, against the sway of money and beyond the protective closeness of their families, 'the only security they could have was one another' (Book 1, Chapter 2) and the myths they exfoliate about each other at the street corner which does duty as 'club-room, mess-deck, mead-hall' (Book 1, Chapter 4). The habit of community follows Mick Docherty into war where he discovers that 'the men were the only identity he had left. He survived only as one of them. The others were the only sanity each of them had' (Book 2, Chapter 13). When Angus Docherty betrays tacit socialist community principles first by the cottage capitalism of independently contracting with his employers for coal, then by refusing to marry his pregnant girlfriend, Tam amalgamates truth of class with the mandate of community in the climactic, idealizing speech of the novel:

> Us an' folk like us hiv goat the nearest thing tae nothin'
> in this world. A' that filters doon tae us is shite. We leeve
> [live] in the sewers o' ither bastards' comfort. The only
> thing we've goat is wan anither. That's why ye never sell
> yer mates. Because there's nothin' left tae buy wi' whit ye
> get. That's why ye respect yer weemenkind. Because whit
> we make oorselves is whit we are. Because if ye don't,
> ye're provin' their case. Because the bastards don't believe
> we're folk! . . . We're wan anither. Tae survive, we'll
> respect wan anither. When the time comes, we'll a' move
> forward thegither, or nut at all. That's whit Ah've goat
> against you, boay . . . You're a fuckin' deserter. Ah don't
> harbour deserters. Ye're wi' the rest o' us or ye go elsebit
> [elsewhere].
>
> (Book 3, Chapter 5)

This is the doomed proletarian, romantic stoicism which Mat Craig's wife, Helen, satirizes in Hind's *The Dear Green Place*: 'Blessed are the meek as long as they don't have any high falutin' ideas' (Chapter 6). *Docherty's* stubbornly autonomous integrity is reincarnated in the character of

McIlvanney's popular Detective Inspector Jack Laidlaw, one of the Glasgow Crime Squad's 'less conventional men' (*Laidlaw*, 1977), and in *The
Big Man* Dan Scoular learns to become like Tam, finally abjuring the
'immorality' of pretending to be different from others (Chapter 8); but it
is the 'five foot fower' miner rather than the philosophizing policeman
or the troubled six-footer who secures McIlvanney's place in the mainstream of the Scottish novel tradition. Unpaternalistic commitment to the
common people, 'a commitment which has an honourable history in
Scottish culture, informs [McIlvanney's] writing at all levels'[15] and readers
of *Docherty* must surely feel, with the men remembering Tam at the
corner of Graithnock's High Street, 'the gratitude always owed to those
who enlarge our sense of ourselves' (Book 3, Chapter 16).

McIlvanney's view of 'the projected radiant future of the working-
class'[16] is anti-Utopian but his nostalgia for place and the nobility he finds
in his characters hold him back from the pessimism of George Douglas
Brown, the bleakness of Grassic Gibbon and the exemplary socialist ferocity of Tom Leonard, Liz Lochhead and James Kelman. The bitterness
of Patrick Doyle, Kelman's school teacher who has become 'totally sickened, absolutely scunnered' and tries in the classroom to 'just make the
weans angry' in *A Disaffection* (1989) infects his job and his relationships,
erupting in outbursts of frustration Graithnock would not have understood. This is not simply because Doyle is a teacher in the 1980s instead
of an early twentieth-century miner, but because he shuts off hope and
belongs to no community, though he does connect his own situation and
state of mind to world-wide oppression:

> . . . I canni understand people who arent awful bitter. I
> aye think there's something up with them; that there must
> be something up with them; as if maybe they've never
> thought things out, otherwise they'd be bound to be
> bitter. It's like being black in Northamerica, if ye meet
> another black person who isni bitter. I think if it was me
> I'd be amazed and I'd just think well here's another silly
> bastard who's never sat down and thought about slavery
> and the way people are still getting totally fucked across
> there and even so much worse in places like fucking
> South Africa or whatever. That's the way I feel here.[17]

Distanced from Patrick Doyle whom he sees as someone 'who thought
there was a possibility of change from within the system . . . a fairly naive
character',[18] Kelman can be identified only with the last stage of Doyle's
descent into hopelessness. For Kelman, the most uncompromisingly socialist novelist Scotland has yet produced, no such change is possible:

The big American corporations and multi-nationals would never allow it, they control most of everything . . . It's a long while since Socialists had any say or power. In the 50s the CIA destabilized the Labour Party anyway. No, there is no possibility of socialist change . . . The fact is that just now people in Britain are being killed in the name of society. That's concrete. That's the reality . . . Everywhere I go in London I'm confronted by Volvos, Mercedes and B.M.W.'s and Rolls Royces – all parked on one street. The wealth down here, the price of a meal and how much it costs for a jacket, say – compared to other parts of Britain just now, it's an obscenity.[19]

Believing that genre writing denies reality, Kelman resists 'becoming "literature" by a fundamental commitment to realism in content and style'[20] and makes the flesh demotically word in a body of fiction lit by 'the great decent socialism of imaginative sympathy with the neglected and previously unseen'.[21] A precedent for Kelman's position is to be found in Alexander Trocchi's *Cain's Book* (1960) whose intellectually restless and questioning protagonist, the dope-addict Joe Necchi, is, like his creator, 'a cosmonaut of inner space',[22] just as alienated from convention as Patrick Doyle is without the agency of drugs. Joe's fixes are attempts to know himself in terms of experience which can only be authentic if liberated from the compartments into which it is conventionally fragmented and falsely classified:

For centuries we in the West have been dominated by the Aristotelian impulse to classify. It is no doubt because conventional classifications become part of the prevailing economic structure that all real revolt is hastily fixed like a bright butterfly on a classificatory pin; the anti-play, *Godot*, being from one point of view unanswerable, is with all speed acclaimed 'best-play-of-the-year'; anti-literature is rendered innocuous by granting it a place in conventional histories of literature.[23]

Kelman portrays the Beckettian inner lives of dangling, marginalized, working-class characters largely in terms of their language in the short story collections, *Not Not While the Giro* (1983) and *The Burn* (1991), as well as in his first two novels, *The Busconductor Hines* (1984) and *A Chancer* (1985). In his more recent writing realism is heightened and spellbound by torrential flows of the vernacular transliterated 'into a phonetic orthography that seeks neither to patronize nor to dignify the actuality of Scottish speech'.[24] Idiomatically Glasgwegian post-Joycean stream-of-consciousness techniques of Kelman's own devising – despite his use of the third person singular he abjures Joyce's literary interferences with the flow of thought – make *A Disaffection* a song of honourable socialist impotence and the controversial Booker Prize-winner, *How Late it was, How Late* (1994), the blinded ex-convict Sammy Samuels's barbaric yawp of survival.

Uses of violence: Frederic Lindsay

With the globally homogenizing effects of easy travel and communications, the internationalizing tyranny of economics and the ubiquitous Americanization of cultures, it became both more plausible and more urgent to see Scotland in terms of supra-national conditions. This is the forte of Frederic Lindsay whose stories are set in Scotland, though only *Brond*, his first, unnervingly surrealist, novel, is ingeniously if enigmatically about the country's socio-political condition. The bewilderment of the unnamed narrator,[25] a first-year Glasgow University student, and his manipulation into kinky sexuality and murder by the inscrutable Brond reflect the disarray, naïveté and want of direction in 1980s Scottish politics. After he has seen Brond push a boy to his death from a bridge over the river Kelvin in Glasgow's Gibson Street the student becomes a metaphor for helpless isolation in a stony place without community:

> I looked round for support and all the million people
> were somewhere else. The other side of the bridge was
> buildings – a blank factory front and a brown tenement,
> its smooth stones stranger than a cliff wall, with not a face
> at any window to share what I felt.
>
> (Chapter 1)

Clearly we have left the warmth of McIlvanney's Graithnock. Referring to the Jekyll-and-Hyde dualism of the relationship between outwardly respectable Professor Maitland Ure and Monty Norman, the neo-Nazi hypnotist, in *After the Stranger Came* (1992), Allan Massie finds the book 'a very Scottish novel', but 'also a novel which would seem significant wherever it had been written'.[26] *Jill Rips* is a 'thriller' only if the term also applies to the majority of Jacobean plays and to such novels as William Styron's *Sophie's Choice* (1979) and Massie's own study of Italian terrorism in *The Death of Men* (1982). Its characters and locale are Scottish, but, detached from the novel's voices, its action would be as idiomatically at home in Los Angeles or Rome as it is shown to be in Glasgow. 'He thinks he's on television in America,' Inspector Peerse says of Murray

Wilson (Book 1, Chapter 6), a gloomy Scottish adaptation of Raymond Chandler's Philip Marlowe with a taste for China tea instead of the office bottle. It may be true that 'they dree their weird with a scabrous differ-ence north of the Border',[27] but violence is its own Esperanto and there is nothing parochial about Lindsay's strategic use of it. The island of Breagda where George Campbell finally becomes a better learner than he has been a husband, father or teacher in *A Charm Against Drowning* (1988) seems based on Scotland's isolated St Kilda, but could be an abandoned island anywhere, and Edinburgh merely gives solid local habitation to the action of *After the Stranger Came* which is based on an account of criminal hypnosis in Heidelberg in the 1930s. Allan Massie comments that Lindsay's 'ability to touch the nerves might consign him to the crime novel section of libraries and bookshops' but that his themes go beyond such rigid classification: 'He is concerned with the violence that lies disturbingly just below the surface of society; that, I should say, is his central pre-occupation.'[28]

Lindsay is another writer who rejects Calvinist doctrine but retains its moral aggressiveness, creating a pressurizing intensity in his novels not only by their violence and his 'rare talent for conveying unpalatable detail'[29] but through his stylish exactitude and narrative economies, his avoidance of obvious literariness, his use of realistically elliptical dialogue and the sustained curiosity he provokes and sharpens in the reader by the slow release of information. His central preoccupation arises from passionately held convictions about the fragility of human well-being, the obstacles life puts in the way of self-knowledge and firm identity, the devastating consequences of cruelty and, particularly in *After the Stranger Came*, the need for kindness. 'This is a sad lady,' says the man from Lewis about Lucy Ure to her husband, 'I hope you look after her with kindness' (Book 5, Chapter 24). *Jill Rips* uses city contract racketeering and Rip-per-style murders by Jill instead of Jack to trace its corruptions back to wartime anti-semitism and the abuse of orphaned children. The gender reversal of the murders invites explanation in terms of the women's movement:

> 'You mean it might be someone who had it in not for the prostitutes but for their clients? . . . A woman who hated what men did to women, the way men exploit them . . . A twentieth-century crime just as the Ripper's belonged so well to the nineteenth. Women's lib instead of Victorian exploitation and hypocrisy.'
> (Book 1, Chapter 7)

Politically correct wishful thinking proves to be an evasion, though such a solution would be a gift to a news-hungry journalist like Billy Shanks.

The root of the novel's evils is more fundamental: 'We want to be kind to one another – but how can we be? Don't blame Jack – or Jill' (Book 5, Chapter 28). Here is the centre of what Douglas Gifford calls 'this ambitious, glittering, horrible book', not 'a cold vision of humanity at the back of all the action'[30] but the heat of anger and moral urging: we must learn to be kind, and to take responsibility.

Virtuoso on a limb: Allan Massie

Like Lindsay, Allan Massie is a stylist; unlike Lindsay he revels in literariness as much as he does in his own post-Evelyn Waugh comedy of manners, in history and in contemplating the moral problems of political power. In *Change and Decay in All Around I See* (1978) his 'nicely raddled cosmopolitan army, an engagingly drunken whoring Earls Court rentamob'[31] flouts traditional values in a fine mist of literary allusions – Housman, T. S. Eliot, Graham Greene, Anthony Powell, with the central, absurdly Adamic Atwater, a 'slow waker' (Chapter 2) who doesn't consider the future, recalling Stevenson's ambiguous Attwater in *The Ebb-Tide* – to make the point that the modernists were phrase-making attitudinizers and connoisseurs of decadence.

Massie's pessimism darkens wittily in the malcontent landed Perthshire plush of *These Enchanted Woods* (1993), a camp divertimento subtitled 'A Comedy of Morals' with updated echoes (homosexuality, lesbianism, racism, money-men with their 'knickers in a twist') of Barrie's know-thyself house-party in *Dear Brutus*. There are, audaciously, two reactionary cheers for the tolerant, even tenor of suburban life (Chapter 6) and amusing oddballs like Sir Gavin Leslie for whom money 'goes up and down of its own accord' (Chapter 9), Colin whose ever-ready quotations, like his conversation in liquor, are 'stale, repetitive and far too often heard' (Chapter 5), an Americanized authoress, originally from Weybridge, who thinks she may have been Mary, Queen of Scots in a previous incarnation – 'When I visited Loch Leven, I was chilled to the marrow. Yes, the marrow' (Chapter 8) – and the Rev. Francis Snaith-Seath who is moved by a contemporary dance called 'The Jazz Hyacinth' performed by a decorative Australian refugee from sexual harassment to declare, 'it really showed you what the church has tried to deny for two thousand years, that Jesus was gay' (Chapter 21). Tony Lubbock, the Thatcherite chauffeur-driven plutocrat of Ukrainian extraction with a passion for Napoleon, merits a smile for observing that 'no matter how high you soared you could never be certain of cigars next year' (Chapter 10), but the key to the novel is Lubbock's unsmiling belief that 'nothing was for the best, that permanence was illusory, that predators prowled around the stockade' (Chapter 14). The shift in tone is typical of Massie and the association with Evelyn Waugh only takes account of one level of his invariably polished writing. Unlike Waugh's his novels achieve moral solidity because he always probes below the level of manners to the causal sub-stratum of values. Politically, he seems non-aligned like Etienne de Balafré, the narrator of his most daring book, *A Question of Loyalties* (1989), who thinks of replacing his South African passport with another:

> People are so often sympathetic. They assume that I have left the Republic because I disapprove of its policies. In fact I am indifferent to them. Apartheid is evil but I have no reason to think any politics other than evil; they are the clearest expression of the truth of the doctrine of Original Sin. That's all. I detest all politics and all politicians.
>
> (Part 1, Chapter 1)

Yet, given Massie's tenuous, conservative nationalism, the refrain on gentry failings and establishment insecurity in *These Enchanted Woods* is, despite the almost invariably saving middle ground of his waspishness, unexpected until the association is made with similar ambivalence in Sir Walter Scott whose life Massie re-creates with scholarly acumen, affection and humour in *The Ragged Lion* (1994).

The ambivalences of power and the relation of private to public lives are his subjects in the adroitly fictionalized histories of *Augustus* (1986) and *Tiberius* (1990). 'History is written from then to now, but understood back to front,' writes Etienne de Balafré in *A Question of Loyalties* (Part 3, Chapter 8), in which Massie's morally clement yet rigorous analysis works back from the glibness of received history into the personal and political complexities faced by Etienne's father, Lucien, to discover the truth about a man who became under-secretary to the Vichy government but, in his devotion to 'that historic civilization of Europe' (Part 2, Chapter 2), was admirable. His treatment of moral and political irony is less successful in the over-elaborate German–Israeli plot of *The Sins of the Father* (1991), but Massie understands such dilemmas as an intellectual who, as Douglas Dunn perceives, writes 'against a psychological background of belonging to a country but being seriously out of step with its contemporary disposition'.[32] From this tension comes Massie's benefit to his culture as a critical watchdog, out on a limb of his own, sceptical of over-simplifying political trends. It is also the source of the personal dilemma alluded to in *The Last Peacock* (1980). Belinda has admitted that Scotland always makes her feel guilty. She and Kenneth drink pints of heavy beer in a graceless, tartan-and-formica Edinburgh pub:

'Why do you always feel guilty in Scotland?'
'Why do you ask? Don't you?'
'I don't often think about Scotland.'
'But you are Scots?'
'Oh yes.'
'Doesn't that answer your question?'
'Does it?'
'I don't know. I can't stand almost anything that
manifests itself as Scots. Tartan and this beer, and Billy
Connolly and Morningside and hard men and football
supporters . . .'
'Well, who can . . . I mean that's not the whole of
Scotland . . .'
'No, but . . . it's terrible to feel ashamed of your family.'

(Chapter 4)

Recoil from kitsch, booze, football chauvinism, patter merchants and the
fabled bourgeois preciosities of Edinburgh's Morningside district is fair
enough, even if it somewhat snootily does less than justice to Billy Connolly's intermittent brilliance as a raconteur who satirizes the same things.

It is clear from his *Edinburgh* (1994) that Massie himself loves the city,
but sometimes he protests too much against the cultural growing pains
of the slicker new Scotland, as in the caricatured back-slapping vulgarity
of his piggy-eyed entrepreneur, Fraser Donnelly, in *One Night in Winter*
(1984) whose most disagreeable feature is his occasional plausibility:

You see . . . the truth of the matter is that a national
movement requires a revolution. It makes nae sense
without it . . . For me Scotland's worth a revolution, and
ripe for one. No' your old-fashioned, wave the red flag
revolution. I'm no thinking of that, it's a load of blethers
too. No, what I'm interested in is a real revolution, a
revolution of consciousness, a revolution of morals. The
hell wi' the auld Scotland of kirk and kailyard. I want a
new Scotland that's free and rich too.

(Part 1, Chapter 3)

Donnelly's plausibility fades when, before turning to the blonde of the
moment, he adds, 'There's no harm in bringing a bit of Texas to Scotland, as lang as we take our new morality from California.' Douglas Dunn
sees the flaw in Massie's theorem: 'It could be salutary to remember that
it was probably the awful likes of Donnelly (but without the Irish name)
who kicked off the wealth and power that set up the withered dyn-
asties.'[33] But it is likely that Massie, a mischief-maker like Muriel Spark

of whom he has written a perceptive study,[34] is well aware of the flaw himself. Provocation generates more mental energy than most theorems, and Massie is a master *provocateur*. Contemporary Scotland is fortunate to be able to claim a writer of such polemical intelligence and virtuosity who, wearing his culture, his learning and his considerable art with distinctive *élan*, can provoke laughter, controversy or depth of contemplation.

Mutability and magic: Alasdair Gray

With accelerating developments in electronics the mid- to late twentieth century became constantly mutable, more accessible and less knowable. Significantly, Trocchi's *Cain's Book*, Archie Hind's *The Dear Green Place* and Alasdair Gray's *Lanark* all feature artists who do not finish their work. Identities blur out of definition into the vacillations of Allan Massie's characters in *These Enchanted Woods* or undergo the Francis Baconesque disfigurements of the boy and girl Duncan Thaw sees in a school refectory in Gray's *Lanark*:

> The skin on the skulls crawled and twitched like half-solid
> paste . . . potatoes with crawling surfaces punctured by
> holes which opened and shut, holes blocked with coloured
> jelly or fringed with bone stumps, elastic holes through
> which air was sucked or squirted, holes secreting salt, wax,
> spittle and snot.
>
> (Book 2, Chapter 21)

In politics, religion and the ethical frameworks of human relations familiar outlines and firm ground dissolve in multiplying but loose or broken connections. Brian McCabe's portrayals of isolation and marital failure make his short-story collection, *In a Dark Room with a Stranger* (1993), a symptomatic text for the times and the space between people is a recurrent theme in the novels of George Friel and Elspeth Davie and the poetry and short stories of Douglas Dunn. The decay of traditional norms is reflected in Muriel Spark's satirical inversions: the dead are haunted by reality in *The Hothouse by the East River*, mock mourning precedes death in *Not to Disturb* and in *The Driver's Seat* the self-appointed victim hunts her killer.[35]

The general condition is expressed in the title and parallel stories of the prodigiously inventive Iain Banks's second novel, *Walking on Glass* (1985), a fable of despair which uses magical realism to split a universe of alienations into three separate planes of reality whose ultimate intersection is disastrous.

Joy, Janice Galloway's heroine on the edge of breakdown in *The Trick is to Keep Breathing* (1990), wonders how other people manage. She considers 'several possibilities':

1. They are just as confused as me but they aren't letting on.
2. They don't know they don't know what the point is.
3. They don't understand they don't know what the point is.
4. They don't mind they don't know what the point is.
5. They don't even know there are any questions.[36]

Joy's problem is '*minding*'. Choosing the fourth possibility, she realizes that she minds 'the resultant moral dilemma of having no answers'.[37] Women's contributions to the war effort both in and out of active service had failed to gain them more than a semblance of equality with men: urgent questions remained about 'the phallocracy in which women have been forced to live since the beginning of recorded history' as Emma Tennant's Scottish solicitor, Jean Hastie, puts it in *Two Women of London: The Strange Case of Ms Jekyll and Mrs Hyde* (Part 1). The apparent death or absence of God, the collapse of institutions and wider acceptance of moral relativities induced writers to find new grids of value and fresh ways of asking the questions. Alexander Trocchi's mouthpiece, Joe Necchi, writes at the end of *Cain's Book*: 'I should not care to estimate what has been accomplished. In terms of art and literature? – such concepts I sometimes read about, but they have nothing in intimacy with what I am doing, exposing, obscuring.'[38] Alasdair Gray and Janice Galloway experiment with form. A. L. Kennedy has developed an arrestingly spontaneous narrative voice combining delicacy, power and deceptive simplicity for expressing female sensibility with an immediacy which is particularly compelling in her first novel, *Looking for the Possible Dance* (1993). Her compassion for others is rooted in a sense of the problematic self yet, as in the title story of *Night Geometry and the Garscadden Trains* (1990), always pushes outward: 'We have small lives, easily lost in foreign droughts, or famines; the occasional incendiary incident, or a wall of pale faces, crushed against grillwork, one Saturday afternoon in Spring. This is not enough.'[39] Many writers turn, like Gray, Emma Tennant, Iain Banks and A. L. Kennedy in *So I am Glad* (1995), to fantasy or to magical realism. Banks is wary of generic compartmentalizing but says that he is 'more at home with science fiction'[40] which he writes under the name, Iain M. Banks. Even when working in a more or less realistic mode, these writers disrupt the ordinary surfaces of life by freakish characters, bizarre situations or idiosyncratic styles of writing.

Alasdair Gray hates exploitation. The 'cunning, straightfaced, pompous men' manipulating the puppet emperor in 'Five Letters from an Eastern Empire' in *Unlikely Stories, Mostly* (1984), a quaint but chilling adaptation of the Orwellian *Nineteen Eighty-Four* situation which also alludes to Kafka's 'The Great Wall of China', are the same people who run the omnipotent Institute in *Lanark* and, down south, perpetuate the class system represented by Harriet Shetland's mother and her artificially liberal headmistress in *Something Leather* (1990). Lanark arrives among these deadly people by becoming symbolically dead himself, swallowed by the Glasgow Necropolis into the black magic of Gray's sinister dream-like subterranean realm. They supply society's authority figures – doctors, teachers, ministers, capitalist plotters and flunkeys – and dump the unmalleable drones in the central Pit where they become food and fuel to sustain those in control. As the court poet, Bohu, puts it in his poem for the Emperor in 'Five Letters', 'It is sad to be unnecessary',[41] a pointer to the Marxist component of Gray's intellectual apparatus.

In *1982 Janine* (1984) the theme of exploitation on the personal level preoccupies the self-recriminatory Jock McLeish. Like William Golding's Sammy Mountjoy in *Free Fall* McLeish needs to find the point in his life where he went wrong. 'We all have a moment when the road forks and we take the wrong turning,' McLeish says (Chapter 1). He finds his crucial moment in Helen's pregnancy, his arranged marriage to her and his 'anti-Denny demolition job' (Chapter 12). Before leaving Denny he teaches her about her position in the great chain of the British exploitative system:

> if you go on strike and demonstrate for better wages (you won't, you have no union, but if you do) then cabinet ministers drawing salaries of twenty-nine-thousand-nine-hundred-and-fifty-a-year (on top of interest on private investments) will appear on television to explain in brave, loud, haw-haw voices that there is not enough money to help you, that your selfish greed is the thing which has reduced Britain to its present deplorable plight . . . The people who manage you, Denny, have been taught to make brazen speeches in firm clear voices, THAT is FAR more important than geography or technology, because RHETORIC RULES, O.K.?
>
> (Chapter 12)

McLeish's guilt comes from recognition that having tutored Denny in the rules of exploitation he has proved them by exploiting her himself. His rhetoric has been as effective and as false as the managers'. Sexual exploitation in a society of user and used is the subject of Bella Baxter's (or Victoria McCandless's) story in *Poor Things*. In the version of events given

in Victoria's letter to posterity Godwin Baxter instructs his fugitive
acolyte with the help of a doll's house, scullery-maid in the tiny kitchen,
daughter of the house at the piano in the parlour:

> *'Tell me, Bella, what the scullery-maid and the master's*
> *daughter have in common, apart from their similar ages and*
> *bodies and this house.'*
> *'Both are used by other people,' I said. 'They are allowed to*
> *decide nothing for themselves.'*
> *'You see?' cried Baxter delightedly. 'You know that at once*
> *because you remember your early education. Never forget it,*
> *Bella. Most people in England, and Scotland too, are taught not*
> *to know it at all — are taught to be tools.'*[42]

Among the controllers and exploiters, the duplicitous banking nations,
the eastern communists, the Ozenfants and Mad Hislops, the English are
the supreme elite, hence the London-based business and media power
structures over which Kelvin Walker briefly triumphs, the Ministry of
Social Stability in *McGrotty and Ludmilla* (1990) which 'had been criticized in the House for employing nobody but Etonians' (Chapter 2), and
the great theatrical producer, Binkie, who 'once owned the whole of
the West End' (*1982 Janine*, Chapter 12). Gray's cheekiest trick is to
exemplify control by blatantly pulling his readers' strings, not only
manoeuvring his hero Jock McLeish into manipulating Denny and
manipulating his fantasized Janine to the point where she realizes she
is trapped in his narrative (*1982 Janine*, Chapter 13), but also gleefully
manipulating us with his stories, his gamesome typography and book
design, his batteries of 'Notes, Thanks and Critic Fuel'.[43] From Gray
himself with his urge to write to Jock with his urge to know and evade,
to Janine stuck in her sexy script, to Denny and Helen caught in their
traps, to the alternative histories of Bella Baxter, to the reader held in
Gray's narrative clutch until the releasing valediction of his habitual 'Goodbye', rhetoric, while always suspect, rules, OK. What else is there in a
morally and politically deliquescent world?

Yet beyond the rhetoric are solidly real human things: poor Lanark,
after his surrealist purgatories, is 'one of us, between heaven and hell, a
survivor of the tyranny of our historical imaginations, waiting the end'[44]
and last glimpsed as 'a slightly worried, ordinary old man' with the dignity of enjoying the light in the sky (*Lanark*, Epilogue, Chapter 44); poor
Jock, chastened by the failure of whisky and pornographic fantasy to provide the needed anodyne, will be kind to his sex-object. *Poor Things*,
which Gray thinks 'the funniest book I've ever written',[45] leaves us with
a liberated woman as well as a satire on the values of 'that most morbid
of centuries, the nineteenth',[46] whether we prefer to believe in Godwin

Baxter as a latter-day Dr Frankenstein, according to the novel's brilliantly imagined *Episodes from the Early Life of a Scottish Public Health Officer*, or in the duller, more plausible story told by the self-righteous Victoria McCandless MD. Even if we opt for Victoria, we will not forget Archie McCandless's insatiable, compassionate Bella, the ultimate whore (when it suits her) with a heart of gold and the brain of her own baby, self-determining feminism incarnate, escaped from the threat of clitoridectomy, sweeping about the world beyond the control of any man including the one who thought he had made her.

Together with James Kelman and Agnes Owens, co-authors of *Lean Tales*, Gray lives 'in a British region containing the greatest number of unemployed Scots in the world, the biggest store of nuclear weapons in Europe, and very large lovely tracts of depopulated wilderness'.[47] If England is the great external enemy, the arch-enemy is the one within, the Scottish character itself:

> Who spread the story that the Scots are an
> INDEPENDENT people? Robert Burns ... The truth is
> that we are a nation of arselickers, though we disguise it
> with surfaces: a surface of generous, openhanded manliness,
> a surface of dour practical integrity, a surface of futile
> maudlin defiance like when we break goalposts and
> windows after football matches on foreign soil and commit
> suicide on Hogmanay by leaping from fountains in
> Trafalgar Square.
>
> > (*1982 Janine*, Chapter 4)

To this diatribe the writer of the festival play about Eustace McGrotty adds the curse of 'wee hard men' who 'hammer Scotland down to the same dull level as themselves' (*1982 Janine*, Chapter 12). As Gray's own place, Glasgow (the surrealist 'Unthank' of *Lanark*) attracts particular criticism. Lanark's wish to leave the city is 'powerful and complete and equalled by a certainty that streets and buildings and diseased people stretched infinitely in every direction' (*Lanark*, Book 3, Chapter 6). One morning in the Cowcaddens district Kenneth McAlpin observes to Duncan Thaw that Glasgow is 'a magnificent city' and asks, 'Why do we hardly ever notice that?' Thaw's answer is, 'Because nobody imagines living here.' He explains:

> if a city hasn't been used by an artist not even the
> inhabitants live there imaginatively. What is Glasgow to
> most of us? A house, the place we work, a football park
> or golf course, some pubs and connecting streets ...
> Imaginatively Glasgow exists as a music-hall song and a

few bad novels. That's all we've given to the world
outside. It's all we've given to ourselves.

(*Lanark*, Book 2, Chapter 22)

Hugh C. Rae, Frederic Lindsay, Jeff Torrington, James Kelman and
Alasdair Gray have made this view of Glasgow obsolete, giving their city
the imaginative life Thaw finds lacking. Their peers in this are the poets:
Edwin Morgan, Tom Leonard and Liz Lochhead. Thaw's comments
were valid some thirty years ago at the time in which the novel is set
and *Lanark*, like any novel, demands to be read in terms of all its codes,
including historical ones. In *Something Leather* Harriet's art dealer asks
Linda to tell her 'about the European Cultcha Capital thing . . . Why
Glasgow? How has a notoriously filthy hole become a shining light?'
(Chapter 10). From the perspective of Glasgow glamorized as European
City of Culture for 1990 *Lanark* still remains valid as an image of any
unreal city. Worthy of a place beside James (B. V.) Thomson's *The City
of Dreadful Night*, the novel confronts the urban waste land made by
political and commercial forces whose impact on the individual is exemplified by the fragmentation of the novel's eponymous hero into Lanark
and Thaw. The two characters are one, yet they cannot coalesce any
more than the shadowy figures of Eliot's desert-city can cohere in *The
Waste Land* except in the device of the ambiguous Tiresias. Here, Tiresias
is Gray himself, not in the book.

In the Utopian Scotland AD *circa* 2230 of *A History Maker* (1994) the
women's movement, the green movement and the peace movement have
triumphed over sexism, monogamy, war and high finance. Wat Dryhope's
longing for the 'bad old days when wars had no rules and bombs fell on
houses and men and women died together like REAL equals' (Chapters
2 and 4) focuses an inspired satirical inversion; but Gray has become too
enamoured of his own whimsies (shades of Barrie) and the destabilizingly
sexy Delilah Puddock is only a sketchy successor to Bella Baxter. The
fable would have been stronger without the intermittently amusing mock-
scholastic pomp of Gray's forty pages of 'pedantical lang-nebbed notes'
(Prologue) and better kept to the scale of his more compressed comic
moralities, *The Fall of Kelvin Walker* (1985) and *McGrotty and Ludmilla*.
Kelvin Walker, a Scottish modification of Denry Machin in Arnold
Bennett's *The Card*, with a hint of Melville's refractory scrivener, Bartleby
(Chapter 4), tries to be a wee hard man, but Calvin and his father won't
let him. Kelvin is from Glaik (trick, prank, deception) but semantically
his derivation also means that he is 'glaikit' (stupid and clumsy). With
his 'blank, nearly characterless face' (Chapter 1) he is clumsily equal
to any situation, behaving by formulae and incapable of following Jill's
advice 'just to act naturally' (Chapter 1). The substitution of Nietzsche's
formulae for God's is merely the temporary replacement of one kind of

self-righteousness with another. Nietzschean or Free Seceding Presbyterian, Kelvin is interested only in power (Chapter 5) and is swiftly cued
back to the foetal position (Chapter 11) and a career in Scottish Church
politics by the Session-Clerk father who represents a power the supremacy
of which was never really in doubt even when posthumous. McGrotty,
just as blank at the beginning of his story as Kelvin is on his first day in
London, succeeds in becoming a wee hard man and scourge of the
smug, dissipated English because he grasps 'the consolations of mere
power, little though he valued them' (*McGrotty and Ludmilla*, Chapter 28)
for the sake of winning Ludmilla. Sexual power yields to deeper feeling
in *Something Leather*. The suggestion 'that forcibly chaining, beating, in-
decently assaulting, depilating and tattooing a woman might be *doing her
a favour* is surely outrageous and dangerous',[48] but possibly less so if there
is an antithesis. In the context of corrupt and corrupting class and sexual
systems June, Senga, Harry and Donalda find, under the kinks and the
comedy of upper-class English phonetically rendered, good old-fashioned
love.

Player of games: Iain Banks

'Me? I'll tell you about me later,' promises the narrator in Chapter 1 of
The Player of Games (1988). His story of Gurgeh, master game-player in
a symbiotically human/electronic society called 'The Culture', may be
read, in part, as a comment by Iain M. Banks on the work of Iain Banks,
his not-so-alter ego. Gurgeh's objection to the infantile destructiveness of
the novel's opening game, a virtual-reality 'shoot' against missiles, is met
by his companion, Yay:

> 'It's hardly destruction,' Yay drawled. 'The missiles are
> explosively dismantled, not destroyed. I can put one of
> those things back together in half an hour.'
> 'So it's false.'
> 'What isn't?'
> 'Intellectual achievement. The exercise of skill. Human
> feeling.'
>
> (Chapter 1)

All Iain Banks's novels are games, intellectually compelling and skilfully
played. Like the satirical novels of Joseph Heller and Richard Condon
they are loaded with wisecracks and black comedy and vary in the degree
of seriousness with which they take human feeling. Moral purpose can be

pre-empted by the ingenuity of the symbolism (*The Bridge*, 1986, which is Banks's own favourite of his novels[49]), attenuated by too assiduously swinging contemporaneity and postmodern quizzery about the status of fiction (*Espedair Street*, 1987), upstaged by *outré* characterization and probings into the nature of reality (*Canal Dreams*, 1989), or, in *The Crow Road* (1992), lost in the exuberance of a plot determined, by Banks's own admission, to convene 'Death, Sex, Faith, cars, Scotland and drink'.[50] Written in 1980,[51] his first published novel *The Wasp Factory* (1984) made his name at once[52] as a voluptuary of the bizarre if not of 'ghoulish frivolity . . . preposterous sadism' and 'exorbitant brutalities'.[53] So much for the book's luridly deviant surfaces, but what lies below them? Even in competition with the surrealist squalors of Irvine Welsh, who seems set to become the newest high priest of patois and *enfant terrible* of Scottish literature, Banks's novel may still appear hideous and intolerable. In the Edinburgh of heroin, loose bowels, pub violence, junk-induced impotence, cot-death and 'psychic vandalism' portrayed in Welsh's *Trainspotting* (1993), horror is alleviated by shaping intelligence, dark laughter, tenderness and the vitality of the language with which Welsh expresses the tenacity of consciousness and the disillusionment of a generation in a loosely constructed parable of corrupting powers. What justifies the unnatural shocks of *The Wasp Factory*? Are they defensible as fable or allegory? Frank, or Frances, Cauldhame gives the answer in Chapter 4, 'The Bomb Circle':

> Often I've thought of myself as a state; a country, or, at the very least, a city. It used to seem to me that the different ways I felt sometimes about ideas, courses of action and so on were like the differing political moods that countries go through. It has always seemed to me that people vote in a new government not because they actually agree with their politics but just because they want a change. Somehow they think that things will be better under the new lot. Well, people are stupid, but it all seems to have more to do with mood, caprice and atmosphere than carefully thought-out arguments.

The novel is a fable whose horrific miniaturizations replicate the falsity and violence of a world 'of fabulous opportunities and awful dangers' (Chapter 9) in which 'mood, caprice and atmosphere' and the craving for change underlie the cosmetic of apparent reason and the fictions of politics. If rhetoric rules for Alasdair Gray, ego rules for Banks. Agnes Cauldhame's ego is responsible for the occurrence of Frank's 'little accident' (Chapter 6); his father's ego is responsible for Frank's belief that he is a boy castrated by a bulldog instead of Frances, her sex suppressed by

344 SCOTTISH LITERATURE SINCE 1707

male hormones; and the collective professional ego of doctors and consultants is responsible for Eric's madness by keeping deformed babies alive (Chapter 9). Like Cameron Colley, strategizing on his computer for 'Despotic Power Level' in *Complicity* (1993), Frank plays the ego game, but admits its pretences. 'There was no *need* to take revenge on the rabbits,' he concedes, 'There never is, even in the big world . . . At least I admit that it's all to boost my ego, restore my pride and give me pleasure, not to save the country or uphold justice or honour the dead' (Chapter 4). Cut off 'from society's mainland' (Chapter 12) on his real and figurative island, Frank's murders of Blyth, Paul and Esmeralda, his secret catechisms and power rituals of the Wasp Factory, the Bunker and the Sacrifice Poles make up a parable of the big world's perverse mumbo-jumbo: territorialism, the Dow-Jones index, the exclusive cabal, the nuclear deterrent. The name 'Cauldhame' not only indicates that Frank and Eric come from a home devoid of human warmth, but also carries an echo of J. D. Salinger's 'Caulfield' in *The Catcher in the Rye* (1951). The palliative cuteness of Holden Caulfield's relationship to his sister, Phoebe, is absent from the twisted lives of Eric and his sister, Frances. There is no gratuitous violence in the book: 'only the squeamish and the humourless need beware'.[54]

An equally purposeful shocker, *Complicity* moves dazzlingly from the first of its graphically described murders to the debate on duty, greed, liability and corruption between Andy Gould and Cameron Colley in Chapter 12. In Chapter 7 it becomes clear that Cameron couldn't be the serial killer in Banks's consistently moral thriller. He is, after all, too much a consumer of drugs, booze, tobacco, kinky sex and news-fixes to take arms against key players in the system which sustains his habits. A veteran of the Falklands War who feels betrayed by Thatcher's Britain, Andy Gould has withdrawn from society to become the 'Real Avenger' or 'Radical Equalizer' called for in Cameron's newspaper article (Chapter 5). Far from being the pornographic 'cultish shock tactics'[55] often attributed to Banks, the function of the repulsive detail in which the retributive killings are described is to induce a nausea commensurate with the enormity of Gould's respectable victims' crimes against humanity. Andy is quite clear about what he has done:

> We all have moral responsibility, whether we like it or not, but people in power – in the military, in politics, in professions, whatever – have an imperative to care, or at least to exhibit an officially acceptable analogue of care; duty, I suppose. It was people I knew had abused that responsibility that I attacked; that's what I was taking as my . . . authority.
>
> (Chapter 12)

To Cameron's objection that he is not God, Andy replies, 'No, I'm not
. . . Nobody is . . . So what?' At the end of a book even more 'compre-
hensively terrifying'[56] than Iain M. Banks's story of 'the crypt' in *Feersum
Endjinn* (1994) the question remains.

Banks's game-playing, genre mixing and moral vision are elegantly
interfused in the three-tiered *Walking on Glass*. On the novel's first, most
normal, plane gullible Graham Park is obsessed by gamine Sara ffitch –
'Not one big "f"; two little ones', Park's apparent friend, Richard Slater,
reminds him, 'Like British industry, our Sara's undercapitalized' (Part 3,
'Amwell Street'). On the second plane Steven Grout is locked into
paranoiac fantasy. While Slater invents exasperatingly far-fetched sci-fi
plots, Grout lives in one of his own making as 'one of the mightiest
warlords in the history of existence' (Part 1, 'Mr Smith'), pursued by 'The
Tormentors' who snipe at him with 'the Microwave Gun' and the 'laser-
axles' of passing traffic. His counter-attack is sawing off car mascots,
starting with Jaguar's leaping cat, and putting sugar in the fuel tanks of
motorbikes. The third plane, presented as matter-of-factly as the first two
but remote from normal reality, introduces Quiss and Ajayi, players of
obscure games in a castle lit by luminous fish under the supervision of a
talking, foul-mouthed, cigar-smoking red crow who tries to incite them
to suicide. Their prize for finishing each game is another chance to
answer the conundrum: 'What happens when an unstoppable force meets
an immovable object?' Their answers are always wrong. There are intimations of contact between the planes like Edwin Morgan's 'Interferences': Steven Grout's room is full of books, 'mostly Science Fiction and
Fantasy', and the castle is made of books (Mervyn Peake's *Titus Groan* and
Kafka's *The Castle* turn up in the last chapter to endorse the novel's
themes as well as the castle's paraphernalia); Grout finds obscure significance in the name of an estate agent, Hotblack Desiato, whose name
Graham Park comes across in Sara's copy of Douglas Adams's *The Res-
taurant at the End of the Universe* (Part 5, 'Half-Moon Crescent').

The convergent crunch comes on 28 June 1983 in a traffic accident
caused by the sugar Grout has introduced into the fuel tank of Sara
ffitch's lover's motorbike. The accident initiates a dénouement in which
Park's infatuation ends in his sexual humiliation by Sara whose leather-
clad lover is revealed as her brother, Richard Slater. A fellow-patient,
strongly reminiscent of the mysterious castle's maleficent crow, gives the
hospitalized Grout pieces stolen from games played by an old man and
an old woman acting out a normalized simulacrum of Quiss and Ajayi's
situation. The final collision of the three planes occurs when Grout finds
an old matchbox that gives the answer to the puzzle Quiss and Ajayi
could not solve: 'The unstoppable force stops, the immovable object
moves' (Part 5, 'Dr Shawcross'). These narrative closures bring aesthetic
satisfaction to Banks's overseeing readers, but none to his floundering

characters who are not in a position to contemplate whatever sense the intersections make. It is surprising to find the American science-fiction writer Samuel R. Delany criticizing Banks's 'formal play' for showing 'no particular insight into the fantasies of any of its three stories'.[57] The social, sexual and psychological elements of the Graham Park–Sara ffitch story are clear, Steven Grout's behaviour is consistent within his paranoia and reasons are given for Quiss and Ajayi's presence in the castle. Banks's purpose is not to explain why Slater and his sister love each other incestuously, how Grout became paranoid, or why a crow can talk; these are the premises that enable him to portray, on all imaginative levels, the tenuous hold we have on reality as well as the madness, exploitation and mental cruelty which make 'Dirt' of the planet Earth and sense of Graham Park's 'total allergy syndrome' (Part 6, 'Truth and Consequences'). Quiss (does the name come from 'quis' meaning 'who?', implying 'you', i.e. everyone?) is driven to attempted suicide by dwelling on the sight the red crow has shown him of the planet's dreaming zombies:

> So many people, so many failed hopes, lost games,
> surrendered dreams; and the castle, a single island of
> warped chance in a frozen ocean of missed opportunities
> . . . In that deep, dark, echoless and echo-filled space far
> beneath him, his mind was already lost; sideless, wall-less
> the place, bottomless his despair . . . He felt like some grain
> of sand inside the place, no more important.
>
> (Part 5, 'Tunnel')

Like Samuel R. Delany, the reader may reject Banks's premises and with them his vision and dark laughter, but if the novel's terms are accepted there is no escape: in a twist that recalls the enmeshing narrative circles of Italo Calvino's *If on a Winter's Night a Traveller* (1981), the last book Ajayi picks up begins with the opening sentence of the novel we thought was about to finish. The stories begin again as the century draws to an end, with most of us walking on glass in the labyrinth of Edwin Muir's dream.

But the isle of Lismore's Bàrr Mòr still watches over the Great Glen of Scotland as it did when the saints and vikings came, and Norman MacCaig's Suilven still 'spouts cool clear water from innumerable springs'.[58] 'Beyond the lochs of the blood of the children of men' and 'beyond hardship, wrong, tyranny, distress' Sorley MacLean's Cuillin rises 'on the other side of sorrow'.[59] The stones of MacDiarmid's raised beach lie there yet, guarding their message of 'stupendous unity'; the people of George Mackay Brown's Orkney have said 'no' to uranium mining; there is Edwin Morgan's optimism about his 'favoured place',[60] A. L. Kennedy's 'possible dance' away from 'irrelevance and defeat',[61] and the 'grace of change'⁶² to be caught in the befriending sea of W. S. Graham's 'The Nightfishing'. It is the artist, as much as the ecologist and always more than the politician, who urges us to love the world well enough to find ways of saving it from consumerism's pollutions, bigotry, the vitiating politics of power and all the depradations of the 'auld enemy' within ourselves. It is from the artist's 'great love' of earth, humanity, mind and language that we may acquire a sensibility militarized against our propensities to self-destruction.

Notes

1. Isobel Murray and Bob Tait, *Ten Modern Scottish Novels* (Aberdeen, 1984), p. 88.

2. Jack Webster, 'Why this rare Scottish talent hides potential classics in a farmhouse drawer', *Glasgow Herald*, 25 June 1984, p. 7.

3. Robin Jenkins, *The Cone-Gatherers*, with an introduction by Iain Crichton Smith (Harmondsworth, 1983), p. 2.

4. Alan Bold, 'The ballad of Miss Jean Brodie's creator', *The Herald*, 30 July 1992, p. 16.

5. Muriel Spark, 'The Go-Away Bird', *Collected Stories I* (London, 1967), pp. 302–59 [314].

6. Charles Alva Hoyt, 'Muriel Spark: The Surrealist Jane Austen', in Harry T. Moore (ed.), *Contemporary British Novelists* (Carbondale, 1965), pp. 125–43 [128].

7. Muriel Spark, 'Miss Pinkerton's Apocalypse', *Collected Stories I*, pp. 163–70 [164].

8. Ruth Whittaker, '"Angels Dining at the Ritz": The Faith and Fiction of Muriel Spark', *The Contemporary English Novel* (Stratford-upon-Avon Studies 18), ed. Malcolm Bradbury and David Palmer (London, 1979), pp. 157–79 [177].

9. 'Talking about Jerusalem', unsigned review of Muriel Spark, *The Mandelbaum Gate*, TLS, 14 October 1965, p. 913.

10. Muriel Spark, *Curriculum Vitae: Autobiography* (London, 1992), p. 113.

11. See John Burns, 'Mastering the Magic Flute', *Cencrastus* (Winter 1990/91), pp. 41–2.

12. Tom Shields, 'Chasing Hemingway on a galloping horse', *The Herald*, 5 September 1992, p. 12.

13. William Blake, *Visions of the Daughters of Albion*, Plate 6, ll. 9–13.

14. Ibid., Plate 2, l. 1.

15. Beth Dickson, 'Class and Being in the Novels of William McIlvanney', in Gavin Wallace and Randall Stevenson (eds), *The Scottish Novel Since the Seventies: New Visions, Old Dreams* (Edinburgh, 1993), pp. 54–69 [69].

16. Keith Dixon, 'Writing on the Borderline: The Work of William McIlvanney', *Studies in Scottish Literature*, 24 (1989), pp. 142–57 [154].

17. James Kelman, *A Disaffection* (London, 1990), p. 320.

18. Kirsty McNeill, 'Interview with James Kelman', *Chapman*, 57 (Summer 1989), p. 1.

19. Ibid., pp. 1–3.

20. Cairns Craig, 'Resisting Arrest: James Kelman', in Wallace and Stevenson (eds), *The Scottish Novel Since the Seventies*, pp. 99–114 [100].

21. James Wood, 'In defence of Kelman; Booker judge James Wood stands by his man', *The Guardian*, 2, 25 October 1994, p. 9.

22. Alexander Trocchi, *Man at Leisure*, with an introduction by William Burroughs (London, 1972), p. 9.

23. Alexander Trocchi, *Cain's Book* (London, 1973), p. 34.

24. Cairns Craig, 'Resisting Arrest', p. 102.

25. He is called Robert in the 1987 television adaptation of the novel for Channel 4 directed by Michael Caton-Jones with John Hannah as the student and Stratford Johns as Brond.

26. Allan Massie, 'Disquieting look into the Scots psyche', *The Scotsman Weekend*, 20 June 1992, p. 6.

27. John Coleman, 'A cast of charismatic cadavers', *The Sunday Times*, 5 April 1987, p. 56.

28. Allan Massie, 'Not drowning, just waving', *The Scotsman*, 16 April 1988, 'Weekender', p. ix.

29. Alan Taylor, 'Upturned morality of a ripping yarn', *Glasgow Herald*, 28 February 1987, 'Weekender 4', p. 11.

30. Douglas Gifford, 'Recent Fiction', *Books in Scotland*, 24 (Spring 1987), pp. 16–19 [17–18].

31. Valentine Cunningham, 'Allusive pimpernels', *TLS*, 18 August 1978, p. 925.

32. Douglas Dunn, 'Divergent Scottishness: William Boyd, Allan Massie, Ronald Frame', in Wallace and Stevenson (eds), *The Scottish Novel Since the Seventies*, pp. 149–69 [158–9].

33. Ibid., p. 160.

34. Allan Mussie, *Muriel Spark: A New Assessment* (Edinburgh, 1979).

35. See Ian Rankin, 'The Deliberate Cunning of Muriel Spark', in Wallace and Stevenson (eds), *The Scottish Novel Since the Seventies*, pp. 41–53 [45].

36. Janice Galloway, *The Trick is to Keep Breathing* (London, 1991), p. 198.

37. Ibid.

38. Trocchi, *Cain's Book*, p. 163.

39. A. L. Kennedy, *Night Geometry and the Garscadden Trains* (London, 1993), p. 34.

40. Andrew Wilson, 'Interview: Iain Banks', *Scottish Book Collector*, 4, no. 9 (February–March 1995), pp. 2–5 [3].

41. Alasdair Gray, *Unlikely Stories, Mostly* (Harmondsworth, 1984), p. 127.

42. Alasdair Gray, *Poor Things* (Harmondsworth, 1993), p. 263.

43. Alasdair Gray, *Ten Tales Tall and True* (Harmondsworth, 1994), p. 168.

44. Cairns Craig, 'Going Down to Hell is Easy: *Lanark*, Realism and the Limits of the Imagination', in Robert Crawford and Thom Nairn (eds), *The Arts of Alasdair Gray* (Edinburgh, 1991), pp. 90–107 [106].

45. Julia Thrift, 'The seamy side of sexless Scotland', *The Independent*, 28 November 1992, p. 29.

46. Gray, *Poor Things*, p. 272.

47. James Kelman, Agnes Owens, Alasdair Gray, *Lean Tales* (London, 1985), book jacket.

48. S. J. Boyd, 'Black Arts: *1982 Janine* and *Something Leather*', in Crawford and Nairn (eds), *The Arts of Alasdair Gray*, pp. 108–23 [122].

49. Wilson, 'Interview: Iain Banks', p. 4.

50. Interview with Iain Banks, *Festival Times*, 17–23 August 1991, p. 57.

51. See Thom Nairn, review of *Canal Dreams*, *Scottish Literary Journal*, S32 (1990), pp. 50–52 [50].

52. Some reviewers found neither positive nor negative distinction in *The Wasp Factory*. According to Banks, 'The archetypal negative review was the one in *The Times* that said that it "soars to the level of mediocrity" . . . Later I found out . . . that [the reviewer's] day job when he wasn't writing reviews for *The Times* was working for Conservative Party Central Office. That was just the icing on the cake – I don't *want* a review from you bastards!' See James Robertson, 'Bridging Styles: A Conversation with Iain Banks', *Radical Scotland*, no. 42 (December 1989/January 1990), pp. 26–7 [26].

53. Patricia Craig, 'Exterminating Agents', *TLS*, 16 March 1984, p. 287.

54. Thom Nairn, 'Iain Banks and the Fiction Factory', in Wallace and Stevenson (eds), *The Scottish Novel Since the Seventies*, pp. 127–35 [128].

55. Helen Birch, 'A troubled news junkie', *The Independent*, 25 September 1993, p. 33.

56. Geraldine Brennan, 'Earthy, seedy and sexy', *The Observer Review*, 19 June 1994, p. 22.

57. Samuel R. Delany, 'In Love with Sara ffitch', *New York Times Book Review*, 91, no. 9 (2 March 1986), p. 37.

58. Christopher Carrell (ed.), *Seven Poets* (Glasgow, 1981), p. 34.

59. Sorley MacLean/Somhairle MacGill-Eain, *From Wood to Ridge/O Choille gu Bearradh, Collected Poems in Gaelic and English* (Manchester, 1989), p. 131.

60. Edwin Morgan, 'The Worlds', *Collected Poems* (Manchester, 1990), pp. 383–4 [384].

61. A. L. Kennedy, *Looking for the Possible Dance* (London, 1994), p. 40.

62. W. S. Graham, *Collected Poems 1942–1977* (London, 1979), p. 93.

Chronology

DATE	POETRY AND DRAMA	PROSE	HISTORICAL/CULTURAL EVENTS
1707			Union of the Parliaments of Scotland and England
1715			Jacobite uprising for 'Old Pretender' (Prince James Francis Edward Stuart, *de jure* James VIII)
1721	Ramsay, Allan, *Poems*		Robert Walpole becomes Prime Minister
1724	Ramsay, Allan (ed.), *The Ever Green*; *The Tea Table Miscellany* (1724–37) including Lady Grizel Baillie, 'Werena my heart licht I wad die' and Elizabeth Wardlaw, 'Hardyknute'	Swift, Jonathan, *The Drapier's Letters* Defoe, Daniel, *Journal of the Plague Year*; *Moll Flanders*	
1725	Ramsay, Allan, *The Gentle Shepherd*		The Black Watch commissioned under General Wade to police the Highlands Shawfield anti-tax riots in Glasgow
1730	Thomson, James, *The Seasons*		*The Grub Street Journal* (–1737)
1736			Porteous riots in Edinburgh Allan Ramsay opens first regular public theatre in Scotland in Carrubber's Close, Edinburgh
1739		Hume, David, *A Treatise on Human Nature*	Formation of Black Watch Regiment First publication of *Scots Magazine*

DATE	POETRY AND DRAMA	PROSE	HISTORICAL/CULTURAL EVENTS
1740	Thomson, James and David Malloch, *The Masque of Alfred*		Ramsay, Allan, *Anne Bayne* (portrait)
1741		Hume, David, *Essays Moral and Political*	Richardson, Samuel, *Pamela*
1745			Jacobite uprising for Charles Edward Stuart ('The Young Pretender')
1746			16 April, Battle of Culloden; Jacobites defeated by army under Duke of Cumberland
1748	Thomson, James, *The Castle of Indolence*	Hume, David, *An Enquiry Concerning Human Understanding* Smollett, Tobias, *The Adventures of Roderick Random*	*Aberdeen Press and Journal* founded as *The Aberdeen's Journal and North British Magazine*
1751		Home, Henry, Lord Kames, *Essays on the Principles of Morality and Natural Religion*	
1756	Home, John, *Douglas*		
1757		Smollett, Tobias, *A Complete History of England from the Descent of Julius Caesar to the Treaty of Aix-la-Chapelle*, 3 vols (–1758)	Ramsay, Allan, 'Margaret Lindsay' (portrait)
1759		Smith, Adam, *Theory of Moral Sentiments*	Voltaire, *Candide*
1760	Blacklock, Thomas, *A Collection of Original Poems* Macpherson, James, *Fragments of Ancient Poetry Collected in the Highlands of Scotland and Translated from the Gallic or Erse Language* ('Ossian')		George III (r. 1760–1820) Sterne, Laurence, *Tristram Shandy*, Vols I–II (completed 1767) Hamilton, Gavin, *Achilles Mourning Patroclus* Kelly, Thomas Alexander Erskine, Earl of, *Symphony in C major* (before 1761)

CHRONOLOGY   353

DATE	POETRY AND DRAMA	PROSE	HISTORICAL/CULTURAL EVENTS
1763		Blair, Hugh, *A Critical Dissertation on the Poems of Ossian* Hume, David, *History of England from the Invasion of Julius Caesar to the Revolution of 1688*, 5 vols (aka *History of Great Britain*)	Peace of Paris ends Seven Years' War 16 May, James Boswell meets Samuel Johnson
1767	Publication of Gaelic poems by Duncan Bàn Macintyre, Dugald Buchanan and John MacCodrum in the 1760s contributes to Gaelic vernacular revival		Allan Ramsay (eldest son of the poet) appointed portrait painter to George III Runciman, John, *King Lear in the Storm*
1768	Ross, Alexander, *Helenore, or The Fortunate Shepherdess* Wilkie, William, *Fables*		Forth & Clyde Canal begun James Cook's first voyage of discovery begins: charts coasts of New Zealand and Western Australia Sterne, Laurence, *A Sentimental Journey*
1769	Elliot, Jean, 'The Flowers of the Forest', in David Herd, *The Ancient and Modern Scots Songs, Heroic Ballads, &c*		First Co-operative Society in Britain founded by weavers in Fenwick, Ayrshire Kelly, Thomas, Alexander Erskine, Earl of, *Trio Sonata in C*
1771	Beattie, James, *The Minstrel*, 2 vols (1771–74)	Mackenzie, Henry, *The Man of Feeling* Smollett, Tobias, *The Expedition of Humphry Clinker*	Transfer of Scottish lowland population in the course of 'improvement' Complete *Encyclopedia Britannica* published in Edinburgh More, Jacob, *The Falls of Clyde: Cora Linn*
1773	Fergusson, Robert, *Poems*	Burnett, James, Lord Monboddo, *Of the Origin and Progress of Language* (–1792) Mackenzie, Henry, *The Man of the World*	16 December, The Boston Tea Party August–November, Boswell and Johnson tour Scottish Highlands and Western Isles

DATE	POETRY AND DRAMA	PROSE	HISTORICAL/CULTURAL EVENTS
1776		Smith, Adam, *An Inquiry into the Nature and Causes of the Wealth of Nations*	4 July, American Declaration of Independence
			Gibbon, Edward, *Decline and Fall of the Roman Empire* (−1788)
1785		Boswell, James, *Journal of a Tour to the Hebrides*	James Watt and Matthew Bolton instal steam engine with rotary motion in cotton-spinning factory in Nottinghamshire
			The Highland and Agricultural Society of Scotland formed in Edinburgh to enquire into the condition and means for improvement of the Highlands and Islands
1786	Burns, Robert, *Poems Chiefly in the Scottish Dialect*, Kilmarnock Edition	Beattie, James, *The Evidence of the Christian Religion Briefly and Plainly Stated*	Mozart, *The Marriage of Figaro*
1787	Burns, Robert (ed.), *Scots Musical Museum*, 6 vols (−1803)		First Scottish lighthouse built at Kinnaird Head, Fraserburgh
1788		Reid, Thomas, *Essays on the Active Powers of the Human Mind*	Death of Young Pretender
1789			French Revolution, Storming of the Bastille
			Blake, William, *Songs of Innocence*
1790	Baillie, Joanna, *Poems; Wherein it is Attempted to Describe Certain Views of Nature and of Rustic Manners* (published anonymously)		Transfer and removal of Highland population accelerates towards the Clearances of the nineteenth century
			Forth & Clyde Canal opened

DATE	POETRY AND DRAMA	PROSE	HISTORICAL/CULTURAL EVENTS
1791	Burns, Robert, 'Tam O' Shanter'; 'Ae Fond Kiss'	Boswell, James, *The Life of Samuel Johnson, LL.D.*	Henry Dundas becomes Home Secretary
			Paine, Thomas, *The Rights of Man*, Part I
			The Observer founded Mozart, *The Magic Flute*
1792		Stewart, Dugald, *Elements of the Philosophy of the Human Mind*, 3 vols (−1827)	Associated Friends of the People for Parliamentary Reform constituted in Edinburgh
			Paine, Thomas, *The Rights of Man*, Part II
			Wollstonecroft, Mary, *Vindication of the Rights of Women*
			Raeburn, Henry, *Sir John and Lady Clerk of Penicuik* (portrait)
1800	Baillie, Joanna, *De Montfort*	Leyden, John, *Journal of a Tour of the Highlands and Western Islands of Scotland*	Bill of Union of Great Britain and Ireland
			Second Edition of *Lyrical Ballads* by Wordsworth and Coleridge, includes Wordsworth's 'Preface'
1802	Scott, Sir Walter, *The Minstrelsy of the Scottish Border*, Vols I–II		Thomas Telford begins building roads in the Scottish Highlands
			Edinburgh Review (−1929) founded by Sydney Smith, Francis Horner and Francis Jeffrey
			Nasmyth, Alexander, *West Loch Tarbert, looking North*
1803	Campbell, Thomas, *Poems* Scott, Sir Walter, *The Minstrelsy of the Scottish Border*, Vol. III	Grant, Ann of Laggan, *Letters from the Mountains*	Caledonian Canal begun Raeburn, Henry, *The Macnab* (portrait) Wordsworth, Dorothy, *Recollections of a Tour Made in Scotland*

DATE	POETRY AND DRAMA	PROSE	HISTORICAL/CULTURAL EVENTS
1804	Brown, Thomas, *Poems*		Napoleon crowned Emperor
			Beethoven, Symphony No. 3 ('Eroica')
1805	Scott, Sir Walter, *The Lay of the Last Minstrel*		Battles of Trafalgar and Austerlitz
			Mungo Park sets off on expedition to trace the course of the river Niger
			The Glasgow Advertiser, founded 1783, changes its name to *The Glasgow Herald*
1807	Byron, *Hours of Idleness*		Wilkie, David, *The Rent Day*
1808	Grant, Anne, *Highlanders and Other Poems*	Hamilton, Elizabeth, *The Cottagers of Glenburnie*	Goethe, *Faust*, Part I
	Scott, Sir Walter, *Marmion*		Beethoven, Symphony No. 5; Symphony No. 6 ('Pastoral')
1809	Byron, *English Bards and Scotch Reviewers*		Raeburn, Henry, *Mrs Spiers* (portrait)
1810	Scott, Sir Walter, *The Lady of the Lake*	Brunton, Mary, *Self-Control*	US reopens commerce with Britain
1812	Byron, *Childe Harold's Pilgrimage*, Cantos I–II		US declares war on Britain
			Napoleon retreats from Moscow
			Weavers' strike in Glasgow and the West of Scotland
			Henry Bell's steamship *Comet* plies on the river Clyde
1813	Byron, *The Giaour* and *The Bride of Abydos*		Austen, Jane, *Pride and Prejudice*
	Hogg, James, *The Queen's Wake*		
1814	Byron, *The Corsair*	Brunton, Mary, *Discipline*	First effective steam locomotive built by George Stephenson
		Scott, Sir Walter, *Waverley*	

DATE	POETRY AND DRAMA	PROSE	HISTORICAL/CULTURAL EVENTS
1814 (cont.)			Highland Clearances in Sutherland begin under the factorship of Patrick Sellar
1815		Park, Mungo, *Journal of a Mission to the Interior of Africa in the Year 1805* Scott, Sir Walter, *Guy Mannering*	Battle of Waterloo Wilkie, David, *Distraining for Rent*
1816	Byron, *The Siege of Corinth*; *Childe Harold's Pilgrimage*, Canto III	Scott, Sir Walter, *The Antiquary*; *Old Mortality*	Byron leaves Britain Sir Walter Scott begins developing Abbotsford (purchased 1811) Patrick Sellar acquitted at Inverness of causing any injury or forced eviction by burning or homicide
1817	Byron, *Manfred* Baillie, Joanna, *The Election* Pringle, Thomas, *The Autumnal Excursion, or Sketches in Teviotdale*		*Blackwood's Magazine* founded *The Scotsman* founded
1818	Byron, *Childe Harold's Pilgrimage*, Canto IV	Ferrier, Susan, *Marriage* Hogg, James, *The Brownie of Bodsbeck* Scott, Sir Walter, *The Heart of Midlothian*; *Rob Roy*	Shelley, Mary Wollstonecroft, *Frankenstein* Hamilton, Thomas, Monument to Robert Burns, Alloway
1820	[Scott] *Ivanhoe*: several stage adaptations	Brown, Thomas, *Lectures on the Philosophy of the Human Mind* Scott, Sir Walter, *Ivanhoe*	Andrew Hardie and John Baird, Glasgow weavers, hanged for treason after the 'Radical Rising' of the weavers Shelley, Percy Bysshe, *Prometheus Unbound* and 'Ode to the West Wind'
1821	Baillie, Joanna, *Metrical Legends*	Scott, Sir Walter, *Kenilworth*	Greek War of Independence begins

DATE	POETRY AND DRAMA	PROSE	HISTORICAL/CULTURAL EVENTS
1821 (*cont.*)	Byron, *Don Juan* (begun 1819), III–V; *Sardanapalus* [Scott] *Kenilworth*: several stage adaptations	Galt, John, *Annals of the Parish*; *The Ayrshire Legatees*	*Manchester Guardian* founded
1824	*The Scottish Minstrel*, 6 vols (includes ballads and songs by Carolina Oliphant, Lady Nairne, under her pseudonym 'Mrs Bogan of Bogan') Byron, *Don Juan*, XV–XVI	Ferrier, Susan, *The Inheritance* Hogg, James, *The Private Memoirs and Confessions of a Justified Sinner* Lockhart, John Gibson, *The History of Matthew Wald* Moir, David Macbeth, *The Life of Mansie Wauch, Tailor of Dalkeith*, serialized in *Blackwood's Magazine* Scott, Sir Walter, *Redgauntlet*	Founding of Royal Society for the Prevention of Cruelty to Animals First performance in Vienna of Beethoven, Symphony No. 9 ('Choral')
1836		Carlyle, Thomas, *Sartor Resartus*	Dickens, Charles, *Sketches by Boz*; *Pickwick Papers*
1837		Carlyle, Thomas, *The French Revolution* Lockhart, John Gibson, *Memoirs of the Life of Sir Walter Scott Bart.*, 7 vols (–1838)	Death of William IV; Queen Victoria succeeds to throne (–1901) Wilkie, David, *The Cotter's Saturday Night*
1840	Baillie, Joanna, *Fugitive Verses* (reprint of anonymously published *Poems* of 1790)		Architectural Institute of Scotland founded Kemp, George, Scott Museum, Edinburgh Lauder, Robert Scott, *David Roberts in Eastern Costume*
1841		Carlyle, Thomas, *On Heroes and Hero-Worship* Miller, Hugh, *The Old Red Sandstone*	David Livingstone discovers Lake Ngami Sir James Ross discovers the 'Great Southern Continent' (Antarctica)

DATE	POETRY AND DRAMA	PROSE	HISTORICAL/CULTURAL EVENTS
1842			Mendelssohn, Felix, Symphony No. 3 ('Scotch') inspired by a visit to Holyrood in 1829
1843		Carlyle, Thomas, *Past and Present*	Disruption of the Church of Scotland: formation of United Free Church
1845		Carlyle, Thomas, *Cromwell's Letters and Speeches*	Lauder, Robert Scott, *Christ Teacheth Humility*
			Wagner, Richard, *Tannhäuser*
1847		Miller, Hugh, *First Impressions of England and Its People*	Chloroform used as anaesthetic by Sir James Simpson
			Brontë, Charlotte, *Jane Eyre*
			Brontë, Emily, *Wuthering Heights*
1848			'Year of Revolutions'; Karl Marx and Friedrich Engels issue *Communist Manifesto*
1849	Aytoun, William Edmonstone, *Lays of the Scottish Cavaliers and Other Poems*	Miller, Hugh, *Footprints of the Creator*	
		Oliphant, Margaret, *Margaret Maitland*	
1850		Carlyle, Thomas, *Latter Day Pamphlets*	
1851		Carlyle, Thomas, *Life of John Sterling*	Melville, Herman, *Moby Dick*
1852			Formation of Highland Emigration Society in London
			Stowe, Harriet Beecher, *Uncle Tom's Cabin*
1854			Crimean War begins
			Society of St Andrews golfers formed
1856		Cockburn, Henry Thomas, Lord, *Memorials of His Time*	

DATE	POETRY AND DRAMA	PROSE	HISTORICAL/CULTURAL EVENTS
1857	Smith, Alexander, *City Poems*	Livingstone, David, *Missionary Travels and Researches in South Africa*	
1858		Ballantyne, R. M., *Coral Island*	
		Carlyle, Thomas, *The History of Friedrich II of Prussia*, 6 vols (1858–65)	
		MacDonald, George, *Phantastes*	
		Ramsay, Edward Bannerman, *Reminiscences of Scottish Life*	
1859		Smiles, Samuel, *Self-Help*	Darwin, Charles, *The Origin of the Species by Natural Selection*
			Chambers's Encyclopedia, ed. Robert Chambers (–1868)
			National Gallery of Scotland founded
1861			Outbreak of American Civil War (–1865)
			Royal Glasgow Institute of the Fine Arts founded to provide annual exhibition of the work of living artists
1862		Miller, Hugh, *Essays*	
1863		MacDonald, George, *David Elginbrod*	
		Oliphant, Margaret, *Salem Chapel*	
1865		MacDonald, George, *Alec Forbes of Howglen*	Salvation Army founded
		Smith, Alexander, *A Summer in Skye*	Caroll, Lewis, *Alice's Adventures in Wonderland*
1866		Oliphant, Margaret, *Miss Marjoribanks*	Dostoevsky, Fyodor, *Crime and Punishment*

DATE	POETRY AND DRAMA	PROSE	HISTORICAL/CULTURAL EVENTS
1867		Oliphant, Margaret, *Dealings with the Fairies*	Arnold, Matthew, *On the Study of Celtic Literature*
1871		MacDonald, George, *At the Back of the North Wind*	Eliot, George, *Middlemarch*
1872	Neaves, Charles, Lord, *Songs and Verses: Social and Scientific*	MacDonald, George, *The Princess and the Goblin*	
1874	Thomson, James (B. V.), *The City of Dreadful Night* (in instalments in the *National Reformer*)		Wagner, Richard, *Götterdämmerung*
1878	Anderson, Alexander, *Songs of the Rail*		Roman Catholic hierarchy restored in Scotland
1879		MacDonald, George, *Sir Gibbie* Stevenson, Robert Louis, *Travels with a Donkey*	Tay Bridge disaster MacKenzie, Sir Alexander, Scottish Piano Concerto
1880	Thomson, James (B. V.), *The City of Dreadful Night and Other Poems*		Bruch, Max, *Fantasie for violin with orchestra and harp, with the free use of Scottish folk melodies*
1881		Stevenson, Robert Louis, *Virginibus Puerisque* Thomson, James (B. V.), *Essays and Phantasies*	Rosebery campaigns for Scottish governmental reforms in response to growing national sentiment McTaggart, William, *The Wave*
1882		MacDonald, George, *Orts* Oliphant, Margaret, *A Little Pilgrim in the Unseen*	The 'battle of Braes' on Skye Highland Land League
1883		Oliphant, Margaret, *Hester* Stevenson, Robert Louis, *Treasure Island*	Melville, Arthur, *Evie, the Flower Girl*
1886		Oliphant, Margaret, *Effie Ogilvie* Stevenson, Robert Louis, *The Strange Case of Dr Jekyll and Mr Hyde; Kidnapped*	Scottish Home Rule Association founded English translation of Karl Marx, *Das Capital*, Vol. I

DATE	POETRY AND DRAMA	PROSE	HISTORICAL/CULTURAL EVENTS
1888		Barrie, J. M., *Auld Licht Idylls*	Scottish Labour Party founded, led by Gavin Clark, R. B. Cunninghame Graham and James Keir Hardie
			Mackenzie, Sir Alexander Campbell, *Benedictus*
1889		Stevenson, Robert Louis, *The Master of Ballantrae*	
		Barrie, J. M., *A Window in Thrums*	
1890	McGonagall, William, *Poetic Gems*	Oliphant, Margaret, *Kirsteen*	Forth railway bridge completed
1891		Barrie, J. M., *The Little Minister*	Pope Leo XIII issues encyclical *Rerum Novarum* on condition of working classes and becomes known as 'the working man's Pope'
		Conan Doyle, *The Adventures of Sherlock Holmes* begins in *Strand Magazine*	
		Oliphant, Margaret, *The Railway Man and His Children*	
1893	Davidson, John, *Fleet Street Eclogues*	Crockett, S. R., *The Stickit Minister*	
1894	Davidson, John, *Ballads and Songs*	Crockett, S. R., *The Raiders*	*The Yellow Book* (1894–97)
		Maclaren, Ian (John Watson), *Beside the Bonnie Briar Bush*	Kipling, Rudyard, *The Jungle Book*
			MacCunn, Hamish, *Jeanie Deans*
		Macleod, Fiona (William Sharp), *Pharais, A Romance of the Isles*	
1895		Crockett, S. R., *The Men of the Moss Haggs*	Marconi invents wireless telegraphy
		Macleod, Fiona (William Sharp), *The Mountain Lovers*	Auguste and Louis Lumière invent the cinematograph
		MacDonald, George, *Lilith; The Lost Princess*	Trial and imprisonment of Oscar Wilde
			McTaggart, William, *The Sailing of the Emigrant Ship*
			Yeats, W. B., *Poems*

DATE	POETRY AND DRAMA	PROSE	HISTORICAL/CULTURAL EVENTS
1896		Barrie, J. M., *Margaret Ogilvy*	Chekhov, Anton, *The Seagull*
		Munro, Neil, *The Lost Pibroch*	McEwen, Sir John Blackwood, *String Quartet in F major*
		Stevenson, Robert Louis, *Weir of Hermiston*	Glasgow underground opened
		Findlater, Jane, *The Green Graves of Balgowrie*	
1897	Barrie, J. M., *The Little Minister* (stage version)		Scottish Trades Union Congress formed
	Davidson, John, *New Ballads*		Rostand, Edmond, *Cyrano de Bergerac*
1898		Munro, Neil, *John Splendid*	Pierre and Marie Curie discover radium
		Grant, Elizabeth of Rothiemurcus, *Memoirs of a Highland Lady*	
		Buchan, John, *John Burnet of Barns*	
1899	Davidson, John, *The Last Ballad and Other Poems*	Clouston, J. S., *The Lunatic at Large*	Anglo-Boer War begins
			Ellis, Havelock, *Studies in the Psychology of Sex* (–1900)
			Elgar, Edward, *Enigma Variations*
1900	Murray, Charles, *Hamewith*	Carnegie, Andrew, *The Gospel of Wealth*	Charles Rennie Mackintosh's work exhibited at the Vienna Secession
		Cunninghame Graham, R. B., *Thirteen Stories*	Scottish Workers' Parliamentary Committee formed
1901	Davidson, John, *The Testament of a Vivisector*; *The Testament of a Man Forbid*	Brown, George Douglas, *The House with the Green Shutters*	Death of Queen Victoria; accession of Edward VII (r. 1901–10)
	Barrie, J. M., *Quality Street*		Freud, Sigmund, *The Psychopathology of Everyday Life*
1902	Barrie, J. M., *The Admirable Crichton*	Bell, J. J., *Wee MacGreegor*	

DATE	POETRY AND DRAMA	PROSE	HISTORICAL/CULTURAL EVENTS
1902 (cont.)		Conan Doyle, *The Hound of the Baskervilles*	
		Jacob, Violet, *The Sheep-stealers*	
1904	Barrie, J. M., *Peter Pan*	Jacob, Violet, *The Interloper*	Charles Rennie Mackintosh designs Willow Tea Rooms, Glasgow
		Geddes, Patrick, *City Development*	
1905	Davidson, John, *Selected Poems*		Abortive Russian revolution
			Albert Einstein formulates his first theory of relativity
1906	Archer, William, translations of the complete works of Henrik Ibsen, 11 vols (1906–7)		Scottish Federation of Women's Suffrage Societies formed
			Bone, Muirhead, *The Great Gantry, Charing Cross* (etching)
1907	Davidson, John, *God and Mammon* (1907–8)	Hay, Ian, *Pip*	Picasso, Pablo, *Les Demoiselles d'Avignon*
			McEwen, Sir John Blackwood, *Coronach*
1908	Davidson, John, *The Testament of John Davidson*	Grahame, Kenneth, *The Wind in the Willows*	
		Findlater, Jane and Mary, *Crossriggs*	
1909		Hay, Ian, *A Man's Man*	Henry Ford's 'Model T' car
			Completion of Glasgow School of Art designed by Charles Rennie Mackintosh
			McEwen, Sir John Blackwood, *Grey Galloway*
1910		Buchan, John, *Prester John*	George V (r. 1910–36)
			Union of South Africa becomes a dominion

DATE	POETRY AND DRAMA	PROSE	HISTORICAL/CULTURAL EVENTS
1910 (*cont.*)			Fergusson, J. D., *The Blue Beads* (portrait)
			Fergusson, J. D., *Les Eus* (1910–13)
1911		Jacob, Violet, *Flemington*	Winston Churchill speaks in Dundee in favour of a Scottish parliament
			Mahler, Gustav, *Das Lied von der Erde* ('The Song of the Earth')
1912		Conan Doyle, *The Lost World*	SS *Titanic* lost on maiden voyage
1913		MacKenzie, Sir Compton, *Sinister Street*	Lawrence, D. H., *Sons and Lovers*
			Stravinsky, Igor, *The Rite of Spring*
			McEwen, Sir John Blackwood, *Quartet for Strings* ('Biscay')
1914		Hay, John Macdougall, *Gillespie*	Outbreak of First World War (1914–18)
		Niven, Frederick, *The Justice of the Peace*	
1915	Jacob, Violet, *Songs of Angus*	Hay, Ian, *The First Hundred Thousand*	
		Buchan, John, *The Thirty-nine Steps*	
		Douglas, Norman, *Old Calabria*	
		Geddes, Patrick, *Cities in Evolution*	
1916		Buchan, John, *Greenmantle*	Sinn Fein Easter Rising in Dublin
			Anti-war demonstration on Glasgow Green
			John Maclean imprisoned for advocating termination of hostilities
			Peploe, S. J., *A Via Dolorosa, Mouquet Farm*

DATE	POETRY AND DRAMA	PROSE	HISTORICAL/CULTURAL EVENTS
1917	Murray, Charles, *A Sough o' War*	Barrie, J. M., *Dear Brutus* Douglas, Norman, *South Wind* Douglas, O., *The Setons*	February and Bolshevik Revolutions in Russia Jung, Carl, *The Unconscious*
1918			End of First World War: the Armistice John Maclean appointed Consul in Glasgow by USSR; tried for sedition Chaplin, Charlie, *Shoulder Arms*
1919		Buchan, John, *Mr Standfast* Smith, G. Gregory, *Scottish Literature: Character and Influence*	Versailles Peace Conference Strike in Glasgow in support of forty-hour week; police and military intervention
1920	Barrie, J. M., *Mary Rose* Murray, Charles, *In the Country Places*	Carswell, Catherine, *Open the Door!* Lindsay, David, *A Voyage to Arcturus*	Prohibition in USA First public broadcasting station in Britain *Northern Numbers* anthologies of contemporary Scottish writing ed. C. M. Grieve (Hugh MacDiarmid) Charles Rennie Mackintosh designs theatre for Margaret Morris
1922	Macgillivray, Pittendrigh, *Bog Myrtle and Peat Reek* Young, Andrew, *Thirty-One Poems*	Barrie, J. M., *Courage* Buchan, John, *Huntingtower* Carswell, Catherine, *The Camomile: an Invention*	Mussolini forms Fascist government in Italy British Broadcasting Company founded Eliot, T. S., *The Waste Land* Joyce, James, *Ulysses* C. M. Grieve edits *Scottish Chapbook* and first uses pseudonym 'Hugh MacDiarmid'

DATE	POETRY AND DRAMA	PROSE	HISTORICAL/CULTURAL EVENTS
1922 (*cont.*)			McCance, William, *Heavy Structures in a Landscape Setting*
			McEwen, John Blackwood, *A Solway Symphony* (first performance)
1923	Brandane, John (John MacIntyre), *The Glen is Mine*	C. M. Grieve, *Annals of the Five Senses* Mitchison, Naomi, *The Conquered*	Scottish Home Rule Association leads protest march of 30,000 in Glasgow USSR established
1924	Buchan, John (ed.), *The Northern Muse*		First British Labour Government Scott, Francis George, 'The Eemis Stane' *Les Peintres de L'Ecosse Moderne* exhibition of works by Cadell, Fergusson, Hunter and Peploe in Paris
1925	Cocker, W. D., *Dandie and Other Poems* MacDiarmid, Hugh, *Sangschaw* Muir, Edwin, *First Poems*	Mitchison, Naomi, *Cloud Cuckoo Land*	Hitler, Adolf, *Mein Kampf*, Vol. 1 McCance, William, *The Engineer, His Wife and Family* (linocut)
1926	MacDiarmid, Hugh, *Penny Wheep*; *A Drunk Man Looks at the Thistle*	Cocker, W. D., *Brave Days of Old* Gunn, Neil, *Grey Coast* MacDiarmid, Hugh, *Contemporary Scottish Studies*	Tory Government under Baldwin upgrades Scottish Secretary to Secretary of State for Scotland General Strike in Britain John Logie Baird invents television
1928	Joe Corrie, *In Time of Strife*	Shepherd, Nan, *The Quarry Wood*	National Party of Scotland founded under the leadership of J. M. MacCormick, aided by R. B. Cunninghame-Graham and C. M. Grieve (Hugh MacDiarmid)

DATE	POETRY AND DRAMA	PROSE	HISTORICAL/CULTURAL EVENTS
1930	Bridie, James, *The Anatomist*; *Tobias and the Angel*	Carswell, Catherine, *Life of Robert Burns* Carswell, Donald, *Sir Walter: A Four Part Study in Biography* Mitchison, Naomi, *The Hostages*	Gandhi begins civil disobedience campaign in India Evacuation of St Kilda
1931	MacDiarmid, Hugh, *First Hymn to Lenin and Other Poems*	Anderson, Willa, *Imagined Corners* Cronin, A. J., *Hatter's Castle* Linklater, Eric, *Juan in America* Macpherson, Ian, *Shepherd's Calendar* Mitchison, Naomi, *The Corn King and the Spring Queen*	Compton MacKenzie elected as Scottish Nationalist to Rectorship of Glasgow University Riots in Glasgow and London *Les Peintres Ecossais* exhibition in Paris of works by Peploe, Fergusson, Hunter, Cadell, Telfer Bear and R. O. Dunlop
1932	MacDiarmid, Hugh, *Scots Unbound and Other Poems*	Gibbon, Lewis Grassic, *Sunset Song* MacColla, Fionn, *The Albannach* Muir, Edwin, *Poor Tom*	Hunger marches in Britain Franklin D. Roosevelt elected US President Scottish Party founded Scott, Francis George, 'Milkwort and Bog Cotton'
1933	Bridie, James, *A Sleeping Clergyman* Campbell, John Lorne (ed.), *Highland Songs of the Forty-five* Young, Andrew, *Winter Harvest*	Anderson, Willa, *Mrs Ritchie* Gibbon, Lewis Grassic, *Cloud Howe* Macpherson, Ian, *Land of Our Fathers* Mitchison, Naomi, *The Delicate Fire*	Hitler becomes German Chancellor; persecution of Jews begins William Johnstone completes his masterpiece, *A Point in Time* (begun 1929; not exhibited until 1938)
1934	Cruickshank, Helen, *Up the Noran Water* MacDiarmid, Hugh, *Stony Limits and Other Poems* Muir, Edwin, *Variations on a Time Theme*	Allan, Dot, *Hunger March* Gibbon, Lewis Grassic, *Grey Granite* Linklater, Eric, *Magnus Merriman*	National Party of Scotland merges with Scottish Party to form Scottish National Party SS *Queen Mary* launched on Clyde

DATE	POETRY AND DRAMA	PROSE	HISTORICAL/CULTURAL EVENTS
1934 (cont.)		Reid, John Macnair, *Homeward Journey*	Hitler becomes Führer Cowie, James, *Falling Leaves*
1935	MacDiarmid, Hugh, *Second Hymn to Lenin and Other Poems* Soutar, William, *Poems in Scots*	Blake, George, *The Shipbuilders* McArthur, Alexander and H. Kingsley Long, *No Mean City* Muir, Edwin, *Scottish Journey*	Scottish National Party contests 8 seats in general election, with an average of 16% Eliot, T. S., *Murder in the Cathedral*
1936	Barrie, J. M., *The Boy David* Young, Andrew, *Collected Poems*	MacDiarmid, Hugh, *Scottish Eccentrics* Macpherson, Ian, *Wild Harbour* Muir, Edwin, *Scott and Scotland*	Spanish Civil War begins Edward VIII abdicates; George VI (r. 1936–52) BBC begins television service IRA declared illegal Saltire Society founded
1937	Corrie, Joe, *Hewers of Coal* McLellan, Robert, *Jamie the Saxt* Muir, Edwin, *Journeys and Places* Young, Andrew, *Nicodemus*	Cronin, A. J., *The Citadel* Gunn, Neil, *Highland River* Mackenzie, Compton, *The Four Winds of Love* (–1945) Niven, Frederick, *The Staff at Simsons*	Scottish National Party pledges itself to oppose conscription except by a Scottish Government Buber, Martin, *I and Thou*
1939		Barke, James, *The Land of the Leal* Mitchison, Naomi, *The Blood of the Martyrs*	World War II begins (–1945) Scottish Government departments transferred from London to Edinburgh with opening of St Andrew's House Joyce, James, *Finnegans Wake*
1941	Fraser, G. S., *The Fatal Landscape and Other Poems*	Buchan, John, *Sick Heart River* Gunn, Neil, *The Silver Darlings*	Germany invades Russia Japanese bomb Pearl Harbor and USA enters the war German blitz on Coventry

DATE	POETRY AND DRAMA	PROSE	HISTORICAL/CULTURAL EVENTS
1941 (*cont.*)			Labour committee publishes *The Plan for Post-War Scotland* pledging a self-governing Scotland with Parliament of Scottish MPs meeting in Edinburgh
1943	Bridie, James, *Mr Bolfry* MacLean, Sorley, *Dàin do Eimhir agus Dàin Eile (Poems to Eimhir and Other Poems)*	MacDiarmid, Hugh, *Lucky Poet*	Russian victory at Stalingrad Germans surrender in North Africa Fall of Mussolini
1947	McLellan, Robert, *The Flouers o Edinburgh* Stewart, Ena Lamont, *Men Should Weep*	Darling, Sir Frank Fraser, *Natural History in the Highlands and Islands* Hendry, J. F., *Fernie Brae* McCrone, Guy, *Wax Fruit* Mitchison, Naomi, *The Bull Calves* Tranter, Nigel, *Flight of Dutchmen; Island Twilight*	First Edinburgh International Festival Elder, Clarence, *The Silver Darlings* (film based on Neil Gunn's novel of 1941) Whyte, Ian, Symphony No. 1
1948	Hay, George Campbell, *Wind on Loch Fyne* Henderson, Hamish, *Elegies for the Dead* in *Cyrenaica* (rev. 1977) Kemp, Robert, *Let Wives Tak Tent*; adaptation of Sir David Lyndsay's *Ane Pleasant Satyre of the Three Estaitis* produced by Tyrone Guthrie at the Edinburgh Festival Smith, Sydney Goodsir, *Under the Eildon Tree* Soutar, William, *Collected Poems*, ed. Hugh MacDiarmid	Gaitens, Edward, *The Dance of the Apprentices* Tranter, Nigel, *Colours Flying*	Labour government under Clement Attlee rejects inquiry into devolution After end of British mandate, Zionist Jews declare State of Israel in Palestine

DATE	POETRY AND DRAMA	PROSE	HISTORICAL/CULTURAL EVENTS
1949	Muir, Edwin, *The Labyrinth* Scott, Francis George, *Songs: Thirty-five Scottish Lyrics and Other Poems Set to Music*	Haynes, Dorothy K., *Thou Shalt Not Suffer a Witch and Other Stories*	Apartheid programme begins in South Africa Republic of Eire proclaimed in Dublin Alexander Mackendrick, *Whisky Galore!* (film based on Compton Mackenzie's novel of 1947)
1950	Reid, Alexander, *The Lass wi' the Muckle Mou'* Young, Douglas, *Selected Poems*	Daiches, David, *Robert Burns*	Korean War begins Scottish Coronation Stone ('Stone of Destiny'), taken from Scotland by Edward I, is removed from Westminster Abbey by Scottish Nationalists (supposedly recovered at Arbroath, 1951)
1951			Conservatives win General Election; Winston Churchill becomes Prime Minister (−1955) Festival of Britain Whyte, Ian, *Donald of the Burthens* (ballet, choreographed by Massine) School of Scottish Studies established at the University of Edinburgh
1953	Reid, Alexander, *The Warld's Wonder*	Tranter, Nigel, *The Queen's Grace*	Coronation of Elizabeth II Korean armistice Mount Everest climbed by Hillary and Tensing Beckett, Samuel, *Waiting for Godot*
1954	Soutar, William, *Diaries of a Dying Man*, ed. Alexander Scott	Muir, Edwin, *An Autobiography*	End of food rationing Mackendrick, Alexander (story and direction), *The Maggie* Minelli, Vincente, *Brigadoon* (film based on play by Alan Jay Lerner)

DATE	POETRY AND DRAMA	PROSE	HISTORICAL/CULTURAL EVENTS
1955	Graham, W. S., *The Nightfishing* MacCaig, Norman, *Riding Lights* MacDiarmid, Hugh, *In Memoriam James Joyce* Tremayne, Sydney, *The Rock and the Bird*	Munro, Neil, *Para Handy Tales*	Launder, Frank, *Geordie* (film based on novel by David Walker) Eardley, Joan, *Children, Port Glasgow*
1956		Gunn, Neil, *The Atom of Delight* Jenkins, Robin, *The Cone-Gatherers* Kennaway, James, *Tunes of Glory* Mackenzie, Compton, *Thin Ice*	Suez crisis Soviet invasion of Hungary Donegan, Lonnie, 'Rock Island Line'
1957	Cameron, Norman, *Collected Poems* Singer, Burns, *Still and All* Young, Douglas, *The Puddocks: a Verse Play in Scots frae the auld Greek o Aristophanes*		CND march to Aldermaston Scottish Nationalist anti-nuclear agitation
1958	Young, Andrew, *Out of the World and Back* Buchan, Tom, *Ikons*	Hanley, Cliff, *Dancing in the Streets* Kesson, Jessie, *The White Bird Passes*	Redpath, Anne, *Landscape, Kyleakin* Relph, Michael, *Rockets Galore* (film based on Compton Mackenzie's novel of 1957)
1959	Brown, George Mackay, *Loaves and Fishes*	Duncan, Jane, *My Friend Muriel; My Friends the Miss Boyds* Fleming, Ian, *Goldfinger*	
1960	Finlay, Ian Hamilton, *The Dancers Inherit the Party* Muir, Edwin, *Collected Poems 1921–1958* MacCaig, Norman, *A Common Grace*	Trocchi, Alexander, *Cain's Book*	Oil discovered in North Sea Shooting of Africans at Sharpeville, South Africa Nigerian independence

DATE	POETRY AND DRAMA	PROSE	HISTORICAL/CULTURAL EVENTS
1960 (cont.)	MacColl, Ewan, *Singing the Fishing*, for radio		John F. Kennedy elected US President (assassinated 1963) Neame, Ronald, *Tunes of Glory* (film based on James Kennaway's novel of 1956)
1961	Smith, Iain Crichton, *Thistles and Roses* Finlay, Ian Hamilton, *Glasgow Beasts, and a Burd Haw, an Inseks, an, Aw, a Fush*	Dunnett, Dorothy, *Game of Kings* Jenkins, Robin, *Dust on the Paw* Spark, Muriel, *The Prime of Miss Jean Brodie* Tranter, Nigel, *Birds of a Feather* Trocchi, Alexander, *Young Adam*	Berlin Wall built Mass CND rally in London South Africa withdraws from the British Commonwealth Soviet astronaut Yuri Gagarin becomes first man in space Ian Hamilton Finlay and Sue Finlay edit the magazine, *Poor. Old. Tired. Horse.* (–1970)
1962	MacDiarmid, Hugh, *Collected Poems* Tremayne, Sydney, *The Swans of Berwick*	Mitchison, Naomi, *Memoirs of a Spacewoman*	Cuban missile crisis End of post-war National Service Stevenson, Ronald, *Passacaglia on DSCH*
1963	Scott, Tom, *The Ship and Ither Poems*	Kennaway, James, *The Bells of Shoreditch* Spark, Muriel, *The Girls of Slender Means*	Profumo scandal; resignation of Harold Macmillan (Prime Minister since 1957) Eardley, Joan, *Stormy Sea No. 1*
1964		Bermant, Chaim, *Jericho Sleep Alone* Dunnett, Dorothy, *Queen's Play* Friel, George, *The Boy Who Wanted Peace*	Forth Road Bridge opened
1965	Smith, Iain Crichton, *The Law and the Grace* Smith, Sydney Goodsir, *Kynd Kittock's Land*	Rae, Hugh C., *Skinner* Sharp, Alan, *A Green Tree in Gedde*	US offensive in Vietnam Scottish poetry magazine, *Akros*, founded and edited by Duncan Glen (–1983)

DATE	POETRY AND DRAMA	PROSE	HISTORICAL/CULTURAL EVENTS
1965 (cont.)	Wright, Tom, *There was a Man*		Paolozzi, Eduardo, *As is When* (screenprints)
1966	Garioch, Robert, *Selected Poems*	Hind, Archie, *The Dear Green Place*	Labour wins General Election
	MacCaig, Norman, *Surroundings*	McIlvanney, William, *Remedy is None*	Aberfan mining disaster
	Mackie, Alastair, *Soundings*	Tranter, Nigel, *A Stake in the Kingdom*	Rise of support for Scottish National Party
	Taylor, C. P., *The Ballachulish Beast*		Bellany, John, *My Father* (portrait)
1967	Conn, Stewart, *Thunder in the Air*	Rae, Hugh C., *Night Pillow*	Legalization of homosexual acts between consenting adults
	Morgan, Edwin, *Emergent Poems*	Urquhart, Fred, *The Dying Stallion*	Anti-Vietnam War demonstrations in Europe
			Winifred Ewing elected for Hamilton as SNP candidate, overturning Labour majority of 16,000
			The Beatles, *Sgt. Pepper's Lonely Hearts Club Band*
			Scottish Arts Council established
1968	Bold, Alan, *To Find the New*	Anderson, Willa, *Belonging*	Edward Heath sets up Scottish Constitutional Committee under former Tory Prime Minister Sir Alec Douglas-Home
	Conn, Stewart, *Stoats in the Sunlight*	Ford, James Allan, *A Judge of Men*	
	MacCaig, Norman, *Rings on a Tree*	Smith, Iain Crichton, *Consider the Lilies*	Oil rigs in North Sea
	Morgan, Edwin, *The Second Life*	Spark, Muriel, *The Public Image*	Martin Luther King and Robert Kennedy assassinated
	Scott, Alexander, *Cantrips*	Urquhart, Fred, *The Ploughing Match*	Ian Hamilton Finlay begins construction of his garden, 'Little Sparta', at Stonypath, Dunsyre, Lanarkshire
		Williams, Gordon, *From Scenes Like These*	
1971	Aitchison, James, *Sounds Before Sleep*	Davie, Elspeth, *Creating a Scene*	Anti-Vietnam War demonstrations in USA
	Brown, George Mackay, *Fishermen with Ploughs*	Dunnett, Dorothy, *The Ringed Castle*	Decimal currency introduced

DATE	POETRY AND DRAMA	PROSE	HISTORICAL/CULTURAL EVENTS
1971 (cont.)	Bruce, George, *Collected Poems 1939–70* Finlay, Ian Hamilton, *Poems to Hear and See*	Rae, Hugh C., *The Marksman*	Work-in at John Brown's shipyard organized by Jimmie Reid
1972	Bryden, Bill, *Willie Rough* Buchan, Tom, *Poems 1969–72* Conn, Stewart, *The Burning* Dunn, Douglas, *The Happier Life* Lochhead, Liz, *Memo for Spring* Morgan, Edwin, *Glasgow Sonnets*; *Instamatic Poems*; *Wi the Haill Voice*	Brown, George Mackay, *Greenvoe* Friel, George, *Mr Alfred M.A.* Spark, Muriel, *Not to Disturb*	Direct rule of Northern Ireland by British Government Miners' strike Stevenson, Ronald, 'Piano Concerto No. 2 ("The Continents")'
1973	McGrath, John, *The Cheviot, the Stag and the Black, Black Oil* MacMillan, Hector, *The Sash* MacMillan, Roddy, *The Bevellers* Morgan, Edwin, *From Glasgow to Saturn* Tremayne, Sydney, *Selected and New Poems*	Brown, George Mackay, *Magnus* Herdman, John, *A Truth Lover* Spark, Muriel, *The Hothouse by the East River*	Cease-fire in Vietnam IRA bombs in England Kilbrandon Commission supports legislative devolution for British historic nationalities Britain joins the EEC
1974	Dunn, Douglas, *Love or Nothing* Fulton, Robin, *Tree Lines* MacCaig, Norman, *The World's Room* Mackie, Alastair, *At the Heich Kirk-Yaird*	Morgan, Edwin, *Essays* Spark, Muriel, *The Abbess of Crewe*	Under Harold Wilson Labour wins General Election; Tory Opposition leader Edward Heath promises indirectly-elected Scottish Assembly US Watergate scandal; President Richard Nixon resigns to avoid impeachment by Congress Bellany, John, *Sea People* Finlay, Ian Hamilton, *Nuclear Sail* (monolith, 'Little Sparta')

DATE	POETRY AND DRAMA	PROSE	HISTORICAL/CULTURAL EVENTS
1975	Smith, Iain Crichton, *The Permanent Island*	Dunnett, Dorothy, *Checkmate* Garioch, Robert, *Two Men and a Blanket* McIlvanney, William, *Docherty*	Labour government under Harold Wilson issues White Paper offering Scotland legislative Assembly with no real economic power Jim Sillars, Labour MP for South Ayrshire, announces intention to found the Scottish Labour Party Third Eye Centre opens in Glasgow
1976	Campbell, Donald, *The Jesuit* Watson, Roderick, *True History on the Walls*	Rae, Hugh C., *Harkfast*	Devolution Bill passes second reading of Commons by majority of 45, with 55 of 71 Scottish MPs in favour; Michael Foot promises referendum John Ogilvie, Catholic martyr of 1617, canonized
1977	Gillies, Valerie, *Each Bright Eye* Graham, W. S., *Implements in Their Places* Greig, Andrew, *Men on Ice* McGrath, Tom, *The Hard Man* MacLean, Sorley, *Reothairt is Contraigh: Taghadh ole Dhàin/ Spring tide and Neap tide: Selected Poems 1932–72* Morgan, Edwin, *The New Divan* Perrie, Walter, *A Lamentation for the Children* Scott, Tom, *The Tree* Taylor, C. P., *Walter*	Daiches, David, *Scotland and the Union* Lindsay, Maurice, *History of Scottish Literature* (revised 1992) McIlvanney, William, *Laidlaw* Spence, Alan, *Its Colours They are Fine* Whyte, Don, *On the Lonely Shore* Williams, Gordon, *The Straw Dogs; Walk Don't Walk*	Devolution Bill destroyed in committee; new Bills introduced for Wales and Scotland become Acts in 1978

DATE	POETRY AND DRAMA	PROSE	HISTORICAL/CULTURAL EVENTS
1978	MacDiarmid, Hugh, *The Complete Poems*, 2 vols, ed. Michael Grieve and W. R. Aitken	Davie, Elspeth, *Climbers on a Stair* Massie, Allan, *Change and Decay in All Around I See* Rae, Hugh C., *Sullivan; The Travelling Soul*	Labour's George Cunningham forces requirement of 40% of Scottish voters to favour Scottish Assembly before pro-Assembly referendum result could be implemented Moffat, Sandy, *Sorley MacLean* (portrait)
1979	Black, David, *Gravitations* Bold, Alan, *This Fine Day* Dunn, Douglas, *Barbarians* Lindsay, Maurice, *Collected Poems* Morgan, Edwin, *Star Gate*	Jenkins, Robin, *Fergus Lamont*	In 1 March referendum Scottish electorate votes by narrow majority for establishment of Assembly in Edinburgh but fails to achieve 40% requirement James Callaghan's Labour government falls in General Election; Tory government under Margaret Thatcher repeals Scotland Act Johnstone, William, *Fragments of Experience*
1981	Dunn, Douglas, *St Kilda's Parliament* Lochhead, Liz, *The Grimm Sisters* Morrice, Ken, *For All I Know*	Calder, Angus, *Revolutionary Empire* Gray, Alasdair, *Lanark* Smith, Iain Crichton, *Murdo and Other Stories*	Riots in London, Liverpool and Manchester Bill Forsyth (story and direction), *Gregory's Girl*
1982	Lochhead, Liz, *Blood and Ice* Morgan, Edwin, *Poems of Thirty Years* Thomson, Derick, *Creachadh Na Clàrsaich/Collected Poems 1940–1980*	Massie, Allan, *The Death of Men* Rae, Hugh C., *Privileged Strangers*	The Falklands War SNP membership falls Federation of Scottish Sculptors founded First Mayfest arts festival in Glasgow
1983		Kelman, James, *Not Not While the Giro*	General Election; second Thatcher victory; Labour still holds Scotland with slight losses Burrell Collection, Glasgow: new building Bill Forsyth, *Local Hero*

DATE	POETRY AND DRAMA	PROSE	HISTORICAL/CULTURAL EVENTS
1984	Kuppner, Frank, *A Bad Day for the Sung Dynasty* Leonard, Tom, *Intimate Voices: Selected Work 1965–83* Lochhead, Liz, *Dreaming Frankenstein and Collected Poems* Smith, Iain Crichton, *The Exiles*	Gray, Alasdair, *Unlikely Stories, Mostly*; *1982 Janine* Kelman, James, *The Busconductor Hines* Lindsay, Frederic, *Brond* Massie, Allan, *One Night in Winter* Watson, Roderick, *The Literature of Scotland*	Miners' strike Bomb explodes during Conservative Party conference at Brighton SNP Conference declares for a Scottish Convention Bill Forsyth, *Comfort and Joy*
1985	Dunn, Douglas, *Elegies* Duffy, Carol Ann, *Standing Female Nude* Lochhead, Liz, *True Confessions and New Clichés* MacCaig, Norman, *Collected Poems* Martin, Troy Kennedy, *Edge of Darkness* (BBC TV) Montgomerie, William, *From Time to Time*	Banks, Iain, *Walking on Glass* Dunn, Douglas, *Secret Villages* Gray, Alasdair, *The Fall of Kelvin Walker* Kelman, James, *A Chancer* McIlvanney, William, *The Big Man*	End of dispute over pit closures Government steps up privatization programme Signature of Anglo-Irish Agreement on Northern Ireland by Margaret Thatcher and Dr Garrett Fitzgerald
1986	Dunn, Douglas, *Selected Poems 1964–1983* Morrice, Ken, *When Truth is Known*	Banks, Iain, *The Bridge*	Explosion at Chernobyl nuclear power station; Europe threatened by radioactive cloud Eduardo Paolozzi appointed Her Majesty's Sculptor in Ordinary for Scotland Currie, Ken, *The Self-Taught Man*
1987	Byrne, John, *The Slab Boys Trilogy* Duffy, Carol Ann, *Selling Manhattan* Jamie, Kathleen, *The Way We Live*	Banks, Iain, *Espedair Street* Herdman, John, *Three Novellas* Lindsay, Frederic, *Jill Rips*	Third Thatcher victory in General Election; Tory vote falls in Scotland British stock market crash Howson, Peter, *The Noble Dosser*

DATE	POETRY AND DRAMA	PROSE	HISTORICAL/CULTURAL EVENTS
1987 (cont.)	Kuppner, Frank, *The Intelligent Observation of Naked Women* Lochhead, Liz, *Mary Queen of Scots Got Her Head Chopped Off* Roper, Tony, *The Steamie*		'The Vigorous Imagination: New Scottish Art', exhibition of work by Howson, Currie, Hardie, Redfern, Wiszniewski and others, Edinburgh
1988	Dunn, Douglas, *Northlight* MacCaig, Norman, *Voice Over* Morgan, Edwin, *Themes on a Variation* Neill, William, *Making Tracks*	Banks, Iain, M., *The Player of Games*	Landslide SNP (Jim Sillars) defeat of Labour in Glasgow Govan Glasgow Garden Festival The Proclaimers, *Sunshine on Leith*
1989	MacBeth, George, *Collected Poems 1958–82* MacLean, Sorley, *O Choille gu Bearradh/ From Wood to Ridge: Collected Poems in Gaelic and English*	Banks, Iain, *Canal Dreams* Davidson, Toni, *And Thus Will I Freely Sing: An Anthology of Gay and Lesbian Writing from Scotland* (includes poetry) Kelman, James, *A Disaffection* Massie, Allan, *A Question of Loyalties* Tennant, Emma, *Two Women of London: The Strange Case of Ms Jekyll and Mrs Hyde* Wagner, John, Alan Grant and Robin Smith, *The Bogey Man*, no. 1	Revolutions in Eastern Europe; beginning of the break-up of the Warsaw Pact Tienanmen Square demonstrations in China SNP Conference calls for a Scottish parliament to restrict majority shareholding of companies holding land in Scotland to those resident and able to work there McGuire, Edward, *Peter Pan: The Ballet* MacLean, Will, *Skye Fisherman: In Memoriam* Runrig, *Searchlight*
1990	Aitchison, James, *Second Nature* Crawford, Robert, *A Scottish Assembly*; (with W. N. Herbert) *Sharawaggi*	Galloway, Janice, *The Trick is to Keep Breathing* Gray, Alasdair, *Something Leather*; *McGrotty and Ludmilla*	Reunification of Germany Nelson Mandela freed in South Africa Iraq invades Kuwait John Major replaces Margaret Thatcher as British Prime Minister

DATE	POETRY AND DRAMA	PROSE	HISTORICAL/CULTURAL EVENTS
1990 (cont.)	Duffy, Carol Ann, *The Other Country* Jackson, Alan, *Salutations: Collected Poems 1960–1989* Lindsay, Maurice, *Collected Poems 1940–1990* Morgan, Edwin, *Collected Poems* Riach, Alan, *This Folding Map*	Kennedy, A. L., *Night Geometry and the Garscadden Trains* Massie, Allan, *The Hanging Tree* Spark, Muriel, *Symposium* Spence, Alan, *The Magic Flute*	Glasgow designated Cultural Capital of Europe MacMillan, James, *The Confessions of Isobel Gowdie, for Orchestra* Leland, David, *The Big Man* (film based on William McIlvanney's 1985 novel of the same title) Weir, Judith, *The Vanishing Bridegroom*
1991	Herbert, W. N., *Dundee Doldrums; Anither Music* Kay, Jackie, *The Adoption Papers* Lochhead, Liz, *Bagpipe Muzak*	Kelman, James, *The Bum* Massie, Allan, *The Sins of the Father*	Gulf War Attempted coup in USSR; Mikhail Gorbachev resigns and Boris Yeltsin oversees break-up of Soviet regions into independent countries
1992	Byrne, John, *Colquhoun and MacBryde* Crawford, Robert, *Talkies* Dunn, Douglas (ed.), *The Faber Book of Twentieth-Century Scottish Poetry* Jamie, Kathleen, *The Golden Peak* Morgan, Edwin, *Cyrano de Bergerac*	Banks, Iain, *The Crow Road* Crawford, Robert, *Devolving English Literature* Gray, Alasdair, *Poor Things* Lindsay, Frederic, *After the Stranger Came* Tennant, Emma, *Faustine* Torrington, Jeff, *Swing Hammer Swing!*	General Election returns Conservative Party for fourth term of office Intensification of IRA attacks on British mainland Bill Clinton elected US President War in the former Yugoslavia MacMillan, James, *Veni, Veni Emmanuel: Concerto for Percussion and Orchestra*
1993	Duffy, Carol Ann, *Mean Time* Graham, W. S., *Aimed at Nobody*	Banks, Iain, *Complicity* Kennedy, A. L., *Looking for the Possible Dance* McCabe, Brian, *In a Dark Room with a Stranger*	UK and Irish Prime Ministers, John Major and Albert Reynolds, sign 12-point 'Downing Street Declaration' setting out general principles for holding peace talks on Northern Ireland

DATE	POETRY AND DRAMA	PROSE	HISTORICAL/CULTURAL EVENTS
1993 (*cont.*)		Massie, Allan, *These Enchanted Woods* Welsh, Irvine, *Trainspotting*	
1994	Duffy, Carol Ann, *Selected Poems* Morgan, Edwin, *Sweeping out the Dark* O'Rourke, Daniel (ed.), *Dream State: The New Scottish Poets* Smith, Iain Crichton, *Ends and Beginnings*	Brown, George Mackay, *Beside the Ocean of Time* Gray, Alasdair, *A History Maker* Kelman, James, *How Late It was, How Late* Massie, Allan, *The Ragged Lion* Welsh, Irvine, *The Acid House*	12 May, death of John Smith, Scottish leader of opposition Labour Party In Northern Ireland IRA announces ceasefire (August) followed by Loyalist paramilitaries (October) Cunningham, John, one-man exhibition in Edinburgh Capercaillie, *Capercaillie*
1995	Leonard, Tom, *Reports from the Present: Selected Work 1982–94* Riach, Alan, *First and Last Songs* Watson, Roderick (ed.), *The Poetry of Scotland*	Dunn, Douglas, *Boyfriends and Girlfriends* Kennedy, A. L., *So I am Glad* McLean, Duncan, *Bunker Man* Welsh, Irvine, *Marabou Stork Nightmares*	At the Conservative Party's annual conference in October Prime Minister John Major affirms Tory opposition to Labour's support for a Scottish parliament SNP wins by-election in Perth and Kinross with over 40% of vote Isle of Skye connected to the Scottish mainland by £30 million bridge

General Bibliographies

i) Bibliographies and reference guides

Aitken, William R. *Scottish Literature in English and Scots: A Guide to Information Sources* (1982) (An extensive though selective bibliographical source comprising six sections: General; to 1660; 1660–1800; 1800–1900; from 1900. Section six deals with popular and folk culture.)

Daiches, David (ed.) *A Companion to Scottish Culture* (1981) (Some 300 articles arranged alphabetically to cover all aspects of Scottish life, from children's street games and the Paisley shawl to the Scottish Enlightenment, Scottish medical history and Scotch whisky. An attractive, helpful compilation which should be the forerunner of an even more useful volume three times its size.)

Glen, Duncan *The Poetry of the Scots* (1991) (An introduction and bibliographical guide to poetry in Gaelic, Scots, Latin and English, with informative commentaries by the compiler.)

Keay, John and Julia Keay (eds) *Encyclopaedia of Scotland* (1994) (Combines a gazetteer, a biographical dictionary which excludes the living, and a basic historical reference work in one volume.)

Macleod, Isebail, Pauline Cairns, Caroline Macafee and Ruth Martin (eds) *The Scots Thesaurus* (1990) (Analyses Lowland Scots, giving insight into the life of Lowland Scotland from the late twelfth century to modern times.)

Robinson, Mairi (ed.) *The Concise Scots Dictionary* (1985; paperback 1987) (Includes an essay by A. J. Aitken, 'A History of Scots'. Based on larger predecessors, sharing their belief that languages and cultures survive because they are at the root of individual lives within a varied national culture.)

Royle, Trevor *The Mainstream Companion to Scottish Literature* (1993) (Updated edition of *The Macmillan Companion to Scottish Literature* [1983]. An indispensable guide including essays on lives and works of the principal poets, novelists, philosophers and dramatists from earliest times to the present who have written in English, Scots and Gaelic.)

Wallace, Gavin and Randall Stevenson (eds) *The Scottish Novel Since the Seventies: New Visions, Old Dreams* (1993) (See below under iii, History and criticism.)

ii) Literary, historical and cultural backgrounds

Aitken, A. J. and McArthur, T. (eds) *Languages of Scotland* (1979) (A collection of essays on various aspects of the Scottish language: historical, linguistic, and literary usage. Includes a survey of current studies in Gaelic and a bibliography.)

Beveridge, Craig and Ronald Turnbull *The Eclipse of Scottish Culture* (1989) (How Scotland has allowed itself to become marginalized.)

Broadie, Alexander *The Tradition of Scottish Philosophy: A New Perspective on the Enlightenment* (1990) (Considers the evolution of Scottish philosophy from the beginning of the fifteenth century, relating pre-Enlightenment ideas to those which followed. Sets Scottish philosophy in an internationalist continuum.)

Calder, Angus *Revolving Culture: Notes from the Scottish Republic* (1994) (Essays on society, politics and literature by one of Scotland's foremost commentators.)

Campbell, R. H. *Scotland since 1707: The Rise of an Industrial Society* (1965) (Considers the transformation of Scotland from an agrarian to an industrial economy in the attempt to suggest the country's unique problems and its contribution to the development of modern British industrial society.)

Campbell, R. H. and Andrew S. Skinner (eds) *The Origins and Nature of the Scottish Enlightenment* (1982) (A collection of essays on the Scottish Enlightenment divided into two parts: essays commenting broadly on institutional matters and the effects of the Enlightenment, and essays concentrating more narrowly on the way developments in philosophy and science served to question theological dogma.)

Chapman, Malcolm *The Gaelic Vision in Scottish Culture* (1978) (Discusses the relationship between 'Gaelic and English spheres of life', suggesting that the popular picture of Gaelic society is formed by the symbolic and metaphorical requirements of the larger society. There are chapters on 'Ossian and the Eighteenth Century' and 'Modern Gaelic Poetry'.)

Chitnis, Annand C. *The Scottish Enlightenment: A Social History* (1976) (The relationship of intellectual enlightenment to economic improvement, with accounts of the Scottish university system and the rise of societies, clubs and other institutions like the *Encyclopedia Britannica* and the *Edinburgh Review*.)

Crawford, Robert *Devolving English Literature* (1992) (Sets 'British' in the context of Scottish literature, questioning Anglocentricity. See in particular Chapter 1, 'The Scottish Invention of English Literature'.)

Crawford, Thomas *Society and the Lyric: A Study of the Song Culture of Eighteenth Century Scotland* (1979) (Considers a general and popular rather than folk tradition and places Burns's lyrics in this context.)

Daiches, David *The Paradox of Scottish Culture* (1964) (Argues that the effects of the Anglo-Scottish Union of Parliaments in 1707 were ambiguous in that, while the Church and legal system maintained Scottish identity, literature and the arts manifested a cosmopolitan influence.)

—— *Scotland and the Union* (1977) (The background to Union debate and an assessment of its effects.)

—— *Literature and Gentility in Scotland* (1982) (A collection of three lectures which deal with the effects on courtly poetry of the loss of the royal court in 1603, and trace the implications for Scottish identity of the failure of the Scots language to sustain itself as a medium reflecting social change. The linguistic dilemma is evident in a 'willed elegance' and a 'prim morality' finally brought to revolt by the achievement of MacDiarmid.)

Davie, George *The Democratic Intellect. Scotland and Her Universities in the 19th Century* (2nd edn, 1964) (A discussion of Scotland's traditional 'general degree' and the arguments for and against specialization which contributes to an understanding of 'Scotland's cultural contribution to the world'.)

—— *The Crisis of the Democratic Intellect* (1986) (A sequel to the above in which Davie considers ways in which the Scots, after the First World War, went out of their way to re-establish the primacy of intellect by preferring a generalist type of university education.)

Dick, Eddie (ed.) *From Limelight to Satellite: A Scottish Film Book* (1990) (Essays by several hands contribute to a history of the film in Scotland. Well illustrated and supplemented by a filmography from 1898 to 1990.)

Donaldson, William *Popular Literature in Victorian Scotland: Language, Fiction and the Press* (1986) (Studies the development of the nineteenth-century Scottish newspaper and weekly press and their miscellaneous offerings of news and original writing. Considers the impact of social and economic views expressed in popular-press fiction and the weekly press's encouragement of vernacular Scots.)

Ferguson, William *Scotland 1689 to the Present, The Edinburgh History of Scotland*, vol. 4 (1968) (In keeping with the conservative aim of the series, covers most aspects of modern Scottish history using factual narrative.)

Fergusson, J. D. *Modern Scottish Painting* (1943) (A painter's ideas about painting and sculpture as means of expressing the human reaction to life itself.)

Fyfe, J. G. (ed.) *Scottish Diaries and Memoirs 1550–1746* (1928)

—— *Scottish Diaries and Memoirs 1746–1843* (1942) (Eminently readable source books for the study of history which provide insights into Scottish life via a series of well-chosen extracts from diaries and memoirs.)

Graham, Henry G. *The Social Life of Scotland in the Eighteenth Century* (1909) (An evocation of a way of life as it is affected by Scotland's movement from social stagnation to energy and widespread wealth.)

Hardy, Forsyth *Scotland in Film* (1990) (A history both of screen representations of Scotland and of the development of the Scottish film industry.)

Hartley, Keith *Scottish Art Since 1900* (1989) (Catalogues with biographies, chronology and colour plates of the 1987 Edinburgh Festival exhibition, *The Vigorous Imagination*. Keith Hartley's essay traces the development of Scottish art in the twentieth century.)

Harvie, Christopher *Scotland and Nationalism: Scottish Society and Politics 1707–1994* (2nd edn, 1994) (A leading work in its field. Hostile to what he sees as the simplifications of nationalist pictures of a martyred nation, Harvie argues that Scotland's past has been forgotten as much by nationalists as by unionists and that its culture 'was the result of a peculiar dialogue between community and enterprise, Calvinism and rationalism, Scotland and "Britain", between the peoples and regions of a complicated, argumentative nation'. Relations between political and literary ideas are discussed in Chapter 3, 'The Intellectuals, 1707–1945'.)

Hay, M. V. *A Chain of Error in Scottish History* (1927) (A Catholic interpretation of Scottish history.)

Hook, Andrew *Scotland and America: A Study of Cultural Relations 1750–1835* (1975) (Evaluates the impact on America of the Scottish Enlightenment and Scottish literary romanticism from Ramsay to Scott and considers America's perceptions of Scotland during the period, particularly illuminating Scottish unpopularity during the Revolution.)

Houston, R. A. and I. D. Whyte *Scottish Society 1500–1800* (1989) (A collection of essays on various aspects of Scottish society in this period, including population mobility, food, continuity and change in urban society, the economic and social roles of women, the Clearances, and ending with an English perspective.)

Kay, Billy *Scots, The Mither Tongue* (1986) (A brisk discussion of the history and problems of the Scots tongue which contends that Scots preserves an older form of English than does the contemporary Standard English beloved of the Establishment.)

Lynch, Michael *Scotland: A New History* (1991; revised 1992) (Highly readable account of the subject from the Picts to the present day which keeps its eye on connections between the past and contemporary Scotland.)

Macafee, Caroline and Iseabail Macleod (eds) *The Nuttis Schell: Essays on the Scots Language Presented to A. J. Aitken* (1987) (Essays by several hands on lexicography, older Scots and modern Scots.)

Macmillan, Duncan *Scottish Art 1460–1990* (1990) (Thorough, well-illustrated survey of Scottish art which links the visual arts to Scotland's history and culture.)

McCrum, Robert, William Cran and Robert MacNeil *The Story of English*, New and Revised Edition (1992) (Chapter 4, 'The Guid Scots Tongue', summarizes the historical circumstances by which the Scots language declined to provincial status, and discusses the fate of Scots exported to America.)

Marr, Andrew *The Battle for Scotland* (1992) (An account of Scottish politics from the collapse of Liberalism, the rise of radical Labour and the securing of power by the Conservatives to more recent Tory insecurities and the complexities of Scottish nationalism. Includes a shrewd assessment of the Scottish National Party.)

Massie, Allan *101 Great Scots* (1987) (A personal selection of influential Scottish people which is worth a shelf of reference books. Massie's sprightly profiles give the salient facts coupled with the learned, provocative opinion of an independent intelligence which refreshes everything that engages its attention.)

Miller, Hugh *My Schools and Schoolmasters* (1854) (A contemporary account of literary, psychological and social tensions.)

Miller, Karl (ed.) *Memoirs of a Modern Scotland* (1970) (A collection of essays which, covering the period from the First World War to just after the Second, follow the course of Modernism in Scotland.)

Muir, Edwin *John Knox: A Portrait of a Calvinist* (1930) (An anti-Calvinist assessment of Knox's thinking and his damaging effect on the imagination. Includes a lucid analysis of Calvinist theology.)

Murison, David *The Guid Scots Tongue* (1977) (A lucid, brief history of the Scots language, well illustrated by examples from Barbour to McIlvanney.)

Pittock, Murray G. H. *The Invention of Scotland: The Stuart myth and the Scottish identity* (1991) (Considers the influence of the Stuart myth on the political and cultural life of Scotland today while offering insight into the radicalism of Scottish Jacobitism and suggesting that the myth gave unity to a nation struggling to retain its identity.)

Purser, John *Scotland's Music, A History of the Traditional and Classical Music of Scotland from Earliest Times to the Present Day* (1992) (Encompasses music from the eighth century BC to the present day with a keen sense of its relation to Scottish culture as a whole.)

Reilly, Patrick 'Catholics and Scottish Literature 1878–1978', *The Innes Review*, 29, no. 2 (Autumn 1978), pp. 183–203 (An introduction to Catholic interaction with Scottish literature which refers to representative figures from the Scoto-Irish descendants of potato-famine refugees, native Catholics from the Highlands and Islands, and converts.)

Rendall, Jane *The Origins of the Scottish Enlightenment* (1978) (Argues that Union, with its challenge to Calvinism among other things, provided the conditions for a Scottish Enlightenment which, unlike its English counterpart, produced a distinct pattern of ideas thanks to such original thinkers as Hume and Adam Smith.)

Scott, Paul H. *Andrew Fletcher and the Treaty of Union* (1992) (A biography which provides a full account of events leading up to Union and analyses of Fletcher's essays and speeches.)

—— (ed.) *Scotland: A Concise Cultural History* (1993) (A scholarly and accessible illustrated guide to all principal aspects of Scottish culture in the form of an introduction and 23 essays by experts in their fields.)

Smout, T. C. *A History of the Scottish People 1560–1830* (1969)

—— *A Century of the Scottish People 1830–1950* (1986) (Scholarly social history at its most readable. The second volume focuses on the working people and the poor. Particularly illuminating on the situation of women.)

Thompson, Harold W. *A Scottish Man of Feeling: Some Account of Henry MacKenzie Esq. of Edinburgh and of the Golden Age of Burns and Scott* (1931) (Not primarily intended as biography; attempts, by reference to the Sentimental Movement, to account for the literature of that 'Golden Age' which produced Hume, Burns and Scott.)

Thomson, Derick (ed.) *A Companion to Gaelic Scotland* (1983) (Organized as an encyclopedia, covering every aspect of its subject with essays from experts in their fields. Comprehensive bibliography.)

Underwood, Robert (ed.) *The Future of Scotland* (1977) (A collection of fourteen esssays about the main isues which have to be taken into account when planning Scotland's future. Particularly valuable are 'The Scottish Identity' by Christopher Smout, and 'The Arts in Scotland' by George Bruce.)

Wallace, Ian *Reflections on Scotland* (1988) (A picture-book tour of Scotland starting at the border with England and moving contemplatively north, with a lively and informative commentary. Fine photography in abundance to give a reader of the literature a feeling for the earth, the places and the lives that have been lived.)

Wendel, François (trans. Philip Mairet) *Calvin: The Origins and Development of His Religious Thought* (1963) (A short biography of Calvin
with a clear account of Calvin's theology.)
Young, Douglas *Scotland* (1971) (A lively discussion of all aspects of Scottish life and culture written at a time when a new spirit of national
identity was 'fermenting among this nation of individualists'. Includes a warning of the dangers of Scotland's 'swirling off into the
Celtic mists'.)

iii) History and criticism

Bold, Alan *Modern Scottish Literature* (1983) (An extensive study of modern Scottish literature which does not attempt synthesis, but devotes
two to three helpful pages to each of a large number of selected
authors.)
Burgess, Moira *The Glasgow Novel: a survey and bibliography*, 2nd edn
(1986) (An introduction to the Glasgow-based novel. Extensive reading list and annotated bibliography.)
Campbell, Ian *Kailyard: A New Assessment* (1981) (A discussion of the
phenomenon of the Kailyard in Scottish literature which does not
restrict itself to the writers of sentimental fiction, but uses the term
to signify particular attitudes to Scottish identity, and suggests that,
while creating a popular version of Scottishness, it may have made
the legitimate functioning of the Scottish imagination possible.)
Carrell, Christopher (ed.) *Seven Poets* (1981) (Essays by Neal Ascherson
on the significance of MacDiarmid and on MacCaig, Crichton
Smith, Mackay Brown, Garioch, MacLean and Morgan. Except for
MacDiarmid, all poets are interviewed by Marshall Walker. Paintings
and photographs of the seven poets by Alexander Moffat and Jessie
Ann Matthew. Selected poems by all poets except MacDiarmid.)
Craig, Cairns (General ed.) *The History of Scottish Literature* (1987–88). (A
four-volume collection of specialist essays by several scholars on
Scottish literature in its cultural and intellectual context. The three
volumes covering the period discussed in this book are listed separ-
ately under their editors.)
—— (ed.) *The History of Scottish Literature, Volume 4, Twentieth Century*
(1987) (Essays range from a discussion of modern poetry in Scots
before MacDiarmid to Scottish theatre from 1950 to 1980, challenging perceptions of Scottish literature as a tributary of the English tradition, showing that such views are at odds with the literature's
demonstrable evolution within its own culture.)

Craig, David *Scottish Literature and the Scottish People, 1680–1830* (1961)
(A 'social history' of Scottish literature which attempts to indicate
those moments in literature when the life of the people reveals itself
most genuinely.)

Fulton, Robin *Contemporary Scottish Poetry* (1974) (Groups contemporary
Scottish poets as individuals – Morgan, Crichton Smith, MacCaig
– and within contexts – Geographical and Social, Private, and Linguistic – in a discussion of poetic motivation.)

Gifford, Douglas *The Dear Green Place? The Novel in the West of Scotland*
(1985) (Fiction from the Glasgow area considered in terms of 'the
dear green place' as 'a metaphor used more than any other in the
twentieth century in Scottish literature'.)

——— (ed.) *The History of Scottish Literature, Volume 3, Nineteenth Century*
(1988) (Essays range from cultural and historical discussions by Paul
H. Scott and Christopher Harvie to Scots and Gaelic poetry and
nineteenth-century drama, providing an overall impression of a
literature which had 'lost its sense of identity and direction by the
end of the century'.)

Glen, Duncan *Hugh MacDiarmid and the Scottish Renaissance* (1964) (Lo-
cates MacDiarmid in a broad historical context of Scottish literature
and examines his role in the Scottish Renaissance of the twentieth
century with reference to contemporaries in poetry, drama and the
novel.)

Hart, Francis Russell *The Scottish Novel* (1978) (Substantial treatment of
the relation of genre to culture in the Scottish novel from Smollett
to Spark. An influential work which considers the paradox that
some Scottish writers have both assimilated and rejected the Scottish tradition.)

Hewitt, David and Michael Spiller (eds) *Literature of the North* (1983)
(Essays on a range of subjects from the fourteenth-century historian,
John of Fordun, to George MacDonald and writers of the Scottish
Renaissance.)

Hook, Andrew (ed.) *The History of Scottish Literature, Volume 2, 1660–
1800* (1987) (Essays consider cultural issues and problems of peri-
odization as well as individual writers and philosophers in the context
of an era which the editor characterizes as tense and uncertain.)

Hutchison, David *The Modern Scottish Theatre* (1977) (A historical and
critical account from nineteenth-century pantomime, variety and
commercial theatre to plays of the 1970s.)

Jack, R. D. S. *The Italian Influence on Scottish Literature* (1972) (Examines
the relationship between Scottish and Italian writing from the medieval period until Sir Walter Scott, concentrating on major figures
including Ramsay, Fergusson, Burns, Urquhart and Smollett.)

——— *Scottish Literature's Debt to Italy* (1986) (Continues the examination of the above volume into a discussion of Renaissance translations, James Thomson, Byron, Smollett and Scott. The last chapter considers twentieth-century writers including Edwin Morgan, Robert Garioch, Norman Douglas, Compton Mackenzie, Muriel Spark, Eric Linklater and Allan Massie.)

Kinsley, James (ed.) *Scottish Poetry: a Critical Survey* (1955) (Ten individual essays by recognized experts make this still an indispensable introduction to poetry from medieval times to the work of Hugh MacDiarmid, Edwin Muir and other poets of the early twentieth-century renaissance. There is 'A Note on Scottish Gaelic Poetry' by Douglas Young.)

Lindsay, Maurice *History of Scottish Literature* (1977; revised 1992) (A very readable survey of the literature from the thirteenth century to the present day by a well-known poet and broadcaster whose life has been devoted to Scottish culture. The revised edition includes comment on contemporary authors such as Liz Lochhead, James Kelman and Janice Galloway.)

—— (ed.) *As I Remember: Ten Scottish Authors Recall How Writing Began For Them* (1979) (Includes essays by George Mackay Brown, Robert Garioch, Norman MacCaig, Iain Crichton Smith and Lindsay himself.)

MacQueen, John *The Enlightenment and Scottish Literature, Volume One, Progress and Poetry* (1982) (Eighteenth-century Scottish literature and philosophy – Gaelic as well as Scots and English – expertly considered in the context of European cultural and intellectual history.)

Millar, J. H. *A Literary History of Scotland* (1903) (An early but elegant and discriminating literary history of Scotland from 1301 to the late Victorian era which gracefully confesses to the 'taint of partiality' and attacks the 'Kailyard' writers fashionable in his time.)

Morgan, Edwin *Essays* (1974) (Part III comprises eleven influential essays on Scottish literature from the work of MacDiarmid and Muir to the novels of Robin Jenkins and Scottish poetry in the 1960s.)

—— *Twentieth-Century Scottish Classics* (1987) (An illuminating choice of fiction published from 1900 to 1984.)

—— *Crossing the Border: Essays on Scottish Literature* (1990) (A collection of 22 hitherto uncollected or unpublished essays on Scottish literary subjects together with five essays reprinted from *Essays* [1974]: 'The Resources of Scotland', 'Dunbar and the Language of Poetry', 'The Poetry of Robert Louis Stevenson', 'MacDiarmid at Seventy-Five', and 'Edwin Muir'.)

Muir, Edwin *Scott and Scotland* (1936; reprinted 1982) (An original and provocative discussion not only of Sir Walter Scott but of the position of the writer in Scotland and the controversial topic of the Scots language.)

Murray, Isobel and Bob Tait *Ten Modern Scottish Novels* (1984) (Detailed readings of 'a selection of novels reasonably spread out over the past fifty years', from Lewis Grassic Gibbon's *A Scots Quair* to Alasdair Gray's *Lanark*.)

Nicholson, Colin *Poem, Purpose and Place: Shaping Identity in Contemporary Scottish Verse* (1992) (Interviews with fourteen poets from Sorley MacLean to Liz Lochhead, Ron Butlin and Ian Abbot, helpfully introduced and interlarded by Nicholson.)

Schwend, Joachim and Horst W. Drescher (eds) *Studies in Scottish Fiction: Twentieth Century, Scottish Studies* (publications of the Scottish Studies Centre of the Johannes Gutenberg Universität Mainz in Germersheim), vol. 10, 1990 (A collection of essays on fiction by several hands from George Douglas Brown to Edwin and Willa Muir.)

Smith, G. Gregory *Scottish Literature, Character and Influence* (1919) (A pioneering discussion of the literature in terms of national idiosyncrasy which includes seminal chapters on Burns and Scott. Ten connected essays deal with the character of Scottish literature and the influence it has exerted on others.)

Thomson, Derick *An Introduction to Gaelic Poetry* (1974; paperback edn 1989) (The best introduction to the range of Gaelic poetry for both those with and without the language.)

Wallace, Gavin and Randall Stevenson (eds) *The Scottish Novel Since the Seventies: New Visions, Old Dreams* (1993) (Essays on writers by several hands from Robin Jenkins and Muriel Spark to James Kelman and Janice Galloway in the context of contemporary issues: gender, postmodernism and political identity. Includes comprehensive bibliography of Scottish fiction since 1970.)

Watson, Roderick *The Literature of Scotland* (1984) (A comprehensive survey of Scottish literature to the 1980s in Scots, Gaelic and English. Scholarly, insightful and accessible.)

Whyte, Christopher (ed.) *Gendering the Nation: Studies in Modern Scottish Literature* (1995) (Five women and four men examine the relationship between gender and nationality, how male and female authors portray women, the treatment of sexuality in Scottish writing, the construction of Scottish masculinity and its relation to class and homophobia. Essays discuss modern fiction, theatre, poetry, film and television.)

Wittig, Kurt *The Scottish Tradition in Literature* (1958) (Written from the conviction that literature 'grows out of the life of the community', and with due respect for 'place and heritage', covers the subject from Barbour to Neil Gunn attending to the moral, aesthetic and intellectual values inherent in the Scottish literary tradition.)

iv) Anthologies

Burgess, Moira (ed.) *The Other Voice* (1987) (An anthology of Scottish women's writing since 1808, edited, with an introduction which argues that Scottish women writers share a tone of ironic detatchment.)

Cameron, Alasdair (ed.) *Scot-Free* (1990; reprinted 1993) (Seven plays, including John Byrne's *Writer's Cramp* [1977] and six works of varying length from the 1980s with an informative historical and analytical introduction by the editor.)

Crawford, Thomas, David Hewitt and Alexander Law (eds) *Longer Scottish Poems, Volume II 1650–1830* (1987) (Includes Elizabeth Wardlaw's 'Hardyknute' and work by David Mallet, William Hamilton of Bangour, Adam Skirving, James Beattie, John Mayne and Charles Keith with introductions and bibliographies.)

Davidson, Toni (ed.) *And Thus Will I Freely Sing: An Anthology of Gay and Lesbian Writing from Scotland* (1989) (Documentary, prose, fiction and verse with an introduction by Edwin Morgan.)

Dunn, Douglas (ed.) *The Faber Book of Twentieth-Century Scottish Poetry* (1992) (A substantial, meticulously chosen unpartisan selection with an informative introduction. The paperback edition of 1993 omits the poetry of Alasdair Maclean who withdrew it on political grounds. The book's only obvious shortcoming is the editor's exclusion of poems by himself.)

—— (ed.) *The Oxford Book of Scottish Short Stories* (1995) (Forty-four stories compiled by a distinguished practitioner of the form who modestly excludes himself. Ranges from traditional tales to work by James Kelman, Ronald Frame, Janice Galloway and A. L. Kennedy. The introduction is authoritative and enlightening.)

Gifford, Douglas (ed.) *Scottish Short Stories 1800–1900* (1971, reprinted 1981) (Eleven stories from Scott's 'The Two Drovers' to Stevenson's 'The Merry Men', chosen to give a wide picture of the Scottish tradition in fiction. Informative introduction and glossary of Scots words.)

Kerrigan, Catherine (ed.) *An Anthology of Scottish Women Poets* (1991) (Poetry from the Middle Ages to the present, from Lowland Scots and Gaelic traditions, reflecting women's experience of aristocratic, rural and industrial life. Meg Bateman supplies parallel translations of the Gaelic poems.)

King, Charles (ed.) *Twelve Modern Scottish Poets* (1971) (Well introduced selections from Edwin Muir, Hugh MacDiarmid, William Soutar, George Bruce, Robert Garioch, Norman MacCaig, Sydney Goodsir Smith, Tom Scott, Edwin Morgan, Alexander Scott, George Mackay Brown and Iain Crichton Smith.)

—— and Iain Crichton Smith (eds) *Twelve More Modern Scottish Poets* (1986) (Introductions are shorter than in the above volume but supplemented by statements from several of the poets, who are G. S. Fraser, George Campbell Hay, Maurice Lindsay, W. S. Graham, Derick Thomson, Alastair Mackie, Burns Singer, Stewart Conn, Douglas Dunn, Tom Leonard, Liz Lochhead and Valerie Gillies.)

Leonard, Tom (ed.) *Radical Renfrew: Poetry from the French Revolution to The First World War by poets born, or sometime resident in the County of Renfrewshire* (1990) (In addition to relatively well-known poets such as Robert Tannahill, Alexander Smith, James [B. V.] Thomson, William Sharp ['Fiona Macleod'] and John Davidson, the editor disinters and introduces forgotten writers from the archives of Paisley Central Library such as the spirited feminist, Marion Bernstein, and the satirist, Edward Polin.)

Lindsay, Maurice (ed.) *Modern Scottish Poetry: An Anthology of the Scottish Renaissance 1925–1985* (1986) (The fourth, updated edition of the anthology originally published as *Modern Scottish Poetry: An Anthology of the Scottish Renaissance 1925–45* [1946]. Selects poems in Scots, Gaelic and English.)

Lonsdale, Roger (ed.) *Eighteenth Century Women Poets* (1989) (Includes selections from Joanna Baillie and examples of poetry written by several Scottish writers whose work is not readily available elsewhere, e.g. Jean Adams, Christian Carstairs, Anne Hunter, Rebekah Carmichael, Janet Little and Isabella Kelly.)

MacDiarmid, Hugh (ed.) *The Golden Treasury of Scottish Poetry* (1940; reissued 1993) (The poet's influential, idiosyncratic selection, designed to show that Scottish poetry 'cannot be confined to a little Anglo-Scottish margin'.)

MacDougall, Carl (ed.) *The Devil and the Giro: Two Centuries of Scottish Stories* (1989; reprinted as a Canongate Classic, 1991) (Fifty stories arranged thematically with brief introductions by the editor.)

Mackenzie, Agnes Mure (ed.) *Scottish Pageant*, Vol. I, 55 BC to AD 1513; Vol. II, 1513–1625; Vol. III, 1625–1707; Vol. IV, 1707–1802 (1946–50) (Collections of passages written by Scots or about Scotland presenting a historical picture of Scottish history and culture as seen by those who lived through it and made it.)

MacQueen, John and Tom Scott (eds) *The Oxford Book of Scottish Verse* (1989; reissued 1995) (A comprehensive selection when first published in 1966. Still useful except for sketchy representation of twentieth-century writing.)

Milton, June (ed.) *Original Prints: New Writing from Scottish Women* (1985) (Two dozen stories with an introduction by Isobel Murray.)

Morgan, Edwin (ed.) *Scottish Satirical Verse* (1980) (Generous selections from the satirical tradition in poetry with an introduction, notes and glossary of Scots words.)

Murray, Ian (ed.) *The New Penguin Book of Scottish Short Stories* (1983) (Twenty stories from Hogg's 'The Brownie of the Black Haggs' to Iain Crichton Smith's 'Survival without Error'.)

O'Rourke, Daniel (ed.) *Dream State: The New Scottish Poets* (1994) (Work from 25 poets, all under 40, in English, Scots and Gaelic, with a helpful introduction by the editor and autobiographical notes by the poets.)

Summerhill, Geoffrey (ed.) *Worlds* (1974) (Selections from seven modern poets including Norman MacCaig and Edwin Morgan. Poems are complemented by statements from the poets about their background, influences and reasons for writing, and by excellent photographs.)

Thomson, Derick S. (ed.) *Gaelic Poetry in the Eighteenth Century* (1993) (A bilingual anthology with Thomson's English translations of Gaelic poems written during 'a time of upheaval and change'.)

Thomson, Geddes (ed.) *Identities* (1981) (An anthology of West of Scotland poetry, prose and drama arranged by theme.)

Watson, Roderick (ed.) *The Poetry of Scotland: Gaelic, Scots and English 1380–1980* (1995) (The most fully representative collection of poetry in the three languages, gathering poems from the earliest times to Liz Lochhead. English translations are given for Gaelic poems. Includes short biographies, concise notes and on-page glossaries. Contents are listed by both chronology and theme.)

Whyte, Christopher (ed.) *In the Face of Eternity: Eight Gaelic Poets/An Aghaidh na Sìorraidheachd: Ochdnar Bhàrd Gàidhlig* (1991) (A bilingual anthology of younger Gaelic poets including work by the editor.)

Whyte, Hamish (ed.) *Mungo's Tongues: Glasgow Poems 1630–1990* (1993) (A revised and expanded edition of Whyte's 1983 anthology *Noise and Smoky Breath*, illustrated by drawings, photographs and prints from the collection in Glasgow's Mitchell Library and a selection of photographs by George Oliver.)

Individual Authors

Notes on biography, major works, and criticism

ALLAN, DOT (1892–1964) Born in Denny near Glasgow; educated privately and at Glasgow University. Worked as freelance interviewer and journalist writing mainly for *The Glasgow Herald*, *The Scotsman* and *The Guardian*. Served as a nurse in the Second World War. Her novels include *Makeshift* (1928), *Deepening River* (1932), *Hunger March* (1934), *John Mathew Papermaker* (1948), *Mother of Millions* (1953) and *Charity Begins at Home* (1958).

> See: Burgess, Moira *The Glasgow Novel: a survey and bibliography*, 2nd edn (1986), pp. 48–9
>
> Elliot, Robert 'Women, Glasgow, and the Novel', *Chapman*, no. 33 (Autumn 1982), pp. 1–4

BAILLIE (*née* HOME), LADY GRIZEL (or GRISELL) (1665–1746) Daughter of the Covenanter, Sir Patrick Home, she married George Baillie, brother of the scholar and scientist Robert Baillie of Jerviswood. Best known for her song 'Werena my heart licht I wad die' (1724) and her collection of memorabilia posthumously published in an edition by R. Scott-Moncrieff as *The Household Book of Lady Grisell Baillie 1692–1733* (1911).

> See: Countess of Ashburnham *Lady Grisell Baillie: a Sketch of Her Life and Character* (1893)
>
> Lady Murray of Stanhope *Memoirs of the Lives and Characters of the Right Honourable George Baillie of Jerviswood and of Lady Grisell Baillie* (1824)

BAILLIE, JOANNA (1762–1851) Born at Bothwell, Lanarkshire, younger daughter of a Presbyterian clergyman who became Professor of Divinity at the University of Glasgow and niece of the surgeons, William and John Hunter. After father's death in 1783 moved to London with her mother and sister. Works include *Poems; Wherein it is Attempted to Describe Certain Views of Nature and of Rustic Manners* (1790), *Series of Plays, in which it is attempted to Delineate the Stronger Passions of the Mind*, 3 vols (1798–1812), *Metrical Legends* (1821).

See: Cameron, Alasdair 'Scottish Drama in the Nineteenth Century', *The History of Scottish Literature*, general editor Cairns Craig, 4 vols (1987–88), III, *Nineteenth Century*, ed. Douglas Gifford, Chapter 23, pp. 429–41 [431–3, 437]

Carhart, M. S. *The Life and Works of Joanna Baillie* (1923)

Norton, M. 'The Plays of Joanna Baillie', *The Review of English Studies*, 23, no. 90 (April 1947), pp. 131–43

BANKS, IAIN (b. 1954) Born Dunfermline, Fife. Educated at Gourock and Greenock High Schools and University of Stirling. Novels include *The Wasp Factory* (1984), *Walking on Glass* (1985), *The Bridge* (1986), *Espedair Street* (1987), *Canal Dreams* (1989), *The Crow Road* (1992), *Complicity* (1993), *Whit* (1995). Author of science fiction as Iain M(enzies) Banks: *Consider Phlebas* (1987), *The Player of Games* (1988), *Use of Weapons* (1990), *The State of the Art* (1991), *Against a Dark Background* (1993), *Feersum Endjinn* (1994).

See: Delany, Samuel R. 'In Love with Sara Ffitch', *New York Times Book Review*, 91, no. 9, 2 March 1986, pp. 37–8.

Nairn, Thom, 'Iain Banks and the Fiction Factory', *The Scottish Novel Since the Seventies: New Visions, Old Dreams*, ed. Gavin Wallace and Randall Stevenson (1993), Chapter 9, pp. 127–35.

BARNARD, ANNE (*née* LADY ANNE LINDSAY) (1750–1825) Eldest child of James Lindsay, 5th Earl of Balcarres. Brought up in Fife with visits to Edinburgh where she met the literary intelligentsia of the time. Wrote 'Auld Robin Gray' in 1771 (published 1776). Accompanied her husband, Andrew Barnard, to South Africa in 1797 when he was appointed Colonial Secretary to the Governor of the Cape of Good Hope. Under the name Lady Anne Barnard her letters give a unique account of the colony at this period.

See: Barnard, Anne *South Africa a Century Ago: Letters Written from the Cape of Good Hope 1797–1801*, edited with a memoir by W. H. Wilkins (1901)

BARRIE, SIR J(AMES) M(ATTHEW) (1860–1937) Born in Kirriemuir and educated at Glasgow, Dumfries and Forfar Academies before studying English at the University of Edinburgh. Began his career as a journalist with the *Nottinghamshire Journal* in 1888 and embarked on his stories of Thrums, a fictionalized Kirriemuir, published as *Auld Licht Idylls* (1888), *A Window in Thrums* (1889) and *The Little Minister* (1891) which, dramatized, brought him his first theatrical success in 1897. After *Quality Street* in 1901, his command of the London stage was assured with *The Admirable Crichton* (1902), *What Every Woman Knows* (1908), *Dear Brutus* (1917), and *Mary Rose* (1920). Among his best one-act plays are *The Twelve-Pound Look* (1910), *The Old Lady Shows Her Medals* (1917) and *Shall We Join the Ladies* (1921). *The Boy David* (1936) is an unsuccessful attempt at religious drama through which Barrie sought to exorcize complex feelings about his dead brother, David, to whom he also refers in his reverential memoir of his mother, *Margaret Ogilvy by Her Son* (1896). His enduring triumph is *Peter Pan, or The Boy who Would Not Grow Up* (1904).

See: Birkin, A. J. M. *Barrie and the Lost Boys* (1979)
Blake, George *Barrie and the Kailyard School* (1951)
Dunbar, J. *J. M. Barrie: The Man Behind the Image* (1970)
Jack, R. D. S. *The Road to the Never Land: A Re-Assessment of J. M. Barrie's Dramatic Art* (1991)

BLAIR, HUGH (1718–1800) Born in Edinburgh and educated at the city's High School and University. In 1762 he was appointed to the University's chair of Rhetoric and Belles Lettres. An outstandingly popular preacher, his five volumes of *Sermons* were published between 1777 and 1801. His *Lectures on Rhetoric and Belles Lettres* (1783) exerted a major influence on the literary thinking of the period.

See: Schmitz, R. M. *Hugh Blair* (1948)

BLAKE, GEORGE (1893–1961) Born in Greenock, educated at the University of Glasgow, he worked as a journalist and director of the publisher Faber & Faber after service in the First World War. His novels include *Mince Collop Close* (1923), *The Wild Men* (1925), *Young Malcolm* (1926), *The Shipbuilders* (1935), *The Valiant Heart* (1940) and *The Voyage Home* (1952). *Down to the Sea* (1937) is autobiography.

See: Whyte, Christopher 'Imagining the City: The Glasgow Novel', *Studies in Scottish Fiction: Twentieth Century, Scottish Studies*, ed. J. Schwend and H. W. Drescher, 10 (1990), pp. 317–33

BOLD, ALAN (b. 1943) Born in Edinburgh where he was educated at Broughton High School and the University. A prolific poet, anthologizer and critic, his volumes of poetry include *To Find the New* (1968), *A Perpetual Motion Machine* (1969), *A Lunar Event* (1973), *This Fine Day* (1979) and *In This Corner: Selected Poems 1963–83* (1983). Notable contributions to Scottish literary criticism are *George Mackay Brown* (1978), *Modern Scottish Literature* (1983), *MacDiarmid: A Critical Biography* (1988) and *A Burns Companion* (1991).

See: Bruce, George 'Alan Bold' in *Contemporary Poets*, ed. Thomas Riggs (1996), pp. 90–93
Dunn, Douglas 'The Poetry of Alan Bold: Hammering on the Lyre', *Akros*, no. 42 (December 1979), pp. 58–76

BOSWELL, JAMES (1740–95) Born in Edinburgh and educated there privately and at its University, completing his legal studies in Utrecht before being called to the Scottish Bar in 1766. His early interests were poetry and the theatre resulting in the publication of Augustan pastiches and *A View of the Edinburgh Theatre* (1759). He first met Samuel Johnson on 16 May 1763 and although he was rebuffed at first, soon won Johnson's confidence. The tour of Scotland made by the two men in 1773 is described in the journal Boswell kept and which was published in an abridged form in 1785. His biography, *The Life of Samuel Johnson*, followed in 1791. The full text of his journal of the Scottish tour was published in 1936 as *Boswell's Journal of a Tour to the Hebrides with Samuel Johnson LL.D. Now First Published from the Original Manuscript*.

See: Clingham, G. (ed.) *New Light on Boswell: Critical and Historical Essays* (1991)

Craik, Roger *James Boswell (1740–1795): The Scottish Perspective* (1994)

Danziger, M. K. and F. Brady *The Great Biographer* (1989)

Pottle, F. A. *The Literary Career of James Boswell* (1929)

BRIDIE, JAMES (O[SBORNE] H[ENRY] MAVOR) (1888–1951) Born in Glasgow and educated at Glasgow Academy and the University of Glasgow. After medical service in France and Mesopotamia in the First World War he practised medicine in Glasgow, writing on the side. In 1938 he became a full-time writer and was increasingly active on behalf of Scottish theatre. His lively wit, at once whimsical and satirical, is already effective in his first plays, *The Sunlight Sonata* (1928), *The Switchback* (1929) and *What It is to be Young* (1929). Later successes include *The Anatomist* (1930) and plays on biblical themes such as *Tobias and the Angel* (1930), *Jonah and the Whale* (1932) and *Susannah and the Elders* (1937). The influence of traditional morality plays is evident in his plays on medical, theological and moral themes, the best of which include *A Sleeping Clergyman* (1933), *Mr Bolfry* (1943), *Daphne Laureola* (1949), *Mr Gillie* (1950) and *The Baikie Charivari* (1952).

See: Bannister, Winifred *James Bridie and His Theatre* (1955)

Low, J. T. *Devils, Doctors, Saints and Sinners: a Critical Study of James Bridie's Major Plays* (1980)

Luyben, Helen L. *James Bridie: Clown and Philosopher* (1965)

Mavor, R. *Dr Mavor and Mr Bridie* (1988)

BROWN, GEORGE DOUGLAS (1869–1902) Born in Ochiltree, Ayrshire, the illegitimate son of a farmer. Educated at his local village school, Ayr Academy, Glasgow University and Balliol College, Oxford, where he was a Snell exhibitioner. Worked as a journalist and tutor in London. Published a boy's adventure novel, *Love and Sword* (1899), under the pseudonym 'Kennedy King' and in 1901 *The House with the Green Shutters* as 'George Douglas'. Two further novels, *The Incompatibles* and *The Novelist*, were left in note form at his early death.

See: Smith, Iain Crichton '*The House with the Green Shutters*', *Studies in Scottish Literature*, 7 (1969–79), pp. 3–10

Veitch, James *George Douglas Brown* (1952)

BROWN, GEORGE MACKAY (1921–96) Born in Stromness, Orkney, and educated at Stromness Academy. After hospitalization with tuberculosis he attended Newbattle Abbey College near Edinburgh, where he came under the influence of the Warden, Edwin Muir, and went on to the University of Edinburgh. His poetry includes *The Storm* (1954), *Loaves and Fishes* (1959), *The Year of the Whale* (1965), *Fishermen with Ploughs* (1971), *Winterfold* (1976), and *Selected Poems 1954–1983* (1991). Short story collections include *A Calendar of Love* (1967), *A Time to Keep* (1969), *Hawkfall* (1974), *The Sun's Net* (1976), *Andrina* (1983), *The Masked Fisherman* (1985), *The Sea-King's Daughter* (1991). His novels are *Greenvoe* (1972), *Magnus* (1973), *Time in a Red Coat* (1984), *The Golden Bird* (1987), *Vinland* (1992) and *Beside the Ocean of Time* (1994).

See: Ascherson, Neal 'George Mackay Brown' in *Seven Poets*, ed.
     Christopher Carrell (1981), pp. 23–5, and Walker, Marshall, 'Six
     Poets' in ibid., pp. 53–6
     Bold, Alan *George Mackay Brown* (1978)
     Murray, Isobel and Bob Tait, 'George Mackay Brown: *Greenvoe*',
     Ten Modern Scottish Novels (1984), Chapter 8, pp. 144–67
     Nicholson, Colin 'Unlocking Time's Labyrinth: George Mackay
     Brown', *Poem, Purpose and Place: Shaping Identity in Contemporary
     Scottish Verse* (1992), pp. 96–113

BRUCE, GEORGE (b. 1909) Born in Fraserburgh and educated at the University
     of Aberdeen. General talks producer with the BBC from 1946 to 1970
     with special responsibility for the arts. His first collection of poems, *Sea
     Talk* (1944), was followed by *Selected Poems* (1947). Later work is collected
     in *The Collected Poems of George Bruce* (1971) and *Perspectives: Poems 1970–
     1986* (1987).

     See: Scott, Alexander 'Myth-Maker: the Poetry of George Bruce', *Akros*,
          no. 29 (December 1975), pp. 25–40
          Smith, Iain Crichton '*Sea Talk* by George Bruce', *Towards the Human*
          (1986), pp. 154–8

BRUNTON, MARY (1778–1818) Born Mary Balfour in Orkney, she lived with
     her husband, the Rev. Alexander Brunton, in Bolton near Haddington,
     East Lothian and in Edinburgh where he was minister of the Tron Kirk.
     Her novels are *Self-Control* (1810), *Discipline* (1814) and *Emmeline* (1819).

     See: Dorothy Porter McMillan 'Heroines and Writers' in *Tea and Leg-
          Irons: New Feminist Readings from Scotland*, ed. Caroline Gonda
          (1992), pp. 17–30 [23–4]

BRYDEN, BILL (WILLIAM CAMPBELL ROUGH) (b. 1942) Born in Greenock
     and educated at its High School. He has directed at the Belgrade Theatre
     in Coventry, the Royal Court Theatre in London and the Royal Lyceum
     Theatre in Edinburgh. In 1984 he became BBC Scotland's head of
     television drama. His plays are *Willie Rough* (1972) and *Benny Lynch:
     Scenes from a Short Life* (1974).

     See: Hutchison, David *The Modern Scottish Theatre* (1977), pp. 140–41

BUCHAN, JOHN (1875–1940) Born in Perth and educated in Glasgow at
     Hutchesons' Grammar School and the University before taking up a
     scholarship to Brasenose College, Oxford. He worked at journalism and the
     law, spent two years in South Africa on the High Commissioner's staff,
     became a director of the publishing company Thomas Nelson and Sons,
     Director of Information during the First World War, and Conservative
     Member of Parliament for the Scottish Universities 1927–35. In 1935 he
     was appointed Governor-General of Canada as first Baron Tweedsmuir of
     Elsfield. The first of his 'shockers', written during an illness, was *The Power-
     House* (1913), followed by *The Thirty-nine Steps* (1915) which introduced
     his popular character, Richard Hannay, who reappears in *Greenmantle*
     (1916), *Mr Standfast* (1919), *The Three Hostages* (1924), *The Courts of the
     Morning* (1929) and *The Island of Sheep* (1936). He edited an influential

anthology of verse in Scots, *The Northern Muse* (1924), wrote the biographies *The Marquis of Montrose* (1928), *Sir Walter Scott* (1932) and *Oliver Cromwell* (1934), and an autobiography *Memory Hold-the-Door* (1940).

See: Buchan, William *John Buchan: A Memoir* (1982; reprinted 1985)
Green, M. *A Biography of John Buchan and His Sister Anna* (1990)
Lownie, Andrew *John Buchan, The Presbyterian Cavalier* (1995)
Smith, Janet Adam *John Buchan* (1965)
Webb, Paul *A Buchan Companion* (1994)

BURNETT, JAMES, LORD MONBODDO (1714–99) Born on the family estate of Monboddo in Kincardineshire, he took the title 'Lord Monboddo' when made a Lord of Session in 1767. Educated at King's College, Aberdeen, he was called to the Scottish Bar in 1737 and became Sheriff of Kincardine in 1760. Famous in his time for his six-volume works *Of the Origin and Progress of Language* (1773–92) and *Antient Metaphysics* (1779–99).

See: Cloyd, E. L. *James Burnett, Lord Monboddo* (1972)
Knight, W. A. *Lord Monboddo and Some of His Contemporaries* (1900)

BURNS, ROBERT (1759–96) Born at Alloway, Ayrshire. Assisted his father, William Burnes, on several farms but received education at home and at school in Kirkoswald. Between 1781 and 1782 he worked as a flax dresser in Irvine. While farming at Mossgiel near Mauchline with his brother Gilbert after the death of his father in 1784 he formed a relationship with Jean Armour whom he married in 1788 despite his involvements with several other women. From 1788 to 1791 he leased the farm of Ellisland near Dumfries and held the position of excise officer from 1789 to 1796. On 31 July 1786 his career as a poet was established with the publication by a Kilmarnock printer of *Poems, Chiefly in the Scottish Dialect*, commonly known as 'The Kilmarnock Edition'.

See: Bold, Alan *A Burns Companion* (1991)
Crawford, Thomas *Burns: A Study of the Poems and Songs* (1960, reprinted 1978)
Currie, James *The Works of Robert Burns with an Account of His Life*, 4 vols (1800)
Daiches, David *Robert Burns* (1950, revised 1960)
Ferguson, J. DeLancey *Pride and Passion: Robert Burns* (1939)
Lindsay, Maurice *Robert Burns: the Man, His Work, the Legend* (1954)
Low, Donald A. (ed.) *Robert Burns: The Critical Heritage* (1974)
MacDiarmid, Hugh *Burns Today and Tomorrow* (1959)
Mackay, James *Burns: A Biography* (1992)
Simpson, Kenneth (ed.) *Burns Now* (1994)
Snyder, Franklyn Bliss *The Life of Robert Burns* (1932)

BYRNE, JOHN (b. 1940) Born in Paisley, near Glasgow. Worked as a 'slab boy' (colour mixer) for A. F. Stoddard, carpet manufacturers, and went on to Glasgow School of Art. Since 1963 he has doubled as painter and writer. Graphic artist for Scottish Television, 1964–6. Exhibitions of art in Glasgow, 1961 and London, 1968. Several designs for theatre include his own *The Slab Boys Trilogy* for Edinburgh's Traverse Theatre in 1982. Other plays include *Writer's Cramp* (1977), *Cara Coco* (1980), *The London Cuckolds*

(1986), *Your Cheatin' Heart* (1990), and *Colquhoun and Macbryde* (1992). BAFTA Award for comedy series *Tutti-Frutti* (BBC-TV, 1987).

> See: Bold, Alan *Modern Scottish Literature* (1983), pp. 310–11
> Cameron, Alasdair 'Introduction', *Scot-Free: New Scottish Plays* (1990)

BYRON, GEORGE GORDON, LORD (1788–1824) Born in London he was found to have a club foot which is thought greatly to have influenced his attitude to life. Educated until the age of ten at Aberdeen Grammar School, he then moved south with his mother, Catherine Gordon of Gight, and succeeded to the family title, with further education at Harrow School and Trinity College, Cambridge. When his first collection of poems, *Hours of Idleness* (1807), was attacked in the *Edinburgh Review* he responded with *English Bards and Scotch Reviewers* (1809) and after travel in Europe and the Near East published *Childe Harold's Pilgimage* (1812, 1816 and 1818) and his romantic narrative poems. His scandalous affair with Lady Caroline Lamb was followed by marriage to Anne Isabella Milbanke, but suspicion of an incestuous liaison with his half-sister, Augusta Leigh, led to his permanent departure from Britain in 1816. In exile he befriended Shelley, settled in Italy and composed *Beppo* (1818), *The Vision of Judgement* (1822) and *Don Juan* (1819–24). Attracted in 1823 to the Greek revolution against Turkey he went to Missolonghi to train Greek soldiers and died there of rheumatic fever.

> See: Calder, Angus (ed.) *Byron and Scotland: Radical or Dandy* (1989)
> Marchand, L. A. *Byron: a Biography*, 3 vols (1957)
> Rutherford, A. *Byron: a Critical Study* (1961)

CAMPBELL, DONALD (b. 1940) Born at Wick, Caithness, but moved to Edinburgh where his play, *The Jesuit*, was first produced at the Traverse Theatre in 1976. Other plays include *Somerville the Soldier* (1978), *The Widows of Clyth* (1979), *Blackfriars Wynd* (1980), *Till All the Seas Run Dry* (1981) and *Howard's Revenge* (1985). Poetry since 1971 is gathered in *Selected Poems* (1990).

> See: Lindsay, Frederic 'The Poetry of Donald Campbell', *Akros*, no. 43 (April 1980), pp. 71–89
> Paterson, Lindsay 'Donald Campbell: Playwright in search of a method', *Cencrastus*, no. 6 (Autumn 1981), pp. 6–8

CARLYLE, THOMAS (1795–1881) Born at Ecclefechan, Dumfriesshire, he was educated at Annan Academy and Edinburgh University where he finally abandoned an expected career in divinity. After schoolmastering and reading in law he set his mind on literary journalism, becoming an expert in the field of German literature through his translations of Goethe and *The Life of Schiller* (1825). In 1826 he married Jane Baillie Welsh whose support of him and his work became legendary. After a short spell in Edinburgh the couple moved for economic reasons to Craigenputtoch, a farm near Dumfries, and in 1834 moved again to 5 Cheyne Row, Chelsea, London. After *Sartor Resartus* (1833–4) he wrote *The French Revolution* (1837) and became known as a public speaker and social commentator resulting in the publication of his lectures *On Heroes, Hero Worship and the Heroic in History* (1841). His other principal works are *Chartism* (1839), *Past and Present* (1843), *Latter*

Day Pamphlets (1850), *Life of John Sterling* (1851), *The History of Friedrich II of Prussia, Called Frederick the Great* (1858–65) and *Reminiscences* (1881).

See: Campbell, I. *Thomas Carlyle* (1974)
Cazamian, Louis *Carlyle* (1913, reprinted 1932, 1966)
Kaplan, F. *Thomas Carlyle* (1983)
Le Quesne, A. L. *Carlyle* (1982)
Rosenberg, J. D. *Carlyle and the Burden of History* (1985)
Seigel, J. P. (ed.) *Carlyle: the Critical Heritage* (1971)

CARSWELL (*née* MACFARLANE), CATHERINE ROXBURGH (1879–1946)
Born in Glasgow and educated at the Park School and the Schumann
Conservatorium in Frankfurt-am-Main. Her first marriage to the mentally
unstable H. P. M. Jackson led to early separation and divorce. She became
drama critic for *The Glasgow Herald* but lost her post after reviewing D. H.
Lawrence's *The Rainbow* without the editor's approval (*The Glasgow Herald*,
4 November 1915, p. 4). In London she became drama critic for *The
Observer* and in 1917 married Donald Carswell. D. H. Lawrence encouraged
her to complete her first novel, *Open the Door!* (1920) which was followed
by *The Camomile: An Invention* (1922). Other major works are *Life of Robert
Burns* (1930), *The Savage Pilgrimage: a Narrative of D. H. Lawrence* (1932) and
The Tranquil Heart (1937), a life of Boccaccio. Her son, John Carswell, has
edited *Lying Awake: An Unfinished Autobiography and Other Posthumous Papers*
(1950).

See: Carswell, John 'Introduction' to Virago edition of Catherine
Carswell, *Open the Door!* (1986)
Pilditch, Jan 'Opening the door on Catherine Carswell', *Scotlands*,
no. 2 (1994), pp. 53–65

CONN, STEWART (b. 1936) Born in Glasgow and educated at Kilmarnock
Academy and the University of Glasgow. Appointed Senior Drama Pro-
ducer for BBC Radio Scotland in 1977. His plays include *Break-Down*
(1961), *The Burning* (1971), *The Aquarium* (1973), *Play Donkey* (1977),
Hecuba (1979), *Hugh Miller* (1988) and *By the Pool* (1988). Poetry includes
Thunder in the Air (1967), *Stoats in the Sunlight* (1968), *Under the Ice* (1978),
In the Kibble Palace: New and Selected Poems (1987) and *The Luncheon of the
Boating Party* (1991).

See: Bruce, George 'Stewart Conn', *Contemporary Poets*, ed. Thomas Riggs
(1996), pp. 179–81
Hutchison, David *The Modern Scottish Theatre* (1977), pp. 137–9
Smith, Iain Crichton 'Towards the Human: The Poetry of Stewart
Conn', *Towards the Human* (1986), pp. 159–66

CORRIE, JOE (1894–1968) Born in Bowhill, Fife. Began writing while working
as a miner, earning comparison with Sean O'Casey, D. H. Lawrence and
Emile Zola. His most enduring play is *In Time of Strife* (1929). A selection
of his work edited and introduced by Linda Mackenney is published as
Joe Corrie: Plays, Poems and Theatre Writings (1985).

See: Hutchison, David *The Modern Scottish Theatre* (1977), pp. 62–3
Reid, Alexander 'Poetry, plays and pacifism: A note on the life and

works of Joe Corrie', *Scotland's Magazine*, 54, no. 3 (March 1958), pp. 43–4

CRAWFORD, ROBERT (b. 1959) Born in Bellshill, Glasgow, and eduated at Hutcheson's Grammar School and the Universities of Glasgow and Oxford, he is currently Professor of Modern Scottish Literature at the University of St Andrews. With David Kinloch he founded the poetry magazine, *Verse*, in 1984. His poetry includes *A Scottish Assembly* (1990), *Sharawaggi* (with W. N. Herbert, 1990) and *Talkies* (1992). Criticism includes *The Savage and the City in the Work of T. S. Eliot* (1987) and *Identifying Poets: Self and Territory in Twentieth-Century Poetry* (1993). See also under 'Literary, historical and cultural backgrounds' in 'General Bibliographies'.

> See: O'Neill, Michael 'Robert Crawford', *Contemporary Poets*, ed. Thomas Riggs (1996), pp. 198–9
> O'Rourke, Daniel *Dream State: The New Scottish Poets* (1994), pp. xxiii–vi, 59–69
> Robertson, James 'Robert Crawford and *Verse*: An International Flavour', *Scottish Literary Journal*, Supplement No. 28 (Spring 1988), pp. 25–8

DAVIDSON, JOHN (1857–1909) Born at Barrhead, Renfrewshire, and raised in Glasgow and Greenock where he attended the Highlander's Academy. After work for Walker's sugar company in Greenock and apprentice schoolteaching he matriculated at the University of Edinburgh but left without a degree, held various teaching posts in Scotland and moved to London where he contributed to the *Yellow Book* and joined the Rhymers' Club. Financial difficulties, frequent ill health and lack of recognition led to a suicidal depression and he took his own life at Penzance, Cornwall. Although he began writing plays while in his twenties it is as a poet that he is remembered, particularly *Fleet Street Eclogues* (1893), *Ballads and Songs* (1894) and his verse 'Testaments'. His unfinished dramatic trilogy *God and Mammon* (1907–8) expresses his Nietzschean but highly personal anti-Christian philosophy. His poems are collected in *The Poems of John Davidson*, ed. Andrew Turnbull, 2 vols (1973).

> See: Lindsay, Maurice (ed.) *John Davidson: A Selection of His Poems*, with a Preface by T. S. Eliot, an essay by Hugh MacDiarmid and an Introduction by the editor (1961)
> O'Connor, Mary *John Davidson* (1987)
> Peterson, Carroll V. *John Davidson* (1972)
> Townsend, J. Benjamin *John Davidson: Poet of Armageddon* (1961)

DAVIE, ELSPETH (1919–95) Born in Ayrshire. After childhood in England she attended the University of Edinburgh and taught in Ireland. Her fiction includes the novels *Providings* (1965), *Creating a Scene* (1971) and *Climbers on a Stair* (1978), and the short-story collections *The Spark* (1968), *The High Tide Talker* (1976) and *The Night of the Funny Hats* (1980).

> See: Spunta, Marina 'A Universe of one's own? Elspeth Davie and the narrative of the "gap"', *Chapman*, no. 81 (1995), pp. 19–26

DOUGLAS, GEORGE NORMAN (1868–1952) Born Thurigen, Vorarlberg, in Austria and brought up at Tilquhillie, Deeside, he was educated at

Uppingham School and at Karlsruhe in Germany. Served in St Petersburg as a Foreign Office diplomat before retiring to the Island of Capri. His works include *Unprofessional Tales* (1901) written jointly with his wife, *Siren Land* (1911), *Old Calabria* (1915), *South Wind* (1917), *Looking Back* (1933) and *Late Harvest* (1946).

See: Greenlees, I., *Norman Douglas* (1957)
Holloway, Mark, *Norman Douglas: A Biography* (1976)

DOYLE, SIR ARTHUR CONAN (1859–1930) Born in Edinburgh. Educated at Stonyhurst and the University of Edinburgh. Medical practitioner at Southsea near Portsmouth, 1882–90. The first novel featuring Sherlock Holmes is *A Study in Scarlet* (1887). Stories about Holmes originally published mainly in the *Strand Magazine* are collected in *The Adventures of Sherlock Holmes* (1892), *The Memoirs of Sherlock Holmes* (1894), *The Return of Sherlock Holmes* (1905), *The Last Bow* (1917) and *The Casebook of Sherlock Holmes* (1927). Stories on various themes in which Holmes does not appear are collected in *The Conan Doyle Stories* (1929). Other fiction includes *The White Company* (1891), *The Exploits of Brigadier Gerard* (1896), *Sir Nigel* (1906), *The Lost World* (1912) and *The Poison Belt* (1913). His experience as war correspondent in the Boer War forms the background to *The Great Boer War* (1900) and *The War in South Africa: Its Causes and Conclusion* (1902). His interest in spiritualism led to *The Spiritualist's Reader* (1924) and *The History of Spiritualism* (1926).

See: Carr, John Dickson *The Life of Sir Arthur Conan Doyle* (1949)
Edwards, Owen Dudley *The Quest for Sherlock Holmes* (1982)
Pearson, Hesketh *Conan Doyle: His Life and Art* (1943)

DUFFY, CAROL ANN (b. 1955) Born in Glasgow, grew up in Stafford and attended Liverpool University. Her poetry includes *Standing Female Nude* (1985), *Selling Manhattan* (1987), *The Other Country* (1990), *Mean Time* (1993) and *Selected Poems* (1994). She has edited *I Wouldn't Thank You for a Valentine* (1992), an anthology for teenagers.

See: Donaghy, Michael 'Carol Ann Duffy', *Contemporary Poets*, ed. Thomas Riggs (1996), pp. 279–80
O'Rourke, Daniel *Dream State: The New Scottish Poets* (1994), pp. xix–xx, 1–10

DUNN, DOUGLAS (b. 1942) Born at Inchinnan, Renfrewshire, and trained as a librarian. Worked in Glasgow and Hull before returning to Fife where he is Professor of Poetry at the University of St Andrews. His volumes of poetry include *Terry Street* (1969), *The Happier Life* (1972), *Love or Nothing* (1974), *Barbarians* (1979), *St Kilda's Parliament* (1981), *Elegies* (1985), *Selected Poems 1964–1983* (1986) and *Northlight* (1988). His short stories are collected in *Secret Villages* (1985) and *Boyfriends and Girlfriends* (1995). See also under 'Anthologies' in 'General Bibliographies'.

See: Crawford, Robert and David Kinloch (eds) *Reading Douglas Dunn* (1992)
Nicholson, Colin 'Dimensions of the Sentient: Douglas Dunn', *Poem, Purpose and Place: Shaping Identity in Contemporary Scottish Verse* (1992), pp. 183–202

ELLIOT, JEAN, OF MINTO (1727–1805) Born at Minto House, Teviotdale, and
is said to have helped her father escape from a party of Jacobites during the
rising of 1745–6. Her song, 'The Flowers of the Forest', appears to have
been written in 1763 or 1764 and was first published in 1769.

FERGUSSON, ROBERT (1750–74) Born in Edinburgh, he was educated
privately and at the High School of Edinburgh, the High School of
Dundee and the University of St Andrews. Worked as legal copyist in the
Edinburgh Commissary Office until ill health forced him to resign in 1773.
He died in the Edinburgh Bedlam after injuring himself by falling down a
flight of stairs. His first distinctive work is the poem 'The Daft Days'
(1772) which was followed by other poems in Scots including 'Auld
Reekie' (1773). Early collections are *Poems* (1773) and *Poems on Various
Subjects* edited by Walter Ruddiman (1779). The definitive modern text is
The Poems of Robert Fergusson, edited in two volumes for the Scottish Text
Society by Matthew P. McDiarmid (1954–6).

> See: Daiches, David *Robert Fergusson* (1982)
> Maclaine, A. H. *Robert Fergusson* (1965)

FERRIER, SUSAN EDMONSTONE (1782–1854) Born in Edinburgh where her
father was a Writer to the Signet and legal agent of the Duke of Argyll.
Recognized by the Edinburgh *literati*, she enjoyed the friendship of Sir
Walter Scott and John Leyden. Her three novels are *Marriage* (1818),
The Inheritance (1824) and *Destiny* (1831).

> See: Grant, Aline *Susan Ferrier* (1957)
> Parker, W. M. *Susan Ferrier and John Galt* (1965)
> Paxton, Nancy L. 'Subversive Feminism: A Reassessment of Susan
> Ferrier's *Marriage*', *Women and Literature*, 4 (1976), pp. 18–29

FINDLATER, JANE (1866–1946); FINDLATER, MARY (1865–1963) Both
sisters were born at Lochearnhead, Perthshire, and educated at home. On
the death of their father in 1886 they moved to Prestonpans but the success
of Jane's most accomplished novel, *The Green Graves of Balgowrie* (1896),
enabled them to move first to Devon, then to London and Rye before
returning to Perthshire. Mary's novels of manners are best represented by
The Rose of Joy (1903). Their most fuitful collaboration is the light-hearted
novel, *Crossriggs* (1908).

> See: Mackenzie, Eileen *The Findlater Sisters: Literature and Friendship* (1964)

FINLAY, IAN HAMILTON (b. 1925) Born in Nassau in the Bahamas and
brought up in Scotland. In 1968 he began the construction of 'Little
Sparta', his garden of sculpture, sundials, symbolic landscape and building at
Dunsyre, Lanarkshire, and became known as a concrete poet. Many of his
poems, often with a strongly visual element integral to the expression, are
published as posters and post cards by his Wild Flounder Press. Early
collections of poems are *The Dancers Inherit the Party* (1960), *Glasgow Beasts,
an a Burd Haw, an Inseks, an, Aw, a Fush* (1961) and *Concertina* (1962).
With Sue Finlay he edited the magazine *Poor. Old. Tired. Horse.* (1961–70).
Short stories are collected in *The Sea-Bed and Other Stories* (1958).

See: Abrioux, Yves *Ian Hamilton Finlay: A Visual Primer* with introductory
notes and commentaries by Stephen Bann, 2nd edn (1992)
Chapman, 78–9 (1994), Special Feature – Ian Hamilton Finlay
Finlay, Alec *Wood Notes Wild: Essays on the Poetry and Art of Ian
Hamilton Finlay* (1995)
Morgan, Edwin 'Early Finlay', *Crossing the Border: Essays on Scottish
Literature* (1990), pp. 292–9
—— 'Finlay in the 70s and 80s', Ian Hamilton Finlay, EVENING
WILL COME/THEY WILL SEW THE BLUE SAIL (1991),
pp. 37–46

FLETCHER, ANDREW, OF SALTOUN (1653–1716) Son of Robert Fletcher
of Saltoun in East Lothian and Innerpeffer. After private education and
travel in Europe he became member for Haddington in the Convention of
Estates in 1678 and opposed the oppressive policies of the Duke of
Lauderdale. The climax of his career as an anti-Unionist was his part in the
struggle for Scottish independence in the parliament of 1703 to 1707. His
most significant political works are *Two Discourses Concerning the Affairs of
Scotland* (1698), *An Account of a Conversation Concerning the Right Regulation
of Governments for the Common Good of Mankind* (1704) and *State of the
controversy betwixt United and Separate Parliaments* (1706).

See: Scott, Paul H. *Andrew Fletcher and The Treaty of Union* (1992)

FRIEL, GEORGE (1910–76) Born in Glasgow where, after education at St
Mungo's Academy and the University of Glasgow, he worked as a teacher,
writing on the side. His novels are *The Bank of Time* (1959), *The Boy who
Wanted Peace* (1964), *Grace and Miss Partridge* (1969), *Mr Alfred M.A.* (1972)
and *An Empty House* (1974).

See: Gillespie, James 'Friel in the Thirties', *Edinburgh Review*, no. 71
(1985), pp. 46–55
Norquay, Glenda 'Four Novelists of the 1950s and 1960s', *The
History of Scottish Literature*, 4 vols (1987–8), general editor
Cairns Craig, IV, *Twentieth Century*, ed. Cairns Craig, Chapter 17,
pp. 259–76 [268–70]

GAITENS, EDWARD (1897–1966) Born in The Gorbals in Glasgow, left school
at fourteen and worked at menial jobs until the First World War when he
was imprisoned as a conscientious objector. Encouraged in his writing by
James Bridie. His short stories, many of which first appeared in the *Scots
Magazine*, are collected in *Growing Up and Other Stories* (1942). His novel,
Dance of the Apprentices (1948), draws on his own experience of the slums,
Glasgow socialism and pacifism.

See: Morgan, Edwin 'Tradition and Experiment in the Glasgow Novel',
The Scottish Novel Since the Seventies, ed. Gavin Wallace and
Randall Stevenson (1993), Chapter 6, pp. 85–98 [85–6]

GALLOWAY, JANICE (b. 1956) Born in Ardrossan and educated at Ardrossan
Academy and the University of Glasgow. Teacher of English for Strathclyde
Regional Council, Ayrshire, 1980–90. Her novels are *The Trick is to Keep
Breathing* (1990) and *Foreign Parts* (1994). *Blood* (1991) is a collection of
stories.

See: Metzstein, Margery 'Of Myths and Men: Aspects of Gender in the
Fiction of Janice Galloway', *The Scottish Novel Since the Seventies*,
ed. Gavin Wallace and Randall Stevenson (1993), Chapter 10,
pp. 136–46

GALT, JOHN (1779–1839) Born at Irvine, Ayrshire, he was educated at Greenock Grammar School and apprenticed to the Greenock Custom House
before taking a clerkship with the local merchant firm of James Miller and
Company while composing his early essays and stories. After an unsuccessful
business venture in London he turned to the study of law, travelled in
Europe where he met Byron, attempted to establish a trading company in
Gibraltar and spent three years in Canada after his appointment as Secretary
to the Canada Company in 1824. He died in Greenock. *Blackwood's
Magazine* advanced his literary reputation by publishing many of his novels
serially before he rejected the magazine's editorial interference and moved
to the publisher Oliver and Boyd. His most enduring fiction is in *Annals of
the Parish* (1821), *The Provost* (1822), *The Entail* (1823), *Ringan Gilhaize*
(1823) and *The Member* (1832). In 1830 he published *The Life of Lord Byron*,
and in 1833 his *Autobiography* followed by *Literary Life* (1834).

See: Gordon, Ian A. *John Galt, the Life of a Writer* (1972)
Lyell, F. H. *A Study of the Novels of John Galt* (1942)
Parker, W. M. *Susan Ferrier and John Galt* (1965)
Scott, P. H. *John Galt* (1985)

GARIOCH, ROBERT (ROBERT GARIOCH SUTHERLAND) (1909–81)
Born in Edinburgh and educated at its High School and University. Until
his retirement in 1964 he taught at schools in Edinburgh, London and
Kent. Writer in Residence at the University of Edinburgh, 1971–3, and
contributed to the compilation of the *Dictionary of the Older Scottish Tongue*.
His experiences during the Second World War with the Royal Signals and
as prisoner-of-war are described in *Two Men and a Blanket* (1975). Most of
his poems and translations (notably of George Buchanan and Giuseppe Belli)
are in Scots, his first collection appearing with work by Sorley MacLean in
17 Poems for 6d (1940). His translations of Buchanan are published as *George
Buchanan, 'Jephthah' and 'The Baptist'* under the name Robert Garioch
Sutherland (1959). *Collected Poems* (1977) is superseded by *Complete Poetical
Works* edited by Robin Fulton (1983).

See: Ascherson, Neal 'Robert Garioch' in *Seven Poets*, ed. Christopher
Carrell (1981), pp. 25–7, and Walker, Marshall, 'Six Poets', ibid.,
pp. 60–67
Chapman, no. 31 (Winter 1981/82), special issue 'In Memoriam
Robert Garioch'
Fulton, Robin (ed.) *A Garioch Miscellany* (1986)
Smith, Iain Crichton, 'The Power of Craftsmanship: The Poetry of
Robert Garioch', *Towards the Human* (1986), pp. 167–70
Watson, Roderick 'The speaker in the gairdens: the poetry of
Robert Garioch', *Akros*, no. 16 (April 1971), pp. 69–76

GIBBON, LEWIS GRASSIC (JAMES LESLIE MITCHELL) (1901–35) Born at
Hillhead of Segget in Auchterless, Aberdeenshire, and educated at
Arbuthnott Village School and Mackie Academy in Stonehaven. At the age

of sixteen he became a junior reporter on the *Aberdeen Journal* before moving to Glasgow to become a journalist with the *Scottish Farmer*. Converted to socialism he joined the Communist Party which led to dismissal from his job and enlistment in the Royal Army Service Corps with whom he served throughout the First World War in the Middle East, Mesopotamia, Palestine and Egypt. Returning to Scotland after the war he subsequently joined the Royal Air Force, serving until 1929. Under the influence of Diffusionist theory which maintained that primitive people lived in a golden age destroyed by civilization, he published *Hanno, or The Future of Exploration* (1928), expressing ideas that reappear in *Niger: the Life of Mungo Park* (1934) and *The Conquest of the Maya* (1934). His first novel, *Stained Radiance* (1930), published under the name of Mitchell, anticipates the setting of the three novels comprising *A Scots Quair* which was published as a whole for the first time in 1946. His other novels are the autobiographical *The Thirteenth Disciple* (1931), *Three Go Back* (1932), *The Lost Trumpet* (1932), *Image and Superscription* (1933), *Spartacus* (1933) and *Gay Hunter* (1934).

> See: Calder, Angus ' "A Mania for Self-Reliance": Grassic Gibbon's *Scots Quair*,' *Revolving Culture: Notes from the Scottish Republic* (1994), pp. 137–51
> Campbell, Ian *Lewis Grassic Gibbon* (1985)
> Gifford, Douglas *Neil Gunn and Lewis Grassic Gibbon* (1983)
> Munro, I. S. *Leslie Mitchell: Lewis Grassic Gibbon* (1966)
> Murray, Isobel and Bob Tait 'Lewis Grassic Gibbon: *A Scots Quair*', *Ten Modern Scottish Novels* (1984), Chapter 2, pp. 10–31
> Young, D. F. *Beyond the Sunset: a Study of James Leslie Mitchell* (1973)

GRAHAM, ROBERT BONTINE CUNNINGHAME (1852–1936) Born in London, the son of a Scottish landowner. Spanish descent on his mother's side earned him the nickname 'Don Roberto'. Spent much of his childhood on family estates at Gartmore, Stirlingshire. Educated at Harrow School until the age of fifteen, then tutored privately. Embarked on business ventures in Argentina, married a Chilean poetess, Gabriela de la Belmondiere, and spent two years travelling and ranching in Texas and Mexico. Liberal MP for North-West Lanarkshire, first president of the Scottish Labour Party and first president of the Scottish National Party. Works include *Mogreb-el-Acksa* (1898), much admired by Shaw and Conrad, *Thirteen Stories* (1900), *A Vanished Arcadia* (1901), *Success* (1902), *Scottish Stories* (1914), *Progress and Other Sketches* (1905) and *The Horses of the Conquest* (1930).

> See: MacDiarmid, Hugh *Cunninghame Graham, A Centenary Study* (1952)
> Maitland, A. *Robert and Gabriela Cunninghame Graham* (1983)
> Tschiffely, A. F. *Don Roberto* (1937)
> Watts, C. and L. Davies *Cunninghame Graham: A Critical Biography* (1979)

GRAHAM, W(ILLIAM) S(YDNEY) (1918–86) Born in Greenock and trained as an engineer. Lived mainly in Cornwall. Achieved his own distinctive voice in *The White Threshold* (1949) and *The Nightfishing* (1955). Later volumes are *Malcolm Mooney's Land* (1970) and *Implements in Their Places* (1977). His work is collected in *Collected Poems 1942–1977* (1979), *Uncollected Poems*

(1990) and *Aimed at Nobody: Poems from Notebooks*, edited by Margaret Blackwood and Robin Skelton with a Foreword by Nessie Graham (1993).

> See: Lopez, Tony *The Poetry of W. S. Graham* (1989)
> Morgan, Edwin 'The Poetry of W. S. Graham' and 'W. S. Graham: a Poet's Letters' in *Crossing the Border: Essays on Scottish Literature* (1990), pp. 251–9, 260–72

GRAHAME, KENNETH (1859–1932) Born in Edinburgh and brought up first in Inverary then in Cookham Dene, Berkshire. Educated at St Edward's School, Oxford. Entered the Bank of England where he became Secretary in 1898. His principal works are *The Golden Age* (1895), *Dream Days* (1898) and *The Wind in the Willows* (1908).

> See: Green, P. *Kenneth Grahame: a Study of His Life, Work and Times* (1959)
> Prince, Alison *Kenneth Grahame: An Innocent in the Wild Wood* (1994)

GRANT (*née* MacVICAR), ANN, OF LAGGAN (1755–1838) Born in Glasgow, the daughter of an army officer with whom she went to North America until 1773 when her father became barrack-master at Fort Augustus where she married the barrack chaplain-and minister of the parish of Laggan. When her husband died in 1801 she wrote for a living. Her most successful book is *Letters from the Mountains* (1803). Other works include *The Highlanders* (1808), *Memoirs of an American Lady* (1808) and *Essays on the Superstitions of the Highlands of Scotland* (1811).

> See: Grant, J. P. (ed.) *Memoir and Correspondence of Mrs Grant* (1844)

GRANT, ELIZABETH, OF ROTHIEMURCUS (1797–1885) Born in Edinburgh, daughter of a Highland landowner and unsuccessful lawyer whom she accompanied to India when he was compelled to flee his creditors. There she married Colonel Hay Smith on whose retirement the couple settled on his Irish estate of Balliboys. Edited by Lady Strachey, her *Memoirs of a Highland Lady* was published posthumously in 1898.

> See: Grant, Elizabeth of Rothiemurcus *Memoirs of a Highland Lady*, edited with an introduction by Andrew Tod (1988)

GRAY, ALASDAIR (b. 1934) Born in Glasgow and educated at Whitehill School and Glasgow School of Art. Has worked as art teacher and scene painter. Retrospective exhibition of art work in 1986. Likes to design his own books. Fiction includes *Lanark*, begun in 1954 and published 1981, *Unlikely Stories, Mostly* (1983), *1982 Janine* (1984), *Something Leather* (1990), *Poor Things* (1992) and *The History Maker* (1994). His poems are collected in *Old Negatives* (1989). *Why Scots Should Rule Scotland* (1992) argues for Scottish political independence.

> See: Acker, Kathy 'Alasdair Gray interviewed', *Edinburgh Review*, no. 74 (1986), pp. 83–90
> Crawford, Robert and Nairn, Thom (eds) *The Arts of Alasdair Gray* (1991)
> Murray, Isobel and Bob Tait, 'Alasdair Gray: *Lanark*', *Ten Modern Scottish Novels* (1984), Chapter 11, pp. 219–39

GUNN, NEIL M. (1891–1973) Born in Dunbeath, Caithness. Educated at the villlage school and privately. Entered the Civil Service in 1907 and moved to London. Customs and Excise officer in Inverness and Kinlochleven from 1911 to 1937 when he settled at Braes, between Dingwall and Strathpeffer. Early work for the theatre was not well received but after his first two novels, *Grey Coast* (1926) and *The Lost Glen* (1932), he achieved financial success with *Morning Tide* (1930). His other principal novels are *Sun Circle* (1933), *Highland River* (1937), *Wild Geese Overhead* (1939), *The Silver Darlings* (1941) and *The Well at the World's End* (1951). *The Atom of Delight* (1956) is autobiography. *Landscape and Light* (1987) is a collection of his essays edited by Alistair McCleery. J. B. Pick has edited his *Selected Letters* (1987).

> See: Gifford, Douglas *Neil M. Gunn and Lewis Grassic Gibbon* (1983)
> Gunn, D. and I. Murray (eds) *Neil Gunn's Country: Essays in Celebration of Neil Gunn* (1991)
> Hart, F. R. and J. B. Pick *Neil M. Gunn: A Highland Life* (1981)
> McCulloch, Margery *The Novels of Neil M. Gunn: A Critical Study* (1987)
> Murray, Isobel and Bob Tait, 'Neil Gunn: *The Silver Darlings*', *Ten Modern Scottish Novels* (1984), Chapter 3, pp. 32–54
> Price, R. *The Fabulous Matter of Fact: The Poetics of Neil M. Gunn* (1991)
> Scott, Alexander and Douglas Gifford *Neil M. Gunn: The Man and the Writer* (1973)

HANNAN, CHRIS (b. 1958) Born in Glasgow. His plays, all first produced at Edinburgh's Traverse Theatre, include *Klimkov: Life of a Tsarist Agent* (1984), *Elizabeth Gordon Quinn* (1985) and *The Orphans' Comedy* (1986).

> See: Cameron, Alasdair 'Introduction', *Scot-Free: New Scottish Plays* (1990)

HAY, JOHN MACDOUGALL (1881–1919) Born and raised at Tarbert, Loch Fyne, Argyll. Established himself as a freelance journalist while a student at the University of Glasgow. After some years of teaching he was ordained as a Church of Scotland minister, serving in Govan and Elderslie. In addition to *Gillespie* (1914) he wrote *Barnacles* (1916) and *Their Dead Sons* (1918).

> See: Spring, Ian 'Determinism in John Macdougall Hay's *Gillespie*', *Scottish Literary Journal*, 6, no. 2 (December 1979), pp. 55–68
> Tait, Bob and Isobel Murray 'Introduction', J. Macdougall Hay, *Gillespie* (Edinburgh, 1979), pp. vii–xvi

HENDERSON, HAMISH (b. 1919) Born in Blairgowrie and educated at Dulwich College and Downing College, Cambridge. Folklorist, poet and translator, his verse is collected in *Elegies for the Dead in Cyrenaica* (1948).

> See: Hunter, Andrew R. 'Hamish Henderson: the Odyssey of a Wandering King', *Cencrastus*, no. 47 (Spring 1994), pp. 3–6
> McNaughtan, Adam T. 'Hamish Henderson – Folk Hero', *Chapman*, no. 42 (Winter 1985), pp. 22–9
> Ross, Raymond J. 'Hamish Henderson: In the Midst of Things', *Chapman*, no. 42 (Winter 1985), pp. 11–18

HIND, ARCHIE (b. 1928) Born in Glasgow, he worked as clerk, labourer, bus driver, machine operator, glass sculptor, data processor and slaughter-house employee. National Service was with the RAMC, 1946–8. He studied writing under Edwin Muir at Newbattle Abbey College and attended WEA lectures by Jack Rillie. He has been writer-in-residence to the Community of Aberdeen. His novel is *The Dear Green Place* (1966).

See: Bold, Alan, *Modern Scottish Literature* (1983), pp. 236–9

HOGG, JAMES (1770–1835) Born at Ettrickhall Farm in the Ettrick Forest, schooled for about six months, and characterized as 'The Shepherd' by John Wilson in the *Noctes Ambrosianae* published in *Blackwood's Magazine*. Failed in several attempts to succeed in farming. Discovered by Sir Walter Scott who became a friend. Early ballads published as *The Mountain Bard* (1807) and made his name as a poet with *The Queen's Wake* (1813). An accomplished writer of short stories, his principal prose works are *The Three Perils of Man* (1822), *The Private Memoirs and Confessions of a Justified Sinner* (1824) and *The Domestic Manners and Private Life of Sir Walter Scott* (1834).

See: Gifford, Douglas *James Hogg: a Re-Assessment* (1976)
    Groves, D. *James Hogg: The Growth of a Writer* (1988)
    Hook, Andrew 'Hogg, Melville and the Scottish Enlightenment',
        Scottish Literary Journal, 4, no. 2 (December 1977), pp. 25–39
    Smith, Nelson C. *James Hogg* (1980)
    Strout, A. L. *The Life and Letters of James Hogg* (vol. 1) (1946)

HOME, HENRY, LORD KAMES (1696–1782) A leading member of the Edinburgh *literati* during the Enlightenment period, he was born in Berwickshire at Kames, trained as an advocate in Edinburgh and called to the Scottish Bar in 1723. His most influential works are *Essays on the Principles of Morality and Religion* (1751) and *Elements of Criticism* (1762).

See: Lehmann, W. C. *Henry Home, Lord Kames* (1971)
    Randall, H. W. *The Critical Theory of Kames* (1944)
    Ross, I. S. *Lord Kames and the Scotland of His Day* (1972)

HOME, JOHN (1722–1808) Born in Leith and educated at the University of Edinburgh. Fought for the government during the Jacobite rebellion of 1745 and wrote *The History of the Rebellion in the Year 1745* (1802). Minister of Athelstaneford, Berwickshire. Famous for his play, *Douglas*, first produced in Edinburgh in 1756 and presented in London by David Garrick with Sarah Siddons in 1757, the year in which he left his ministry to become Lord Bute's private secretary. Other plays written for the London stage are *The Siege of Aquileia* (1760), *The Fatal Discovery* (1769), *Alonzo* (1773) and *Alfred* (1778). A modern edition of *Douglas* is edited with a critical introduction by G. D. Parker (1972).

See: Backsheider, Paula R. 'John Home's *Douglas* and the theme of
        unfulfilled life', *Studies in Scottish Literature*, 14 (1979), pp. 90–97
    Colville, James 'Home and his *Douglas*', *Scottish Art and Letters*, 3,
        no. 2 (1904), pp. 157–60
    Gipson, A. E. *John Home: A Study of His Life and Works* (1917)

Simpson, K. G. 'Rationalism and romanticism: the case of Home's *Douglas*', *Scottish Literary Journal*, 9, no. 1 (May 1982), pp. 21–47

HUME, DAVID (1711–76) Born and educated in Edinburgh. Rejecting law and commerce he retired to France and wrote *A Treatise of Human Nature* (1739). His philosophical ideas incubated during periods of service as diplomat in Europe and librarian to the Faculty of Advocates in Edinburgh. His philosophy is contained in his *Philosophical Essays Concerning Human Behaviour* (1748) which developed into his crowning achievements, *An Enquiry Concerning Human Understanding* (1758) and *An Enquiry Concerning the Principles of Morals* (1751).

See: Capaldi, Nicholas *David Hume, The Newtonian Philosopher* (1975)
Mossner, E. C. *The Life of David Hume* (1954)
Price, J. V. *David Hume* (1968)

JACOB (*née* KENNEDY-ERSKINE), VIOLET (1863–1946) Born in Montrose, daughter of the Laird of Dun, she married an army officer, Arthur Otway Jacob, with whom she spent her early married life in India. Returning to north-east Scotland she contributed poetry in Scots to Hugh MacDiarmid's *Northern Numbers* and to John Buchan's *The Northern Muse*. Her Scots poems from several volumes are collected in *The Scottish Poems of Violet Jacob* (1944). Her fiction is best represented by her historical novels, *The Sheep-stealers* (1902), *The Interloper* (1904), *The History of Aythan Waring* (1908) and *Flemington* (1911).

See: Caird, Janet 'The Poetry of Violet Jacob and Helen B. Cruickshank', *Cencrastus* no. 19 (1984), pp. 32–4.
Hendry, Joy 'Twentieth-century Women's Writing: The Nest of Singing Birds', *The History of Scottish Literature*, general editor Cairns Craig, 4 vols (1987–8), IV, *Twentieth Century*, ed. Cairns Craig, Chapter 19, pp. 291–309 [292–5]
MacDiarmid, Hugh 'Violet Jacob', *Contemporary Scottish Studies*, ed. Alan Riach (1995), pp. 27–34

JENKINS, ROBIN (b. 1912) Born in Cambuslang, Lanarkshire; educated at Hamilton Academy and the University of Glasgow. He has taught English in schools in Scotland, Spain, Borneo and in Afghanistan which becomes the 'Nurania' of his novels, *Some Kind of Grace* (1960), *Dust on the Paw* (1961) and *The Tiger of Gold* (1962). His novels set in Scotland or dealing with Scottish themes are *So Gaily Sings the Lark* (1950), *Happy for the Child* (1953), *The Thistle and the Grail* (1954), *The Cone-Gatherers* (1955), *Guests of War* (1956), *The Missionaries* (1957), *The Changeling* (1958), *Love is a Fervent Fire* (1961), *A Love of Innocence* (1963), *The Sardana Dancers* (1964), *A Toast to the Lord* (1972), *A Would-be Saint* (1978) and *Fergus Lamont* (1979).

See: Morgan, Edwin 'The Novels of Robin Jenkins', *Essays* (1974), pp. 242–5
Murray, Isobel and Bob Tait, 'Robin Jenkins: *Fergus Lamont*', *Ten Modern Scottish Novels* (1984), Chapter 10, pp. 194–218
Norquay, Glenda 'Disruptions: The Later Fiction of Robin Jenkins', Gavin Wallace and Randall Stevenson, *The Scottish Novel Since the Seventies* (1993), Chapter 1, pp. 11–24

Thompson, Alastair R. 'Faith and Love: An examination of some themes in the novels of Robin Jenkins', *New Saltire*, no. 3, Spring 1962, pp. 57–64

KAY, JACKIE (b. 1961) Born and brought up in Glasgow. Her *The Adoption Papers* (1991) won several awards and was broadcast on Radio 3 as part of the *Drama Now* series. Plays include *Chiaroscuro* (1986), *Twice Over* (1988) and *Every Bit of It* (1992). *Two's Company* (1992) is a collection of poetry for children.

See: Calder, Angus 'Jackie Kay's *Adoption Papers*', *Revolving Culture: Notes from the Scottish Republic* (1994), pp. 209–16

KELMAN, JAMES (b. 1946) Born in Glasgow and educated at Hyndland Secondary School. Fiction includes *An Old Pub Near the Angel and Other Stories* (1973), *The Busconductor Hines* (1984), *A Chancer* (1985), *A Greyhound for Breakfast* (1987), *A Disaffection* (1989), *The Burn* (1991) and *How Late It was, How Late* for which he was awarded the Booker Prize in 1994. A collection of his plays is published as *Hardie and Baird and Other Plays* (1991). *Some Recent Attacks: Essays cultural and political* (1992) collects talks, speeches and political and literary comment.

See: *Chapman*, 57 (Summer 1989), Special Feature – James Kelman
Craig, Cairns 'Resisting Arrest: James Kelman', Gavin Wallace and Randall Stevenson (eds), *The Scottish Novel Since the Seventies* (1993), Chapter 7, pp. 99–114
Klaus, H. Gustav 'James Kelman: a Voice from the Lower Depths', *London Magazine*, 29, nos. 5 and 6 (August/September 1989), pp. 39–48
McLean, Duncan 'Interview with James Kelman', *Edinburgh Review*, no. 71 (1985), pp. 64–80

KENNAWAY, JAMES (1928–68) Born in Auchterarder, Perthshire. Educated at Glenalmond and, after the Second World War, at Trinity College, Oxford. Commissioned into the Cameron Highlanders in 1947, he served with the Gordon Highlanders in Germany. Killed in a motoring accident caused by a heart attack. His novels are *Tunes of Glory* (1956), *Household Ghosts* (1961; adapted for the stage in 1967 and screen in 1969 as *Country Dance*), *The Mind Benders* (1963), *The Bells of Shoreditch* (1963), *Some Gorgeous Accident* (1967), *The Cost of Living Like This* (1969) and *Silence* (1972).

See: Kennaway, James and Susan *The Kennaway Papers* (1981)
Murray, Isobel and Bob Tait 'James Kennaway: *Tunes of Glory*', *Ten Modern Scottish Novels* (1984), Chapter 5, pp. 78–99
Royle, Trevor *James and Jim: A Biography of James Kennaway* (1983)

KENNEDY, A. L. (b. 1965) Born in Dundee, she now lives and works in Glasgow. Her first collection of stories, *Night Geometry and the Garscadden Trains* (1990), won several awards including the Saltire Award for Best First Book. *Now That You're Back* (1994) is a second collection of stories. Her novels are *Looking for the Possible Dance* (1993) and *So I am Glad* (1995).

See: Birch, Diana 'Warming My Hands and Telling Lies', *London Review of Books*, 3 August 1995, p. 17

Smith, Sarah 'A nose for injustice', *New Statesman and Society*, 26 May 1995, p. 25

KERMACK, ALISON (b. 1965) In 1994 she said: 'av rittin poyitry aw ma life, mare or less, bit ah nivvir shode it tay naybiddy till a cupply yeer back . . . ah rite coz ah hufty. beein published iz an ucayshinil boanus.' Her poems are collected in *Restricted Vocabulary* (1991) and *Writing Like a Bastard* (1993).

> See: O'Rourke, Daniel *Dream State: The New Scottish Poets* (1994), pp. xxxv–vi, 191–6

KESSON, JESSIE (1916–94) Born in an Inverness workhouse, brought up in a depressed area of Elgin and, between the ages of nine and sixteen, in an orphanage. Left Scotland in 1954. Worked in Woolworths, and with delinquent and spastic children and in homes for the elderly. Films have been made of her best-known novels, *The White Bird Passes* (1959) and *Another Time, Another Place* (1983). Other novels are *The Glitter of Mica* (1963) and *Where the Apple Ripens* (1985).

> See: Anderson, Carol 'Listening to the Women Talk', *The Scottish Novel Since the Seventies*, ed. Gavin Wallace and Randall Stevenson (1993), Chapter 12, pp. 170–86 [171–5]
> Bold, Alan *Modern Scottish Literature* (1983), pp. 213–15
> Kesson, Jessie 'My Scotland', *The Scottish Review*, no. 35 (August 1984), pp. 39–41

LEONARD, TOM (b. 1944) Born in Glasgow and educated at Lourdes Secondary School. Worked in a bookshop before further education at the University of Glasgow. Writer-in-residence positions have included Renfrew District Libraries, Glasgow and Strathclyde Universities and Bell College of Technology. From the archives of Paisley Library he has compiled *Radical Renfrew: Poetry from the French Revolution to the First World War* (1990), an attempt to reconstruct and reclaim the region's literary past. (See under 'Anthologies' in 'General Bibliographies'.) Best known as a poet and political commentator, his work is collected in *Intimate Voices: Selected Work 1965–1983* (1984) and *Reports from the Present: Selected Work 1982–94* (1995). Other publications include *If Only Bunty was Here* (1979), *Satires and Profanities* (1984), *On the Mass Bombing of Iraq and Kuwait, Commonly Known As 'The Gulf War'* (1991) and *Places of the Mind: The Life and Work of James Thomson (B. V.)* (1993).

> See: Boddy, Kasia and Barry Wood 'Interviews with Tom Leonard', *Edinburgh Review*, no. 77 (1987), pp. 59–71
> Kirkwood, Colin 'Vulgar eloquence: Tom Leonard's *Intimate Voices, 1965–1983*', *Cencrastus*, no. 20 (Spring 1985), pp. 21–3
> McGrath, Tom 'Tom Leonard: man with two heads', *Akros*, no. 24 (April 1974), pp. 40–49

LINDSAY, DAVID (1878–1945) Born and educated in London but spent much of his childhood in Jedburgh with Scottish relations. Worked as an underwriter at Lloyds and served with the Grenadier Guards in the First World War. After *A Voyage to Arcturus* (1920) he published *The Haunted*

Woman (1922) in which there are elements of a sequel, the autobiographically based *Sphinx* (1923), *The Adventures of M. de Mailly* (1926) and the Nietzschean *Devil's Tor* (1932).

See: Fulton, Robin (ed.) *Lines Review*, no. 40, March 1972 (David
    Lindsay special issue with a note by J. B. Pick and extracts from
    Lindsay's unpublished works)
  Sellin, B. *The Life and Works of David Lindsay* (1981)
  Wilson, C., E. H. Visiak and J. B. Pick *The Strange Genius of David
    Lindsay* (1970)

LINDSAY, FREDERIC (b. 1933) Born in Glasgow and educated at the Universities of Glasgow and Edinburgh. Teacher and lecturer in English and Linguistics at Annan Academy, 1960–66, and Hamilton College of Education, 1966–78. Novels are *Brond* (1984), *Jill Rips* (1987), *A Charm Against Drowning* (1988), *After the Stranger Came* (1992).

See: Gifford, Douglas 'Recent Fiction', *Books in Scotland*, no. 24 (Spring
    1987), pp. 16–19 [17–18]
  Hendry, Joy 'After the Stranger Came', *Scottish Literary Journal*,
    Supplement no. 37 (Winter 1992), pp. 36–8
  Massie, Allan 'Not drowning, just waving', *The Scotsman*, 16 April
    1988, 'Weekender', p. ix

LINDSAY, MAURICE (b. 1918) Born in Glasgow and educated at Glasgow Academy and the Royal Scottish Academy of Music. After service with the Cameronians in the Second World War he worked as journalist and critic before becoming Controller of Border Television. His *Collected Poems 1940–1990* (1990) supersedes *Collected Poems* (1979) and prints poems from collections published between 1981 and 1988 along with 'final revisions' and new poems. His considerable influence as a critic has been chiefly through *Robert Burns: the Man, His Work, the Legend* (1954, revised 1971), *History of Scottish Literature* (1977, revised 1992) and *Francis George Scott and the Scottish Renaissance* (1980). See also under 'Anthologies' in 'General Bibliographies'.

See: Campbell, Donald 'A Different Way of being Right: The Poetry of
    Maurice Lindsay', *Akros*, no. 24 (April 1974), pp. 22–6
  Macintyre, Lorn M. 'The Poetry of Maurice Lindsay', *Akros*, no. 42
    (December 1979), pp. 44–53

LINGARD, JOAN (b. 1932) Born in Edinburgh she was brought up in Belfast where she was educated at Bloomfield Collegiate School, returning to Edinburgh for teacher-training at Moray House College of Education. Her work includes fiction for adults and children. Among her adult novels are *The Prevailing Wind* (1964), *The Second Flowering of Emily Mountjoy* (1979) and *The Women's House* (1989).

See: Bold, Alan *Modern Scottish Literature* (1983), pp. 229–30

LINKLATER, ERIC (1899–1974) Born in Penarth, Wales. Spent much of his childhood and later life in Orkney where his father had ancestral roots. Educated at Aberdeen Grammar School and University. After service with the Black Watch in the First World War he worked as a journalist, academic assistant and broadcaster. After his romantic first novel, *White Maa's Saga* (1929), he developed his own vein of comedy in *Poet's Pub* (1929), *Juan in America* (1931) and *Juan in China* (1937). Other fiction includes *The Men of Ness* (1932), *Laxdale Hall* (1933), *Magnus Merriman* (1934), *Private Angelo* (1946), *The House of Gair* (1953), *Position at Noon* (1958) and *A Man Over Forty* (1963). Short fiction is collected in *The Stories of Eric Linklater* (1968). *The Wind on the Moon* (1944) is an adventure fantasy for children and *The Man on My Back* (1941) is autobiography.

See: Parnell, Michael *Eric Linklater: A Critical Biography* (1984)

LOCHHEAD, LIZ (b. 1947) Born in Motherwell, Lanarkshire, and educated at Dalziel High School and Glasgow School of Art. Has taught art in schools in Glasgow and Bristol. Poetry includes *Memo for Spring* (1972), *Dreaming Frankenstein, and Collected Poems* (1984), *True Confessions and New Clichés* (1985), *Bagpipe Muzak* (1991). Her plays include *Blood and Ice* (1982; revised 1984), *Dracula* (1985), *Mary Queen of Scots Got Her Head Chopped Off* (1987), *Quelques Fleurs* (1991).

See: Crawford, Robert and Ane Varty (eds) *Liz Lochhead's Voices* (1993)
Lochhead, Liz 'A Protestant girlhood', *Jock Tamson's Bairns: Essays on a Scots Childhood*, ed. Trevor Royle (1977), pp. 112–25
Nicholson, Colin 'Knucklebones of Irony', *Poem, Purpose and Place: Shaping Identity in Contemporary Scottish Verse* (1992), pp. 203–23

LOCKHART, JOHN GIBSON (1794–1854) Born at Cambusnethan, Lanarkshire, and educated at the Universities of Glasgow and Oxford before moving to Edinburgh to enter the Faculty of Advocates. Co-edited the conservative *Blackwood's Magazine* with John Wilson ('Christopher North') and with Wilson and James Hogg published the 'Chaldee Manuscript' (21 October 1817) attacking the Whig publishers of the *Edinburgh Review* in the language of the Old Testament. His sketches of social life in Edinburgh and Glasgow, *Peter's Letters to His Kinsfolk*, were published by Blackwood in three volumes in 1819. In 1820 he married Sir Walter Scott's daughter, Sophia, and in 1837–8 published his seven-volume *Memoirs of the Life of Sir Walter Scott Bart*. His four novels are *Valerius* (1821), *Adam Blair* (1822), *Reginald Dalton* (1823) and *Matthew Wald* (1824).

See: Hart, F. R. *Lockhart as Romantic Biographer* (1971)
Lochead, M. *John Gibson Lockhart* (1954)

MacCAIG, NORMAN (1910–96) Born and educated in Edinburgh, where he attended the High School and the University. Worked as a schoolteacher and also taught at the University of Stirling from 1970 to 1979 (Reader in Poetry from 1972). The style of his early poetry published in *Far Cry* (1943) and *The Inward Eye* (1946) reflects his affiliation to the New Apocalypse Movement, but he found his true voice in *Riding Lights* (1955). The poetry he wished to preserve from *Riding Lights* and subsequent volumes is gathered in *Collected Poems* (1985), followed by *Voice Over* (1988).

See: Ascherson, Neal 'Norman MacCaig' in *Seven Poets*, ed. Christopher
Carrell (1981), pp. 19–21, and Walker, Marshall, 'Six Poets',
ibid., pp. 33–41
Hendry, Joy and Raymond Ross (eds) *Critical Essays on Norman
MacCaig* (1991)
Nicholson, Colin 'Such Clarity of Seeming: Norman MacCaig',
*Poem, Purpose and Place: Shaping Identity in Contemporary Scottish
Verse* (1992), pp. 37–56
Rillie, Jack 'Net of Kins, Web of Ilks: MacCaig's Phantasmagoria',
Chapman, no. 66 (Autumn 1991), pp. 46–51

MacCOLLA, FIONN (pen name of THOMAS DOUGLAS MACDONALD)
(1906–75) Born in Montrose, Angus, trained as a teacher in Aberdeen and
worked in Wester Ross and Palestine. Studied Gaelic at Glasgow University
and occupied several positions as headmaster in schools in the north-west of
Scotland. His novels are *The Albannach* (1932), *And the Cock Crew* (1945),
Scottish Noël (1958), *Ane Tryall of Heretiks* (1962) and *The Ministers* (1979).
His theories of Scottish history and culture are published in *At the Sign of
the Clenched Fist* (1967). *Too Long in This Condition* (1975) is autobiography.

See: Gorak, I. 'Too Long in This Condition: The Metaphysics of Region
in MacColla's *The Albannach*', *Scottish Literary Journal*, 15, no. 1
(May 1988), pp. 82–96
Herdman, John 'Fionn MacColla: Art and Ideas', *Cencrastus*, no. 13
(Summer 1983), pp. 11–13
Murray, Isobel and Bob Tait, 'Fionn MacColla: And the Cock
Crew', *Ten Modern Scottish Novels* (1984), Chapter 4, pp. 55–77

MacDIARMID, HUGH (CHRISTOPHER MURRAY GRIEVE) (1892–1978)
Born in Langholm, Dumfriesshire, he trained as a teacher but became a
journalist in Edinburgh and Wales. After service with the RAMC in the
First World War he settled in Montrose, abandoned attempts at neo-
Georgian poetry and launched the Scottish Literary Renaissance movement,
intending to dissociate Scotland from Victorian sentimentalism and to align
Scottish culture with modernist and European developments. Co-founder of
the National Party of Scotland in 1928, he became estranged from his first
wife and family, moving from London to the Shetland Islands with his
second wife and young son and surviving a period of poverty, isolation and
physical and mental breakdown. In 1934 he joined the Communist Party of
Great Britain while advocating separatism for Scotland. The 'First Hymn to
Lenin' was followed by *Stony Limits and Other Poems* (1935) and the
autobiography, *Lucky Poet* (1943). After work during the Second World
War in a munitions factory in Glasgow and on boats on the Clyde, he and
his wife settled in a cottage near Biggar, Lanarkshire, in 1951. While in the
Shetlands he had started work on a poem of epic scale dealing with the
relations between language, poetry and imperialism, parts of which were
published as *In Memoriam James Joyce* (1955) and *The Kind of Poetry I Want*
(1961). He stood as a Communist candidate against the Conservative Prime
Minister, Sir Alec Douglas-Home, in the general election of 1964, the year
in which critical recognition of his poetry began to grow internationally.
The first edition of his *Complete Poems* was published in two volumes in
1978. See also under 'Anthologies' in 'General Bibliographies'.

See: Bold, Alan *MacDiarmid* (1988)
Buthlay, Kenneth *Hugh MacDiarmid (C. M. Grieve)* (1982)
—— (ed.) Hugh MacDiarmid, *A Drunk Man Looks at the Thistle,
Annotated Edition* (1987)
Crawford, Robert 'MacDiarmid and His Makers', *Identifying Poets:
Self and Territory in Twentieth-Century Poetry* (1993), Chapter 2
Gish, Nancy (ed.) *Hugh MacDiarmid: Man and Poet* (1992)
Glen, Duncan *Hugh MacDiarmid (Christopher Murray Grieve) and the
Scottish Renaissance* (1964)
—— 'Special Double Hugh MacDiarmid Issue', *Akros*, vol. 12, nos.
34–5 (August 1977)
McCarey, Peter *Hugh MacDiarmid and the Russians* (1987)
Morgan, Edwin *Hugh MacDiarmid* (1976)
Riach, Alan *Hugh MacDiarmid's Epic Poetry* (1991)
Watson, Roderick *MacDiarmid* (1985)

MacDONALD, GEORGE (1824–1905) Born at Huntly, Aberdeenshire, the son
of a farmer, educated at King's College Aberdeen and Highbury
Theological College and admitted to the Congregationalist ministry in 1850.
When his liberal doctrine brought him into conflict with his superiors he
resigned his charge and turned to journalism and lecturing. The best of his
conventional novels are *Alec Forbes of Howglen* (1865), *Robert Falconer* (1868),
Malcolm (1875), *The Marquis of Lossie* (1877), *Paul Faber, Surgeon* (1879) and
Sir Gibbie (1879). His most original works are *Phantastes: a Faery Romance for
Men and Women* (1858) and *Lilith* (1895). His fairy-tales for children include
At the Back of the North Wind (1871), *The Princess and the Goblin* (1872) and
The Princess and Curdie (1888).

See: Auden, W. H. 'Introduction' to *Visionary Novels of George MacDonald*
ed. Anne Fremantle (1954)
Lewis, C. S. 'Preface' to *George MacDonald: An Anthology* (1946)
MacDonald, Greville *George MacDonald and His Wife* (1924)
Phillips, Michael R. *George MacDonald: Scotland's Beloved Storyteller*
(1987)
Raeper, William *George MacDonald* (1987)
—— *The Gold Thread: Essays on George MacDonald* (1990)
Reis, Richard H. *George MacDonald* (1972)
Robb, David S. *George MacDonald* (1987)
Saintsbury, Elizabeth *George MacDonald: A Short Life* (1987)
Wolff, Robert Lee *The Golden Key: A Study of the Fiction of George
MacDonald* (1961)

McGONAGALL, WILLIAM (c. 1825–1902) The son of an immigrant Irish cotton
weaver, he was probably born in Edinburgh in 1825 and spent his childhood on the Orkney island of South Ronaldsay before moving with his
family to Dundee where he spent the rest of his life. While working as an
amateur actor with travelling groups of players he began writing the verses
which earned him fame as the world's greatest bad poet, selling his poems
in broadsheets and giving public readings. *Poetic Gems* (1890) has been
reprinted regularly and *More Poetic Gems* were published in 1962 with 'The
Autobiography of Sir William Topaz McGonagall, Poet and Tragedian'.

McGRATH, JOHN (PETER) (b. 1935) Born in Birkenhead, Cheshire. Educated at Alun Grammar School and St John's College, University of Oxford. National Service with British Army 1953–5. Wrote for BBC Television series *Z Cars* and worked as writer at Royal Court Theatre. *Events While Guarding the Bofors Gun* (1966) filmed as *The Bofors Gun*. Founded 7:84 Theatre Company in 1971 and Scottish 7:84 Theatre Company in 1973, the year of *The Cheviot, the Stag and the Black, Black Oil*. Later Scottish productions include *The Game's a Bogey* (1974; radio version 1979) and *Little Red Hen* (1975).

> See: Itzin, Catherine 'John McGrath', in Simon Trussler (ed.), *New Theatre Voices of the Seventies* (1981), pp. 98–109
> McGrath, John *A Good Night Out. Popular Theatre: Audience, Class and Form* (1981)

McGRATH, TOM (b. 1940) Born in Rutherglen, Lanarkshire, and educated at the University of Glasgow, he was founding editor of the underground newspaper *International Times* (London) and served as director of the Third Eye Centre, Glasgow. Writer-in-residence positions at the Traverse Theatre, Edinburgh, and the University of Iowa. Since 1990 associate literary director, Scottish Arts Council. Plays include *Mr Laurel and Mr Hardy* (1976), *The Hard Man* (with Jimmy Boyle, 1977), *The Android Circuit* (1978), *The Innocent* (1979), *1–2–3: [Who are You Anyway?; Very Important Business; Moondog]* (1981), *Kora* (1986), *Trivial Pursuits* (1988).

> See: *The Riverside Interviews: 6 – Tom McGrath* (1983)

McILVANNEY, WILLIAM (b. 1936) Born in Kilmarnock; educated at Kilmarnock Academy and the University of Glasgow. Schoolteacher from 1960 to 1975. His fiction includes *Remedy is None* (1966), *A Gift from Nessus* (1968), *Docherty* (1975), *Laidlaw* (1978), *The Papers of Tony Veitch* (1983), *Strange Loyalties* (1991). *Walking Wounded* is a set of related short stories and *Surviving the Shipwreck* (1991) a collection of his journalism. *In Through the Head* (1988) is a selection of poems from two earlier books with some new poems.

> See: Dickson, Beth 'Class and Being in the Novels of William McIlvanney', Gavin Wallace and Randall Stevenson (eds), *The Scottish Novel Since the Seventies* (1993), pp. 54–69
> Dixon, Keith 'Writing on the Borderline: The Works of William McIlvanney', *Studies in Scottish Literature*, 24 (1989), pp. 142–57
> Murray, Isobel and Bob Tait 'William McIlvanney: *Docherty*', *Ten Modern Scottish Novels* (1984), Chapter 9, pp. 168–93

MACKAY, JOHN HENRY (1864–1933) Born in Greenock and brought up in Germany. Studied philosophy, art history and literature at the universities of Kiel, Leipzig and Berlin. After residence in London and Switzerland he returned to Berlin in 1892 and wrote under both his own name and the pseudonym, 'Sagitta'. Works include *Die Anarchisten* (The Anarchists, 1891), *Der Schwimmer* (The Swimmer, 1901), *Der Freiheitsucher* (The Freedom-seeker, 1920), *Der Puppenjunge* (The Toy-boy, 1926; translated by Hubert Kennedy as *The Hustler*, 1985).

See: Kennedy, Hubert *Anarchist of Love: The Secret Life of John Henry Mackay* (1983)
——— 'A Preface to John Henry Mackay' in Toni Davidson (ed.), *And Thus Will I Freely Sing: An Anthology of Gay and Lesbian Writing from Scotland* (1989)

McKAY, JOHN (b. 1964) Began writing and performing in 1985 with the Scots comedy group, The Merry Mac Fun Show. His play, *Dead Dad Dog*, was premiered at the Edinburgh Traverse Theatre's 'Scottish Accents New Writing' season in 1988. His other work includes *Hellbent on Christmas* (1988), *Stubborn Kinda Fellow* (Channel 4 Television, 1989), *Onan* (written and performed with Robert Llewellyn, 1989), and *Up with Bob and Jessie* (1990).

See: Cameron, Alasdair 'Introduction', *Scot-Free: New Scottish Plays* (1990)

MACKENZIE, SIR (EDWARD MONTAGUE) COMPTON (1883–1974) Born at West Hartlepool as Edward Montague Compton but took his family name Mackenzie to affirm his Scottish lineage. Educated at St Paul's School, London, and Magdalen College, Oxford, where he studied law but turned to writing with the publication of *Poems* (1907) and his first novels, *The Passionate Elopement* (1911), the highly successful *Carnival* (1912) and the autobiographical *Sinister Street* (1913). Known to a wide public as a broadcaster and as founding editor of *Gramophone*, he lived at various times on Capri, where he was associated with Norman Douglas, the Channel Islands and in Scotland, converted to Roman Catholicism in 1914 and spent his last years in Edinburgh. His most ambitious fiction is the quartet of novels, *The Four Winds of Love* (1937–45), and he won popularity with his comedies of Scottish life and manners, *The Monarch of the Glen* (1941), *Whisky Galore* (1947) and *Rockets Galore* (1957). His autobiography, *My Life and Times*, was published in ten volumes between 1963 and 1971.

See: Linklater, A. *Compton Mackenzie: A Life* (1987)
Robertson, L. *Compton Mackenzie: an Appraisal of His Literary Work* (1954)

MACKENZIE, HENRY (1745–1831) A lawyer, born in Edinburgh and educated at its University, he became a leading attorney in taxation. His writing career began with the contribution of sentimental poems and romantic ballads to the *Scots Magazine* and *General Intelligencer* and he became famous with his novel, *The Man of Feeling* (1771), which was followed by *The Man of the World* (1773), *Julia de Rubigne* (1777) and a play, *The Prince of Tunis* (1773). A founder of the Royal Society of Edinburgh, he edited two periodicals, *The Mirror* (1779) and *The Lounger* (1785–7).

See: Crane, R. S. 'Suggestions towards a Genealogy of the "Man of Feeling"', *ELH*, 1 (1935), pp. 205–30.
Humphreys, A. R. 'Friend of Mankind', *Review of English Studies*, 24 (1948), pp. 203–18
Thompson, H. W. *A Scottish Man of Feeling* (1931)

MacLEAN, SORLEY (SOMHAIRLE MACGILL-EAIN) (b. 1911) Born on the island of Raasay, raised in the township of Osgaig and attended the Raasay school and Portree High School before reading English at Edinburgh

University. A schoolteacher all his professional life except for war service during the Second World War. His works include *17 Poems for 6d*, with Robert Garioch (1940), *Poems for Eimhir and Other Poems/Dàin do Eimhir agus Dàin Eile* (1943), *Poems to Eimhir*, translated from the Gaelic by Iain Crichton Smith (1971), *Spring Tide and Neap Tide, Selected Poems 1932–72/ Reothairt is Contraigh, Taghadh de Dhàin 1932–72* (1977), *Ris A' Bhruthaich: The Criticism and Prose Writings of Sorley MacLean*, ed. William Gillies (1985), *From Wood to Ridge/O Choille gu Bearradh: Collected Poems in Gaelic and English* (1989).

See: Ascherson, Neal 'Sorley MacLean' in *Seven Poets*, ed. Christopher Carrell (1981), pp. 29–30, and Walker, Marshall, 'Six Poets', ibid., pp. 68–77

Campbell, Angus Peter (ed.) *Somhairle – Dàin is Deilbh: A celebration on the 80th birthday of Sorley MacLean* (1991)

Crawford, Robert 'Somhairle MacGill-Eain/Sorley MacLean', *Identifying Poets: Self and Territory in Twentieth-Century Poetry* (1993), Chapter 3

Neat, Timothy *Hallaig: The Poetry and Landscape of Sorley MacLean*, commentary by Iain Crichton Smith and Seamus Heaney, poetry read by Sorley MacLean (film, 1984; video, 1990)

Nicholson, Colin 'Against an Alien Eternity: Sorley MacLean', *Poem, Purpose and Place: Shaping Identity in Contemporary Scottish Verse* (1992), pp. 1–18

Ross, Raymond J. and Joy Hendry *Sorley MacLean: Critical Essays* (1986)

McLELLAN, ROBERT (1907–85) Born at Linmill, Kirkfieldbank, Lanarkshire, he grew up and was educated in the vicinity of Glasgow. In the belief that period plays in Scots are viable for present-day theatre he produced three volumes of collected plays including *Jeddart Justice* (1933), *Tarfessock* (1934), *The Changeling* (1934), and his most successful work, *Jamie the Saxt* (1937). Later plays include *Torwatletie* (1946), *The Flouers o' Edinburgh* (1946) and *Young Auchinleck* (1962). *Collected Plays* (1981) is edited by Alexander Scott. Short fiction is collected in *Linmill and Other Stories* (1977), and the poem *Arran Burn* (1965) portrays life on the Isle of Arran, McLellan's home from 1938.

See: Campbell, Ian and Ronald D. S. Jack (eds), *Jamie the Saxt, A Historical Comedy by Robert McLellan* (1970)

Cording, Alastair 'A dramatic life: Robert McLellan', *The Scottish Review*, no. 9 (1978), pp. 27–32

Hutchison, David *The Modern Scottish Theatre* (1977), pp. 36–42

MacMILLAN, HECTOR (b. 1929) Born in Glasgow. Has served as Chairman of the Scottish Society of Playwrights. His plays include *The Sash* (1973), *The Rising* (1973), *The Royal Visit* (1974), *The Gay Gorbals* (1976) and *Oh What a Lovely Peace* (1977).

See: Hutchison, David *The Modern Scottish Theatre* (1977), pp. 139–40

MacMILLAN, RODDY (1923–79) Born in Glasgow, trained as an aero-engineer, and began his acting career with the Glasgow Unity Theatre in 1948.

Especially remembered for the part of Para Handy in the television series based on Neil Munro's stories. Author of two plays: *All in Good Faith* (1954) and *The Bevellers* (1973).

See: Hutchison, David 'Roddy McMillan and the Scottish Theatre', *Cencrastus*, no. 2 (Spring 1980), pp. 5–8

MACPHERSON, JAMES (1736–96) Born at Ruthven, Inverness-shire, educated at King's College and Marischal College, Aberdeen, and the University of Edinburgh. Abandoned a planned career in the ministry when he became a schoolteacher and published his wordy epic *The Highlander* (1758). Encouraged by John Home he published to the acclaim of the *literati* his alleged translations from Gaelic, *Fragments of Ancient Poetry Collected in the Highlands of Scotland and Translated from the Gaelic or Erse Language* (1760) in which he claimed that a major Gaelic epic existed which he could recover with financial assistance. Commissioned to visit the Highlands to undertake the search, Macpherson produced in 1761 *Fingal: an Ancient Epic Poem* and in 1763 *Temora*, an epic in eight books. His work is often regarded as fake because he altered his original material and expanded it with passages of his own, falsely offering the whole as authentic. Hoax or not, the impact of Macpherson's 'Ossian' on European romanticism was immense.

See: Clark, S. H. *Mark Akenside, James Macpherson & Edward Young: Selected Poetry*, with an Introduction and Notes (1994)
Stafford, Fiona *The Sublime Savage: A Study of James Macpherson and The Poems of Ossian* (1988)

McWILLIAM, CANDIA (b. 1955) Born in Edinburgh and educated at Girton College, Cambridge. Has worked for *Vogue* magazine and in advertising. Her novels are *A Case of Knives* (1988), *A Little Stranger* (1989) and *Debatable Land* (1994).

See: Mitchison, Amanda 'The Folding Starlet', *The Independent Magazine*, 4 June 1994, pp. 14–18

MASSIE, ALLAN (b. 1938) Born in Singapore, brought up in Aberdeenshire and educated at Glenalmond and Trinity College, Cambridge. Novelist, political commentator and literary critic. Novels include *Change and Decay in All Around I See* (1978), *The Last Peacock* (1980), *The Death of Men* (1981), *One Night in Winter* (1984), *Augustus* (1986), *A Question of Loyalties* (1989), *The Hanging Tree* (1990), *The Sins of the Father* (1991), *Tiberius* (1991), *These Enchanted Woods* (1993) and *The Ragged Lion* (1994), a re-creation of the life of Sir Walter Scott. *101 Great Scots* (1987) is Massie's personal selection of influential Scottish men and women from St Ninian to the great football manager, Jock Stein.

See: Douglas Dunn, 'Divergent Scottishness: William Boyd, Allan Massie, Ronald Frame', *The Scottish Novel Since the Seventies*, ed. Gavin Wallace and Randall Stevenson (1993), Chapter 11, pp. 149–69
Paterson, Lindsay 'Language and Society: The Novels of Allan Massie', *Cencrastus*, no. 10 (Autumn 1982), pp. 34–6

MILIER, HUGH (1802–56) Born in Cromarty and largely self-taught, he developed his interest in geology while an apprenticed stonemason, published his early verse, *Poems Written in the Leisure Hours of a Journeyman Mason* (1829), and went on to write *The Old Red Sandstone* (1841), *Footprints of the Creator* (1849) and *The Testimony of the Rocks* (1857). In Edinburgh he edited the evangelical newspaper, *The Witness*, from 1840 until his death by suicide. A collection of his essays were published posthumously in *Essays* (1862). His enquiring mind and powers of description are particularly evident in *Scenes and Legends of the North of Scotland* (1835) and *First Impressions of England and Its People* (1847).

See: Bayne, P. *The Life and Letters of Hugh Miller*, 2 vols (1871)
Mackenzie, W. M. *Hugh Miller: A Critical Study* (1905)
Rosie, G. *Hugh Miller: Outrage and Order* (1981)
Waterston, C. D. *Hugh Miller, the Cromarty Stonemason* (1966)

MITCHISON, NAOMI MARGARET (HALDANE) (b. 1897) Born in Edinburgh. Educated at the Dragon (boys') School and St Anne's College, Oxford. Labour candidate for the Scottish Universities' Constituency, 1935; member of the Argyll County Council, 1945–66, and the Highland and Island Advisory Council from 1966. Active in the women's movement, the peace movement and the Labour movement. In the late 1950s became tribal mother to the Bakgatla of Botswana. Novels include *The Conquered* (1923), *Cloud Cuckoo Land* (1925), *The Corn King and the Spring Queen* (1931), (with Wyndham Lewis) *Beyond This Limit* (1935), *The Blood of the Martyrs* (1939), *The Bull Calves* (1947), *The Big House* (1950), *Memoirs of a Space Woman* (1962), *Solution Three* (1975), *Not by Bread Alone* (1983). Other publications, spanning seven decades, include a large body of writing for children, e.g. *The Young Alexander the Great* (1961) and *The Vegetable War* (1980), and works on miscellaneous subjects, e.g. *Comments on Birth Control* (1930), *Naomi Mitchison's Vienna Diary* (1934), *A Fishing Village on the Clyde* (1961), *The Africans* (1970), *The Cleansing of the Knife* (poems, 1979), *Mucking Around: Five Continents over Fifty Years* (1981).

See: Calder, Angus 'Naomi Mitchison', *Revolving Culture: Notes from the Scottish Republic* (1994), pp. 173–7
Gifford, Douglas 'Forgiving the Past: Naomi Mitchison's *The Bull Calves*', *Studies in Scottish Fiction: Twentieth Century*, ed. Joachim Schwend and Horst W. Drescher (1990), pp. 219–55
Nicholson, Colin 'For the Sake of Alba: Naomi Mitchison', *Poem, Purpose and Place: Shaping Identity in Contemporary Scottish Verse* (1992), pp. 19–36

MORGAN, EDWIN (GEORGE) (b. 1920) Born in Glasgow, where his father rose to directorship of a firm of iron and steel scrap merchants, he was educated at Rutherglen Academy, the High School of Glasgow and Glasgow University. In the Second World War he served with the RAMC, mostly in the Middle East. After graduating in 1947 he lectured in English at the University of Glasgow where he was made Titular Professor in 1975. After early retirement in 1980 he maintained academic involvement through visiting professorships and a busy schedule of reading and lecturing throughout the UK. He has published or exhibited concrete/visual poems, has written opera libretti, and has worked as translator, editor and anthologist. His poetry is collected in *Poems of Thirty Years* (1982), *Collected Poems* (1990) and *Sweeping Out the Dark* (1994). His essays are gathered in *Essays*

(1974) and *Crossing the Border: Essays on Scottish Literature* (1990). See also
under 'History and criticism' and 'Anthologies' in 'General Bibliographies'.

See: Ascherson, Neal 'Edwin Morgan' in *Seven Poets*, ed. Christopher
Carrell (1981), pp. 30–31, and Walker, Marshall, 'Six Poets',
ibid., pp. 78–87
Calder, Angus 'Morganmania' in *Revolving Culture: Notes from the
Scottish Republic* (1994), pp. 178–85
Chapman, 64 (Spring/Summer 1991), Edwin Morgan: A Celebration
Crawford, Robert and Hamish Whyte (eds) *About Edwin Morgan*
(1990)
Nicholson, Colin 'Living in the Utterance: Edwin Morgan', *Poem,
Purpose and Place: Shaping Identity in Contemporary Scottish Verse*
(1992), pp. 57–79
Whyte, Hamish (ed.) *Edwin Morgan: Nothing Not Giving Messages –
Reflections on Work and Life* (1990)

MUIR, EDWIN (1887–1959) Born in the parish of Deerness, Orkney, and
brought up in the islands until he was fourteen when his family moved to
Glasgow. Largely self-educated, he worked in a beer-bottling factory and a
bone-processing factory at Fairport. Began to write for A. R. Orage's
journal, *The New Age*. In 1919 married Willa Anderson with whom he
translated European literature including the works of Franz Kafka, settled in
London and travelled in Europe. Worked for the British Council in Prague
and Rome before appointment in 1950 as Warden of Newbattle Abbey
College for residential education near Edinburgh. Norton Professor of
English at Harvard University in 1955, and returned to residence in the UK
near Cambridge until his death. His critical writing became widely respected
– see *Scott and Scotland* (1936), *Essays on Literature and Society* (1949) and
The Estate of Poetry (1962) – his three novels less so, and it is as a poet that
he is chiefly remembered. Early poems are collected in *First Poems* (1925).
His strongest volumes are *The Labyrinth* (1949) and *One Foot in Eden*
(1956). *An Autobiography* (1954) is a reprint of *The Story and the Fable*
(1940) with some revisions and seven additional chapters. The authoritative
collection of his poetry is *The Complete Poems of Edwin Muir*, an annotated
edition for the Association for Scottish Literary Studies prepared by Peter
Butter (1991) who has also edited *Selected Letters of Edwin Muir* (1974).

See: Aitchison, J. *The Golden Harvester: The Vision of Edwin Muir* (1988)
Butter, Peter *Edwin Muir* (1962)
—— *Edwin Muir, Man and Poet* (1966)
Knight, Roger *Edwin Muir: An Introduction to His Work* (1980)
MacLachlan, C. J. M. and D. S. Robb *Edwin Muir: Centenary
Assessments* (1990)
Morgan, Edwin 'Edwin Muir' in *Essays* (1974)
Wiseman, Christopher *Beyond the Labyrinth: a Study of Edwin Muir's
Poetry* (1978)

MURRAY, CHARLES (1864–1941) Born in Alford, Aberdeenshire, he trained as
an engineer, emigrated to South Africa in 1888, worked with a gold-
mining company and served with the Railway Pioneer Regiment during
the Boer War. In 1912 he became Secretary of Public Works for the
Government of the Union of South Africa. His first successful book of

poems, largely written in the dialect of the north-east of Scotland, is *Hamewith* (1900) which was reissued several times with additional poems from subsequent collections, *A Sough o' War* (1917) and *In the Country Places* (1920). His *Complete Poems* were edited in 1979 with an introduction by Nan Shepherd.

> See: Milton, Colin 'Modern Poetry in Scots Before MacDiarmid', *The History of Scottish Literature*, general editor Cairns Craig, 4 vols (1987–8), IV, *Twentieth Century*, ed. Cairns Craig, Chapter 1, pp. 1–36 [26–9]

OLIPHANT, CAROLINA, LADY NAIRNE (1766–1845) Daughter of Laurence Oliphant, a fervent Jacobite supporter, she was born at Gask, Perthshire, and married her cousin, Major William Murray Nairne, who, in 1824, was restored to his forfeited estates and the accompanying peerage. Under the pseudonym 'Mrs Bogan of Bogan' she wrote songs to traditional Scottish airs.

> See: Rogers, Charles *Life and Songs of the Baroness Nairne; with a memoir and poems of Carolina Oliphant the younger* (1869).

OLIPHANT (*née* WILSON), MARGARET (1828–97) Born at Wallyford, East Lothian, her early years were spent in Glasgow, Liverpool and London. After the success of her first novel, *Margaret Maitland* (1849), she became associated with William Blackwood's publishing house and contributed regularly to *Blackwood's Magazine*. Marriage to her cousin, Frank Wilson Oliphant, ended after two years when he died in 1859 leaving her with three children. Author of over 100 best-selling novels, she produced *The Chronicles of Carlingford*, a series of novels dealing with English provincial life, between 1861 and 1876, and novels of Scottish life, the best of these being *Effie Ogilvie* (1886) and *Kirsteen* (1890), as well as historical and critical work including *Francis of Assisi* (1868), *Literary History of England in the End of the Eighteenth and Beginning of the Nineteenth Century* (1882) and two volumes of *Annals of a Publishing House: William Blackwood and His Sons, Their Magazine and Friends* (1897). Her interest in the supernatural yielded *A Beleaguered City* (1880) and *A Little Pilgrim in the Unseen* (1882) and Margaret K. Gray has edited *Selected Short Stories of the Supernatural* (1985). Her incomplete autobiography and letters are available in a modern edition edited and introduced by Elisabeth Jay as *The Autobiography of Margaret Oliphant: the Complete Text* (1990).

> See: Coghill, H. (ed.) *Autobiography and Letters of Mrs Margaret Oliphant*, with an introduction by Q. D. Leavis (1974)
> Jay, Elisabeth *Mrs Oliphant: 'A Fiction to Herself' – A Literary Life* (1995)
> Williams, M. *Margaret Oliphant: A Critical Biography* (1986)

PRINGLE, THOMAS (1789–1834) Born in Teviotdale, Roxburghshire, and educated at Kelso Grammar School. After a brief spell as co-editor of the *Edinburgh Monthly Magazine* he emigrated to South Africa where he was outspoken in opposition to the slave trade. His works are *The Autumnal Excursion, or Sketches in Teviotdale* (1817), *Ephemerides, or Occasional Poems Written in Scotland and South Africa* (1828) and *African Sketches, Narrative of a Residence in South Africa* (1834).

See: Calder, A. *Thomas Pringle: A Scottish Poet in South Africa* (1983)
Thomson, D. H. *The Life and Work of Thomas Pringle* (1961)

RAE, HUGH C. (b. 1935) Born in Glasgow and educated at Knightswood
School before working as an antiquarian bookseller. Full-time writer since
1966. Has also published crime thrillers, war fiction, science fiction and
historical romances under the names Robert Crawford, R. B. Houston,
James Albany, Stuart Stern and – in earlier titles collaborating with Peggy
Coghlan (b. 1920) – Jessica Stirling. Novels published under his own name
include *Skinner* (1966), *Night Pillow* (1967), *A Few Small Bones* (1968; in the
USA titled *The House at Balnesmoor*), *The Interview* (1969), *The Saturday Epic*
(1970), *The Marksman* (1971), *The Shooting Gallery* (1972), *The Rock Harvest*
(1973), *The Rookery* (1974), *Harkfast* (1976), *Sullivan* (1978), *The Travelling
Soul* (1978), *Privileged Strangers* (1982).

See: Bold, Alan *Modern Scottish Literature* (1983), pp. 248–9
Henderson, Lesley (ed.) *Twentieth-century Crime and Mystery Writers*,
3rd edn (1991), pp. 897–8

RAMSAY, ALLAN (1684–1758) Born at Leadhills, Lanarkshire, he was brought
up by his farmer stepfather, educated at the local school and apprenticed to
an Edinburgh periwig maker. Abandoning wig-making he opened a
bookshop and established the first British circulating library in 1725. In
1736 he opened a playhouse which was closed under the Licensing Act of
1737. His earliest poems were written for members of the Easy Club of
which he was a founding member and collected in *Poems* (1721). In 1724
he produced his anthology of early Scottish poetry, *The Ever Green*, and the
first part of his five-volume collection, *The Tea-Table Miscellany* (1724–37).
His play, *The Gentle Shepherd* (1725), was made into a ballad opera for the
boys of Haddington Grammar School in 1729. The authoritative edition of
his work is *The Works of Allan Ramsay* in six volumes, edited for the
Scottish Text Society by John Burns Martin, John Walter Oliver, Alexander
Manson Kinghorn and Alexander Law (1945–74).

See: Crawford, Thomas '*The Gentle Shepherd*', *Society and the Lyric:
A Study of the Song Culture of Eighteenth-century Scotland* (1979),
pp. 70–96
Martin, J. B. *Allan Ramsay: a Study of His Life and Works* (1931)
Smart, A. *The Life and Art of Allan Ramsay* (1952)

REID, THOMAS (1710–96) Born at Strachan, Kincardineshire, he was educated
at Marischal College, Aberdeen. Between 1726 and 1737 he worked as
minister and librarian. In 1751 he became Professor of Philosophy at King's
College, Aberdeen, and in 1764 succeeded Adam Smith as Professor of
Moral Philosophy at the University of Glasgow. With his pupil, Dugald
Stewart, and Sir William Hamilton he belonged to the 'Common-Sense
School' of Scottish philosophy, his most influential work being *An Inquiry
into the Human Mind on the Principles of Common Sense* (1764).

See: Stewart, D. *The Life of Thomas Reid* (1803)

RIACH, ALAN (b. 1957) Born in Airdrie, Lanarkshire, and educated at the
Universities of Cambridge and Glasgow, he lectures in English, Scottish and

post-colonial literatures at the University of Waikato in New Zealand. Author of *Hugh MacDiarmid's Epic Poetry* (1991), he is general editor of the projected fourteen-volume edition of MacDiarmid's collected works for Carcanet Press. His poetry is published in *This Folding Map* (1990), *An Open Return* (1991) and *First and Last Songs* (1995).

> See: Morgan, Edwin 'This Folding Map', *Landfall*, no. 179 (September 1991), pp. 382–4
> O'Rourke, Daniel *Dream State: The New Scottish Poets* (1994), pp. xxix–xxx, 31–8
> Smith, Anna 'Alan (Scott) Riach' *Contemporary Poets*, ed. Thomas Riggs (1996), pp. 908–9

ROPER, TONY (b. 1941) After working as a miner, shipbuilder and brickie's labourer, he studied at Glasgow's Royal College of Music and Drama. His play *The Steamie* won the Glasgow Mayfest Award in 1987. He has also written the *Rab C. Nesbitt* series for BBC Television.

> See: Cameron, Alasdair 'Introduction', *Scot-Free: New Scottish Plays* (1990)

SCOTT, ALEXANDER (1920–89) Education at the University of Aberdeen was interrupted by the Second World War during which he served with the 5th/7th Gordon Highlanders and was decorated with the Military Cross. Developed the Department of Scottish Literature at the University of Glasgow. Poetry, mainly in Scots, is best represented by *Selected Poems 1943–74* (1975). His best-known critical writing is the biography, *Still Life: William Soutar, 1898–1943*. His edition of Soutar's diary is *Diaries of a Dying Man* (1954).

> See: Bruce, George 'The Poetry of Alexander Scott', *Akros*, no. 19 (August 1972), pp. 30–33
> Macintyre, Lorn 'Alexander Scott, Makar Extraordinary', *Akros*, no. 25 (August 1974), pp. 71–8

SCOTT, TOM (1918–95) Born in Glasgow; educated there and in St Andrews before attending Newbattle Abbey College and the University of Edinburgh. Poetry in Scots includes: *Seeven Poems o' Maister Villon* (1953), *The Ship and Ither Poems* (1963), *Tales of King Robert the Bruce* (1969), *Brand the Builder* (1975), *Tales of Sir William Wallace* (1980) and *The Dirty Business: A Poem about War* (1986).

> See: *Chapman*, nos. 47–8, Spring 1987, special feature on Tom Scott
> Crawford, Thomas 'Tom Scott: From Apocalypse to *Brand*', *Akros*, no. 31 (August 1976), pp. 57–69
> Harris, T. J. G. 'The Creature's Love of Creation', *P.N. Review* 95, 20, no. 3 (Jan.–Feb. 1994), pp. 63–5

SCOTT, SIR WALTER (1771–1832) Born in Edinburgh he contracted infantile paralysis at the age of eighteen months and convalesced at his grandfather's farm in Tweeddale where he acquired an early grounding in Border legend before returning to Edinburgh at the age of four. Educated at Edinburgh's High School and University, he joined his father's legal practice in 1786 and was called to the Scottish Bar in 1792, later becoming Clerk to the

Court of Session. During the summer of 1792 he collected the ballads for *The Minstrelsy of the Scottish Border* (1802–3). With the success of *The Lay of the Last Minstrel* (1805) he embarked on a series of ballad-epics whose popularity commended him as an author to his friend James Ballantyne, the printer, and to the publisher Archibald Constable who published the first of his Scottish historical novels, *Waverley; or 'Tis Sixty Years Since* (1814) which gave its name to the series known as *The Waverley Novels* which Scott published anonymously, although his authorship became an open secret before he publicly admitted to it in 1827. Embroiled in a complicated business relationship with Ballantyne and Constable, their financial crash in 1826 led to his bankruptcy, with Scott contracting to pay off his debt by writing.

See: Calder, Angus and Jenni *Scott* (1969)
Cockshut, A. O. J. *The Achievement of Sir Walter Scott* (1969)
Crawford, Thomas *Scott* (1982)
Daiches, David *Sir Walter Scott and His World* (1971)
Devlin, D. D. *The Author of Waverley: A Critical Study of Sir Walter Scott* (1971)
Ferris, Ina *The Achievement of Literary Authority: Gender, History, and the Waverley Novels* (1991)
Hayden, John O. (ed.) *Scott: The Critical Heritage* (1970)
Hillhouse, J. T. *The Waverley Novels and Their Critics* (1936)
Hogg, James *Familiar Anecdotes of Sir Walter Scott* in Mack, Douglas S. (ed.) James Hogg *Memoir of the Author's Life and Familiar Anecdotes of Sir Walter Scott* (1972)
Jeffares, A. Norman (ed.) *Scott's Mind and Art* (1969)
Lockhart, John Gibson *Memoirs of the Life of Sir Walter Scott Bart*, 7 vols (1837–8)
Lukács, Georg 'Sir Walter Scott', *The Historical Novel* (1962, reprinted 1969)
Muir, Edwin *Scott and Scotland* (1936, reprinted 1982)
Pritchett, V. S. 'Scott', *The Living Novel* (1946)
Scott, Paul Henderson *Walter Scott and Scotland* (1981)
Shaw, Harry E. *The Forms of Historical Fiction: Sir Walter Scott and His Successors* (1983)
Sutherland, John *The Life of Sir Walter Scott* (1995)
Welsh, Alexander *The Hero of the Waverley Novels with New Essays on Scott* (1992)

SHARP, ALAN (b. 1934) Born in Alyth and educated at Greenock High School. Apprentice joiner in shipyards, trainee private detective, English teacher in Germany, construction labourer, dishwasher, night switchboard operator for burglar alarm firm, packer for carpet factory, novelist and screenwriter. *A Green Tree in Gedde* (1965) and *The Wind Shifts* (1967) are the first two novels of a projected trilogy of which the third part, provisionally titled *The Apple Pickers*, has not yet appeared.

See: Norquay, Glenda 'Four Novelists of the 1950s and 1960s', *The History of Scottish Literature*, general editor Cairns Craig, 4 vols (1987–8), IV, *Twentieth Century*, ed. Cairns Craig, Chapter 17, pp. 259–76 [266–8]

SHARP, WILLIAM ('FIONA MACLEOD') (1855–1905) Born in Paisley, he was educated at Glasgow Academy and the University of Glasgow. After a year in Australia he worked in London as banker, journalist and editor, travelling in Europe and North America. While in Rome in 1890–91 he invented his literary persona, 'Fiona Macleod', author of his most successful works, the novels *Pharais, A Romance of the Isles* (1894), *The Mountain Lovers* (1895) and *The Washer of the Ford* (1895).

> See: Alaya, F. *William Sharp: 'Fiona Macleod'* (1936)
> Halloran, William F. 'W. B. Yeats and William Sharp: The Archer Vision', *English Language Notes*, 6, no. 4 (June 1969), pp. 270–80
> Janvier, Catherine A. 'Fiona MacLeod and Her Creator', *North American Review*, 184 (April 1907), pp. 718–32

SHEPHERD, ANNA ('NAN') (1893–1981) Born in Aberdeenshire and educated at the University of Aberdeen after which she became a lecturer in English at Aberdeen College of Education. Her three novels are *The Quarry Wood* (1928), *The Weatherhouse* (1930) and *A Pass in the Grampians* (1933). *In the Cairngorms* (1934) is a collection of poems. *The Living Mountain* (1977) is non-fiction.

> See: Shepherd, Nan *The Quarry Wood*, introduced by Roderick Watson (1987)

SMITH, ADAM (1723–90) Born in Kirkcaldy, Fife, he was educated at the Universities of Glasgow and Oxford. After making his mark as a public lecturer on rhetoric, history and economics in Edinburgh he was appointed Professor of Logic at the University of Glasgow and transferred in 1752 to the Chair of Moral Philosophy. *The Theory of Moral Sentiments* (1759) brought him to the attention of Lord Charles Townshend who appointed him tutor to the young Duke of Buccleuch in 1763, and in 1764 he went with his charge to France where he met Voltaire and the group of social reformers and theorists known as the physiocrats, headed by François Quesnay. Returning to London he was elected a fellow of the Royal Society and met Edmund Burke, Samuel Johnson, Edward Gibbon and perhaps Benjamin Franklin. In 1767 he settled back in Kirkcaldy where he completed *The Wealth of Nations* (1776). His complete works are published definitively in *The Glasgow Edition of the Works and Correspondence of Adam Smith*, 6 vols in 7 (1976–83). Vol. 4 is his *Lectures on Rhetoric and Belles Lettres* edited by J. C. Bryce (1983).

> See: Campbell, T. D. *Adam Smith's Science of Morals* (1971)
> Hollander, S. *The Economics of Adam Smith* (1971)
> Jones, P. and A. S. Skinner (eds) *Adam Smith Reviewed* (1991)
> Werhane, P. H. *Adam Smith and His Legacy* (1991)
> Winch, Donald *Adam Smith's Politics: An Essay in Historiographic Revision* (1978)

SMITH, IAIN CRICHTON (IAIN MAC a'GHOBHAINN) (b. 1928) Born on the island of Lewis. Educated at the Nicolson Institute, Stornoway, and the University of Aberdeen. Teacher in schools in Clydebank and Oban until 1977. Bilingual in Gaelic and English and writes poetry and prose in both languages. His principal works in English include *Collected Poems* (1992) which reprints selections from his previous volumes of poetry, the novels *Consider the Lilies* (1968), *The Last Summer* (1969), *An End to Autumn* (1978), *A Field Full of Folk* (1982) and *The Dream* (1990), and several collections of short stories including *The Black and the Red and Other Stories* (1973), *Murdo and Other Stories* (1981), *Selected Stories* (1989) and *Thoughts of Murdo* (1993). *Towards the Human* (1986) gathers autobiographical and critical essays.

See: Ascherson, Neal 'Iain Crichton Smith', *Seven Poets*, ed. Christopher Carrell (1981), p. 23, and Walker, Marshall, 'Six Poets', ibid., pp. 43–51
Gow, C. *Mirror and Marble: The Poetry of Iain Crichton Smith* (1992)
Morgan, Edwin 'The Raging and the Grace: Some Notes on the Poetry of Iain Crichton Smith', *Essays* (1974)
Nicholson, C. (ed.) *Iain Crichton Smith: Critical Essays* (1992)
—— 'To Have Found One's Country: Iain Crichton Smith', *Poem, Purpose and Place: Shaping Identity in Contemporary Scottish Verse* (1992), pp. 114–32

SMITH, SYDNEY GOODSIR (1915–75) Born in Wellington, New Zealand, he went to Edinburgh in 1927 and was educated at the Universities of Edinburgh and Oxford. His reputation as a poet in Scots rests chiefly on *Under the Eildon Tree* (1948) and *Figs and Thistles* (1959). His novel, *Carotid Cornucopius* (1947), was admired by Hugh MacDiarmid. His poetry is gathered in *Collected Poems 1941–1975* (1975).

See: Buthlay, Kenneth 'Sydney Goodsir Smith: Makar Macironical', *Akros*, no. 31 (August 1976), pp. 46–56
Gold, E. *Sydney Goodsir Smith's 'Under the Eildon Tree'* (1975)
MacDiarmid, Hugh *Sydney Goodsir Smith* (1963)
—— *For Sydney Goodsir Smith* (1975)

SMOLLETT, TOBIAS (GEORGE) (1721–71) Born at Dalquharn in Dumbartonshire, he was educated at Dumbarton Grammar School and the University of Glasgow where he read medicine. Failing to attract a London producer for his play, *The Regicide, or James I of Scotland* (1749), he embarked as ship's surgeon in the abortive Cartagena expedition and lingered in Jamaica before returning to London where he lived by journalism and translation. His first novel, *The Adventures of Roderick Random* (1748), was an immediate and lasting success but *The Adventures of Peregrine Pickle* (1751) proved too astringent for popular taste and Smollett toned it down in a second edition (1758). His translation of Cervantes's *Don Quixote* received little attention in his own time but has since been recognized as a distinguished English version. His farce, *The Reprisal*, enjoyed a successful run at Drury Lane in 1757, and from 1756 to 1763 he edited the *Critical Review* with acknowledged flair. In 1771, shortly before his death, *The Adventures of Humphry Clinker* emerged as his masterpiece.

See: Adamson, W. R. *Cadences of Unreason: A Study of Pride and Madness in the Novels of Tobias Smollett* (1990)
Bold, Alan (ed.) *Tobias Smollett* (1982)
Goldberg, M. A. *Smollett and the Scottish School* (1959)
Kelly, L. (ed.) *Tobias Smollett: The Critical Heritage* (1987)
Knapp, L. M. *Tobias Smollett, Doctor and Man of Letters* (1949)

SOUTAR, WILLIAM (1898–1943) Born and educated in Perth, he served in the Royal Navy during the First World War, matriculated at the University of Edinburgh to read medicine but transferred to Arts, read English literature and graduated in 1923. By 1929 he had lost the use of his legs through ossification of the spine and was permanently invalided a year later. By 1931 he had begun to write in Scots and published his first book of Scots verse, *Seeds in the Wind*, for children in 1933, followed by *Poems in Scots* (1935), *A Handful of Earth* (1936), *Riddles in Scots* (1937), *In the Time of Tyrants* (1939), *But the Earth Abideth* (1943) and *The Expectant Silence* (1944). *Collected Poems* edited by Hugh MacDiarmid (1948) includes his 'whigmaleeries', short poems for children. W. R. Aitken has edited *Poems of William Soutar: A New Selection* (1988). His diary is edited by Alexander Scott as *Diaries of a Dying Man* (1954).

> See: *Chapman* no. 53 (Summer 1988), special issue, 'On William Soutar'
> Scott, Alexander *Still Life: William Soutar 1898–1943* (1958)

SPARK, MURIEL (b. 1918) Born Muriel Sarah Camberg in Edinburgh where she was educated at James Gillespie's School for Girls. Employed in the Political Intelligence Department of the Foreign Office, 1944–5. General Secretary of the Poetry Society and editor of *Poetry Review*, 1947–9, then converting to Roman Catholicism and becoming full-time writer based in New York and Rome. Her fiction includes *The Comforters* (1957), *The Go-Away Bird* (1957), *Robinson* (1958), *Memento Mori* (1959), *The Ballad of Peckham Rye* (1960), *The Bachelors* (1961), *The Prime of Miss Jean Brodie* (1961), *The Girls of Slender Means* (1963), *The Mandelbaum Gate* (1965), *The Public Image* (1968), *The Driver's Seat* (1970), *Not to Disturb* (1971), *The Hothouse on the East River* (1972), *The Abbess of Crewe* (1974), *Territorial Rights* (1979), *Loitering with Intent* (1981), *A Far Cry from Kensington* (1988), *Symposium* (1990).

> See: Bold, Alan *Muriel Spark* (London, 1986)
> —— (ed.) *Muriel Spark: An Odd Capacity for Vision* (1984)
> Massie, Allan *Muriel Spark: a New Assessment* (1979)
> Murray, Isobel and Bob Tait, 'Muriel Spark: *The Prime of Miss Jean Brodie*', *Ten Modern Scottish Novels* (1984), Chapter 6, pp. 100–22
> Rankin, Ian 'The Deliberate Cunning of Muriel Spark', Gavin Wallace and Randall Stevenson (eds), *The Scottish Novel Since the Seventies* (1993), Chapter 3, pp. 41–53

SPENCE, ALAN (b. 1947) Born in Glasgow where he was educated at Allan Glen's High School and the University of Glasgow. Writes poetry, fiction and plays for stage, radio and television. Runs the Sri Chinmoy Centre in Edinburgh. Works include *Plop!* (1970), *Ah!* (1975), *Its Colours They are Fine* (1977), *Glasgow Zen* (1981), *Sailmaker* (1982), *Space Invaders* (1983), *Changed Days* (1991) and *The Magic Flute* (1991).

> See: Burns, John 'Mastering The Magic Flute', *Cencrastus*, no. 38 (Winter 1990–91), pp. 41–2

STEVENSON, ROBERT LOUIS (LEWIS BALFOUR) (1850–94) Born in Edinburgh, he was sickly as a child with the bronchial condition that afflicted him all his life. He studied engineering and law at the University of Edinburgh but gave up both for a writing career which he began by contributing essays and criticism to the *Cornhill* magazine and *London Magazine*. His reputation was established by *An Inland Voyage* (1878), *Travels with a Donkey* (1879), *Edinburgh: Picturesque Notes* (1879), the miscellaneous pieces collected in *Virginibus Puerisque* (1881), the stories of *The New Arabian Nights* (1882) and *The Merry Men* (1887), and the poems of *A Child's Garden of Verses* (1885). His essays, short stories, sketches of travel and autobiography were generally well received but real fame came with his adventure novels, beginning with *Treasure Island* (1883) and *Kidnapped* (1886), and he became a celebrity in Britain and America with *The Strange Case of Dr Jekyll and Mr Hyde* (1886) which offset the disappointment of his failure to succeed as a dramatist in collaboration with W. E. Henley. The search for a climate congenial to his fragile health took him with his American wife, Fanny Osbourne, to the southern Pacific where they settled in 1889 at Upolu, Samoa. The best work of his last years is 'The Beach of Falesa' (1892), *The Ebb Tide* (1894) and the unfinished *Weir of Hermiston* (1896).

See: Balfour, Graham *The Life of Robert Louis Stevenson* (1901)
Bell, Ian *Dreams of Exile – Robert Louis Stevenson* (1992)
Calder, Jenni *RLS: A Life Study* (1980)
Chesterton, G. K. *Robert Louis Stevenson* (1927)
Daiches, David *Robert Louis Stevenson and His World* (1973)
Hennessy, James Pope *Robert Louis Stevenson* (1974)
McLynn, Frank *Robert Louis Stevenson: A Biography* (1993)
Smith, Janet Adam *Robert Louis Stevenson* (1937)

STEWART, ENA LAMONT (b. 1912) Educated at Glasgow's Woodside School and Esdaile College in Edinburgh. While working as librarian and medical secretary she wrote for radio and stage. Her plays include *Distinguished Company* (1943), *Men Should Weep* (1947), *Towards Evening* (1975) and *High Places* (1987).

See: Hutchison, David 'Scottish Drama 1900–1950', *The History of Scottish Literature*, general editor Cairns Craig, 4 vols (1987–8), IV, *Twentieth Century*, ed. Cairns Craig, Chapter 11, pp. 163–77 [175–6]

TENNANT, EMMA (b. 1937) Born in London but brought up mainly in Peebleshire until the age of eight. Educated at St Paul's Girls' School, London, and a finishing school for young ladies in Oxford and studied the history of art at the Ecole du Louvre in Paris. Novels include *The Colour of Rain* (under pseudonym Catherin Aydy, 1963; reprinted under name Emma Tennant, 1988), *The Time of the Crack* (1973; published as *The Crack*, 1978), *The Last of the Country House Murders* (1975), *Hotel de Dream* (1976), *The Bad Sister* (1978), *Wild Nights* (1979), *Woman Beware Woman* (1983; published in USA as *The Half-Mother*, 1985), *The House of Hospitalities* (1987), *A Wedding of Cousins* (1988), *The Adventures of Robina, By Herself: Being the Memoirs of a Debutante at the Court of Queen Elizabeth II* (1988), *Two Women of London: The Strange Case of Ms Jekyll and Mrs Hyde* (1989), *Faustine* (1992), *Tess* (1993).

See: John Haffenden (ed.) 'Emma Tennant', *Novelists in Interview* (1985), pp. 281–304
Kenyon, Olga (ed.) 'Emma Tennant', *Women Writers Talk: Interviews with 10 Women Writers* (1989), pp. 173–87

THOMSON, DERICK (RUARAIDH MACTHÒMAIS) (b. 1921) Born on the island of Lewis, son of the Gaelic poet, James Thomson, he studied at the Universities of Aberdeen, Cambridge and Wales. After war service in the RAF he taught at Edinburgh and Aberdeen Universities before appointment to the Chair of Celtic at the University of Glasgow. Founder and editor of the Gaelic quarterly *Gairm* and editorial director of Gairm publications. In addition to academic works in the field of Gaelic and several earlier volumes of poetry he has published his collected poems in bilingual format as *Plundering the Harp: Collected Poems 1940–1980/Creachadh Na Clàrsaich: Cruinneachadh De Bhardachd 1940–1980* (1982).

> See: Smith, Iain Crichton 'The Poetry of Derick Thomson', *Towards the Human* (1986), pp. 136–43
> Whyte, Christopher 'Derick Thomson: Reluctant Symbolist', *Chapman*, no. 38 (Spring 1984), pp. 1–6

THOMSON, JAMES (1700–48) Born at Ednam in Roxburghshire, educated at Jedburgh and at the University of Edinburgh where he read divinity. Moving to London to tutor the Earl of Haddington's son he met Pope, his friend, the Scottish physician John Arbuthnott, and David Malloch with whom he collaborated on *The Masque of Alfred* (1740). His plays have not worn well, but, despite its mannered poetic diction, his long poem, *The Seasons* (1926–30), heralded views of nature associated with the Romantic movement. His allegorical poem, *The Castle of Indolence*, was published in 1748.

> See: Cohen, R. *The Unfolding of 'The Seasons'* (1969)
> Grant, D. *James Thomson: Poet of the Seasons* (1951)
> Scott, M. J. W. *James Thomson: Anglo-Scot* (1988)

THOMSON, JAMES (B[YSSHE] V[ANOLIS]) (1834–82) Born at Port Glasgow, he moved to London when his merchant-seaman father died of a stroke in 1840. Within two years his mother also died and he was brought up at the Royal Caledonian Asylum for the children of indigent Scottish servicemen, completing his education at the Royal Military Asylum in Chelsea before joining the army to serve as a schoolmaster. Service in Ireland and England was followed by a period in the 1870s when he worked as secretary to a mine company in Colorado and as war correspondent in Spain. In Ireland in 1851 he met Charles Bradlaugh, publisher of the *National Reformer*, in which his major work, *The City of Dreadful Night*, was published in instalments in 1874. The work first appeared in its entirety in *The City of Dreadful Night and Other Poems* (1880). The poem is available in a modern edition introduced and annotated by Edwin Morgan (1990). Thomson's health was broken by depression, poverty and drink and he died of an internal haemorrhage in University College Hospital, London.

> See: Dobell, B. *The Laureate of Pessimism* (1910)
> Leonard, Tom *Places of the Mind: The Life and Work of James Thomson (B. V.)* (1993)
> Salt, H. S. *The Life of James Thomson (B. V.)* (1889)

TROCCHI, ALEXANDER (1925–84) Born in Glasgow and studied at the University of Glasgow before moving to Europe and America. Founder-editor of the avant-garde literary review *Merlin* published in Paris during the

1950s. His works often appeared first under a pseudonym and were reissued under his own name. Novels published under the name Trocchi include, in order of first appearance, *Helen and Desire* (1967), *The Carnal Days of Helen Seferis* (1967), *Young Adam* (1961), *School for Sin* (1967), *Thongs* (1967), *Sappho of Lesbos* (1960), *Cain's Book* (1961). *Man at Leisure* (1972) is a collection of poems.

See: Campbell, James 'Alexander Trocchi', *London Magazine*, 32, nos. 1 and 2 (April/May 1992), pp. 45–59
Morgan, Edwin, 'Alexander Trocchi: A Survey', *Crossing the Border: Essays on Scottish Literature* (1990), pp. 300–11
Scott, Andrew Murray *Alexander Trocchi: The Making of the Monster* (1991)

WATSON, RODERICK (b. 1943) Born in Aberdeen where he was educated at the Grammar School and University before going on to Cambridge. He is Professor of English at the University of Stirling and Director of the Stirling Institute for International Scottish Studies. Critic, broadcaster, anthologizer and poet, his own poetry includes *Poems* (Parklands Poets, 1970), *Trio* (1971), *True History on the Walls* (1977) and *What Your Look Meant Then: Four Poems for Hugh MacDiarmid* (1987). See also under 'History and criticism' and 'Anthologies' in 'General Bibliographies'.

See: Glen, Duncan 'A New Harmony? Younger Scottish Poets Today', *Akros*, no. 27 (April 1975), pp. 51–65
Vinson, J. and D. L. Kirkpatrick, *Contemporary Poets*, 4th edn (1985), pp. 907–8

WELSH, IRVINE (b. 1958) Born in Leith and brought up on Edinburgh's Muirhouse estate, he left school at sixteen and spent most of the 1980s in London as a punk and drug addict. Began writing as a sideline while studying for an MBA at Heriot Watt University. His fiction includes *Trainspotting* (1993; stage adaptation 1995), which reached the final ten in competition for the Booker Prize, *The Acid House* (1994) and *Marabou Stork Nightmares* (1995).

WILSON, JOHN ('CHRISTOPHER NORTH') (1785–1854) Born in Paisley, Renfrewshire, he was educated privately and at the Universities of Glasgow and Oxford. An Advocate, he is remembered neither for his law nor for his undistinguished poetry but for the literary consequences of his association with William Blackwood. Co-editor of *Blackwood's Magazine*, he was co-author of the 'Chaldee Manuscript' (see under John Gibson Lockhart) and co-author or author of the 71 imaginary conversations which appeared in *Blackwood's* as the *Noctes Ambrosianae* (Wilson was mainly responsible for numbers 19 and 21 to 71). A selection of the *Noctes* is published in a modern edition as *The Tavern Sages: Selections from the Noctes Ambrosianae*, edited by J. H. Alexander for the Association of Scottish Literary Studies (1992). Wilson published two novels, *The Trials of Margaret Lyndsay* (1823) and *The Foresters* (1825). From 1820 to 1851 he held the Chair of Moral Philosophy at the University of Edinburgh.

See: Gordon, M. *A Memoir of Christopher North* (1862)
Swann, E. *Christopher North* (1934)

Index

Mackintosh, Charles, 37
MacLean, Alistair, 243
MacLean, Sorley, 1, 11, 100, 285,
  290–4, 346
McLellan, Robert, 21, 84, 249, 257–8
MacLennan, David, 268
Macleod, Fiona, 230
McMillan, Dorothy Porter, 53
MacMillan, Hector, 6, 268
MacMillan, James, 18
Macmillan, Roddy, 268
Macpherson, James, 73
MacQueen, John, 38
Macrae, Duncan, 258
McWilliam, Candia, 219
Machiavelli, Niccolò, 155
Mailer, Norman, 320
Manzoni, Alessandro, 113
Martin, Troy Kennedy, 11
Marx, Karl, 41, 113, 238
Mary, Queen of Scots, 4, 269, 333
Massie, Allan, 16, 23, 33, 41, 319, 331,
  332, 333–6
Mavor, Ronald, 261, 262
Mayakovsky, Vladimir, 303
Melville, Herman, 156, 189, 207
Mill, John Stuart, 167
Miller, Hugh, 34, 36
Milne, A. A., 176
Milton, John, 18, 92, 104, 117
Mitchison, Naomi, 325
Moir, David Macbeth, 158
Moluag, St, 3
Monsarrat, Nicholas, 320
Moore, George, 197
Morgan, Edwin, 16, 18, 19, 20, 22,
  23, 83–4, 117, 142, 263, 278, 285,
  302–12, 341, 345, 346
Morris, William, 167
Muir, Edwin, 100, 104, 271, 285–8,
  304, 346
Munro, Neil, 112, 217, 240
Murray, Charles, 9, 80–1, 84, 306

Nabokov, Vladimir, 211
Napoleon, Bonaparte, 45, 173
Neaves, Charles, Lord, 6
Newman, John Henry, Cardinal, 34
Nietzsche, Friedrich Wilhelm, 14, 170,
  173, 186, 284, 286, 341
Norris, Frank, 135
Novalis (Friedrich Leopold von
  Hardenberg), 168, 174, 176, 178, 185

O'Casey, Sean, 270, 284
Oliphant, Carolina, Lady Nairne, 50
Oliphant, Margaret, 11, 19, 167,
  180–5, 218, 225, 233
Olson, Charles, 304
Orwell, George, 21, 338
Osbourne, Lloyd, 196, 200, 201, 203
Owen, Robert, 10
Owens, Agnes, 340

Paine, Thomas, 10
Peake, Mervyn, 176, 345
Percy, Thomas, 114
Pinter, Harold, 151, 253
Poe, Edgar Allan, 151, 207, 208, 241,
  310
Pope, Alexander, 19, 40, 59, 68, 281
Potter, Dennis, 176, 203
Pound, Ezra, 19, 117, 284, 291
Powell, Anthony, 333
Prickett, Stephen, 145
Priestley, J. B., 222
Pringle, Thomas, 47
Pritchett, V. S., 127

Quilter, Roger, 95

Rabelais, François, 103
Rae, Hugh C., 319, 325, 326–7, 341
Raeburn, Henry, 37
Ramsay, Allan, 10, 16, 47, 68–72, 73,
  75, 76, 77, 84, 88, 93, 114, 249
Ramsay, Allan, Jr, 37
Reid, Alexander, 257, 258
Reid, Thomas, 35, 43
Riach, Alan, 33–4, 113, 285
Richards, I. A., 117
Richardson, Samuel, 67, 92
Richter, Johann Paul Friedrich, 168
Rilke, Rainer Maria, 302
Robertson, William, 77
Roper, Tony, 249, 271–2, 326
Rosa, Salvator, 63
Rostand, Edmond, 303
Rousseau, Jean-Jacques, 10, 173
Ruskin, John, 167
Russell, Bertrand, 39

Said, Edward, 12
Sainte-Beuve, Charles-Augustin, 113
Salinger, J. D., 344
Saurat, Denis, 256–7